Private
Justice

Shadow
of Doubt

Books by Terri Blackstock

Soul Restoration
Emerald Windows

Restoration Series
1 | *Last Light*
2 | *Night Light*

Cape Refuge Series
1 | *Cape Refuge*
2 | *Southern Storm*
3 | *River's Edge*
4 | *Breaker's Reef*

Newpointe 911
1 | *Private Justice*
2 | *Shadow of Doubt*
3 | *Word of Honor*
4 | *Trial by Fire*
5 | *Line of Duty*

Sun Coast Chronicles
1 | *Evidence of Mercy*
2 | *Justifiable Means*
3 | *Ulterior Motives*
4 | *Presumption of Guilt*

Second Chances
1 | *Never Again Good-bye*
2 | *When Dreams Cross*
3 | *Blind Trust*
4 | *Broken Wings*

With Beverly LaHaye
1 | *Seasons Under Heaven*
2 | *Showers in Season*
3 | *Times and Seasons*
4 | *Season of Blessing*

Novellas
Seaside

TERRI BLACKSTOCK

#1 bestselling suspense author

Private
Justice

NEWPOINTE 911 BOOKS 1 & 2

Shadow
of Doubt

ZONDERVAN.com/
AUTHORTRACKER
follow your favorite authors

This book is lovingly dedicated to the Nazarene

ZONDERVAN®

Private Justice/Shadow of Doubt Compilation Lifeway
Copyright © 2007 by Terri Blackstock

Private Justice
Copyright © 1998 by Terri Blackstock

Shadow of Doubt
Copyright © 1998 by Terri Blackstock

Requests for information should be addressed to:

Zondervan, *Grand Rapids, Michigan 49530*

ISBN-10: 0-310-61026-5
ISBN-13: 978-0-310-61026-7

Published in association with the literary agency of Alive Communications, Inc., 7680 Goddard Street, Suite 200, Colorado Springs, CO 80920.

Interior design by Jody DeNeef

Printed in the United States of America

08 09 10 11 • 25 24 23 22 21 20 19 18 17 16 15 14 13 12 11 10 9 8 7 6 5 4 3 2 1

Private Justice

Lower Louisiana

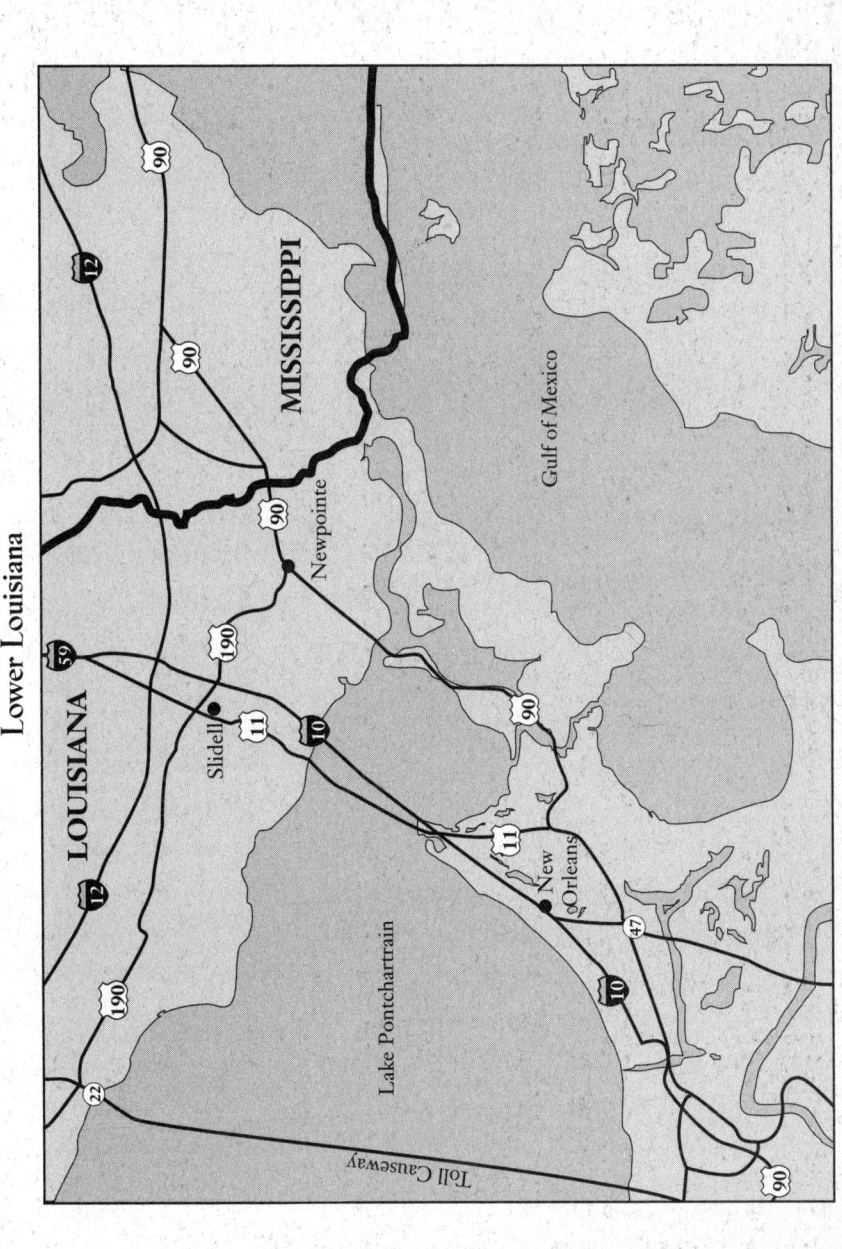

Newpointe, Louisiana

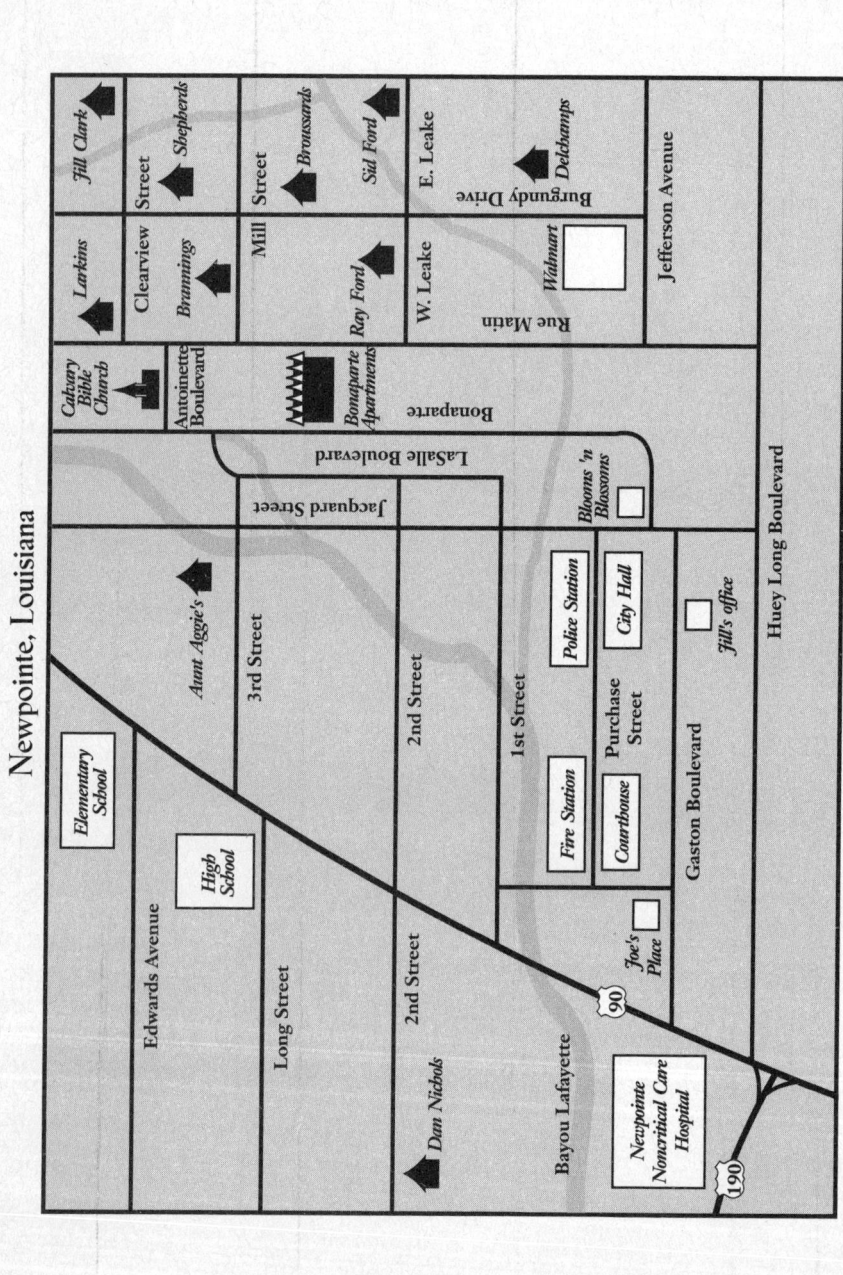

Acknowledgments

In March of 1996, my neighboring town of Jackson, Mississippi, was shaken to the core when one of our firemen walked into Central Fire Station and killed four district chiefs. He then wounded several other firefighters and a cop in his effort to get away. Shortly thereafter, police discovered that he had also murdered his wife.

The event was a tragic one for our community. A gaping hole was left in the Jackson fire department, and suddenly the town became aware of how important those men and women in our protective services can be.

It gave me the idea for the Newpointe 911 series, in which the close-knit community of firefighters, paramedics, and police officers in my fictitious town of Newpointe struggle together against the dangers that threaten their town. I wanted my readers to have a new appreciation for the individuals who make up these forces—individuals with families and friends and beliefs and values. Individuals who hurt and grieve and bleed like we do, but who must go on, because they've sworn to protect us. This series is a salute to those real individuals who live from emergency to emergency, and often put our lives before their own.

Thanks to my stepfather, Bill Weathersby, retired Jackson firefighter, who fought fires because it was what he loved to do. He gave me answers to many questions—both simple and complicated. I couldn't have written this if he hadn't been just a phone call away.

Also, thanks to Dr. Harry Kraus, who doesn't report me to the FBI when I ask him questions like, "How could I shoot a person in the head without killing him?" Being a novelist himself, he patiently talked me through the scenarios I needed to set my story up. I hope I can someday return the favor.

Thanks to my agent, Greg Johnson, for not putting money above the calling. How wonderful to work with someone who shares my vision.

Thanks to Mike Hoffman, Zondervan webmaster, who gave me a map of cyberspace and opened a whole new world of research for me.

And finally, a huge thanks to the best fiction team in publishing today—Dave Lambert, Lori Walburg, and Sue Brower—for their tireless work to make my books something we can all be proud of. I probably put us all through the wringer on this one!

Chapter One

The competing sounds of brass bands, jazz ensembles, and zydeco musicians gave Newpointe, Louisiana, an irresistibly festive atmosphere, but Mark Branning tried not to feel festive. It was a struggle, since he stood in a clown suit with an orange wig on his head, preparing to make the long walk down the Mardi Gras parade route. Already, Jacquard Street was packed with tourists and townspeople here to chase beads and candy being thrown by drunken heroes. In moments, he and his fellow firefighters, also dressed as clowns, would fall into their sloppy formation on the town's main drag, followed by the fire truck that carried even more painted firemen.

It was what promoters advertised as a "family friendly" parade—unlike the decadent bacchanalian celebrations in New Orleans, only forty minutes away. But Fat Tuesday was still Fat Tuesday, no matter where it was celebrated, and it always got out of hand. It was the time of year when the protective services in Newpointe had to be on the alert. Last year, during the same "family friendly" parade, a man had been stabbed, two women had been raped, and they'd been called to the scene of four drunk-driving accidents. It seemed to get worse every year.

Just days ago, Jim Shoemaker, police chief of the small town, and Craig Barnes, fire chief, had appealed to the mayor that the town was better served if their forces remained on duty on Fat Tuesday. Mayor Patricia Castor insisted that the community needed to see their emergency personnel having fun with everyone else. It fostered trust, she said, and made the men and women who protected the town look more human. At her insistence, and to Shoemaker's and Barnes's dismay, only skeleton crews were to remain on duty, while the rest of the firemen, police officers, and paramedics were to dress like clowns and act like idiots. "It's a religious holiday," she drawled, as if that sealed her decision.

Mark slung the shoulder strap of his bag of beads and candies over his head, and snickered at the idea that they would call Fat Tuesday a religious *anything*. The fact that it preceded Lent—a time for fasting and reflection as Easter approached—seemed to him a lame excuse for drunken revelry.

A police squad car pulled up beside the group of wayward firefighters, and Stan Shepherd, the town's only detective—still unadorned and unpainted—grinned out at him. "Lookin' good, Mark," he said with a chuckle.

"So how'd you get out of this?" Mark asked him, ambling toward the car. "I thought Newpointe's finest were supposed to dress like demonic bikers."

"Makes a lot of sense, doesn't it?" Stan asked with a grin. "Pat Castor wants us to show the town how human and accessible we are, so she makes us wear makeup that could give nightmares to a Marine."

"Hey, what can you say? It's Mardi Gras. You still haven't told me why you're not made up."

"Because I refused," Stan stated flatly. "How's that for a reason?"

Mark leaned on the car door and stared down at his friend. "You mean that's all it took?"

"That's all. Plus I read some statute to her about how it was illegal for someone out of uniform to drive a squad car."

"You're not in uniform, Stan."

"Yes, I am. I'm a plainclothes cop. This is my uniform." Stan looked past Mark to the others milling around, waiting impatiently for their chance to ruin their reputations. "Speaking of nightmares, check out George's costume."

"You talkin' 'bout me?" George Broussard asked, coming toward the car. Mark grinned at the Cajun's gaudy three-colored foil wig and the yellow and purple-polka dot shirt he wore. It was too little for him, and the buttons strained over his protruding gut. His hairy belly peeked out from under the bottom hem of the ill-chosen blouse, and someone had drawn a smiling pair of lips under his navel and crossed eyes above it.

"Yep. The stuff that bad dreams are made of," Mark agreed.

"Yeah, and you got lotsa room to talk," George returned. "Just 'cause you don't got the canvas I got to work with . . ." He patted his bare belly again, and Mark turned away in mock disgust.

Mark was glad he had lost weight since he and Allie had split up. The wives gleefully wielding the face and body paint were particularly cruel to those midlife paunches. His costume did, at least, cover all of his torso without accenting any glaring flaws, though he could have done without the flapper fringe that some sadistic seamstress had applied in rows to the polyester shirt.

"Is Allie gonna be here today?" Stan asked Mark.

Mark glanced at George, wishing Stan hadn't asked that in front of him. He hadn't broadcast the news of his separation from his wife and figured there were still some in town who didn't know about it. That suited him just fine. George, who had only been in Newpointe for the past year, wasn't a close enough friend for Mark to air his dirty laundry with.

As if he sensed Mark's discomfort, George wandered off and blended back into the cluster of clowns.

"How would I know what Allie's gonna do?" Mark asked.

"Don't give me that garbage," Stan said. "You keep closer tabs on your wife now than you did before."

"Estranged wife. I don't know if she'll be here. I doubt it. It's not her thing." He straightened, unwrapped a Jolly Rancher, and popped it into his mouth. "Then again, I did kind of think she might swallow some of her self-righteousness today to come help the wives paint us up. It's a power thing, you know. They love to make us look ridiculous. Allie's devoted her life to it."

"At least you're not bitter."

The barb hit home. "Bitter? Why should I be bitter? Actually, I feel great. I love my new bachelor life. Did I tell you that I picked up some great furniture at Kay Neubig's garage sale? Mid-century relics complete with the original stuffing coming out from the tears in the authentic vinyl. And my apartment has ambiance. The building's foundation is going, so the whole place slants. It's hard to keep gravity from pulling the kitchen cabinets open, and I worry a little when the train that comes by at two A.M. every night makes the building sway and vibrate—but like I said, ambiance. You know how I live for ambiance."

"So you're ticked about the apartment. Do you miss your wife?"

Mark was glad his face was painted so the heat moving to his cheeks wasn't apparent. Stan was a good friend, but he was crossing the line. He decided to change the subject. "Let's just say I'm aware that she's not here. I'm also aware that *your* wife isn't here. Why isn't Celia wielding a paintbrush today with the other cop wives?"

"Because we're boycotting the whole makeup idea. She's here. I'll pick her up when the procession gets up to Bonaparte, and she'll ride the rest of the way with me."

"I thought only uniformed cops could ride in the squad cars."

"She's dressed just like I am—in plainclothes." Stan grinned and winked, then put the car into drive and skirted the band and the motorcycles up ahead.

Mark turned back toward the firemen and saw George dancing to the jazz band. That face painted on his stomach gave him a comical double-decker look that had the women among them doubling over in laughter.

"If Martha could see you now!" one of the wives yelled.

"She will, darlin'," George said. "She's bringin' the baby. They're probably in the crowd as we speak."

"Poor kid," Mark muttered with a grin. "Only six months old, and he has to see a thing like this."

• • •

The noise of the sirens, revving motorcycles, and brass bands playing three streets over almost drowned out the screams of the six-month-old baby in the Broussard house, but Reese Carter, the old man who lived next door, pulled himself up from his little rolling stool in his garden and wondered why the baby's mother hadn't quieted him yet. The parents—George Broussard, a local fireman, and his pretty wife, Martha—were attentive, and he rarely heard the baby crying for more than a few minutes. But this had gone on since the parade had started—probably more than half an hour now.

Not one to intrude where he wasn't invited, he tried to mind his own business and concentrate on the weeds he pulled from his garden. He wished the parade would end, so that he could have peace again. The conflicting sounds of jazz and marching bands, drum corps from the high school, tapes playing on floats, and sirens blaring were making him wish he'd picked today to visit a relative out of town. But most of his people lived here in Louisiana, and he doubted there was a place in the state that was immune to Fat Tuesday.

Despite the parade noise, he could still hear the baby screaming. He pulled his gloves off with a disgusted sigh, trying to decide whether to go inside where he couldn't hear the baby's cries, or check to see if things were all right next door. His first instinct was to go inside, but then he remembered that last Christmas, after his wife died, when he'd expected to spend the day alone mired in self-pity, Martha Broussard had knocked on his door and invited him over to share Christmas dinner. He hadn't wanted to go—hadn't been in a festive mood and didn't want to pretend he was—but she had insisted. So he had gone, and several hours later he realized that the day was mostly over and he hadn't had time to feel sorry for himself.

If something was wrong next door now, he owed it to them to see if there was anything he could do. Maybe the baby was sick, and he could go to the drugstore for some medicine. Or maybe Tommy just had colic and couldn't be comforted, in which case Reese could show Martha some of the tricks that his wife had used on their children and grandchildren.

He dusted off his hands, then rinsed them under the faucet on the side of his house and dried them on his pants. He caught a faint whiff of smoke in the air. Someone must be breaking the city ordinance about burning limbs in their yard. Fat Tuesday seemed to give people license to do whatever they wanted, he thought with disdain as he headed down his driveway, cut across the Broussard yard, and trudged up the porch steps to the door. He rang the bell and waited. No answer.

Now that he was closer, he could hear that the baby wasn't just crying—he was screaming wildly. Reese leaned closer to the door and called, "Martha? Are you there?"

He knocked hard, hurting his arthritic knuckles, then raised his voice. "Martha! It's Reese Carter, next door. Martha, are you there?"

But all he heard in reply was the baby's gasping wails against the background of jazz music three blocks away.

• • •

The jazz band in front of Mark and the other firemen changed tunes, and some accordions launched into a zydeco tune. Trying to keep himself and the rest of the firemen in the spirit as they waited for their turn to march out onto the parade route, Mark led some of the others in an absurd chorus-line kick dance that fit perfectly with their attire. As he clowned, he scanned the other firemen and wondered how much beer they—and the rest of the parade participants—had already guzzled in the spirit of the festivities. It was only ten o'clock in the morning, yet trays and trays of drafts in plastic cups had been doled out to those waiting to participate.

Some of the wives still milled among the firemen, finishing up the outlandish makeup jobs. Jamie Larkins, with a cup of beer in one hand and an eyeliner pencil in the other, was swaying to the beat as she painted Marty Bledsoe's face. Susan Ford, a pretty black woman who wouldn't touch alcohol even if she were dying of thirst, finished Slater Finch's bare back—on which she'd drawn Betty Boop eyes and lips and applied a fake nose. She saw Mark horsing around and said, "You better stop that sweating, Mark Branning, you hear me?" The sweet demand cut through the laughing voices as Susan approached him with her makeup tray. "Look at you. Your smile is dripping. Our king of choreography is losing his looks."

"Me? Never," Mark deadpanned. "You may note that I have the least amount of face paint on. They knew not to mess with a good thing."

"Either that, or you already fit the bill without it."

Mark looked wounded. "Susan, you slay me. I believed you when you said I looked like George Clooney."

"Loony, Mark, not Clooney. And I never mentioned a George."

He grinned as she reached up with a tissue and wiped the smear from his mouth. "You're a mean woman, Susan Ford."

"You bet I am. And don't you forget it." Her smile faded as she touched up his face. "By the way, I saw Allie yesterday."

"Speaking of mean women?" he asked.

She wasn't amused. "She looked awful lonesome, Mark."

Again, he was glad that his face paint hid the heat rushing to his cheeks. He didn't know why every conversation these days seemed to lead directly to Allie. If Allie looked "lonesome," it was because she'd chosen to be alone. They'd been separated for over two months now, and although neither of them had made a move to file for divorce, there was no movement being made toward a reconciliation, either.

Susan seemed to realize she'd hit a nerve. Reaching up to press a kiss on his painted cheek, she whispered, "Sorry, honey. Didn't mean to bring you down."

"It's okay. No problem." A bone-thin majorette passed with a tray of beer, and he eyed it this time, wondering if he should drink just one to keep his mood from deflating completely. But Susan was there, as well as others from his church who would pass immediate judgment. He let the tray pass and wished the parade would hurry up and move so he could get the morning over with.

• • •

At Midtown Fire Station on Purchase Street, where all of Newpointe's protective services were located side by side, right across from city hall and the courthouse, Nick Foster paced the bunkroom and rehearsed his sermon for his little church's midweek service. It was tough being a bivocational pastor, juggling practical and spiritual duties. Sometimes it was impossible to separate his ministry from his profession. Today was one of those times. Whenever he dared to buck the mayor's authority and refuse to participate in something he believed to be immoral—as he had today—he risked losing his job as a fireman. Without it, he wouldn't make enough to pay his rent. Though Calvary Bible Church had its share of supporters, there weren't many families in the body who had much to give. Newpointe, as a whole, was not a wealthy town. Most of the tithes and offerings went to pay for the building they'd built two years ago, plus the missions projects he'd started. There wasn't much left over for him, which was fine as long as he had firefighting to keep his refrigerator stocked. He lived in a trailer across the street from the church. "The parsonage," his church called it, even though neither he nor the church owned it.

He got stuck on one of the points in his sermon, went back to his notes, made a quick change, then began pacing again. What did you tell a town whose residents had been brought up on voodoo and Mardi Gras? Even though he'd made it a point to preach a series of sermons on idolatry in the weeks preceding Mardi Gras, he was still astounded at the number of his church members who made themselves part of the infrastructure that upheld the holiday. Half of his congregation was in the parade, and the other half was watching.

He stumbled on the words again and sank onto a bunk, feeling more frustrated than usual. Did it really matter if he got the words right, if no one really listened?

Taking off his wire-rimmed glasses, he dropped his head and stared down between his feet for a moment, feeling the burden of all those souls weighing on his heart. Finally, he closed his eyes and began to pray that God would make him more effective, that he'd open their hearts and ears, that they would see things clearly . . .

He heard the door slam shut and looked up to see Dan Nichols, one of the other firefighters holding down the skeleton crew.

The tall blonde man was drenched in sweat and breathing hard, but to Nick's amusement, he went straight to the mirror and checked the receding hairline that seemed such a source of preoccupation to him.

"Has it moved any?" Nick teased.

Dan shot him an annoyed look. He slid the towel off of his neck and began wiping his face. "I wasn't looking at my hair."

Nick forced back his grin. Though he knew that he and Dan were considered two of the most eligible bachelors in town, Dan was by far the first choice of most of the single ladies. He was athletic and physically fit, something no one could say about Nick. And Dan had something else Nick didn't have. Money. Lots of it. He was one of the rare breed of firefighters who didn't have to work a second job to make ends meet. Dan had come from a wealthy family, had a geology degree, and could have been anything he wanted. But all he'd wanted was to be a fireman.

"You been out jogging?" Nick asked, a little surprised that he'd risk being away from the station when they were understaffed.

"I didn't go far," Dan said. "If we'd gotten a call, you would have seen me as soon as you pulled out."

"So is it crazy out there yet?"

"Gettin' loud, I'll say that." He dropped down on the bunk across from Nick, still panting. "You know—" He hesitated, as if carefully weighing his words. "I know it was right for us to take a stand and not participate in Mardi Gras, but part of me feels like a stick-in-the-mud."

"Sure, I know," Nick said. "It's just a parade, right? No big deal, just a day of fun that's no harm to anybody. Don't buy into that lie, Dan."

Dan grinned. "It's just that everybody's there. I'm human. I grew up on Mardi Gras. It feels weird not being part of it."

Nick fought his disappointment. "Tell you the truth, I was surprised you stood with me on this. Why did you?"

Dan patted his shoulder and grinned. "Because you're right. You know you are." He stood up. "I think I'll go take a shower."

The door opened again as Dan headed for the bathroom, and Craig Barnes, the fire chief, shot in.

"Hey, boss," Nick said. "Thought you were at the parade."

"Yeah, I'm going," he said. "I'm hoping to avoid the blasted makeup. You won't see Mayor Castor prancing down the street with floppy shoes and a big nose. No, she gets to ride in a convertible and hang on to her dignity, and she expects me to hoof it with a bunch of drunken firefighters whose goal it is to make this department the laughingstock of the town."

Nick thought of echoing the sentiment, but in this mood, he doubted Craig would appreciate it. The chief wasn't one to pal around with his subordinates. He rarely vented, but when he did, it was usually meant to be a monologue.

"Where's everybody, anyway?" Craig demanded as he went to his locker and pulled out his cap. "Don't tell me you're the only one here."

"Dan's in the shower, and Junior is sweeping out back. You know, Craig, if you didn't show up, it might make a nice statement."

"With all those other bozos falling all over themselves to be in the parade? Some statement. No, I've got to grin and bear it." He slammed the locker and started out. "If anybody calls looking for me, tell 'em I'm on my way."

"Sure thing," Nick said.

As the fire chief headed back out the door, Nick sighed. So much was being made of so little. The mania itself ought to be a wake-up call to those who made themselves a part of the custom.

But all he could do was preach and pray, and hope that someday, they would start listening.

• • •

The city employees' float, decorated like a pirate's ship, pulled into the street several positions in front of the firemen, cueing them that it was time to get into formation. Laughter erupted from some of the wives milling among the firemen, some already tipsy, others sober yet giddy as they prepared their husbands for the parade.

Lonesome, Mark thought with contempt. He couldn't say why Susan's description had ruined his mood.

He remembered another parade: the July Fourth parade last year, when Allie had been there among them, part of the fire family and the other half of himself. She had dressed like Martha Washington, and he'd been Uncle Sam. It had been a fun day, even in the sweltering heat.

He winced as Jamie Larkins, another fire wife, was swept away on a gale of raucous laughter. Cale, her husband, had been stealing sips from her draft, too, and Mark wondered if the effects would wear off before Cale went on duty tonight. He hoped so. A drunk or hungover firefighter was the last thing they needed on Fat Tuesday.

As the parade began to move, the brass band in front of them kicked into a newer, faster cadence and began dancing their way toward Jacquard Street. The firemen all looked at each other with comical dread before following. Some of them were jollier clowns than others, having been siphoning the beer that had been circulating like water since they'd gotten there that morning. It was the one day each year when the mayor footed the bill for something that wasn't an absolute necessity. Nick Foster, Mark's pastor, had protested the use of funds and asked her to spend it on much-needed bulletproof vests for the cops, a new pumper for the fire department, or updated rescue units for the paramedics. But as usual, she paid no attention.

Mark had considered taking Nick's stand and refusing to be in the parade, but part of him *wanted* to join in the fun, even though he'd voiced his righteous indignation just for the record. Part of him felt like a hypocrite—pretending to be spiritually offended by the parade even though, as everyone knew, he hadn't attended church since he and Allie had separated. It wasn't that he didn't want to—it was just that it was too uncomfortable with his wife there, all tense and cold, and with all of the members who had been his close friends offering advice that he neither needed nor wanted. If Mark had chosen to follow his pastor's lead, he was sure Nick would have used their time alone at the station to lecture him, again, about the mistake he was making in letting his marriage fail—as if that were his choice.

In a whirlwind of noise, the siren on the ladder truck behind them went off, and the motorcycles carrying the cops with faces painted like demonic rock stars roared louder. Another siren farther back, presumably from a rescue unit, moaned at migraine-level volume. Mark tried to shake himself out of the depression threatening to close over him; impulsively, he reached for one of the passing trays. He grabbed a draft and threw it back, then crushed the cup in his hand and dropped it to the ground. It did nothing to improve his mood, but he noticed Susan Ford and her husband, Ray—one of Mark's closest friends and the captain on his shift—watching him with sober, concerned faces. He wished they would both just mind their own business.

As the parade moved, the firemen scuffed onto Jacquard Street in their oversized shoes and undersized ruffled shirts, waving and tossing beads and candy to the cheers and pleas of hyperactive children and intoxicated adults, begging, "Throw me some beads!"

For the sake of goodwill in his community, Mark plastered on a smile and tried to have a good time.

Chapter Two

The baby's vibrato cries grew hoarse, but the level of urgency in his tone seemed to heighten as Reese Carter banged once again on Martha Broussard's door. Should he go around back? Maybe Martha was hanging laundry or working in the yard with one of those carry-around stereos with those despicable headphones that young people seemed to love these days. That wasn't like her, though. Martha wasn't that young, and she wasn't that irresponsible.

The smell of smoke grew stronger, and finally his fear that something was terribly wrong overcame his reluctance. He tested the knob, found it unlocked, and pushed the door open.

Feeling as if he were intruding in a place where he had no right to be, he stepped hesitantly inside. "Martha? Is anyone here?"

The baby's hoarse voice choked out louder and more desperately, so he headed down the hall to the baby's room.

Martha wasn't there. The baby's face was crimson and wet, and his eyes were swollen from the tears. It had been a long time since Reese had picked up a baby, and again he worried that Martha would think he was intruding, but something was obviously wrong. He leaned over the crib and lifted the baby out.

Tommy had been crying too hard to stop, so his pattern changed from screams to hiccup sobs as the old man rocked him. "Martha?" Reese called again.

He carried the baby back down the hall and peered into the living room. There was no sign of her, but a packed diaper bag lay on the floor, some of its contents spilled out. He stepped toward it, peering from the living room into the kitchen. "Martha?"

It was then that he saw the splatters on the blue carpet, the brownish-red spray that was easy to miss at first, then the darker red blotches. He caught his breath.

His heart began to pound painfully against his chest. The baby still cried, and Reese held him tighter as he followed the drops across the carpet and into the kitchen, toward the back door that stood open. His mind raced with possibilities. Maybe she had fallen and hit her head, then gotten up, confused, and wandered outside, where she had passed out in the yard.

He stepped carefully around the blood and pushed open the screen door.

The yard was filling with smoke, and he doubted that it was coming from someone burning tree limbs. He turned back into the kitchen and, with trembling hands, set the baby in the swing and locked the seat belt. As Reese stumbled outside, the baby began to wail again, but he couldn't go back. There was an old storage building at the back of the Broussard yard, and flames were shooting out of the roof.

The door to the structure was partially open, and thick smoke poured out. Coughing, he kicked the door open and tried to see inside. Between the lawn mower and a bicycle, he could barely make out the shape of a woman's legs.

"Martha!" Stomping out the flames over the threshold, he stepped in, reached for her feet, and pulled her out. It wasn't until she was out of the reach of the flames, lying on the grass, that he was able to see her face.

Martha Broussard had a bullet hole through her forehead.

Reese fell back in horror, then turned and ran, tripping on the step as he rushed into the house for the telephone. The baby kept screaming as he grabbed the phone and dialed.

"911, may I help you?"

He tried to speak, but the words choked in his throat. "Uh . . . yes . . . please, help. Martha . . . Martha Broussard . . . has been shot . . . and there's fire."

Clutching the telephone in his shaking hands, Reese gradually became aware of the raucous strains of "When the Saints Come Marching In" mingling with the screams of the baby whose mother lay dead.

Chapter Three

Stan Shepherd's wife Celia leaned out the passenger window of his squad car, tossing "What Would Jesus Do?" bracelets and gospel tracts to the frolicking onlookers as he drove slowly along the parade route. It had occurred to Stan that he could get fired for sharing his faith from a squad car. But he had decided to allow himself that freedom to make up for having to be in the parade in the first place. Besides, Celia wouldn't have taken no for an answer.

The roar and clash of the parade almost drowned out the radio call from Dispatch, but he heard the name Martha Broussard and just enough more to make his face go pale. He reached across the front seat for Celia's shoulder and pulled her back into the car. "Honey, you've got to get out."

"Why?"

"I've got a call. Possible homicide."

Celia got out, closed the door, and trotted alongside, asking through the open window, "Who was killed?"

He didn't want to alarm her—and besides, he still hadn't confirmed the identity of the victim—so he didn't answer. "I don't know how I'll get out of here," he said instead. His siren and lights were already on for the parade, so there was nothing he could do to let the crowds know he had a real emergency.

"Stan?" Celia asked again. "Who is it?"

"I don't know yet," he shouted over the noise. "Get back now. I have to find a way through."

Celia fell back, and he tried to inch his way to the side of the road—but there were people crowding the roadside. Up ahead, one of the motorcycle cops had heard the call and was turning his bike around and ordering people out of the way. He yelled something to the other cops in the parade, who stopped their parade maneuvers and skirted the side of the parade up to where the firemen clowned.

Up ahead, Stan saw the fire truck pull out of the line and make a path through the crowd toward an intersection that wasn't on the parade route. He wondered if anyone who'd heard the call had told George Broussard yet.

He picked up the radio mike and told the dispatcher he was on his way. As he inched his way through the crowd to the next intersection, where he could escape the parade route, he saw George Broussard standing stock-still in the middle of the parade, his face painted in a surreal smile and his belly poking out from under his shirt with a face painted on it. One of the cops straddled his bike next to George, shouting into his ear, breaking the news. George's face went slack as he reached up and pulled off the foil wig he wore, then spotted Stan in the approaching squad car and launched toward him.

The music played on, festive and upbeat, as the distraught fireman reached Stan's squad car and dove into the passenger seat. "My wife!" he cried.

"We're on our way, buddy," Stan said. Finally reaching the intersection, he stomped the accelerator.

• • •

At the Midtown Station, Nick Foster, Dan Nichols, and Junior Reynolds pulled the pumper out of its stall and raced to the address the dispatcher had given them. Something about Martha Broussard—had the dispatcher said she'd been shot?

Nick pulled on his oxygen tank and set the mask over his head as the truck approached the Broussard house. As the truck slowed and he leaped off, he prayed that Martha Broussard wasn't this year's first casualty of Fat Tuesday.

Chapter Four

The fire at the Broussard house had been small; the crew on duty had put it out quickly. In no time, the modest home had been converted into a crime scene. Yellow tape cordoned off the yard and the street for a block in either direction, and a handful of cops in clownwear came and went from the front door, most with smeared paint on their faces, since none had taken the time to remove it.

Mark Branning, still dressed in his flapper fringe and baggy ruffled pants, stood back among the firemen awaiting further instructions. None of the usual post-fire policies could be observed, since the blaze was connected with a shooting. The police department was in charge now.

Nick, who'd been one of the first firefighters to reach the scene, had told him that Martha Broussard had been found in the fire with a head wound from a gunshot. Two paramedics were still in the backyard—saving her life, Mark hoped, but as time passed and they didn't rush her out to the ambulance to be helicoptered to the hospital in Slidell, his fears rose that the news wasn't good.

The faces were sober as cops and crime photographers came and went from the house. The air was charged with smoke and apprehension.

"She's dead, don't you think?" Ray Ford asked him in a dull monotone.

Mark shook his head in sympathy. "Poor George. Who could have done this?"

"Could be anybody," Ray said. "We don't really know them that well."

That was true. The Broussards had lived in Newpointe for only a year. George had grown up here, but had lived in Monroe for most of his adult life. They had moved back to be closer to his aging parents. The fire department had accepted George's experience with wide-open arms, making him a shift captain. They had seemed like nice people—kept their yard neat, went to church, minded their own business . . .

But this murder changed everything.

"You don't think they was runnin' from somethin' when they come here, do you?" Ray asked him.

Mark glanced at him, surprised. "I thought Susan and Martha were friends. Wouldn't she know?"

"She thought the world of Martha. Loves that baby. She gon' be sick."

Mark stared back up at the house as Stan came out the front door, got behind the wheel of the car he'd driven in the parade, and radioed something in. The baby's cries grew louder, and Mark looked back at the front door. George stood in the foyer with that stupid clown shirt hanging open, his burly chest and the face on his belly exposed as he stared into space.

Mark wondered if Allie would be frightened when she learned that there was a killer on the loose. He thought of asking Stan if Martha was, indeed, dead, and if they knew who did it. But Stan was busy.

"I still say they was runnin' from somethin'," Ray Ford muttered. "George's got some enemy did this. Maybe a gamblin' debt."

"Does George gamble?"

"I don't know. But it makes sense."

Mark glared at the black man who was one of his closest friends. "Anybody ever tell you you watch too many movies? You don't even know if the man gambles, and you're convinced that his wife was murdered because of a gambling debt. If you leave here and tell *anybody* that, so help me, I'll strangle you."

Ray looked offended. "I ain't no gossip, Mark. I'm just sayin'—it looks a little suspicious."

"Hey—maybe George did it," Mark muttered sarcastically.

Ray's eyebrows shot up. "No! You don't think—"

Mark rolled his eyes. "Stop speculating, Ray. The man's wife was killed. That doesn't make him a gambler *or* a murderer, and it doesn't mean he was in the Witness Protection Program, and it doesn't mean he's an underworld spy. It's Fat Tuesday, and bad things *always* happen on Fat Tuesday. Leave it at that and let the cops do the detective work."

Ray bristled and ambled back to the fire truck.

Chapter Five

Allie Branning put the finishing touches on the last purple Mardi Gras centerpiece she had made for the Krewe of Janus Ball tonight at the Newpointe High School gym. Sweeping her blonde hair behind one ear, she checked her list to see which hospital arrangements she needed to do first. She couldn't make any deliveries until after the parade, because it cut through the center of town, making it impossible to get from her little flower shop, Blooms 'n' Blossoms, to the tiny noncritical care hospital on the other side of town. At least she could take consolation in the fact that the steady stream of customers she'd had yesterday had stopped, if only for the duration of the parade.

The bell attached to the front door clanged as someone came in, and she peered from the back room to the front. It was Jill Clark, her closest friend. "Come on back, Jill," she called. "I've got a ton of things to do. These Mardi Gras parties are killing me."

"Enjoy it and just *make* a killing," Jill said, purloining one of the peppermint sticks that Allie kept in a container beside the cash register. Peeling off the wrapping, she stuck the tip in her mouth and strolled to the back room. The candy gave her a youthful, pixie look that belied the fact that she was the most respected attorney in town. "You know, I think you're the only business in all of Newpointe that's open today," Jill said.

Jill was wearing jeans and tennis shoes rather than the usual dark suit that seemed to be her dress code in the courtroom.

Her short brown hair looked more relaxed and less polished than usual.

"Did you take off today?" Allie asked.

"Well, not really, but when no one made any appointments and court wasn't even in session, I figured I might as well kick back and take it easy. You want to have lunch?"

"Can't," Allie said. "Too many deliveries to make after the parade is over, and no help. I've called every part-timer who's ever worked for me, and they all considered it cruel and unusual punishment to make them work on Fat Tuesday. Last year, I had Mark to help me. But things were different then: Pat Castor didn't force the firemen to observe this oh-so-solemn religious holiday, and we weren't in the middle of a divorce—"

"Divorce?" Jill took the peppermint from her mouth. "Allie, you said that wasn't an option, that you didn't believe in divorce."

"Well, I've been thinking about it, and I've decided that it believes in me," she said, clipping the flower stems with a vengeance in the sinkful of water. "I have biblical grounds."

"What biblical grounds?"

"Adultery."

Jill stepped up to the table where Allie stood and touched her wet hands, stopping her work. Allie met her eyes.

"Allie, I know you. Biblical grounds or not—*adultery* or not—divorce will make your life worse, not better."

Allie held her gaze for several moments. Outside the shop, she heard the upbeat music of the parade passing by, children shouting and revelers laughing. She wondered if Mark was at the beginning of the procession or the end—and if he'd even give her a second thought as he passed the business they had built together.

"What choice do I have?" she asked Jill. "What am I supposed to do? There haven't been any grand gestures or any noble attempts to reconcile."

"From you *or* him," Jill pointed out.

"I'm the one who was wronged."

"You aren't even *sure* about that, Allie."

"Oh, I'm sure, all right. Jill, the ball's in his court, and he's not going to play it."

"Do you really *want* him to play it?"

"I don't know." She smiled sadly. "Maybe I just want to ram him in the head with it."

"He's a stubborn man," Jill conceded. "But I don't really think you want to lose him."

"I have already." Allie picked up a long-stemmed rose and tapped the white petals against her lips. They'd had white roses shaped in a cross as the centerpiece of their wedding, when they'd vowed to love each other until death. The death of what, she wondered now. "Problems can be worked out, but when your husband just stops loving you . . ."

Jill took the rose out of Allie's hand. "See, I don't think he really has stopped loving you. Not entirely. It's a miserable, unhappy man that I see walking around town these days. He covers it with jokes and barbs, and all that Branning sarcasm and charm, but there's a lot of pain in his eyes."

"He's not proud of our failure," Allie said. "Neither am I."

"Then don't fail."

Allie met her friend's steady, pull-no-punches gaze. Jill would never change.

The front door jingled again as someone came in. "Allie, are you here?"

Allie and Jill came out from the back room and saw Celia standing at the door, perspiring as if she had just run two miles, and gasping to catch her breath. Outside, the jazz of the parade mixed with jubilant shouts and motorcycle engines and horns honking. "Celia, what is it?"

"There's been a murder," she said, trying to catch her breath. "They're saying it's Martha Broussard."

Allie's eyes widened. "Really?"

Celia went to the small water tank and filled a paper cup with water. She took a drink, then tried to go on again. "The whole crew left. Cops, firemen, paramedics. The parade was gutted."

Allie looked at Jill, then back at Celia. "Celia, are you sure?"

"No," Celia admitted, "not about who the victim was. But Ray Ford told Susan that the call had been to the Broussard address, and that Martha had a gunshot wound. I'm telling you, it gets worse every year. I just hope Stan can figure out who did it before the creep gets away. All we need is to have a killer loose on the night of Fat Tuesday."

"Poor Martha," Allie whispered. "I can't imagine . . ." She looked at the other two women. "Did either of you know her very well?"

Celia shook her head. "I kept meaning to have them over."

"Yeah, me, too," Allie said. "But with Mark and me separated . . ."

"Maybe it's not too late. I'll hear from Stan as soon as he gets back to the station," Celia said. "Maybe she's still alive. You know how news can get distorted in this town."

A while later, Allie tuned to the Newpointe radio station as she returned from her deliveries. Details about the shooting were sketchy, but the announcer seemed certain that Martha had been murdered, that there were no leads on the killer, and that someone with a gun and a heart to kill was still roaming the streets. Allie drove back from the high school gym by rote, down Second Street, then right on Jacquard to Bonaparte. The parade was over, and broken beer bottles, cigarette butts, plastic cups, and confetti of every shape and color lined the streets. She pulled into the parking lot in front of Blooms 'n' Blossoms, turned off the van's ignition, and sat there for a moment.

She had never been one to enjoy being alone, and this murder wouldn't make things easier. As it was, she had trouble sleeping nights. Every creak in their old house, every whistle of the wind, every car that drove by woke her.

Tonight she'd probably be up all night, listening for killers.

Summoning the numbness that had anesthetized her for the past two months, she got out of the van and hurried in, tied her apron back on, and began to furiously design the last of the arrangements that had been ordered. If she could just keep busy, keep her hands working and her mind racing, keep her schedule full and hours packed, she wouldn't have to let the horror of the news sink in. She would finish the arrangements, make the deliveries, then come back and clean up here. The floor in the front of the shop needed mopping, and it was time to clean the bathroom, even though no one but employees ever used it. And those curtains in the windows were getting dusty. She should wash them tonight, then iron them and hang them back up. There was so much to do that it would be hours before she stopped hurrying and settled into the quiet. After that, maybe she'd be exhausted enough to sleep.

The telephone rang, startling her; she knocked a glass vase off her work table, and it shattered all over the floor. She stood still, staring down at the sharp fragments as if they formed a picture of her life blowing apart.

She made no move to answer the phone. She couldn't talk right now, not about Martha or George, not about murders or marriages, not even about parades or flowers.

Eventually, the phone stopped ringing, but she remained frozen. *I've got to move*, she told herself. *Got to keep busy. No time to think.*

But she *couldn't* move, couldn't organize her thoughts enough to clean up the glass or find another vase or arrange the flowers.

She heard the bell on the front door as someone came in, and she wished she had put the "Closed" sign out and locked the door behind her.

"Allie?"

Mark's voice startled her again, but there was nothing nearby to knock over.

"Allie, are you in back?"

"Here," she said, surprised at how hollow her voice sounded. "I'm here."

He came into the doorway.

"Stop!" she said. "You'll step on the glass. I broke a vase."

He looked down at the pieces all around her feet. She realized it must look odd to him, the way she just stood there, not making any attempt to clean it up, but she still couldn't manage to make herself move. "I . . . have so many deliveries to make. So many arrangements still . . . and now this."

She realized how absurd it sounded, as if in the course of her busy day a broken vase rated higher than a murder.

She made herself look at him, at the redness in his eyes and the remnants of white face paint around the edges of his unshaven face. He was wearing a pair of jeans and a pullover golf shirt. Despite the paint, he looked good—as good as he had when she'd first met him. And he stood silently looking at her, as if he had something to say but couldn't find the words. Looking away from those eyes that seemed to see straight into her, she tried to make a list. Get broom, sweep up glass, finish the arrangement, load the van . . .

As if he sensed her distress, he got the broom and the dustpan and began to sweep up the glass. She stayed where she was, watching him empty the dustpan into the trash, then come back for a second round of sweeping. "There," he said quietly. "No harm done."

She nodded like a robot. "Thank you."

He regarded her carefully. "You heard about Martha Broussard, didn't you?"

She nodded again. "How is George?"

"Not too good. You're not either, are you?"

She felt her face flushing and reached for another vase. "All this business about murder," she said. "It's just shaken me a little."

"I thought you might be afraid." He got the vase and held it under the sink, filled it halfway with water. He set it back down in front of her.

She began to stick the flowers in the vase, with no regard for color or symmetry.

She looked down at her watch, but the time didn't register. "I have to get back to the high school. They're already decorating for the Krewe of Janus Ball. I've taken one load over there already. They're probably waiting."

"I thought you'd decided not to sell to them. Idol worship, you said, since Janus was a mythical god and all."

She might have known that he'd throw her words back in her face. "I had to do it anyway," she said. "I needed the money. It's not easy maintaining two households. You said you were going to boycott Mardi Gras," she told him. "Guess neither of us is too good at following our convictions."

"Or keeping our commitments."

Her eyes whiplashed up to his as she wondered how he dared make a comment like that when *he* was the one who had broken his vows. "Like I was saying," she bit out, "they're waiting for me at the high school."

"The Krewe can wait, Allie. I need to talk to you."

Not today, she thought. *Not now.* The last thing she wanted was to cry in front of him.

He rubbed his face and took a deep breath, but kept his eyes on the floor. "I was wondering something, Allie. I was wondering if you would go to the funeral with me."

She felt transparent and wondered if he saw the million conflicting emotions battling on her face. "Why?" she asked. Though the question seemed confrontational, Allie couldn't help asking it. Did he want her with him for image control—so people who didn't already know about their breakup wouldn't find out now?

He swallowed. "I just thought we could put our differences aside for George's sake. And . . . well, it's not going to be an easy day."

Maybe he needed her, she thought. He was certainly closer to George than she was to Martha. But that idea raised questions.

"Is she going to be there?"

"Who?" he asked in a flat voice, but she didn't doubt for a moment that he knew.

"Isabelle Mattreaux. Oh, that's right. You call her Issie." She said it so bluntly that she surprised even herself. For so long, they had talked *around* the name, as if uttering it would somehow unleash things that were better left contained.

He looked slightly indignant. "Everybody calls her that. And I would imagine she'll be there. The whole town will be there. What difference does it make?"

She tried to think. *Did* it make a difference if she was there? Wouldn't Allie go anyway? Would she rather be *with* Mark or *without* him when she faced her? Would she rather look like the independent, strong woman who'd gone on with her life, or the wife who still hadn't quite let go?

Mark watched the struggle on her face. Finally, he said, "Never mind, Allie. Just forget it. I thought it would be nice if we went together, for George's sake, but never mind." He started for the door.

For a moment she thought of letting him go, but something told her that, if she did, it would become one more thing to add to her list of regrets.

"Mark?"

"What?"

"I'll go with you."

He swung around. "Don't do me any favors, Allie."

"Do you want me to go, or not?"

"Yes! That's why I came here. That, and to see if you were all right. To tell you to lock up carefully, and not answer the door if you don't know who it is."

The tears that had threatened her, that she had managed to hold at bay, pushed into her eyes now. She turned away and closed her eyes, pressing her tear ducts to keep her tears from falling.

He stepped slowly back into the room.

"Do they know who did it?" she asked, not sure if real curiosity triggered the question or if she was merely trying to get the focus off her feelings for Mark. "Do they have any idea?"

"No. There are very few leads." His words were delivered in a soft monotone, all business. "We know that it wasn't a forced entry. Her back door was wide open, and the killer probably just came in through the unlocked screen. He didn't take anything, so robbery isn't the motive, and there was no rape. They took fibers and prints and blood samples, and they're all at the crime lab now."

"So there's somebody out there who could walk in and shoot a woman in the forehead for no good reason."

"Probably somebody who came to town for Mardi Gras. The whole holiday seems to bring out the absolute worst in society. Wouldn't bother me if Newpointe refused to celebrate it."

"We'd be evicted from the state of Louisiana."

He shrugged sarcastically. "A murder here, a rape there—small prices to pay to boost the economy."

She wasn't amused, but she knew he didn't mean for her to be.

"Well, I'll let you know if they find out anything. And we'll make firmer plans when the time for the funeral is set."

She nodded. "Yeah, okay."

He gazed at her a little longer, then finally looked away. "Are you gonna be all right?"

"You know me," she said without much feeling. "I'm always all right."

He started to respond to that, then stopped himself. Finally, he said, "Keep everything locked, okay? Even the shop. I'll lock up on my way out and put out the 'Closed' sign. You have enough to do without any new customers today, anyway."

She nodded agreement. "Are you on duty tonight?"

"Unofficially. It's not my shift, but I'm gonna go in and help out for a while. We're expecting a little more activity tonight."

They held each other's gaze for a moment longer, and finally, Mark headed out of the shop.

As she heard him locking the door, Allie sank down onto her stool and covered her face with her hands.

Chapter Six

As expected, the 911 lines stayed lit up the evening of Fat Tuesday as brawls broke out in barrooms and drunk drivers rammed trees. Some addict on PCP tried to fly from a two-story building and wound up breaking his back and both legs. A group of pot-smoking teenagers gathered leaves and sticks to start a campfire in the elementary school's playground, only to find that the wind was too strong and caught the school on fire. The firefighters had put out the fire before too much damage was done, while the police dispatched to the scene had arrested the youngsters and the paramedics had treated them for smoke inhalation and a few minor burns. Almost every call required a collaborative effort among the town's emergency teams, and tonight, they were all hopping.

But none of the emergency personnel in Newpointe wanted to answer these emergency calls when there was a killer on the loose. Every one of them wanted to be out searching the town for the man who had killed Martha Broussard.

Since Mark wasn't officially on duty, he left the station just after ten and headed to the bar a couple of blocks away, where many of the cops and firemen hung out after work. It was unusually crowded as the Fat Tuesday-ers crushed in to celebrate. Their cigarette smoke left a haze over the room, and the low roar of voices competed with the jazz band playing in the corner.

There had been a time when Mark had hated this place. But then he and Allie had begun having problems, and he'd dreaded going home. He had started coming here after work with Cale

Larkins, one of the firemen on his shift. He hadn't come to drink—he'd always gotten a soft drink while his buddies indulged in their choice of spirits. Now, looking back, he couldn't remember exactly when he'd made the transition from Sprite to vodka, but it had happened some time after he and Allie split up. Now his visit to Joe's Place was almost a nightly event.

He took a stool at the bar and looked around. Some of the off-duty cops sat at a table, probably talking about the murder. He wondered if they'd learned anything about the killer yet.

Joe Petitjean, the proprietor, pointed to him. "Where y'at, Mark?" It was the typical Cajun greeting, and even non-Cajuns like Mark responded appropriately.

"Awright," Mark said. "Vodka, straight up. Double."

Joe turned back, unfazed, and poured the drink. "Was you at the Broussard's house today when they found her?" he asked, leaning across the counter to be heard when he handed him the drink.

"Yeah," he said.

"Ever'body's talkin'."

"Anybody saying who could have done it?" Mark asked.

"Not yet. No leads, what I hear."

Joe went back to work, and Mark swiveled on his chair and scanned the patrons. He sipped on his vodka, let the liquid burn down his throat, and told himself that soon he wouldn't be thinking about the murder or his marriage, or any more of a million things that could keep him awake nights.

The door opened and cool air spilled inside, providing a little relief from the smoke. He glanced over his shoulder and saw Issie Mattreaux coming in with two girlfriends. She saw him immediately, said something to her friends, and started toward him.

She wasn't in uniform, the way he usually saw her, and in her jeans and sweater she looked almost like a teenager. Her nickname suited her well. No one could ever call her Isabelle with a straight face. Her silky black hair hung straight to her shoulders, and she wore a small barrette on one side to hold it back from her face. But around her eyes were tiny lines, lines that belied her youthful look and gave away the fatigue and worry on her face since the murder. He wondered if Allie would still be threatened if she could see Issie now.

She came up behind him, set a hand on his back, and leaned around him to Joe. "Give me a Diet Coke, Joe," she said.

Mark lifted an eyebrow and looked back at her. "Diet Coke? On Fat Tuesday?"

She knew him well enough to know that his question was sarcastic. "I'm not in the mood to drink," she said, pulling up onto the stool next to him. She nodded at the glass in his hand. "I see you are, though."

He grinned. "Whatever gets you through the night."

She turned so that she was facing him, and asked, "You okay?"

"Sure, why?"

"Well, it was a rough day. Martha and everything . . ." Her voice trailed off. "I saw your car at the florist this afternoon. Is Allie all right?"

"I guess." He looked down at the bar and tried to rub a spot off the wood. He knew she wasn't really concerned about Allie's state of mind. More likely, she just wanted to get the scoop on what had happened between them today. But he couldn't blame her—before his separation from Allie, he'd accommodated that curiosity plenty.

"So . . . are you two trying to work things out?"

It annoyed him that she would ask such a thing.

"You don't have to answer if I've hit a nerve," she said, starting to get up. "I know it's none of my business."

"No, that's not it," he said. "I mean . . . I'd talk about it if I had any answers. I just don't."

He felt her gaze on him, but he didn't dare meet it. He had managed to keep his distance for the past few weeks, even though he saw her frequently at the fire station. But he kept her at arm's length, didn't look her in the eye, and avoided any heartfelt conversations that he'd feel guilty about later.

"Has either of you filed for divorce?"

He shook his head. "I don't believe in divorce."

"Just separation?"

He rubbed his eyes. "No, I don't believe in that, either. But sometimes you don't have a choice."

"Are you still going to counseling?"

He knew he should never have told her about that in the first place, but she had been there when no one else had, and he'd needed to talk. "No. When she threw me out, she refused to go back. Said I wasn't being honest and it was a waste of time." He took a gulp of his drink, then grinned up at her, trying to shift the conversation away from such serious matters. "Speaking of wasting time, can we talk about something else?"

"Honest about what?" she asked, ignoring his question as she sat back down.

He couldn't tell her that it was all about her, but he knew she realized it. That was why she questioned him so hard. She wanted him to state the obvious, so that their relationship—or whatever it was—could move to a higher level.

Either that, or she was just genuinely interested in seeing him reunite with his wife.

Yeah, right.

"You don't really care about this. It's too sad for a stand-up act and too boring for a country song."

"Come on, Mark," she said, leaning toward him. "It's me you're talking to. What did she think you weren't being honest about?"

He turned away from her and scowled, frustrated. He didn't like being put on the spot. "Got me."

She leaned forward on the bar and took a sip of her drink, pondering what he'd said. He glanced up at her, saw her expression. "What?" he asked. "You have something on your mind. What is it?"

She shook her head. "Just something I've wanted to ask, but haven't had the nerve." Their eyes locked. Was this where he was supposed to tell her to go ahead and ask? No, no need. She would find the nerve somewhere.

"Mark, this may come out sounding like a real arrogant question, and if it does, then I'll just have to look like a jerk."

"You should become an ambassador, Issie. You're the queen of diplomacy. All those great lead-ins ... I want to ask, but I don't have the nerve ... this may come out sounding real arrogant, *but* ... I can hardly wait for what all these lead-ins are leading up to."

"It's about Allie," she said, ignoring his sarcasm—which she had said she found charming anyway. "I've run into Allie a few times, and I feel a little bit of a chill from her, and I was wondering ..."

His stomach tightened, and he brought the glass to his lips, seeking the burn it could bring.

"Mark, are you sure your breakup doesn't have anything to do with our friendship?"

"Are you kidding?"

She frowned. "Mark, I'm serious."

He set the glass down hard, and Issie jumped. Mark took a deep breath, trying to calm himself, then looked her in the eye. Lowering his voice so they wouldn't be overheard, he said, "My wife caught me with my arms around you in the bunk room at the fire station. She drew a conclusion—a mistaken one, but it had some pretty serious repercussions."

"But the breakup came weeks later, and you said it had nothing to do with me."

"I lied. I didn't want you to feel bad, when nothing really happened."

"She should have trusted you enough to know that. Even I know you better than that."

He looked into his glass, recalling how Issie had cried on his shoulder about being jilted by her pseudofiancé. He had closed the door so she could cry in private, and they had sat on the bunk while she bared her soul to him. She'd told him he was her best friend, the only one she trusted, and when she'd been overcome with emotion and grief, he had held her to let her cry.

So much for being a nice guy.

Just his luck that Allie had surprised him with a visit to the fire station, that the other guys had innocently directed her to the bunk room, that she had walked in on that little scene. He had tried to explain, but she wasn't interested in explanations. Only in what she thought she had seen.

The fact that Issie seemed so concerned now galled him. She hadn't cared that much at the time.

"I could talk to her," Issie said. "I mean, if it would help."

He almost laughed. "Trust me. Having you call Allie is the fastest way I can think of to get the divorce wheels turning. Allie would turn the wheels, and they'd run right over me."

"Don't worry, Mark. I'd be there to rescue you."

He met her eyes and saw that she meant exactly what he thought she did. Something about that pleased him.

The door opened, and several other off-duty firemen spilled in and made a beeline for him. *Talk about rescue*, he thought. They just might be rescuing him from himself.

Chapter Seven

Jamie Larkins was already nursing a hangover at 10:30, about the time most of the town was getting their second wind. She was also cursing herself for getting ripped so early in the day. She took two Tylenol and tried to sleep. It had occurred to her that she could keep drinking—even that she should, since she planned to give up alcohol for Lent tomorrow and needed to get the partying out of her system—but the murder had doused her plans. Her girlfriends who had planned to go out partying with her tonight after Cale reported to work had all backed out, mostly out of fear because a murderer was on the loose.

She went to her purse and dug out the vial of cocaine, and with a great sigh dropped it into a drawer in the end table next to the couch. She had hoped to talk Cale into sharing it with her tonight, even though he was so paranoid about random drug testing and losing his job. But she knew that he liked a good time as much as she did, and with the right coaxing, he would come around. It didn't matter now, though, since he'd had to work and she felt too lousy right now to waste it.

Unable to sleep, she sat on her bed and turned on the television with the remote control. She combed her fingers through her hair to pull it out of her eyes and flipped channels until she came to channel 4, a New Orleans station doing a live broadcast from Bourbon Street. The reporter seemed to be living it up himself, and in the background drunken, laughing partyers crowded in behind him while music from street musicians kept the mood upbeat.

If Cale hadn't had to work tonight, the two of them would be there now, right in the middle of things as they had been so many times before. Mardi Gras was her favorite time of year, and the Southshore—New Orleans—was her favorite place to celebrate it. That far from home—over forty miles—they needn't worry about his reputation as a public servant. Besides, she knew they wouldn't be doing drug testing for a while yet, since they had just tested Cale's shift last week.

But Cale had wound up working tonight, and her friends had all backed out. She couldn't believe she was sitting at home alone on Fat Tuesday. The phone call they'd shared half an hour ago was no substitute for his being here.

She picked up the phone and dialed the number of the fire station, hoping Cale was available and would have a minute to talk. The phone rang unanswered, and she guessed they were out on a call.

She hung up the phone and leaned back on her pillows, watching longingly as the television cameras zoomed in on Pat O'Brien's, where revelers in bawdy costumes brandished Hurricanes in their trademark glasses. As she watched the cameras pan the French Quarter, she heard a noise in the living room. She sat up, wondering if Cale had sneaked away and come home to check on her, or if he, too, was feeling so hungover that he'd convinced someone from another team to swap shifts.

She cut off the television and listened. "Cale? That you?"

There was no answer, and a chill of apprehension shivered down her back. But then her cat came strolling in and leaped up on her bed. Relieved that the noise hadn't been an intruder, she reached for the cat. She could have sworn she had let him out, but with her hangover and pounding headache, she had probably forgotten letting him back in.

She heard a sound again. Her hand stilled on the cat's back, and she felt its fur rise. "Cale?" she called again. "Cale, this isn't funny."

"No, it's not funny." The voice was not Cale's, and she screamed and grabbed the empty beer bottle on her bed table.

The man was hidden in the shadows of the hallway as the first shot rang out, shattering the bottle in her hands. The second hit her in the chest, knocking her back against the headboard.

Fog closed over her as she struggled to catch a breath. Her last grasp of awareness was the smell of diesel fumes, but she was powerless to move or escape the death that had come to take her before she was ready.

Chapter Eight

The A Shift had just returned to the station from a wreck on Bonaparte, one that hadn't really required their help, when the alarm sounded again. Still dressed in their fire gear, they headed back to the pumper, listening to the dispatcher's orders as they took their places.

"Fire reported at 1302 Clearview Street . . . a neighbor reports that someone may be in the house . . ."

Cale Larkins reacted immediately. "That's *my* house, man!"

Though they would have hurried for any call, the team made a special effort to screech out of the firehouse and fly to the scene.

"Is Jamie at home?" Nick asked, leaning forward in his rear seat as he slipped on the shoulder strap for his oxygen tank.

"I think so," Cale shouted. "She was when I called around ten. What if she's in there? What if she's sleeping?"

"Take it easy," one of the guys yelled over the siren. "She'll probably have the fire out by the time we get there."

• • •

Mark and Issie heard the sirens heading past the bar, and instinctively they threw down their tab and hurried out to the parking lot. Mark had a scanner under his dashboard and turned it on to listen as Issie stood at the driver's side door. The dispatcher was still giving orders to the cops on duty. "Clearview Street," Mark said. "I'm going."

"Me, too." She jumped in, and he pulled out of the parking lot and headed in the direction the trucks had gone.

Mark flew, and they caught up to the trucks and pulled up to the curb right behind the pumper. With a shock, Mark realized that it was Cale's house. By then, one side of the house was dancing in flames, and that side of the roof was engulfed. Cale leaped from the pumper before it had stopped completely and bolted inside. Mark slipped on his bunker coat and tank, which lay on the back seat of his car, and followed Cale as the rest of the crew unwound the hose and began dousing the flames.

"Jamie!" Cale shouted as he ran from room to room. "Jamieeee!"

He headed for the bedroom, which was black with smoke and popping with flames, and Mark knew that nothing in that room could have survived.

Cale screamed his wife's name as he bolted into the bedroom, and the anguished wail that followed shook the house even more than the flames. Mark rushed in after him. Cale had found his wife and was rolling her in the bedcovers to smother the flames. When they were out, he lifted her and carried her from the house.

The ambulance was there, as were several squad cars, and Issie ran up the walk with the other two paramedics to take Jamie from his arms. They laid her on a gurney and unrolled the blanket, but her burns were so severe that she was nearly unrecognizable.

"Do something!" Cale screamed. "She's not dead! She can't be dead!"

But Mark could see from Issie's strained face that she was. "Cale . . . I'm sorry. . . ."

"No she's not!" he screamed again. "Do—" He gestured hopelessly. "Something!" He reached for his wife and lifted her up. Her hair was seared and her skin was charred, but as he crushed her against him, Mark saw the blood soaking her back.

"Issie," he said, and she, too, saw the exit wound the bullet had made.

"Oh, no," she whispered.

Chapter Nine

The house at 1302 Clearview Street was handed off from the fire department to the police department and marked as a homicide scene. Stan Shepherd, the detective who had been the first cop on the scene at the Broussard house earlier that day, stepped through the wet, smoldering rubble of the bedroom, looking for empty shells or lodged bullets, while in the part of the house that hadn't burned, others dusted for prints and vacuumed the carpet for possible hair follicles.

As the only detective on the Newpointe police force, Stan considered this second murder to be a personal failure. If he'd caught the guy who'd killed Martha earlier today, Jamie would still be alive. But Stan had mistakenly assumed that the killing was an isolated event.

He picked up some of the charred wood from the wall and smelled it. The faint scent of diesel confirmed how the fire had started. From the evidence they'd already collected, he knew there was a psychopath out there somewhere with a .38, a can of gasoline, and a deadly intent that could not be predicted. He was glad Celia had gone to stay with her Aunt Aggie tonight. He didn't want either of them to be alone.

He heard Cale wailing in the yard and cursed the fact that a homicide investigation called for such cruelty. He would rather have let the ambulance take Jamie Larkins away, but instead, they had to leave her there, in the front yard where the paramedics had put her, until they'd recorded all of the evidence.

And Stan knew that Cale wouldn't leave—not until the medical examiner came to remove her body from the scene.

"The two women were friends," Jim Shoemaker, the police chief who had just gotten to the scene, said. "This can't be a coincidence."

"No," Stan said. "No coincidence. Can't be."

"Stan?" Officer Anthony Martin called from the living room, which hadn't entirely burned. Though everything had been damaged by smoke and water, most of the living room was still intact.

"Yeah," Stan asked.

"I just found something you might want to see."

Stan stepped through the wet, smoldering rubble, and Jim followed, until they were back on the smoke-stained carpet. Anthony showed them the vial full of white powder still lying in the drawer of an end table.

Stan frowned. Cale liked to drink, but he wasn't a druggie. If he had been, he could never have kept his job at the fire department. They had random drug testing every few weeks. Cale had never had a trace of it in his system.

Jamie, on the other hand, had been through drug rehab a couple of years ago. Apparently, she'd slid back into her old habits.

"Tag it," Jim said. "That just might be the key to what's going on here."

"What?" Stan asked. "You think it was a drug deal gone bad?"

"Might be."

"But what about Martha Broussard? You don't think *she* was buying coke."

"No telling."

"No way," Stan said. He went to church with the Broussards, and there wasn't a doubt in his mind that George and

Martha were both devout believers. "Not Martha. Jim, you knew her."

"Not that well, Stan. There's got to be a connection. Maybe Martha knew something. Maybe she saw something. Maybe Jamie told Martha something she wasn't supposed to, and somebody had to shut them both up."

"A lot of speculation; no real evidence."

"We have to start somewhere."

Stan looked around him as the other cops took pictures and videos and collected what evidence they could find amid the soggy, charred rubble. "I don't know, Jim. But I do know that whoever it is has got to be found, and fast."

"We've already called in every cop in town to set up road-blocks."

"It's Fat Tuesday, man. All we're going to find is a bunch of drunk drivers and dopers, and we'll be backed up until November with paperwork to process."

"Can't help it. We can't let 'em go."

"No, we can't. And maybe we'll find him." He looked through the damaged wall into the front yard. Ray Ford, Mark Branning, Craig Barnes, Dan Nichols, Nick Foster, and the others were clustered around Cale, trying to keep him calm as two cops questioned him.

"Yeah, if he's a tourist, we'll catch him in the roadblocks," Jim said.

"And what if it wasn't a tourist?" Stan asked quietly.

Jim looked up. "No way," he said.

The men locked eyes briefly. If it wasn't a tourist, then the person who had done this was someone from Newpointe, someone they all knew. Unable to deal with that possibility, Stan turned and continued sifting through the rubble.

Chapter Ten

Mark Branning felt as though he hadn't slept in days. The combination of alcohol and murder had seeped the energy right out of him, and if there had been an extra bed at the station, he would have stayed and slept there tonight. But the shift was fully staffed, and it seemed that all of the firemen felt as he did, though many of them had grumbled about the futility of trying to sleep on a night when Newpointe seemed to be at its worst.

At three A.M. he was too tired to stay and help out anymore, but the unease in his soul made him dread going home to his barren, lonely apartment. With finances so tight now that he and Allie were maintaining two separate homes on already meager incomes—and because he'd originally thought it would only be temporary—he'd furnished the apartment with just a twin bed, a forty-year-old couch that someone had been about to throw away, a couple of chairs, and a half-dozen cardboard boxes that served as end tables, cupboards, and ottomans.

The bar usually provided a comfortable transition between the depression following a long shift and his lonely return to the apartment, but in the wee hours of the morning, he wasn't in the mood to return to that smoke-filled room and all the noise and gossip.

The truth was, he longed for his real home, the home he'd shared with Allie. It was a tiny little house, only two bedrooms, one bathroom, a kitchen, and a den, but it had been all they could afford on a fireman's salary and the pittance they got from the florist shop after all the bills were paid. It had been the most desirable place on the planet for him at one time, though, because of Allie's knack for decorating. Flowers and plants bloomed all over the house, casting a pleasant and soothing scent. The furnishings, too, though inexpensive, were inviting and comfortable; they had saved for years to buy them. He supposed that, if their marriage ended in divorce, they would find some way of dividing the spoils, but for now, he'd chosen to leave them in their home. He didn't know why, since the separation had been Allie's idea. He should have taken at least half of what they'd accumulated together. But Allie was more materialistic, and she would probably fight tooth and nail for the things she had coveted for so long. He just wasn't up for that kind of fight.

Still, he missed the house, the things they'd filled it with—and worst of all, he missed his wife. He didn't like that, didn't want to acknowledge it. But having seen George grieving over Martha and Cale mourning over Jamie, he'd felt a sick void in his heart, a smothering despair.

What if he'd answered a call to his own house and found his own wife shot to death and surrounded by flames?

Suddenly he wanted to see her, despite the hour. He wanted to touch her and talk to her, tell her about Jamie, make sure she was all right.

He headed out the back room of the fire station and pushed through the kitchen door on his way to the parking lot—then stopped dead in his tracks. Issie was hunched in a chair in the corner of the kitchen, still wearing blue jeans and that teenager blouse she'd been wearing earlier, but there was blood and soot on it from Jamie's body. She looked tiny sitting there, staring off into space, her skin pale and her eyes vacant.

"Issie?" he asked. "Are you all right?"

She looked up at him and managed to nod. "Yeah. I was just thinking."

"About what?"

"I was thinking . . . what a horrible way to die."

Her eyes were dry, though clearly distraught. He stepped toward her. "Why don't you go home? Get some sleep?"

"I'm a little scared," she whispered.

He could understand that. As soon as the town found out about the second murder, there would probably be a panic among all of the women of Newpointe.

"Look, I'll be glad to follow you home, if you want. Make sure you get into your apartment all right."

"Would you?" she asked, looking hopefully up at him with tear-filled eyes that had a little too much power over him. She reached for his hand.

He knew he should have recoiled and stepped back out of her reach. This was how it had started before—tears, need, a touch . . .

His marriage was ending over it.

But he didn't disengage his hand.

"I mean, I can do it alone," she whispered. "I just . . . this has kind of got me strung out. You know, like there's a murderer lurking in every shadow . . ."

"Come on," he said, pulling her to her feet.

She grabbed her bag, and he walked her out into the night. The stars were brilliant, as was the moon, lending a false sense of security to the night.

"My car's still at Joe's Place," she said. "Will you walk me over?"

He walked her across the street to her car, opened the door for her, and locked it before he closed it. Then he trotted back across the street and got into his own.

His mind raced as he followed her the few blocks to her apartment. He had avoided this in the past, worried that getting this close to her home might be too tempting. Tonight was an exception, though—any of the guys at the station would have wanted to watch out for her. It was a Good Samaritan thing, he told himself. Not a lust thing.

She parked in the parking space in front of her apartment, and Mark got out of his car to walk her up to her door. She locked her car carefully, then looked nervously up at him and headed for her door.

He walked a step or two behind her. Wanting to look at her in the moonlight, he forced himself instead to walk with his hands in his pockets and his head cast down—just a good guy doing his masculine duty to protect the fairer sex. She stopped when she reached the door and unlocked it, then turned back to him. "Mark, come in for a few minutes. We could have a drink and talk . . ."

It seemed so innocent, so tempting. Just a few minutes in a warm apartment, talking with a good friend over a glass of wine that would relax him and help him to sleep later . . .

But something inside him resisted. Until now, he'd denied Allie's accusations of being involved with Issie by insisting that nothing had ever happened between them. And until now it had been true. But if he stepped through that door . . .

"I can't," he said, wishing he could. "I need to go."

She looked up at him, her doleful eyes meeting his, and for a moment, he wished she'd coax him, persuade him, ask him one more time. They were both lonely, and it had been a traumatic day. What could be more natural than two people who'd shared such experiences winding down together and talking things over?

"I'm not going to beg, Mark," she said softly. Silence passed as she waited, and he waited, thinking, weighing, wondering . . . Finally, she sighed, releasing him from the decision. "Thanks for following me home," she said matter-of-factly, breaking the mood.

Deflated by the disappointment that she hadn't tried harder, he said, "Sure. Lock up good, okay?"

She nodded and went in, closing the door between them.

He stood in the darkness for a moment, his heart pounding, wondering what he had let slip through his fingers—then wondering what he had escaped.

Allie. I need to see Allie.

The irrational need drew him back to his car, and the soul-deep fatigue and confusing emotions made him sit and stare out the windshield for a moment. He didn't know what he wanted tonight, didn't know where he belonged.

But as he cranked the car and pulled back out into the street, he drove by rote to his own home, where Allie lived, where things had once seemed so secure and so clear, where he'd known right from wrong and love from hate and security from fear.

He pulled into the driveway, turned off the ignition, and sat still for a moment, wondering what he would say when he woke Allie up and she came to the door. Would he tell her about Jamie? Or could he somehow put that off until morning, and just convince her to let him stay here where he could make sure she was safe, where he could *feel* safe, not from the killer, but from the world that seemed to be tugging at him, tearing him apart?

He didn't know, and didn't wait for answers. He made his way to the side entrance, pulled open the screen door, and rang the bell. He still had the key and knew that he could just go in, but he had to offer her some degree of respect since they were no longer living as man and wife.

He knocked. Knowing she was probably afraid to answer or to even call "Who is it?" he leaned close to the door and said, "Allie, it's me."

She still didn't answer, and he rang again as a sense of sick dread fell over him. Where was she? Had someone gotten her, too? Could she be lying in there, another victim of the psychopath who didn't give his targets a chance?

Trembling, he sorted through his keys, trying to find the right one. He tried to insert it into the dead bolt, but his hand was shaking too badly.

Suddenly, the knob turned and the door opened. Allie stood inside the kitchen, her long white cotton robe pooled around her bare feet. In the dim glow cast from the night-light on the stove, she looked angelic, sweet, innocent in contrast to the ugliness he had seen tonight.

"Mark? What is it?"

He couldn't stop the pounding in his heart, and he stumbled in and closed the door behind him, quickly turning on the light to make sure that she was safe and whole, unharmed.

"Mark, what's going on?" She sniffed—of course, she would smell the smoke from the bar, the alcohol on his breath. Why hadn't he thought of that? She stepped back, putting distance between them. "Mark, have you been drinking?"

"It's not about that, Allie," he said quickly, defensively. He shook his head and tried to find the right words, then gave up and just blurted it out. "There was another murder."

Her face showed no expression. She was bracing herself, marshaling her energy, processing the words. "What do you mean, another murder?"

"Jamie Larkins."

She caught her breath and took another step backward. "Oh, no."

"She was shot, just like Martha, and there was a fire."

"Oh, dear God." The words caught in her throat as she asked, "Who's doing this?"

"They didn't know anything when I left," he said. "But I'm sure everything's being done to find the killer."

She lifted her chin and tried to think it through. "Why Martha and Jamie?"

"They found some cocaine in Cale and Jamie's house. Cale seemed genuinely surprised to see it. I don't think he knew it was there. They're thinking maybe a drug deal went bad, and that Martha might have known something. There's no telling."

"Jamie wouldn't have confided in Martha. They were too different, and Martha was at least fifteen years older than Jamie. It's not like they hung around together."

"I know. It doesn't make sense. But until they find him, I don't think anyone is safe. Allie, I'm not going home tonight. I'm staying right here, with you, just to make sure."

He could see the protest forming on her lips, but just as quickly, it died. She was as frightened as he was, and she didn't want to be alone.

"I'll sleep on the couch," he said.

She stared at him for a long moment, and he felt a dread coming over him, coupled with an urgency that he didn't think she'd understand. Was she going to be so stubborn that she'd send him home?

The telephone rang, startling them both. She reached for it, keeping her eyes on him, and he felt exposed, transparent, as if she could see right through him. Sometimes he thought she really could.

"Hello?" she said tentatively. She kept the phone far enough from her ear that Mark could hear the voice on the other end.

"Allie, honey, this is Susan. You're not gonna believe what just happened! Jamie Larkins—"

"I know," Allie cut in. "I've already heard."

"Allie, this is getting scary, and Ray and I got to thinking about you being there all by yourself with a killer on the loose, and honey, we want you to come stay with us tonight. Ray will come and get you, but you don't need to be by yourself—"

"I'm not alone right now, actually," she said, and her eyes locked with Mark's.

"You're not?"

"No." She swallowed, and Mark took a step toward her. The alcohol on his breath seemed to hit her again, and she looked away. "But I do appreciate the invitation, and if you don't mind, I think I will come over. I don't really want to sleep here alone, and the alternative seems—" Her eyes shot up to Mark's again, and he waited for her to finish her sentence. "Well, there really isn't an alternative."

The remark stung him, as it was meant to, and he took the phone out of her hand. "Susan, this is Mark. I've already told Allie that I would stay here tonight. I don't want her here alone, either, so thanks—"

She grabbed the phone back and twisted away from him. "Susan, I'll come right over. But you don't have to send Ray."

"Honey, I don't want to interfere with you and Mark—"

"No, no," Allie said. "Really, I'd rather stay with you."

Mark was almost too angry to talk. "At least tell her that I'll bring you."

Allie put her hand over the phone. "No, Mark, I'd rather drive myself. You've been drinking."

"Allie, for pete's sake, I had one drink! I didn't even finish it. You're just using that as an excuse—"

"I'll drive myself, I said!"

"Fine, then!" he shouted. "You can drive yourself in my car, but I'm going with you!" He jerked the phone back from her and tried to calm his voice. "Susan, I'll bring her over. She'll be there shortly."

Susan's voice was dripping with apology. "Mark, I'm so sorry if I interfered. I didn't know you were there."

"It's okay, Susan," he said. "She'd rather face murder than have me in the house. I'm glad you called."

He hung up the phone and looked down at her, standing in her white robe tied at the waist, with her bare feet peeking out beneath it. She had no makeup on, and her hair was sleep-mussed, and something about the whole picture made his anger melt. He was still drawn to her, no matter how their ardor seemed to have cooled. But he couldn't act on it, not when her tongue was so sharp with accusations and allegations.

"Go get your stuff," he said quietly. "I'll wait for you."

She started into the bedroom, but he stopped her. "Allie, I did drink tonight, but it was only because it's been a lousy day."

"There've been a lot of lousy days lately, Mark." She looked down at the carpet beneath her feet. "I remember when they were about to build Joe's Place, and you were one of the loudest opponents in the meetings at city hall, protesting the fact that it was being built too close to the church. They made him build it somewhere else. Who would have thought that you'd become a regular patron?"

"That's not what I am, Allie. I just stop in there now and then, when things are really rough."

"Maybe things wouldn't be so rough if you didn't stop in there," she said. Her eyes were direct, clear, penetrating as she nailed him with her next question. "Tell me something, Mark. Was Issie there tonight?"

That anger rose again, and he looked away. "What if she was?"

"That's what I thought."

"I didn't go there with her, Allie. It was Fat Tuesday. Everybody in town was at that bar."

"Not everybody," she said.

"Don't be self-righteous, Allie."

"I'm not, Mark. I'm just stating a fact. Did you take her home?"

He looked away again, indignant. "Actually, we were called away by Jamie's murder," he said, hoping his words had the same sting hers did. "And I'm here, aren't I? Not with her, but here." The fact that he evaded her question only bothered him a little. So he had followed Issie home. It didn't mean a thing. He was still innocent. In fact, he probably deserved a trophy for not succumbing to temptation on a night like tonight. If Allie just weren't so bitterly pious, she'd realize it.

"So why *are* you here?" she asked.

"Because I was worried about you. No underlying motive, Allie, as evil and deceptive as you think I am. I wanted to make sure you were all right."

They stared off for a long moment, and finally, he said, "You'd better hurry. No need to keep the Fords up any longer than we have to."

She nodded quietly and went to pack.

• • •

At the Fords' house, Allie climbed out of Mark's car, then waited while he dragged her bag out of the trunk and carried it to the door where the porch light was on. Mark set the bag on the porch. She felt him looking down at her, but she didn't look back. Instead, she focused on a button on his shirt.

"Well . . . thanks for bringing me."

"I didn't bring you," he reminded her. "You brought me."

"Well, anyway. Thanks."

"Don't mention it," he said, and she heard the sarcasm in his voice. They were behaving like strangers. Part of her wanted it that way; the other part despised it.

"Allie . . ."

She looked up at him, finally, but the moment she did, he looked away and seemed to lose his train of thought.

She started to knock, knowing that inside, Susan probably waited for her, not wanting to break the moment between them. Poor Susan, she thought. She had such hope for their reconciliation. More hope than Allie had.

But Mark caught her hand, and she hated the fact that his touch still caused a little electric jolt to shoot through her, as it had when they'd first met. "Allie, don't always think the worst of me. I haven't done anything wrong."

"That's exactly the problem," Allie said.

"What? That I haven't done anything wrong?"

"No, that you won't admit it." She felt her cheeks growing hot, and hoped he couldn't see them reddening in the dim light.

"Allie, I can't admit to something that I haven't done. Do you want me to lie?"

"Why not?" she asked. "You've been doing it for months." The words weren't uttered in anger, but in deep sadness, and she looked away as she said them, hoping he wouldn't see the tears filling her eyes.

He lifted her chin, made her look at him. "Allie, I've never lied to you."

She moved her chin away from his fingertips and took a step backward. "No, Mark, it's yourself you lie to, mostly. That way you can convince yourself that what you tell me is the truth."

He rubbed his stubbled jaw and looked up at the night sky, as if he could find some logic, some rationale there. "I remember when you thought the best of me."

"I remember when you *were* the best."

The implication that he no longer was seemed to pierce him, and the pain on his face brought a pang to her own heart. She didn't enjoy hurting him. But for some time now, their conversations seemed to consist of both of them saying things that hurt.

He turned his back and stood on the edge of the porch, looking out into the night. He smelled of smoke, as he often did, and his big shoulders, normally so strong and capable, looked slumped beneath the weight of all that had occurred that day. For a moment, she thought of touching his back, or reaching up to press a kiss on his stubbled cheek. But she wouldn't allow herself to. Several silent moments passed, and finally he turned and said, "Make sure you aren't alone in the store tomorrow. It's easy to let your guard down in daylight, but don't forget Martha was killed in the morning."

She nodded.

"And if you need me, you know where I'll be."

Their eyes met again, and this time, he leaned over and kissed her cheek. "Good night, Allie."

"Night." She waited for him to leave, then realized he wasn't going to until she was inside. She rapped lightly on the door, and Susan answered it.

"Hey, honey, come on in."

Allie stepped inside as Mark trotted down the porch steps and back out to his car.

Susan closed the door and locked the dead bolt. "Is everything all right?"

Allie shook her head. "No, not really." She pulled in a deep sigh. "I really appreciate your inviting me over."

"Isn't it awful about Jamie? And Martha . . . oh, Allie."

The two women hugged. Ray, who was usually jovial, came into the room looking more solemn than she had ever seen him, and as tired and shocked as Mark.

"Ray, have you heard any more about Jamie's murder? Any leads?"

"No, 'fraid not. I just got off the phone with my brother Sid."

Sid was a lieutenant on the Newpointe police force, and likely to know how the investigation was going.

"He said they're pretty sure the murders have somethin' to do with the drugs they found. They've set up roadblocks and are hopin' to catch the guy leavin' town."

"But that doesn't make sense," Susan cried. "Martha would never have touched cocaine. And she wouldn't have known anything about Jamie taking it, either."

"How is Cale?" Allie asked.

"Stunned," Ray said. "He wasn't even s'pose to work tonight. Swapped with somebody at the last minute. Wonder if anything woulda been different if he'd been home."

"Maybe he would have been killed, too," Allie suggested.

"Maybe."

Susan wiped her eyes, breathed deeply, then released it. "Well, we'd better turn in. Tomorrow's gonna be a long day. I made up Ben's room for you, Allie," she said, referring to her son who was away at Louisiana State. "Just make yourself at home, hear?"

Allie went into Ben's room and dropped her bag on the bed. The room was decorated with posters of sports heroes and pennants of his favorite colleges; a basketball hoop hung on the wall. She caught a glimpse of herself in the mirror as she scanned the room, and quickly turned away. She didn't like seeing herself lately.

The fact that Mark had wanted to protect her confused her. What did it mean? She couldn't believe he still loved her, not after two months of separation, when he'd made so little effort to set things right again. He didn't seem to care how she felt about his "friendship" with Issie—or anything else. Why, now, did he suddenly care?

She went to the window and peered out. His car was gone, and she wondered whether he'd go back to the bar or to his apartment. Would he go to see if Issie was all right, since she, too, lived alone?

The thought sickened her. Trying to shove down the emotions welling up inside her, she sat down in the chair across from the bed. Closing her eyes, she cried out to God.

She prayed for Mark, that he would be safe tonight, and that the thoughts he had of her as he drifted into sleep would not be cold, angry thoughts. She hoped they were tender thoughts, the way they used to be.

Where had they gone wrong?

She asked that question of God, but no answer came. Troubled and confused and frightened and exhausted, she finally fell into a shallow sleep.

Chapter Eleven

Jill Clark was awakened from a sound sleep at four A.M. by a ringing telephone. Reaching blindly for it, she managed to bump the touch-me lamp, and the light came on. Squinting from the sudden, unexpected brightness, she picked up the phone. "Hello?"

"Jill, you gotta help me."

The man's voice was not familiar, so she sat up in bed, trying to clear her brain. "Who is this?"

"Joe Petitjean," he said.

For a moment she struggled to put a face with the name, then remembered—he was the owner of Joe's Place, the town's favorite bar. "What is it, Joe?"

"I need a lawyer. I'm down to the po-lice station, and they questionin' me 'bout Jamie Larkins's murder. Jill, I don't have nothin' to do with that, and I did *not* sell her the bag of cocaine she had in the house."

"Jamie Larkins was murdered?" she asked, sitting straight up. "Joe, it's Martha Broussard who was killed—not Jamie."

"Both of 'em, Jill. I'm tellin' you, they tryin' to pin somethin' on me, even though they said they just brought me in for questionin'. And I ain't the only one."

She had her pants on and was reaching for a pullover sweater. "What do you mean?"

"I mean they got at least twenty others in here. They got some kind of roadblock set up and they catchin' every pot-smoking, beer-drinkin' yo that tries to leave this town. You come down here, you better be ready to stay a while. I ain't the only one gonna need a lawyer."

Jill hung up and hurried to the bathroom. She washed her face and brushed her teeth, then grabbed her shoes and hopped as she put on one at a time on her way out.

It wasn't until she was in the car that the horror of what Joe had told her finally penetrated. Jamie Larkins was dead?

She wondered if Allie knew. Digging her cellular phone from her purse, she punched in Allie's number with her thumb as she drove, hoping Allie would have a few details Jill might need. The phone rang five, six, seven times before Jill pushed "end," terminating the call attempt. Where could Allie be?

She tried to think. She needed some background information before she burst into the police station. Someone at the fire department would know something, she thought, since they were usually dispatched to all of the calls at the same time the police were.

She dialed information, got the number for the Midtown Fire Station, and waited as it rang. The voice that answered was subdued and muffled.

"Hello?"

"This is Jill Clark. Who's speaking, please?"

"This is Dan Nichols, Jill," the voice said, and she had an instant image of the tall blond fireman with bright blue eyes.

"Dan, I'm on my way to the police station, but I needed a little information about Jamie Larkins's murder. Can you tell me anything about it?"

"I can tell you what I know," he said. "I wasn't on duty when they got the call. I just came in an hour ago to take Cale's place. But whoever did it shot her through the chest, then set the house on fire."

Jill's stomach jolted, but she tried to stay calm. "What's this about cocaine?"

"They found it in her house—in the part that didn't burn down. They're thinking that maybe there's a connection."

"Okay, that makes sense," she said, thinking out loud. "So now they're rounding up anyone who saw her today, trying to find witnesses. Dan, do they have any leads at all?"

"I couldn't say, Jill. But for now there is a killer on the loose, and I wouldn't be out there alone if I were you."

She turned onto Purchase Street, where the police station and fire station were located. "Thanks, Dan. But I'm almost there."

"I'll meet you outside and walk you in," he said.

She smiled. "I don't think that's necessary. No one's going to attack me right outside the police station."

"It's four-thirty in the morning, Jill, and we know for sure there's a killer in town. I'll meet you outside," he said.

He hung up. Smiling, she clicked off the phone and dropped it back into her purse. As she pulled up to the front of the police station, she saw him coming out of the open garage of the fire department adjacent to the building. Grabbing her purse and briefcase, she got out.

"I appreciate this, Dan," she said.

"Not a problem."

He walked her up the steps to the police station doors and opened the glass door for her. "If you want me to walk you out when you leave, just holler," he told her. "Unless I'm on a call, it's no problem to pop over here."

She touched his arm in thanks. She had heard that he was arrogant, vain, and self-centered. But to her he just seemed like a nice guy, and she hadn't had much experience with nice guys lately. "Thanks, I will."

He disappeared back into the night.

Jill stepped through the next set of glass doors, surprised at the amount of activity in the usually sleepy station. It looked as if every police officer in Newpointe had been called in to work tonight and half the town had been dragged in for questioning.

She spotted Joe sitting outside one of the interrogation rooms. Before she could reach him, though, someone else called her name.

"Jill, thank goodness. I've been trying to call you."

She stopped as she saw Lisa Manning, Jamie Larkins's best friend. Her eyes were swollen, and she was wiping her nose with a wadded tissue. "Lisa, what are you doing here?"

"They came and got me for questioning," she said. "I already told 'em everything I knew, but they won't let me go home yet. I didn't think to call you until a few minutes ago."

Joe was standing now and waving impatiently across the room at her, but she touched Lisa's shoulder. "What did you tell them, Lisa? What *do* you know?"

"*Nothing.* At least, nothing about the murder. I want the killer caught as much as anybody. All I knew was about the coke. She bought it this morning—or yesterday morning—at the parade. She saw some guy she knew and bought it right there on the spot, in front of God and everybody. I didn't even know what it was until later, I swear."

"Did you know the guy?"

"No, I've never seen him before. He had like a black buzz cut, and this gross tattoo of a spider on his neck. Really gave me the creeps. He was about five eleven, I guess, early twenties. She said she knew him from when she used to party on the Southshore a lot. That's all I can remember, but I told them I'd recognize him if I saw him again. Jill, should I have called you first?"

She glanced toward the interrogation room from which two cops were coming, and she shook her head. "I think you're all right, Lisa. You're a witness, that's all. They're trying to get as many leads as they can so they can catch the guy."

"Do I need a lawyer?"

"If they want to talk to you any more, I'll go in with you," she said. "Just sit tight and wait. I have to go talk to Joe."

Lisa sank back into her seat, among the others who had been brought in. Some were handcuffed and leaning back drunkenly against the wall. Most were out-of-towners; she recognized few of them. They were probably people who lived too far north of New Orleans to make the trip all the way in, so they'd come here to do their partying. Some of the bars in town had advertised special events tonight to draw the crowds. Apparently, it had worked.

She made her way to Joe and saw the fear in his eyes. "They wanted to question me, but I told 'em to wait till you got here."

"All right," she said, sitting down. He did the same. "Joe, they must think you know something or saw something. Had Jamie Larkins been in your bar tonight?"

"Not tonight, but she was in this afternoon, all shook up about the murder. She wound up tyin' one on."

"Did you see her talking to anybody?"

"Couple of her girlfriends. She's a wild one, but I never seen her with any men except Cale."

Jill looked Joe in the eye, carefully trying to phrase her words so she wouldn't set him off. "Joe, I have to ask. Is there any reason for the police to believe that she might have gotten the cocaine from you or someone who works for you?"

"No! You kiddin'? I sell booze, not dope."

"All right." She stood and looked around for the nearest cop. Stan Shepherd was just coming out of the interrogation room. "Stan?" she called.

Stan nodded. "Hey, Jill. I see Joe called you."

"Yeah. You want to question him?"

"Sure do."

"All right, let's get this over with. It's late."

He ushered them both into the interrogation room, called in another cop, and set up a tape player in the middle of the table. Jill coached Joe through Stan's questioning for the next hour.

Chapter Twelve

Just outside of town, miles of traffic at the junction of Highway 90 and I-59 sat backed up as police checked each car for a man who fit the description Lisa had given them. If they could come up with any reason to legally search a vehicle, they made the driver pull over and checked for drugs and guns—specifically a .38 caliber handgun, which had killed both Martha and Jamie. A dozen cars had been pulled over to the side, and officers were arresting their passengers. Several had been caught with drugs, from marijuana to heroin, though they were all possession cases since the quantities of the drugs were small. One guy had been caught with a handgun that they'd determined was, indeed, registered to him, and three others had been caught with illegal weapons. Several others walked invisible lines, trying and failing to prove that they were not too drunk to drive. Though all eight of Newpointe's squad cars were on the scene, fifteen cops had been called to work the roadblock.

As they filed those arrested into the van that was quickly filling up for the third time, they still had gotten no closer to finding the suspected killer. Drunken revelers stewing in their stalled cars were getting angrier, and some were yelling out the windows at the cops who, undaunted, continued going from one car to the next.

Vern Hargis waved a carload of college-aged girls past, and stopped the next car in line, a gray Plymouth that looked as if it had seen better days; the driver was the only one inside. Vern shone his beam into the car as he stepped close to the window. The man had a buzz cut, just as Lisa Manning had described. But so had a couple dozen other guys who'd come through tonight.

"May I see your drivers' license, please, sir?"

The man pulled out his wallet, slid out his license, and handed it to him. "Rounding up all the drunk drivers?" he asked.

Vern noticed the spider tattoo on his neck. "Please get out of the car," he said. The driver opened the door and stepped out. Vern snapped the cuff on one of his wrists. Before the man could react, he had the other one on, and yelled across the roof of the car, "Captain, I've got something!"

Two cops came running as Vern spread-eagled the suspect against the car and began to frisk him.

"What is this? I'm not *drunk!* Can't you see that I'm as sober as you are?"

"He fits the description!" Vern said. "Check out the tattoo." He reached into the man's pocket and slid out three vials of cocaine. "Look at this!"

The other two cops began to search the car. When they found a backpack in his trunk holding at least twenty grams of cocaine and $4,000 in cash, they knew they had their man.

"You're under arrest, pal," Vern said, jerking him over to his squad car, which was parked in the grass on the side of the highway.

"For *what?*"

"Take your choice. Possession with intent to distribute, or murder one."

"*Murder?* Hey, I didn't kill *anybody!* Is this about that Broussard woman?"

That was as close to a confession as Vern needed. This guy was as guilty as the serpent in Eden. "Radio back to the precinct and tell 'em we've got our man."

Chapter Thirteen

The smell of something cooking in the kitchen woke Allie just as the first light of dawn softened the gray outside. She quickly showered in the hall bathroom, then dressed and headed for the kitchen. Susan was busy stirring something in a mixing bowl as her fifteen-year-old daughter, Vanessa, gathered her books for school. "Mama, please!" Vanessa argued. "What good is it to have your learner's permit if you never get to drive?"

Not wanting to interrupt their discussion, Allie stopped just short of the kitchen doorway.

"Not today," Susan said. "Ride with your car pool."

"But Mama! *I* can drive the car pool! My friends never seen me drive before. I been waitin' my whole life to drive and you won't *ever* let me!"

"You're gon' have to wait one more day."

"If it wasn't for the murders you'd let me."

"Young lady, I said *no!*"

"But Mama, don't let these murders get you all unreasonable and paranoid. Some of us still have a life!"

Thinking she'd waited long enough, Allie reluctantly stepped into the room. "Good morning."

Susan looked up from her mixing bowl. "Hey, girl. I hope Vanessa didn't wake you. If she did, she's sorry, ain't you, Vanessa?"

"She didn't wake me," Allie said before the girl had to answer. "Good morning, Vanessa. I love your hair."

The compliment changed the girl's tone, and she ran her fingers through the long weaves that gave her a movie star look. "Thanks. It took hours. Allie, how old were you when your parents let you drive?"

"Uh . . ."

A horn sounded outside, and Susan grabbed Vanessa's sack lunch and thrust it at her. "Your ride's here. Go."

"Shoot!" Pouting, she took the lunch and rushed out the door without saying good-bye to either of them.

Allie grinned, and Susan chuckled lightly. "She's got a tough life. And to think we were both awake all night worrying about murderers running loose . . ." Her smile faded, and she went back to stirring. Susan's eyes were tired, and Allie wondered if her friend had slept at all last night. From the looks of the casseroles cooling on the stove, she doubted it. But it was Susan who asked, "Did you sleep okay?"

"As much as can be expected," Allie said. She went to one of the dishes and pulled the tin foil back to see what was in it. A broccoli casserole that smelled like heaven. "How long have you been at this?"

"Oh, a couple hours. I couldn't sleep." She kept stirring, harder and longer than Allie thought she needed to. "I thought I'd make myself useful and take some casseroles over to George and Cale, so they wouldn't have to worry about what to eat."

"George is with his parents, isn't he?"

"I'll take it to them," she said. "Heaven knows they'll have enough on their minds without having to think up meals to fix."

Allie gazed at Susan. She was so pretty and petite that Allie had always envied her, and she seemed to have unlimited energy and enough compassion to comfort the whole town. "That's sweet of you, Susan."

"Well, it's the least I can do." She drew in a deep breath and kept stirring. "I just don't know what George is gon' do. With that little baby . . ." Her eyes filled with tears, and she looked up at Allie. "Allie, I just don't understand this. I know God's in control, but George and Martha prayed fifteen years for that baby, and it was to God's glory when Tommy was born. How can Martha's murder be for good? How can it be part of the plan?"

"Maybe it isn't part of God's plan," Allie said weakly as she sank into a chair and stared down at the floor.

"But that would mean that God's *not* in control."

"He's in control," Allie said, thinking it through as she went along, "but he allows some things to happen."

"Why?" Susan's voice cracked with the question. "Why something like this? That's what I don't understand."

Allie's own emotions began to well up in her throat, burning her eyes, and she shook her head and got up. "I don't know, Susan."

Susan abandoned her bowl and came to Allie, and the two women embraced and held each other for several moments.

"Well, I guess that's where faith comes in," Susan said finally, stepping back and wiping her eyes. "We just have to pray that God'll help us understand."

"We may never understand," Allie whispered. "Maybe the best we can hope for is peace about it."

"Peace," Susan said, turning back to the bowl. "That seems so impossible right now, with some maniac on the loose and two friends dead." She pulled out a pan that she had already greased and poured the batter into it.

Ray came to the door of the kitchen, just wakened, though he was fully dressed in khakis and a pullover knit shirt. "I just got off the phone with Sid. He's still at the police station," he said. "He been there all night. Says they caught the perpetrator."

"What?" Allie asked, spinning around. "Really?"

Susan stopped pouring the batter. "Who was it, Ray?"

"Some dope dealer they caught on his way out of town. He's from Bogaloosa. Name's Hank Keyes. Been I.D.'d by one of the witnesses who saw Jamie making the deal with him yesterday."

"And they think he's the one who killed Martha and Jamie?"

"They do."

Allie breathed a huge sigh of relief, and turned to Susan, who was staring at Ray with a poignant look on her face. "Do they know why yet, Ray?"

"He's denyin' everythin'," he said. "They can't get nothin' out of him."

Susan pulled out a chair and wilted down. "I wish I could talk to him."

"What would you tell him, Susan?" Allie asked.

"That he blew a terrible hole into this town yesterday. That he didn't just hurt the husbands and the little baby, but he hurt all of us."

"He wouldn't care," Ray said.

"No, he wouldn't," she said. She drew in a deep breath, got back up, and returned to her cooking. "I'm gonna ask Brother Nick to open up the church today," she said. "We need to pray for that man."

Allie didn't say anything. But she didn't think she could pray for a killer.

Chapter Fourteen

Hank Keyes's apartment in Bogaloosa looked as though it had been ransacked, but it was soon apparent to Stan Shepherd and the other officers with him that Keyes had left it this way. Dishes in the sink in the kitchen had week-old food dried on them, and the half-filled glasses scattered around the room looked like science experiments Stan had done in high school—green fuzz covered the contents and climbed up the sides. The apartment reeked of decay and neglect.

They stepped over dirty laundry and wadded papers on the floor, looking for a place to start the search that might prove definitively that Hank was their man.

Before they'd gotten past the living room, the door opened and a bearded, greasy-looking man came stumbling in wearing a black T-shirt with the sleeves cut off. His eyes were blood-shot, and he smelled of vomit, booze, and body odor. He didn't look surprised to see strangers, only mildly annoyed. "You friends of Hank's?" he asked.

"Police officers," Stan said, flashing his shield. "We're from Newpointe, but Officer Cockrell over there is from the Boga-loosa P.D. We're going to have to ask you to leave. We're in the middle of an investigation, and we can't allow any of the evi-dence to be disturbed."

"I can't come into my own apartment?" the man bellowed.

"You live here?" Stan asked.

"Yeah, I live here. Who'd you *think* lived here?"

"We were told that Hank Keyes lives here."

"Well, he does. We share it." Aggravated, he rubbed his eyes, as though it would somehow clear his thinking. "Who'd you say you were?"

"Police officers," Stan repeated. He noticed the spider tattoo on the man's neck—just like the one their suspect had. "What's your relationship to Hank Keyes?"

"We're roommates," he said. "You got a warrant? 'Cause if you ain't got a warrant—"

"We've got one, pal." Stan showed him the warrant, and the man wilted.

"*Man!* What'd he *do* to get the cops to swarm this place?"

Stan ignored him. "Do you own any guns of any kind?"

"No. None. Come on, man. Whatever you're lookin' for, we ain't got it."

One of the cops who'd started perusing the closets cleared his throat. Stan turned around and saw the guns sitting on the top shelf. "Want to change your story, pal?"

"Man . . ." The guy shook his head. "I thought you meant unregistered guns. Those guns are registered."

"To who?"

"To me."

The same cop who had found the guns began riffling through some boxes on the floor in the same closet. "Man, that stuff's personal. Don't open that!"

The cop on the floor opened the box and looked up at Stan. "It's personal, all right. His personal stash. There's enough cocaine here for every high school kid in Newpointe High."

"That's Hank's stash, not mine. I didn't even know that was there!"

"Right." Stan snapped his handcuffs on the man, and hoped he didn't have to be the one to take him back. He'd never get the smell out of his car. "You weren't by any chance in Newpointe with your buddy last night, were you?"

"No, man. I been in New Orleans all night. Why? Wha'd he do?"

"He killed two women."

"*Hank?* No, man. He couldn't have. I had nothin' to do with that, man. I have witnesses who saw me in the Quarter. A girl I was with can tell you. Her name was Wanda something. I was with her all night."

Stan gave a dry laugh as he led the man to the door. "Hey, Cockrell. Look up Wanda Something in New Orleans. That ought to clear things up."

Chapter Fifteen

Before he headed back to Newpointe, Stan Shepherd stopped in at the only tattoo parlor in Bogaloosa, where he surmised that Hank and his roommate may have gotten their tattoos. The eight-foot-square waiting room was furnished with two split vinyl love seats that looked as if they'd been rescued from someone's garbage pile. On the walls were sketches of hundreds of tattoos to choose from.

Stan scanned the pictures carefully, looking for the spider.

"Be right with you." The voice was deep and phlegmy, and Stan turned to the curtained doorway separating the waiting room from whatever was behind it. A man who must have weighed four hundred pounds stood holding the curtains out of his way with one pudgy hand, a cigarette hanging from his mouth. "Know what you want?"

"I'm looking for something in particular," Stan said. "A spider."

The man pushed the curtain back and came through, giving Stan a once-over. "Spider, huh?" He pointed to one that Stan hadn't noticed yet. "Like that there?"

"Yes." Stan stepped closer to examine the lines of the drawing. "You do many of those?"

"What are you, some kind of cop?"

Stan studied the man, wondering why his simple question would have led him to that assumption. He pulled his shield from his pocket. "Stan Shepherd, Newpointe P.D. Do you do many tattoos on necks?"

"Newpointe? Ain't you a little out of your territory?"

"I'm investigating two homicides we had there last night."

"Blacks?" the big man asked.

Stan frowned. Why would he ask that? "No, actually. Both white women. Why?"

The man shrugged. "You lookin' at spiders and talkin' about necks and murder investigations. They usually only kill blacks. They can't get the spider 'til they do."

Stan didn't want to appear ignorant, but he needed information. "*They* being some kind of white supremacists?"

"You might call 'em that," the fat man said.

"How many of these have you done?"

"That's privileged information."

Stan smirked. "There's no law protecting tattooer confidentiality."

"No written law, maybe. But there's a law, all right, and if you violate it, you get dead. Besides, I don't keep lists. They come in and pay me, I do my job, and I never see 'em again."

"Do they talk when they're here?"

"Some do, some don't."

Stan pulled out a copy of Hank Keyes's mug shot and showed it to the man. "Remember doing one for this guy?"

"All the faces just blend together after a while."

Stan smirked, reached into his back pocket, pulled out his wallet, and held out a twenty-dollar bill. "Does this help your memory?"

The man took the bill. "It's coming back to me. Still a little blurry, though."

Stan handed him another twenty, then closed the wallet and slid it back into his pocket.

"What do you want to know?"

"What kind of gang it is he belongs to. The name of it, the code they have, anything you can give me."

"That's easy. Why didn't you just ask?" The man began to laugh, a wet, phlegmy laugh that ended in a coughing fit. Stan considered calling an ambulance before the coughing finally subsided. "They're called the Slashers, and they're mostly former military dudes. Hate blacks, and they have to kill one to earn their spider."

"What about women? Do they have anything against white women?"

"They like 'em." Amused, the man laughed again, which once more threw him into a round of coughing.

After that Stan got nowhere. Fearing reprisals, the tattooer wasn't about to give Stan any specific information about the Slashers—where they met, the names of any other members, anything that would be useful to Stan in his investigation. As he drove back to Newpointe, he struggled to make sense of things. Why would a skinhead—who'd killed at least one black person to earn his spider—want to kill two white women? Was there anything in what he'd just learned that supported the theory that these murders were just a drug deal gone bad? Had the Nazi-like group decided to start killing off Caucasian women, or were these murders unrelated to the Slashers? If the murders were gang-related, then he'd have to charge Keyes—and maybe his roommate, too—with conspiracy, as well as murder one.

He was bone-tired. He hadn't slept all night. Maybe he should get some sleep and let someone else interrogate Hank's roommate, now that they had the killer off the streets.

No, he thought. Not yet. He wanted to make sure no one dropped the ball. This was too important, and he didn't want Keyes to slip through their fingers just because something wasn't done right.

Chapter Sixteen

The funeral services were scheduled for two days later, back to back in Calvary Bible Church, the little nondenominational church in the heart of Newpointe. Brother Nick Foster sat at the big table in the firehouse kitchen and stared with tears in his eyes at the telephone in front of him, on which he had just spoken to Cale Larkins. Cale wasn't one of his church members, nor had Jamie been, but since the Larkins had no church home, Cale had asked his friend Nick to officiate at Jamie's funeral. Earlier, George Broussard had made the same request for Martha's funeral, but George's request had been natural, expected. From the Sunday they'd joined Calvary, Martha and George had been active members of the small church, and Nick would have much to say about the woman who had so often demonstrated tireless service and devotion to God.

But Jamie was another story. Nick hadn't known her well, which meant that he would have to find people who had and ask them for things to share at her funeral, good things about the woman that would make them smile or nod, that would give them hope or encouragement. On the phone, he had asked Cale a question that had been plaguing his mind since her death. "Cale, where was Jamie spiritually?"

"Oh, she was a real spiritual person, Preacher," Cale said. "Really. She was real interested in angels and swore she had her own personal guardian angel. She talked to her sometimes, right out loud. And she wore that cross around her neck most of the time, with a little crystal right next to it, because she said it had healing powers, in case she ever got sick."

Nick had groaned inwardly. "Cale, did Jamie ever pray, that you knew of? Did she study Scripture?"

"Everybody prays sometimes, don't they, Preacher?" Cale asked. "She wasn't much of a reader, though." His voice had cracked then, and there was a long moment of silence. "I know what you're gettin' at, Nick. I've been to church enough in my life to see what you're leadin' up to. You're tryin' to decide whether she went to hell or not."

Nick was speechless, something that didn't happen often. Quickly, his mind searched for some type of verbal Band-Aid. "Not at all, Cale. That's not up to me to decide. I just didn't know her very well, and I'm trying to find out as much as I can about her."

"Still . . ." The silence hung like a cloud over the phone line. "Don't you think the way she died would have been hell enough? I mean, wouldn't a lovin' God—the kind you preach—have mercy on somebody who was . . ." His pitch rose and his voice cracked. ". . . murdered like that?"

Since he'd become a preacher, Nick had often wished that he didn't have to be bivocational, that he could devote all of his time to shepherding his flock. But right now, he wished the opposite—that he were just a fireman, and not a preacher at all. He was supposed to give honest truths to people who asked him spiritual questions, but this was a tough one. The man was in the depths of grief and needed comfort desperately. And Nick wasn't sure he could give him any.

"Cale, where are you? I'm on duty right now, but as soon as I get off, I'd like to come talk with you, face-to-face."

"That's it, then, huh? You do think she's in hell, but you don't want to say it over the phone."

"Cale, I can't pretend to know where Jamie's soul is."

"You know where Martha's is, don't you, Preacher?"

"I knew her better than I knew Jamie." It was a lame, weak response to a complicated question, and he wished he'd studied more, gotten deeper into Scripture this week, prayed harder this morning . . .

"It all boils down to the sentence, don't it, Preacher?"

"Sentence?" Nick asked. "What sentence?"

"The prayer sentence. The one where you say you accept Jesus as your Savior. I grew up in church, Preacher. I know all the rules. And you expect me to believe that if my Jamie didn't say that one sentence some time in her life, that she's burnin' in hell right this minute?"

Nick rubbed the tears from his eyes and realized that his hands were trembling. He closed his eyes and asked the Lord for an extra helping of wisdom. "Cale, the gospel has little to do with a bunch of words strung together. It's a heart's commitment, an emptying out of self, and being filled, instead, with the Holy Spirit. It's not about repeating a sentence. I don't know what condition Jamie's heart was in, and I would never pronounce her to be in hell. Besides, Cale, neither of us knows what might have happened in her heart and soul in her last moments."

"That's right," Cale said. "We don't know." He grew quiet again, then asked, "Preacher, do you think if I got my heart right, that I could pray and ask God to put her in heaven, just in case she ain't there, after all?"

"We're each responsible for our own souls, Cale," he said sadly. "The only person you can pray out of hell is yourself."

"Yeah, that's what I figured." Cale drew in a deep, shaky breath, then sniffed hard, and said, "She was a good person, Preacher. She loved me. She had a lot of friends, and loved to laugh. She was a good person."

"I know she was, Cale. I know she'll be missed."

"You don't know the half of it." Cale was sobbing now, and Nick wished they were face-to-face so that he could offer the man more than hollow words. Handling needs such as this over the telephone made Nick feel so awkward, so helpless.

"Cale, I'm so sorry this all happened." Nick's own voice cracked, and he rubbed his face. "If there's anything more I can do for you—if you need to get away, I can borrow my uncle's boat, and we can go sit out in the middle of the lake for a few hours, and think and talk . . ."

"Yeah, I'll keep that in mind," Cale said. "I'll get back in touch."

Now, sitting in the kitchen of the firehouse, Nick wondered what Jesus would have done. He closed his eyes and tried to think. Jesus wouldn't have pulled any punches with the truth, he thought. He would have told Cale exactly like it was. Then maybe he would have taken Jamie's hand, brought her back to life, and forgiven her sins.

But Nick wasn't Jesus. He was just a man, and he'd never healed anyone, much less raised anyone from the dead. Today, he couldn't even provide the simplest comfort. Maybe he was just fooling himself into believing he was called to be the shepherd of this little church in this little town. Maybe he should resign, and just fight fires.

As he always did when his soul cried out, he opened his Bible and began to search for God's answers to the painful questions that plagued him.

• • •

It was getting close to lunchtime when Aggie Gaston got out of her big lavender Cadillac. As she opened the back door to retrieve the groceries she'd bought on her way there, she saw the front door of the firehouse open. Mark Branning hurried out.

"Aunt Aggie, I'll get that."

They pampered her here, as if she were an old lady, but she didn't mind. To most people, eighty *was* old. But most eighty-year-olds didn't walk five miles a day, or have the entire fire department as their adopted sons. Those things kept her young. She reached for a hug as Mark got to the car, and gave him an extra pat because of the bad news.

"Where y'at, Mark?" she asked in her thick Cajun accent.

"Awright, Aunt Aggie."

"You okay?" Still holding him and examining his face, she said, "You lookin' mighty tired, *mon ami*."

"I'm fine," he said. "We're all a little shaken up."

"With good reason." As he bent in to get the groceries, she said, "Careful with dat, now. I'm makin' a gumbo for tonight— a little lagniappe to cheer everybody up."

"You're a princess."

Aggie beamed and followed him in. As she cut through the firehouse, each of the firemen greeted her with a hug and asked what was for lunch, and she told them just enough to whet their appetites before she started cooking.

Like Aunt Bea in Mayberry, who cooked all the meals for the residents of the town's jail, Aunt Aggie had a reputation for mothering the firefighters, but that was where the similarity ended. Though she seldom mentioned it herself, it was well known around town that she had been Miss Louisiana back in 1938, and she had held onto her figure and good looks. She still watched her weight and carried herself as if she had an Amy Vanderbilt book of etiquette balanced on her head. When she was sixty, she'd had a face-lift that made her look forty, and now that she was eighty, and looked sixty, she wanted to have another one. But she couldn't find a doctor who would perform it on a woman of her age—a fact that she considered quite an insult. Despite her efforts to cling to her youth, she had long ago allowed her hair to turn white, but only because it was a pure white that looked glamorous—and because she secretly hated the humiliation of sitting for an hour in the chair at the beautician's with her hair all pasted on top of her head while peroxide burned her eyes and color trickled down her temples.

Besides, the men she served each day seemed to like her hair the way it was. They told her daily how good she was

looking, and she never ceased to believe it. They also compli-
mented her taste in clothing and her exquisite talent for creating fine cuisine. It was the only payment she required. Every
day, including weekends, she pampered the firefighters with
crawfish bisque, lobster tails, and a million other Cajun con-
coctions that had brought a little culture into the otherwise
boring little firehouse. It had started over forty years ago, when
she'd tired of hearing her husband complain about the meals
other men cooked in the firehouse, so she had begun then to
bring meals so often that they stopped cooking entirely and
came to depend on her. They never worried about how much
money she spent on the food—she was independently wealthy,
having first inherited her father's money and then made a substantial ground-floor investment in a little company called
Microsoft. Besides, she considered this the closest thing she
had to a "calling." Had she believed in God, she would have
sworn this was the job he had foreordained for her.

But she didn't believe in God. She considered herself a fine
example of someone with strong moral fiber and a good life,
none of which she attributed to church, an institution she considered a waste of time. She proudly boasted that she hadn't
darkened the doors of any church in four years, not since Celia,
her great niece—the only one in town who had a blood right to
call her Aunt Aggie—had married Stan Shepherd. Still, she fed
Nick Foster, Celia's preacher, when he was on duty at the firehouse, and treated him as kindly as she did any of the others,
even though she thought he was probably no better than a car
salesman peddling his congregation a weekly bill of goods. Still,
she liked Nick, and she was glad he'd kept his day job so he'd
have something to fall back on when his proselytizing got old.

As if her very thoughts had conjured him, she found him
sitting at the table in the kitchen when she went in, looking as
if he'd seen better days. The books all spread out on the table
in front of him, Bibles and notebooks and whatnot, didn't seem

to be offering him much help. She stepped over the phone cord and gave him a hug. "You awright, *mon petit?*"

"I'm okay, Aunt Aggie. How are you?"

"Dandy. I'm gonna cook you some good eats, make you feel better."

Nick gave a faint smile. "I'm looking forward to it."

Mark left the groceries on the counter, pulled out a chair, and sat down with the preacher. "Was that Cale you were talking to?"

"Yeah," Nick said, rubbing his eyes. "It wasn't an easy conversation." He looked up at Mark. "He wanted to know if I thought Jamie was in hell."

"Oh, heaven's sake," Aggie spouted. "I hope you didn't say yes!"

"Of course not," Nick said.

"Then you told him she was in heaven or wherever it is he wants to believe people go?"

Both men looked up at her, and she realized she'd stepped on some toes.

"No, I couldn't tell him that, either, Aunt Aggie," Nick said. "I would never just tell someone what they want to hear to make them feel better."

She pursed her lips and decided to bite her tongue, though she didn't know how long she would manage it. "Whatever happened to preachers havin' compassion, what I want to know," she muttered under her breath.

She heard a chair scraping back, and Mark appeared beside her, that charm-your-socks-off grin on his face. "Aunt Aggie, Nick has compassion. And he believes the things he preaches."

"How would you know?" she asked, looking up at him. "Accordin' to Celia, you ain't been to church in months."

Mark's smile crashed. "It hasn't been that long." He glanced self-consciously back at Nick. "Nick, tell her it hasn't been that long."

The preacher's gaze locked on the small Cajun woman. "What are you getting at, Aunt Aggie?"

"Just that all these *grande* convictions do get shaky when times get rough."

"Aunt Aggie—you're saying I'm a hypocrite," Mark said, with the same hurt-little-boy look on his face he'd have had if she'd spat on him.

She considered him for a moment. He was a handsome man, always had been, even when he was fourteen on the junior-high football team, scoring touchdowns and driving the girls crazy. He had been one of her husband's favorite local athletes, and now he was one of her favorite young men. "*Mon petit*, I'd never call you somethin' that mean. I just don't understand all the rules, and all the mumbo jumbo. No better'n voodoo, y'ask me. Seems to me at a time like this, when a friend needs a little comfort, you'd just give the comfort any way you could."

"Just because I fail, Aunt Aggie, doesn't mean what Nick preaches isn't true."

She patted his back with affection, and began unloading the groceries. "Awright, darlin'. It's just . . . Cale is one of *mes enfants*, too, and I hate to see him hurtin'."

"What about George?" Nick asked, catching her attention again. She turned back to him. "Aren't you concerned about him and the baby?"

"Of course I am," she said. "I just know Cale's all by hisself. Not like George."

"Why do you say that?" Nick asked, and she knew he was trying to make a point.

"Okay," she said, giving him his little victory. "Because of his church, that's why. He has all them folks rallyin' 'round him, bringin' him food, keepin' him company, offerin' him hope and comfort. He won't be shunned like Cale will."

"Shunned?" Mark asked. "Why would Cale be shunned?"

"Because he ain't one of you."

Nick looked down at his Bible for a long moment, then began to nod. "Thank you, Aunt Aggie," he said. "You've just given us a challenge. We need to make Cale one of us, even if he wasn't before. We need to bring him into the fold and love him and minister to him, just like we would to George. That's what Jesus would do."

Aunt Aggie smiled and turned back to her food. She hoped they would do just that, even if she didn't believe in Jesus or heaven or any of those other things. There were some good things about church. It had done a lot to heal Celia, her niece, after some great tragedies in her life, and she'd seen more than once how it embraced members of the community in times of crisis, and helped them through it. She knew they could help Cale. False hope, she supposed, was better than no hope to people at some points in their life. She didn't begrudge anyone the chance to lessen their grief.

Mark kept standing beside her, staring down at the counter with pensive brown eyes that almost broke her heart. She looked up at him and asked, "What is it, Mark?"

He seemed to shake out of his reverie. "Nothing," he said. "I just hate that I'm coming across as a hypocrite. I admit things haven't been quite right since my marriage broke up, but my beliefs haven't changed." He turned back to Nick. "You realize that, don't you, Nick?"

Nick looked as if the day was getting too heavy for him. "There are a lot of dynamics going on in your life right now, Mark. I understand that."

Whatever that means, Aggie thought with disdain as she turned back to her cooking. That was why she didn't trust preachers. They could never be counted on to say the right thing.

Patting Mark's hand, she put on her biggest smile. "Quit worryin', Mark, darlin'. You're as fine a Christian as anybody walkin' the streets of Newpointe."

But she could tell that her words didn't do anything to improve his mood as he pushed off from the counter and left the kitchen.

●   ●   ●

Outside, Mark found a tree stump and sat on it, looking out over the bayou that snaked through the back lots of the city property. It was a well-maintained bayou, not like the serpentine swamps covered in algae that characterized so much of south Louisiana. In the summer, a stretch of it further down was used for water skiing, but in this part, fishermen often drifted down the narrow channel in their boats, seeking both a catch and a little solace.

Mark glumly scanned the trees draped with long Spanish moss and tangled with catalpa webs, and watched a squirrel run from one of them up toward the city jail on the other side of the police station. Several hundred yards down, from the windows at the top of the basement cells of the city jail, he could hear inmates yelling and cussing. The jail was overcrowded because they'd brought in so many lawbreakers from the roadblocks the night before, and now they didn't know how they were going to process them all. Eventually, he suspected, they would have to let most of them go.

Funny that he felt as imprisoned as them, even though his separation from Allie was supposed to have given him freedom. He'd never felt so constrained, so much in bondage. He'd never had such anxiety, such dread, such hopelessness.

And now Aunt Aggie's comment had dragged him even deeper into his abyss of self-pity and self-deprecation. She hadn't called him a hypocrite, had even gone out of her way to deny that she'd meant that. But the comment about his church attendance from someone who watched from a distance—it had shaken him, made him realize that maybe he had fallen farther than he'd imagined. Were there others out there—other nonbelievers—who were watching his example, seeing him in the bars, following his marriage woes, recording his transgressions? Were they using him as an example of their conviction that Christian zeal was a temporary thing, that it always faded eventually, that it was an emotional exercise that waxed and waned as seasons changed?

Was he being punished for all of that?

The thought, itself, seemed so arrogant, so selfish, that he hated himself all the more. All of this intended as punishment for him? As if God would take two women so that Mark's resulting fears and anxieties would bring him back into step. There were bigger things going on here, and he doubted God even had time to notice his insignificant little lapses.

He heard the back door squeak open and looked over his shoulder to see Ray Ford coming toward him. "Aunt Aggie sent me to get you. Said it's time for lunch."

"I'm not hungry," Mark said. He looked up at his friend, whose dark skin was impressed with lines that hadn't been there days before. "Ray, the truth, no holds barred. What do you and Susan think about me these days?"

Ray looked genuinely surprised by the question. After a moment, he dropped down on the dirt in front of a pine tree across from Mark and looked him in the eye. "Where'd that come from?" he asked.

"Just wondering," Mark said. "Allie's opinion might be contagious."

"If we caught an 'opinion,' Mark, it was from you, not her."

Mark felt himself tensing, growing angry, even before Ray had answered the question. "And what would that opinion be?"

"That maybe, just maybe, you've forsaken your first love."

It wasn't an indictment, wasn't even said in bitterness, but still Mark reacted defensively. "The separation wasn't my idea, Ray. She threw me out over something I didn't even do. She's not interested in counseling; she doesn't want to talk about rec-onciliation—I don't know *what* she wants, Ray. Maybe blood. But don't condemn me because of things I can't control."

Ray only stared at him for a long moment. "How long since you been in the Word?"

Mark rolled his eyes. "What's that got to do with it? I've been busy, okay? Things haven't exactly been smooth sailing lately."

Ray nodded and got back up, dusted off the back side of his uniform. "Maybe that's why," he said, and started back up to the firehouse.

"What does that mean?" Mark called after him. "Really—what does that mean?"

Ray spread his arms innocently, then motioned for him to come on in. "It means I love you, bro, and I think you know better. Aunt Aggie's waiting."

But Mark didn't go in. He had no appetite.

Chapter Seventeen

The morning of the funerals, Blooms 'n' Blossoms buzzed with activities as patrons stopped in or telephoned by the dozens to send flowers to the church for both families. Allie had called in everyone who had ever worked part-time for her during Valentine's or Mother's Day—all three of them—and had them running deliveries for her or taking orders, while she worked feverishly in the back to finish in time for Mark to pick her up.

She heard the front door open and the bell jingle, then Jill Clark appeared in the doorway of the back room. "I had a feeling you'd be up to your elbows in funeral sprays."

"You were right." She put the finishing touches on the spray she was working on, attached the card, then moved it to the side of the room where five other sprays waited to be loaded onto the van. "I figured you'd be up to your elbows processing all those reprobates they threw in jail the other night."

"You were right, too," Jill said, leaning against the doorway. Allie looked up and realized that Jill looked more exhausted than she'd ever seen her. It seemed that everyone in town had aged a decade over the past few days. "I was interviewing clients all night at the jail, and I've been in court all morning, but fortunately the judge wants to go to the funerals, so he recessed for the rest of the day. I just wondered if you wanted to ride with me."

Allie stopped what she was doing and stared down at the flowers in her hand. "Can't. I'm going with Mark."

"With Mark?"

Allie looked up again and saw the surprise in her eyes. "Yeah, he asked me to go with him. I'm not sure why, but it seemed like the right thing to do."

"Well, that's interesting." Jill came further into the fragrant room and leaned on the table, which was covered with cut stems. "You think he's coming around?"

"I don't know," she said. "He's in this protective mode, all of a sudden. Acting real concerned about me, worrying ..." She let the words trail off, and released a long sigh. "It's kind of confusing."

Jill considered that for a moment. "Well, maybe it took the murders to make him realize what he was giving up."

"Don't get your hopes up," Allie said. "I'm not."

"Yes, you are."

Allie met her friend's eyes and saw that she was smiling. But Allie couldn't muster a smile of her own. "Jill, if we got back together out of fear over a couple of murders, how long do you think that would last?"

Jill got quiet. "I don't know, Allie, but you didn't get married out of fear. There was something else there."

Allie's face softened, and she looked back down at the flowers. "We got married because we couldn't stand to be apart. No matter where I was or who I was with, I would rather have been with him."

Jill leaned back against the door casing and smiled. "I remember when he announced your engagement, back when he was leading our singles Sunday school class. He said, 'In one of the greatest acts of kindness known among humans, that beautiful lady in the back has agreed to marry me.'"

Allie almost smiled, but refused to let herself get nostalgic. "Yeah, Mark's always had a way with words. I'm sure Issie appreciates it. I ran into her the other day, you know. She was all smiles. No remorse at all. Superior, like she knew she'd won."

Jill frowned. "Allie, he's not just a bowling trophy or something. She can't win if he doesn't let her."

"But he has. That's just it."

Jill shook her head. "I'm not buying that, Allie. Not yet. I'm just not convinced that Mark can so easily set aside his Christian—"

"People justify their sins all the time, Jill. And that serpent is just waiting, saying, 'Surely you will not die.' Mark's lost his focus. As Nick would say, he believes the lie."

Jill looked disturbed. "Still—if he liked her better, how come he's taking you to the funerals?"

Allie went back to working on her spray. "You act like he's taking me on a date."

"He didn't *have* to ask you, Allie. He could have gone alone."

"He's trying to nip the gossip in the bud."

"Too late for that. Everyone in town already knows you're separated."

Allie breathed a sardonic laugh. "Thanks, Jill. You always know what to say."

"You can't keep secrets in Newpointe. I say he's taking you because he wants to be with you. You said yourself that he's been worrying about you. All symptoms of love, Allie. Not the signs of a man whose heart is somewhere else."

Allie closed her eyes, trying to sift through the signs and signals—and the contradictions.

Just then, Jesse Pruitt, a retired teacher who had come in to help her this morning, breezed into the room, slightly out of breath and sweating. "You ready for me to take these?" She started gathering up the funeral sprays Allie had finished.

"Yes," Allie said. "Two are for Martha, the rest for Jamie."

As Jesse began moving them out to the van, Jill asked, "Is there anything I can do to help?"

Allie looked down at herself. "I had hoped to change clothes before Mark picked me up, but it doesn't look like I'll get to."

"You look fine," Jill said, then smiling slightly, added, "and you smell like the Garden of Eden." Jill touched her friend's cheek, a look of concern on her face. "I would say 'cheer up,' but under the circumstances, I won't. I'll see you at the funeral. Call me if you want to talk afterwards."

Allie waved good-bye, then went into the rest room and looked at herself in the mirror. Would Mark see the fatigue, the depression, the despair on her face, or would he see whatever it was that he used to like about her? Did it really matter? And should she even think about such things when they were on their way to bury the wives of two of Mark's friends?

She got her purse, dug into it for her lipstick, applied some, then powdered and tried to lighten the dark circles under her eyes. But even as she did, she felt the futility of it.

She wasn't sure there was any hope for the two of them.

Chapter Eighteen

When Mark pulled into the parking lot, Allie was just putting the "Closed" sign in the window. He thought of waiting in the car for her, but then decided against it. When they were dating, she had refused to come out unless he came in to get her. To not do so today would seem like an insult, and he didn't want to annoy her now, not when their emotions were already so frayed. Besides, he liked going into the shop. It was fresh and bright, and it smelled like Allie, and he never went through the doors without remembering the way they had dreamed of it and worked for it, and finally made it a reality. It had been as much his dream as hers—a great supplement to his insubstantial fireman's salary, and a place to work on his off-days.

But now it wasn't his anymore. Not really. He supposed that, if there was going to be a divorce, he would let her have the shop in the settlement. She could run it just fine without him—she had for the past two months—but he couldn't run it without her.

He went through the front door, making the little bell ring, and saw her across the floral arrangements. "You ready?" he asked.

"Just a minute," she said, looking preoccupied at the cash register. When she'd finished locking it, she got her purse. "Okay, I guess I am."

He stood there looking at her for a moment, wanting to tell her that she looked like a million bucks, that the blue in her dress brought out the stark blue of her eyes, but something stopped him. Was it pride? Fear of more rejection, like he'd suffered with her the night of the murders? He honestly didn't know.

His perusal seemed to make her feel self-conscious. "I didn't want to wear black," she said, her voice strained and hoarse. "Martha was a Christian, and we're not supposed to grieve as those who have no hope."

"No, we're not," Mark said.

"But then I thought of Jamie, and I wasn't sure if I'd be offending Cale if I didn't wear black."

"You're fine," he said. "I'm sure Cale won't be offended."

"But his parents . . ."

"If you'd feel more comfortable changing . . ."

"Do you think I should?"

"There's not much time, but if you want . . ."

She checked her watch and shook her head. "No, no. That's all right. I'll just wear this." Finally, she met his eyes. "I guess I'm just stalling."

He didn't blame her.

"Let's go," she said. She closed the shop's door behind them, set the dead bolt, and followed him to the car.

A steady stream of cars threaded into the already crowded lot at Calvary Bible Church. They saw Patricia Castor, the mayor, getting out of her car and shaking hands with others as they headed for the door.

Mark pulled into a space beside Ray Ford's car, then sat for a moment, straightening his tie.

"This is awful," Allie whispered. "We're supposed to say good-bye to old people and those who've been sick. Not healthy women in the prime of their lives."

Mark gave up on his tie and took a deep breath, then let it out slowly. "I guess we'd better get in there."

She nodded, and glanced at the car next to theirs. "The Fords are already here."

He took her hand as she got out of the car, and like nervous children who borrowed from each other's strength, they walked into the church where they had been married four years before. Ray Ford met them at the door, acting as usher, and Allie reached up to hug him. "Where's Susan?" she asked.

"She'll be here shortly," Ray said. "I came early to usher."

"We'll save you a place," she said. "Just point her to us when she gets here."

But several minutes later there was still no Susan, and the organist began playing. As the church filled up, Allie had to surrender her saved seats to those pressing in. By the time the service began, she assumed that Susan had found a seat of her own further back in the crowd. Forgetting Susan for the moment, Allie concentrated instead on this quiet moment of closeness in the midst of grief—Mark was sitting beside her, and he was holding her hand.

• • •

Across town at the Ford house, Susan's phone rang, waking her up. She had sat down for just a moment to rest before getting ready for the funeral, but sleep, which had seemed so scarce lately, had overtaken her. She looked at the clock on the wall, and gasped when she realized the funeral had started long ago.

Just then she heard the side door open.

"Ray?" she called. "Ray, I fell asleep. I'm so sorry."

There was no answer.

She started for the kitchen, then felt a chill come over her, and fear traveled through her veins like a drug. Someone was in the house, and it wasn't Ray.

Turning, she bolted toward the back of the house. She took one quick look back over her shoulder—and a muffled gunshot *whoofed* through the air. Her back exploded with scorching, ripping pain. The impact threw her forward, and she hit the floor. *I've been shot*, she realized in terror. *But I'm not dead. Not yet.*

She lay motionless in her own blood, face down, afraid to make a sound for fear that he would finish the job.

And then she heard him crying. At first it was a soft whimper, then it grew louder, more sloppy, more anguished, until the killer was sobbing. She heard him moving around her as he did; she smelled the gasoline . . .

Still she lay motionless, not breathing . . .

"I'm so sorry," the man sobbed in a high-pitched voice. "I'm so sorry, Mary. So sorry."

She heard the match striking, heard the quiet whoosh of the fire igniting in a circle around her. She felt her energy seeping out in the puddle of blood beneath her, felt her life slipping away. She began to pray, even as darkness overtook her.

• • •

Martha's funeral, though sad, was a celebration of a saint going home. The church choir, of which Martha had been a part, sang "It Is Well with My Soul," and Nick Foster told stories of Martha's devotion to Christ, her sacrificial acts of mercy around the town since arriving in Newpointe, her selfless acts of service to her church in the short time she'd been a member. He told of the miracle of the baby she and George had prayed for, and reminded the congregation that, reckoned in eternal time, she would only be separated from that baby and her husband for "a few minutes" before they would be reunited in heaven. He promised that some good would come of this death, whether the killer intended it or Satan wanted it, because God promised that all things would "work together for good to those who loved the Lord and were called according to his purpose."

After the service, they assembled at the grave site in the small cemetery adjacent to the church. There, George held Tommy in his arms and wept as they lowered the casket into the ground. He and his parents and Martha's parents stood accepting condolences from those who chose to give them. As friends and neighbors and church brothers and sisters hugged George or shook his hand or cried with him, they offered words intended to comfort and support—but those words often fell far short.

"Consider it joy," Sue Ellen Hanover, one of the clerks at the local post office, told him, and George swallowed and nodded mutely. Standing nearby and watching, Allie knew that regarding his wife's murder with joy was one of those God-sized tasks George hadn't yet grasped.

"Think how many were led to the Lord through this funeral today," Joyce Drake, who owned the cleaners, told George.

He bounced little Tommy and said, "Martha led lots of folks to Christ when she was alive."

"But maybe more will come through this," the woman insisted.

It was a nice thought, and most likely true, but Allie doubted that George's heart was ready for that kind of speculation.

When she and Mark worked their way close enough to George, Allie reached up to hug him tight, choosing not to say anything. "She's in heaven, man," Mark said with tears in his eyes. "And as hard as it is for you to be separated from her, it's not that long before you will see her again."

George glanced self-consciously at those in line behind them, then lowering his voice, said, "Wonder if she's really there, or just asleep 'til . . ."

Mark stepped closer and touched George's shoulder. "He said, 'Today you will be with me in paradise.' Not hundreds of years from now, but today."

Allie shot him a look, surprised that he still had any spiritual impulses.

George let his words soak in. "He did say it, didn't he?"

"She's there, buddy."

George tightened his lips and looked down at the baby, who was just nodding off in his arms. "We gon' be okay, you know. Tommy's a miracle baby, and God ain't gon' forsake us now."

Allie struggled to hold back her tears, but she failed. Wiping her eyes, she asked, "Is there anything we can do for you, George? Anything at all?"

George's face changed, and his eyebrows lifted. "Yeah, matter of fact. There is."

"What?" Mark asked. "Anything, man."

"Put yo' marriage back together. Some of us don't got a choice. Don't just th'ow it away."

Allie looked down at the floor, avoiding Mark's eyes. "We're doing the best we can, George," Mark said.

"You ain't doin' enough," the grieving man said. He patted Mark's shoulder, then forced a smile. "I can say these things 'cause I know you won't deck me today."

Mark breathed out a strained laugh, then his smile quickly faded as he looked at Allie. Squeezing his friend's arm, he took Allie's hand and led her back to the church.

They were silent for a long moment, then finally, Mark said, "Leave it to George to nail us like that today of all days."

"He just doesn't know all the facts," she said in a flat voice.

"No, he doesn't."

So they did agree on something, Allie mused miserably.

She looked up at the parking lot, and saw a whole new string of traffic pulling in for Jamie's funeral. While most of the town had come for both funerals, some had known Jamie better than Martha and had only come for the second one. "How long before the next funeral?" she asked.

Mark checked his watch. "About half an hour."

"I'm gonna go try to repair my makeup," she told him. "I'll meet you inside the church."

Chapter Nineteen

Susan struggled in and out of consciousness as the flames grew hotter around her and the smoke grew more smothering. As her consciousness returned, she forced herself to move. She was still bleeding, and her hand slipped through the wet puddle beneath her. Summoning all her strength, she turned her head—and saw the flames creeping across the carpet toward her. She had to move. She had to get out of the house while she still could.

She pushed with her feet, triggering unimaginable pain, until she managed to rise up on her knees. Blackness overtook her again, and she fell. But her consciousness hung on, and she pulled herself into a weak little ball and forced herself to roll with all the momentum she could gather—right through the flames that surrounded her.

She felt them singeing her hair and scorching her back, but she managed to keep rolling until she was out of the circle of fire the killer had made for her.

The flames were catching hold of the curtains and climbing the couch. Susan pushed with her feet and clawed with her hands until she reached the table next to the couch. She groped for the telephone cord, found it, and jerked the phone down. The phone fell off the table with a crash and a ring, and she dragged the cord until she had her hands on the base.

Darkness was coming again, sucking her under, but she managed to punch out 911. She couldn't reach the receiver, didn't know where it was. Smoke was filling the room, choking her, burning her lungs, and she felt the heat of flames licking close to her again.

"911, may I help you?"

She knew that the dispatcher could help her, but she couldn't get the words out.

"Hello? May I help you?"

"Help ..." The word was too faint, and she knew the dispatcher didn't hear. She groped for the coiled cord to the handset and pulled the receiver closer. "Help ..."

The darkness was too thick and the smoke too smothering, and she couldn't get a breath. Finally, the darkness closed in on her, leaving her no escape.

Chapter Twenty

Ray Ford grew concerned when the crowd had thinned out and Susan was still nowhere in sight. He wondered if she had fallen asleep at home and missed the funeral. She hadn't been sleeping well since the murders, and he wouldn't be surprised if she'd lain down for a few minutes and failed to open her eyes again in time.

He went to the church office to call home, but someone was using the phone. No problem. He had time to run home and get her up before Jamie's funeral began.

He trotted out to his car, pulled out of the packed parking lot, and headed down the street between the rows of cars parked on the sides of the streets. When he reached his house, he saw that Susan's car was still there.

A dull buzzing noise sang from inside the house, and as he realized it might be the smoke alarm, he broke into a run. He reached the back door and flung it open. Smoke billowed out.

He yelled for his wife as he stumbled into the kitchen. His heart jolted when he saw the flames dancing in the living room. He grabbed the tablecloth from the kitchen table and the fire extinguisher they kept under the sink, ran into the living room, and began smothering the flames, yelling, "Susan! Susan!"

Then he saw her, lying facedown in a pool of blood in the only part of the room that wasn't yet engulfed.

"No!" His scream shook the house. He dropped the extinguisher, gathered her up, and crashed out the front door. As he collapsed with her on the grass, he saw that her face was blood-splattered and her chest was soaked with blood. He heard a siren as he searched her neck for a pulse. "Susan, hang on, darlin'. Don't leave me, baby."

Finding a pulse, he bent his head and began praying as the sirens grew closer. A fire truck stopped in front of his house, then an ambulance, and the paramedics rushed to take her from him. "She's not dead," he told them. "She's not dead." His voice cracked as he tried to speak. "You've got to save her. Please."

But as they tried to stabilize her for rapid transport, he wondered if it was too late.

Chapter Twenty-One

Because no one knew for sure whether Jamie Larkins was a believer—and from her behavior, most assumed she was not—hers was a funeral of despair. Though Nick tried to offer hope, it was a floundering attempt at best. Nick had confided to Mark before the service that, as hard as he'd tried to come up with kind, hopeful words to say about her, most of what he'd heard from her friends and family had been wild stories about how "carefree" she was, how she loved life, how she would rather spend a night on the town with good friends than just about anything.

Empty sentiments for a life that would leave little legacy, Mark thought as he watched the pastor struggle with the eulogy. The difference between Cale's face now and George's at the previous funeral was profound. Though both were in agony, and neither could boast of much peace, George seemed to hold together better than Cale did.

Mark wished now that he had felt more concern about the Larkins's relationship to God, but all those nights he'd gone to Joe's Place and shared drinks with them, it had never crossed his mind that their need to find God might be urgent. He wasn't sure where his mind *had* been, but he knew it hadn't been on spiritual life—his own or anyone else's. Not for a long time. He felt as guilty as if he'd had something to do with Jamie's death himself. He'd moved a long way since his last Promise Keepers rally, he thought. An awful long way. In the wrong direction.

Allie was crying. Instinctively, he put his arm around her. She didn't recoil, as he'd half expected, and he wished he could take her home and hold her through the night, comfort her and let her comfort him . . .

But these moments—sitting here so close to her, holding her, touching her—were no longer reality. And when reality set back in, he and Allie would once again go their separate ways, despite George's admonitions.

After the service, they headed to their car for the procession to the grave site on the other side of Newpointe, which was not in the churchyard since the Larkins weren't members there. Mark opened the door and helped Allie into his car, then got in and pulled into the procession forming in the parking lot. At the front of the line, just behind the hearse, was Johnny Ducote, another fireman, driving the big limousine—his "moonlighting" job when he wasn't on duty. He had offered his services free for both families today, but Mark doubted that it gave them much comfort.

Before the hearse began to move, Mark saw Slater Finch pull out of the procession and make a quick U-turn. Several cars back, another car pulled out.

"Must be something going on somewhere to pull them away from this," Mark said, reaching to turn on the scanner he kept under his dash. He kept it on most of the time, as many of the firemen and police officers did, to the chagrin of their wives and families, but he had turned it off before he'd picked up Allie.

"You'd think they could let the on-duty guys handle it," Allie said. "It's not like this is a football game. It's the funeral of their colleague's wife, for heaven's sake."

"Shhh. Listen." He turned it up and tried to tune to an active frequency.

He found a police frequency first, heard an excited cop practically yelling into the radio. "The fire department is working on the fire, and we've got the ambulance taking Susan to meet the Medicoptor so they can get her to the hospital in Slidell. But I don't know, the gunshot wound was pretty bad. If Ray hadn't come home when he did and found her ..."

"Susan and Ray?" Allie shouted, turning the radio up. "Not the Fords. Not Susan!"

"Oh, no." Mark closed his eyes and covered his face. "Not again. They caught the guy! He's still in jail."

Someone behind him in the procession tapped his horn. Mark jumped and opened his eyes. The cars ahead were moving, and he was holding the line up. Jerking his steering wheel hard to the right, he pulled out of the line.

"Where should we go?" Allie's voice was high-pitched, panicked.

"I don't know. House or hospital?"

"The hospital," she cried. "Oh, Mark. Hurry!"

Chapter Twenty-Two

Television vans were rapidly filling the parking lot at Slidell Memorial Hospital. Technicians scurried around setting up for live broadcasts as camera crews and reporters hurried toward the emergency room, providing a morbid sense of melodrama as Mark and Allie tried to find a parking space. The case was no longer just another murder, so common in south Louisiana. Now it was a serial killing, and the whole nation would follow the story.

Mark finally parked on the street, took Allie's hand, and headed into the emergency room. It wasn't easy—photographers and reporters were already crowded in elbow to elbow, some taping already, others calling in stories on the two pay phones or their own hand-held cell phones. The handful of people who'd come for treatment—a man with a cut arm, an asthmatic baby wheezing in his mother's arms, and a woman who appeared to be close to passing out—seemed incidental to the news the reporters sought.

Mark and Allie pushed through the crowd to the information desk where a frazzled nurse sat. He started to ask her if Susan had made it to the hospital, then overheard a reporter taping for the six o'clock news: ". . . here in Slidell Memorial Hospital, where this bizarre serial killing, targeting only wives of firemen in the Northshore town of Newpointe, is taking a new twist. We're told that Susan Ford, the newest victim, has a serious chest wound. She came very close to being burned as well, and if her husband had not found her when he did, she may have lost her life. She remains unconscious . . ."

The haggard nurse pulled a pencil from her beehive hair. "Sir, if you're a reporter, I'm going to have to ask you to move over there."

Mark swung his attention from the news anchor. "No, I'm a friend of Susan and Ray Ford. Do you know where Ray is?"

"Yes, sir, he's here," the woman said in a nasal twang. "But everyone here wants to see him. We're not allowing anybody back."

"Oh, please," Allie said, bracing her hands on the reception desk. "He shouldn't be alone through this. We're close friends, and he needs someone with him."

The nurse sneered at them. "You reporters are reprehensible. I don't know how you sleep at night."

"We're not reporters!" Mark insisted. "I'm a fireman in Newpointe and I work with Ray."

Her face changed, and she crossed her big arms and chewed on her pencil for a moment. "A fireman, huh?"

He pulled out his wallet and showed her his I.D. "Yes. Mark Branning. And this is my wife, Allie."

It was as though he had changed channels on the woman's personality. Instantly, she softened. "Oh, you poor thing. You must be scared to death that you'll be next."

Mark looked at Allie, and she looked back. He put his arm around her shoulders. Three firemen's wives shot. He'd worried before that there was a killer on the loose in Newpointe. For the first time, he realized the killer was actually targeting—

"Excuse me!" The loud voice turned them around, and a reporter stuck a microphone in Mark's face. Blinding lights were suddenly on them. "I'm Clive Southerlyn from WDSU-TV in New Orleans," the man said in his familiar broadcast voice. "Did I hear you say you're on the fire department with Ray Ford?"

"That's right," Mark said.

"Sir, why do you think this killer is targeting your wives?"

He started to answer, but other reporters began to gravitate toward him, sticking more mikes in his face. "Uh . . . well, I didn't realize until Susan was shot that he was . . . that is . . ."

"Do you know who could be doing this?" someone shouted.

"No . . . uh . . ."

A reporter jabbed a mike in front of Allie's face, almost hitting her in the mouth. "What's your name, ma'am?"

"Allie Branning," she said, trying to back away.

"How do you feel about being a target for this killer, Mrs. Branning?"

"I'm not sure that's what I am."

"Are you going to stay at home tonight?"

"Were you friends with the other three women?"

"Do you know if Susan Ford was involved in drugs, as well?"

As Allie burst into tears, Mark struggled with the anger moving red-hot through his veins. He pushed away the cluster of mikes. "Please! We just want to know how our friend is doing."

He pulled Allie along with him toward the double swinging doors leading to the examining rooms. No one stopped them as they burst through, but when the reporters tried to follow, two security guards appeared and held them back.

They stopped in the corridor. Allie was shaking, and she wiped her eyes with a trembling hand. "Are you all right?" he asked.

"I'm scared, Mark," she whispered.

"Me, too."

"What does this mean? What's going to happen? Is he really targeting *us*?"

Mark shook his head. "I wish I knew. We have to find Ray," he said. He looked past her down the long antiseptic hallway, and saw Ray slumped over in a folding chair. "Ray!" He let Allie go, and they both ran to their friend's side. Still wearing his dress blues from the funeral, though they were soaked with blood, Ray stood up and accepted their fierce hugs.

"How is she?" Allie asked.

"Alive," Ray said. "I went in and saw the smoke, and she was layin' there ... fire all 'round her ..."

"Thank God you found her."

"I have thanked him, believe me." He wiped his rough face and shook his head as he sank back down. "But she ain't conscious yet. They got her in surgery, and they're tryin' to see how much damage the bullet did to her lungs." He looked up at them, his lips thin as he bit the words out. "Shot her through the back, you know. Poured gas in a circle around her. But the fire spread away from her instead of toward her." He looked up at Mark, his eyes tormented and anguished, and he asked, "Why, Mark? Who *did* this?"

"I don't know."

"It ain't the guy they got locked up, that's for sure. And it don't have nothin' to do with drugs. It's us, Mark. Somebody's comin' after our wives!"

The double doors opened again and the nurse came back escorting a distraught Vanessa, the Ford's fifteen-year-old daughter. Behind her was Sid, Ray's brother, still in his cop's uniform, who looked as if he, too, had wept all the way from Newpointe.

"Daddy?" Vanessa cried when she saw her father. "Is she dead, Daddy?"

Ray got up and she ran into his arms. "No, honey," he said. "No, she ain't dead. But she's in bad shape. We're waitin' to hear how her surgery comes out."

Vanessa wailed against her father's shoulder.

Sid patted his brother's back. "I called Ben. He's on his way from Baton Rouge."

Ray nodded, still clinging to his daughter. Finally, he looked back at the rest of them over Vanessa's head. With pleading eyes, he said, "Don't waste your time here, Mark. Take Allie and go back to Newpointe. Call a meetin' of all of the firefighters and their wives, and brainstorm 'til you figure this thing out. Somebody knows somethin'. Somebody will have some idea who might be doin' this. Mark, we can't let him get any of the other wives."

"You're right," Mark said. "But I'd rather stay here until I know how Susan is."

"I'll call the station and let y'all know," Ray said. "But time's wastin', Mark. We have to *do* somethin'."

Reluctantly, they left Ray with hugs and empty words of comfort. Then, hand in hand, they pushed back through the reporters. Other firemen and their wives had come in by now and were surrounded by cameras and microphones. As Mark pushed through the doors leading out, one of them called, "Mark, what did you find out? How's Susan?"

"Still in surgery," he said. "Ray wants us back in Newpointe. He wants us to call a meeting with all the firefighters and their wives, and figure out some kind of strategy."

"How are you going to protect your wives, Mr. Branning?" one of the reporters asked.

Without answering, Mark pushed out through the double doors, pulling Allie beside him.

Uneasy now that they were out into the open, he found himself with his arm around Allie, holding her close as they walked. Yes, all three wives had been at home alone when the killer had gotten to them, but now he must know that they were onto him, and that it wouldn't be so easy anymore. What if he got desperate or overconfident or anxious and started coming after them wherever he could find them? His eyes scanned the cars in the parking lot as he headed to his own.

Allie picked up on it immediately. "He wouldn't come after us in broad daylight out in a parking lot, Mark. He's doing this in secret."

"You're assuming he's consistent," he said, "This guy's too unstable to be predictable. Anyone who would murder a woman and then set her on fire has a loose wire somewhere. There's no telling what he might do."

He opened the driver's door of his car, guided Allie in first, and then slid in next to her. He checked the rearview mirror for anything out of the ordinary, then turned his key in the ignition.

"I wonder if he'd count me," she said in a flat, pensive voice as he pulled out of the parking space.

"What do you mean?"

"As a wife," she said. "Maybe I'm safe because we're not married anymore."

That almost sent him over the edge. "We *are* married, Allie."

"On paper," she said miserably as tears filled her eyes again. "Maybe he knows that. Maybe that exempts me from all this madness."

"Maybe," he conceded. "We can hope."

She covered her face with a hand, and her shoulders shook as she wept quietly.

He could feel her trembling next to him as her tears came harder. "I never thought there would be a blessing in our separation," she whispered.

He swallowed the emotion in his throat, but couldn't find a response to that. So he said nothing.

He concentrated on breaking into the traffic on Highway 90. They traveled for several miles in silence before he finally turned on the radio.

They listened to the news of Susan's shooting and the fires and the two other wives. Mark gritted his teeth. To the reporters, these women were just statistics—not real people with husbands, children, friends. When he realized that they were just repeating the same information over and over, he turned the radio off.

"As soon as we hit town, we'll go by the fire station and ask the chief to schedule a meeting. Then we'll go home and pack our bags."

"Bags?" she asked. "What for?"

"We can't be where he expects us to be tonight. I'm supposed to go on duty at five, but I'll get somebody to cover for—"

"Mark, every fireman in town is going to want to take off tonight. They're not going to let you."

"Then they'll have to fire me," he said. "I'm not leaving you alone tonight."

He wasn't sure what to make of her silence. "Mark, this isn't necessary," she said finally. "Believe me, I'm scared to death. I'm not going to stay at home alone. I'll stay with Jill or something."

"Two women alone could be just as bad as one. No way."

"Then I'll stay with Celia and Stan. What better place to be than with the detective who's investigating the murders?"

"He won't be home. Celia will be looking for a place to stay, too. She'll probably stay at Aunt Aggie's, and that's no help."

"Maybe we could *all* stay together. All the wives of the men who are on duty tonight. We could rent a hotel suite somewhere and hide until they catch him."

"No. Too easy. He could get you all in one swoop."

She shivered. "Don't be so morbid, Mark. I'm trying to find a solution."

"The solution is that I'm going to stay with you. We'll go get a room on the Southshore, where he won't be looking for us. I'm not going to leave your side until this is over."

Instead of relieving her, his insistence seemed to make her angry. "That's very touching, Mark, but I don't think it's a good idea. I don't want you suddenly caring about me because someone's trying to kill me. If you can't care about me every day, then it doesn't mean anything. There are other people who can protect—"

He slammed his hand against the steering wheel. "I *do* care about you, Allie," he shouted. "Every day. You're just too blind to see it."

As soon as the words were out of his mouth, he regretted them. They wouldn't help his cause. But he couldn't pull them back.

"And I suppose falling in love with another woman was one of the caring acts I was too blind to see?" she cried.

"I did *not* fall in love with another woman!" he shouted. "How many times do I have to tell you?"

"Don't tell me, *show* me," she yelled. "That's all I've been asking all along. And what I've seen is just the opposite. I'm not blind, Mark, you just wish I were."

"So you want me just to throw you to the wolves and pretend like you're not my wife?"

"You've been pretending it just fine for the past two months, Mark. I have friends, lots of them. I can stay with some of them, and I'll be fine."

"But *I won't*," he rasped. "*I won't!* Every time we get a 911 call I'll worry that it's you. Every minute I'll wonder if he's seeking you out, if he's found you. I'm not working tonight, Allie, and I'm not letting someone else do the job that I'm supposed to do. I promised to honor and protect you, and I intend to do that."

"You fell way short of the honor part," she cried. "Why is the protection part so important? Does it make you feel more like a man?"

He opened his mouth to shout a reply, then stopped. He breathed deeply a couple of times, then lowered his voice to a barely controlled monotone. "You won't insult me out of this, Allie. When you decided our marriage was over, I left. When you told me you wanted to quit going to counseling, we stopped. Until now, you've called most of the shots, but now *I'm* telling *you!* You're going home and packing a bag, and you're coming with me to New Orleans tonight, if I have to physically carry you."

"So you're going to protect me if it kills me?"

"That's right," he said.

To his relief she said nothing else. It wasn't until they passed the "Welcome to Newpointe" sign that he realized that he'd meant every word he'd said. Nothing on this planet could keep him from staying with her tonight. He just wasn't sure what her stubbornness was going to cost him.

Chapter Twenty-Three

As soon as Aggie Gaston had heard about the meeting for the firefighters and their wives that evening, she'd started working to prepare enough food for all of them—and she'd been at it all day. She'd had no way of getting it all into the courtroom at city hall, where the mayor had suggested they hold the meeting, since none of the rooms at either the fire station or police precinct were big enough. One of the firemen had suggested that she borrow a gurney from one of the ambulances to cart the food on—an idea that had seemed distasteful at first, but after she'd wiped it down with Lysol and gotten all the food loaded on, she had found it quite a handy thing to have. She even toyed with the idea of buying one herself, in case the need ever arose again. She unloaded the pots and bowls onto the defense table, then set all of her china on the prosecutor's table, complete with silverware and cloth napkins folded in the shapes of swans. She had to admit that it had exhausted her to do all this, and she would no doubt sleep like a baby tonight, but it was worth it, because she knew it would be appreciated. They must all be starving to death, what with the murders and the fires, and that poor little Susan lying up in the hospital fighting for her life. And she should know, of all people, since she knew their appetites better than anyone else.

The courtroom smelled like a Creole restaurant by the time the firemen and their wives began arriving. In another room in the courthouse, Lynette Devreaux, a rookie cop, baby-sat their children. The courtroom filled up as they filed in, all eighteen married firemen and their wives, as well as the seven bachelors. Craig Barnes, the fire chief, was among them, as well as Jim Shoemaker, the police chief, and Patricia Castor, their esteemed mayor who liked to be at the center of everything important in the town, if for no other reason than to campaign for the next election. Stan and Celia were there, too—Stan, to answer questions and help with the brainstorming process as the detective working on the case, and Celia, because she was Aunt Aggie's great niece and a friend to everyone there—and because she had insisted on helping to clean up.

To Aunt Aggie's chagrin, few of those who came seemed to have appetites, and over half of them took their places without even looking at the food. She briefly considered taking the leftovers down to the jail, but changed her mind when she realized that that's just what Aunt Bea would have done.

When Patricia Castor finished her plate of crawfish etouffee and took her place in the judge's seat, as if she were in charge here instead of the police chief or the fire chief, Aunt Aggie took a seat in the defense attorney's chair, turned it so that she could see everyone in the room, and waited for Jim Shoemaker to tell them who was killing the firemen's wives.

- - -

Mark and Allie sat side by side in the courtroom—with several inches between them, since both were still angry over their fight in the car. In the end, she had capitulated—they had gone by the house and she had packed a bag. But, to Mark's annoyance, before they had settled into their seats in the courtroom, she had looked for someone else to stay with. It wasn't to be, however, since none of the wives intended to stay in their homes that night. All of them had plans to go into hiding until the culprit was caught. Allie was stuck with him, Mark thought angrily.

As if she were the judge reading out a verdict, Patricia Castor, in a pullover cable-knit sweater and a pair of khaki pants, banged the gavel on the judge's desk and insisted it was time to get down to business. "Now, I know ya'll are upset by these killings," she drawled, raising her voice since she didn't have the microphone she usually had when she spoke in public. "We all are. But we cannot panic. I've been hearing some of you men saying that ya'll refuse to go on duty until the killer is caught, but that is simply out of the question. We have to have firefighters on duty. We can't leave Newpointe without its protective services. That would present a crisis for our town. So the shifts will proceed as scheduled."

Jim Shoemaker, the plump, bald-headed police chief who leaned on the railing in front of the jury box, rolled his eyes. "We've taken care of it, Patty. The unmarried firemen on the force have agreed to work until the killer is caught, so that the married firemen can tend to their wives. Newpointe won't go up in a blaze of smoke, and you won't come out with egg on your face. Don't worry—if you lose the next election, it won't have anything to do with this."

The mayor's face reddened, and she leaned forward condescendingly. "Jim, I'd suggest that you start looking for the killer instead of worrying about our firefighters' schedules or my next election." She glanced at Craig Barnes, the fire chief. "Craig, do you always let the police chief do your job?"

Craig Barnes, whose eyes and nose were red, as if he'd had a weeping bout of his own over the killings, bristled at the accusation. "No, Patty, I do not. And I, personally, don't like the idea of keeping the same crew on duty until this person is caught. It could take weeks, and my men would be exhausted. I've tried to think of alternatives, and to me, the best solution is to let the wives whose husbands are working stay together with a twenty-four-hour guard. You can handle that, can't you, Jim?"

"No way," Mark called out, looking around at the others. "I don't want Allie anywhere near the other wives. No offense, but she's not gonna be a sitting duck."

"The wives could leave town," Patricia said. "Just take a vacation until it all blows over. Visit relatives or something. Why should the bachelors work consecutive shifts without a break?"

"They can sleep when they're not out on a call, Mayor," Mark said, "and they'll eat better than ever while they're at the station anyway."

Aunt Aggie beamed.

"I don't care," the mayor said. "There has to be another alternative. We will not jeopardize the protective services in this town."

"And *I* will not jeopardize my wife's life!" Mark yelled, jumping to his feet.

Everyone got quiet, and the mayor, who hadn't given Mark the time of day since her last campaign, pinned him with a look. But Mark would not back down.

"Two women are dead and another is fighting for her life. I don't give a rip about schedules and shifts. I am not going on duty tonight when some maniac wants to see my wife dead!"

Stunned, Allie looked up at him.

The mayor banged her gavel again. "It appears to me that your wife is the least endangered, since you don't even live together!"

Mark breathed an exasperated laugh and shook his head dolefully. "And here I thought that the mayor had too much to do to worry about all the town's gossip."

Pastor Nick Foster, always the peacemaker, stood up. "Mayor, as one of the unmarried men in the department, I can say that I'm more than willing to work as long as necessary, provided I can get off for a couple hours on Sunday morning to preach. There's not a lot I can do, but at least I can do that."

"That's nice of you, Preacher," Patricia said, "but you're not the only bachelor we're talking about."

Dan Nichols cleared his throat, getting the mayor's attention. "Uh, Mayor, I'm one of those single men, too, as you know, and I'd very much like to work in my friends' places while they take care of their wives. It's no problem. We get plenty of sleep on most normal nights. These women are my friends, too, and it would do me good to know that I was helping in some way."

"Me, too," Jacob Baxter, a young widower, added. "I'd feel a lot better about it. Don't seem right these women should be in danger just because their husbands are city employees."

The other two bachelors chimed in, and finally, Shoemaker tried again. "It makes the most sense, Mayor. And Craig, no offense intended, but if you force these men to leave their wives and work tonight, you might be asking for mass mutiny. If you make these husbands work, and then something happens to one of the wives, well . . ."

Craig looked at Jim as if he'd like to step outside and settle the matter with his fists. His jaw popped as he turned back to his men. "You're firefighters. *My* firefighters. And firefighters are public servants—which means they do their jobs when their jobs need to be done. Without good firemen, people die. Now, this is a critical time in Newpointe. If people hear that our firefighters are turning tail and running—"

Mark stood up, his heart pounding in anger and frustration. He concentrated on regaining his cool. "Look, Chiefs, Mayor—I know all three of you have a ton on your shoulders because of these murders. You're at the top of the protection chain in this town, and you have to think of the whole town, not just us." If anger wouldn't work, he would try flattery and charm. He didn't want to see Allie—or any of the other wives—jeopardized just because of a clash of egos among those at the top. "I understand that you don't want to start a panic, and that it's important for everything to look normal. I understand about job commitment and scheduling and public confidence. I love my job. I've wanted to be a firefighter since I was a kid. And I've given this job and this town everything I've had since the day I was hired, without complaining about the low pay and the toll it can take on my personal life." He glanced at Allie. She was watching him skeptically, and he knew that she wondered if this speech was sincere or just a means of manipulating her. He suddenly felt defeated—she always jumped to the wrong conclusion.

He forced himself to continue. "But I'm asking for a favor now. Let me protect my wife. Let all of us. You can't possibly believe we should make our work schedule a priority over the lives of our wives. Not in a family-friendly town like this. Mayor?"

Pat Castor's expression had softened during his speech, and now she looked torn. "Family-friendly" was one of the most-used phrases in her last campaign, so she couldn't dismiss Mark's point. "Well, I always do say that this is a family town. And of course I don't expect you to prioritize like that. That wasn't our intent. We do care what happens to your wives."

He turned to Craig, his arms spread, palms up. "Chief?"

The fire chief, who had never been married, stared back for a long moment, then looked around at the grieving, frightened couples in the room. "All right," he said, almost grudgingly. "You can have some time off. Jim, you'd better find this guy quick, because I can't work with one crew indefinitely."

"I'll do my best."

"Why don't you tell us how you plan to do that?" Pat Castor asked.

Jim nodded to Stan Shepherd. "Stan, you're the detective working on these cases. Tell us what you know."

Stan stood up from his front-row seat and turned to face the crowd, his back to the mayor. "Well, I hate to say it, but it does look like we got the wrong guy when we arrested Hank Keyes. We transferred him back to Bogaloosa this afternoon, where he's being held on drug charges. But he's no longer a suspect in the murders."

"No!" Marty Bledsoe bellowed, and a murmur went up over the room. "Why would you go and do a thing like that?"

"Because he couldn't have gone after Susan Ford while he was in jail."

"But the paper said he was in a gang," Mark argued. "Maybe his roommate did it, or another gang member."

"These murders don't fit that gang's profile," Jim Shoe-maker said. "They're known for race crimes."

"So Susan Ford is black!"

"But Martha and Jamie aren't," Stan said. "Or—weren't," he corrected himself awkwardly. "We're beginning to think that Jamie Larkins's purchase of that cocaine from Hank Keyes had nothing to do with the murders. We searched his car and didn't find the murder weapon, and while we did find some guns in his apartment, they were registered and none of them was what we were looking for."

"If it isn't him, who is it?" Mark demanded.

"That's where we need your help," Stan said. "Everything is speculation at this point."

"You don't have any leads at all?" Craig Barnes asked.

"Few," Stan said, and a murmur rose from the crowd. "Our killer has been pretty good at burning all the evidence. We don't know if he's setting the fires to do just that, or whether it's some kind of statement or signature. And at this point, we have to consider everyone a suspect. If any of you has reason to think anyone could be connected with this, we need to know."

The room got uncomfortably quiet as each of them tried to identify plausible suspects among their neighbors and friends.

"We're not expecting anyone to point a finger right here, right now, but if you have any hunches we hope you'll come to us in private and let us know as soon as possible. You don't have to be right. But just bringing up the name could help. We'll rule him out if he's the wrong guy."

"Sounds like a witch hunt to me," Dan Nichols said.

"It's not a witch hunt," Jim Shoemaker piped up. "We just have to start somewhere."

"Meanwhile, we need to talk logistics," Stan added. "Do's and don'ts. Listen carefully, people, because these things just might save your lives."

Chapter Twenty-Four

Mark and Allie were on their way out when Stan and Celia Shepherd stopped them. "Can I talk to you two for a minute?" Stan asked.

"Sure," Mark said.

Celia, a pretty woman with hair so fair and blonde that it looked like baby hair, touched her husband's arm. "I'll just stay here and help Aunt Aggie clean up."

Stan regarded the gurney on which Aunt Aggie had loaded the food. "I think she's got it under control, and some of the guys are helping her. Why don't you come with us?"

"But isn't this police business?"

He looked uneasy at the question, then said, "Look, I'm feeling as uneasy right now as the firemen are about leaving my wife alone. Just come with me, okay?"

Celia looked from Stan, to Mark, then to Allie, and finally said, "Okay."

"You're worried he's going to cross over to the police wives next?" Mark asked softly as they walked out of the courthouse and crossed the street to the police station.

"I don't know what his motive is, or why he's targeting the fire wives. The truth is, we can't be sure that we *know* what his pattern is yet—he could be targeting city employees' wives, or wives of emergency personnel. Who knows? I'm not willing to take the chance."

Celia took in a deep breath and put her arm through Allie's. Arm in arm, the two friends followed their husbands into the interrogation room.

When they had sat down, Allie beside Mark and Celia beside Stan, Mark asked, "So what's this about, Stan?"

Stan rubbed his face and looked at his friends for a moment. He was tired, Mark could see, and he realized that Stan had probably gotten even less sleep than the rest of them in the past few days. He, after all, was the one on whose shoulders this whole investigation fell.

"I have a favor to ask."

"What?"

"I want to use your house tonight. See if we can trap the killer."

Mark sat stiffer in his chair, and gaped across the table at the detective. "You've got to be kidding."

"I can't see any other way, Mark," Stan said. "We haven't caught him, and we don't have any serious leads. But we might be able to trap him. Now that we can see that he has an agenda—"

"To kill our wives," Mark added.

"Looks that way. And now that we can see his agenda, I'm thinking that maybe we can start trying to think like him. Anticipate his next move."

Allie's face was pale as she stared at Stan through fear-stricken eyes. "And you think *I'm* going to be his next move?"

"Not necessarily," Stan said. "But so far, all of the shootings have been very close to each other. Houses just blocks from city hall, right in the heart of Newpointe. All of the other families live a little farther out. You're the only one left who lives in the center of town. Whether that means something to him or not, I can't say. But if it does, and he hits your house, we'll be there."

"No way," Mark said, standing suddenly and pulling Allie to her feet beside him. "No way are you going to use my wife for a decoy. This guy isn't playing. He sets fire to houses and puts bullets into defenseless women. He doesn't wait to make sure there aren't cops hiding in the other room."

"You're getting me all wrong," Stan said. "Sit down, okay? Sit down and let me explain what I'm suggesting."

Allie wiped her eyes with a trembling hand. After a moment, Mark took his seat again beside her. This time he reached for her hand and held it, as if through their hands he could communicate that no one on this earth was going to endanger her. Not while he was still breathing.

Stan tried again. "What are your plans for tonight? Were you going to stay in town?"

"Nope," Mark said, brooking no debate. "We're leaving town, so you'd better find someone else's house to use."

"Fine. Go. That's what I want you to do. Just give me the key to your house, so we can make it look like Allie is still home. Turn on some lights, leave the car in the driveway, turn the sprinkler on in the yard. All signs that someone is home. We'll be waiting for him."

"What if he burns down my house?" Allie asked. "What if he kills one of you?"

Celia turned her worried eyes to her husband, but said nothing.

"I'm a cop, Allie," Stan said. "I know what I'm doing. As for your house, his MO seems to be that he shoots first and then sets fire. If we catch him before there's a victim, there will never be a fire. Guys, it's the only way I can think of right now to catch him quickly. We have to draw him out."

Mark looked at Allie again. "What do you say, Allie? It's really your house now."

She looked down at the table. "The thought of him coming anywhere near my house . . ." Her voice cracked, and she swallowed hard. "But he's got to be caught, or I can never go back there myself." She rubbed her eyes, long ago tear-washed free of any vestiges of makeup. "Oh, what he did to Susan. And Martha, and Jamie." Her voice got higher in pitch with each word. "I want him caught, Mark. If this is the way . . ."

"It's the fastest way, if it works," Stan said. "And it may not. He may not come. Or, like the mayor said, he may not count you, Allie, since you two are separated. It's a sick mind we're dealing with, so we can't know for sure. But it's a start."

Allie wiped her eyes again, then dried her hands on her skirt. "The thought that I might be next ..." Her voice broke off. "Let's do it."

Stan fixed his eyes on Mark. "Are you okay with this?"

Mark didn't like it. None of it. But if it worked ... "I guess so."

"This means that you can't tell anyone you're leaving town. No one. Understood?"

"Stan, I just announced in that meeting that I'm not leaving Allie's side. So no one will expect her to be home alone."

"Then let's make him think you had another falling out. Allie can storm out of here with you right behind her, Mark, where everyone can see. You can say something like, 'Okay, then protect yourself! I've had it!'"

"Man, they'll think I'm such scum."

"We'll clear it up later, Mark. For now, I need your help. We can leave lights on at your apartment, and the television, too. If he checks, he'll think you're home. He'll buy it. Everybody in town knows you're separated."

Mark bit his lip. The idea that the trouble in his and Allie's marriage was apparently so widely discussed infuriated him, but he supposed he deserved it. He hadn't made a secret of his maintaining a separate residence, or of his nightly visits to Joe's Place.

"What do I need to do?" Allie asked.

"Nothing. Just give me the key, then fake a fight as you both run out of here, and I'll take care of the rest," Stan said. "You two slam into the car and screech away. They'll think you're taking her home, Mark, but go ahead and leave town instead. Allie, we'll get your van home, since it's still at your shop."

"What about the press people out on the sidewalk?"

"I'll pick the moment you leave to give them a statement," he said. "It'll distract them."

Allie reached into her purse for her key chain and handed it across the table. Stan dropped the keys into his pocket, then crossed his arms on the table. "Look, a lot of people in town are praying for you," he said. "Both of you, and all of the other families. Do me a favor, though, would you? Pray for me, too. I really want to find this guy." He took Celia's hand, squeezed it, and said, "He's got to be stopped."

"We will," Allie said. She got up and hugged Stan tightly, then Celia. "Be careful, okay? Both of you."

Celia clung to her, her body shaking with a renewed onslaught of tears. "I love you guys. And I know this'll all be over soon."

Chapter Twenty-Five

Are you okay?" Mark looked at Allie as he drove. Her head leaned against the window, and she nodded mildly. Their orchestrated argument at city hall had gotten the attention of several of the firefighters and their wives, but it seemed to have taken a lot out of her.

"Yeah. I was just thinking."

"Thinking what?"

She hesitated, and a few minutes passed. "About what George said to us at the funeral."

"About getting back together?" he asked.

"Yeah. And I know it isn't going to happen. But it would be nice if we didn't have to air our dirty laundry in public the way we just did."

"I'm not crazy about it, either, especially since I came out looking like a major-league jerk. But like Stan said, we'll clear it all up after this is over."

"Will we?" she asked. "As we go our separate ways, we'll let the town know that we weren't really at each other's throats? We were just helping Stan? You think that'll really change their opinion of you, Mark?"

He bristled. "*You* threw *me* out, Allie. I was in it for the long haul."

"Till death do us part?" she asked cynically.

He started to retaliate, then stopped, watching her out of the corner of his eye as the lights of passing cars and street-lamps cast her face in light and shadow. For a long time, the silence held. Finally, Mark spoke again. "I don't want death to part us, Allie."

Her face had turned back to her window, and he knew she was crying. He hated it when he made her cry. "Look, we're tense," he said quietly. "Our nerves are frayed. Let's just try to get along, okay?"

"You don't have to stay with me tonight, Mark."

"Yes, I do. You're my wife."

A tense silence caught them again. Finally, Allie asked, "Where are we going?"

He shrugged. "New Orleans," he said. "We can get lost there."

•   •   •

The long drive on I–10 over Lake Pontchartrain was quiet, and Allie leaned her head against the window and watched the shadows and lights dancing off of the water. Something told her that her life had taken a drastic turn, that things were never going to be the same again. She'd never go into her house without locking the door again, and she'd never feel comfortable alone. She would never take for granted any of her friends. And she'd never take her own life for granted again.

She looked at Mark and saw that he, too, was lost in his thoughts. What was he thinking? Was he wondering what he was going to do with her? It was clear that he worried about her safety, something that surprised and gratified her. But there was still Issie Mattreaux. Where was she, and was Mark worried about her, too?

The thought filled her with that familiar mixture of pain and outrage, and she looked out the window again.

"Do you have any place in particular that you'd like to stay when we get there?" Mark asked.

The only place she had ever stayed on the Southshore was the Marriott, where they'd shared their honeymoon four years ago. They'd gone back occasionally to see a Broadway traveling show or celebrate a birthday or anniversary. In fact, on previous trips, there'd never been any question of where they would stay; it was always the same.

But this time, *they* weren't the same.

"I'm thinking the Marriott," Mark said when she didn't answer. He gave her a moment, then glanced at her. "It's secure and safe. At least, it feels that way. And we're familiar with it."

"It's expensive," she said.

"I think there's a little room on our credit card. No, wait—if we check in with a credit card, we can be traced. I'll swing by an ATM machine and get a cash advance on the card."

"Fine," Allie said quietly. "But Mark, get something with two double beds, instead of one king-sized."

He stared out the windshield. "We're married, Allie."

"Not really," she said.

He didn't protest, and her gaze drifted out the window again. Her eyes misted over. How sad—they would be sleeping in the same room, but yards apart. She had missed sleeping next to him, feeling his warmth when she was cold, touching him for reassurance when she woke in the middle of the night. She would miss it even more tonight, so near and yet so far. It would be better—if she'd been brave enough—to insist that they get separate rooms. But she wasn't that brave. There was, after all, a killer on the loose. Despite her protests, she wanted Mark to be there, in the same room, watching over and protecting her.

But they couldn't touch—not if she was going to hold on to her sanity. They couldn't pretend to be man and wife, love each other, cling together, then go back to their separate lives and their separate homes. She couldn't let her heart find hope in him—not when he was sure to let her down, as he had before.

They got cash from an ATM and checked into the hotel under fake names—just in case the killer was looking for them—then rode the elevator up quietly and found their room.

"We should call home and see if Stan is there, and if he needs to know where anything is," she said as she set her purse on one of the beds.

Mark dropped the bags. "I'll call him. I'd like to know if anything's happened yet, anyway. Want me to order room service first?"

She shook her head. "No, I'm not hungry. I think I'll just get ready for bed."

He nodded, then picked up the phone.

•　•　•

Hours later, in Newpointe, Stan Shepherd sat at the table in Allie's house looking glumly at Sid Ford—Ray's brother, who therefore had a personal stake in the investigation—and Lynette Devreaux, a rookie cop who had Allie's coloring and hairstyle, making her a good decoy. While they waited for something to happen, they were going over everything they knew about the murderer. There were too many missing pieces, too many problems with every lead they'd followed. Although they had lifted quite a few fingerprints from all three houses, they still knew little. The same firemen and police officers had been in and out of all three homes, and even though they'd been careful not to disturb evidence, some of them had touched things inadvertently. The same caliber bullet had been used for each of the women, and in all three homes, according to the fire inspector, the fires had been started with diesel fuel. Diesel fumes didn't rise the way gasoline fumes would have, which had allowed the killer time to get out of the house unscathed after he'd set fire to it. There had been several shoe prints found—all belonging either to the residents of the homes or to the fire and police personnel who had come in afterward. The crime lab had examined all of the fibers vacuumed from the carpet of the Broussard house—since it hadn't been set on fire, there was more evidence to collect—but again, the only supposed clues wound up being related to the Broussards or to the firefighters and police officers who had responded to the call.

"What we don't know," Stan said, rubbing his tired eyes and staring down at the lists on Allie's kitchen table, "is whether he rang the bell and was invited in—in which case, he's someone they knew—or whether he picked the lock."

Sid stared quietly down at the papers spread out on the table. "My gut tells me there was an element of surprise. Susan was shot in the back, as if she was running away. Jamie was in bed. I can't see her getting up to let someone in, then getting back in bed."

"And that diaper bag in the middle of the floor at Martha's. Like she dropped it," Lynette added.

"Okay, then. Where does that leave us?" Stan asked wearily. "He may or may not know the victims. May or may not have been invited in. May or may not have worn gloves or shoe covers to keep from leaving prints."

"We know he's not afraid of being seen," Lynette pointed out. "Twice he entered homes in broad daylight."

"But both times there was some major event going on in town, so neighbors weren't as likely to be home. The parade and the funeral."

"We need the guest books at both funerals," Sid said. "We could at least use them for elimination. Whoever's on those lists isn't guilty."

"I'll get George's," Stan said. "You're right. But we need more than a process of elimination—we need a list of active suspects. And other than Hank Keyes, we don't have a single name."

"Hank Keyes may still be guilty."

"I don't think so," Stan said. "It doesn't fit. He's just a punk who thinks he's a big shot. Sure, he needs to be locked up for something, but I don't think it's this."

The radio they had turned down low on the table gave out a burst of static, and Stan reached to turn it up. "Yeah, this is Stan," he said into the mike.

"We might have some activity," came the low voice of Anthony Martin, who was sitting in the car parked in the garage across the street, keeping an eye on the outside of Allie's home. "Somebody's walking up the driveway. He left his car four houses down at the vacant house."

Stan and the others sprang up and reached for their weapons. "Can you get a picture?" he asked.

"No, the streetlight's out and I can barely see him. He's almost to the door."

Lynette was shaking as she went into the kitchen and pretended to wash the dishes she had put there earlier. Though the curtains were closed, they wanted the noises inside to be authentic, to make the killer feel sure that she was home, and alone. Stan and Sid got on either side of the door and held their breath, waiting.

The doorbell rang, and a tentative knock followed. Lynette froze. "What do I do?" she mouthed.

Stan shook his head, warning her to do nothing. Then he watched as, breathing hard, she pulled her gun with a trembling hand and held it at the ready, aimed toward the ceiling, as the bell rang again. He felt a bead of sweat trickle from his temple, down the side of his face.

They heard the knob rattle slightly. Although the volume on his radio was turned down so that its static wouldn't be heard, he whispered into it, "Back us up, Anthony."

The knob jiggled. They heard a key being inserted. Stan's heartbeat flew into triple-time. A bead of sweat trickled down his temple.

Then the knob turned. The door began to push open. Stan and Sid both stood back, guns drawn and ready.

The second the intruder's foot stepped over the threshold, Stan heard Anthony Martin's voice outside. "Freeze! Put your hands over your head and get down on the floor!"

The suspect jerked, startled, at the sound of Anthony's voice, then did as he was told. Anthony followed him in.

The intruder was face-down wearing a fireman's hat and bunker coat. Sid frisked him roughly while the others kept their guns trained on him.

"It's me, you idiots." The voice was muffled against the carpet. "It's just me!"

Stan grabbed the man's hair and pulled his head up to get a look as Sid kept up his search for weapons.

Craig Barnes's face was crimson, and he was gasping for breath. Stan turned him all the way over and gaped down at him. "What are you doing here?"

"I was checking on Allie, you fool!" Craig cried. "I just came from a call and was feeling nervous about her after their fight at the courthouse today."

Sid pulled a .38 automatic out of Craig's coat pocket. The fire chief sat up, cursing. "Yeah, I'm carrying a gun. Everybody and his dog is carrying a gun tonight."

"I asked what you're doing here," Stan bit out.

"And I told you! I'm on duty tonight. I was coming from a call and I thought I'd drive by and check on Allie. This is as much on my mind as it is on yours, Stan, maybe more, because it's *my* men who are losing their wives." They let him up, and he slipped out of the hot bunker coat and tried to catch his breath. "When I came by here I saw Allie's car and the lights on. I got concerned and drove around to Mark's apartment, and it looked like he was home, too. I figured he had meant it today when he said she could fend for herself. I wanted to check to make sure she was all right, and see if I could help her find an alternative to staying here alone." He looked around at them, one by one. "What are *you* guys doing here? Staking the place out?"

"Yes." Stan was getting confused, so he tried to shake his head free of the conflicting signals. "Craig, how did you unlock the door?"

"With a key!" he said, opening the door and showing them the key that was still in the lock. "When she didn't answer the door, what was I supposed to think? She could have been lying dead in here. I decided to look for the key and come on in, but I have to tell you I was nervous. I know this guy is just killing women, but I didn't want to wind up dead myself if I happened to catch him in the act. So I came in as quietly as I could—and then you guys scared the livin' daylights out of me."

"Why'd you park so far down the street?" Anthony asked, obviously not convinced. "Why wouldn't you want anyone to see your car here?"

Craig gaped at them, as though in disbelief. "You guys think *I'm* the killer? Chief of the fire department? I just lost seventy-five percent of my force because of this. You think I'd orchestrate all that and put myself in this kind of bind? You've got to be kidding."

"Answer the question about your car," Stan said.

Craig rubbed his hand through his hair. "The sprinkler was running—getting the whole driveway wet, and the street in front, too. I didn't want to get wet, so I parked in that driveway. I figured if I parked in front of any of the other houses, somebody would see me and call the police." He sat down and slumped wearily. "Look, we're all tired. We're all a little on edge. I need to get over to Eastside, because they've only got two of the usual three on a shift over there."

Stan looked from one of the cops to another, and saw that they had relaxed and were buying the story. Even Anthony Martin. Stan still wasn't sure, but after a moment, he nodded. "All right, Craig. But don't go breaking into anybody else's home, or I'll haul you in."

"Believe me, I'll never pull that again."

"You could have gotten your head blown off."

"Tell me about it." He got up, dusted off his uniform, then started for the door. "I hope you catch the real guy tonight. I'm ready for this to be over."

They watched him go out and closed the door behind him.

For a moment, all four cops stood looking at each other. "What do you think?" Stan asked.

"I believe him," Lynette said. "It made sense. Everybody's so strung out about all this, I guess nobody's really acting all that rationally."

"He's got to be concerned about his men and their families. I buy it," Sid said.

Stan looked at Anthony, who had gotten a distant look in his eyes. "Anthony?"

Anthony shook his head. "I don't know. He sure did look suspicious walking up to the house. But he's right about the sprinkler."

Stan had his doubts—but he needed more than doubts to justify an arrest. "All right, Anthony. Go back across the street, and let's try it again. Let's just hope that little fiasco didn't scare off the real guy, or we'll have wasted this whole night."

Chapter Twenty-Six

Because Mark was unwilling to take a room any higher than a ladder truck could reach in the event of a fire, their room at the Marriott was on the third floor, making all of the ground noise of Canal Street audible during the night. Allie lay awake in her bed on her side of the room as flashing blue lights occasionally colored the walls and sirens screeched by. Now and then, she could hear a jazz band somewhere in the Quarter, its music fading in and out like a dream.

Across the room, Mark lay in his own bed, tangled in the covers. He wore a T-shirt and white boxer shorts, and his hair was in disarray. He appeared to be sleeping soundly, though he didn't make the soft, snoring noise he usually made when he slept. It had taken her three weeks after he'd moved out to get used to sleeping without that sound. Now she longed for it. She turned on her side and watched him in the moonlight spilling in through the window. It was the first time she'd known him to sleep in a T-shirt, but she supposed their estrangement had created an unnatural modesty between them. She had always slept in his T-shirts, but tonight she wore a big LSU jersey and white leggings. Now she wished she'd worn something a little more attractive. As angry and hurt as she was at him, it hurt her to think that all of the attraction and chemistry were gone.

She got up quietly, went to the big picture window, and peered out into the night. She could see the lights of cars passing by on Canal Street, and establishments lit up in neon. Some were raunchy, decadent places that sold unspeakable things, and as she often had before, she asked herself how one city could have so much beauty and so much ugliness at the same time.

She heard a siren not far away and wondered if someone had been murdered. How often did those police cars have to rush to the scene of a homicide? Was life less valuable here than it was anywhere else? Was it growing less valuable in Newpointe?

She tried to picture what Martha, Jamie, and Susan must have gone through. Had they seen his face? Had they spoken to him, pled for their life? Had the two deaths been instant, or had they suffered that lingering awareness that it was all about to end and there was nothing they could do?

She covered her face with both hands and tried to muffle her sobs. Then she heard the creaking of the mattress behind her. She didn't turn around.

Warm, familiar, comforting arms turned her around, and she let herself relax into them. Mark held her for a long time, letting her weep against his chest, letting her cry out all the fear and rage and confusion that plagued her. After a while, the fear and rage were gone, and she cried, instead, out of grief, not for her friends, but for her husband. Even as he held her, she missed him.

When he kissed her, she had no power to resist, and all the old feelings came rushing back on a tidal wave of memory. The campfire where they'd first kissed, being carried in his arms to their car after the wedding, her long veil dragging the ground, the overwhelming love she'd felt for him as they'd moved into their first home and set up housekeeping, the conversations and plans and anticipation of children . . . all of those things were still there, in that desperate kiss, and her heart raced with hope. But there was sadness, too. And that sadness was grounded in reality, whereas the hope seemed as empty as a child's balloon.

When the kiss broke, she looked up at him, her face wet and her eyes swollen, and she felt more vulnerable than a toddler standing in rush-hour traffic. She knew she should say something, but nothing came to her.

"It's been a long time," Mark whispered, his fingertips cupping her chin. "I've missed you." There was deep emotion in his face as he spoke, and she wanted to trust him. But Mark had always been a charmer. He had charmed her when she'd met him at a youth camp her senior year of high school. He had told her he loved her then, and had held her just this way when she'd had to go back home to Georgia. He had whispered that he would miss her, just as he whispered it now.

She had been swept away then, certain that he was her life partner, the one God had chosen for her. But God wouldn't choose a man who could forsake his vows so easily. He wouldn't have set aside a man who professed to be a Christian but drank too much and avoided the church they had both loved. She had made a mistake in marrying him. Somehow, without realizing it, she must have deposed God and followed her own agenda. And now she was paying with the deepest pain she'd ever felt.

She backed away, grabbed a tissue, and blew her nose, deliberately breaking the mood. He stood in his boxer shorts and T-shirt, watching her, waiting for the response she wasn't able to give. She pressed the wadded tissue to the inside corners of her eyes, trying to stop the tears. But she couldn't speak, and she couldn't look at him.

Finally, he moved into the bathroom. She heard water running, and in a moment he was back at her side, holding out a glass for her. "Here," he said softly. "Drink this."

She took it gratefully, drank it until it was empty, then set the glass down on the table next to her bed. She sat down, looking at the floor. Mark stooped in front of her and looked up into her eyes. He, too, seemed to be at a loss for words. Gently, he swept her hair behind her ear.

"Do you think you can sleep now?" he asked finally.

She drew in a deep breath and decided to lie. "Yes."

"If you can't, tomorrow we'll see about getting something to help. Maybe a mild tranquilizer just at night."

She nodded and slipped back into the bed. It seemed so big, so cold, without him beside her. She realized as he covered her that she would like nothing more than to have him slip in beside her and hold her until she fell asleep. But she couldn't let that happen. Not when their marriage was nonexistent. Not when there was another woman in the picture.

She closed her eyes and listened as he got back into his own bed. She couldn't wait for morning.

• • •

Across the room, Mark lay in his bed with his back to her, fighting the longing to climb into her bed and hold her so tight that the memories of the last two months would flee. That kiss had been a mistake, he thought. It had almost done him in. As if it had opened the floodgates, it had brought back a rush of feelings that he wasn't sure he could control.

He had felt her reaction, too, but then he'd felt the hesitation, the despair, then the separation.

Confusion dominated his mind as his heart mourned for the woman who was within his grasp, yet so far away that he feared he would never reach her again. Had their marriage been ruined beyond repair? In the words of the ceremony that had bound them, had they been torn asunder? Or were they still one, as his heart seemed to claim?

He honestly didn't know.

He thought of turning over, looking to see if she was still awake, hoping that maybe she was still distraught and needed him again. Only then could he go to her. Unless he knew that she needed and wanted him too, his fear of rejection was too great.

But he didn't hear her crying, didn't hear her wrestling with the bed covers ...

She didn't need him, he thought miserably. Without that, he couldn't go to her. They were destined to spend this time together ... all alone.

And as the night ticked by, he realized that he already knew the answer to his question about whether they were still one. He felt as though his soul had been ripped in two. Yes, they had been torn asunder. And it was probably too late to put them back together again.

Chapter Twenty-Seven

At two-thirty A.M., Officer R.J. Albright, who was patrolling Newpointe, drove down Purchase Street, which housed the Midtown fire station, police department, city hall, and courthouse, then turned onto Jacquard Street, where the Blooms 'n' Blossoms shop was. Allie's flower van was there, and a dim light shone from the back room. He turned into the parking lot. Had the rumors been true, about Mark abandoning her tonight? As his headlights lit up the small gravel parking lot, he saw someone coming from behind the building.

He radioed his location to the dispatcher, then pulled his car further in to get a better look. He got out, his hand on his gun, his heart pumping hard, and saw the man stop in the shadows, waiting for him.

"Hello, R.J." It was Dan Nichols's voice, and as the tall man walked out of the shadows, he saw that he was dressed in his fireman's uniform and carrying a crowbar. "I was just about to call you guys."

"Yeah?" R.J. asked. "What for?"

"Somebody tried to break in here," Dan said. He sounded excited, out of breath. "I was down the street at the station, and I came out for some fresh air. I could have sworn I saw someone moving around the door, but when I ran down here, I guess I scared him off."

R.J. examined the door. The lock was scratched, as if it had been tampered with. The dead bolt inside kept the door from opening, but someone had tried to pry it open. He turned back to Dan and regarded the crowbar.

"I found this in the back," Dan explained. "I was looking around, and I saw it lying a few yards from the shop. He probably dropped it as he ran away."

R.J. was mildly suspicious, despite his years of friendship with Dan. "So you're sayin' you *saw* someone? What did they look like?"

Dan hedged. "It's not that I saw anybody, just movement. I *thought* I saw something."

"Why didn't you call us right then?"

"I don't know," he said. "Didn't want to take the time to run back in, I guess. I saw Allie's light on and thought maybe she was inside, so I wanted to get over here quick."

"And when you got here, you didn't see nothin'?"

"No. Like I said, I think I scared him off."

R.J. stared at him for several seconds.

"Well, are you just going to stand there, or are you going to call in some other patrol units to search the woods back there?" Dan asked, irritated.

"Why ain't you sweatin'?" R.J. knew the question seemed to come from left field, but he had to ask it.

Dan frowned. "What?"

"I asked, why ain't you sweatin'? You said you ran down here. If you did, why ain't you sweatin'?"

"It's less than a block, R.J., and it's cold out here. Are you suggesting I'm lying?"

"Just askin'."

"Terrific. Remind me not to get involved the next time I see someone's business getting broken into." He flung down the crowbar and headed back up the street toward the station. "Glad you boys have so much time on your hands that you'd suspect fellow public servants instead of looking for the real killer."

But R.J. wasn't listening. Deep in thought, he went to his car and grabbed the radio mike.

Chapter Twenty-Eight

Jill Clark had just sat down with her first cup of coffee of the morning when the telephone rang. "Hello?"

"Jill, this is Dan Nichols. I'm sorry to call so early, but I thought you'd want to know."

A sick feeling washed over her, and setting her coffee cup down, she braced herself. "Not another murder."

"No, not that," Dan said quickly. "But last night there was almost a break-in at Allie's shop. I thought I saw someone over there and I apparently scared them away. But to me it indicates that Allie's definitely in danger. She might even be next on this guy's list."

Jill's skin turned cold, and she got to her feet and began to pace. "Are you sure, Dan? I mean, did they go in?"

"No, but they used a crowbar to try to pry open the door, since it was dead-bolted."

"But maybe it was just a simple robbery. I mean, it was apparent that she wasn't there, wasn't it?"

"Not really. Her van was parked there, and there was a light on in the back. He may have thought she was inside."

Jill closed her eyes and sat back down. "Have you heard anything? Are they any closer to finding this guy?"

"Haven't heard, and they're not really telling me anything. I think R.J. even suspects me, since I was at the shop when he got there last night. But we had a real quiet night at the station. Only a couple of calls, and those were for minor things. So I was out in the garage lifting weights, and I walked out into the fresh air. That's when I saw."

"Quiet night? At least there were no more murders."

"All the wives are out of town. Makes you wonder how bad he wants them dead, and if he's going to start going after them where they are."

She shivered.

"Look, do you know where I can reach her and Mark to let them know?" Dan asked.

"No, I don't. They didn't tell me where they were going."

"Well, if you hear from them, tell them what I said. They need to really be on guard. And hey, if they need a place to stay, tell them they can use my house. It's out in the country, and no one will look for them there."

"All right, Dan. I'll tell them."

After she hung up, Jill sat praying that Allie could somehow escape this madness. Someone insane enough to try to kill three women—two in broad daylight—might not stop until he had finished the job, regardless of what obstacles they threw in his way. Did he even care about getting caught? Was he rational enough to lie low?

Quickly, she started to get dressed. She would go to the police station and find out what they knew. Maybe something would give her—and Allie—a little hope.

●　　●　　●

While Mark was in the shower, Allie called her best friend in Newpointe.

"Hello?"

"Jill, it's me. Did I wake you up?"

"No. Allie, I'm so glad you called. I wanted to get in touch with you, but I didn't know how."

Allie stood up. "What's wrong? Is it Susan? Did something happen?"

"I don't know," Jill said. "I haven't heard a word about Susan. But I just talked to Dan Nichols, and he told me that someone tried to break into your shop last night."

"*What?*"

"Dan scared him off, so he didn't get all the way in, whoever it was—but Allie, he probably thought *you* were in there. The light in the back was on."

Allie's heart began racing. "I've gotta go, Jill. I've gotta call Stan Shepherd and see what he can tell me."

"Allie, don't come back here. Wherever you are, stay there. I'm scared to death for you. This guy's getting bold, and he isn't going to give up."

"I know," she said. "Look, I'm thinking about going to Georgia, to stay with my parents until this blows over."

"Do it. Get as far from here as you can."

"You be careful, too, Jill. Don't stay alone."

Jill hesitated. "I'll do what I can. But I'm not married to a fireman."

"If he can't get to us, he might start on others," she said. "Don't take the chance, Jill."

She hung up as Mark came out of the bathroom, his hair wet and a towel flung around his neck. He was wearing a pair of jeans and a clean T-shirt and smelled like soap. She felt rumpled and frumpy and wished she had gotten up earlier to put herself together. She'd be willing to bet that Issie Mattreaux never looked like this in the morning.

"Who was that?" he asked.

"Jill. Mark, the shop was broken into last night."

He stared at her in amazement, then grabbed the phone from her hand. "I'm calling Stan."

As he dialed, she said, "Mark, I want to go to Georgia. I think it would be a good time for me to visit my parents."

"Maybe you're right." He was quiet for a moment. "Stan Shepherd, please. This is Mark Branning." Turning toward Allie, he said, "Pick up the phone in the bathroom so you can hear."

Allie had often chuckled at the oddness of bathroom phones in hotels. Now she was grateful for it as she sat on the toilet lid and waited for Stan to pick up.

"I heard about the break-in," Mark said when Stan was on the line.

"Which one?"

Mark was stunned into silence.

"What do you mean, which one?" Allie asked.

"Well, there was the attempt at the shop. If Dan Nichols had called the police instead of trying to be a hero, we might have caught the guy. And then there was the one at your house when we were there, but it turned out to be Craig Barnes, checking on Allie. If your friends would stay out of our way, we could do our job."

Mark was getting impatient. "Stan, was the shop broken into or not?"

"It was an attempted break-in, and yes, there's plenty of evidence. A broken door, for starters, scratches on the knob, a crowbar that just happens to have Dan Nichols's fingerprints all over it, since he found it and didn't take precautions to protect it—"

"What about the house?" Allie cut in. "You said it was broken into?"

"Like I said, Craig Barnes was just checking on you. He heard the fight you two faked and worried that you were alone. When you didn't answer the door, he decided to come in and see if you were all right."

"But whoever broke into the shop was probably the killer," Mark said. "Does this mean Allie is supposed to be his next victim?"

"Might have been if she'd been here last night. Then again, it could have been just a routine burglary."

"No, too coincidental."

"Not really. Any fool kid looking for drug money would assume that the fire wives are all out of town."

"Were any other homes or businesses broken into that you know of?"

"No. We did a check of all of their homes this morning, and didn't find anything."

Allie heard Mark swallow. "Look, Stan, Allie and I have decided to get her out of the state. The farther the better."

"Good idea," Stan said.

"I'll call you later and see if you've come up with anything."

He hung up, and Allie came out of the bathroom and stood looking at him, fear and frustration illuminating her eyes. "I'm coming with you," he said.

"To Georgia? No, Mark, that wouldn't work."

"Why not?"

"Because . . ." She hesitated to tell him the real reason, then had to admit to herself that lying would be futile. "My parents are so angry at you right now."

His face changed instantly. "Why? What exactly have you told them?"

"I told them the truth, Mark."

"And just what is your version of the truth? That I was sleeping around?"

"No . . ."

"Then what? I haven't done anything wrong, Allie. There is nothing you could have told them about me to turn them against me—not anything true. What *did* you tell them?"

"I told them about my walking in on you and Issie at the fire station. I told them you moved out, that you were interested in someone else, that you'd started drinking and quit going to church, and didn't care about our vows anymore. I told them the truth, Mark!"

She turned away and started packing her suitcase. She could feel him standing there behind her, watching her, angry and so hurt—but denying nothing. Finally, he said, "You're wrong about what you saw at the fire station, Allie. But we've been through all that. I'm here right now. I'm sticking by you. Doesn't that count for something?"

"Don't do me any favors," she said. "Other people are watching over me, too. Dan Nichols, apparently, and Craig Barnes, and who knows who else. I can do without you, Mark."

She knew that stung him, and she was glad. But the satisfaction only lasted a moment. She knew Mark well enough to know that he might just leave her out of pride now, and then she would have to face all of this alone. She turned back to her bag and zipped it up.

Behind her, she heard him packing, too, and then he picked up the phone and dialed again.

"Econojet Airlines," he said. He wrote the number down, dialed it, then waited again. "Yes, I'd like to make reservations for two on the next flight from New Orleans to Atlanta this afternoon."

She swung toward him. "Mark, I *told* you! We only need one ticket."

He put his hand over the phone, and through his teeth said, "And I told *you*. I'm not leaving you."

"You already left me! You're only with me now because you're afraid I'm going to be killed. I don't want you staying with me out of duty!"

"Reservations for two," he repeated into the phone again. "Mr. and Mrs. Mark Branning."

She threw up her hands and went back into the bathroom and began brushing her teeth with a vengeance. In the other room, she heard him say, "No, it has to be today. Don't you have *any* seats? Yes, they have to be together."

She closed her eyes in frustration.

"All right, tomorrow then. Yes, that'll be fine. What time?"

When he hung up, she came out of the bathroom. "They were booked up today?"

"Yes," he said, staring down at his shoes.

"What about Delta or American or—"

"We can't afford them, Allie. Our credit cards are almost maxed out. We can only afford Econojet."

"My parents will pay for me."

"But not me."

"What about your dad? Maybe he could give you a loan."

Mark's laughter was bitterly sarcastic. "You've got to be kidding. My father hasn't got two dimes to rub together. Allie, we're just going to wait until tomorrow and take Econojet and pay for it ourselves. Meanwhile, we'll check out of here and go to Slidell, and see about Susan. We'll stay someplace else tonight. It isn't wise to stay in the same place two nights, anyway."

She sighed. She knew he was right, and the truth was, she didn't want to travel alone. "All right," she said finally. "I guess we have no choice."

Chapter Twenty-Nine

Jill got little information from the police department regarding the attempted break-in at the florist, so she walked over to the fire department to see Dan Nichols. Aunt Aggie stood in front of the stove making Monte Cristo sandwiches for the firemen. Jill watched her drop the batter-covered turkey sandwiches into the hot oil to fry them, then scoop them out and smother them with powdered sugar. A side dish of marmalade went on every plate for dipping. She wondered how any of them managed to keep from looking like Pillsbury Dough Boys. Actually, most did show a little pudginess from the rich food Aunt Aggie made them each day, but Dan remained thin. Why had no one in town snatched him up yet?

"Can I talk to you privately?" she asked him quietly, and he looked at the other firemen sitting around the kitchen.

"Sure," he said. "Let's walk out back."

She followed him outside, walked to a bench halfway across the lawn, and sat down. "I talked to Allie this morning," she said.

"Did you tell her what I saw?"

"Yeah. She was pretty upset."

"Where is she?"

"Headed to Georgia to stay with her parents until this blows over."

"Georgia? I didn't know she was from there. What part?"

"Atlanta."

"When's she leaving?"

"Today sometime, I think."

"Is Mark going with her?"

"She didn't say." She looked up at him, her eyes wide and pensive. "I called the hospital in Slidell this morning, and they're saying that Susan's still comatose. They don't know if she's going to come out of it or not."

"Yeah, I heard."

"Dan, last night when you saw the guy at the florist—why didn't you chase him down? Why didn't you call the police right away?"

"I was trying to get a look at the guy when R.J. pulled up. In his patrol car, he probably still could have caught the guy on the other side of the woods, but he was so busy trying to make me out to be the culprit that he let him get away."

Jill frowned. "They suspected you?"

"Yeah, you believe that? They stopped because they saw *me*. I might need a lawyer before this thing's over."

"Well, you know how to reach me. But I don't think you have anything to worry about. I'm just glad you ran the guy off."

"I would rather have caught him."

"Yeah, well. Don't beat yourself up."

"You know, with all these media people around, some people in this town might not want the killer caught. Apparently murder is good for business."

"Yeah, every motel in town is full, and the restaurants are bursting at the seams. Give me our sleepy little town any day of the week," Jill said. "This kind of attention we don't need."

Aunt Aggie came to the door and called out, "Eats is ready, *mon ami*. Jill, stay. There's plenty."

She stood up. "Are you sure?"

Aunt Aggie laughed with delight. "Where else can you enjoy the company of six bachelors at one time?"

"Six?"

"Sure. The chief is one, too."

Jill grinned and glanced at Dan. "How can any self-respecting woman pass up an invitation like that?"

• • •

Before they left New Orleans, Mark and Allie went to Pat O'Brien's for lunch. Though it was quiet now, this was one of the hot spots at night, when tourists and local party animals packed in to guzzle Hurricanes and dance to the band whose equipment was set up in a corner of the open brick courtyard. Now, only a guitarist, a bass player, and a saxophone player droned out a New Orleans flavored jazz medley that made them almost forget their troubles for a while.

When the waitress came to take their order, Allie saw Mark hesitate over the wine list. He looked up, apparently sensed her disapproval, and closed it again. "I'll just have a Sprite," he said, then told the waitress his lunch order.

When the waitress had gone, he met Allie's eyes again. "I don't drink that much, Allie. I just thought a glass of wine might relax me a little."

She let her eyes drift to the ensemble in the corner. But she could feel him watching her, could sense his frustration and his desire to launch into a conversation that she knew would prove both unproductive and unpleasant.

"Allie, I don't like you thinking I'm a drunk."

"I never said you were a drunk," she said, keeping her eyes on the musicians.

"You might as well say it. You act like I'm an alcoholic or something, and that's not true."

She looked at him again. He was asking for it. "Mark, remember when we started seeing each other, and I lived in Georgia and you lived here, and you had been to visit my parents, but you never wanted me to come home and meet your father?"

He lowered his eyes to the wrought iron table and traced the pattern with his finger. "Yeah, so?"

"I was hurt, because I thought you didn't want him to meet me. And then I found out that the real reason you wouldn't bring me home was that you didn't want *me* to meet *him*. When you finally told me the real reason, do you remember what you said?"

"No, Allie, I don't," he said on a note of sarcasm. "Why don't you tell me?"

"You said that your father drank too much, and you were embarrassed by him. You said that he was an alcoholic, and that your poor mother had to live with the stigma of being a drunk's wife until the day she died. You said that he wouldn't admit he had a problem, that he claimed he didn't drink that much and could stop anytime he wanted to."

"All right, Allie. You've made your point."

"No, I haven't," she said. "You also told me that you would never drink as long as you lived, because you saw how easy it was for alcohol to get its claws into you—because it had ruined your father's life, and your mother's life, but it wasn't going to ruin yours."

He compressed his lips and stared across the tables to the musicians on the stage. "Alcohol isn't ruining my life, Allie. It's a result of our problems, not the cause of them."

"So when you started going to Joe's Place with your buddies after your shift, when you started having those long heart-to-hearts with Issie, you were doing it because we were having problems?"

He hesitated, started to speak, then stopped and shook his head as if the argument was too futile to continue.

"Because I distinctly remember that our problems started *after* you made Joe's Place and Issie your daily habit."

"I wasn't drinking then, Allie. I just went to be with my friends. If coming home had been more pleasant, I wouldn't have found other places to go."

The blow was low, and she almost flinched with the force of it. She stared at him for several seconds, fighting the rage that seemed so familiar these days. "And why was coming home so unpleasant?" she bit out.

"Because you kept harping on the fact that you wanted to have a baby but we didn't make enough money for you to sell the shop and stay home, that you wanted me to get a better job, that you were having to work so hard to make up for the money that I didn't make, that the shop was barely breaking even—on and on and on. It was always the same. But you knew when you married me that I wanted to be a fireman, had always wanted to be a fireman. You don't go into that job for the money."

"So you were justified in going to bars every night with your friends?"

When he didn't answer, she added, "I wonder if that's how it started with your dad."

She knew that would hit him where it hurt, for his father had been a fireman, too, as his father before him had been. The realities of the job, particularly the low pay, had to have caused problems in their marriages, too.

"It's not the same, Allie. I'm not a drunk. I told you, when I first started going to Joe's Place, I didn't even drink. I just wanted some pleasant conversation, some companionship."

"And you chose to have that with another woman?"

He rolled his eyes. "And here I thought we were talking about drinking."

Tears welled in her eyes, but she wouldn't let them spill. She focused on a schefflera plant hanging from the ceiling. A soul-deep sadness filled her heart, weighing her down, and she wondered where things had gone wrong. Had she really turned into a nagging wife that made life so unpleasant that her husband had to seek out comfort in other women? Was it really her fault?

These were all issues that they hadn't been able to deal with in marriage counseling, primarily because either of them had the option to leave when things got too hot. Now they seemed stuck together by grim circumstances, trapped, unable to leave.

Their food came, and they both picked at it as the jazz music played on. Neither of them had anything to say.

"I should call my parents," she said finally. "Tell them we're coming."

"Warn them *I'm* coming."

She slid her chair back and dug into her purse for her calling card. "I'll be right back."

"No, I'm coming with you."

"But we haven't paid the bill."

"Then wait," he said. "We're not that far from Newpointe, Allie. I don't want you to be alone."

She bit back her objection and waited for their bill, amazed at his unwavering determination to protect her, even when being around her seemed painful to him. She regretted bringing up his dad's drinking; she wished she had tried to be more pleasant, more fun to be with, but there was nothing pleasant or fun about their circumstances. It was bad enough that their marriage had come to a halt. But the added stress of the killings made things a dozen times more confusing.

She looked up at him and met his eyes—and wished she didn't see contempt, guardedness, and anger there. Last night, when he had held her and kissed her, when she had melted in his arms, it hadn't been there then. But that moment had had little to do with reality.

The waitress brought their bill and Mark paid it, then they both walked to the nearest pay phone.

He stood close to her as she dialed, and in her peripheral vision she noted the fatigued slump to his shoulders and the tired lines around his eyes. This was hard on him—and he didn't have to do it. He could be in Newpointe working his shift, near Issie, but he had chosen to stay here with her. Warmth flooded through her, but she tried to shove it away.

Her mother answered on the first ring. "Mom? It's me."

"Allie, where have you been? We've been hearing all the reports about the murders, and we've tried to call, but we couldn't get you—"

"I'm fine, Mom. I'm in New Orleans right now, just trying to keep low until they catch the killer, but I'm catching a plane tomorrow to come there. I think I need to be out of the state for a while."

"Yes," her mother agreed. "Yes, this is exactly where I want you to be. But honey, be careful. If this man wants you dead—"

"Mark's with me," she said, not certain if that would put their fears to rest or not.

"Mark? Why?"

"He's worried." She met his eyes awkwardly, then looked away. "He hasn't left my side since this whole thing started. He's coming with me to Georgia, Mom."

"Are you two back together?"

"No. Nothing like that. It's just a safety thing."

"What about the woman?"

Her mother was blunt, as always, but Allie hoped Mark hadn't heard. "We'll talk about it later, Mom."

"So do I need to make up one bed or two?"

He'd heard that, and now he watched her, waiting for an answer. "Two, Mom, if you don't mind."

"I'll tell you what, I'm going to give him a piece of my mind when I see him. You should have divorced him already, and then maybe you wouldn't be on that maniac's list."

"Mom, we're not coming to fight. Please, we've been through enough lately."

"Then I have to bite my tongue?"

"I'd appreciate it."

"Oh, really, Allie, you can't be serious."

"Mom, there are more pressing issues to deal with right now. Be glad that I'm not coming alone."

"All right," her mother conceded at last. "I'm glad. But I still might tell him what I think of him if I get the chance."

When she hung up, Allie turned back to Mark. She could tell from the look on his face that he'd heard what her mother had said.

"So, is she going to let me in?"

"Not without telling you off first. Mark, if you want to back out, I'll be fine. Really."

"No way. I'm going with you and that's final. I can deal with your parents."

"All right," she said, "but I warned you."

He seemed thoughtful, and she knew that he dreaded the confrontation tomorrow. They both needed something to distract them. "Let's go to Slidell and check on Susan," she said. "At least we'll feel like we're accomplishing something."

Chapter Thirty

Television vans filled the parking lot of Slidell Memorial Hospital, and a crowd of reporters waited outside the front door for a story. CNN was among those lined up at the edge of the lot. "CNN? This is making national news?" Allie asked.

"Take a look over there," Mark said. "NBC, CBS—I guess it's big-time. 'Serial killer hitting all the wives of the firemen in a sleepy little southern town.'"

"I think I'm gonna be sick."

He stopped the car, let it idle for a moment. "We don't have to go in there."

"Yes, we do. I have to see Ray. I have to know about Susan."

"Look at all the reporters still here—that must mean she's alive."

Allie's face went from dejected to hopeful. "Do you think so?"

"Of course. They wouldn't hang around here if there wasn't a story. They'd be back in Newpointe."

She studied the crowd. "I don't know if I have the strength to walk through them again."

"Don't talk to them. Just stick close to me and keep your eyes on the door. It looks like the security guards are keeping them out of the hospital now, so once we're inside we should be all right."

She pulled down the visor and took a look at herself in the mirror. She had dark circles under her eyes and wore little make-up. "I look terrible. I don't want to wind up on national news."

Mark reached across the seat and touched her cheek. "You look pretty good to me."

Her eyes met his, and they locked there for a moment. Finally, he looked away. "Come on. Let's get this over with."

They got out of the car, and he took her hand and led her toward the door at the far end of the building, away from the crowd of reporters. Some correspondents doing stand-ups in front of their cameras noticed them, and Mark and Allie hurried faster to avoid them.

Once inside the doors, they navigated the halls until they were at the front desk where two elderly volunteers sat. "May I help you?" one of them asked.

"Yes. We were wondering about Susan Ford. Could you tell us where she is now?"

The gray-haired woman eyed them suspiciously. "Reporters?"

"No, ma'am," Mark said. "I'm a fireman with Ray Ford in Newpointe, and this is my wife."

"I have to ask for I.D. before I give you any information," one of the ladies said. "Our hospital administrator wants the media kept out."

"Sure." He reached into his wallet and pulled out his driver's license, as well as his firefighter I.D.

"All right," the woman said. "ICU is on the fourth floor, and Captain Ford is waiting in there."

They thanked her and took the elevator up. In the ICU waiting room, dozens of people waited in various stages of weariness. They saw Ray in a little cluster of people at the back of the room and hurried through.

Craig Barnes was there, along with George Broussard. Mark slowed as he reached them, and Ray looked up at them. His eyes looked as if he'd wept an ocean of tears in the last few hours, but he managed a smile. "You two back?"

"Yeah," Mark said. "How is she, Ray?"

His bloodshot eyes misted over again. "She ain't out of the woods. She's still unconscious."

Allie turned to George and hugged him. "It's nice of you to come here, George, when you've got griefs of your own."

He swallowed. "I thought nothin' would take my mind off my troubles like bein' here to help a brother with his. My folks got Tommy."

"It's gotta be hard for you," Allie said.

"Yeah." George sank down onto a vinyl chair. "At least Martha didn't suffer."

Allie sat down next to him. She took his big hand and held it tightly as she looked back up at Ray. "Has she come to at all?"

"No," Ray said. "Not at all. But I ain't leavin' here, and they promised me that if she does wake up, they'll call me. Other than that, I have to wait until six o'clock tonight to see her again." He blinked back the fresh tears in his eyes. "Anybody talked to the preacher?"

"He was at the meeting," Craig said. "He can't come, Ray, because all of our unmarried men are working to give the rest the chance to protect their wives."

"Good idea," Ray said. "Yeah, that's a better use of his time than bein' here with me."

"I know he's praying, Ray," Allie said. "Lots of people are."

Ray nodded. "I've tried, but it just seems like a chant or somethin'. I can't seem to concentrate."

"I've had the same problem," George said softly. "I know who can give me comfort. I know who can give me peace. But I can't seem to let go of all the anger and confusion long enough to talk to him about it."

"We could pray with you both," Allie offered.

Something about that suggestion made Mark uncomfortable. It had been a long time since he'd prayed with others . . . in fact, he hadn't done a lot of praying alone lately, either. Still, he did what he knew he should do, and nodded. "Sure, we could."

Ray sat slowly down, and Craig Barnes looked for a moment as if he might find an excuse to leave. But Mark sat down next to Ray, and after a moment, Craig followed.

For a moment, they sat there quietly, reverently, while the noise of the waiting room continued around them. Telephones rang, the intercom blared, people talked . . .

Mark looked at Allie; she was looking at him, waiting for him to lead them. He swallowed the lump in his throat and suddenly felt dirty, unrighteous, though he wasn't sure why. Knowing that it was cowardly, he passed the baton to his wife. "Allie, will you lead us?"

He could see her disappointment in him, but he also saw that she wasn't surprised. She bowed her head, closed her eyes, and began to pray.

None of their eyes were dry as she entreated God to intervene on Susan's behalf, prayed for peace for Ray and George, and asked the Almighty to stop the killer from killing again, and to aid the police in finding him.

When the amens came, all of them were weeping. Craig Barnes was so overcome that he had to excuse himself and head for the men's room. Allie dug into her purse and handed each of them a tissue.

"Thank you, Allie," Ray whispered.

"Yeah, *merci*, darlin'," George added. "I needed that."

In a moment, Craig came back, his face dry, but his eyes still glassy and red. "I guess I'd better get back to the station," he said. "I'm short on captains, so I need to be available."

Ray shook his hand and patted his shoulder. "Thanks for coming by, man."

"I'll be back tomorrow," he said. Craig turned to Allie. "You take care, okay?"

"I will," she whispered. "We're flying to Georgia tomorrow morning. Seems right to get out of town."

"I think you're right," Craig said. "But why are you waiting?"

"Econojet," Mark said. "They were booked till then. Anyway, we wanted to come here."

Craig shook Mark's hand. "See you later. Let me know if you need me."

Mark appreciated the sentiment—but he also remembered Craig's objection to the husbands taking off work, so he took those words with a grain of salt.

· · ·

Moments later, Allie moved to sit in the empty chair next to Ray. "Where are the kids?" she asked him.

"Ben's takin' a shower," he said. "We been here all night. And Vanessa . . ." He nodded toward a window across the room, and Allie saw the girl sitting on the sill, staring out. "She's takin' it real hard," he said. "Think you could talk to her, Allie? I ain't been able to do much good."

"Sure, I will."

She zigzagged between chairs and clusters of people until she came to the pretty teenager whose only concern just days ago had been getting permission to drive. She touched Vanessa's shoulder, and the girl looked back.

"You okay, Vanessa?" she asked.

She moved her gaze back to the window. "She gon' die."

"We can hope not. They're taking good care of her here—"

"It's my fault."

"*What?* How?"

"Because I'm bein' punished. God's fed up with me so he's teachin' me a lesson."

"What lesson?"

"That if I don't value my mama he gon' take her away." She broke into a sob and turned back to Allie. "Yesterday I called her Ms. Hitler. I said I had the worst mama I knew of. I didn't know those'd be the last words I'd ever say to her, Allie! I didn't know she'd die thinkin' I hated her guts! They was just words."

"Vanessa, there hasn't been a single moment in your life when your mother thought you hated her." Allie's mind drifted back to all the hateful words she and Mark had exchanged—

words of contempt and bitterness. "Words can be pretty powerful, though, can't they?" she asked weakly.

"I just want another chance," the girl whispered. "Just one more chance, to tell Mama I love her. I don't care if she never lets me drive."

Allie pulled the girl into a hug and held her tightly, and they both wept.

"I can't pray for her," Vanessa cried. "God won't hear me, 'cause he gon' teach me a lesson."

"He does hear you, Vanessa. And what happened to your mom was not to punish you, honey. There's a sick man out there, and he's not doing God's business for him. You can pray for your mom, and I know God will listen."

The girl wiped her eyes and flipped her long black weaves back over her shoulder. "You really think so?"

"I know so."

Again they embraced, long and hard.

• • •

From across the room, Mark watched. The gentle way Allie spoke to the girl made him remember how he had wanted to have children with her, how strongly he had believed that Allie would be a wonderful mother. He had almost forgotten.

Now it came back to him how those discussions had led to Allie's desire to stay home with their children, which inevitably led to their conclusion that it was impossible because of his low income, which caused her to work extra hours at the florist to pay the bills, which caused him to feel inadequate and frustrated ...

It was an endless cycle of discontent, all of it diverting them from their original course: loving and being committed to each other. It was what had made Joe's Place—and ultimately Issie—so attractive to him.

Ben, Ray's son, came back from his shower, and Mark smiled weakly and shook his hand. The boy's eyes were red, and he looked more like a scared little boy than a college track star.

"Any word?" Ben asked his father.

"No, son. No word."

Nor was there any change all that afternoon.

Chapter Thirty-One

Since money was getting low, Mark and Allie stayed in a less expensive, more obscure hotel near the French Quarter that night and ate hamburgers that they'd picked up on the way back. The room came with only one bed, which infuriated her.

"I'll sleep on the floor," she told him when they unlocked the musty room and spotted the one bed.

"That's a little silly, don't you think, considering that we shared a bed for four years? It's not like I'm going to attack you in your sleep."

"I don't want to sleep in the same bed with you," she bit out.

They were both irritable, and he hadn't shaven. Thick stubble shadowed his face, and he looked as if he hadn't slept in days. "Allie, the minute my head hits that pillow, I'm gonna be out. It'll be just like you're alone, if that makes you feel better."

"But I don't think it's right, Mark. Sharing a bed is a privilege between a husband and wife, and we are not husband and wife. We haven't been in eight weeks."

"For heaven's sake, Allie. I'll sleep on the floor then!"

He grabbed the pillow off the bed and threw it onto the stained carpet. She jumped when she saw a roach migrating across the room. Mark stepped on it, then threw it away.

"Long way from the Marriott, huh?" he asked.

He went to the closet for a blanket and threw it down on the floor next to the pillow. The thought of roaches crawling on him while he slept sickened her. "Mark, you can't sleep down there."

"Watch me. I could sleep anywhere right now. There's no choice, anyway."

"All right, sleep on the bed," she said finally.

He sighed, then leveled his red eyes on her. "I'll sleep on top of the bedspread so we don't accidentally touch. How would that be?"

She recognized the sarcasm, and it made her angrier. "Sounds good to me."

"Fine."

She went into the bathroom to take a bath and brush her teeth, and when she came out, Mark was already asleep on top of the covers, facing the window. She got in on the other side and lay still for a long moment.

When he began to snore, she tried to feel irritated, but some secret part of her found comfort in that. Turning her back to him, she closed her eyes and tried to sleep.

●　　●　　●

A thud against their door woke her. She sat bolt upright in bed and listened. The glowing clock beside her told her several hours had passed since she'd fallen asleep.

She heard footsteps in the hall.

"Mark," she whispered. "*Mark!*"

He didn't hear, so she reached for the lamp on the bed table to turn on the light, but she knocked over a glass.

Mark woke up. "What is it?" he muttered.

"I heard something outside."

He got up and padded across the room to the door. She followed him, listening.

They heard the sound again, footsteps, then a thud, and a scraping sound.

Mark went to the door and looked out through the peephole.

Allie came up behind him and touched his back, as if that could protect her. He turned around. "Come look," he whispered, then pulled her toward the peephole.

She stood on her toes and peered out. A man was standing at the door across the hall from them. He was obviously drunk and barely able to stand, repeatedly trying and failing to get his key into his door.

As she watched, someone opened the door, and he almost fell into the room.

"Where have you been?" a woman shouted.

He muttered something about a bar downstairs, and she slammed the door behind him.

Allie turned around. Mark was leaning on one arm against the door, close, too close, and she looked up at him in the darkness. "Guess it was a false alarm. I'm sorry I woke you."

"It's okay," he whispered. "No problem. I'm sorry he woke *you.*"

The kindness in his voice almost did her in. She realized that her coldness gave him reason to treat her with contempt— which, ironically, she was better able to handle.

"Well, no point in standing here. Let's go back to bed."

He took her hand, as if he sensed that she was still frightened, and led her to the bed. She slid in, and he covered her up, then went around to his side.

She lay there on her side, shivering.

"Are you cold?" he asked, his voice a gravelly baritone against her ear.

"No. Just still shaking from the scare. But you must be cold."

"A little," he said.

She knew he waited for her to invite him under the covers, but something inside her, some hurt, self-protective part of her, refused. Finally, he did it without asking. Before she could object, he had slid up behind her, set his knees at the back of hers, and slid his arms around her.

"Mark . . ."

"Shhh," he said. "I'm just trying to warm you up and make you stop shaking. Just relax and quit trying to be mad at me. Close your eyes."

Trying to be mad at him? The thought almost made her smile. It sometimes did take an effort, when things were going well and he was so much like he used to be. But then she remembered walking in on him holding Issie, remembered him lying his way out of it, remembered the sick despair that had crushed her as she'd tried to decide what to do.

She stiffened. "I can't sleep with you touching me," she said.

He let her go and backed away. "You used to sleep like a baby when I was holding you."

"I've gotten used to sleeping alone."

A moment passed, and then she felt him turn over, slide out from under the covers, and drop back on top of the spread. Not another word was spoken until morning.

Chapter Thirty-Two

Mark stood inside the airport looking out onto the tarmac at the aircraft they were about to board, a small commuter jet that looked tiny compared to the massive airliners around it.

It was starting to rain, and he wished they had thought to bring an umbrella. He looked at Allie and saw the distant, worried look on her face.

"What's wrong?"

"Nothing," she said. "I just had this sick feeling. I don't know if I'm more afraid of getting on that little plane in a storm or of taking my chances with the killer."

"The plane is fine, Allie. It's all we could afford."

"If it weren't raining, I wouldn't be worried."

"We could wait. But the tickets are nonrefundable."

Chilled, she rubbed her arms, and he fought the urge to put his arm around her to warm her. After last night's rebuff, he had decided she would have to make the next move. "I'll be all right," she said.

"Are you sure? You didn't eat much breakfast. Maybe you need something in your stomach."

"No, there's no time."

"I don't want you to get—"

"I *said* I'll be all right!"

He sighed, disgusted, and turned back to the window. What was he doing here with a woman who didn't want him near her? His very presence seemed to keep her so tense that she couldn't eat or sleep. So far, he hadn't really protected her from anything. Was all of this wasted effort?

Their flight number was called, and Mark picked up their bags. Allie started for the gate, and he followed.

A handful of others trotted down the steps onto the tarmac ahead of them. The rain was picking up; thunder boomed above the sound of the jet engines; the scent of fuel and exhaust washed over them as they hurried toward the plane. Allie walked rapidly in front of him, carrying her purse in one hand and a small bag in the other.

Mark heard a crack from his left, and the bag flew out of Allie's hand. She screamed and spun around. *A bullet!* he thought. *Someone shot at Allie!* He dropped the suitcases and hurled himself forward.

Allie fell beneath him, still screaming.

He covered Allie entirely with his body. "It's okay, baby, it's okay," he chanted, trying to reassure her. But it wasn't okay. Another shot cracked the air. The bullet hit him, whiplashing his head sideways.

Lord, protect her, was the last conscious thought that cried through his mind before blackness overtook him.

•   •   •

Allie's screams shrilled into a higher, more desperate pitch as she felt the impact of the bullet move Mark's body. Then he went limp, and she saw the blood dripping onto the concrete. Screaming in a voice that seemed distant, apart from her, she rolled him over. Forgetting the threat of being struck by another bullet, she knelt beside him and tried to wake him.

Chaos surrounded them as people screamed and ran for cover. "Help me!" she screamed. Mark lay limp, lifeless, blood gushing from the side of his head and pooling on the asphalt.

"Somebody please help me!" She clutched his head with trembling hands, trying to stop his bleeding.

Time seemed frozen, and no help came. Finally, security guards appeared, then a rescue unit and police officers. Someone pried her hands from his wound and tried to pull her away, but she fought them. Even so, she soon found herself sitting on the ground a few feet from him. "I have to stay with him. He needs me!"

"You can, ma'am. But we need to check you first. Were you hit?"

She watched them working desperately on Mark. "Please, you've got to save him! Please."

"Ma'am, are you hurt?" they asked, examining the scrapes and bruises she'd received from being thrown to the ground.

"No!" she shouted, pushing their hands away. "Help *him!*"

But there *were* people helping him. It just wasn't enough. He was going to die. She knew it.

An officer with a badge that said Jefferson Parish Sheriff's Office bent down to her. "Ma'am, did you see the shooter?"

"No."

"Then you can't say how far away he was?"

"No. I . . . I think it came from over there." She pointed in the direction from which the bullet had come. "My bag . . . got hit first."

Several other officers clustered around the bag, and she turned back to Mark. "Is he alive?" she asked.

"Yes, ma'am."

That was all she could get out of them as she watched them lifting him onto a gurney.

She got to her feet and found that her legs were weak. She followed as they loaded him into a rescue unit. "It was meant for me," she told them, as if they would realize the mistake and clear the whole mess up. "*I'm* the fire wife."

"Fire wife?" A cop was in her way at once, but she pushed him aside and climbed in next to Mark. "Guys, she's a fire wife!" he shouted.

The paramedic closed the doors. Allie sat out of the way as they worked on him, putting tubes down his throat, an IV in his arm, applying pressure to his wound. One paramedic barked out vitals on the radio to the online physician at the hospital where they were headed.

He was still alive; she clung to that reality, and from somewhere she found the strength to pray. She reached between the paramedics to touch Mark's hand. Hers was still covered with his blood. His was warm, though limp. Sobbing, she closed her eyes and sent up her pleas to God, offering him bargains and promises and sacrifices, all peppered with terror and rage and confusion and desperation.

They were at the hospital in moments, and she followed them out of the ambulance as if in a fog, only dimly aware of the handful of reporters who shouted questions that she ignored.

They whisked him away from her before she had time to tell them how urgent it was that they save him, how she needed another chance with him, how good a man he was . . .

And they whisked her into an emergency room stall where they began to check her scrapes and bruises, her blood pressure, her temperature, asking her questions that she couldn't understand, couldn't answer, couldn't think about . . .

All she could think of was her husband, and the fact that she might never have the chance to make things right with him.

Chapter Thirty-Three

The television set in the living area of the Midtown Station in Newpointe blared the news report as WVUE-TV broadcast live from the New Orleans airport. Nick Foster, the room's only occupant, looked up from the notes he was making for Sunday's sermon, his attention caught by the urgent tone of the news correspondent. "John, the airport is teeming with police and airport security personnel as they comb the area from which the bullet seems to have been fired. Just over my left shoulder is the area where the shooter probably stood, although there doesn't seem to be any witnesses. The Jefferson Parish Sheriff's Office responded to the call, just after the shooting, but we're told that the Kenner Police Department is investigating the case. Police have determined that the shooter did not come through security; otherwise his gun would have been found. Instead, they believe he came through the gates leading to the tarmac and found a place on which to perch that would give him a clear shot of his victim. He is believed to be the Newpointe serial killer, since the victim was a Newpointe fireman."

Nick threw his notes aside; they fluttered across the floor. "Slater! Dan! Hey, anybody!" he yelled.

"Witnesses say that the first bullet hit Allison Branning's bag, at which point her husband, Fireman Mark Branning, flung himself over her to protect her."

"No, not Mark," Nick whispered, slowly rising to his feet.

"The second bullet fired, and he was hit in the head. It's clear that both bullets were intended for Mrs. Branning. Fortunately, she was not injured, but we have no word on Branning's condition. We'll have more for you later, John, as this bizarre case continues to unfold."

Nick almost tripped on his chair as he rushed to the door. "Mark's been shot!" he shouted to anyone who could hear. "He got Mark!"

He found Slater Finch lying on a bed napping, and Slater sat up and squinted at him. "What?"

"Mark Branning's been shot!"

He ran to the bathroom where there was a light under the door, and banged for whomever was in there. "Mark Branning was shot at the airport!"

Frantic, he searched for others. *Where was everybody?*

Slater was on his feet now, following Nick. "How do you know? Where did you hear this?"

"On the news." Nick's hands were shaking, and he rushed around a corner and ran into Junior Reynolds. "Mark Branning—"

"I heard you," Junior said, breathless. "Is he dead?"

"I don't know," Nick said, rushing to the phone. "I'll call."

He started dialing information as Bob Sigrest and Issie Mattreaux came in from the garage. "What's going on?" Bob asked.

"Mark's been shot."

Issie uttered a loud curse, then dropped slowly into a chair.

By the time Nick had been connected with East Jefferson Hospital's intensive care unit waiting room, all of the firemen and paramedics on duty, except for Dan Nichols, were in the room. He asked for Allie, but no one came to the phone. Nick hung up, frustrated and desperate. Some of them were now gathered around the television waiting for updates, while others ran next door to tell Stan, in case he hadn't heard. Issie just sat motionless, staring into space.

"I've got to get up there," Nick said, picking up the phone and dialing Craig Barnes's beeper. "I've got to go sit this out with Allie."

"You can't, man. You've got to stay on duty," Slater said. "That was the deal."

"But I'm their pastor! This is the kind of thing I'm supposed to be there for!"

"Craig is never gonna let you off. Not unless you get a replacement. Pat Castor will have a fit if she thinks we're operating with less than a full crew."

"Then I've got to call someone else in."

"They're all gone with their wives. You think they're gonna leave their wives alone after they hear about this? It means he knows, man. He knows where they are. What they're doing. He can find them."

Nick was feeling nauseous. "I'll call George Broussard."

"George? After what he's been through?"

Nick put the phone back down. "You're right." He stood motionless for a moment, lost in thought, then grabbed the phone again and tried the ICU waiting room. "But Allie can't be there alone. This guy will stop at nothing."

But despite how much he wanted to go, he knew he wasn't going to get to. He had a job to do, and he was stuck with it.

• • •

A little over an hour later, Dan came jogging back in, drenched from head to foot in sweat. He saw the others clustered around the television set, and stopped cold. "What's going on?"

Nick looked up at him. "Where have you been?"

"Out jogging," Dan said. "What happened?"

Issie wiped the tears on her face. "Mark's been shot."

"Mark *Branning?*"

"Yes, Mark Branning," Nick said. "He was shot at the airport as he and Allie were about to get on a plane."

Dan dropped his towel and gaped at his pastor. "Is he dead?"

"I don't know."

Dan's face reddened, and his mouth fell open as if in a silent groan. "I don't believe this," he muttered finally. "It can't be happening. What hospital is he in?"

"East Jefferson. I tried to call but couldn't find out anything."

Dan's eyes were misting over, and his cheeks were mottled now in blotchy patches of red. Sweat ran from his wet blonde hair down his face. "You couldn't find out if he was dead or alive?" he yelled. "Don't they know?"

The door opened and Craig Barnes ran in, his face twisted with emotion. "Did you guys hear about Mark?"

All eyes turned to him. "Yes," Slater Finch said. "We were just listening to the news. Do you know anything?"

"Is he dead?" Dan demanded.

"The news reports didn't say. But he got shot in the head. Doesn't sound good."

"In the *head?*" Dan shouted. "He got shot in the head? Man, I've gotta go there! Chief, you've got to let me go!"

"No," Nick said firmly, taking off his glasses and wiping his own eyes. "I've got to go be with Allie, Craig. I'm her pastor. She needs me. Dan, you know she does."

"He's my best friend!" Dan yelled.

"You can't both go," Craig shouted over them. "Only one of you. Now calm down."

Nick turned to Dan, entreating him. "Dan, I need to pray with Allie. I need to calm her down. She's bound to be a wreck, and you know it. You can't help right now. You're as upset as she is."

Dan knocked a chair over with a clash and kicked it. "I want to be there!"

Craig picked up the chair, and Nick could see that he, too, struggled with the emotion on his face. Compassion wasn't an emotion they commonly saw in their chief's face, but today none of them seemed able to fight it. "Dan, Nick's right," Craig said. "Let him go."

Dan banged his fist on the wall then leaned back hard against it. "No offense, Nick, but I'm in better shape to guard Allie. That bullet wasn't meant for Mark. This guy's getting desperate. He's not going to give up now."

Nick bristled. "Just because I don't spend most of my waking hours working on my body like you do, doesn't mean I can't defend Allie Branning."

Dan took a menacing step toward him. "I stay in shape, which is more than I can say about you. There's a killer out there, Nick! Do you really think you're ready to take him on?"

Junior Reynolds popped up from his seat in front of the television and stepped between them. "That's enough. Why don't you both just shut up?"

Craig intervened then. "Allie doesn't need either one of you protecting her. She's safe in the hospital, and if she did need protection, it wouldn't be from a fireman. Dan, you go get back in uniform before I dock your pay, and Nick, you get out of here before I change my mind."

Dan wilted and picked his towel up off the floor. "Tell Allie I wanted to come," he said.

Nick suddenly hated himself for being drawn into such a childish exchange. Pride wasn't supposed to be one of his weak points. He was supposed to be immune. He set his hands on his hips and looked apologetically at his friend. "I will, Dan. I'm sorry for what I said, okay?"

Dan drew in a deep breath, then let it out quickly. "Yeah, me, too," he muttered.

"I'll let you know the minute I know Mark's condition."

Dan couldn't speak, and Nick glanced with shame at Craig and saw the red rims of his eyes and the tears he was fighting to hold back.

Nick could have kicked himself as he headed out the door, praying that God would overlook his little display of spiritual bungling and still give them a miracle. He wasn't up to conducting his third funeral in a week.

• • •

On her way to meet Stan at the police station, Celia Shepherd rushed into Jill Clark's office to tell her what had happened. Jill's secretary tried to stop her, but Celia ignored her and burst in.

"Jill, have you heard about Mark and Allie?"

"No, what?"

"Mark's been shot! He's in surgery at East Jefferson Hospital in Metairie, and Jill, they're saying it was a head wound. I'm headed to the Southshore right now to be with Allie. Do you want to go?"

"Yes." She closed the file on her desk and came around it. Tears were already filling her eyes.

"Stan had the key to her house, so he went by to get some of her things. He's meeting us at the station. He's coming with us."

Jill grabbed her purse and headed out the door, shouting back to her secretary, "Cancel everything. Don't know when I'll be back."

Chapter Thirty-Four

M rs. Branning?"

Allie gasped, startled. She looked up into the compassionate eyes of the nurse who, sometime before, had brought her coffee and a blanket. Lost in thought, Allie hadn't heard her approaching.

"Mrs. Branning, there are some police officers out front who need to speak to you about what happened. Do you feel up to seeing them now?"

"Yes," Allie said, trying to hold the now-lukewarm coffee without spilling it. "Yes, please. They have to catch him. They have to catch him before he kills all of us."

The nurse disappeared, and in moments, two Kenner detectives—Peter Blanc and Lou James—came in and introduced themselves as homicide detectives.

"Homicide?" she asked, still shivering. "He's not dead. It wasn't a homicide."

"We know, ma'am, but we got to assume it was an attempted homicide. This person's killed before."

She listened, then focused inward as thoughts whirled in her mind. "You think he's going to die, don't you?" she asked, her mouth twisting as she tried to control her tears. "What have they told you? I have a right to know."

"Nothing, ma'am. Really."

She spilt her coffee and one of the men took it from her, set it down. She covered her face with both hands and let her sobs rise up into her throat, reddening her face and threatening to explode out of the top of her head. "He was shot in the *head!*" she cried. "People don't survive things like that! Of course he's gonna die!"

She forgot about the two men as she wept, thinking only of Mark and of their lost chances, but sometime later she glanced up and saw the two men looking awkwardly at one another. Remembering how important it was to catch the person who did this, she tried to pull herself together. Still sobbing, she wiped her face. "We were headed to Georgia, to stay with my parents until they caught the killer. I can't think who we told . . . who knew that we were going . . . what plane we'd be getting on." She shook her head, trying to clear her thoughts. "I told my parents, and then I told my best friend Jill that we were going, but I didn't say when or which flight. And Mark told Stan, our detective in Newpointe. Maybe Jill or Stan told someone, and they figured out which flight." She drew a deep, painful breath. "It was meant for me. That bullet should have hit me instead. But he threw himself over me." She fixed her pleading eyes on them. "Did they find him? Did they find anything?"

"No, ma'am. He never went in the airport. Came through a gate to the runways and climbed to where he shot from. But we can't figure out how he got past security. We're wonderin' if maybe he had some kind of airport employee identification, or a uniform that looked like the ground crews—somethin' that woulda kept someone from asking for his I.D. We're checkin' with the security agents on duty now."

"It all happened so fast," she said. "I didn't see anyone. All I saw was Mark, lying—" She shook her head sharply, then said, "You should call Stan Shepherd in Newpointe and compare notes with him. He's been around for the last three shootings. And now Mark . . ."

One of the detectives scooted to the edge of his chair, his long legs making him seem uncomfortable. "We're doing the best we can, Mrs. Branning, and I'm sure the Newpointe P.D. are, too. Just take care of yourself until we can find him."

Feeling hopeless, she shook her head. "There's no stopping him. He goes where he wants to, shoots whoever—"

But the detective held up a hand to stop her. "Mrs. Branning, you'll be safe here. There's security at the entrances. No one with a weapon can get in here."

She looked wearily back at them. They just didn't understand. Security at the entrances—it wouldn't make any difference. There'd been security at the airport, too.

The two men got up to leave, and Allie got to her feet, too, still clutching her blanket around her. She started out behind them, but the nurse stopped her. "Mrs. Branning, what can I get you?"

"My husband," she said. "I want to see my husband."

"He's in surgery, and I've made sure that the surgeon knows to call you as soon as he has any information. If you'll just wait in there, there's a phone, and it'll ring right to you. Plus, you can call out if you need to."

Gently, she led Allie back into the room. "My parents," she said. "I need to call my parents. And my pastor. People have to pray. There's no time to waste." She broke down weeping again, and the nurse pulled the blanket more securely around her. "Call your parents first," the woman suggested gently. "Here, I'll dial the number for you if you want."

Allie nodded weakly and told her the number.

Chapter Thirty-Five

Self-recriminations, white-hot and scalding, lashed through Allie's mind as she sat in the small waiting room. She was being punished, she thought, for rebuffing Mark's efforts, for resisting his advances. She was being taught a horrible lesson, though she wasn't sure what it was.

She pulled her feet up onto the vinyl sofa and hugged her knees as she cried out to God, pleading with him to let the judgment be hers alone, begging him to spare Mark. As her mind turned her own judgment inward, she felt smaller and smaller, less significant, rabidly infected by her own thoughts.

A sound startled her, and she looked up as Jill, Celia, and Stan rushed into the room. She fell into their arms, weeping with them, as she tried to tell them what had happened in broken sentences that she knew made no sense. Moments later, Nick Foster came in, his presence providing a fragile peace.

After only a few minutes, Stan left to go to the police department to see what they knew. Nick organized them all into a circle near the telephone—in case the surgeon called—and started them praying earnestly for Mark's recovery. Allie couldn't pray—not while her thoughts and emotions and fears were tangled in such a terrible knot—but she listened gratefully as the others prayed for her. When each of them had prayed, Nick led them in Psalm 23, offered as a prayer. "Yea, though I walk through the valley of the shadow of death, I will fear no evil. Thy rod and thy staff, they comfort me ..." Allie quoted it with them, trying to let that peace which transcends all understanding fall over her, trying to cling to the words that she knew gave life itself.

When they were finished praying, Nick stooped in front of her and made her look him in the eye. "Who's in control, Allie?"

"Feels like Satan," she admitted.

"Feels like it," Nick acknowledged. "But who do *we* know has already won the victory?"

"God."

"And if God is in control, what's going to happen?"

She wilted. "I don't know."

"He's going to watch over those he loves. He's going to make all things work together for good to those who love him and are called according to his purpose."

"That's just it!" she cried. "We weren't acting like people who loved him. We weren't doing much of *anything* according to his purpose. He's punishing us. He's judging me!"

"Allie," he said, not allowing her to look away from him. "God loves you, and he loves Mark. Do you believe that he *sent* some maniac to punish *you?*"

She couldn't answer, just hiccuped her sobs as she stared at him. After a few moments, she whispered, "You're right. Why would he have even bothered? I'm not that important."

Nick gripped her tighter. "You're his *child*, Allie. That's how important you are. And so is Mark. Jesus grieves over your pain. Allie, what does the Bible tell us about Christ interceding for us?"

She couldn't answer, just shook her head.

"That he prays for us . . ." He paused to let her finish, but she didn't. "With what, Allie? Romans 8:26. You know the verse. He prays for us with what, Allie?"

"Groans that words cannot express," she whispered.

"If he were the kind of God who sent an assassin to gun you or Mark down, would he be the kind of God who prays for you with groans that words cannot express?"

"No," she whispered. She tried to let that sink in, but her heart rejected the comfort.

What if Mark's death now was part of God's plan?

• • •

After a while, Nick offered to go to the cafeteria to get her some tea. Jill and Celia stayed behind, holding her hands.

Allie checked her watch. She had been there for almost three hours, and still there was no word.

Celia got up, took Nick's seat across from Allie, and looked her in the eye. "Allie, I've been sitting here asking the Lord if I should tell you something I've never told anyone else in New-pointe, except for Stan and Aunt Aggie. I've decided that it would help you to know."

Jill got up. "I'll let you two talk alone."

Celia took her hand to stop her. "No, Jill. I know I can trust you both."

Jill sat back down.

Breathing deeply, Celia leaned forward, her elbows on her knees. Her baby-fine blonde hair fell into her eyes, and she swept it behind an ear. Celia's eyes were smeared with mascara from her tears, but Allie didn't suppose she looked any better herself.

"See, I've been in your place before, Allie. I was married before Stan. And my husband was murdered."

Allie's mouth fell open, and Jill leaned closer to her friend. "Celia, I never knew . . ."

Tears came to Celia's eyes. "He was poisoned," she said. "They never caught the killer." Her mouth trembled as she smeared the fresh tears away. "I remember sitting in the hospital up in Jackson, waiting, praying, wondering who would do such a horrible thing. I know how you feel, Allie. I kept trying to bargain with God. I kept wanting to throw myself on the altar as a sacrifice, to convince him to let Nathan live. It was one of the worst nights of my life."

Something about that shared experience gave Allie comfort. Celia had come through the pain. She had found light again after wandering through the same darkness Allie wandered through now. Allie put her hand over Celia's. "Celia, I'm so sorry. I remember when you came to town. You seemed so broken, so sad. But no one knew anything about you, and Aunt Aggie wasn't talking."

"She was so good to me," Celia said. "I found healing here, and I know God led me here so I could meet Stan. But I didn't tell anyone for a lot of reasons, one of them being that I didn't want to talk about it."

"I know that feeling," Allie whispered.

"I'm just telling you this, Allie, so you'll know that you can talk to me. I've been here, where you are. I've felt that kind of pain. I've prayed those prayers."

"But yours weren't answered," Allie said weakly.

"Yes, they were," she said. "Nick was right. God is still in control. He didn't answer them the way I wanted him to, but he did make things work together for good. I miss Nathan, but he was a Christian. I know I'll see him again. And God provided."

Allie leaned back in her seat and put her head against the wall. "I don't want God to provide anything but Mark. I don't want to have to get used to him being dead." She started to cry again. "All this time, he's been staying with me, and I've been so cold to him. I made him sleep in a separate bed most of the time, and every time he's tried to touch me I've pulled away. I wouldn't have blamed him if he'd left me to fend for myself. But he didn't. Why didn't he?"

"Because he loves you," Jill whispered.

Allie nodded. "I kept wondering how much. Now I know. Enough to take a bullet for me. He saw it coming, and he took it on purpose. He chose to take it."

"If that's a picture of his love for you, Allie, then it's some picture," Celia said.

Allie covered her face as she wept.

· · ·

Not long after, the doctor came in. The very sight of him in his scrubs, with his blue mask pulled loosely down under his chin, alarmed Allie. "They said you were gonna call. Please, he's not—"

"He's good," the doctor said gently, cutting into her anticipation. "He's a lucky guy."

She caught her breath and looked up at him, not believing. "Really? He's alive?"

"Yes. The bullet didn't penetrate his brain; it was a glancing shot. It looked bad and he lost a lot of blood, but the damage may be minor in the long term. We've had a plastic surgeon patching up the damage to his face—his right temple and half of his forehead—so he has quite a few stitches. The bullet did cause a concussion, which is why he's unconscious. We're going to keep him in ICU until he's awake, and we'll watch closely to make sure no infection sets in. We're also concerned about his brain swelling from the impact. In head trauma such as this one, sometimes the brain can be shaken so hard that some damage occurs. That's why he's not entirely out of the woods yet. But I'm optimistic."

She burst into tears again, but this time they were tears of gratitude. Throwing her arms around the doctor, she said, "Thank you. Thank you so much."

The doctor looked awkward at the embrace, and patted her back. She let go of him, then turned to her friends.

They all clung together as if the very force of their embrace could keep Mark alive.

Chapter Thirty-Six

Mark's father, Eddie Branning, made it to the hospital before they allowed Allie to go see Mark. He sat with her in the waiting room, his hands shaking. She knew he longed for a drink, but she was thankful that he had abstained today, of all days. His leathery face was wrinkled beyond his years, and he was skinny to the point of emaciation. Since his wife's death and his retirement from the fire department, he hadn't taken very good care of himself. Most days, he sat in his recliner drinking the day away, watching talk shows and game shows and forgetting to eat.

His relationship with Mark had not been good, and although they lived in the same town, Allie knew that Mark hadn't spoken to him in nearly a year. Had he even heard that she and Mark had been separated? He must have—he often ventured out at night to a little hole-in-the-wall bar called the Pop-A-Top Lounge, where he drank with his buddies; someone would have told him. Even so, as he sat with her now, he didn't mention it.

For the first time since she'd met him during her engagement to Mark, she felt compassion, rather than disgust, for the man who had raised her husband. It hadn't been easy for him to come here, but Mark was, after all, his only son. She pictured him hearing about the shooting during an episode of Jenny Jones, thought of him stumbling around the filth and clutter of his decaying house to find something clean to wear to the hospital, forcing himself not to take the drink that would have made things easier to bear . . .

When the doctors finally allowed her to go in to see Mark, she leaned over to her father-in-law and touched his shaking hand. "Eddie, would you like to come in with me?"

He shook his head. "No, that's okay. He's your husband."

"He's your son."

Tears filled those red eyes that looked so much like Mark's, and he wiped them quickly. "He won't want me there."

"Please, Eddie," she said. "*I* want you there."

He looked up at her, stricken with emotion, and she wondered how long it had been since anyone had shown him compassion. She had failed as a daughter-in-law. She should have been drawing him into their family, instead of avoiding him as if his presence would contaminate their marriage. Funny how they'd managed to contaminate it without him.

Eddie cleared his throat, then stood up and nodded toward the door. "Okay," he said. "You lead the way."

Filled with trepidation, she headed out of the waiting room, wondering what condition she would find her husband in. A nurse met them at the double steel doors of ICU and escorted them back to the three-walled room where Mark lay, still unconscious, under a tangle of wires and monitor cords.

For a moment, she thought they had led them to the wrong room. The man on the table had little resemblance to Mark. His eyes were bruised, and she could see the bare, bristly skin of his shaved scalp above the bandage that covered one side of his face. His color was deathly pale against the black of the bruises. Looking down at him, she went numb.

"He's very lucky," the nurse said as she made some notations on his chart. "If that bullet had changed its direction by even a centimeter . . ."

"But . . . he looks so different. It doesn't look like him."

"It will."

Allie stood paralyzed, staring, unable to grasp the idea that this helpless, wounded, unconscious stranger was her husband, who had been so protective of her just this morning. She heard a garbled sound behind her and turned to see that her father-in-law was doubled over, his hand covering his mouth as he muffled his own sobs.

Quickly, she went to embrace him. "I . . . can't," he said. "I'll . . . I'll be in . . . the waitin' room."

"Okay," she whispered. "I understand."

She let him go, and he fled from the unit.

She turned back to Mark and touched his face, then bent down to kiss his cheek. His skin felt warm, and the stubble was thicker than it had been earlier. It felt rough, familiar, beneath her lips. She closed her eyes and kept her lips there, wishing she'd had the grace to make such a move when he was awake, wishing the kiss could stir him to life. But Mark didn't move.

"If he's doing so well, why isn't he conscious?" she asked the nurse. "Is he in a coma?"

"No," the nurse said. "He's been awake for a minute or so a couple of times since the surgery. The concussion is the main reason he's out."

Allie looked hopefully up at her. "Did you talk to him? Ask him questions?"

"He wasn't talking yet," she said. "He was very groggy. But if he wakes while you're here, ask him questions like who he is, where he lives, what your birthday is, things like that. We'll be able to tell a lot about his condition when he wakes up."

The nurse began to describe the purpose of all of the machinery in the room, and a heaviness came over Allie's heart. So many instruments waiting for something to go wrong. So many things that *could* go wrong.

"I have to go talk to some other families now," the nurse said, "but if he wakes up while I'm gone, let me know, okay?"

"Should I try to wake him up?"

"Yes. It's important that I evaluate his progress."

Allie held her gaze. "He could still die, couldn't he?"

The nurse hesitated to answer. "Everyone in here is in pretty critical condition, Mrs. Branning. But we have a high success rate."

She left them alone, and Allie stood beside his bed, gently stroking her fingers along the side of his face. "Mark?" she asked, close to his ear. "Mark, wake up. Wake up and let me see that you're all right."

He didn't stir, so she tried shaking his arm.

"Mark? Wake up, Mark."

The silence and limpness of his body made her despair even more, and as a sob rose to her throat, she dropped her forehead to his chest. The terrible, irrational fear that he would die without knowing that she loved him overwhelmed her. "Why did you do it?" she whispered against his face. "Why didn't you take cover?"

He didn't have to answer. She knew why. It was because he loved her. From the beginning of this ordeal, he had been there, worrying and protecting and watching over her. If he'd loved Issie, he would have been watching over her, but he'd given no indication that he'd even thought about Issie in days. And Allie hadn't made it easy for him.

It was so simple, despite all the pain, and the betrayal, and the fact that she had biblical grounds for divorce. The Bible never mandated divorce in the case of adultery. It only allowed for it. The simple fact was that Mark loved her, despite how he had strayed. He had spent the past two days proving it.

A tear rolled down her cheek and dropped onto his. "I love you, too, Mark," she whispered. "I do. And I'm so sorry for all the things I've said and done. How I've acted toward you. I do love you."

There was no change in the expression on his face or in the position of his body.

In a broken voice, she whispered, "Oh, Lord, please let him wake up."

It occurred to her that she had almost no right to ask for that, when she had been willing to throw her wedding vows away without a fight. She had behaved as if her vows were contingent on his. But her vows hadn't included "as long as you keep your vows to me." In their wedding ceremony, she had said, "Till death do us part." And now that there was a real chance of that very thing happening, she realized that she didn't want it to end. Could God hear her prayers now, when she'd been so out of touch with him that she'd almost broken the most important earthly commitment she'd ever made?

She pressed her face into the sheets, muffling the words that she knew God heard clearly. "Forgive me, oh, God. Please forgive me for letting my marriage fall apart. Lord, if you'll just give me one more chance, I'll make my marriage work, I promise. I'm committed now, Lord, whether he is or not, whether he does what he should or not, whether he admits to me that he had feelings for Issie or not. Even if he doesn't change anything, I'll change, Lord. Please, just let me have one more chance."

She was wiping her eyes, trying to pull herself together, when she noticed the other families beginning to leave. Her time was up, and it wasn't enough.

The nurse came in, and Allie asked in a heartbroken voice, "Can't I stay? He never woke up."

"No." The nurse touched her shoulder and met her eyes with compassion. "But I'll tell you what. If he wakes up before I get off tonight, I'll let you come in for an extra visit."

"Will you?" she asked, wiping her tears. "You promise?"

"Yes. And if that doesn't happen before you come in for the eleven o'clock visit, let one of the new nurses know that you haven't seen him awake yet, and she'll do the same thing."

She took in a deep cleansing breath. "All right. I'll be right out there. I won't leave."

"You need to eat," the nurse said. "It won't do him any good if you get sick."

"I can't eat," she said, and went back into the waiting room.

She saw with some relief that her parents had arrived and were talking with Celia, Jill, and Nick. They were waiting for her to return, but she dreaded telling them how bad things were. Eddie sat off to himself, still obviously distraught, but unable to speak to anyone. Her heart welled with love and compassion for the man she had never gotten to know very well. She wished she had some good news for him.

When they spotted her, Allie's parents rushed to intercept her from the crowd coming back from ICU. They pulled her into a family hug, and she clung to them with all her might.

"We got here as soon as we could," her mother said as they broke the hug. "How is he?"

"I don't know," she said. By now, Celia, Nick, and Jill had joined their cluster, waiting eagerly for some positive word. She racked her brain for something to tell them. "His vital signs are good." There. That was it. The only positive thing she could think of.

"Is he awake?"

"No."

"Has he been?"

"Only for a second. They're gonna call me if he wakes up again."

Allie's mother, Mattie Miller, had given birth to Allie when she was eighteen years old. She was only forty-three now, and people often marveled at how young she looked. Her father, still handsome at forty-five, didn't have a gray hair on his head, and he worked out to avoid the paunch that many men his age carried.

Though they looked more like yuppies than potential grandparents, when it came to their daughter, they both behaved like typical parents.

"Honey, your mother and I talked about this all the way down here," her father, Robert, said. "We're worried. Someone is trying to kill you. Coming to Georgia was a good idea, and we still want you to do it."

She looked up at them, surprised. "Now?"

"Yes," her mother said emphatically. "There's a killer out there, and he's after you, Allie. There's nothing you can do for Mark here."

She stiffened. "No way. I'm not leaving him."

"He's the one who left *you*. Two months ago."

"*Today* he took a bullet for me!"

Her mother shot her father a look, and he sat down next to Allie, set his hand on her shoulder, and stared intently into her face. She could see that he struggled with his words. "Allie, what Mark did was admirable. I'm grateful to him for it. You'll never know how grateful. But right now, for his action to have any meaning, you have to think of your own safety."

"You don't have to feel any guilt, honey," Mattie piped in. "You're not even really married anymore. You have no obligation to stay here with him."

Allie closed her eyes and told herself to stay calm. They meant well. She knew they did. "We *are* married until we have divorce papers, and neither of us has filed," she bit out. "I'm not leaving."

Eddie looked up from his stooped position a few seats down, and Allie saw the pain on his face.

"Allie." Jill's voice stopped her mother's reply, and Allie saw that Jill was staring, stricken, toward the door. "What is it?" Allie asked.

Jill looked as though she didn't quite know what to say. "Uh—looks like you have a visitor."

Allie looked through the doorway. Issie Mattreaux stood at the desk. Allie's heart crashed like a lead ball. She didn't have the energy to deal with this now.

"Who is it?" her mother asked cautiously.

Allie hesitated. If she told her mother who was waiting outside, Mattie would launch out of her chair to "give that woman a piece of her mind."

Celia and Nick, both of whom knew of Issie's role in the Brannings' marital problems, stood up as if to divert whatever confrontation was imminent. Nick started toward her. "Allie, you just sit and rest. I'll do it."

It was tempting to let her pastor handle it, but something reminded Allie that she had made a commitment to God, despite what Mark had done or what had happened with Issie. Now that she was committed to her marriage again, she felt a sense of compassion for Issie, instead of the rage and resentment she might have felt earlier. Had God empowered her already? "No, Nick, that's okay," she said, getting up. "I'll go talk to her."

Allie was dimly aware of everyone's surprise as she walked toward the front. The receptionist, who was still talking to Issie, pointed back toward her. Issie turned and saw Allie coming toward her. Looking unsure of herself, she met her halfway.

For a moment, the two women stared at each other. Allie saw the trepidation in Issie's eyes. She didn't know whether Issie's coming here showed an incredible amount of gall or an incredible amount of courage. Breathing a silent prayer for strength and wisdom—and an extra measure of gentleness—Allie reached her.

"I had to come," Issie said. "I just wanted to see how he is. And how you are."

Issie's eyes were red, and Allie knew she had been crying. People cried when their friends were in trouble. It didn't really reveal anything about her relationship with Mark.

"Mark's still unconscious," she said. "But the bullet didn't penetrate his brain. He's got a bad concussion, but they're expecting him to recover—or at least that's what they say. We'd appreciate your prayers. Until he wakes up, we can't be sure how he is."

Issie looked at her hands, where she clutched a shredded tissue. "I don't know how effective my prayers will be, but I'll give it a shot."

Allie swallowed and followed her eyes to the floor between them.

"I'm glad you weren't hurt," Issie said. "It must be awesome knowing your husband loves you so much he'd give his life for you."

Allie looked up, soaking in the words, the meaning, the intent. Did Issie even know that she was the main reason for their breakup? Or was she in denial, too? Was she, like Mark, pretending that nothing had ever happened between them?

Her heart began to stray down that dangerous path, and she jerked it back, reminding herself of her commitment just moments earlier. Regardless of Mark's feelings, regardless of his behavior, regardless of his admitting or denying his relationship with Issie, Allie was committed to her marriage.

The silence stretched, and eventually Issie said, "I probably shouldn't have come."

"No, no, it's nice that you did." Allie locked eyes with Issie again. "I'm sure it'll mean a lot to him."

Issie was quiet, probably sifting Allie's words for some sign of sarcasm, but Allie had intended nothing malicious. Issie's coming *would* mean a lot to Mark.

"Not as much as you might think," Issie whispered.

Allie held Issie's gaze, looking deeply, and seeing the sincerity there, and reassurance, and even promise. Issie was not out to steal her husband away, Allie realized suddenly. At least, not anymore.

The thought made Allie uncomfortable, for it had been easy to think of her as the malicious other woman, the one who had finagled her way into Mark's affections, the woman who had rejoiced when she'd heard that Mark had moved out. Now Allie saw a different picture—one that confused her.

"Why don't you come sit down and wait with us?" Allie asked. "They're going to call me when he wakes up."

Issie looked over Allie's shoulder to the people in the back corner. Allie glanced back and saw that her parents were watching, arms crossed like judges. They had figured out who Issie was, and she didn't blame them for their feelings. She had vented to them so much about the woman that it wouldn't surprise her now if they stormed over and ordered Issie out. Guiltily, Allie realized that she had created their hostility, giving them a bitter play-by-play of what she'd seen and heard and thought. No wonder they felt no allegiance to Mark.

Issie forced a smile and blinked back the tears in her overbright eyes. "No, I really need to go. I just wanted to come by for a few minutes."

Allie didn't mention that Issie had driven almost an hour just for those few minutes. She knew Issie wouldn't be comfortable staying.

"I'll have someone call you and give you a report when he wakes up, okay?" Allie didn't know what had made her say that, but now she would have to do it.

Issie gave her a surprised look. "I would appreciate that."

The two women stood with eyes locked for a moment longer. Finally, unable to keep her tears at bay any longer, Issie leaned forward and hugged Allie. Reflexively, Allie hugged her back—a tight, warm hug that somehow felt like an apology. When Issie let her go, she looked embarrassed, then took a step back. "I'll talk to you later, Allie. Hang in there, okay?"

"You too."

Issie headed back down the hallway and disappeared.

• • •

Nick Foster watched from his seat across the room, moved at how gracious Allie had been to the woman who had almost destroyed her marriage. He had expected such a different reaction. Perhaps one like he'd experienced earlier when Dan had insulted him.

And Issie seemed to have no ill will toward Allie, either. Though he wouldn't have advised her to come had she asked him, he saw that it might have been for good. He saw Issie struggling with tears, saw her hug Allie . . .

And then he watched her walk out.

He didn't know why, but he felt the need to go after her, to comfort her in some small way. He didn't know her that well. What he did know about her was that she was unchurched and uninterested, that she spent a lot of time at Joe's Place, that she did have an unhealthy interest in a married man.

But if she was lost, then why should he expect her to act any differently?

He excused himself and followed her out into the hall. She had already stepped onto the elevator and the doors were just closing behind her. He pressed the button, and the elevator next to it opened.

He rode it down, and as the doors opened, he saw her walking out across the lobby.

"Issie," he called. She turned around.

Tears mixed with mascara stained her face, and she wiped them away self-consciously, then dried her hands on the pants of her uniform. She looked at him suspiciously, as though she expected him to lecture her about having the gall to show up here. "I know, I know," she said. "You don't have to preach me a sermon, Nick. I know I shouldn't have come."

"No, no," he said softly. "That's not why I came after you."

"Then why?" she asked.

She looked up at him, and he searched his mind for a reason. "I just . . . wondered how I could pray for you."

"*Pray* for me?" She looked at him as if he'd just offered to read her palms. "Why would you pray for *me*?"

"Because . . . I know that you and Mark . . . well, I mean . . . I just know that you cared for him, and—"

"And you want me to think that doesn't disgust you?" she returned.

He realized he was digging himself into a deep hole. "Well, no, actually, it does. I care a lot for Mark and Allie, and I want to see them work things out. I don't think you've helped much with that."

She nodded while he was speaking, as if she might have expected that exact speech from him.

"But I also don't think you set out to break up their marriage. I don't see you as a malicious person, Issie. I see you in emergencies all the time. You do care about people."

She was growing more agitated, and her eyes filled with tears again. "What do you want, Nick?"

He racked his brain. What *did* he want? "I don't know. I guess . . . I just wanted to tell you that I appreciate what you did up there. It took a lot of courage."

She swallowed. "Yeah, well. Nothing ever happened between us, you know. I mean, nothing physical. And before you go putting me on some list for sainthood, I should tell you that it wasn't because I didn't want it. But Mark loves Allie. Enough to take a bullet for her." She wiped the tears spilling over her lashes. "Nobody ever loved me like that."

"Oh, yes, they did. Somebody loved you just like that."

She looked at him like he was nuts. "Who?"

"Jesus."

She breathed a laugh, shook her head, then looked back up at him. "I should have seen that coming."

He grinned. "Yeah, I guess so. But it's true." He cocked his head and gazed down at her. "You know, that smile looks pretty good on you. Even when it's mocking."

She couldn't seem to shake it from her face as she looked up at him. Finally, she reached up and took his wire-rimmed glasses off of his face. The surprisingly personal act made his heart jolt, and he asked, "What are you doing?"

"Cleaning your glasses," she said as she wiped them on her shirt. "You're not seeing clearly."

He laughed then, and realized he was, once again, behaving like a teenager instead of a minister. He wondered if she could see the heat climbing his face.

"You know what Dan said earlier? About you being out of shape?" Issie asked.

His smile crashed and he made a mental vow to start a diet immediately.

"You look just fine to me. For a preacher, that is."

She reached up and shoved his glasses back on, and he stood stock-still, too pleasantly moved to know how to react. She gave him a wink, then turned and headed out the door.

Nick stood frozen until she was out of sight. He told himself that he'd better stay as far away from her as he could in the future. It was a bad sign when a preacher reacted to a woman with wet palms and a runaway heartbeat. A real bad sign.

• • •

In the ICU waiting room, Allie saw that her parents were staring at her with shock. Feeling more peace than she'd felt all day, she started back toward them.

"What was *that* about?" her mother asked. "What did she want?"

"Just to see how Mark was doing." She sat down and looked at Jill and Celia. Both women offered her sweet smiles that told her they admired what they had just witnessed.

Her mother was livid. "Honey, are you sure you're okay? You're not thinking clearly." She looked at the others. "Has she eaten today?"

"No, not since she's been here," Jill said.

"That explains it. Her blood sugar is so low that it's paralyzing her brain cells."

Allie almost smiled. "I've always had a problem with sluggish brain cells, Mom. It has nothing to do with food."

Jill tried to hide her grin. "Allie, do you want to go down to the cafeteria and get a bite?"

"No," she said, serious again. "I'm going to fast until I know for sure Mark's okay."

"I'll join you," Jill said, and Celia agreed to do so, as well.

Her father looked at them all as if their neurons had collectively misfired. "Are you crazy? Allie, you *have* to eat."

"No, I don't."

"Why not?"

"Because praying and fasting is all I can do for Mark right now, and I'm going to do it. God will honor that."

"God doesn't need you to fast. That's an Old Testament thing. People don't do that anymore."

"Well, maybe they should."

"He could stay unconscious for a week!"

"Then I'll go a week without eating."

Her mother shifted in her seat and huffed out a sigh. "I'm going to ask the doctor for a sedative for you."

"And risk paralyzing more brain cells?" Allie asked with a half-smile. "Mom, I'm glad you're here, but I really need you to support me, not challenge me at every turn."

Her parents shot each other eloquent looks. Finally, her father patted her hand. "How about if we shut up?"

Allie smiled.

They all sat quietly, awkwardly, for a while, flipping through magazines, until the receptionist called Allie's name over the intercom. They sprang to their feet and together headed for the front desk.

"Yes?" Allie asked.

"The nurse just called to tell me your husband is awake." The receptionist smiled warmly as Allie caught her breath. "You can go on back."

Without another word, Allie shot for the door.

She pressed the button that opened the double metal doors leading into ICU, and saw a nurse waiting for her. "He's awake?" she asked.

"Yes, and asking for you."

Allie laughed softly and hurried to his bedside.

His eyes were closed, but a nurse stood over him, talking gently. "Mark, your wife is here."

His eyes opened as Allie went to his side and took his hand. He squeezed it, and she wilted into tears.

"Hey, what's wrong?" he whispered with the slightest hint of a grin.

"Oh, nothing," she said, laughing quietly as she wiped her tears. "So what do you mean going and getting shot?"

He closed his eyes. "Is that what happened?"

"Yes."

He was silent for a moment, and it looked as if he'd drifted back off to sleep. Allie looked up at the nurse. "How is he?"

"Doing very well," she said, keeping her voice low. "He had appropriate answers to everything we asked. Knew his birthday, your birthday—but he doesn't remember what happened to him."

"Yes, I do," he whispered, surprising them both.

Allie touched his face. "You do?"

"Most of it," he said. "I saw the bullet knock the bag out of your hand." His voice was weak, losing energy with each word.

"You saved me," she told him. "You threw me down and covered me, and the next bullet hit you."

"Gave me a raging headache," he said, barely audible, and Allie smiled. He closed his eyes again, but this time, the calm look on his face vanished, and his mouth twisted. She saw the tear rolling from his eye.

"What is it, Mark?" she asked.

He squeezed her hand harder. "I'm so glad . . . you're all right."

"He thought you were dead," the nurse whispered. "It was his first question."

Overcome, Allie rested her face on Mark's chest. "I'm glad you're all right, too," she cried. "I'm so glad."

She looked up at him. One slick, wet line went from the corner of his eye into his hair, and she smeared it away.

"I'm sorry, Allie," he whispered.

"For what?"

"For not being able to protect you now."

"I don't need protection. I'm safe here. They have security at the doors."

"No," he whispered. "You need to go somewhere else. Somewhere that he won't look for you. You need to—"

"No, Mark," she cut in emphatically. "I'm not leaving you. Nick's here, and your father, and my parents, Jill and Celia, and Stan's in town and will be back soon."

"I want to see him," he said. "I want to see Stan."

"All right," she told him. "If he's back at the next visiting hour, I'll let him come in with me."

"No, now," he said. "I need to see him now."

"What for?"

"Just call him."

"Okay," she said, trying to placate him. "I will."

"When's the doctor coming?" he asked the nurse. "I need to see the doctor."

"He'll be in shortly," the nurse said. "Why do you need to see him?"

"Because I need to go home. I have to get out of here. I have to protect my wife."

"You can't get out tonight, Mark," Allie said. "You're in ICU. You have to be still. Just relax . . ."

"Have to . . ."

He was getting weaker but more agitated. Allie stroked his forehead. "Mark, shhhh. You need to rest. Calm down."

Her gentle touch and soft words seemed to have the effect she wanted, and his eyes closed again.

"Shhhh. Get some more sleep, honey. Rest so you can get better."

His lips moved again as he tried to speak, but no sound came out. Finally, his breathing settled, and she knew that he was asleep.

"We'll be rousing him every hour," the nurse whispered. "He won't like it, but we have to do it. But we'd prefer you waited until visiting times to come back. We'll try to get him good and awake before the next one."

"Okay." Allie knew that was her dismissal, but she wasn't ready to leave. "Could I have just a minute alone with him before I go?"

"Sure," the nurse said. "Just don't be too long."

She watched the nurse leave, then laid Mark's limp hand on his stomach and set her hand on top of it. Closing her eyes, she thanked God for letting him wake up, for the possibility that she might get that second chance. And she prayed that he would continue to heal Mark—and take divine vengeance on the killer who had done this.

Feeling as if a million pounds had been lifted off her shoulders, she headed back into the ICU waiting room to tell the others that things were looking up.

Chapter Thirty-Seven

The Homicide Unit at the Kenner Police Department was as depressing as Stan had expected. The huge dry erase board on the wall had columns headed by the names of each of the homicide detectives. Beneath each name, listed in red ink, were all of the active homicide cases he had been assigned, the date of the crime, the name of the victim, the means of death. As the crimes were solved, the ink color was changed to blue—incentive for each detective to solve his crimes as quickly as possible, for those red cases were a source of shame and aggravation.

For the first hour Stan had been here today, Peter Blanc, the Cajun detective assigned to the airport shooting, had bemoaned the fact that he'd been given a case that wasn't really a homicide, since Mark Branning wasn't dead. He didn't appreciate having another red name on his list. He was quite familiar with the Newpointe killings, and immediately wanted to send someone to interview Hank Keyes in the Bogaloosa jail. Despite Stan's insistence that Keyes was no longer a suspect, Blanc was intent on proving he could be. He wanted to solve this crime, and soon. He had other cases—cases involving dead bodies, cases that really were in his jurisdiction, cases in red that he needed to change to blue.

Realizing that he wasn't going to get far with Peter Blanc, Stan haunted the crime lab for the rest of the afternoon. He learned the bullet that had hit Allie's bag had been retrieved from the concrete a few yards from where Mark was hit, and from that they had determined that the gun had been a .38—the same caliber used in the other three shootings. The ballistics report, evaluating the angles at which the bullets had struck Allie's purse and Mark's head, identified the possible areas from which the gun could have been fired. Kenner P.D. had also collected tape from the security cameras just inside the airport in that area, in the hope that the killer could be seen through the window. Stan viewed all of the tapes during that time, only to find that none of the cameras covered the exact area in question.

However, Stan noticed in the file that there was a witness—a guy who'd been loading luggage onto the small plane Allie and Mark would have gotten on, who claimed he had seen a man in uniform running down a ladder that led up to an air conditioner unit, and that the man had cut across the tarmac and around the airport terminal. The witness had taken cover behind the plane and peered out from under it to see if he could spot the source of the gunfire. While everyone else was scurrying out of harm's way, the man in uniform had been running the wrong way.

Thirty minutes after reading the report, Stan was at the airport interviewing the witness himself. "What kind of uniform was it? Did it belong to a ground crew worker?"

"Nope," the man said, spitting on the ground. "Wasn't a jumpsuit like mine. No, I think it was blue or gray. Might have been a pilot without his coat."

"A pilot?"

"No, come to think of it, the pants weren't black like a pilot's. The pants were, like, gray or something. Like a cop or a mailman."

A cop or a mailman? Ordinarily, he would have found the comparison amusing. But nothing about this was funny to him.

He climbed up the ladder to the air conditioner unit that the witness had pointed out. It was a perfect perch from which to fire at someone. Easily accessible, yet inconspicuous. Was the uniform an air conditioner repairman's uniform? Is that how he had gotten in without being stopped? Or was he, indeed, a cop, which would have kept anyone from asking questions? Or could he actually have been a mailman?

He went back to the homicide unit, hoping once more to put his head together with one of their detectives, even the cynical, hardened Blanc. To his frustration, none of them took him seriously enough to give him the time. He was, after all, the only detective on a small-town force—a small town which, until last week, averaged zero to one homicides a year. Stan had once taken pride in that, as though it somehow reflected well on him. Now, seeing the contempt and disinterest of the Kenner cops, who each had up to a dozen cases at a time in red, all murders within the last month, he couldn't help feeling inferior.

Stan pulled out his case file again, and sat down with a pen and paper to list all of the clues they had. Fibers from the Broussard and Larkin houses, though they had no one to match them to. A generic shoe print that could have matched a million size-ten feet. No fingerprints. No weapon. No motive . . .

"Stan Shepherd?" a detective called from across the room. He turned around and scanned the desks and faces of the dozens of people milling around the room.

"Yeah?"

"Telephone," the man yelled out, as if he hated being bothered.

Stan closed the file and carried it to the man's desk. "Hurry up, I've got work to do," the man bit out.

Stan ignored him. "Stan Shepherd," he said into the phone.

"Stan, it's me. Allie."

Stan stiffened, bracing himself for news of Mark's death. A sense of defeat and dread fell over him. "Allie."

"Mark woke up, and he's asking for you."

His heart jolted. "He's awake? All right!" He looked around for someone to tell, but no one was interested. "He wants me?"

"Yeah," she said. "He made me promise to tell you that he wants to see you. The next visiting hour is at eleven tonight, and they promised they'd rouse him for it. If you want to go in with me, you can."

"I'll be there. Allie, how is he?"

"He's great," she said, her voice cracking. "He looks like he's been in a train wreck, but he's talking and making sense, worrying."

"Thank God."

"You said it. God was watching over him, Stan. He's still in ICU. Anything could go wrong, but they're keeping a close watch on him."

"Is Celia okay?"

"Yeah, she's right here. Wanna talk to her?"

"Yeah." He told his wife he loved her and to stay right there, not to leave the waiting room under any circumstances, and not to allow Allie to. When he hung up, he felt a chill. His wife was so close to a marked target, someone the killer wanted dead. He hoped the security in that hospital had been reminded of the danger. Selfishly, he thought how glad he'd be to take Celia home after he saw Mark tonight.

Chapter Thirty-Eight

Because Mark insisted on it, the nurses called Allie for a visit at eight-thirty instead of making her wait until eleven. Since Stan had just arrived, she let him and Nick come in with her.

The nurse met them at the door. "He's doing much better than I would have predicted," she said with a smile. "But remember—let him rest."

The two men, shocked by Mark's appearance, hesitated at the door, but Allie went right to his side and hugged him. He hugged her back weakly, the gesture giving her a world of hope.

"Did you bring Stan?" he asked.

She had wondered if, with the concussion and head trauma, he would forget. Apparently he hadn't. "He's right here. Nick, too."

They came on each side of the bed, and Mark took both of their hands and squeezed them. "Thanks for coming, guys," he said in a gravelly voice that reminded her of the way he sounded when he woke up in the mornings. She had missed that voice.

"You don't look so good," Stan said with a grin.

"What can I say?" Mark asked weakly. "I've always wanted a cleft in my chin, but I didn't expect one across the side of my head."

The men laughed with relief—he still had his sense of humor, and Allie felt an overwhelming joy. He was still Mark, the Mark she'd fallen in love with once, the Mark she had married, the Mark who had, once upon a time, been able to make her laugh—until the fears and anxieties and disappointments of the last few months had interfered.

"So," Stan probed, growing more serious. "Did you remember something about the killer?"

Mark shook his head. "I wish. No, I'm worried about Allie, man."

Allie blinked back the mist in her eyes. "Why, Mark? What do you mean?"

"I've been watching over you since the murders started. Now I can't, and I don't like it. So Stan, I wanted to ask you a favor."

"What?" Stan asked. "You know I'm doing whatever it takes to find the killer."

"I know. But I want you to find Allie a bodyguard. I'll pay him whatever it costs. I'll sell my car if I have to. I can ride my ten-speed to work, or walk. But I want someone watching over my wife while I'm in here."

Allie took his hand, and he closed his fingers around hers and pulled it to his lips.

"I can do that, buddy," Stan said. "No problem. I'll call T.J. Porter. He's always looking to make some extra dough, and he's got a bunch of debts to pay off. Besides that, he's a giant, and looks menacing enough to scare off the meanest scumbag."

"Yeah, he'll do fine."

Allie wasn't sure she liked the idea of someone being with her twenty-four hours a day. "Mark, don't you think I'll be okay as long as I'm here?"

"No, I don't," he said. "You aren't safe anywhere." He looked up at Stan. "Hire him, and get him here tonight, okay? I know it'll be late, but you're a big, important cop, and you can coax security into letting him in, right?"

"I'll do my best. I'm more worried about getting him to come on such short notice. He may even be on duty."

"I'll be forever beholden, Stan. Think if it was your wife."

Stan had thought of that. "You got it. Somebody'll be here, even if it's me. But Mark, they won't allow a gun in here."

"Not even for a cop?"

"For an on-duty cop, maybe, but not for a Newpointe off-duty bodyguard."

Mark looked distressed. "Well, a gun wouldn't have done me any good today. But I managed to keep him from hitting Allie. I want someone who'll do that."

"T.J.'ll do it, if I can get him. I'll do my best."

Mark seemed to rest at that idea. "Okay. I'm counting on you." He turned to Nick. "So, Nick, are you gonna pray with me, or what?"

Nick grinned. "You bet I am."

Holding hands, they all prayed together for God's victory in all of this.

Chapter Thirty-Nine

They were on their way back into the waiting room when Stan's beeper began to vibrate. He checked the number. It was the Kenner Police Department where he'd spent the afternoon, and the extension was for Peter Blanc. He quickly went to the phone and called the detective back.

"Blanc," the man barked.

"Blanc, Stan Shepherd. Did you page me?"

"Yeah. We gotta witness, called in just a while ago. Said she remembers lettin' in a man in uniform right before the shootin'. Said he was a fireman and was answerin' a call, so she let 'im right in."

"A fireman? Did you check with the fire department to see if they really had any calls?"

"I know how to do my job, Shepherd. Yeah, I checked, and there was no calls from the airport today, 'cept in regard to the shootin'."

"A fireman," Stan repeated, incredulous.

"Said he was wearin' a bunker coat hangin' open and fireman's hat with that clear mask down."

"She didn't think that was odd?" Stan asked.

"Said she was busy and took 'im at his word."

"What was his description?"

"Average height, she says, somewhere 'tween five-eleven and six-two. Didn't notice eye or hair color under the hat and mask. Says she prob'ly couldn't ID him."

"Did she see him again after the shooting?"

"Nope. Says she was distracted and takin' cover. One thing," Blanc said. "She said his shirt under the bunker coat was gray. Our firefighters wear blue. What they wear in Newpointe?"

Stan closed his eyes, letting the horror sink in. "They wear gray." He felt nauseous. "How come the other witness didn't mention the bunker coat?"

"I was gettin' to that," Blanc said. "We searched that air conditioner unit he was on again, and found a bunker coat and hat wedged down between the unit and the building. He prob'ly ditched it before he started shootin'. Guess what fire department was identified on the hat?"

Stan didn't want to know, but he forced himself to ask. "What?"

"Newpointe," Blanc said. "Our man may be one o' your firefighters."

Stan couldn't speak. "Look, do me a favor, will you, Blanc? Don't leak this. We don't have that big a fire department in Newpointe. If the media gets hold of it, they'll blow it for us. I have to be careful, or we'll spook him and lose him. Can I have your word that you'll keep this just between us?"

"You think you can narrow it down?"

"Yes. Do I have your word or not?"

"All right, you got it. I got better things to do than start a frenzy."

Stan hung up and tried to think. His head was beginning to throb, and he was shaking. Someone touched his shoulder, and he jumped. He turned around and saw his wife. "Celia."

"Honey, are you all right?"

"Yeah, fine. I have to call T.J. Mark wants a bodyguard for Allie. But I have to get back to the Northshore. I've got a lead on the killer."

Nick was standing nearby. "A lead? Really?"

"Yes." Stan tried to remember if he'd eaten. He felt light-headed. Vaguely, he remembered eating something ... lunch? Breakfast? He wasn't sure. "Look, Nick, can you stay until T.J. gets here, assuming I can get him?"

"I think so."

He dialed information to get T.J.'s number.

Moments later, Stan headed back across the waiting room to Allie. "T.J. is coming, Allie. I called down to security, and they said the doors will stay open until ten. He should be here before that, although he might be cutting it close because he's on duty and has to wait for a replacement."

"Okay," she said.

"I'll stay with you until he gets here," Nick said. "Then I'll head back to the station."

Stan fought the urge to tell Nick what he knew, so that he'd be careful whom he trusted. But he couldn't. Everyone was suspect.

As he and Celia left, Stan had the feeling that his real work was just beginning.

• • •

A few minutes later, while Allie was saying good-bye to Eddie, who was shaking so badly he would undoubtedly head straight to the nearest bar, the waiting room phone rang and someone called out, "Branning family."

Jill was closest to it and took the phone. "Hello? This is Jill Clark."

"Jill, hi. Dan Nichols. I just wanted an update."

She smiled. "Hi, Dan. Well, let's see. Mark is conscious, and there doesn't seem to be any apparent brain damage. He's talking a lot, making demands, worrying about Allie."

"You're kidding. He's doing that well?"

"Yes. God was really with him."

He let out a heavy breath. "Man, I thought it would be—I don't know. A whole lot worse." His voice cracked.

"We all did."

"Cale and George just came in to relieve some of us. I'm about to get off for the night."

"Really?" she asked. "Are they ready to come back this soon?"

"Said they needed to get back to work to get their minds off their problems. George said Tommy's already asleep and his parents are baby-sitting, and he says he hasn't been sleeping so well. Anyway, they insisted, so I thought I'd come down there and hang out for a while."

Her heart leapt slightly, but she told herself that was silly. He was just a man. "Well, okay. You'll have to hurry, because I think they lock the doors at ten. And I'm not sure you can get out if you're in past that time."

"So I'll stay all night. I can sleep anywhere. Besides, I've worried about Allie all day. She shouldn't be alone, not with this guy out there still running loose. If he'd shoot in broad daylight at a crowded airport, he could be capable of anything."

"Already taken care of. Mark got Stan to hire T.J. Porter to be her bodyguard. He'll come as soon as he can find a replacement. He's on duty right now."

"Well, why don't I call and tell him he doesn't have to come? I could stay with her all night, and he could come in the morning. I wouldn't have a weapon or anything—"

"They wouldn't let you, anyway."

"Well, right. But my presence might be a deterrent if the creep tried to pull anything tonight. I'm no Hulk Hogan, but I don't think your average Joe would want to take me on."

Jill grinned. Maybe the rumors about his vanity were true.

"I know Allie would appreciate it, Dan. And Mark would feel good knowing you were the one here. Frankly, I'd appreciate it, too. I was planning to stay all night with Allie, but I've been a little concerned, too. I'm not much protection. Nick's here now, but he plans to go back to work tonight."

"Tell him help is on the way. I'll be there in half an hour."

"It takes at least forty, Dan."

"Not the way I drive," he said.

It was the first time Jill had laughed in days.

Chapter Forty

Dan looked like a breath of fresh air when he blew into the ICU waiting room wearing his gray firefighter's uniform. Just having him here made Allie feel closer to Mark, for Dan was his closest friend.

She noted the unusual grin on Jill's face when Dan came in, and she wondered if there was some interest developing there that her friend hadn't confided.

"Thanks for coming, Dan," Allie said, kissing his cheek. "When Mark asked for a bodyguard, I really dreaded it. I like T.J. and everything, but I don't know him that well. I'm glad you came instead."

"No problem," Dan said. "I should have changed clothes, though. This uniform caught a lot of attention from the press downstairs. Guess all us Newpointe firefighters are celebrities now, whether we want to be or not." He sat down and crossed an ankle over his knee. "CNN called the station a while ago. Wanted to interview some of us. I couldn't go on national television until I'd had a haircut though, so I passed."

Allie was surprised. "Your big chance to be discovered, Dan, and you passed?"

He winked. "I figured I'd let the others have a chance. Maybe after the haircut. Anyway, thank goodness for Cale and George or I couldn't have come."

"How are they?" Jill asked.

"Down. But they're okay. Cale really needed to get back to work, be around his friends, get his mind off of things. And

George just wanted to help in some way." He gazed down at Allie. "So how are you doing?"

"I'm okay."

"Have you eaten?"

She shook her head. "I'm not hungry."

"Allie, you have to eat."

"She's fasting," Jill said. "It's okay. She knows what she's doing."

Jill didn't mention that she was fasting, too, but Allie understood why. Somehow, the privacy of the decision lent more reverence to it—something that was just between God and them.

• • •

At eleven P.M., the families were called in for their last visit of the night. Dan walked Allie to the door of ICU, then he and Jill went to the window looking down onto the small courtyard behind the hospital.

"It's gonna be a long night," Jill whispered, looking out on the lights flickering off the surface of the pond. It all seemed surreal—her being here, knowing that today her best friend's husband had been shot in the head.

"You'll make it shorter," Dan said. "I'm sure Allie appreciates your friendship right now. How long have you two been friends?"

"About five years," Jill said. "Since she and Mark got engaged." She smiled at the memory. "You know how it is. Most of my friends from high school moved away. I got to know Allie at church, and we just hit it off. She and Mark were constantly trying to fix me up with some friend or other."

"Really?" he asked. "Wonder why they never fixed you up with me?"

She laughed. "Maybe because I put a stop to it after the third or fourth time. I convinced them I could wait for Mr. Right to find me."

His grin was so disarming she had to look away. "And has he?"

"Nope," she said. "Still waiting."

"So how'd you feel when they split up?"

"Depressed," she said. "I always thought if there was ever a couple whose marriage was made in heaven, they were it. I haven't given up yet, though."

"I've wondered if you were planning to represent Allie if they had a divorce."

"I would, of course, but I really hate for it to come to that."

"Yeah, me too," he said. "Maybe this shook them up enough to change things."

"I don't know. I gotta tell you, I've been amazed at the way he's tried to protect her through all this. Maybe we all need a glimpse of life without someone we love once in a while, just to teach us not to take them for granted."

"So you think they'll get back together when this is over?"

"Who knows?" she said. "A woman doesn't fast and sit in a waiting room all night keeping vigil for her husband if she doesn't love him. She doesn't fall apart the way I saw Allie do today if she's lost her feelings for him. And a man doesn't take a bullet for just anybody."

"Well, no one ever thought they didn't love each other. But they had some pretty fierce differences. He got to where he didn't like to go home anymore. Said she was always nagging him about things."

Jill bristled. "He called it nagging. But she had a right to confront him about his time in bars with his friends from work, about the fact that he wasn't pulling his weight in the shop on his days off from the fire department, about his relationship with other women—"

"Boy. She didn't leave anything out, did she?"

Jill was a little embarrassed that she'd said so much. "We're close. We talk a lot."

"Yeah, well." Dan crossed his arms and looked at his reflection in the window. "That's one of the reasons I'll never get married. The minute you tie the knot, you've got that other person telling the world every little thing you do in private. Your life is thrown out there for everyone to criticize."

"Oh, come on. Don't tell me Mark didn't talk to you about Allie."

He abandoned his reflection and turned back to her. "Of course he did. That's what I mean. They did it to each other. One of them did something wrong, and the next thing you know, they're telling their friends what a jerk the other one is. And a guy like me, who's never been married, stands back and watches, and thinks they'd all be better off if they were single."

"Single isn't all it's cracked up to be," Jill said. "Before their breakup, there weren't many days when I wouldn't have traded places with Allie in a minute. Not to be married to Mark, but just to belong to someone, to have that hope of having a family."

"A family would be nice," Dan said with a soft chuckle, "if it weren't for that pesky marriage thing."

Jill looked seriously at him, wondering if she'd misjudged him all those times she'd seen him in church.

"No, don't get me wrong," he said. "I'm thinking of Paul, and his encouragement to stay single. He felt marriage distracted people from God's work. That's why it was preferable not to be married."

"But that wasn't God's instruction to his children," she said. "It was Paul's opinion, that was all. The whole point of that passage was to tell us how focused and devoted we should be to Christ—not to tell us that marriage is wrong. God loves marriage and family. Even in Eden, his first commandment was to be fruitful and multiply."

"True. But the earth is populated now. We don't have to fill the earth with our offspring anymore."

"So marriage is obsolete?" she asked with a smirk.

He shrugged. "No. I just think it's a lot less complicated to be single. Look at all these guys in the fire department. Most of them are going nuts protecting their wives, scared to death of losing them—and they might. It may be a good thing that there's nobody I can lose that would make me grieve like that."

"And you're determined to keep it that way?"

"Well, yeah, sort of. I like being unattached. Hey, if I want to take off for a trip on my days off, I can. I don't have to make arrangements, leave instructions, call home every night . . ."

"Don't you ever wish you had someone to call home to—or better yet, take with you?"

He laughed, and she noted the laugh lines crinkling out from his eyes. "Sometimes. But then I remind myself that there are strings attached in every relationship. Conditions. Expectations."

"And you stop wishing?"

"Something like that."

She didn't know why that disappointed her so. "I'm glad it's so easy for you," she said.

Dan got quiet for a moment. "So if you wanted to get married, Jill, why didn't you?"

She shrugged. "I could have. I was serious about someone in college. But I had dreams of going to law school, and we broke up, and he married someone else. Since then, I've been in a few relationships, but they're either self-centered, or they're sports-centered, or they're big around the center . . ."

Dan laughed.

"None of them were Christ-centered. Really, I don't know. Guess I never found the right person."

"Like me."

"No, not like you," she said. "I'm looking. You're not."

"I thought most professional, independent women denied that they were looking."

"Well, I could lie. But there's nothing I'd like better than to fall head over heels in love and get married and have children and live happily ever after. I know it isn't politically correct, but I don't make apologies for it. All my life I've wanted that, and someday I'm going to have it."

He turned back to her and met her eyes. She saw the gentleness there, the sweetness, and her heart reacted despite her better judgment. "Well, I hope you do," he said.

She leaned her face back against the glass and looked out on the courtyard again. A man and woman, both in scrubs, sat on a concrete bench. The woman leaned her head on his shoulder, and he held her and stroked her hair. Jill yearned for that kind of human warmth. It was too bad Dan felt the way he did. He had seemed so gallant, so masculine, so caring. And he wasn't too hard on the eyes, either.

Which was exactly why he wasn't her type. He went for anorexic blondes with beauty titles, she mused. Not plain-Janes with law degrees.

The doors to ICU opened, startling her, and she looked up and saw the others milling out, some with tears in their eyes, others laughing in relief and joy. Allie trailed at the end, her eyes tired but hopeful.

"He's awake," she said. "Dan, he wants to talk to you."

"Me?" Dan asked. "Why?"

"I told him that you came instead of a bodyguard, so I guess he wants to give you instructions or something." She grinned and lifted her eyebrows. "I'm trying to humor him. You just have a few minutes."

"All right," Dan said, and started through the doors.

"I have to go with you," she said. "That's one of his rules. Come on, Jill. You come, too."

Jill felt awkward as they went through the doors and around to the cubicle where Mark lay. She caught her breath at the sight of him, then told herself that a man who'd been shot in the head probably had a right to look pretty rough. His eyes were closed.

She hung back and let Dan go to his bedside, as Allie took the other side. "Mark, here's Dan," she said. "And Jill."

Mark opened his eyes and saw Jill at the foot of the bed. "How's it going, Jill?" he asked weakly.

She smiled. "Great. You feeling okay?"

"Been better." He looked up at Dan and reached for his hand. "Hey, buddy."

Dan leaned over and lowered his voice. "Man, I thought you were ugly before, but I think you could win the championship tonight."

Mark laughed. "You try a one-on-one with a bullet, see how you look."

"No thanks, man."

Mark's face sobered, and his eyes grew more serious. "Well, you hang around us long, brother, and you might wind up doing it. No kidding."

"I'm okay with that," Dan said.

"I appreciate it. And I'll pay you, man."

"No way."

"Yes way. I'm paying you, or I'll call T.J. myself. I know *he'll* take my money."

Dan laughed. "What are you gonna do? Get up and go to a pay phone?"

"Don't test me," Mark said. "I can do it. Now do we have an understanding?"

"Whatever you say."

"And you gotta promise me that you won't leave her side, not for a minute. I know you've got to sleep, but if you sleep out there in the waiting room, keep one eye open, will you? No kidding. He's after her. I don't even think he's afraid of getting caught. You've got to watch over her, man, because I can't."

"Don't worry. I've got this under control. I'm not going to sleep tonight at all. I brought a book to read, and I'll sit right next to her and keep my eyes on the door."

"And the windows. Are there windows? What floor are we on, anyway?"

"We're on the third floor. I won't let anything happen to her, buddy."

"Promise me."

"I can do that. I promise."

Mark seemed to relax. "What about the killer. Have they got any leads yet?"

"I don't know. I haven't talked to Stan today."

"Man, they've got to. Pray, okay? Pray hard. With your eyes open."

Dan chuckled. "I will. Now get some sleep. We expect to see you looking a lot better in the morning."

Allie kissed him good night, and they all headed back into the ICU waiting room, where they were given blankets. The lights were turned down, and Jill took a seat and tried to get comfortable in her recliner.

Dan sat between her and Jill, reading a novel.

As she drifted into a light sleep, Jill told herself that no harm could come to Allie here. Dan was watching over them both.

Chapter Forty-One

Our man may be one of your firefighters.

The words played over and over in Stan's mind as he took Celia to stay with her Aunt Aggie. Once he was sure they were both safe and settled in, he drove back to the police station and sat at his desk. *Not one of our firemen*, he thought. *It couldn't be.*

The bunker coat could have been stolen. It didn't mean that the killer was one of theirs.

Besides, why would the killer wear something so identifiable? What was the logic? He rubbed his eyes, trying to focus his thoughts. Maybe the uniform gave the killer anonymous access to places he couldn't normally go. It *had* gotten him onto the airport tarmac without a security check. After he'd fired on Mark and Allie, he had escaped during the confusion. Anyone who'd seen him probably thought he was responding to the emergency and ignored him.

But that didn't mean he was a firefighter. It only meant that he owned a uniform. These days, any yahoo off the street could walk into a specialty shop and buy any uniform he wanted, without authorization.

Stan needed advice. He needed to know what kind of person he was dealing with. Maybe his old friend Jake Logan, a psychology professor at Tulane who specialized in criminal behavior, could help. Jake had helped New Orleans police with profiles of murderers before. He could help Stan put together some kind of psychological profile on this killer. Stan dialed information and got the man's number.

He checked his watch. It was nearing midnight, but he couldn't wait. The phone rang once, twice—

"Hello?"

"Jake, this is Stan Shepherd. Hope I didn't wake you."

"No, Stan. In fact, I've been wanting to talk to you. I was going to call tomorrow to see if I could offer any help on this serial killer case."

"You sure can, man. I don't know what I've got on my hands here. That's why I'm calling."

"I've been following the case," Jake said. "I'm particularly interested in the pattern of the murders—he kills them first, then sets them on fire. My guess is he's trying to tell us something with that pattern. It means he's a thinking man, and in my experience, I'd say that he feels some sort of high purpose for what he's doing."

"High purpose? Like what? How can anybody justify what he's doing?"

"I didn't say he was thinking rationally. Just that he's thinking, planning. It's very important to him to follow the murder up with a fire."

"I figured he just wanted to destroy the evidence."

"Then why didn't he burn the Broussard house down? No, I think it's more than that. It could be that he's involved in the occult in some way, and that he considers these to be sacrificial murders. When you find him, you're likely to find evidence of obsession of some kind. A collection, maybe, of clips and articles about the fire department, or pictures of the women he's targeted, or some sort of evidence of occultism, or books on a certain subject. I studied a case once where a guy killed six 7–11 workers in three states, because he believed in his heart that 7–11 stores were part of a conspiracy for Iran to take over our country. He believed he was killing for his country. At his home, they found stacks and stacks of articles from the Internet about conspiracies and attempts to overthrow the government. He felt he had a mission to fulfill, and he set out to do it."

"Would people know about this obsession?" Stan asked. "I mean, would the people he's around every day think he's strange? Would there be clues?"

"Maybe not. Serial killers often live very normal lives, and later their friends and acquaintances are stunned to learn that they've done such brutal things. But in this guy's case, I'd say he's going to start making mistakes soon. One would almost think that he *wants* to be found out, judging by the way he went after that couple in broad daylight at the airport. If I were you, I'd be worried: his carelessness means that he intends to keep his agenda, whatever the cost to him."

Stan rubbed his forehead, trying to process all of this. "There's one new development, just between you and me," he said. "It seems that the guy at the airport was wearing a New-pointe firefighter's uniform. I'm trying to figure out if he's one of our guys, or if he's just using the uniform. I know all of our firemen, Jake, and I can't think of one that would do something this bizarre."

Jake was quiet for a moment. "I don't know, Stan. It doesn't make sense that he'd steal or buy a uniform, unless that was one more piece in the puzzle. Part of the statement he's making, if you will. Is there any other evidence that it really could be a firefighter?"

"Well, he uses diesel fuel to start the fires, which is safer for the arsonist, because the fumes don't rise as fast as gasoline. Not everybody knows that, but firemen do. He knows when the husbands won't be home. And today he knew where to find Mark and Allie. Seems like it's someone who knows them well. And why are the firemen's wives the target? Why no one else?"

"Do you have any bitter widowers who've lost their wives, so they want to deprive everyone else of theirs?"

"Well, yeah. We have a couple of widowers."

Jake was getting excited. "Were either of their wives shot or burned to death?"

Stan frowned. "No, I'm sure they weren't."

"Oh." Stan could almost hear the wheels turning in Jake's brain. "That blows that theory. I thought maybe these were murders of revenge—a firefighter who had a vendetta, and wanted his coworkers to pay for something. Maybe not." He thought for a moment. "Did the fire department lose anyone in the last couple of years? Fire victims, I mean. Anyone they didn't save?"

Stan thought for a moment. "Yeah. Three people. A few months ago two kids died of smoke asphyxiation before the fire department got to the scene. And before that, probably a year ago, a woman burned to death in a fire."

"The father of the children!" Jake said. "Where is he?"

Stan saw where Jake was going with this and shook his head. "The mother was single—as in, father unknown."

"Okay, what about the husband of the woman who died?"

"Dead. Was killed a few months ago, too, in a car accident. I think we're barking up the wrong tree."

Stan wondered if he was any closer than he'd been when he made the call. "Look, I appreciate your help, Jake. Can I call you back if I get anything new? Maybe you can help me brainstorm some more."

"I hope you will," Jake said. "This is fascinating. Simply fascinating."

"Yeah, well. Look, keep that bit about the fire uniform between us, okay? I don't want that leaked."

"You mean, don't make this a case for my classes to solve?" He could hear the smile in Jake's voice.

"I'd appreciate it if you'd hold off."

"Will do. I won't say a word until you've locked the guy up."

When Stan hung up, he walked out the back door of the police station, where a full moon painted the bayou behind them in grays and blacks. He looked into the yard behind the fire station. Two of the guys were out there now, one of them smoking a cigarette. He watched the red, glowing ember blaze more brightly, hang in the darkness as the man puffed, then drop to the grass where it was ground out with the toe of a foot.

Not a fireman, he thought. *It couldn't be a fireman.*

He went back to his desk. Closing his eyes, he tried to reconstruct the events on the day of Martha's and Jamie's murders. There was the parade first ... He got a pen and began to jot down the names of all the firemen he remembered seeing in the parade. That was difficult since they'd been made up like clowns, so he moved his thoughts to Martha Broussard's house, and the people who had been on the scene while they were sifting through the rubble. He had seen Mark Branning and Cale Larkins and Ray Ford, all men whose lives would be irrevocably affected by the events that began on that day. He remembered seeing Craig Barnes, and Nick Foster had been there—without makeup, since he'd been on the skeleton crew at the fire station that day—and Dan Nichols and Junior Reynolds had been with him. He closed his eyes tighter and tried to remember the others—which ones had gotten there sooner, which ones later, who they were standing with, whether they were in uniform, civilian clothes, or dressed like clowns.

Could one of them have been the one who'd shot Martha Broussard, dragged her out to a storage house, and set fire to her? Could one of them have been the one who came into Jamie Larkins's house at night and killed her, then buried her in flames? Had one of those men shot Susan? Then Mark?

The thought made him shudder, so he tried to think clearly, despite the fatigue that made his entire body ache. Since most of the firemen were accounted for on Fat Tuesday, he discarded the process of elimination. He tried a different tack: Did the evidence point to anyone in particular?

And then he remembered the other night, when Dan Nichols had been caught with a crowbar in his hand at Allie's shop, and the building had almost been broken into. Had Dan lied? Had *he* been the one breaking in?

And then there was Craig Barnes, who had gone into Allie's home the night of the stakeout. Had he lied about what he was doing? Did his suspicious behavior make him a suspect?

He rested his face in his hands and tried to think. First, he needed the personnel records of all of the firemen on the force. Maybe just examining their histories, their job performance, their beefs, their reprimands, could help him finally eliminate some of the firemen and target others as possible suspects. The first two files he would look at would be Dan's and Craig's—with the hope that he could rule them out.

But how would he get those files quietly? If the press heard that the detective on the case was asking for firefighters' personnel files, they'd have a field day. It would destroy the whole investigation and jeopardize their search for the killer. Even if he did it in private, he'd have to get those files through Craig Barnes.

He looked around the room. Ah—LaTonya Mason, the skinny little rookie cop who was always looking for something important to do. He slid his chair back, went to her desk, pulled up a chair, and sat close enough to her to speak in a low voice without being overheard. "I need your help," he said.

She looked up at him, her black eyes suspicious. "Oh, yeah? Whatchu want?"

"I need for you to get some files for me first thing in the morning. I want the personnel files of all the firefighters in town. But I don't want anyone to know who requested them. I want it to seem routine. Tell the chief we're ready for another round of drug testing, and we need the files so we can decide who to test. Got that?"

"Sure." She wrote down what she was to say, then looked up at him, folding her fist and propping her chin on it. "So what's the real reason? Somethin' to do with these murders?"

"I can't say just yet," he said. "But this is all confidential. You're not to talk about this with anybody, even another cop. That clear?"

"Sure."

"And whatever you do, don't let Barnes know that I requested it. If he asks you, just say that you don't know who will be doing the testing. That'll be evasive enough."

"Do we always request all the files before we do drug testin'?"

"I haven't got the foggiest idea," Stan said. "But if we don't, we should. Tell him we've decided to start."

"Will do."

"Thanks, LaTonya. Put them in a closed box on my desk, and I'll see them when I come in tomorrow."

"Yeah, if you go home in the first place. Everybody worked like you, we wouldn't need shifts."

Stan headed back to his desk. What LaTonya had said was true. But it was hard to go home and sleep comfortably when two friends were fighting for their lives in the hospital, and at least a few more were on some killer's hit list.

Still, he was exhausted. Since he couldn't get those files until morning, maybe he should go home and sleep. Besides, he was worried about Celia. Even though she wasn't a fire wife, he was uneasy. Presumably, the killer knew Stan was on the case. What if he decided to hit Celia, too, just to slow Stan's investigation? The thought, as unlikely as it seemed, plagued him.

He went home, punched in the phone code that would forward calls to his cellular phone, and went to Aunt Aggie's to be with Celia.

Celia was already in bed in the guest room. Stan got undressed, set the phone on the bed table, and climbed in beside her. She snuggled up to him, her warmth giving him more comfort than he'd had in days. Slowly, he drifted off to sleep.

• • •

The phone chirped, startling Stan out of sleep. Forgetting where he was, he glanced groggily to where the clock should be. How long had he slept? It rang again, and Celia stirred. "I'll get it."

"No, I've got it." It was still dark, not morning yet. Fumbling, he reached for the cell phone.

"Shepherd." He reached for the light, turned it on. His watch read three A.M.

"Sorry to wake you, Stan, but I thought you'd wanna know." The voice belonged to LaTonya Mason at the precinct. "There's been another murder."

His heart plummeted, and a wave of dizziness passed over him as he got slowly to his feet. "Who?"

"Marty Bledsoe's wife, Francis."

Another fire wife. He sat down on the side of the bed, and Celia slid her arms around him from behind. He took her hand. "They were in hiding," he said. "They weren't even in town."

"They was in Slidell stayin' at her mama's. He broke in and shot her in the head, while Marty was lyin' in bed right next to her. Must have had a silencer, because Marty didn't even wake up till a few minutes later, when he found the room on fire."

Stan reached for his clothes hanging over a chair. "When did you hear?"

"Just now. It all happened within the last hour."

"All right, give me the address. I'm headed to Slidell."

Chapter Forty-Two

By the time Stan arrived at the crime scene in Slidell, the media had descended. Armed with cameras and microphones, they stood just outside the area marked off by police tape. The moment he drove up, they surrounded him, as if he were a celebrity arriving on Oscar night.

Vultures, he thought, shoving them back with his car door as he got out of the car.

"Detective Shepherd, has tonight's murder produced any new leads on the Fire Wife Killer?"

"Excuse me," he said, trying to find an opening in the crowd around him.

"How many wives are left, Detective?"

"Are any measures being taken to protect the others?"

"Wouldn't it seem that the killer knows the victims, since he was able to find this one's hiding place?"

He shoved himself between two of them and ducked under the crime scene tape. He quickly flashed his badge at the officer standing there trying to keep order. "Stan Shepherd, Newpointe P.D. Who's in charge here?"

"Detective Madison is the supervising officer, sir. He's inside."

Stan ignored the questions being shouted at him and headed for the door.

He was stopped by the logging officer before he entered the house. He showed his identification and asked for Detective Madison. Madison, who had worked with him on an occasional case that crossed from one town to the next, seemed glad to see him. "I figured you'd be showing up soon, Stan."

Stan stepped into the house and looked around at the handful of officers collecting evidence. "Where's Marty?"

"Out back. He's pretty strung out. We had to take his mother-in-law to the hospital. Her blood pressure was stroke level. She took the twins with her, and Marty's parents are supposed to go get them."

"Did Marty see anything?"

Detective Madison shook his head. "He woke up, saw the fire, and tried to get her up. That was when he realized she'd been shot."

"Right there beside him? He didn't feel her body jerk or anything?"

"Claims he sleeps like the dead. Didn't know firemen could sleep like that."

Stan rubbed the back of his neck, wondering how they got Marty up at the station when they had a call in the night. "Well, truth is, none of us from Newpointe have slept all that sound lately. He was probably so tired he just zonked out. I was almost that way myself tonight."

He went into the bedroom, where one of the evidence technicians was photographing the scene. The body was still lying on the sheets, apparently untouched. Stan had last seen Francis at the meeting at the courthouse, looking as worried and scared as the rest of them. She looked oddly peaceful now, pretty even, as though someone had arranged her hair on her shoulders and folded her hands across her chest. He swallowed and fought the urge to look away. He needed to look. Maybe there was something there, something that would help him get to the bottom of this.

He made himself step closer and examine the bullet hole in her forehead. ".38?" he asked Joe Madison, who had come in behind him.

"Yep. Fired at pretty close range."

Stan leaned back against the wall that hadn't yet burned and looked up at the ceiling. A char pattern from the flames had shot up the other wall and climbed across. "They were hiding. How could he have known where? Marty didn't even tell *me* where they were."

"Stan, I think you need to start looking at someone who knows all of these victims. Someone who knows them real well. And the first place to start is by asking Marty who he told. It's probably a short list."

"You're right," Stan said. He thought of telling Joe about his suspicions that it was another Newpointe firefighter. But someone might overhear. If that word got out, the resulting panic would render the fire department useless in Newpointe—people would rather let their houses burn than call 911. "Look, don't say that to the vultures out there, okay? I don't want them to start speculating."

"I'm not talking to them," Madison said. "I know better."

Stan turned away from Francis's body and headed back through the house to the patio where Marty sat with his head hanging down between his knees. He touched his friend's neck, and Marty looked up at him.

"How's it goin', buddy?"

Marty rubbed his eyes. "How could this happen?" he asked. "How, Stan? We was hidin'. How did he find out where? He come in and shot her right next to me. How could I have slept through it?"

"That's what we have to figure out," Stan said. He found a chair and pulled it up to face Marty. Sitting close, he asked, "Who did you tell where you were?"

"Nobody!" Marty said. "I didn't tell nobody. We just came."

"All right, did anyone know where Francis's mother lived?"

He closed his eyes. "Well, yeah. I mean, lotsa folks knew she lived in Slidell. I guess if they knew her maiden name it wouldn't be that hard to find out the address. And then my car was in the driveway."

"All right, let's think, Marty. Can you think of anyone, say, in the fire department, who knows Francis's maiden name and that her mother lives here?"

He thought for a moment. "Well, it wasn't no secret. Few months ago when her daddy died, I took off work a week or so while he was in the hospital. I reckon everybody in the department knew where we were, and why."

"How about flowers?" Stan asked. "Did any of them send you flowers when he died?"

He tried to think again. "I don't know. I can't remember. There were so many flowers. They might have. Why?"

"If they did, then we know they knew your wife's maiden name. It wouldn't be a stretch to think they could have found out the address."

Marty began to stiffen, and looked at him as if he'd just suggested something ludicrous. "You're thinkin' this guy is somebody in the department?"

"I didn't say that. Don't you tell anyone I said that."

"Then what? Why would one of us be doin' somethin' like this? Instead of lookin' at us, you need to be out there findin' the real killer."

Stan looked from side to side, to make sure they hadn't been overheard. "Marty, do you have any idea where Francis's mother might have kept the guest book for the funeral, or the list of people who sent flowers?"

He rubbed his eyes again, trying to think. "Uh ... maybe. Yeah, in there in the dinin' room. She keeps lots of stuff like that in the drawers of the hutch. Pictures she hasn't put in albums, that sort of thing. She mighta stuck it in there."

"Okay. I'll go look."

"Stan?" Marty grabbed the lapel of Stan's sport coat as he started to stand up. "When are they gon' do somethin' with her? They can't just leave her lyin' there. It's wrong. All those pictures they're takin', and all those cops gawkin' at her. Please, can't you tell 'em to leave her alone?"

Stan sighed. "They're taking the pictures for evidence, Marty. It might keep anyone else from getting killed the same way. And when we catch this creep, the pictures'll help us nail him."

Marty dropped his head back into his hands. "Oh, why didn't he shoot me, too? Havin' t' see all this—it's cruel, man."

Stan couldn't answer. It did seem cruel. Almost intentionally so. Was the whole thing for that purpose? To somehow make the firemen suffer when they found their wives dead? If so, why? Why *hadn't* the killer shot Marty, too, or his mother-in-law? Why had he not hurt Tommy Broussard?

He went into the dining room and found the hutch. He pulled on the latex gloves he'd brought and began to go through each of the drawers until he found the guest book from Marty's father-in-law's funeral. There was a stack of cards stuffed inside it in a ziplock bag. He pulled them out and began to thumb through them. Some of them were small florist's cards. He went through the cards one by one, noting who from Newpointe had sent them. There was one from Nick Foster. One from all the guys at the Midtown Station, signed by each of them individually. He checked the address on the front, then compared the handwriting to the signatures. It looked as if Dan Nichols had been the one to address the card. Where had he gotten the address? He flipped a few more cards, found one from Mark and Allie Branning, one from Craig Barnes, one from the Fords.

Joe came into the room. "Got something?"

"Maybe, maybe not. I'm gonna take this bag of cards for evidence. It might help me figure out who in Newpointe knew where Francis's mother lived."

"All right, Stan. Just log it in, so we'll know where it is."

A uniformed cop came in and said, "Detective Shepherd?"

"Yes," Stan said.

"Someone from your office is looking for you. They said to tell you that Susan Ford just came out of her coma. She wants to talk to you."

Stan's heart leapt. "All right, now we're getting somewhere."

"That the woman who survived the shooting?"

"That's right," Stan said, dropping the ziplock bag into a paper sack and pulling off his latex gloves. "And she just might be able to tell us who's doing all this."

Chapter Forty-Three

Back on the Southshore in the ICU waiting room, Jill woke up and felt the pangs of hunger, the chill of the room, and a slight disorientation. She looked around. Allie was lying two chairs down from her, her vinyl recliner back as far as it would go. She thanked God that Allie was sleeping. She needed rest, and the energy that would come from it.

She stretched and tried to move into a more comfortable position, but there weren't many choices. Dan, who had been between them when they'd fallen asleep, wasn't there. She looked around, trying to adjust her eyes to the dim light, to see where he'd gone. Surely he hadn't gone far—not when he'd promised Mark he wouldn't leave Allie's side. Her eyes strayed to the doors marked "Men" and "Women." He must have gone there.

Closing her eyes, she let her consciousness drift as sleep came back over her.

A while later, she stirred awake again, this time to see Dan ambling slowly back in with a canned drink in his hand. He smiled when he saw that she was awake, and sat back down between Allie and her. Leaning close, he whispered, "Hi."

"Hi," she said. "Where'd you get that?"

"In that little kitchenette area over there. I know every nook and cranny of it. There are some stale muffins in there if you want some."

"No," she whispered. She didn't tell him she was fasting. "Is that where you were? I woke up a while ago and you were gone."

"I was over at that window overlooking that courtyard. I was bored and didn't want to read because the light might disturb someone. So I took my book out there and read for a while. If anybody had tried to get into the waiting room, they'd have walked right past me, so you and Allie were safe. If I'd stayed in here, I would have just fallen asleep. I promised Mark I'd be alert."

She lay the side of her head on the back of her recliner, but it wasn't comfortable, so she shifted again. "Come here," he whispered. He put his arm around her and guided her head to his shoulder. He was warm, and his uniform had the faint scent of aftershave and a lingering hint of smoke. He'd probably put out a fire today—he must be exhausted. Yet he was willing to give up his sleep to come here and guard Allie. The thought warmed Jill.

It wasn't long before sleep overtook her again, but this time, instead of cold, she felt the deep, soul-stirring sense of warmth that Dan had given her.

Chapter Forty-Four

Even though it was four-thirty A.M., the security guard at the Slidell Hospital let Stan in as soon as he showed him his identification. Stan rode the elevator to the second floor, where Susan Ford's room was. The moment he stepped off the elevator he saw Sid, Ray's brother, sitting in the corridor beside the door, still wearing his Newpointe P.D. uniform.

"How's it going, Sid?" Stan asked in a low voice, taking Sid's hand in a casual shake. "I hear she woke up."

"Yep," Sid said. "And she got some stuff to say. You ain't gon' believe this."

Stan looked past him into the room and saw Ray sitting on the side of Susan's bed, holding her hand and kissing it and talking softly to her. Vanessa and Ben stood on the other side, leaning over the rail, their expressions poignant. At the foot of the bed, two nurses spoke softly and recorded pertinent information for her chart.

Stan stepped inside the door and rapped lightly, and Ray looked up.

"Hey, Stan. Thanks for comin', man. How'd you get here so fast?"

Stan hated to tell him that he'd already been in Slidell because of Francis Bledsoe's murder. "I was already here working on the case when I got the call," he said. "I hear she woke up."

"She sho' did," Ray said with a chuckle, then turned back to his wife.

Stan went to the bed rail and looked down into Susan Ford's face. She had an oxygen mask on and looked frail, but her eyes focused on him as soon as he came into her view.

"Stan." Her voice was weak, so weak he almost couldn't hear, so he braced his elbows on the rails and leaned over her. She groped for her mask and pulled it off her face. "Need to . . . talk to you."

"She been askin' for you ever since she woke up," Ray said softly. "Stan, she remembers gettin' shot."

Reluctant hope surged through Stan, and he told himself to stay calm. "What do you remember, Susan?"

"He . . . he came in . . . I couldn't see his face . . . he was aimin' for my head, but I swung around and ran—"

"You couldn't see his face?" Stan asked.

"No . . . a mask."

Stan leaned closer, trying to hang on every word. "Mask? Like a Mardi Gras mask?"

"No," she whispered. "No, not that. Like Ray's mask. The oxygen mask."

Stan looked up at Ray, questioning. "What does she mean?"

"The face piece they . . . wear in fires," she said before Ray could answer. "Had on that face piece, that mask, and a bunker hood that covered his head."

Stan looked up at Ray again. "Does she mean . . . like a fireman's hood? The mask you wear in fires?"

"Sounds like it," Ray said.

Stan's heart was hammering. "Susan, you didn't see his eyes? Any identifying marks on his body? What he was wearing?"

"Bunker coat," she said. "I just ran . . ."

Tears rolled out of her eyes, and Ben wiped them away. "It's okay, Mama."

Vanessa turned away and began to sob, and Ray got up to embrace his daughter. "Honey, you want to go out and talk to Uncle Sid?"

Vanessa shook her head. "No, I'm stayin' with Mama. I wanna hear."

Susan took her hand and squeezed it. "My baby. Thank goodness . . . you weren't home."

"Put the mask back on, Mama," Vanessa coaxed. "Please put it back on."

Susan put the oxygen mask back on and closed her eyes for a moment, resting. Stan stepped back from the bed, his mind racing. So it *was* a fireman, without a doubt. But which one?

"He cried," Susan said after a moment, her eyes opening again.

Stan wasn't sure he'd heard right. "He what?"

She pulled the mask down again. "He cried. After he shot me . . . and I was layin' there . . . he thought I was dead . . . I wanted him to think so . . . and he cried, and started prayin'."

"Praying?" Stan asked. "He was *praying?*"

"Some kind of Catholic prayer, I think," she said. "He was prayin' to Mary. Sayin', 'I'm sorry, Mary. I'm so sorry.' I thought . . . he might have me . . . mixed up with somebody named Mary . . . but now I think he was prayin'."

"Why would he cry?" Vanessa asked, her eyes full of tears. "Why would some maniac shoot my mama and then cry about it?"

"I don't know," Stan said.

Ray's face was confused. "Stan, do you think this killer is one of our firefighters? Somebody I sleep and eat and go to church with?"

"I don't know, but I'm gonna find out," he said.

"Hurry up, will you?"

"I'll do my best. Look, you can all do me a big favor by keeping quiet about this. If it is a fireman, and I'm not saying it is, we don't want to start a panic. And we sure don't want to clue the guy in that we've got his number and risk having him disappear."

"I won't say nothin', man," Ray said. "Look, how's Mark? I been wantin' to call, but I been so busy here—"

"He's gonna be fine. The Lord must've had an army of angels around him when he got shot."

"Him and Susan both."

Stan squeezed Susan's hand. "I appreciate your calling me. I needed to know this."

"You be careful, Stan, you hear?" she whispered.

"I will," he said. "Now you get some rest."

He left them all there, then stepped out into the hall. Sid got to his feet. "So what'd you think o' that?"

"I think it confirms some leads I've already gotten," Stan said quietly. "I didn't want to believe it was a fireman, but I can't ignore the evidence. Sid, I didn't want to tell Ray, but something else has happened."

Sid looked as if he wasn't sure he wanted to hear this. "What?"

"Marty's wife was shot this morning."

Sid backed against the wall. "Not Francis. Where was she?"

"Here in Slidell. Whoever it was came in and shot her in bed without ever waking Marty. He's in pretty rough shape. The killer knew where they were, Sid. And Marty didn't tell anyone."

"Wait a minute." Sid narrowed his eyes and stared at Stan. "Somebody shot her and Marty didn't wake up? That don't seem possible."

"It happened," Stan said.

Sid obviously wasn't buying. "But the bed woulda jerked, and the body woulda flailed at least a little." He frowned. "Was there a fire this time?"

"Sure was. That's what woke him."

"A bullet didn't wake him, but a *fire* did? Huh-uh, Stan. I don't think so."

"He must have used a silencer," Stan said. "Come on, Sid. You aren't suggesting that Marty's our man. What did he do? Set up the whole serial killer thing so nobody'd suspect him when he killed his own wife?"

Sid lifted his eyebrows, as though that was a possibility.

"No way," Stan said. "You don't know Marty. He's not a killer."

"Name somebody in the fire department who is," Sid challenged. "Can you, Stan?"

"No," Stan said. "I can't."

"Gotta be somebody, man. And I don't buy this business about your wife gets shot while you're sleepin' in the same bed and you don't even wake up."

Stan hadn't considered Marty to be a suspect—not the man he'd just seen grieving over his wife, who worried about her body and all the pictures being taken. But then he also couldn't explain why a killer would weep and pray, as Susan had said.

"I don't think it's Marty," he said finally. "I think he's covered during at least some of the other murders. But listen: I found cards that some of the firemen had sent when Francis's father died, so some of them had known earlier where her mother lived. It wasn't a big stretch to figure out they'd be hiding there. And there's something else, too. Yesterday, after Mark was shot, they found a Newpointe bunker coat at the scene."

Sid dropped his head back against the wall again and closed his eyes. "We gotta find him . . . stop him before he comes back for Susan. He might think she can identify him." He opened his eyes and fixed them on Stan. "Okay, look, if it ain't Marty, look at Dan Nichols. He's the one got caught at the flower shop the other night, walkin' around with a crowbar in his hand."

"I'm considering him," Stan said. "And Craig too. He's the one who got lured in with our bait the other night. But he's also the one tap-dancing to keep both stations running."

"Question all of 'em, Stan. Just take ever' one of 'em in and question 'em one at a time."

Stan knew that Sid's insistence came from fear and frustration, not from doubts about his ability to do his job. "Well, I'll get back to you. I need to get back to the office and put all this together. Let me know if Susan remembers anything else, will you?"

"Stan, you find him! 'Cause if I find him first, I ain't gon' be askin' no questions!"

"I'm working as fast as I can, Sid," Stan promised.

Chapter Forty-Five

Good news came that afternoon, when the doctor evaluated Mark and decided that he could be moved into a private room. There was a cot in there for Allie, so she could sleep beside him that night. Dan had gone home, and T.J. had come to replace him. The hulking cop had set up a chair outside the door in the hallway, where he could screen everyone who tried to come in.

As Allie tried to make Mark's room as comfortable as she could, she felt much the way she'd felt when they'd bought their first house together. Flowers had begun arriving early that morning, so she quickly reworked the arrangements to her satisfaction and placed them around the room where Mark could see them. Then she fluffed his pillow and filled his pitcher with ice water.

Because they all felt that Mark was out of the woods, Jill had broken her fast, and Allie intended to as soon as Jill brought something back for her to eat. As they waited for Mark to be brought from ICU, her parents sat on the couch, watching her do her best to domesticate the sterile little room. They had something to say, she realized, but their reluctance in saying it warned her that it was something she didn't want to hear. Finally, she sat down on the bed and regarded them both. "What is it, Mom? Dad?"

Her parents looked at each other and seemed to silently agree to tell her what was on their minds. "We just hate for you to have your heart broken."

"What do you mean?" she asked.

Her father seemed to consider his words carefully. "We understand why you would be so devoted to Mark after such a trauma," her father said. "Really, we do understand. But now that he's going to get better, we hate to see you acting like everything is fine between you. Like you're still married—"

"We *are* still married."

Her mother took the baton. "But honey, as soon as he gets out of here, he's going to go back to his apartment and that woman, and you're going to go back to yours."

She sighed heavily. "I really don't want to talk about that."

"We just want you to be safe, honey. We don't want your heart broken, or your life threatened by some killer. We were thinking . . ."

Her father touched her mother's hand, taking over again. It was uncanny how they finished each other's sentences, completed each other's thoughts. "We were thinking, honey, that you should fly back with us this afternoon. Mark will be fine. He has all sorts of friends who can take care of him, and that father of his—"

"I'm not going," she cut in. She couldn't find anything else in the room to do, so she reached for the remote and turned on the television. She hadn't seen the news since yesterday in the hotel room; the ICU waiting room had no television. "I'm staying here with my husband."

"And what if he just uses you until he's better?"

She couldn't believe their persistence. "Uses me? How?"

"To take care of him. He's not exactly in a position to tell you to hit the road."

"He's never told me to hit the road," Allie said with weariness. "I told *him* to, so he did."

"But that woman—"

"Mother," she said, using the name she called her only when she was getting angry. "I'm tired of hearing about this. I never should have told you all those things. It's my fault that you feel the way you do about him, but—"

"*. . . identified as Francis Bledsoe . . .*"

The name blaring from the television grabbed Allie's attention, and she quickly stood, gaping up at the set in the corner of the room. "Oh, no," she whispered.

"*. . . victim number five in the bizarre case of the Fire Wife Killings. Victim number four, Mark Branning, himself a firefighter at Newpointe's Midtown Station, is still hospitalized after a bullet to his head, and victim number three, Susan Ford, is still in critical condition. Francis Bledsoe was found shot through the head in her mother's home, while her husband, firefighter Marty Bledsoe, slept beside her. The killer is purported to have started a fire, as he did in almost every other case. Sources tell us that Bledsoe woke after the fact and saw the fire. It was moments later that he realized his wife was dead in their bed.*"

"Oh, God, what is happening?" Allie cried, sinking to the floor. "Not another one! Not Francis! She had kids! She had those sweet little twins!"

Her parents were at her side in an instant, kneeling beside her and holding her while she wailed out her anguish and pain.

"What's happening? He's killing us all!"

"You're coming home with us today," her father said. "I won't take no for an answer. Mark will want it, too, if he really cares about you."

She shook away from them, got up, and tried to pull herself together. "I'm not going *anywhere*, do you hear me? He found her! He found her at her mother's. He found *us* at the airport. He'll find me wherever I go, so I might as well be here, with my husband!"

"Oh, for heaven's sake, Allie, listen to us!" her mother shouted. "Stop being a martyr. You won't do Mark any good if you're dead!"

"I have a bodyguard!" she argued, red-faced. "I'm doing what's necessary. But I made vows to my husband, and I intend to keep them. He took a bullet that was intended for me, Mom. Don't you understand that? I wouldn't be alive if it weren't for him. I'm going to stay with him and take care of him, and nothing—not you or Dad or some stupid wild killer—is going to make me leave him now. So either get that through your heads, or go on home. I have enough to deal with!"

Her parents backed away, and finally, her mother said, "Let's go for a walk."

Her father nodded. "We'll leave you alone for a while, honey. Eat something, okay? You'll feel a lot better."

She watched, sobbing, as they walked out of the room. Wilting on the bed, she began to pray—short, disjointed prayers that she feared made no sense, but she knew God heard. He knew she prayed for Marty Bledsoe and their little twins, for Mark to get well so they could renew their vows, for her parents to understand, for herself to cope, for Stan to find the killer, for the killer to have a conscience . . .

When she had finished, she washed her face, brushed her hair, and tried to hide the evidence of her tears before Mark was brought in. He didn't need to know about Francis Bledsoe. He needed to concentrate on getting better.

Not long after, they wheeled Mark in and moved him onto his bed. He saw Allie and smiled. "Hey . . ."

"It's not much," she said, her eyes glimmering, "but it's home."

"You mean they're actually gonna let us be together for more than fifteen minutes at a time?"

"That's what they tell me."

He grinned. His voice was gravelly, groggy, as he asked, "You think we can handle that? I'm better in small doses, they tell me."

She knew he was kidding, playing with her, but the challenge made her feel awkward. When he reached out for her hand, she took it and came close to the bed. The nurses worked around her, hanging his IV bag, taking his blood pressure.

He smiled up at her, but suddenly his smile faded. "Your eyes are red. Is that from fatigue, or have you been crying?"

"Fatigue," she said quickly.

"You slept in a chair last night, didn't you? Man, that's cruel. With all the beds in this place, you would think . . ." His voice faded out, and he began to shake his head. "No. That's not fatigue. Your nose doesn't turn red when you're tired. You *have* been crying."

She feared that the tears would come again. Desperately, she tried to blink them back. "I was just thinking about everything that's happened," she said, giving him a half-truth. "I guess now that I know you're out of the woods, I was able to let go and have a good cry." She reached over and stroked the hair that started behind his bandage. "Wonder what you're going to look like when the bandage comes off?"

"It won't be pretty."

The nurse left them, and his eyes grew serious as he looked up at her. "I really appreciate your staying here with me, Allie. I didn't know for sure if you would."

"Of course I would."

"So how's T.J. treating you? You two getting along?"

"Sure, we're fine. He mostly sits out there flipping through magazines, but he's careful not to let just anybody in. Dan was more fun."

"You just know him better. But T.J. will do a good job. Make sure you don't go anywhere without him."

"I'm not going anywhere at all. I don't want you left alone."

"Hey, the killer is after you, not me. I got in the way, remember?"

She swallowed the lump in her throat. "Still, I think I'll just stay here."

"Fine with me. Come here."

When he opened his arms, she bent down and went willingly into them, and clung to him for several moments, basking in the warmth of his strength. Tears filled her eyes again as she thought about how close she had come to losing him. "I'm glad you're going to be okay," she whispered.

He loosened the hug, letting her pull back enough to look at him. His eyes were soft, sweet, as he gazed up at her, and she wondered what he was thinking. Did he, too, want to renew his commitment to their marriage vows?

"I'm sorry you ever married me," he whispered.

Her expression crashed. "What?"

"I'm sorry," he repeated. "If you hadn't married me, you wouldn't be in this mess. Maybe you'd be off happily married to some rich guy with a big house, a minivan, and a couple of kids by now."

"What about you? Where would you be?" she asked soberly.

"Probably right where I am, since that maniac wants to kill my wife no matter who she is. On the other hand, there's probably nobody else in the world I'd ever take a bullet for but you."

"Sure there is," she said sadly. "That's the kind of guy you are. There are probably lots of people."

"Nope. Just you, kiddo." His eyes locked with hers for a long moment, and he reached up and stroked his finger through her hair, pushing it back from her face, sweeping it behind her ear.

The overwhelming urge to kiss him swept over her, drawing her toward him. Her heart pounded, and that old chemical ache that had drawn them together when they met began to pump through her again. She felt the slightest pressure of his hand on the back of her head, pulling her down to him . . .

Their lips met, and her heart soared like a bottle rocket in a fourth of July celebration, as all the love she'd felt for him and stifled, all the misery of their separation, all the joy of his survival, all the regrets of her part in their marriage, culminated in a moment of bliss even more poignant than their first kiss. The kiss lingered for several moments. Neither wanted to end it, and his fingers stroked the roots of her hair, as her knuckles moved across his stubbled jaw.

When at last the kiss ended, she pulled back a fraction of an inch and looked into eyes that were dark with longing for her. Joy burst through her heart that he could look at her that way again.

"How do you manage it?" he asked in a whisper.

"What?" she whispered against his lips.

"To give me a coronary workout when I'm flat on my back?"

She grinned, but his eyes remained serious.

"I meant it the other night," he said. "When I told you that I'd missed you. I know you didn't believe it then, but it's true, Allie. I've missed you."

He pulled her into another kiss, and a sense of supreme well-being, intense contentment, filled her.

"Knock, knock." It was her mother, back from her walk, and Allie sprang up as if she had been caught at something.

"Hey there, Mom, Dad," Mark said, surprised to see them. "Allie didn't tell me you were here."

Her mother assessed the situation, then shot her father another of those wordless, but eloquent, looks. "Uh . . . yes. We've been here since yesterday," her father said in a cool tone.

Her mother stepped closer to his bedside, but still hung back a noncommittal distance, as if she didn't want to be mistaken for someone who cared too much. "We're glad you're feeling better," she said, as if he'd had a head cold.

Allie hated the chill coming from her mother, the chill she didn't want Mark to feel, so she changed the subject. "Mark, can I get you anything? Water? A popsicle? I could call the nurse, and get her to bring one."

"No, I'm fine. Thanks." He looked back at her parents, who still stood there, so cold and uncommunicative. "Why don't you guys sit down? The remote control's probably around here some—"

"No!" Allie said, too quickly. "No television, Mom. Please."

Mark gave her a suspicious look. "Why not?"

"Because ..." She felt like a thief caught in the act of stealing. But she didn't want Mark to know about Francis Bledsoe, not until he was better. "I just want some peace and quiet."

"But I'd like to watch the news," Mark said. "They might have some word on the hunt for the killer."

"They don't," she lied. "Mark, don't you want to rest?"

He stared at her for a moment, then looked at her parents and saw the volumes written on their faces. "What's going on? Has something happened? Was someone else shot?"

Allie glared at her parents to keep them quiet.

"Allie, tell me! What's going on?"

She wilted. "Mark, you really need to ignore the news. You need to concentrate on getting better. You can't do anything about the killer from in here, so there's no point in—"

"Who?" Mark asked, turning to her parents. "Who's the latest victim?"

Her father started to speak, but Allie stopped him. She took a deep breath. "It's Francis Bledsoe," she said, her mouth trembling with the words. "She was killed last night."

"Aw, no!" He closed his eyes and brought his hand to his eyes. "No, Allie, not another one. How many is that?"

"Including you and Susan, five. But there is good news, Mark. Susan woke up, and T.J. said that she's been able to give them some pertinent information about the identity of the killer. He won't say what that information is, but it must be a strong lead."

He let out a heavy breath, then slid his hand down his face. "Well, good for Susan. I'm glad she's gonna pull through. But how's Marty?"

"I don't know. I just heard about it all myself."

"His kids," he whispered in horror. "Those poor little kids."

Her mother got up and stepped close to the bed, her face suddenly softer. "Mark . . . we're worried about Allie."

"That makes three of us."

"We want her to come home with us. Today."

Allie's eyes filled with fire as she turned on her mother. "Mom, I've already told you," she said through her teeth. "I'm not going."

Mark took Allie's hand and made her look at him. "Maybe you should."

"Why? I have T.J. here, and you. The killer found Francis Bledsoe at her mother's in Slidell. What makes you think he wouldn't find me in Georgia?"

Mark closed his eyes and let that sink in for a moment.

"Mark, I'm not leaving, no matter what you say. I'm staying, and that's final."

He seemed to be undergoing some supreme struggle. She laid her hand on his chest. "Mark, I mean it. Don't even think about it."

Mark looked at her mother, then her father, who had approached the bed himself. Mark's eyes were deep with thought. For a moment, she thought he would agree with them and insist that she leave, and she wondered how in the world she would convince all three of them that her place was here.

But Mark surprised her. "She's right. She's really probably safer here, where there's a mob of press people downstairs and a bodyguard outside the door."

Her father's teeth came together, and through compressed lips, he said, "That's selfish, Mark! You want her here taking care of you, so you're letting your selfishness endanger her life. She's my daughter. I want her to be safe."

"She's my wife," Mark said. "And I want that, too. If I thought she'd be safer in Georgia—"

Her mother's tough facade shattered, and she turned away. "You don't even love her, Mark. You were going to divorce her just a few days ago. Why should we believe now that you'll do everything in your power to protect her?"

Allie's face was hot, and tears stung her eyes. "Mother, please—"

"You're right," Mark said, closing his hand possessively over Allie's. "My power is pretty limited right now. And there's no good reason you should believe me when I say that I'll make sure she's protected."

"Yes, there is, Mark!" Allie shouted. "There *is* a good reason." She swung around to her parents, her face raging red. "He almost died protecting me! He almost died! The least I can do—the very least—is to stay here with him now."

Mark tugged on her hand and turned her back around. She saw the pain on his face, and realized that he'd misinterpreted her words. "You don't owe me anything, Allie."

"No, Mark, that's not what I meant. But they can't pretend that you haven't protected me. That you haven't done everything in your power—"

"We appreciate what Mark did," her father said, more softly now, as if trying to appease her. "We do. But now it's our turn—"

"No, it's not! I've made my choice."

"You're our only daughter," her mother cried. "We don't want to leave you." Her voice broke, and she began to sob. In a high-pitched voice, she cried, "We may never see you again."

Suddenly, Allie understood the reason for her parents' domineering stance in this. They were terrified. Maybe even more terrified than she was. Melting, she whispered, "Oh, Mom," and went to her mother, hugged her, then pulled back and hugged her father. "Dad—I'm gonna be all right. Really. Please. Just go home. I'll call you every day."

"You promise?" her mother asked through her tears.

"Yes. You can pray for us, and trust that God is still watching over us."

Her mother, who had been the one to teach Allie to pray, nodded her head, unable to speak. Her father struggled with his own tears as he turned to Mark. "Don't let anything happen to our little girl, do you hear me?"

"Yes, sir."

He settled his gaze on his daughter.

"We'll go home," her father said. "We're just getting in the way here, and we're not going to see things eye to eye. But we love you, sweetheart."

"I love you, too." She hugged them again, and finally, he took her mother's hand and escorted her out.

She turned back to the bed and met Mark's eyes. Though they were still bruised, she saw clearly the longing in them.

"You know, you don't have to stay," he said quietly. "You don't have to take care of me. If you want to go with them—"

"I want to stay, Mark."

"Why?" The question seemed important, but she was too tired, too hungry, too depressed to answer it eloquently.

"For the same reason you want to take care of me."

The quiet seemed to bond them in some unspoken way as they gazed at each other with sad, questioning eyes. Questions needed to be asked, questions about where they stood in each other's hearts, what their next step would be, whether there would still be a marriage when all the dust settled. But those questions were never asked, because Jill came hurrying in with a Styrofoam plate in her hand.

"Allie, I'm so sorry it took so long to bring this back, but the line was long."

"It's okay," Allie whispered. But her eyes stayed locked with Mark's in sweet anticipation and fragile hope.

Chapter Forty-Six

Two days later, Aunt Aggie puttered in the kitchen at the fire station, making a thick gumbo that she didn't really have the heart for. These funerals were wearing her out. It was one thing saying good-bye, one by one, to people her own age who'd led long lives and were ready for the fat lady to sing, but it was another watching them bury a beautiful young woman with twin girls who would need their mama. The sight had broken her heart; it almost made her want to stay at home in mourning today. But her boys had to eat, and they, too, were in mourning. They needed some comfort, even if she could only offer it through their stomachs.

Nick had come in after the funeral and a visit to Susan Ford in Slidell, looking drained and sober. He looked worn and aged, too, she thought, even though he was only thirty. He needed a wife to take care of him and keep that soft heart of his pumping. He was a good man, even if Aunt Aggie didn't believe a word of the stuff he preached.

Dan Nichols hadn't gone to the funeral. He had stayed behind on the skeleton crew that kept the fire station open, as had Cale Larkins, who said he couldn't bear the thought either of attending another funeral or of staying in a lonely house. One by one, they had all returned to the station. It was quiet, deathly so—there hadn't been a call in hours, they'd said, not even a cat up a tree. She wished someone would turn on music or something, to break the quiet. She thought of humming as she prepared the meal, but she just had no hum in her.

She heard footsteps in the doorway and turned around to see George Broussard standing there in a pair of worn jeans and a gray sweatshirt, holding that little baby, Tommy, on his hip. The little boy looked freshly bathed, and his hair was slicked over like that of an older child. His face was so clean it shone.

"Oh, let me see *mon enfant*," Aunt Aggie said, rushing to his side. "Oh, George, how is he, bless his heart?"

George pressed a kiss on his cheek. "He's good, Aunt Aggie. He's gon' be awright."

"My heart break for him. And for you, too."

He swallowed and looked down at the baby, then asked, "Is Nick here, by any chance?"

"He in the back changin'."

"I need to talk to him," he said.

"I'll baby-sit for you," she said, "soon's I get the table set. Y'eat?"

"No, but I ain't hungry."

"Y'have to eat, George. You look like nothin' but skin and bones." She'd meant it to make him smile, since it was so obviously untrue. But it didn't work.

"I ain't been hungry."

"Neither has nobody." She hurriedly set the table, then reached for the baby. "Come here, darlin'."

Tommy puckered up like he was going to cry, and George shifted him to the other hip. "I b'lieve I'll just keep him with me."

"You sure?"

"Oh, yeah. No problem."

Aggie watched them disappear to the back. She heard a knock, and turned to see Celia standing in the doorway. "Aunt Aggie? What's wrong?"

She dabbed at her eyes with a corner of her apron. "Just George," she said. "And that poor little orphaned boy."

"He's not an orphan, Aunt Aggie. He has his daddy."

"But not his mama. We could set up a whole school full of young 'uns lost their mamas in the last week." She dabbed her eyes again. "How many is that monster gonna kill before Stan stops him?"

"He's doing the best he can, Aunt Aggie. You know he is."

She waved a frustrated hand. "Ah, it's takin' forever." She pulled a tissue from a box on the corner of the counter and blew her nose. "So what bring you here? You smell my gumbo all way across town?"

Celia smiled. "No. I was just talking to Allie Branning, and she said that Mark is doing so well that they might let him go home tomorrow."

"Really? After gettin' shot in the head?"

"The Lord was really looking out for him."

"Then why he got shot in the first place?"

"He was protecting Allie."

"No, no," Aggie said with frustration. "I mean, why did somebody go t' shootin' at him? If the Lord was lookin' out for him, why he got shot? And was the Lord not lookin' out for Martha and Jamie and Susan and Francis?"

She knew that her niece wasn't fooled. Everyone in town knew she didn't believe in the Lord, nor any other supposed higher being, and she sure didn't believe in divine intervention of any kind. Aggie was making a point, and she hoped she'd made it well.

"Aunt Aggie, I can't pretend to know what God is doing, or why he's doing it. I just believe that he is working somehow. Now, the reason I came is to ask you a favor."

"What favor, darlin'?" Aggie asked, suddenly contrite that she'd offended her niece. If she hadn't been so grouchy and irritable from the funeral, she wouldn't have.

"Well, I was just thinking. Allie was a little worried about where she and Mark would go when he gets out. They can't go home for obvious reasons. In fact, the farther from Newpointe they are, the better. And it's a little hard to recover in a hotel. They need a place with a kitchen so they don't have to go out. That got me to thinking about your apartment in the French Quarter."

Aggie's eyebrows arched. "You think they'd want to stay there?"

"I'm not sure, but we could offer. Oh, Aunt Aggie, it's such a romantic little place. It's just what they need. It was heaven for Stan and me on our honeymoon. I could stock the kitchen and get it all ready for them. That is, if there's not a tenant in it already."

Aggie had kept the apartment for her frequent visits to the Southshore. She rented it out through a real estate agent who specialized in tourism, but only for a week at a time. This time of year, between Mardi Gras and Easter, tourism was slow, so the apartment was vacant. "It's a good idea," she said. "I'll call the realtor and tell her we'll be usin' it ourselves 'til further notice. And I'll get the cleanin' lady I use down there t' go by and give it a once-over. Oh, and I'll have some fresh flowers sent over, to freshen it up a little, since Allie loves flowers. Me and you can go down there tomorrow mornin' and spruce the place up before they get there."

"Okay," Celia said with a smile. "What about feeding the guys?"

Aggie looked back at the food, still sitting on the table, cooling. "Nobody 'round here has much appetite, noway. Let 'em order pizza for a coupla meals; they'll appreciate my eats a little more when I get back."

Craig Barnes came in just then, his face as tired and preoccupied as all of the other firefighters today. He glanced at the table. "Where is everybody?"

"Nick's in back talkin' to George Broussard. Dan, Slater, and Cale's washin' the ladder truck. Jacob and Junior is out back shootin' hoops. Sit down if you hungry. Food's gettin' cold."

"No thanks," he muttered. "Not hungry." He disappeared into the back.

"Heaven's sake," she said. "Guess I'll be glad to get out of town tomorrow and do somethin' with my time that's worthwhile."

Celia set a time for them to meet, then rushed out to call Allie.

• • •

In the back room where the television set and a couple of recliners and rockers were, George rocked his baby. Nick sat across from him, elbows on his knees, his eyes locked into his friend's.

"I just wondered, Nick," George said, his voice cracking as he got the words out, "if you have any advice ... on, you know ... how to stop feelin' like I'm smotherin' in the dark."

Nick prayed silently for an answer. He'd counseled people before about dealing with death, but never after a murder. He felt helpless, inadequate. "Trust God," Nick said. "That's all I know. It's normal to grieve, George. Jesus grieved over Lazarus. But you have to trust God and know that things are working together for good, and that this grief will just be a memory some day when you're reunited with Martha."

Little Tommy's eyes were drifting shut as George rocked, the steady rhythm of the rocker the most soothing sound Nick had heard in days. "I do trust God," George said, stroking the baby's cheek with his rough knuckle. "I just wish he'd let me in on what he's up to."

"Don't we all?"

"I wish it didn't have to hurt so bad. I wish—" His voice broke, and he dropped his head and squeezed his eyes shut as a

sob broke from his throat. "I wish Tommy would stop lookin'
around me for his mama." He drew in a deep, wet breath, and
wiped his face with a hard hand. "I wish I'd spent more time
with him before it happened . . . so's he'd be more used to me.
But she was nursin', so I couldn't do the feedin's, and I was here
every third night, and she changed most of the diapers and did
most of what had to be done. I shoulda helped her more. I
shoulda been there instead of actin' the clown in some stupid
parade."

Guilt. It was a natural stage of grief, yet knowing that didn't
give Nick a clue how to make it easier to deal with. Again, he
prayed for strength. An idea came to him, and he sat back in his
chair.

"Let's think about Martha for a minute, George," he said.
"About where she is right now."

George brought his grieving eyes back up to Nick's. "She's
in heaven. No question."

"What do you think she sees there? What's it like for her?"

George thought about that for a moment. "I couldn't say."

"All right," Nick said, taking it one step at a time, though
he realized he was going way out on a limb. "Let's just think
about it. If when we get there, we're reunited with loved ones,
who do you think would have come to greet Martha?"

George was quiet for a long moment, and Nick began to
think this line of thought might have been a mistake. Finally, the
man said, "Her parents. She'll be glad to see 'em. Especially her
mama. She just lost her last year, and it really hurt her. She
wanted so much for her mama to see her as a mama herself."

"Wonderful. She's reunited with her parents. Who else?"

"Grandmaws and grandpaws, I reckon. And her sister who
died when she was a teenager. I never knew her, but she was in
a car wreck, and Martha always missed her."

"She's with her sister!" Nick exclaimed. "What a wonderful
homecoming she must have had. Anyone else?"

George struggled with his thoughts for a moment longer. "Yeah." He looked up at Nick with a look of surprise as the thought came to him. "Martha had two miscarriages. Reckon those babies'll be there, too?"

Nick's eyes filled with tears. "I'm certain they are."

George managed to get out a smile, then a soft, poignant laugh as he wiped the tears from his face. "What do you know 'bout that? She'll get to be a mama, after all. And her mama *will* see it." He laughed again, and shook his head. "She'll have her work cut out for her, what with two babies and me not there to help her."

"But she's got her parents there, and her sister. And you've got your family here."

He nodded. "Yeah, I do. Maybe that's why the good Lord didn't let the killer take Tommy, too. He left one for me."

"And one day, you'll have them all together."

George looked down at the little baby, a sweet smile on his face. "Wonder if she has cellulite there?"

Nick didn't think he'd heard right. "Has what?"

"Cellulite," George said, chuckling and leaning his head back on the rocker. "She always said that she hoped when she got to heaven she wouldn't have no cellulite. Reckon she has any?"

Nick laughed softly. No matter how hard he tried, he couldn't think of a single scriptural reference to cellulite.

• • •

When no one had come to the table, Aggie had gone looking for them, one by one, insisting that the boys eat so that her gumbo wouldn't go bad. When she'd gone after George and Nick, she had heard the conversation going on in the TV room, and had hung back, listening quietly.

All that talk about heaven irritated her. It was a nice thought, but she didn't see the point in getting a man's hopes up about some fairy-tale future. Then she'd heard them laughing, and she'd peeked around the door and had seen the beginning of joy in George Broussard's eyes, and she decided that, fairy tale or not, it had chased the shadows from the grieving man's face. She didn't know how he was as a preacher, but Nick Foster would make a great shrink. Empty fairy tales or not, if hope made the man feel better, then she supposed she wasn't against it.

Miscarriages, two babies, the Lord leaving Tommy behind, the idea of reuniting a family of five when on earth it had only been a family of three . . .

Funny thing about Christians, she thought. They always managed to see good in the most awful circumstances. At least, some of them did. It beat everything she'd ever seen. Either they were master pretenders or master self-deceivers.

She went back into the kitchen, only to find the other men at the table with their heads bowed as Dan Nichols led them in a prayer of thanks for the food she had cooked. Shaking her head in frustration, she took off her apron, grabbed her sweater, and decided to go for a walk before she came back to do the dishes.

Chapter Forty-Seven

Allie was amazed at how quickly Mark had been able to bounce back from his run-in with the killer's bullet. He had gotten up and walked around the day after they'd moved him into a room, had eaten a full meal that afternoon, and had visited with his father who had come to visit. It was clear that Eddie had been drinking, but Mark was used to it, and didn't even let that bother him. Though he complained of a headache only when asked, he had insisted repeatedly that he felt well enough to go home.

The doctor told her that the minimal damage caused by the bullet did indicate a quick recovery, and that, under the circumstances, he thought Mark might actually recover more quickly if he and Allie were in a safer, less public location than a hospital. But he cautioned her not to let Mark get carried away—he had lost a lot of blood and was still in danger of infection. He needed rest, lots of it, and a stress-free environment.

But he didn't sleep well that night and seemed tired the next day as she loaded the car with their suitcases and flowers. Allie told herself his fatigue had more to do with his insomnia than with the trauma itself. His head was still bandaged, but the bruising around his eyes was clearing to yellow patches.

They said good-bye to T.J., who needed to get some rest before his next shift as a cop. They had agreed not to hire a replacement, since they had a good hiding place. Money was a problem—they just couldn't afford to keep a bodyguard. Still, Allie hoped they were doing the right thing.

Allie was jumpy as she drove across New Orleans, heading for the French Quarter apartment Aunt Aggie had loaned them. She watched her rearview mirror for some sign that they were being followed.

When they reached Canal Street, Mark told her to pull over.

"What?" she asked.

"Pull over. Right up there, next to that purple sign."

"But the apartment is still a few blocks over."

"I know. But I need to stop here. There's something I want to buy."

She did as he told her, even as she protested. "Celia stocked the apartment, Mark. We don't need to buy anything."

"Yes, we do."

As she pulled over next to the purple sign, she saw that they were parked in front of a pawn shop. She looked at him, confused. "Mark, what do you want here?"

"I'm buying a gun," he said, his tone brooking no debate.

She hated guns, always had, and the thought of having one in their possession frightened her. "Why a pawn shop? This isn't the best place to buy a gun."

"Because there's a seven-day waiting period in this state, Allie, and I don't have seven days to wait."

"So you're going to buy one illegally?"

"Yes. And if they want to lock me up for protecting my wife and myself—especially after I've been shot in the head—more power to them."

"Mark, are you sure? I don't like it."

"Yes. I'm going to protect you, Allie. And the only way to do it is to be armed, just like he's armed."

She let out a heavy breath. "But I don't know if I even believe in guns. It doesn't seem like Christians ought to be pistol packers. Jesus said, 'He who lives by the sword, dies by the sword.'"

"That's right. But look." He opened her purse, and pulled out the small Bible he knew she carried there. She waited as he flipped through to Nehemiah. "I was thinking about this yesterday, and praying about it, and I ran across this passage. Look here at chapter 4, verses 13 and 14. Nehemiah knew that the enemies of the Israelites were going to attack them to keep them from rebuilding the wall, and he says, 'Therefore I stationed some of the people behind the lowest points of the wall at the exposed places, posting them by families, with their swords, spears and bows. After I looked things over, I stood up and said to the nobles, the officials and the rest of the people, "Don't be afraid of them. Remember the Lord, who is great and awesome, and fight for your brothers, your sons and your daughters, your wives and your homes."'"

Tears came to her eyes as she watched him studying those verses again. Was her husband praying again? Was he searching the Word for his answers? As much as the thought moved her, she found it hard to believe that the Holy Spirit had led him to break a law.

He brought his soft eyes back up to her. "They can have my home, and my brothers can fend for themselves, and I don't have sons and daughters. But I plan to fight for my wife, Allie. I plan to fight with all I've got."

An unbridled warmth gushed through her. She reached across the van and touched his face.

"We need a gun, Allie. I'm not gonna go off the deep end and start waving it at everything that moves. But I need a defense."

"Okay," she whispered.

He swallowed and held her eyes for a moment longer. "It's not that I think we won't be safe there. We will be safe. He won't know where we are."

"I know."

"I'll just sleep better tonight."

She nodded. "I understand."

"Good." He opened the door and, weakly, got out. She hurried around the van to help him, but he waved her off.

"I'm okay."

She opened the door for him, and she tried to shove back her doubts as they both went in to buy the gun that they hoped would defend them from any more attempts on their lives.

Chapter Forty-Eight

If she had custom-ordered a perfect little romantic getaway, Allie could not have found an apartment more pleasing. Located on the outskirts of the French Quarter, away from the sleazy shops and loud bars, the apartment was on the second story. It had a sweet balcony that was covered in blooming jasmine, with antique wrought-iron chairs and a little round table.

Celia had left a fire in the fireplace—for effect, Allie imagined, since there was only a touch of chill in the air and no need for a fire. But it lit the romantically decorated living room in a yellow glow, and the little lanterns around the room accented that light. Hanging baskets of ferns and schefflera, and pots of vinca and impatiens in every shade of the rainbow colored the small rooms. The place was fragrant with floral scents, much like Allie's shop.

"This is perfect," Mark whispered, sinking down on the overstuffed couch that faced the fire. He pulled off his shoes and socks and let his bare feet slide across the lush carpet. "Absolutely perfect. We owe Aunt Aggie one."

Allie crossed the living room to the two doors on the opposite wall. She felt Mark's eyes watching her as she opened a door and peered in. "The bathroom," she told him. "It's lovely. An antique tub with claw feet, and a separate shower." She went to the next door and opened it.

It was the one and only bedroom, with a four-poster bed with a canopy, and lacy mosquito curtains hanging to the ground from the canopy and draped back with satin ribbons.

The bedspread, too, was made of satin and lace, as were the curtains.

She stepped into the room, taking in the sight of the scented candles around the room, the bright throw rugs on the floor, the Tiffany lamps.

"Beautiful." The voice came from behind her in a whisper, and she turned and saw that Mark had followed her in.

She swallowed. "It sure is."

He went to the bed, sat on the edge, then after a moment, pulled his feet up and lay down. His eyes slowly closed. "This sure beats a hospital bed."

She stepped up to the bed and ran her hand along the bedspread. "Yeah, and that couch sure beats that hospital cot. Maybe we'll both get some sleep tonight."

She started to walk away to check out the kitchen, but he reached out and caught her hand. His reflexes were quick for a wounded man, she thought, but she didn't tell him so. She found that she couldn't speak at all.

"You must be tired," he whispered. "Sleeping in a chair in the waiting room, and then on some vinyl cot."

"Yeah, a little."

"You're not sleeping on any couch tonight," he said. "That's silly."

She didn't know what to say. "I don't mind. That way you can stretch out. You need your rest, Mark."

He scooted over on the bed and pulled her on it beside him. She sat on her knees for a moment, looking down at him. "I can't rest unless you're beside me. That's the only way I can be sure you're safe."

That was true. She hadn't thought of the safety issue, but her heart's safety was what worried her now.

"Lie down," he coaxed in a voice that mesmerized her. "Come on. Just lie here with me for a minute."

282

She felt silly arguing with him about it, especially when she really was so tired, and the bed seemed so inviting. Slowly, she stretched out and lowered her head to the pillow.

He slid his arm under her neck, and pulled her onto her side until they were facing each other. Their eyes locked in longing, but neither of them could speak of it.

"I should fix you something to eat," she whispered. "You must be starving."

"No," he said, closing his eyes. "I'm not. Just stay here. Be still."

He scooted closer, until their knees were touching, and their faces were centimeters apart. He wrapped his arms around her.

She watched him as his eyes drifted shut, as his breathing slowed, as his body slowly relaxed next to her.

Such love burst through her that she thought she might weep at the very thought of it. As tears came to her eyes, she closed them, and felt the anxiety and stress and tension seep out of her, as well. For the first time in over two months, she felt as if she was truly home.

Safe in his arms, she let herself fall asleep.

Chapter Forty-Nine

The boys at Midtown Station were glad to see Aunt Aggie when she arrived that afternoon to make dinner. As if she'd been gone a week, they convened in the kitchen to find out where she'd been during the lunch hour that day, when they'd wound up having to order pizza.

"Was on the Southshore," she announced as she began to chop celery. "Girl needs culture ever now and then, you know."

Craig Barnes sat at the table with a clipboard, studying some paperwork he'd brought from his office. He looked tired, worn; they all did. Nick looked tiredest of all, and she pitied him. Dan Nichols had dark circles under his eyes, and she wondered if he was getting any sleep at all.

"Did you see Mark while you were there?" Dan asked her, sliding out a chair and sitting in it backwards.

She glanced at him over her shoulder. He had folded his arms over the back of the chair and propped his chin on it. She had long considered him the best-looking firefighter of the bunch, but he was looking a little worn around the edges, if you asked her. "Yep. Just before they let him out."

"He's out?" Craig Barnes asked, looking up. "This soon? How can that be?"

"You know them hospitals," she said. "They slap a Band-Aid on you and send you home."

"So is he back in Newpointe?" Craig asked.

"Not home, home. They stayin' in my apartment there. Me and Celia, we fixed it up, stocked the kitchen. They'll be fine there."

"You have an apartment in New Orleans?" Craig asked. "I didn't know that."

"There's a lot about me you fellas don't know. I got a life, you know. I like to go to the city ever now and then and take in a show or the opera. Don't just spend all my time cookin' for the likes of you, you know."

"Where in New Orleans?" Dan asked.

It wasn't until then that she realized she had said too much. Should she have told anyone that Mark and Allie were staying in her apartment? Could she really trust everyone here?

"Never mind. Mark and Allie are hiding, don't forget. I ain't gonna go around spoutin' out where they are to nobody who asks. Not with that killer runnin' loose shootin' people at airports and in their mothers' homes. Just makes your skin crawl to think about it."

"How are Allie and Mark getting along?" Craig asked, getting up and flipping with preoccupation through his papers.

"Nothin' like a bullet in the head to bond a couple. They might just work things out." Aggie nodded her head emphatically. "Yep, they just might."

Chapter Fifty

Mark woke at eight P.M. and found the apartment bathed in darkness. Both of them had apparently slept so deeply that they hadn't even awakened to eat. He opened his eyes and tried to let them adjust to the night. It took a moment for him to orient himself to the big four-poster bed with the white lace mosquito netting—and his wife lying beside him. She was on her side facing him, deep in sleep, and she looked angelic in repose. Though she was still fully dressed, as he was, all of the tense lines seemed to have melted from her face, and she was completely relaxed, her rhythmic breathing making her shoulder rise and fall. He smiled at the way one fingertip touched her lip in sleep. She probably didn't even know she did that. He had forgotten, but now it brought back such warmth, such personal truth, that his eyes filled with tears.

He didn't know how long he lay there watching her sleep, but eventually he realized that he was not going to be able to go back to sleep himself.

He reached for the gun he'd set on the table beside the bed, slid it into his pocket, and sat up on the edge of the mattress. His head ached, and he felt a little dizzy, but he got up and felt his way to the door. Closing it quietly behind him, he groped in the darkness for a lamp, found one, and clicked it on.

It bathed the room in a soft yellow hue and calmed the unease stirring in him. He padded across the lush carpet to the kitchen, looked in the refrigerator, and saw all the treasures Celia and Aunt Aggie had put there. He pulled out some cold cuts, lettuce and tomato, found the bread, and made a sandwich. It was the best thing he'd eaten since the killings had begun.

When he finished, he cleaned up, then went to the window and peered out between the blinds. The street was quiet, and a damp fog hung around the street lanterns, lending an eerie feel to the night. He saw their car parked on the street, and he suddenly wished they had rented a different one in case the killer was out looking for them, searching for their car in parking lots.

He shivered and abandoned the window.

He needed to go back to bed and bury himself in sleep, but suddenly he was too tense. He needed a drink. Just one drink would relax him, and then he could lie back down with Allie and sleep until morning.

He went to the refrigerator, sifted through the contents, and found a bottle of Chablis back in the corner. Good old Aunt Aggie. She'd known just what he needed. He pulled the bottle out and began searching the drawers for a corkscrew.

He moved quietly, so he wouldn't wake Allie; he didn't want her to catch him with the wine. It wouldn't help the already fragile situation. They had come so far in the past few days, and he never again wanted to see that look in her eyes he'd seen when they'd been at the diner before they'd gone to the airport the other day, when he'd perused the wine list, and she'd acted as if he was ordering up a syringe of heroin.

Unbidden, from somewhere in left field, thoughts of his childhood came to his mind. He remembered waking up in the night and going to the bathroom. He'd heard his father milling around in the kitchen. Rubbing his eyes, Mark had gone to see what he was doing. Entering the kitchen, Mark had startled his father so badly that he'd dropped the bottle of bourbon he was drinking from, which had shattered all over the floor, along with the bitter-smelling liquid. His father had cursed and sent him back to bed, and then he'd heard his mother getting up to see what had happened, and the fight had begun . . .

It had always been the same. His father was always the wounded party, misunderstood, not trusted. And his mother would apologize meekly to keep the peace, and pretend the next day that nothing had ever happened.

Had his father once been like him, drinking only occasionally, but getting up in the middle of the night and searching the kitchen for something alcoholic?

His heart sank, and he closed the drawer, abandoning the search for the corkscrew, and returned the wine bottle to the refrigerator. He didn't need it. He wasn't like his father.

He sank onto the couch and tried to think. They said that alcoholism was genetic, but he'd never believed it. Weakness could be genetic. Self-pity might even be inherited. And what about cowardice? Wasn't that what really led his father to drink? A fear of confronting the real issues of life that plagued him and everyone else on the planet?

He was different than that, he told himself. He knew better. He knew Christ. But maybe Christ had turned his back on him. Wasn't there a place in Revelation that talked about God spitting us out of his mouth?

Suddenly, he felt the overpowering urge to find that passage, study it, and determine whether God had already done that with him. Maybe that was why he'd been shot. Maybe he was being punished . . . or maybe God's protection had been lifted from him. Maybe the Lord was trying to teach him something.

He took Allie's little Bible from her purse. Going back to the lamp next to the couch, he flipped through the book until he came to Revelation. He scanned the letters to the churches and paused at chapter two, at the beginning of the red letters denoting Christ's words, and read the letter to the church in Ephesus. Praise, commendation, approval. But then he came to the rebuke, and he sat up straight and read the words out loud, realizing they were meant for him, that God had led him to this page tonight.

"Yet I hold this against you: You have forsaken your first love."

Sitting out behind the firehouse just a few nights ago with Ray—it seemed a lifetime ago—he had asked his friend what he thought of him now. And Ray had answered Mark with those very words.

"Maybe, just maybe, you've forsaken your first love."

And Mark had totally misunderstood. He grimaced, touching his forehead. That just showed how far from God he had truly strayed. He had thought Ray meant only that he had forsaken Allie. But Ray had been commenting on much more than that. It was his relationship with Christ that Mark had forsaken.

Mark turned the page and read on.

"Remember the height from which you have fallen! Repent and do the things you did at first."

What were those things? For one, Mark had abstained from alcohol, not wanting to repeat his father's mistakes. He had worshiped regularly. He had loved God and others. He had cherished his wife.

He read on, each of the letters to the churches, both the praise and the reprimands. He read God's warning that he would spit them out of his mouth, and he read that God rebukes and disciplines those he loves. Was the Fire Wife Killer God's way of rebuking Mark? Had God raised up a murderer—snuffing out lives, taking mothers from their babies, wives from their husbands, daughters from their parents—just to punish Mark for straying from his walk with Christ?

In his confusion, he cried out to God, and he felt the still, peaceful voice of his Savior whispering that the consequences Mark had created himself were discipline enough. Separation from God, the darkness of divorce, loneliness, regret, fear— those were disciplines that would teach him to follow Christ. But the evil wrought by a murderer's bullets were not part of some avalanche of judgment by an angry God. The father had not sent hit men to torment the Prodigal Son. He had allowed him the suffering he'd brought on himself, but all the while, he'd been watching, waiting, hoping for his return.

Wiping tears from his eyes to clear his vision, Mark read on, praying that God would show him his way back, that he would have the strength to get things right. There were things in his heart he had to pull out and hold under the light, things he had made into lies that had rubbed calluses on his heart.

Issie. Allie had accused him, and he'd hidden behind his righteous indignation, telling himself and Allie and even God that he'd been falsely condemned. He'd comforted himself with that thought when she'd asked him to leave. It had been his self-acquittal, his excuse for not keeping his commitment to love and honor her.

What had Allie ever really wanted from him? Fidelity. And he had sworn that he had been faithful to her.

But she had known better.

He wept harder as he closed his eyes and recalled the late-night talks with Issie, when they had bared their souls, even if their bodies had been clothed. He had shared intimacies with her in the form of conversation, had told her unflattering things about Allie, had told her just how unhappy he was in his marriage. He had enjoyed the attentions the pretty woman had shown him, had enjoyed the flutter of his heart when she had smiled at him or flirted with him, had appreciated that she wanted to spend time with him.

For so long, he had told himself they were just friends. But now he realized how deeply he had wounded Allie with that friendship. What would he have felt if he had walked in on Allie in another man's arms? Would he have listened if she'd told him it had been innocent? Would the fact that nothing more physical had happened really matter to him if she'd been unfaithful in her heart?

Lord, show me what to do, he prayed through his tears. *Help me get it right.*

And for the first time in his life, he read the Bible like a starving man, searching for words addressed to him, and answers that could restore him.

Chapter Fifty-One

Even though it was only eight-thirty, Aggie had shut off all the lights and was upstairs in bed reading when she was startled by the sound of a door closing quietly. For a moment, she thought she had dreamed it, but then she heard something else: the sound of a drawer closing, the floor creaking as someone moved across it . . .

She sat up in bed, listening, and didn't hear anything for several moments. Maybe it had been her imagination. But she'd never imagined anyone in her house before.

Quickly, she got up, grabbed the poker from the fireplace in her bedroom, and started down the stairs.

She heard a sound again, the sound of the drawer closing in her study. Someone was in there, she thought as she waited halfway down the staircase. The killer? The thought made her heart flip into triple-time, and she reached out for the banister to steady herself.

She heard another drawer close quietly; the sound of the rollers moving in and out on her file cabinet drawers was unmistakable. Summoning all of her courage and hoping her heart could stand it, she tiptoed toward the study, her poker raised, and saw that the door was closed.

She never closed that door.

She wanted to scream, wanted to run and call the police, wanted to burst into that room and catch whoever had had the gall to break into her home. But what if he had a gun aimed at the door, waiting for her? She would wind up the next victim, dead on the floor as he set fire to her house and burned it down around her.

She froze, unwilling and unable to move. She heard papers rustling. What was he looking for? Then she heard the sound of the window being raised, then shut again.

Silence followed, and she waited, still not moving. Had he gone out the window? Is that how he had come in?

Of course he had. Anyone who drove by could see that her front windows were usually open an inch or two this time of year, before it got too muggy and she had to depend on air conditioning. What if he came back?

Forcing herself, she slowly, carefully, pushed the study door open. The room was just as she had left it.

The windows were slightly open, as usual—except for one, which was closed. Was that the one he had gone out?

Quickly, she slammed all of the windows down, locked them, then rushed for the telephone. She dialed Stan and Celia's house.

"Hello?" It was Stan, wakened from sleep, but she made no apology.

"Stan, he was here. Somebody—maybe the killer. He come in my house, and he went out a window, and I didn't see him, but I heard him—"

"Whoa, wait a minute. Aunt Aggie, is that you?"

"Yes! Stan, come over here. Maybe there's fingerprints on the window or on my desk. I heard drawers openin'. Maybe the file cabinet. Maybe you could catch him now before he get too far."

"Aunt Aggie, I'll be right over. Meanwhile, don't let anyone in until I get there, okay? Don't touch anything. And lock those windows."

"Already did. What he wants with me? He killin' the wives of dead firemen, too?"

"If it was the killer and he wanted you dead, you'd be dead."

Aggie shivered at the realization of how close she had come.

Chapter Fifty-Two

By 9:30 Mark had managed to read all of First, Second, and Third John, as well as Jude, James, and First and Second Peter ... when the lamp began to flicker.

He checked the bulb to see if it was screwed in tightly, found that it was, then went back to his reading.

The lamp flickered again, and this time went out. He got up and fumbled for the cord, followed it in the darkness to the plug, and found that it was still plugged in.

Feeling his way to the bedroom door, he slid his hand across the wall until he found the light switch. He flicked it up, but there was still no light.

Had they somehow tripped a breaker? He stood in the dark for a moment, wondering where the breaker box was. Maybe the kitchen. He began working his way toward it. He stubbed his toe on a table he didn't remember being there, tripped on a cord, knocked over a plant. Finally, he made it to the kitchen and tried the switch there. Still no light. Was this entire apartment on a single breaker? He wished for a flashlight, but didn't have a clue where Aunt Aggie might keep one.

He was sliding his hand across the wall, feeling for the breaker box, when he heard a sound outside. Someone was at the door, scratching on the lock.

He pulled the pistol out of his pocket and groped for the telephone he'd seen hanging on the wall. Miraculously, his hand closed over it, and he jerked it up.

No dial tone.

His heart jolted, and he thought of running to the bedroom, waking Allie up, putting her out through the window onto the fire escape. But there was no time. The doorknob was turning, the door was pushing open—

He raised the gun, and in the darkness watched and waited for someone to come through. He smelled the faint scent of diesel as a shadowy form came into the room and bent over to set something down. A canister of some sort? A gas can?

His hand trembled, his head ached, and he felt dizzy as he stood frozen, holding that gun on the man who seemed unaware that he stood there, watching him. The man straightened and, like a shadow in the dark, started to steal through the room.

"Hold it right there, pal." The words sounded alien, distant, but Mark knew he had uttered them. A strange peace fell over him—whether from God's strength or from his own weakness he wasn't sure—but as the man twisted quickly toward him, a dim ray of light from a street lamp outside partially illuminated him. A fire mask covered the man's face. He was wearing bunker pants and boots, a bunker coat, and carrying oxygen on his back—all the things a firefighter would wear when fighting a fire.

The sight was staggering, and he almost lowered the gun— until he saw the man go for his own. Mark had no time to think, only to react, and his finger closed over the trigger, smoothly, quickly, without hesitation.

The gun went off, and the man fell backward.

He heard Allie scream behind the closed bedroom door, and he yelled, "Go out the fire escape, Allie, and call the police!"

If there was a response from Allie, Mark had no time to hear it. The man got to his feet and launched himself at Mark, knocking him to the floor. Mark's head jarred slightly with the impact, but he managed to stay conscious and keep fighting. The man's right arm was slick with blood, and he no longer held his gun. He lunged for Mark's gun, an ironclad grip on his wrist cutting off his circulation, challenging him to let it go.

Mark kicked him in the groin with his knee, making the bleeding man recoil. Still on the floor, Mark kicked him again in the right shoulder. The anguished groan that followed told Mark that his kick was aptly aimed, and the man loosened his grip on Mark's wrist, allowing Mark to roll away from him. Mark fired the gun again, but he knew even as he pulled the trigger that his shot would miss.

The man rolled away. Mark sat up and tried to shake the dizziness away. He heard a clattering. Something cold splashed against Mark's legs. He recognized the smell of diesel fuel. Mark could hear it gurgling out of the can, soaking into the carpet, into his jeans. He fired again in the darkness, but the bullet smashed into the wall. He heard a match striking, saw the flame ignite, saw it being thrown his way—

The carpet in front of him ignited, throwing him back. Flames erupted on his legs—

He fired the gun at a shadow on the far side of the flames, then hit the ground again and rolled, trying to put out the fire on his skin. He grabbed an afghan draped over the couch and smothered the flames on his body. Scalding agony charged through his body, but he tried to find the man through the flames again, to aim the gun and finish the job he had started.

He was gone.

"Allie!" Mark screamed, staggering back to his feet and running into the bedroom as the fire raged behind him. If Allie had gone out the fire escape, as he'd told her, the killer might have caught her by now. *"Allie!"*

The window was open, and she was gone.

Chapter Fifty-Three

The moment the gunshot woke her, Allie had heard Mark yelling for her to escape. Without hesitation, she had done what he'd said and gone to the window. After several tugs she managed to get it open, hurled herself out, and half-ran, half-tumbled down the steps of the fire escape to the ground. She tore around the building to the front doors and banged on the first one she saw with a light on. A couple of doors down, a man came out, and other neighbors emerged. She grabbed one of them and pleaded for their telephone.

Even as she spoke to the 911 operators, she saw the killer running down the steps of Aunt Aggie's apartment, dressed like a fireman answering the call. He headed up the sidewalk, blending into the shadows until she lost him. "He's running up Bienville in a fireman's hat and mask, and full bunkers like a fireman wears. Please—you've got to catch him. He's the Fire Wife Killer from Newpointe. Please hurry!"

"Ma'am, there's smoke coming from your apartment," the neighbor shouted. "I think there's a fire up there. We have to wake everyone in the building!"

Her heart raced as she told the operator to send a fire truck and ambulance, too, then took the fire extinguisher the neighbor thrust at her, and hurried up the stairs, praying that Mark was all right.

The apartment door was open when she got there; flames engulfed the carpet. From somewhere, she heard Mark's voice screaming for her. "Allie! *Allie!*"

"Mark, I'm here!" she called as she pulled the pin on the fire extinguisher and began to spray the flames. "Are you all right?"

"He got away!" Mark cried as he came out of the bedroom. "But I shot him. He's wounded. Maybe there's a blood trail."

He grabbed the extinguisher from her and quickly doused the flames. Dropping it, he stumbled back against the wall.

"Mark, are you okay?" She touched his face with both hands, trying to examine his bandage in the darkness and smoke.

He was weeping. "Thank God. Thank God he didn't get you."

He pulled her against him and held her, sobbing, until the police arrived. They came up the steps with flashlights, several of them shining their beams on the charred carpet as firefighters pushed into the apartment to make sure the fire was completely extinguished.

A paramedic stepped in front of them. "I need to look at those burns."

"Mark, you're hurt!" Allie cried, seeing the burns for the first time.

"I'm okay," he said. "I put it out real quick." Wiping the tears from his face, he raised his voice so the police could hear. "I shot him in the right arm or shoulder. There's got to be a blood trail—enough for a DNA test. This is the guy who's killing our wives."

The paramedics rolled in a gurney. "We need to take you to the hospital for these burns," they told him.

"No," Mark said. "I'm not going back to the hospital. I just got out. Treat the burns here with whatever you've got, and I'll be fine. I have to talk with Stan Shepherd. He'll want to hear what I've got to say."

Chapter Fifty-Four

Stan searched Aunt Aggie's house for evidence of the burglar's identity, but found none. There were no fingerprints, no footprints, and nothing taken—nothing except a few missing files from Aunt Aggie's file cabinet. She had determined that the files were nothing more than paid bills for everything from credit cards to her utilities.

He was looking for something, Stan thought, racking his brain for what that could be. A credit card number, or a bank account, or . . . an address.

His heart began pounding. Could it be that he knew Mark and Allie were staying in Aunt Aggie's apartment in New Orleans? If so, they were in serious trouble.

"Aunt Aggie, what's the number of your apartment in the Quarter?"

She rattled off the number, and he quickly dialed it.

"You think he was after that?" she asked. "You think he goin' after them?"

The phone began to ring, and he waited. "Was there anything in those files that would have that address?"

"I don't know. Well . . . yes. The records of them realtor fees. It would have the address. Oh, Stan!"

The phone kept ringing, unanswered. "Why aren't they answering?" he asked. "Is there a phone in the bedroom?"

"Yes. You don't think the line was cut—"

He finally hung up and dialed the number for Blanc's office at the Kenner Police Department. Blanc wasn't in. Quickly he dialed the number for the New Orleans police. "This is Detective Stan Shepherd, Newpointe P.D. I need for you to get a patrol car to this address." He gave them the address of the apartment, and explained his fears. They told him they'd check on Mark and Allie and get back to him.

He took Aunt Aggie to stay with Celia at his own house. Celia had a gun and had been instructed on how to use it. Then he headed back to the police station, a terrible sense of dread making him feel helpless and useless.

His cellular phone rang, and he jerked it up. "Stan Shepherd."

"Stan, this is Mark. You're not gonna believe what's happened."

"Mark, are you all right? I tried to call. I think the killer may know where you are—"

"You think right. I had a run-in with our man tonight, but he got away. Stan, he was wearing a complete bunker suit with a mask. I think you need to consider that this guy is a fireman."

"I already have," Stan said. "Mark, what happened?"

"I got him before he got me. Shot him through the arm or shoulder, and then he threw diesel fuel on the carpet and set fire to it. He got away, but the police are looking for blood evidence now. I'm at the station—Eighth District on Royal Street."

"Is Allie all right?"

"Yes, thank the Lord. She's fine."

"Were you burned?"

"Yeah, but not bad. Stan, did you say you'd already considered that this guy is one of us?"

"Yes. We have other witnesses who saw a guy dressed in Newpointe bunkers. Susan told me she saw the guy wearing a bunker coat and mask, and an airport employee saw a man in a gray fireman's uniform."

There was a stunned silence. Finally, Mark said, "Stan, don't you think that information might have been pertinent to those of us hiding for our lives?"

"Of course it was pertinent, Mark, but I couldn't start a scare. I didn't want the press stringing up some poor innocent guy and keeping us from nailing it down to the real one."

"I'm not the press, Stan. I needed to know this!"

"Mark, I'm doing the best I can. It was against my better judgment—"

"So do you know who the killer is?" Mark cut in, his voice teetering on the edge of rage. "Or are you going to keep that to yourself, too? You think you might let me in on it before I'm six feet under?"

Stan closed his eyes. "No, Mark, I don't know. Not yet, but I've managed to narrow it down a little."

"Stan, if you don't tell me *something*, so help me—"

"I will, but not on the phone, Mark. In fact, if you're feeling up to it, I need you and Allie here. I'll arrange a squad car to get you here."

"Fine," Mark said. "Whatever it takes to get this guy locked up. I don't care who he is."

"You might when you hear my hunches."

Mark got quiet again.

"Look, put one of the cops there on the phone so I can set up your trip home and compare notes with those guys."

"All right," Mark said. "You'll be there when we get there?"

"I'm not going anywhere," Stan said. "I've got a job to do."

Chapter Fifty-Five

The highway patrolman who drove Allie and Mark back to Newpointe was fascinated with the "Fire Wife Killer" case. He grilled them—and, since he had nothing to do with the case, Allie felt that his questions were based on mere morbid curiosity. He would get a lot of great gossip out of this.

"So you got brain damage from that bullet?" he asked around the tobacco stuck in his bottom lip.

"No," Mark said, trying to be patient. "I'm fine."

"You think fine now. But you still gon' be as sharp as you was before?"

"I don't know," Mark said. "I guess I wasn't all that sharp before. Probably won't be able to tell a difference."

Allie grinned.

"I mean, you cain't get shot in the noggin without havin' somethin' wrong with you afterwards."

"He's really fine," Allie said. "Please, he needs to rest."

Gratefully, Mark laid his head back on the seat and closed his eyes.

The patrolman peered at her in the rearview mirror. "I reckon you must be scared t' death, ma'am. Dude poppin' off them wives one by one, tryin' t' get t' you. You don't have no idea who it might be?"

"No idea," she said.

"Some psychopath from up north. They like to come south to do their killin'. Them Jeffrey Dahmer types."

"Dahmer didn't come south," Mark said.

"May have," the patrolman said. "Maybe they just ain't found the bodies. What kind of crazy would wanna leave a trail of dead firemen's wives? Downright bizarre. I heard he tortured 'em first, at least the ones he killed. Fed 'em dope and made 'em drink diesel—"

"That's not true," Allie said hotly.

"What I heard." The man spat into a Styrofoam cup on the seat next to him. "Don't know why my sources at N.O.P.D. would lie. They'd know, since they're investigatin' the case."

Mark's face was turning red, the most color Allie had seen on it in days. "The only part of this case *they've* investigated had to do with me, so why don't you just shut up and drive?"

Allie tried to suppress her grin as the patrolman muttered a benign apology, then did just what Mark suggested.

The car was quiet for a while, except for the roar of the engine, the crackle of the radio, and the occasional call that came through it.

"You okay?" Allie whispered to Mark.

"Yeah," he said.

"Tired?"

"Yeah. Thinking about what Stan said."

"About it being a fireman?" she whispered.

"Yeah," he said quietly. "That, and the possibility that I might be close to the killer."

She stiffened in surprise. "He said that?"

"Not in so many words."

"Then what?"

"He said I might not like hearing who he's narrowed it down to."

She got quiet a moment, her mind running over the men at the station, assessing them one by one. The thought that it could be a good friend gave her chills. "You're close to Ray, and it couldn't be him, since Susan was one of the victims. Nick isn't a killer. And you're best friends with Dan, but it obviously isn't him."

Mark was too quiet, too pensive, and she watched his face as he struggled through the possibilities. "Mark, you don't think it's one of them, do you?"

"Let's just see what Stan says," he told her.

• • •

It was 11:30 when Allie and Mark arrived in Newpointe. Stan was waiting for them in the interrogation room with a stack of files spread out on the table in front of him. He leapt to his feet when they came in, giving Mark a once-over from the smoke-stained, bloody bandage on his head to the charred remains of his jeans and the burns visible through the holes and rips. "Mark, you look awful."

"Thanks, man. You don't look so hot yourself."

"You should be in bed, if not the hospital."

"I want this guy caught first, Stan. Then I'll go to bed." He sank carefully into a chair, and Allie poured him a glass of water, then took the seat next to him.

"Stan, Mark said that you'd narrowed it down," she said. "Who are the suspects?"

Stan set both hands palm-down on the table. "I spoke to the detective at N.O.P.D. a few minutes ago, and they collected some blood samples from the carpet, the stairs, and the sidewalk. I'm about to send some of our uniforms out to bring three guys in for questioning. First thing we're looking for, of course, is the wound. That with hair fibers and a blood sample should satisfy any jury and get us a conviction."

"Just arrest him," Mark said weakly. "Get him off the street. Then worry about getting a conviction. My wife has been through enough."

Amazed, Allie looked at her husband—at the bandage on his head, at the pale cast to his skin and the burns on his legs. And he thought that *she* had been through enough?

"I need to ask you and Allie a few things," Stan said, rubbing his red, fatigued eyes. "First, who did you tell where you were staying?"

"No one. Absolutely no one. Only Aunt Aggie and Celia knew."

"I've already talked to them. Aunt Aggie said she did mention to some of the firemen that she had loaned you her apartment. But she didn't say where it was. Tonight, her house was broken into. Nothing was stolen except a couple of files from her file cabinet. My guess is they were looking for an address."

Mark leaned forward, his face intense. "Who was in the room when she told them?"

"Nick Foster, Dan Nichols, Slater Finch, Craig Barnes, Cale Larkins, Jacob Baxter, and Junior Reynolds."

"Seven people?" Mark asked, growing angry again. "Stan, if you'd *told* her it was a fireman, she wouldn't have spouted off like that. What were you thinking, keeping this information to yourself?"

Stan bristled and raised a cautionary hand. "I didn't know for sure. Now, do you want to hear the rest or not?"

Mark took a deep breath and nodded for him to go on.

"She said a couple of them asked her where the house was, but she wouldn't tell."

"A couple of them? Who?"

"Dan and Craig."

"Well, they were probably concerned. Both of them. Maybe they went out and mentioned it to someone else, who then broke into Aunt Aggie's house and came after us. It's not Dan—he's my best friend. He was with Allie all night when I was in intensive care, the night Francis Bledsoe was killed. And the chief of the fire department? Give me a break. These killings have caused him a ton of problems. Why would he do something like this?"

"There's another suspect," Stan said. "Marty Bledsoe."

Mark's mouth fell open, and Allie gasped. "Stan, you can't be serious," she said. "His own wife was a victim."

"But his account of her murder is suspicious," Stan said. "He didn't see or hear anything, didn't feel her body jolting when it was hit. Don't you find that odd?"

"Why would he kill the mother of his twins?" Mark asked. "Stan, *think*. It doesn't make sense. None of these guys could have done it!"

"I've checked everybody's whereabouts for each murder," Stan went on. "Around the time of Martha's murder, Dan was out jogging, and no one can confirm it. Marty and Craig both showed up at the parade late. When Jamie was killed, no one's sure where Craig was, and Dan claims he was home alone—no one can confirm that—and Marty was supposedly at home, but since Francis isn't here to confirm it, we can only take his word for it. We aren't sure who was at the funerals when, so we can't say if any of them could have left or come late after shooting Susan."

"What did you do? Ask them all for alibis?"

"No. I asked for an account of who was on duty during each emergency, and where they were if they were off duty. I told them the prosecutor might need to call some of them as witnesses. No one questioned it. Once I had their answers, I tried to confirm them."

Allie still looked disturbed. "Stan, what about the night Francis was killed? Dan was at the hospital with me that night."

"Allie, are you sure that Dan didn't leave at any time during the night that he stayed with you? Even for a couple of hours?"

"Positive. Both Jill and I were there. He didn't leave."

"Didn't you sleep at all?"

"Well, yeah. But not deeply. I would have known if he'd left for that amount of time." But even as she spoke, a memory seemed to come back to her.

Mark saw the change on her face.

"What?" he asked.

She looked at Mark, shaking her head. "He didn't do it," she said. "He's not a killer. But I was just thinking—one time when I woke up, he was coming back from somewhere, and he told Jill he'd been outside the door in the hallway, reading. Jill and I had both been sleeping. I didn't think anything of it, just went back to sleep."

"And you don't know how long he'd been gone?"

"Not long."

"How do you know, if you were asleep?"

She thought about it for a long moment. "Well, if it was him, why didn't he just kill me then? Why would he sit up with me all night? It doesn't make sense."

"No, it sure doesn't," Mark said. "I trusted him with my wife. He wouldn't have hurt Allie, or me for that matter. But neither would Craig or Marty."

"Mark, Allie, remember the night that we set up the stakeout in your house, hoping to lure the killer?"

"Yes," Allie said. "You said Craig Barnes showed up, that he was worried and was checking on me."

"Right. But he parked his car down the street, and he was wearing his bunkers, like he'd just come from a fire. Only I just did a check on emergency calls for that night, and there wasn't a fire within two hours of his showing up there."

Mark and Allie stared at him in disbelief.

"On the same night, Dan Nichols was caught sneaking around your shop with a crowbar in his hand, and there was evidence that someone had tried to break in there. Both men thought Allie was inside."

"Okay, but Dan was on duty when I got shot at the airport," Mark said. "He was on the clock. He couldn't have just left. And Craig was running both Midtown and Eastside. He couldn't have left town, either."

"Yet no one knows where Craig or Dan were at that time. Craig claimed he was at the other station, but no one at either station saw him during that time. At least, not that they can remember, and I have to leave some room for error since these have been hard days and people aren't thinking that clearly. But no one could find Dan, either. He came in some time later, all sweaty, and claimed he'd been out jogging."

"That's possible. He jogs every day," Mark said.

"But isn't it a coincidence that he did it right at the time when he'd need an alibi? And I can't find anyone who saw him."

"Well, what about tonight? Wasn't he working tonight?"

"He was, but he left early. And I sent someone to bring him in for questioning, but he wasn't home. At this hour of morning, where would he be?"

"What about Craig?"

"Not home, either, and not at either station. And Marty's not home, either. His parents live in Metairie, though, so I've sent some men to see if he's there."

"You're kidding."

"Wish I were."

Mark looked as if he was going to be sick, and Allie's eyes filled with tears. Finally, he rubbed his face. "All right, there's one easy way to tell. The killer has a gunshot wound in his arm or shoulder."

"It's none of them, Stan," Allie said. "You're wasting your time, and meanwhile, the killer may be going after someone else."

Chapter Fifty-Six

At first, the banging was part of his dream, a *whop, whop, whop* of a fireman's ax, chopping at wet, smoldering wood ...

Then the dream was gone, and Dan shifted in his bed. The *whop, whop, whop* was coming from the other room, and he raised himself up and looked at the clock. Midnight.

Only then did he realize that someone was banging on his door. Feeling as if he'd just slept off a three-day drunk, he slid out of bed, pulled on the jeans he'd dropped on the floor beside his bed when he'd fallen into it, grabbed a sweater and pulled it on, and stumbled to the door.

"Who is it?" he called through the door.

"Police. Open up!"

Frowning and squinting in the lamplight, he unlatched the door and pulled it open. The two cops standing there were old friends—he'd played football with both of them in high school. "Chad, Vern—what in Sam Hill—do you know what time it is?"

"Why didn't you open the door earlier?" Vern asked him.

"I was asleep. I've been on duty for days and haven't slept much. I haven't caught up yet. How long have you been here?"

"Long enough to think you weren't home."

"Have you been here all night?" Chad asked with a tone of suspicion.

"Well, yeah. Since about seven or so. I was working but I cut my hand—"

Chad and Vern exchanged eloquent looks.

"So they let me come home. What?" Dan asked. "What's going on?"

"We came by earlier and you weren't home."

"When?"

"About an hour and a half ago."

"No way. I was here. I was sleeping. Didn't you see my car? Anyway, what did you want?"

"We have to take you in for questioning," Vern said. "Stan needs to see you."

Dan stared at them for a moment, groggily assessing their faces. "Am I under arrest for something?"

"No. We just need to question you about some things."

"What things?"

Vern stepped into the house and looked around. "We also have a warrant to search your house and your car."

"Search—for *what?*" His eyes followed Vern as he walked from room to room. "Chad, what's going on? Has there been another murder or something?"

"Not a murder, but another attempt."

"Another—who was it?"

"Allie Branning."

"*What*—how is she?"

Chad looked at him suspiciously. "She's fine. They're both okay."

Dan paused for a breathless moment. "And they think *I* did it?"

"They're not jumping to conclusions of any kind, Dan. We just want to ask you some questions."

"Fine. Then ask. Why do you have to search my house and car?"

"Do you have an objection? Something to hide?"

"No!" he yelled. "Search all you want. I have nothing to hide. I just don't understand why you'd think it was me. I've been at the station for the past several days, practically nonstop, except for when I was at the hospital with Mark and Allie. How could I be out killing people?"

Vern looked down at the bloody bandage on Dan's hand. "What's wrong with your hand, Dan?"

"I told you, I hurt it at the station tonight. Cut it on some glass. That's why I called Cale in to replace me."

Chad looked at Vern, again exchanging silent observations. "Dan, would you mind taking off your sweater?"

"My sweater? What for?"

"Just take it off."

Agitated, Dan pulled the sweater off, wondering what in the world they were looking for.

"No wound," Chad said with a note of relief.

"Okay, but remember," Vern said, "people have been known to get overconfident about where and how they wounded someone. It was dark, and his adrenaline was pulsing, and he could have gotten it way wrong."

"Yeah, I know."

"Wounded?" Dan asked. "You think I did it, don't you? You think I've been killing those women. You can't be serious!"

"You're not the only one we're questioning, Dan. You can put your shirt back on now and calm down."

Dan pulled the sweater over his head, shaken and sweating now. "I want to call my lawyer."

• • •

The phone woke Jill on the first ring, for she hadn't been sleeping well. She had been too worried about Mark and Allie, and her dreams all night had been plagued with shadows chasing her, chasing Allie, chasing Mark, chasing Martha and Jamie and Susan and Frances.

She lifted up on one elbow and picked up the phone. "Hello?"

"Jill, it's Dan Nichols. I need a lawyer."

"Dan, what's wrong?"

"Vern Hargis and Chad Avery are here to take me into the police station for questioning, but they have a warrant to search my house and car. Jill, I think they're trying to pin these murders on me."

"That's ridiculous!"

"Tell me about it. Can you meet me at the station?"

"I'll be there," Jill said, already getting out of bed. "And Dan, don't say anything at all until I get there, okay?"

"Don't worry," he said. "I won't."

Chapter Fifty-Seven

Jill made it to the station moments after they had brought Dan in, just after one in the morning. She found a haggard Mark Branning slumped in a chair next to Allie. She caught her breath and rushed to them. "Allie, what happened?"

Allie looked wearier and more defeated than Jill had ever seen her. "The apartment where we were staying was broken into tonight. Mark fought the guy off and he got away—but not before he'd started a fire."

Jill's face drained of all its color. "Was either of you hurt?"

"Mark was," Allie said. "His legs . . ."

Jill saw the burns and winced.

"Jill, they've just brought Dan Nichols in for questioning."

"I know," she said. "He called me. That's why I'm here. Why are they interested in him?"

"Because the man who broke into the apartment had on a firefighter's bunker suit and a mask. The other day, at the airport, they found a Newpointe bunker coat. Stan's been trying to narrow it down."

"And he's narrowed it down to *Dan?* That's ludicrous. Didn't you tell him it couldn't have been him? He was with us all night the night Francis was killed."

"We told them," Allie said quietly. "But there's that time I woke up and he was coming back in from the hall. You were talking to him—you remember. They're saying that maybe he wasn't in the hall, maybe he had been to Slidell and back."

"Give me a break!"

"The guy who broke into our apartment tonight is wounded," Mark said weakly. "I shot him somewhere in the right shoulder or arm. It'll be easy to rule Dan out, if he's innocent."

"*If* he's innocent? Mark, you can't really think there's a possibility—he's your best friend!"

"Of course he is," Mark said wearily. "I didn't mean that."

She looked down at them for a moment, frustrated. Then she realized how painful those burns must be, and how tired and sapped for energy Mark was, just out of the hospital. His head was wrapped in a fresh bandage, but the yellow bruises around his eyes reminded her just how miserable he must feel. "Mark, you don't look so good. Shouldn't you be in bed?"

"What bed?" he asked. "We can't go home or we'll be killed in our sleep. We can't go back to where we were hiding. We can't get on a plane."

"Maybe they could find a place for you to lie down, at least."

"Forget it," Mark said. "I'm not closing my eyes until this man is caught."

A few minutes later, Jill found Dan in the interrogation room with Stan Shepherd, Chief Shoemaker, Vern Hargis, and Chad Avery. She walked in with an air of disgust, dropped her briefcase into a chair, and took the seat beside Dan. "All right, guys, let's get down to business so my client can go back home and get some rest."

"We just want to know where he was between seven and twelve tonight."

"I *told* them," Dan said. "I cut my hand around seven, then went home and went to bed. No witnesses. Can't prove a thing."

"Yes, you can," Jill said, looking directly at Stan. "Stan, surely you've checked him for that gunshot wound Mark says he inflicted on the killer. Does he have one?"

"He has a wound on his hand," Stan said. "Mark could have been mistaken about where the bullet hit."

She looked down at the small bandage wrapped around his hand. "Take the bandage off, Dan. Let us see it."

Dan unwrapped the gauze bandage and showed them the cuts on his hand. "Glass," he said. "Not a bullet—glass."

The cops weren't convinced. "Did anyone see you break the glass?"

"Absolutely. Nick did. He disinfected it and wrapped it for me."

Stan nodded for Vern to go and check, and he dismissed himself from the room.

While they waited, Dan looked at Stan. "Mark was in a gunfight with that guy? What happened? Was Mark hurt?"

"He was burned," Jill said. "But he seems okay. I just saw him outside." She glanced back at the detective and chief of police. "Surely you guys have other suspects. If you know it to be a fireman—"

"A fireman?" Dan cut in. "Is that what this is about? The killer is a fireman?"

"If you know him to be a fireman," Jill went on, "you must have a whole list of suspects."

"We have two others we're questioning tonight, Jill. We just haven't been able to locate them yet."

"Well, maybe one of them has a gunshot wound. Maybe you'll find him soon, and you'll see. Meanwhile, you must realize that Dan is not your man."

"I don't want to think he is," he said. "But Dan, there are pieces that don't fit. You can't prove where you were when Mark was shot at the airport."

"I was *jogging*, Stan. People saw me—"

"We can't find anyone who did."

"Stan, if I'd gone to New Orleans, shot Mark, then driven back to Newpointe, I'd have been gone two hours, at the very least. I wasn't jogging that long."

"Like I said, we can't confirm that. Besides, everybody knows you drive like Mario Andretti. And you weren't home when they came to get you earlier tonight, and the night Francis was killed, you were allegedly at the hospital with Allie and Jill, but you disappeared for an unspecified period of time ..."

"*What?* I did *not*. I was there all night."

Stan focused in on Jill. "Jill, did you or did you not wake up to see Dan coming back from somewhere?"

Dan gaped at her. "Did you tell them that? That I left?"

Jill couldn't believe Stan had breached professionalism this way. "No, Allie did. Stan, he wasn't gone long. He was just in the hall. And I'd appreciate it if you wouldn't question me like a witness when I'm trying to defend my client!"

Stan wilted. It was pure exhaustion that had motivated him, she thought. They were all worn out.

"Can you prove that you were in the hall, Dan?" Stan asked.

"Prove that I didn't sneak out and kill Francis Bledsoe in another town? Yes, I can prove it! You bet I can prove it!"

"How?"

"Well ... there were others in the waiting room that night. Some of them had to be awake. Somebody saw me, Stan. Somebody had to."

Stan looked doubtful. "Dan, Vern and Chad found a bunker suit in your trunk."

"Yeah, so?"

"So why did you have it with you?"

"Because I keep scanners in my car and my house. Sometimes I hear a call and I go to help. I keep the suit in case I need it when I'm off duty." He gaped at each of them. "Oh, come on, Stan. Most of the guys keep suits in their trunks, and you probably have a scanner at home, too."

"Even Mark has a bunker suit in his car," Jill cut in. "I saw one in his car just yesterday."

"Yeah," Dan said. "Even Mark."

"What about the night at the florist, when you had a crowbar—?"

"Aw, man." He sat back hard in his chair and rubbed his face roughly. "It happened exactly like I said. I saw somebody, Stan." He banged his hand on the table, then winced at the cut as it started to bleed again. Tipping his hand up to keep the blood from dripping, he said, "Here. You must have blood samples from the killer. Take some of mine, Stan. It'll rule me out. And give me a lie detector test, truth serum, whatever you want. I'm innocent."

Stan reached for the phone to call someone to do just that, when Vern came back in. "I just talked to Nick, Stan. He says he did see Dan cut his hand, and he bandaged it up himself. But I asked him if he was sure Dan hadn't left the station before that, and he said he didn't know, because he was sleeping. I asked him if Dan could have already had the wound and broken the glass after the fact—"

"*What?*" Dan shouted. "Why would I do that?"

"To cover for a gunshot wound," Vern said, raising his voice over Dan's outburst. "The killer wouldn't have to be a genius to go back to where he was supposed to have been all night, make a big deal out of breaking a glass and cutting his hand, and then he's got an alibi."

Dan just stared at him for a long moment. "You ought to be writing movies, Vern. Your talents are wasted here."

"Oscar caliber," Jill agreed. "Stan, if this is a bullet hole in his hand, how come it doesn't come out on the other side? It's on his palm, for heaven's sake, so it couldn't have been grazed. It's a *cut! Look* at it!"

"I have O positive blood, Stan," Dan threw in. "What kind did the killer have?"

"I don't know. I'll have to call New Orleans and see if they have any results yet."

"Do it," Dan said. "I don't like being in the hot seat."

• • •

Less than fifteen minutes later, the telephone in the interrogation room rang, and Stan picked it up. He listened and jotted down something on the pad on his lap, then brought his eyes back to Dan and Jill. Gravely, he hung up the phone.

"What is it?" Jill asked. "Is it the results of the blood test?"

Stan rubbed his eyes, thinking, then focused on them again. "They found two types of blood in Aggie's apartment," he said. "O positive was one of them."

Dan jumped up from his chair, knocking it over. "I don't believe this."

"The other one was Mark's blood type."

Dan picked the chair up and slammed it down on its legs, then plopped back into it and dropped his head into the circle of his arms.

Jill was silent for a moment. Then she spoke up. "Stan, O positive is the most common blood type. What about the DNA tests?"

"Not ready yet."

"So where does that leave us?"

Stan turned his bloodshot eyes to Dan. "I'm afraid we're going to have to book you, Dan."

Dan looked up, his face burning. "Stan, you must know you're making a mistake. You know me, man. We go to church together. I was in your wedding."

Stan nodded glumly as he looked down at his hands. "Go ahead and book him."

Vern got Dan to his feet again.

"Vern, we played football together. You know me, man!"

Vern didn't answer as he led him to the door.

"Dan, I'm going to get you out of here as soon as I can," Jill said. "I won't rest until I do."

Dan turned to her. "You believe me, don't you, Jill? I didn't do this!"

"Yes," she said without hesitation. "I believe you. And I'll make sure they do, too, before it's all over."

•   •   •

Dan was distraught as Vern led him out of the interrogation room. In the waiting area a few feet down, Mark sat in a chair with his bandaged head leaning back against the wall. Allie sat next to him. His pant legs were burned, and Dan could see blistering burns on his friend's calves. Dan's anger melted, and he took a step toward them.

"You don't think I did this, do you, Mark?" he asked.

"No!" Mark got to his feet. "Vern, what's going on?"

"We're booking him," Vern said reluctantly.

"Why? Dan, we both said that it couldn't have been you."

"So how come they weren't convinced?" He looked at them both with a misty heaviness in his eyes. "Allie, you told them I disappeared when I was guarding you in the ICU waiting room. How could you tell them that? How could you even think it?"

"Dan, that's *not* what I said. I told them you were with Jill and me all night. That you didn't leave. They just asked me if there was ever a time when I woke up and you weren't there, and I told them about when you had walked back in from the hall. I believe you, Dan. But I had to answer their questions. I want the killer caught."

"Well, I'm not him!"

"We know you're not," Mark said. "Vern, I shot the guy in his right arm. Dan isn't shot."

Vern lifted Dan's bloody hand. "It was dark, Mark. You could have just thought it was his arm."

Mark's fight drained out of him, and he stared, stricken, down at Dan's hand.

"Mark, I broke a glass. Nick was there; he'll tell you. It doesn't even *look* like a gunshot wound."

Dan jerked the bandage off and held out his hand. "You tell me, Mark. It's just a stupid cut—doesn't even need stitches. Does that look like a bullet did it?"

Mark couldn't answer. Dan weighed and analyzed the confusion on Mark's face, and realized that even his best friend had some doubts.

"Aw, man," he said. "I don't believe this."

He turned away from all of them and started up the hallway, where he would be booked as the serial killer that had terrorized the town.

Chapter Fifty-Eight

Marty Bledsoe's parents lived in a mobile home near Metairie, right outside of New Orleans. It took R.J. Albright and Anthony Martin an hour and a half to find the trailer park. When they finally did, they saw a Metairie police officer waiting to make the arrest with them, since they had no jurisdiction there. They pulled up beside his squad car and rolled the window down. "Thanks for comin'," R.J. said. "Sorry it took us so long to get here."

"No problem," the officer said. "You said it was about the Newpointe killin's. You think the serial killer's hidin' out here?"

"We ain't sure," R.J. said. "We just need to take him in for questionin'."

"Well, the trailer you want is up that-away to the right. I'll foller ya'll up."

R.J. pulled up ahead and turned into the driveway.

When he saw that Marty's pickup truck was parked out front, he knew they'd hit pay dirt.

A brisk wind swept up, chilling them, as they reached the door. R.J. knocked hard. It was after 1:30 A.M., so they waited, then rapped again.

R.J. was about to knock again when something metal touched the back of his neck. He jumped and reached for his gun.

"Don't neither of you move." It was Marty's voice, and R.J. realized he had a gun pointed at him. Next to him, Anthony stood frozen, as well. The Metairie officer cursed and spat.

"It's me, Marty—R.J. Put the gun down. Me and Anthony just want to talk to you."

"You didn't hunt me down at 1:30 in the mornin' just to talk to me," Marty said, his voice quivering. "What'd you come for? You gonna kill me and my kids now, too? You gonna kill my folks?"

"We ain't gonna kill nobody!" Anthony shouted. "Marty, we're here on police business. Put the stinkin' gun down!"

"Turn around."

The three cops turned slowly around and saw the fireman standing barefoot in nothing but his Fruit of the Looms. R.J. would have been amused if he hadn't had a deer rifle pointed at his head.

"Did we get you out of bed?" Anthony asked.

R.J. almost laughed at the polite question. Didn't Anthony realize Marty could blow them away?

"I come out the back way when you knocked," Marty said. "I ain't gon' sleep through another killin'. This time I'm ready."

R.J.'s amusement faded as he heard the pain and self-recrimination in Marty's voice.

"Marty, I don't blame you for bein' nervous. But Stan sent us. We have to take you in for questionin'." He kicked himself. How absurd, to tell Marty that when his finger was over the trigger.

"Me?" Marty asked. "Why would you wanna take *me* in? I'm one of the victims."

"We just want to ask you some questions. You aren't the only one."

The porch light came on, and Marty's father peered out. "I called the po-lice, son. They're on their way."

"These *are* police," Marty said. "They're sayin' they have to take me in. Do me a favor, Pop. Call the Newpointe P.D. and see if they sent 'em."

Marty's father disappeared, and they waited while Marty kept his gun on them.

"No wound," Anthony noted.

R.J. nodded. "I see that."

"What are ya'll talkin' about?"

"Mark Branning got into a scuffle with the killer tonight," Anthony said. "Mark wounded him, but he got away."

Marty's face twisted, and R.J. saw the tears reddening his eyes. "Did he get Allie?"

"No, she's okay."

His mouth quivered. "You think *I'm* the killer?"

"No," R.J. said honestly.

"Why would I *do* that?" He wiped at his eyes with the back of his hand. "Why would I want to do somethin' like that?"

Flashing blue lights lit up the trees around the trailer as another Metairie police car approached. About that time, Marty's father stepped out onto the porch. "They confirmed it, son. Stan Shepherd sent 'em. Put the gun down."

Slowly, Marty lowered the rifle as another Metairie cop got out of his car.

R.J. relaxed. "Why don't I go with you to put some clothes on, Marty, while Anthony fills him in. Then we'll take you in and get this cleared up."

Marty nodded, wiped his eyes again, and led R.J. into the house.

Chapter Fifty-Nine

With Dan Nichols locked up and Marty Bledsoe in inter- rogation—though they had ruled him out—Jim Shoe- maker ordered Vern Hargis and Chad Avery to wake the judge to get a warrant to search Craig Barnes's home and patrol truck, while Stan tried to find Craig.

Stan tried to shake the misery as he stepped out onto the front steps of the police station at two A.M. Several cameras were setting up there, and a reporter dashed up the steps to meet him. "Detective Shepherd, we're told that you've made an arrest in the Fire Wife Killings."

"No comment," Stan said and trotted on down the stairs.

"Detective, can you confirm that it's a local firefighter?"

"No, I cannot." He reached his car and locked himself in, then tried to get his bearings as he cranked it and pulled away from the curb.

As he drove, his mind raced. As much as the evidence pointed to Dan, Stan didn't want to believe it. But he didn't want to believe Craig or Marty had done it, either, and the evi- dence suggested that it was one of the three.

He remembered Dan's face as Vern had taken him to be booked. Part of him hoped they'd done the right thing, or Stan would never be able to live with himself. The other part, the bigger one, prayed for some turn of events that would prove Dan's innocence. After all the prayer groups Stan had attended with him, all the Promise Keepers rallies . . .

He drove to Craig's house and found Vern and Chad already there. "He's not home," Vern said. "We're gonna have to bust in."

Stan thought that over. "No. Let me go back to the fire station one more time. I'll wake everybody up and see if anybody knows where he went. Meanwhile, you two go to the Eastside station and do the same thing."

They headed out in separate directions, and Stan prayed that they would find him. Maybe by now Craig was back at the station. Maybe he had sacked out there, and didn't have a clue that people were searching for him.

Stan cruised past the Midtown station; reporters still clustered around the door. He parked a block down the street, then cut through the yards until he reached the back door of the station.

The door was unlocked, so he went in and saw Nick and George Broussard sitting at the kitchen table. "Hey, guys."

They both sprang up when they saw him. "Stan, what's this about Dan getting arrested?" Nick asked. "I told you guys—he cut his hand on glass. I still have the broken glass in the wastebasket to prove it."

Stan didn't want to talk about it. "Look, can you tell me if you've seen Craig Barnes? Has he been here?"

"I haven't seen him," George said. "Stan, Dan would never have hurt Martha. You've got the wrong guy."

Stan went through the kitchen and into the back room, where three other guys slept. He turned on the light. "Wake up, guys. Come on, get up. I need to talk to you."

One by one, they woke up—Cale, Slater, Lex.

"What is it, Stan?" Cale asked, sitting on the edge of his bed and squinting into the light. "Has something else happened?"

"They've arrested Dan," George said. "Ain't that the most ridiculous thing you ever heard?"

"Dan?" Cale asked, standing up. "Is that for real?"

Stan wanted to evade as many of the questions as he could. He'd only come to find out one thing. "Look, I need your help. We're trying to locate Craig Barnes. Did he say anything to any of you about where he would be tonight?"

"Not me," Cale said.

He asked each of them individually, and all said no.

"How long since any of you has seen him?" Stan asked.

"I haven't seen him since supper," Nick said wearily. "Stan, why are you looking for him?"

"I just need to ask him some questions."

"About Dan?" Nick asked.

"No. Are you sure none of you has seen him since supper?"

"Absolutely," Cale said.

"Well, do you know of any place he might be? A favorite hangout, or maybe a woman—"

All of the men shook their heads. Did they really not know, or were they just covering for him?

"Look, guys, we're on the same side here. Are you being straight with me?"

"The same side?" George asked. "When you've already locked up one of us?"

"I'd give anything to prove Dan didn't do it," Stan said. "I don't like my job much right now, but I'm sworn to do it. All I'm trying to do is keep any more of our townspeople from getting murdered, and you can help me or you can stand in my way!"

"Stan, we don't know where Craig is," Cale said quietly. "But if we see him, we'll tell him you want to talk to him."

"Does Dan have a lawyer?" Nick asked as Stan headed to the back door.

"Yes, Nick. He has Jill." Unwilling to answer any more questions, he headed back out to his car.

Vern and Chad came up empty, too, and radioed Stan that they would meet him back at Craig Barnes's house. They were waiting there for him when he pulled up to the curb.

"He's still not answerin'," Chad said. "Time to break in?"

Stan thought for a moment. Barnes wasn't one to take it lightly if they did any damage to his house. If they broke the lock and splintered the door, they'd better be dead sure he was the killer. If he just had a key. . . .

A dim memory came to him of another key. The key Craig claimed he'd gotten under Mark and Allie's mat, the night he'd broken in.

"Just a minute, guys," Stan said, getting back into his car and grabbing his cell phone. He dialed the number of the police station and told them to get Mark to the phone.

Mark's voice was strained and hoarse as he answered. "Yeah, Stan. What is it?"

"I need to ask you something. Do you and Allie keep a house key hidden?"

"No, why?"

He wasn't surprised. "Not even under the doormat?"

"Especially not under the doormat. That's the first place anyone would look. Why?"

"I'll tell you later." Stan clicked off the phone and sat staring for a moment. Craig had lied. He'd already had the key. Did he have the Broussards', the Larkins', and the Fords' keys, too?

Despite the chill breeze, he was beginning to sweat as he got out of the car. "Let's do it," he said.

Vern got a crowbar from his patrol car and Stan broke the inner edge and splintered it until the door opened. Guns drawn, they went cautiously inside.

Stan turned all the lights on, and began to search the premises—for what, he wasn't sure. The house was clean, everything in its place, and it smelled of strawberries or apricots . . . A woman's picture—the only picture in the living room—sat on a table beside the recliner.

"Hey, that's Amanda Marigrove!" Chad exclaimed, bending over to get a closer look. "She died last year when her house burned down."

"Yeah, I remember," Vern said. "Pretty lady. Kind of quiet. Why would he have her picture?"

"Good question," Stan said.

"Wasn't she married?" Vern asked.

"Yes. Her husband worked offshore on an oil rig. He died a few months ago, though. He had moved to Gulfport. I heard he was in a bad car wreck."

Vern shot Stan a look. "Do you think she had a thing going with Craig?"

Stan shook his head. "No telling." He stood frozen for a moment, remembering the tragic circumstances of her death. Her house had caught fire in the middle of the night, and it was blazing out through the roof by the time a neighbor had reported it. The firefighters were told no one was home—the husband was out of town, and the neighbor thought Amanda was visiting her mother in Gulfport. Still, they had tried to search the house where it was possible, but by the time they had found Amanda, it had been too late.

The firemen at the scene had taken it hard, and Craig Barnes, who had not gotten there until after the body was found, had been outraged. But no one had suspected that his feelings were any more significant than those of the other firemen who grieved their failure. It was his department, after all, and everyone assumed he had taken the brunt of the guilt.

Could it be that, instead, he was grieving the death of his lover, and biding his time until he could take vengeance on the men who should have saved her?

Chad and Vern were checking out the other rooms now, and Stan went into the hall. There was a door there, and he nodded to the others to back him up as he opened it.

He swung the door open, and they saw a set of stairs leading up to the attic. The scent of strawberries seemed more pungent there.

Stan slid his hand on the wall until he found a light switch. When he flicked it on, a dim yellow bulb lit up the room above their heads, enough to see to climb the stairs.

Stan went first, his gun in one hand as he used his other hand to steady himself on the shaky banister. The smell of strawberries was getting stronger, and a strange sense of fore-boding fell over him. He reached the top of the stairs and froze.

"I don't believe it."

Vern and Chad came up behind him, and they all froze, gaping at the scene: a shrine, built of tables and shelves, with a kneeling bench in front of it, and scented candles of all shapes and sizes sur-rounding the large portrait of Amanda Marigrove in the middle.

"Weird," Vern whispered.

Stan stared at the altar as a million fragments of the same puzzle whirled through his mind.

"He was prayin' to Mary. Sayin', 'I'm sorry, Mary. I'm so sorry...'"

Could it be that he wasn't praying to the Virgin Mary, but to someone else? Amanda Marigrove? Had he called her Mari?

A chill swept over him as he saw an ashtray full of keys, and a clipboard with a list on the altar. His heart hammered as he walked toward it. "It's a list," he said. "A list of women." He looked up at the other two men. "Fire wives."

"You're kidding."

With gloved hands, Stan picked up the clipboard, and he saw the list with women's names marked through. Martha and Jamie and Francis were all marked out. Susan was marked through with a question mark beside her name. And Allie was last on the list. "What do you bet these keys are to their houses? He probably had them copied while the firefighters slept at the station."

"It's him," Chad said without a doubt. "Craig Barnes is the killer."

Vern bolted down the stairs. "I'll call an APB on him. If we can get everybody on it, we'll find him before daylight."

Chapter Sixty

A hospital was a luxury Craig Barnes could not afford. But it didn't matter much anyway. Yes, the pain was great, and the blood loss had been significant. He was finding it hard to operate that right arm, and since he was right-handed, that presented a dilemma when he tried to drive.

He turned down rural roads and saw old man Radcliff's farmhouse sitting out in the middle of its acreage. The old man was half deaf, decrepit, and lived alone. As he drove past the house, Craig hoped he was a heavy sleeper as well. There was the big barn in the back, just as he remembered.

He left his car idling as he got out and opened the wide door on the side of the barn. The door was big enough to drive a tractor through—but the mayor had forced the old man to sell off his tractor after one too many accidents that had come close to killing him or others. Craig drove his car in, cut off the engine, and closed the door behind him.

Breathing more calmly in the safety of the barn, he unbuttoned his uniform shirt, peeled it off, and carefully removed the towels he had pressed over the wound, front and back, to stop the bleeding. The towels were soaked, and still he bled.

He was getting dizzy. Quickly, he reached into the glove compartment for the bottle of iodine he had borrowed from a rescue unit. He'd found the unit parked in the Delchamps parking lot a few hours ago and had simply driven up beside it and asked the attendants for some iodine. Because he was their boss, they had simply handed it over, no questions asked.

By now, Jim Shoemaker and his crew probably knew that Mark had shot someone. Too bad he'd left Mark alive to describe what he'd been wearing. It would lead them to him. He'd known that he would be caught eventually; he had long since adjusted to that idea. But now time was running out, and he wasn't finished. They would catch him and lock him up, and Susan Ford and Allie Branning would continue to live, and Mark and Ray would never know the pain that George or Cale or Marty had experienced—the pain that he, himself, had experienced over a year ago. They had to know. They had to understand the pain.

He poured the iodine over his wound, front and back, and screamed at the intensity of the pain.

It was a while before the pain from the antiseptic eased, leaving only the raw pulsating agony that had come with him from New Orleans. He wished he had some clean towels. He opened the car door and stumbled out. There was a bale of hay against one wall, and he staggered to it. He had to lie down. If he could just rest for a few minutes, he'd get a second wind. He could then go after Allie, and finish off Susan—and then they could catch him, because it wouldn't matter anymore.

Chapter Sixty-One

The safe house where Jim Shoemaker put Mark and Allie at 2:30 A.M. was guarded by four police officers. It was a small house that had once been owned by Patricia Castor, the mayor. She had long ago vacated it for a bigger place more in keeping with her image of authority and power. Though she'd tried to sell it, the furnished house had been vacant for some time, and Stan had gotten her to loan it to the department.

Mark was waning as Allie walked him in, and she realized that the things he'd been through tonight would have worn out a healthy person. In Mark's condition, it had to be agony. He complained of a headache, and walked with a limp. She was sure his burns were causing a lot of pain.

The house was dusty, but Allie told herself she'd take care of that later. Her first priority was to get Mark to bed.

That didn't take much persuading. As soon as he was horizontal, his eyes closed. In no time, he sank into a deep sleep.

Allie was tired, too. Climbing in beside him, she was soon asleep herself.

• • •

Less than an hour later, a killer headache woke Mark. He opened his eyes and found his wife beside him, her finger touching her lips again. The sight of her filled him with warmth, and he ached to reach over and pull her against him. But she needed her sleep.

He got up, feeling as sore as a man who'd been beaten. The blistered skin on his legs stung, the pain competing with his headache. He wished he had taken a pain pill. Then again, it was better that he hadn't. He needed a clear head in case anything happened. He padded into the kitchen and opened the back door. "Hey, R.J.," he said.

His old friend looked up at him, smiling. "Hey, Mark. You get enough sleep?"

"I think so," Mark said. "Listen, heard anything from Stan? Are they still holding Dan?"

R.J. looked as though he didn't want to disclose the information. "I think so. But they're lookin' for somebody else now."

"Who?" Mark asked. "Marty or Craig?"

The cop hesitated. "I think you'd better call Stan for information, Mark. I'm really not authorized to disclose it."

"Okay," he said. "But is the phone working in here?"

R.J. nodded. "The mayor never had it cut off."

Mark went back in and dialed Stan's number.

"Stan Shepherd." His voice was fatigued and gravelly, and Mark knew it had been a long time since he'd slept.

"Stan, what's the latest?"

"Who is this?" Stan asked.

"Me, Mark. I heard you were after someone besides Dan."

Stan was quiet for a moment. "Mark, we're still holding Dan. But we have strong reason to believe that Craig Barnes is the killer."

"No way."

"'Fraid so. And since we put the APB out on him, we've heard from two paramedics who said he came by their rescue unit and borrowed some iodine last night."

Mark let that sink in. "Was he bleeding?"

"They couldn't see. He didn't get out of the car at all, and it was night. He just pulled up to their window and asked them for it."

"Still . . . Craig Barnes? Why, Stan? It doesn't make sense."

"There was something interesting in his attic, Mark. A shrine set up to Amanda Marigrove—remember her?"

Mark thought for a moment. "Yeah. The woman who died in the fire last year. He didn't even know her, did he?"

"Must have. He had a shrine to her, complete with candles and a kneeling bench, and a list of some of the fire wives with lines crossed through the ones who've been killed."

"You're kidding."

"Wish I were. Mark, tell me something. Do you remember much about the fire Amanda Marigrove died in?"

Mark struggled to think back to that night, but it was so long ago that the memory was blurry. "I remember that the neighbor told us he had seen her leave, that she wasn't home. We still searched the rooms, but some of them were so engulfed that we couldn't get all the way in. If we'd had reason to think she was there, we might have tried harder to get to her. But I think she was dead before we ever got there."

"What was Craig like that night?"

He closed his eyes and tried to remember. Craig had shown up late after hearing of the fire on his scanner. He had been rabid when they'd told him about Amanda. "Oh, he was furious. Ranting and raving that we'd dropped the ball, that we'd let a woman die . . . real emotional. He disappeared and didn't come back to work for several days. We didn't know what was going on with him, except that he was so angry at us for letting it happen. Believe me, we felt plenty of guilt, but I don't think there was anything we could have done. The house was so far gone when we got there."

"Apparently, he was obsessed with her," Stan said. "Tell me something, Mark. Who was on the shift that went to the fire that night?"

Mark thought. "Well, I guess that's obvious, isn't it? Me, Ray, George, Cale, and Marty. And Barnes has targeted all of our wives."

"Guess we've got our motive. That's why the fire. He wants you to know what it's like to have the woman *you* love burned in a fire. Only it was hard to keep them there unless he shot them first. He's getting desperate to get Allie," Stan said. "The thing at the airport proves that. Just seeing her dead would have been enough, and even if he'd gotten caught it would have been worth it to him."

The realization washed like a black tide over Mark. Dizzy, he felt for the chair behind him and sat down. "Find him, Stan."

"That's not so easy. We have an APB out on him, and chances are, he's listening to his scanner to find out what we know. We're having to be real careful. But you're safe, Mark. He's not going to get past the guards we've posted there."

Mark realized he was drenched with sweat, and his hand trembled as he clutched the phone. "Stan, go out and find him. Don't let another minute go to waste. Come up with a plan. Draw him out somehow. I don't care how you do it, but keep him from finishing the job."

When Mark hung up the phone, his head was throbbing harder. He went back to the bedroom door, opened it quietly, and looked in on his wife. She still slept peacefully.

To his frustration and dismay, he began to weep as his exhaustion and the horror of Barnes's betrayal of them all washed over him. He closed the bedroom door and sank down on the plaid couch in the living room, covered his face with his hands to muffle the sound, and wept for several minutes. Finally, he leaned back and looked up at the ceiling, as if he could see God through it. "Don't let me lose her, Lord. Please don't let me lose her. I want my wife. Forgive me for treating my marriage lightly. Forgive me for ignoring my vows."

He wiped his wet face with both hands, then his body shook once again with the force of his remorse. He had forsaken Christ, he had forsaken Allie, and worse, he had blamed her for his indifference.

He'd had choices—and he'd made bad ones. He'd had chance after chance to set things right—and he'd ignored them. Even in counseling, when Allie had pleaded with him to tell the truth about his feelings for Issie so that they could put this chapter behind them, he had continued to deny it. He'd even told her that his marriage vows said nothing about choosing each other's friends.

And then he'd told Issie that Allie didn't want to work on their marriage, that she was materialistic and a workaholic, that their marital problems were Allie's fault. Maybe Allie was right—maybe his friendship with Issie *had* been building toward a sexual affair. It was the natural progression for a relationship like theirs, after all. And she'd made no secret of her willingness.

How far he had fallen, how despicable he had become. He hated himself—and for a moment, he wished that Craig Barnes had succeeded in killing him at the airport. Allie deserved so much better. Allie, who had not taken the easy way out and gone home with her parents. Allie, who had suffered so much grief and fear.

And now, the threat to her life only reminded him that his marriage was still too precious to lose. It was a viable, sacred union under God.

He fell to his knees, folded his hands in front of his face, and pleaded with God to forgive him. "I love her, Lord," he whispered. "I love her. Please give me one more chance. Keep her alive so I can convince her to stay with me, so we can have kids—and help us to teach them not to make the same mistakes we've—"

The door opened, and he looked up to see Allie, standing in the doorway.

"Mark? Are you all right?"

"No," he said, wiping his face. "No, I'm not all right."

She stooped beside him, her face panicked. "Do you need to go to the hospital? Do you need me to call an ambulance?"

"No," he said, almost laughing. "No, it's not my body. It's my soul."

"Your what?"

"Allie, can you ever forgive me?" he cried.

"For what?" she asked. He moved her up onto the couch, and knelt in front of her. His eyes were still full of tears as he looked up at her. "You were right, Allie. My relationship with Issie, though it was never physical—it was too close. It was out of line."

She touched his face. "Mark, you don't have to—"

"Shhh," he said. "I have to say this. It was wrong. And I should have distanced myself from her the minute you got uncomfortable with it. *I* should have gotten uncomfortable with it! I had no business having long intimate talks with another woman, and I had no business lying about it, and I had no business leaving you and our marriage and blaming you. That night at the station, when you walked in on us—we hadn't done more than hug, Allie, I swear it. But in our hearts, well—it was heading that way, Allie. You were right. In your eyes and the eyes of God, I was being unfaithful. But I'm so sorry. I love you, Allie, and I don't want our marriage to end."

He laid his head down on her knees, and she stroked the back of his head.

He looked up at her again. "Maybe it took the danger of losing you permanently for me to realize how much I love you, but I need your forgiveness, Allie. And I need another chance. I want to go home with you when this is over, and be your husband, and grow old with you. And you don't have to worry about the drinking, because it's over."

He reached for her, and she went willingly into his arms. For the first time, he had a full understanding of the concept of grace. "You have another chance," she whispered. "You've had it for some time. I promised God when you were in the hospital that I would make our marriage work, even if I had to do it by myself. I'm committed to this marriage, Mark. I'm committed to being your wife."

Gratitude seeped through him like warm honey, filling him with joy and peace. He kissed her then, a kiss that was like a gift, a wonderful gift that he neither expected nor deserved. When the kiss broke, he led her back into the bedroom.

There, they renewed their vows to one another and consummated the reunion that they both intended to last the rest of their lives.

However long—or short—that might be.

Chapter Sixty-Two

Craig Barnes tried to sleep in the hay in the big barn that smelled of manure. But sleep would not come. Even though he had bled out most of his energy, he could not sleep. The pain from his wound was too great, and he was alternately feverish and chilled. He needed a hospital, but that was out of the question. He'd be okay if he could just find enough energy to finish off Susan Ford and Allie Branning. He couldn't leave the job unfinished—he owed it to Mari. He had to let their husbands experience the horror of knowing their loved one died a painful, screaming death.

He had listened all night to the scanner crackling and police and firemen talking about the APB on him, and he'd heard someone calling in from the "safe house" where Allie and Mark were being kept. If he listened long enough, he might get some clue as to where that was. Then he would go there, kill Allie, and set her on fire. He would love to tie Mark to a tree out front, to make him watch the fire blaze and the building fall around his wife. Yes, that would be justice. That would be retribution.

The hospital would be trickier, but he would get to Susan somehow. He hadn't figured out a way yet, but he would.

Yes, they would catch him. That was inevitable. But it didn't matter to him as long as he got the job done. Then he could join Mari.

"I'm coming soon, Mari," he said to the empty barn. "I'll be there when I finish the job."

He looked forward to the end for himself. If they didn't catch him first, he would somehow get back to his house, up to his attic and the shrine to his beloved, and he would take his own life right there on the altar. He couldn't wait to see her again. The thought filled him with renewed vigor, and he got up, shivering from his fever.

In the shadows cast by the moonlight playing through the window of the barn, he saw a form taking shape, and Craig stared at it, trying to focus. It looked like the filmy shape of a woman, smiling and reaching out for him.

His eyebrows lifted, and he staggered toward her. "Mari? Is that you?"

It *was* her, he thought as he drew closer. He took her in his arms and held her. He heard music—their song, "Unforgettable," the old Nat King Cole version, sweet and mellow, and he began to dance with her. "I've missed you, Mari. But I've made them pay. Did you see how they paid?"

But he sensed that she wasn't happy, for he had not finished his job. Two of the wives were still alive.

"I was just going out to get them, Mari. They'll be dead tonight. And I'll be coming home to you."

She faded. Like an image sucked away in a vacuum, she retreated, slowly, quietly, fading out of view until he could no longer see her.

He wept at her disappearance, but he kept dancing to the song that played in his brain, swaying as if he held her, as if she'd never left.

He shivered again, and suddenly saw flames coming up through the hay, but he smelled no smoke, nothing burning. The building still smelled of cows and chickens. But he could see the flames, could see Mari right through them, standing in the center of them, screaming. "Save me, Craig! You're a fireman. You can save me! Please! Help, Craig! *Please!*"

"I would have, Mari!" he cried. "But I wasn't there. I didn't know until it was too late!"

She kept screaming, shrinking from the flames, and he stood helpless, watching her burn. If only he had been on duty and heard the call. If only he'd been with her when it happened. If only he had gotten there moments sooner.

But he hadn't, and she had died, and all those firemen who had been on the scene had as good as murdered her. They had pretended to be remorseful, had attended her funeral with sober faces and dry eyes, had recounted the events as if nothing more could have been done. But he had known better.

"I'll show them, Mari," he whispered. "I promise, I'll show them."

Staggering to the barn door, he opened it cautiously. He couldn't take his own car; they would be looking for it. He retrieved the scanner from his car and then made his way out the door, holding onto the building for support, and saw the dust-covered pickup truck old man Radcliff kept parked under the trees beside the house.

He crossed the pasture to the truck. He got in, leaned over, and with his left hand he pulled out the crucial wires and hot-wired the truck.

As he hoped, it cranked, and he backed out of the spot it had occupied next to the house for so long, leaving a rectangle of tall grass where it had been.

His right arm had grown virtually useless. He drove with his left hand. He knew all the back roads, and took them as he listened to the scanner, trying to figure out where Allie could be. *Someone* knew where she was—someone who could lead him to her.

Jill Clark? Did she know where the safe house was? If he followed her, would she eventually lead him to Allie?

Not likely. Surely they realized by now how important it was to keep the Brannings' location secret. No, it was more likely that only a handful of police officers knew where they were.

Which ones, though? He tried to think like the cops he had known for years, tried to imagine which ones Stan would entrust to guard Allie. It was difficult to guess. Stan, himself, was the only one Craig was certain about.

He would have to follow Stan Shepherd.

Chapter Sixty-Three

The moment the press learned who the suspect was, Craig Barnes's picture flashed all over the nation. It was just a matter of time before they caught him, Stan thought as he headed out of the station to his car at 4:30. The problem was, they didn't have time. Judging from the level of psychosis apparent in his shrine to Amanda Marigrove and the desperate urgency with which he had tried to commit the final two murders, time was running out.

But he had a plan.

In the car, he turned on his scanner as he switched on his engine. Routine calls came across the radio, and an occasional report from a cop who'd sought Craig Barnes at one location or another, to no avail.

There was still time to carry out his plan if Mark would go along with it. He had Sid Ford guarding them, along with R.J. Albright, two of the finest, most trustworthy officers on the force. Allie would be safe with them.

He checked his rearview mirror before he made the turn-off to the safe house, and wondered briefly if the pickup truck behind him had followed him all the way from the station. He turned onto the street where the safe house was and watched to see if the truck followed. It did not.

He breathed a sigh of relief.

He pulled into the driveway of the house where Mark and Allie were staying, looked out all of his windows to make sure no one had followed, then hurried in.

• • •

Craig Barnes turned the pickup truck around, and turned onto the street where Stan Shepherd had gone. He cut off his lights as he drove past the houses there, looking for Stan's car.

There it was, parked at the fourth house on the left. Mayor Castor's old house, before she'd decided that she needed something a little more opulent. He might have guessed.

He drove down the street and pulled his truck into the driveway of a house for sale, the Krafts' old house before Alex Kraft had been transferred to Houston. There he waited for the right time to make his move.

• • •

So what's this plan?" Mark asked Stan as they all sat around the kitchen table.

Stan hated to ask for his cooperation in anything, with his head all bandaged up, and those burns on his calves and hands. He looked tired and sick, but there was a strange peace about him as he sat next to his wife, his arm protectively around her. At least something good had come of this—it might have saved the Brannings' marriage.

"My plan is to use your flower shop to draw Barnes out. He's probably listening to the scanner. We can let something slip about you and Allie staying at the shop. Then you go there, Mark, and we send Lynette with you as a decoy for Allie. If he's listening, he'll go there, and we'll have the place staked out from every angle. We'll get him the minute he shows up."

Mark just stared at him for a moment, and Stan could see this might be a tough sale. "So what about Allie? Where will she be?"

"Here," Stan said. "With Sid and R.J. It's the safest place for her."

"But it isn't safe for Mark to be at the shop," Allie argued. "I don't want him there. Couldn't you set up a decoy for him, too?"

"No. If Craig's watching, he needs to see one of you, so it'll look authentic."

"But I don't want him there. He's still recovering, Stan, and I don't want him to risk getting shot again."

"He won't get shot. We'll never let Barnes get near him."

"Then let me go with him," Allie said. "Don't make me stay here. If it's so safe, let me be there instead of the decoy."

"No way," Mark said. "She's not coming. I don't want her anywhere near Craig Barnes."

"And I don't want *you* anywhere near him!"

"Allie, you're the one Craig wants," Stan said. "He'll stop at nothing to get to you. It's my job to protect you, and I want you here. Mark will be protected. The person who'll be in the most danger is Lynette, but she's willing. She's a good cop."

Mark sat stone still for a moment, thinking. He looked up at his wife, his eyes gentle as he touched her cheek. "If this might end this terror tonight, baby, I say we do it."

"But Mark, you need to be in bed—"

"I'm fine. I can rest a whole lot better after Barnes is caught."

Allie followed Mark to the door, and as Stan went out to his car, the two stood in the doorway and embraced for a short eternity. "I love you, Allie," he whispered.

Tears came to her eyes. "I know you do. I love you, too." She breathed in a sob. "Please be careful. Please don't do anything stupid or heroic. Don't stand in front of any windows. Just promise—"

"Shhh," he whispered, touching her lips. "Calm down. I'm gonna be fine. It's time to trust the Lord. He's taken care of us so far."

"But I don't know what his plan is," she whispered. "I don't know how he wants this to end. I don't know what he wants to teach us."

"Whatever it is, it's right. We have to trust in that."

He kissed her then, a long, gentle, familiar kiss. "I don't want you to go," she whispered.

"But I have to so that we can go back to our own home and start that family we both wanted when we got married, and get on with our lives. I have to, Allie, so you'll be safe again."

He hugged her tightly again, then with tears in his eyes, said, "I'll keep in touch on the phone, okay?"

She swallowed hard and breathed in another sob. "Okay." Then she hurried back inside to keep from seeing them drive away.

•   •   •

From his driveway down the street, Craig Barnes watched the scene. At first, he thought that Allie was going out to the car with Mark and Stan, but at the last moment, she had stayed.

On his scanner, he heard Stan ask a car to patrol the Branning florist shop, and he laughed lightly, realizing that they were trying to draw him out by making him think that was where Mark and Allie were. It was a trap. But it wouldn't catch him.

It couldn't be more perfect. Even though Allie was guarded by at least two cops, he could get to her—even if he had to take both of them out. Then while all the commotion continued in Newpointe, he would drive to Slidell and finish off Susan Ford. He didn't care if he had to take half of the hospital along with her.

Then he would go back to his own house, to his altar in front of his picture of Mari, and he would sacrifice himself to her, once and for all. Then he would be redeemed.

Chapter Sixty-Four

An hour had passed and it was 5:30 A.M. Allie had spoken to Mark by phone twice, only to learn that nothing had happened. Craig Barnes hadn't shown up. Maybe he had the trap figured out. Maybe he wasn't going to bite.

Or maybe she just needed to be patient.

Sid and R.J. stuck so close to her that she felt claustrophobic, and she wished there were a television set to distract her. But Pat Castor hadn't left much in the house when she'd moved out. All they had was the police scanner, which Sid had brought in from his car to keep in touch with the outside world as they hid.

The smell of fumes drifted on the air, and she looked up at R.J. "Do you smell something?"

R.J. sniffed the air, and his face changed. "Diesel." He shot Sid a look. Sid looked around as he drew his own weapon.

Allie grabbed the telephone. "I'm calling Mark and Stan."

She brought it to her ear, but it was dead. She felt her skin grow cold, felt her heart race, felt herself growing dizzy. "He's out there," she whispered. "He found me."

Sid took the phone and listened, then slowly set it in its cradle. "She may be right," he told R.J. "Why didn't we have this house staked out, too? We knew he was smart."

"Calm down," R.J. said again. "We still don't know—"

The lights flickered, and all the power went out.

Allie screamed.

Chapter Sixty-Five

Mark was getting impatient. He'd been sitting at the shop with Lynette for over an hour, and nothing had happened. Sweating from anxiety, he paced the room back and forth, back and forth.

"You should sit down," Lynette said. "You need to rest."

"Where is he?" Mark asked. "Stan was so sure he would come."

"Maybe his wound has slowed him down. Maybe it was even fatal. We'll find him eventually, dead or alive, Mark."

"That's not good enough," he said. "I want Allie out of danger now."

"She is out of danger. She's safe."

"Wish I was as sure of that as you are." He picked up the phone and dialed the number again. Just hearing her voice would give him some peace. But this time, he got an obnoxious honking sound, more abrasive than a busy signal. The phone was out of order.

He suddenly felt nauseous. "The phone isn't working. Something's wrong over there." He slammed the phone down and frantically punched out Stan's number.

"Shepherd," Stan answered.

"Stan, the phone is dead at the safe house. I want to get over there right now."

Stan hesitated for only a second before he said, "All right, Mark. I'll be there to pick you up in less than a minute."

• • •

Allie heard a faint pop, then the sound of a bullet smashing through the wooden front door. She hit the floor. Sid fell virtually on top of her, his gun drawn, guarding her with his body. R.J. was in front of them, aiming his gun with one hand while, with the other, he reached for his radio.

There was another shot and the door flew open, letting in a dim ray of light from the streetlight at the end of the driveway. Allie screamed, scooted out from under Sid, and crawled to the bedroom nearest them. She flattened herself under the bed and slid as far back against the wall as she could, knowing even as she did that it was one of the first places he'd look, since there weren't that many places to hide. She hoped the darkness would shelter her, that dawn wouldn't come soon and bring deadly light to expose her. Panicked, she closed her eyes and began praying.

She heard another gunshot, and someone's body thudded on the floor. She closed her hand over her mouth, muffling a sob. Another shot, another thud.

She heard footsteps coming into the room, saw a flashlight beam scanning the hardwood floor. From under the bed she could see the fire boots and bunker pants he wore, and the fumes grew stronger as he poured more diesel around the room.

Suddenly the bed slid, and she was exposed against the wall. She looked up into the light blinding her and closed her eyes, waiting for the gunshot that had been meant for her all along.

• • •

A convoy of police cars headed with sirens blaring and lights flashing to the street where Pat Castor's old house was. Mark sat in the front seat of Stan's unmarked car, holding onto the dashboard to keep from being flung around the car as Stan tore through town.

They had heard R.J.'s frantic radio call that he'd been shot, and that he needed backup, and now Mark prayed desperately that Allie would be spared. But did Craig have her already? Had he already shot her and started the fire that would consume her?

They rounded the corner in a power slide, and came to a stop in front of the house. "Stay here!" Stan ordered Mark.

"No way!" Mark said. "I'm going in with you."

• • •

In the bedroom, Craig heard the sirens. He cocked the pistol. It wasn't too late to shoot Allie and start the fire. In fact, it would be perfect. Mark was probably standing out there now, and he'd have to watch while the house burned down around her. Craig couldn't have planned it better.

But what would he do about Susan?

He was sweating and shaking—not from fear but from weakness, for he'd lost too much blood. His whole side ached from the festering bullet wound, and he didn't have much energy left. He needed to get Allie and Susan both, and quickly, or his redemption would be forever lost.

But if he killed Allie here, the police would descend on him, and he'd never get to Susan. He froze for a moment, thinking.

"Don't do it, Craig," Allie pleaded. "Amanda wouldn't have wanted it. She was a good person. It won't bring her back."

The fact that she knew who he was, though the light blinded her, registered vaguely in his mind. She was crying, sobbing, and he wondered if Mari had cried when she'd realized her house was on fire. Maybe she'd never awakened at all. His energy revived when he thought of how casually the firefighters had fought the fire, as if there wasn't a human life involved, as if Amanda had meant nothing to anybody. He wondered if they'd treat this fire as casually.

Or the one at the hospital.

He heard more sirens, heard tires squealing to a halt outside, and through the windows saw the reflection of dozens of flashing blue lights. No, this wouldn't work. He should have gotten Susan first. But then they might have caught him at the hospital, and he wouldn't have gotten to Allie. He had to get them both. There had to be total redemption.

"Get up." His words were weak, breathless, and he hoped they didn't make him seem less in control. Allie had to fear him. "Get up!" he shouted, and she scrambled to her feet.

"Craig, please. I trusted you. I never would have thought—"

"Shut up!" He looked out the back window and saw cops scrambling into position. The house was surrounded. "You're coming with me," he said.

"Where?" she cried.

"To the hospital," he said. "I'm taking you with me. I can't let them stop me before I get there. If I have you as a hostage, they'll let me go."

Her face flashed on and off like a blue strobe light, flashing like the lights on the cars outside, and he felt as if he was about to pass out.

"Yes," she said. "The hospital. You need a hospital. I'll help you get there. Just give me the gun."

He managed to laugh and didn't lower the gun. "Not for me. I need to get there for Susan."

He put the gun in his right hand, which was growing weaker, and grabbed her with the other. "We're going outside," he told her. "We're going to get into one of the cars out there and head for the hospital. And I'm going to hold you close. They won't dare shoot me, or you'll die, too."

He pulled her against him and hoped she didn't sense how weak he was. "They're going to kill you," she said.

"Come on." He pulled her toward the front door. "If you make a move to get away, I'll blow your head off."

He could feel her trembling. That was good. She would be too frightened to try anything.

They reached the living room, and in the flashing blue lights still coming through the window, he could see the two cops he had shot, still lying there. He stepped over them, making her do the same, and headed for the door.

He pushed the door open with his foot and yelled, "I'm coming out!"

He could almost taste the tension in the air as he pushed her through the doorway ahead of him. Dozens of police officers stood with guns drawn, waiting. "I have a hostage!" he shouted. "Don't make a move or she's dead."

"Allie!" It was Mark's voice, and he heard the struggle behind one of the cars as someone wrestled Mark down.

"We're going to go out to get in one of your cars," Craig yelled. "And if anybody makes a move, she's dead."

He held her tightly beside him, as he headed out toward a squad car at the outer edge of the cluster of cars—the one that seemed easiest to get out. He moved slowly as cops with guns drawn and trained on the two of them slowly fell back and took new cover. When they finally reached the car, he opened the passenger door and pushed Allie in first. "You're driving," he said, closing the door behind him. "Crank it up."

She did as she was told, and he leaned close to her and pressed the gun against her ribs. "Head to the hospital," he said. "As fast as you can drive."

She put the car into drive and skidded forward. He looked back and saw Stan and the others jumping into their cars and pulling out. They would follow him all the way—but that was all right. As long as he had Allie, they wouldn't try to stop him.

• • •

In the safe house, Sid Ford heard the cars pulling away. The blue flashes faded. Had they forgotten him? Had they assumed he was dead?

The door flew open, and Issie Mattreaux and Bob Sigrest burst in, carrying flashlights. "Sid?" Issie asked. "Sid, where are you?"

"Here," he groaned.

Behind her, two more paramedics ran in.

"R.J.?"

No answer. He prayed that R.J. wasn't dead.

Issie fell to her knees beside him and began checking out his wound. "Were you shot more than once, Sid?"

"No," he managed to get out.

"R.J.'s alive," Bob yelled. "But he's losing a lot of blood."

Issie had a cuff around Sid's arm and was taking his blood pressure. He grabbed her shirt and pulled her down to him. "Susan. He's goin' after Susan."

"Calm down," she said. "We're gonna get you to the hospital. Your BP is real low."

"Susan," he said again. "Radio. He's headed for the hospital."

Issie hesitated. "Are you sure?"

"Yes. Radio. Have to warn Ray."

She pulled her radio out of its sheath on her hip. "Simone, this is Issie," she said to the dispatcher. "We have two police officers down at 232 West Lake Avenue. Sid Ford is conscious, and says that Barnes is headed for the Slidell Hospital to get to Susan Ford."

There was a moment of static, then, "Copy, Issie. I'll get the word out."

Before Sid could be sure that Ray had been warned, they were moving him onto the gurney and carrying him out to the waiting ambulance.

• • •

Traffic seemed to part for Allie as she drove down Highway 90, headed for Slidell. Craig kept that gun in her ribs, and she feared that it would go off at any moment, if only accidentally. Behind her was a convoy of police cars with flashing lights, and she worried that one of them would try to shoot Craig and hit her instead.

Next to her, Craig seemed to be getting weaker, and she prayed that she'd be given an opportunity to disarm him once they got to the hospital. Somehow, she would have to stop him from shooting Susan.

Perspiration trickled down her temples, and her hands trembled as she gripped the wheel. "Craig, you don't think they're going to let you waltz into that hospital and kill Susan. Every cop in Newpointe is behind us, and probably every one in Slidell will be waiting for us. They'll kill us both to stop you."

"No, they won't." He was panting hard. "They've lost too many already. They won't risk losing you."

She hoped he was right. She glanced at him, saw how pale he was, how he shivered with chills. His bullet wound must be causing him significant pain. Maybe if she just talked to him . . .

"I understand what you're doing, Craig," she said, tempering her voice. "I understand how angry you were that Amanda was killed. It wasn't fair."

"No, it wasn't. But I'm making it fair."

"What's fair about three women dead? Five if you kill Susan and me? How will that even things up, Craig?"

"That's how it has to be," he said. "It's the only way I can redeem myself to her."

"She's dead, Craig. You're not thinking clearly. She can't give you redemption."

"But I can get it for myself," he said.

"No, you can't. You'll only multiply your guilt. Craig, you're sick. You need help." She tried to calm her voice, tried to sound like a friend who cared. "No one knew how upset you were about her, how much you loved her. No one knew she was in that house. Killing those women hasn't helped, has it? It hasn't brought you peace."

"It wasn't peace I was looking for," he said in a dull monotone. "It was revenge. Retribution. An eye for an eye." He began to weep, a deep, guttural, wailing sound, and she found that she felt compassion for him even while she feared him.

"Craig, I'm sorry for your pain."

Her kind words seemed to calm him somewhat, and he wiped his tears away. "It's not personal, Allie," he moaned. "It's not about you. This is to hurt Mark. I'm not a cruel man. I'll make it be over quick for you. Not like it was with her."

Tears pushed to her eyes again, and she realized that there might not be a way out. He fully intended to kill her.

"What if you turned things around?" she asked, her voice quivering. "What if you found that peace you're looking for by giving Susan and me a way out—just what you would have wanted for her? What if you changed the ending, Craig—if you were the hero who saved lives instead of the killer who destroyed them?"

He was still weeping, but he kept the gun aimed at her. "If it was just you, I would. But then Mark would never learn. Ray would go on feeling no remorse."

"They've seen what it feels like, Craig. They've been afraid. You put them through it. You did. And you shot Mark and Susan. They've felt the pain. You accomplished what you set out to do. Isn't that what you really wanted?"

He was quiet, looking out the windshield, and she wondered what he saw. Was he weighing her words? Thinking about listening?

She saw the hospital up ahead. Her time was running out. "Craig? You don't have to go through with this. You can rest. You can go into that hospital and have them treat your wound. You can turn over your gun—"

"Pull up to the emergency room door," he said.

She didn't know if that meant that he was going to heed her words and get himself some help, or if that was just the only entrance he knew would be open.

The parking lot was noticeably clear of people, and she saw the scattering of police cars waiting for them. She put the car in park and closed her eyes, praying that God would watch over all of them, that no stray bullets would hit the innocent, that no one else would have to die . . .

"Craig, if you give me the gun right now, no one will have to know. We can go in, just like I'm your hostage, and once we're in, we can get you treatment. Don't you want help?"

He grabbed her arm. "Open your door."

She was trembling so badly that she could barely grasp the handle. "Craig—"

"Open it and get out."

She opened the car door and slid out, Craig's fingers still tight around her arm. Dozens of police officers crouched behind their cars, weapons drawn. Someone was going to shoot—some trigger-happy rookie would fire, and then Craig would fire, and there would be bloodshed all around.

Craig got out of the car, keeping his gun pressed into her ribs. As he put his arm around her neck, she tried reaching him again.

"Give me the gun, Craig. Give me the gun, and I'll walk you in. You don't have to kill anyone else, and you don't have to die. You know you're not ready."

He stood frozen beside her for a moment, holding her in an embrace of terror. For a split second, she felt how weak he was and thought he might drop the gun or give it over to her. Then she saw him shaking his head. "I have to keep my promise to Mari," he said. "I have to finish my list."

• • •

Mark crouched behind Stan's car, watching as Allie stepped out of the car. Then Craig came out beside her, staggering like a drunk man.

"He's weak," Mark said. "Somebody could get that gun away from him."

"He's expecting something like that. He'll be ready for it." Stan lifted a megaphone to his mouth. "Craig, this is Stan Shepherd. Don't go any further."

Craig didn't listen. He kept walking toward the entrance, with Allie tight against him.

Mark knew that if they disappeared inside that hospital, Craig would kill her. He looked around at the cops staked out in firing position, and realized that not one of them had the means to protect his wife once they were inside.

But he could.

Still crouched, he ran from one car to another, hiding to keep Craig from seeing him. As soon as he reached the building, he skirted the corner so that he was out of Craig's sight, and ran around to the admissions doors.

He burst through, and two police officers stopped him. "Don't go any further," they warned him.

"I'm Mark Branning," he said. "My wife is the hostage. What's the fastest way to the emergency room from here?"

"You can't go any further," one of them said.

"Watch me," he said, and headed down a hall.

He followed the maze of corridors from admissions, to the lab, to the radiology department, past a number of other doors and a dozen other halls. Finally, he saw a sign that said "ER," and an arrow pointing east.

There were several police officers already up ahead crouched in the corridor, watching the emergency room doors for Craig to come in with Allie. Mark tried to think. If Craig had come here to kill Susan, he would have to go to her floor. He wouldn't dare take the elevator—someone might cut power to it. No, he would take the staircase. He looked around for an exit sign, and saw it near the elevators.

Quickly, he ducked into the stairwell and waited.

●　●　●

Allie waited for something to happen. A gunshot, or another warning from Stan's megaphone . . .

Craig was leaning partly on her as he held her with one arm and kept the gun against her waist with the other. The emergency room doors opened automatically, then closed behind them, cutting her off from those outside who could have saved her. The security people normally stationed at the door were conspicuously absent. They had been warned to stay out of the way or risk getting shot, she realized. She hoped the police were hiding, waiting to disarm him.

"Where are we going?" she asked.

"Stairwell," he said. "Third floor."

She looked down at the gun pressing into her side. Craig kept that elbow against his side. He was clearly in a lot of pain, and Allie realized that he couldn't move his arm very well. If she hit him in that arm, it would send pain radiating through him, and maybe he would drop the gun . . .

But his finger was over the trigger. Just a slight nudge could make it to go off.

She headed for the stairwell, but stopped at the door.

"Open it," he said.

Dread rose up in her. They would climb those stairs to Susan's floor, and no one would stop them. Didn't they realize that they *had* to stop him? If he got to Susan, he would kill them both! Didn't they understand?

She opened the door and shuffled into the dark stairwell, wondering where the light switch was.

"Turn the light on!" he said in a panicked voice. "Find the switch!"

He moved with her as she felt around for the switch.

Suddenly she was hurled against the wall, and she spun as Craig was knocked away from her.

"Run, Allie!" It was Mark's voice, and she groped for the stair rail and began running up, as fast as she could, stumbling in the darkness as the staircase turned. Below her, she heard the sounds of a struggle, heard bodies thudding and curses and groans. She found the light switch at the top of the stairs and flicked it on, bathing the place in light—just as she heard the *whoosh* of Craig Barnes's silenced gun.

Allie screamed and threw herself back against the wall.

Chapter Sixty-Six

Allie slid to the floor, her hands covering her head, screaming hysterically. But over her screams she heard footsteps
coming up the stairs, and then there were hands on her shoulders, pulling her out of her fetal position, and a soft, soothing
voice saying, "It's okay, baby, he's dead. It's over, Allie. Come
here. It's over."

She surged upward and fell into Mark's arms. She wept as
he held her with all his might. Below them, she heard the many
voices of cops revved up with adrenaline, checking for a pulse,
shouting loud enough to wake the dead. One of them said,
"Forget it. He's dead."

Craig's plan for achieving his own redemption, doomed
from the start, would never be completed.

She heard paramedics rushing up the stairs, and the door
behind them opened as Ray Ford dashed in. He looked from
Allie to the body at the bottom of the stairs. He put a hand on
the wall to steady himself and sat slowly down on one of the
stairs.

"He's dead," Mark told him as he kept holding Allie. "It's
over."

She tried to control her sobs, but they came like hiccups as
Issie Mattreaux rushed up the stairwell. She touched Ray's
shoulder. "Ray, I just brought Sid in. He was shot, but I think
he's gonna be all right."

In shock, Ray looked up at her and nodded his head. "I
thought he was dead," he said. "They made it sound like—"

"He's asking for you," she said.

Ray got clumsily to his feet and went back out the door he'd come through. Issie came the rest of the way up. She stooped down next to them. "Let go of her, Mark. I need to check her, make sure she's not hurt."

"No," Mark told her. "Leave her alone. I've got her."

"But she could be injured. I need—"

"She was," he choked out, "but it's nothing you can fix, Issie. She's my wife, and I'll take care of her."

Issie stared at them, a dozen emotions passing over her face. "I understand," she said quietly. "I'm glad you're both all right."

Issie went back down the stairs. Allie realized that Mark seemed entirely uninterested. His only interest right now seemed to be in her, and in the words he muttered in her ear.

"Thank you, Lord, thank you . . . thank you so much . . ."

And she let that gratitude seep into her own heart as well. Gradually, the realization came that she was alive, and her marriage was renewed, and her life had a new start. It was a new day.

Chapter Sixty-Seven

Dan Nichols lay on the hard cot in the Newpointe jail cell, staring at the ceiling and wondering how on this green earth he had wound up in such a mess. The betrayal gnawed at him like a mole tunneling through his heart. Stan, Vern, Chad, Mark, Allie . . .

He heard his name and looked up to see Vern standing at the cell door. "Dan, you're free to go," he said, unlocking the door. "We found Craig Barnes. He's the killer, so we owe you an apology."

Dan hesitated. Were they going to make someone else the scapegoat now? "Just because Craig has a bunker suit doesn't mean he's a serial killer."

"He's dead, Dan."

Dan's face changed. "Craig Barnes is dead? How?"

"He shot Sid and R.J. and took Allie as a hostage. He was headed for the Slidell Hospital to finish Susan off, but Mark managed to get his gun away from him."

Dan slowly lowered back to the cot. "I can't believe it."

"Me, either," Vern said. He leaned in the doorway of the cell, then pushed off from the bars and stepped closer to Dan. "Look, man, no hard feelings, huh? We were strung out. We didn't know which end was up. We were desperate."

Dan shook out of his reverie and got to his feet. "You say I'm free to go?"

"You can walk right out." Vern held out a hand to shake, but Dan ignored it and pushed past it.

"Dan, come on. You have to understand—"

Dan spun around. "How could you think that I was a serial killer?" Dan stared him down. "No, I don't think I *can* understand that."

"But, Dan—"

Dan walked up the hallway, between the other cells, where drunk drivers slept it off and vandals waited for their parents.

Jill was waiting at the end of it. She'd been crying, he could see. Her eyes glimmered and her nose was red. "Dan, I'm so glad you're free. You're not going to believe what's happened. Allie almost got killed, and Craig—"

"I heard," he said coldly. "Where's my stuff?"

"Over here." She led him to the booth where he could pick up his watch, his wallet, the cross he wore around his neck. "Dan, are you all right?"

He looked down at her as he slipped his watchband on. "No, I'm not, Jill. I feel like the whole town betrayed me."

"I know, Dan. I'd feel the same way. But put yourself in their places."

"I don't care what their place was. If I'd been in the same position, I wouldn't have suspected Vern or Chad, or Stan, or Mark or Allie."

"You also wouldn't have suspected Craig. It was an unusual circumstance, Dan. The town doesn't know how to deal with so much tragedy. It went on for too long."

He headed out the door. Thankfully, all of the reporters had fled to the scene of the shooting, so he and Jill were alone on the steps, squinting in the morning sunlight. "Oh, great."

"What?" she asked.

"I don't have my car. They brought me in a squad car."

"I'll take you home, Dan," she said. Wearily, he walked her out to her car, took her keys, and unlocked her door. Then he got in on the other side.

He was quiet as she drove to the outskirts of town, where he lived. When she reached his driveway, she looked at him expectantly. "Guess I'll see you later."

"Yeah. Thanks for the ride." He got out and started up to his house, then stopped suddenly. Jill was the only person in town who had come to his defense, and he'd treated her like he was angry at her, too. Slowly, he turned back around.

She was still sitting there, waiting for him to go in. He went back, opened the passenger door again, and got in.

"Uh—I meant to tell you how much I appreciate you going to bat for me. It means a lot that you didn't seem to have any doubts about my innocence."

"Why would I doubt, Dan?"

"Mark and Allie did." She started to object, but he went on. "And you didn't. You went in there with both barrels loaded, like you knew beyond a shadow of a doubt that I wasn't the guy. I really appreciate that, Jill."

She was quiet for a moment as she regarded him. "It was easy," she said. "I'm a good judge of character."

He sat, thinking, as he gazed seriously at her. "Do you think, after this is all over, that you might like to have dinner with me some night? Maybe someplace nice on the Southshore?"

Her smile broke through the fatigue and tension on her face. "I'd love to."

"Okay then." He squeezed her hand, then got out of the car. "I'll call you."

"Get some sleep. And take care of that hand."

"Yeah, I will."

He went into his house and watched from the window as she drove away. He felt warm around her, close to her—a strange feeling for a man who dated widely but avoided feelings that might lead to something deeper than mere dating. He tried to shake it away, along with the fatigue and the distress, as he headed back to his bedroom.

Chapter Sixty-Eight

Nick Foster waited until Susan was out of the hospital—four weeks after Craig Barnes's death—before he held the memorial service the town so desperately needed to begin its healing after all of the deaths. Mark expected the whole town to turn out—except for Dan, who hadn't been to church or spoken to him at work since he'd been wrongly arrested.

He had left a dozen messages on Dan's machine, all of which had gone unacknowledged and unreturned, and had tried to convince Ray, who had taken Craig's place as fire chief, to assign them to the same shift, but Dan had managed to evade even that. He feared that Dan would never understand or forgive him.

"Who are you watching for?" Allie whispered, sitting on the pew next to him.

He started to deny he was watching for anyone, but then worried that she might think he was looking for Issie. "Dan," he said. "I sure wish he'd come."

"He'll come around," she said. "I know he will."

The service started, with Susan, Ray, Ben, and Vanessa sitting in the front row with Marty Bledsoe and his twins, George and Tommy Broussard, Cale Larkins, and Mark and Allie. Much of the town packed in behind them, until there was standing room only.

Mark held Allie's hand as Nick preached on healing, pressing on, looking forward instead of behind, and finally, forgiveness.

There wasn't a dry eye in the house when he was finished, and as each of them said a word to the crowd, the emotions grew even more intense. Mark wondered if he could even find his voice as he went to take his turn behind the microphone.

He cleared his throat—then simply stood quietly for a moment, looking out on the loving faces in the crowd, the people who were part of his family . . .

Allie's parents, who had forgiven him after he'd proven his remorse to them, were sitting on the second row. His father, dead sober though he trembled miserably, sat next to them.

There were firemen and cops, schoolmates and teachers . . .

And then he saw Dan, standing at the back in the crowd.

He cleared his throat again, and tried to find the words he'd been wanting to say. "As Nick said, bad things aren't all bad. I wish we could do some of it over. I wish I hadn't hurt one of my best friends because I was so panicked that anything seemed possible. I wish he could forgive me. Me and all the others— because we do know that he's incapable of such a horrible crime. We do know that, now that we can think clearly."

He saw Dan push through the crowd to the nearest door, and he was gone.

Disheartened, Mark tried hard to go on. "But some good came, too. I realized that I didn't want to live apart from Allie anymore. That I wanted to share a double rocking chair with her someday in that nursing home where our children would send us."

The crowd chuckled.

"I guess I owe that to Craig Barnes—or more likely, to the Lord. He can make something good out of something bad. And today, it's my pleasure to tell you, that Allie and I just found out we're expecting our first child. A Thanksgiving baby."

A round of applause went up over the congregation, and everyone cheered. Allie got up and came to his side, and Mark kissed the wife whom God had taught him to cherish. They had so much to look forward to. So many things to be thankful for. So much to rejoice in.

He only wished that Dan could rejoice with them.

•   •   •

Dan stood just outside the door to the small sanctuary, fighting his wildly conflicting feelings while Mark spoke. When the announcement about the pregnancy came, he smiled, surprisingly glad for Mark and Allie despite how he wanted to hang onto his anger.

Confused, he just stood, his mind shifting from his brief time in jail to the years he'd spent as Mark's friend. The amount of time he'd spent in jail wasn't the issue—it was the principle of the thing. He had the right to be angry.

Yes, he had the right. But he didn't *want* to be angry anymore.

The choir sang the final song, and then the memorial service broke up, and the crowd began to pour out of the small building.

He worked his way through the crowd back into the sanctuary. Mark and Allie stood at the front, hugging well-wishers with so much joy on their faces that he longed to share it with them.

He pushed toward the front, through the people, weaving back and forth against the flow of traffic.

Mark looked up, and their eyes met. Mark excused himself and started toward him.

They grasped hands first, then pulled each other into a tight hug, one that lasted much longer than either of them would normally have allowed. When Dan let Mark go, Stan was waiting, and Dan hugged him too. Then Vern and Chad grabbed him, then Nick, then some of the firemen—as if *he'd* been one of the injured ones.

And when he was done, Jill was standing nearby, looking so beautiful and so happy. He pulled her into a hug too, and laughed in her ear. Surprised, he found he didn't want to let her go. "So how about that dinner you promised me?" he asked, still holding her.

"Tonight?" she asked.

"Yes," he said. "Right now."

She laughed heartily against his shoulder, and made no attempt to get out of his embrace. "All right," she said. "Let's go."

• • •

Allie beamed as she watched two of her favorite people head out of the church together, and she breathed a silent prayer that something important would blossom between them. They both deserved so much happiness.

Celia touched her arm, and Allie turned and hugged her.

"I'm so excited for you," Celia said, her voice shaking. Allie pulled back to look into her friend's face.

"Celia, what's wrong?"

She tried to laugh off the tears. "I'm just so jealous," she said. "Stan and I have been trying to have a baby, too."

"You will," Allie said with excitement. "And they'll play together, and we can join some hokey mom's group and take our kids to the park. I'm selling the flower shop so I can stay home with the baby. We're going to have to cut way back, but it'll be worth it. And you and I can exchange recipes and babysit for each other ..."

Celia threw her head back and laughed. "Oh, if it would only hurry and happen."

"It will," Allie said, as Mark walked up behind her and put his arms around her. "I know it will. And there's no rush. We have all the time in the world."

Or so it seemed—and that was good enough for them.

Afterword

As a Christian writer, I struggle with the balance between the message and the story. I don't want to preach to any of my readers, nor do I want to read stories that preach to me. But each time I finish a book, I experience the very real fear that someone will read my book and be spiritually moved, but not know where to go from there. Will they know they need something, and follow a false doctrine that might come along at just that time, a false doctrine that temporarily fills some void in their life, but keeps them from ever walking through the door that leads to salvation?

It's possible. So I include this page, to let you know that there is only one way to God, and that is through Jesus Christ, who is the way, the truth, and the light. There are many counterfeit religions, and they're dressed up in pretty packages. They promise great rewards. Some promise license to live as you want; others exalt *you* as God; others tickle your ears through psychics and New Age thinking; others lead you to angel worship and offer "spiritual guides" who seem safe but are, in reality, demonic. But perhaps the most counterfeit religions of all is the one in which you sit in church Sunday after Sunday and tell yourself you're a Christian, when you've never entered into a sacred covenant with Christ, never died to yourself, never lived for Christ, and never borne fruit. All of these counterfeits offer cheap hope, temporary pleasure, shallow fulfillment. They also offer a miserable eternity.

That wonderful salvation through Christ is not cheap, temporary, or shallow! Our doctrine deals with sin—my sin, your sin—and only through dealing with that can we come to understand why Christ had to die. Only then can we have the promise—not of feeling good and important and guilt-free and unaccountable while on this earth—but of having *abundant* life on earth, and *eternal* life in God's presence. The most wonderful worship experience I've ever had is just a sample of what my everyday life will be like in heaven!

But I'm like a prisoner on death row who's been pardoned. All I have to do is accept the pardon and walk out. I have a choice. Why would I deny a pardon that came at such a high price—in fact, at the cost of someone else's death—and insist on finishing out my sentence? I don't know. But day after day, millions and millions of people choose to do just that.

Don't be one of them.

Tell Christ you accept that pardon today, and walk out of your prison into freedom. And if you've already done that, tell someone else, so that they can be pardoned, too.

God bless all of you!

Terri Blackstock

Shadow of Doubt

Chapter One

The thing about upset stomachs was that, eventually, they got better, but Stan Shepherd's stomach was proving that theory wrong. He hadn't slept a wink all night. First he'd had stomach cramps, and then it had turned to nausea, so he'd spent half the night in the bathroom standing over the toilet, but that brought no relief. His T-shirt and boxer shorts were soaked with sweat, but he was too weak to change clothes. A cold shower might help—except that the prospect of walking those few feet to the bathroom again was more than he could bear. He was tired, and his head ached. Still, there had to be something he could do. He grabbed the corner post on the bed for support and tried to pull up. His heart raced, and his breathing accelerated as if he'd just climbed ten flights of stairs. Wearily, he fell back onto the bed with a bounce.

Celia woke up and squinted at him in the darkness. "Stan, what's wrong, honey?"

"I'm sick." The words came with great effort between short raspy breaths.

He knew his retching in the bathroom had already awakened her twice, and both times she had scurried around getting cold compresses and glasses of water. Each time he had convinced her he felt better, and she had managed to go back to sleep. Now it was evident that he had lied.

She crawled across the bed and slipped her bare feet to the floor. The lamp came on, and she bent over him, touching his head, looking into his eyes, feeling for his pulse. "You're worse.

Stan, this isn't just a little nausea. I'm taking you to the emergency room!" She tried to pull him up, but he resisted.

"No, I'll be okay. I must've eaten something . . ."

"What?" she asked urgently. "I ate everything you ate tonight, and I'm not sick."

"There must've been something. Just . . . find me some Pepto Bismol. Baking soda. Something. And more water. My throat's on fire. Help me get in the shower first."

She slipped her arm under his and tried to help him pull up, but she was only five-three, and his six-foot, two-inch frame was too big for her. He managed to sit, but then dizziness assaulted him again. She struggled to pull him into a standing position. Instead, he collapsed onto the floor, worrying even as he fell that he would pull her down with him.

"Stan, I'm calling 911!" She was crying now. He hated making her cry. He tried to tell her just to help him back into bed, that he didn't want her to get all nervous and upset. Tomorrow was her birthday, and he'd made so many plans. She needed her rest.

He heard her talking to the dispatcher, Newpointe's busybody who would have the word of his illness all over town before the sun even came up. He wished Celia would just go for the Pepto. If she'd just get him some Pepto . . .

"Stan, can you hear me? Stan? Stan?"

He couldn't seem to respond, nor could he breathe, and the pain in his throat and gut felt like a knife probing around, but he was too weak to double up with the pain. She was pulling on him, trying to revive him, trying to make him sit up, and he kept wishing for the pink stuff . . .

He wanted to throw up again, but it wouldn't come, and he prayed for a breath, just a breath that could go all the way into his lungs, and for the room to stop spinning, and for something to stop the nausea.

And then he stopped praying as he felt her pulling him up. He fell forward again, this time into a deep hole, where it was dark and he couldn't find the end, and there was nothing to reach out for that would stop his fall, and he didn't know where the darkness would take him . . .

• • •

Mark Branning's fire truck was the first one on the scene. Though Celia's panicked call had been for a rescue unit, all of the emergency services of Newpointe responded to the call. That was policy, so even when there wasn't a fire, the fire truck headed out. Because they'd been two blocks over at a call for Mrs. Higgins, a lonely old lady who managed to set a grease fire at least once a month, they'd arrived at Stan's house before anyone else.

As he ran up Stan's driveway and banged on the locked door, Mark wondered what could have happened to the town's only detective to make his wife call with such urgency. Stan was in perfect health, or so it seemed. He wasn't much over thirty, and he lacked the "spare tire" that seemed to be a by-product of a happy marriage. Wasn't Stan too young for a heart attack?

He could hear Celia inside screaming, and he glanced back at the firemen behind him, George Broussard, his shift captain, and Dan Nichols, his best friend. George jabbed the doorbell and shouted, "Celia, open up! Fire department!"

In seconds she was flinging the door open, and she fell into Mark's arms. "Mark, help him! He's dying! Hurry! Please hurry!"

They bolted in as the sirens of the rescue unit and police squad cars grew closer.

"Celia, what happened?"

"I don't know!" She was sobbing too hard to get the words out clearly. "Do CPR, Mark! George, do something! Somebody has to help him!"

They got to the bedroom and saw Stan lying on the floor on his back.

George and Dan stooped beside him, but Mark stayed with
Celia, knowing either of them could administer CPR if it was
needed. "Celia, tell us what happened so we can help him."

She nodded. "I woke up and he was sick, and I tried to get him
to the bathroom, but he was too weak, and he just passed out ..."

The paramedics raced in with a gurney, and Issie Mattreaux
dropped to Stan's side and began checking his vital signs.
"What symptoms was he having before he passed out, Celia?"
she asked as Steve Winder, her partner, began recording Stan's
vitals.

"He mentioned stomach cramps, and he was breathing real
fast and he was dizzy ... He thought it was something he ate."

"How long since he ate?"

"Um ... what time is it?"

"Twelve-thirty."

"Six hours, then. Nothing since dinner, but we ate the same
things. But he didn't eat much because he wasn't feeling very
well before dinner. Said his stomach had been upset all afternoon. Please, can't you help him breathe?"

Sid Ford, dressed in his police uniform, came running in,
and stopped cold when he saw his friend lying unconscious on
the floor. Two other cops, R.J. Albright and Chad Avery, filed
in, and Mark wondered how long it would be before every cop
in town was here. Even the off-duty ones. The emergency personnel in Newpointe were a close-knit group, and they all worried when one of their own was in trouble.

"What's goin' on?" Sid demanded loudly, as if Stan's collapse had offended him personally.

"Sid," Issie barked out quickly. "Go get samples of whatever
you can find that he may have eaten tonight. Celia, is he on any
medication?"

"No. None."

"Any allergies?"

"No."

"Has he been drinking tonight? Wine, beer, anything?"

"No, he doesn't drink!"

"The truth, Celia," Issie demanded. "I know some of these guys are your church friends, but it won't leave this room. We have to know what he ingested."

"I *am* telling the truth! Stan doesn't drink!"

"Has he vomited at all?"

"Yes. Several times."

"Chad, go get some samples from the bathroom."

Chad hesitated. "Samples of *what?*"

"Anything you can find," she said. "I'll get graphic if you want. We need something we can examine for whatever's made him sick. Hurry!"

Chad dashed into the bathroom. Mark set his arm around Celia's shoulder, offering her feeble reassurance.

"I'm gonna be sick," she said.

He dropped his arm as her hand came to her mouth. Her face had drained of its color, and she shot out for the bathroom.

"Not in the same bathroom, Celia!" Issie shouted. "You'll contaminate the samples. Guys, help her. She must have the same thing he has."

Mark followed her through the small house, and she barely made it to the tiny bathroom off the kitchen. He stood at the door, embarrassed and slightly repulsed, as she retched into the commode. She grabbed the hand towel next to the sink and turned the water on.

"You've got it, too," Mark said.

"What *is* it?" she cried.

"My guess is food poisoning, but it could be some kind of virus."

She splashed water on her face and washed her mouth out, then hurried back into the bedroom. They were feeding a tube down his throat, but he still wasn't conscious.

"When is he gonna come to?" Celia asked.

"I don't know." They put an oxygen mask over his face.

"Why do you have the oxygen mask on him? Is he breathing at all?"

"There's evidence of cyanosis," Issie said as she worked rapidly to stabilize him.

"Cyanosis," Celia repeated, taking a step back. Mark watched her pale face change. "Blue skin. I hadn't noticed in this light." It was as if the word had triggered something frightening, something that horrified her. Mark started to ask her what it was, but the paramedics' rapid-fire exchange overrode him.

"Set up an IV of LR, TKO rate," Issie told Steve. "He's dehydrated."

"Blood pressure's dropping," Steve said. "I'll set up the IV in transport. We don't have time to waste."

They lifted him onto the gurney. Quickly, Issie checked his blood pressure again. "Dropping fast!" she said. "Call for the medi-copter to Slidell and I'll set up the IV. There isn't time to drive."

"Guys, whatever this is, Celia must have it, too," Mark yelled over the voices. "She just threw up in the other bathroom."

"Go get a sample, Mark, and make sure you mark it."

"But shouldn't that be taken by an evidence technician, instead of a fireman?"

"They're not investigating a crime, Mark," she said impatiently. "We just have to get to the bottom of this. The other guys are busy, so you do it. Celia, how are you feeling?"

"Fine, now," she said almost absently as she stared down at Stan. "Nothing like Stan was."

"Well, if his condition is any indication, you'll be getting worse. You might want to get dressed."

But Celia stood still as that look on her face grew more pronounced, that look that said something was cooking in her mind, something triggered by the word *cyanosis*. Finally, she flung open a drawer and pulled out some clothes. As she disappeared into the bathroom, Steve radioed for the medi-copter and Mark ran from the room to get the sample.

Issie shouted, "Have you got those samples, guys?"

"A bag of all the prescription bottles I could find," R.J. yelled across the house. "And the samples from the bathroom. Sid's still workin' on the food in the fridge."

"Even at the hospital they won't know what to do if they don't know what's made him sick," Issie said as they wheeled Stan toward the front door.

Celia was running out behind them. "Issie, you said he's showing signs of cyanosis. That's . . . that's a symptom of poisoning. I've heard of it in connection with . . . with arsenic poisoning. Tell them to test him for that."

"Arsenic?" asked Sid Ford, who had just come back into the room with a grocery sack full of jars and bottles. "That's Hollywood stuff. Why would you think that?"

"Because . . . I've seen these symptoms before. Real similar. I didn't think of it until you mentioned the cyanosis."

"I'll tell them to test him for it at the hospital," Issie said.

"Copter's on its way," someone shouted from the front door. "They're landing in the street."

Issie rolled the gurney out as Steve ran beside it, holding the IV bottle up.

A boisterous wind whipped up as the helicopter landed, and lights in other houses blinked on as neighbors began to spill out of their homes. They got Stan into the helicopter and gave orders to the medics on board, then Issie turned back to Celia. "Celia, I'll take you in the rescue unit," she yelled over the noise. "There isn't room in the copter."

"No, I have to go with him!" she shouted, trying to climb in. "Please! Please, I can't leave him." Steve and Mark wrestled her back. "What if he dies on the way?" she screamed. "You've got to let me go!"

But even as she struggled to get past them, the helicopter pulled back into the night sky, its wind whipping her hair wildly into her face. She doubled over with misery and wailed, but the sound was lost in the wake of the helicopter.

"Come on, Celia," Issie shouted over the noise. "We'll get you to Slidell as fast as we can."

As she got into the ambulance, Mark saw her staring up at the helicopter lights as they faded from sight.

Chapter Two

The shrill ring of the telephone pulled Allie Branning from a deep sleep, and she slit open her eyes and waited for Mark to answer it. It took two rings for her to realize that Mark wasn't there—he was on duty tonight. Wearily, she rolled over to his side of the bed and groped for the telephone on his bed table. Her free hand automatically went to her eight-month pregnant belly as she brought the phone to her ear.

"Hello?"

"Allie, it's me. I'm sorry I woke you, but something's happened."

She reached for the lamp and turned it on, squinting against the light. Slowly, she sat up. "Mark, what is it?"

"It's Stan Shepherd. He's come down with some kind of illness, and he's in a coma. They're helicoptering him to Slidell."

"A coma? I just saw him yesterday. He was fine."

"It happened during the night. The thing is, Celia's showing a few symptoms, like she may have whatever it is, too, and they're taking her in the ambulance. She's really strung out, Allie. I'd go there myself if I wasn't on duty ..."

"I'm getting dressed right now," Allie said, sliding out of bed and pulling the phone cord into the closet with her. "Mark, what kind of illness is this?"

"I think it must be food poisoning," he said. "We're not sure. I'm gonna call Aggie Gaston next. She'll want to be there with her niece. She may want to ride with you."

Allie pulled on a pair of maternity jeans, then stopped and held the phone with both hands. "Mark, is Stan going to be all right?"

"I don't know, Allie. Pray on the way, okay? I'll be doing it from this end."

"I love you," she said, suddenly stricken at how fragile life could be.

"I love you, too. Call me from the hospital when you know anything. And be careful."

Mark punched off the cell phone he kept with him in case Allie, in her delicate condition, needed to reach him, and called information for Aggie Gaston's phone number. When there wasn't a listing for Aggie herself, he asked for Dugas Gaston, her husband who had died over twenty years earlier. As he'd suspected, it was still listed under his name. Aggie, the eighty-one-year-old Cajun spitfire who played "Aunt Bea" to the firemen by bringing them at least two meals a day, was one of the town's staple citizens.

"Who you callin' now?" George asked him as he drove the fire truck back to the station.

"Aunt Aggie," Mark said. Though Celia was the only one in town truly related to Aggie Gaston, everyone in town referred to her as Aunt Aggie, for she seemed like family to them all. "I hate to wake her up, old as she is."

"You just afraid she'll be too tired to bring you some good eats tomorrow."

Mark grinned. "And you don't care a whit about that, I guess."

"Hey, I can cook 'em up myself."

"Right. That's why you show up at mealtime even when you're off duty."

The big Cajun laughed.

Mark dialed the number and listened as it rang once, twice, three times. Despite Aunt Aggie's vast wealth due to an inheritance that she'd invested in Microsoft before anyone knew who Bill Gates was, it was just like her to keep only one phone in the house. He pictured her getting up and pulling her robe on, as if anyone on the phone could see her, then turning on the light and making her way downstairs to the telephone in the hallway. As if he'd imagined it all just right, she answered on the fifth ring.

"Hello?"

"Aunt Aggie, this is Mark Branning," he told the Cajun woman. "I'm terribly sorry to wake you, but I thought you'd want to know that Stan and Celia are being transported to the Slidell Hospital. They've come down with some kind of illness, and Stan is in a coma."

"Oh, me, no!" she shouted. "Mark, how my Celia is?"

"Not that bad yet," he said. "Look, I don't know that much, but I thought you'd want to go over there. I'm on duty, but if you call Allie, she can drive you."

"I call her right now."

The phone clicked, and he slipped it back in his pocket.

Dan came into the garage, a barbell in his hand. "Hey, Mark, do you know what Celia was talking about? Saying she'd seen arsenic poisoning before?"

"No. I don't have a clue. She hasn't been in Newpointe but a few years, and she doesn't talk much about her life before she came here. She must have had some experience with it then."

"Yeah, I guess. Just seemed weird. Did you call Aunt Aggie?"

"Yeah," he said. "She and Allie are on their way over there."

He only hoped that it wouldn't be too late.

Chapter Three

Not for the first time, Issie cursed the fact that Newpointe didn't have more than a noncritical care hospital and that they had to drive over twenty minutes to Slidell for any serious medical problems. But that, she supposed, was better than driving the forty miles to New Orleans. She hoped that Stan had awakened by now, that he was feeling better.

"How are you feeling?" she asked Celia, checking her blood pressure again as Steve drove.

"Fine," Celia said. "I really don't think I'm sick. It was probably just nerves."

"But this could be how it started with Stan." She listened for a moment, then pulled the tips of her stethoscope out of her ears. "Your vitals are good. Blood pressure's fine. Stan was soaked with sweat, but you're not. Any stomach cramps?"

"No, none."

"Good."

"Issie," Celia said, touching her shoulder and making her look at her. "Is Stan going to be all right?"

"I hope so."

"Even if it's arsenic?"

That question again. Issie stared into her face, trying to read her eyes. "I'm real doubtful that it's arsenic, Celia. But even if it is, they can save someone who's been poisoned with arsenic, depending on how much he ingested and how long it's been in his system."

"It could have been in his system for hours and hours," Celia said. "Arsenic doesn't work immediately."

Issie shook the chill that came over her. "Celia, how do you know about arsenic? Was that in a book you read?"

"No. Nothing like that." Looking distressed, she raked her fingers through her fair hair and looked away. "I just knew someone . . . He had . . . real similar symptoms, and he died."

Issie kept her eyes locked on Celia's. "But lots of things cause stomach cramps, nausea, diarrhea . . ."

Celia wiped her tears away with a shaking hand. "Lots of things don't cause respiratory problems, burning throat, coma . . . and cyanosis."

Issie wondered if Celia's trembling had more to do with her own symptoms than Stan's. "Celia, I want you to lie down. We're almost there, and I'll wheel you in."

"No!" she said, as if that was ridiculous. "Issie, I'm not sick. I want to be with Stan."

"But you might be *getting* sick. We need to run a few tests."

"*After* I've seen Stan."

"No, Celia. Now! I don't want to wait until you've gone into coma, too."

The ambulance stopped. Steve got out of the rescue unit and opened the back doors. Celia didn't wait for the gurney. Instead, she jumped out and headed inside.

"Celia!"

"I'll give them whatever they want, Issie!" she called back. "But first I'm going to see my husband!"

Chapter Four

Allie and Aunt Aggie rushed into the emergency room and looked around for Celia. She wasn't there, so Allie went to the front desk and asked about Stan.

"He's being examined," the uninterested receptionist told them. "Just take a seat and we'll let you know something soon."

Aunt Aggie wasn't easily dismissed, so she pushed Allie aside and leaned over the desk, her eyes only inches from the receptionist's. "Take me to him," she ordered. "I wanna see him."

"I'm sorry, ma'am. That's impossible."

"Then where my niece is? Celia, his wife. You don't take me to her, you gon' be all over this floor."

The receptionist got to her feet and seemed to struggle with whether or not to take this elderly spitfire seriously. Allie would have been amused if the situation weren't so grave.

"Mrs. Shepherd is in an examining room," the receptionist said. "I guess you can go on back."

Aunt Aggie didn't wait for directions. She headed through the double swinging doors with missile-like speed, and Allie followed on her heels.

Celia was having blood drawn in an examining room, but other than looking pallid, she seemed okay. "T-Celia! There you is!" Celia looked up at her aunt and eagerly accepted her desperate embrace. The *T* prefix—Cajun for little—was one she used only on those she loved the most.

Allie touched her chest and breathed a sigh of relief. "Thank God you're all right."

But she wasn't, not really. Allie could see the terror in her red eyes as she looked up at them. "He's dying."

"Is that what the doctor said?" Allie asked.

"No," Celia said. "They haven't told me anything."

"Then you don't know that he's dying. The question right now is, how are you?"

Celia rolled her eyes as if that was incidental. "I'm fine except for a little nausea that comes and goes. But Stan can't breathe, and he's in a coma." Aunt Aggie's bony hand reached out to grip hers as the nurse finished drawing her blood, and Celia turned her troubled eyes to the old woman. "Aunt Aggie, what if he dies?"

The old woman pulled her niece against her as if she were a child and stroked her pale blonde hair. "He won't," she said.

"God wouldn't do that to me twice, would he?"

"If there was a God, I know he wouldn't," Aunt Aggie evaded.

Allie's heart melted with compassion as she remembered that Celia had lost a husband before. "Celia, I forgot you lost your first husband. I know that makes you more afraid that you'll have to suffer that again. But he's in good hands."

"Nathan was in good hands, and he died."

Allie didn't know how to answer that. She assumed Nathan had been her first husband, but since she didn't know how he'd died or why, she was at a loss for words. How could she comfort Celia? She didn't know. At this point, she could only pray.

Chapter Five

Sid Ford found Celia, Allie, and Aggie in the waiting room when he arrived at the hospital. He was just trying to get an update on Stan when a doctor dressed in scrubs came through the double doors and found them.

"Mrs. Shepherd?" he asked, and Celia sprang to her feet.

"How is he?"

"Still critical. But I wanted to let you know that we have been able to confirm that your husband's been poisoned with arsenic."

"*Arsenic?*" Aunt Aggie's reaction resounded in the big waiting room, and the handful of others waiting to be treated turned to look. "You tellin' me *this* is arsenic? *Celia!*"

Stunned, Sid watched Celia sink back into her chair and cover her face with both hands.

"What about Celia?" Allie asked the doctor. "Was she poisoned?"

Sid looked up at the doctor, waiting for the crucial answer.

"No, she wasn't. We didn't find any traces of arsenic in her blood or urine. Just in his."

"Then look again," Aunt Aggie insisted. "She been throwin' up. Don't take a genius."

"We're running some other tests on her, but the lab isn't very well staffed at night, and they're concentrating on Stan right now."

"Yes," Celia blurted. "That's what they should do. You can save him, now that you know, can't you? There's got to be an antidote . . ."

"We're giving him dimercaprol to bind the arsenic, and we're treating him for dehydration, shock—"

"Shock?" Sid cut in.

The doctor looked back at Sid over his shoulder, seeing him for the first time.

"His body's been traumatized," the doctor explained. "We're also treating him for fluid on the lungs, and we're watching his kidneys because arsenic will sometimes cause kidney failure. It's too early to tell. We may have to put him on dialysis before it's over. There's also a danger of liver damage, but we're monitoring that, as well."

"Doctor, is he going to die?"

Sid held his breath, waiting for the verdict on everyone's mind.

"We're doing everything we can, Mrs. Shepherd."

It wasn't the answer Sid had hoped for, and his heart plummeted. The idea that his friend could die was too much to bear. He choked back the emotion in his throat as the doctor left them. Arsenic. Stan had been poisoned. As the truth sank into his heart, he understood that the case had just changed from personal illness to attempted homicide.

Someone had tried to murder Stan Shepherd.

He turned his eyes back to Celia and watched her lean back against the wall. Aggie seemed to be in shock since hearing that it was arsenic, and now she stared at Celia with eyes that said there was more to this than Sid knew.

A million questions rushed into his mind, but one seemed to flash urgently in neon colors, demanding an instant answer. How had Celia known? Sid stooped in front of Celia. His voice trembled. "Celia, I need to ask you a few questions. And I need you to be honest with me."

There was a certain resignation in her expression, an expectation that disturbed him.

"Celia, how did you know he was poisoned with arsenic?"

"I *didn't* know." She wiped her tears and squeezed her eyes shut. "Not for sure. But I've seen this before. All the symptoms . . ."

"That's what you said." He tried to keep his voice gentle, realizing it wouldn't pay to put her on the defensive. But his heart was pounding, and his breath was rapid. "When, Celia? When have you seen someone else poisoned with arsenic?"

Celia's mouth twisted as she tried to hold back her tears. She averted her eyes, unable to look at him.

Allie was sitting on one side of her, stroking Celia's hair, waiting for a response that made some sense, but even she seemed to be struck by Celia's struggle. Aunt Aggie, on the other side of Celia, looked as miserable, as expectant, as her niece.

"Tell him, *sha*." Her voice broke on the Cajun endearment that bore little resemblance to its French root, *chere*. "He gon' find out anyway."

Celia covered her face with both hands and sat frozen for a moment. Sid waited, holding his breath, trying to imagine what it was she had to tell him. It took more physical effort to wait, motionless, than it would have to throw her across the room. The force of his will prevailed.

Slowly, she slid her hands down her face, swallowed back her tears, and looked Sid in the eye. "I was married before," she said. Her lips quivered as she got the words out. "My first husband died . . . of arsenic poisoning."

Sid's face went slack as he stared at her, and Allie caught her breath. For a moment, he couldn't speak, but somehow he managed to find his voice. "Who poisoned your first husband?" he asked finally.

She closed her eyes again, and Aunt Aggie's face got tighter. Allie seemed to wait for a pat answer that Sid suspected would not come. "I don't know."

"You don't know?" he prodded. "They never arrested nobody? They never had a suspect?"

"No," Aunt Aggie interjected. "Now, leave her alone. She upset. Can't you see?"

Sid forgot his resolution to speak gently. Through his teeth, he said, "Aunt Aggie, there's been a murder attempt on a Newpointe police officer. I wanna know who did it, and I wanna know as soon as possible. Now if this is connected to the first murder, I need to know everything. I either have to ask her here, or at the station. Which do you want, Celia?"

"I'm callin' a lawyer," Aunt Aggie said, getting to her feet. "I'm callin' Jill Clark."

Sid looked up at her, frowning. "Why would she need a lawyer?"

"Because I see where this is goin', and she—"

Celia grabbed Aggie's hand to stop her. "Aunt Aggie, I can handle this!" She turned her big, pale blue eyes back to Sid. "There was one suspect," she said as her face reddened. "And one arrest."

"And was there a conviction?" Sid asked.

"No. The suspect didn't do it. It was all a mistake. There was never a conviction."

"Mistakes don't repeat theirselves like this, Celia." Sid's tone was growing louder. "Who was it? Maybe they're at it again."

"Apparently they are!" she cried, getting to her feet and moving away from him. Crossing her arms across her stomach, she sucked in another sob. "But not the person who was tried for it. Maybe the person who really did it, but since the police stopped looking and never found the real killer, we never knew . . ."

Sid was losing his patience. He stood up and faced her. "Celia, who was tried for killing your husband?"

She turned away from him. There was a moment of silence as he stared at her back, fighting the urge to shake her until the truth spilled out. "Celia, I'm askin' you a question. I need a answer!"

She spun back around. "Me, okay?" she yelled. "I was the suspect! But I ... didn't ... do it ..."

Sid felt as if he'd been poled in the stomach.

"*What?*" Incredulous, Allie got to her feet. "*You* were?"

Aunt Aggie put her arms around Celia and sat her back down. "She didn't do nothin', Sid," she said. "Stan knew, 'fore he married her. Celia was a victim, and they pinned her with the crime. The killer was never caught, and now it happened again."

Sid stood frozen, letting the words sink in.

"Celia," Allie said in a disbelieving whisper. "Why didn't you tell me? When Mark was in the hospital, you told me about your first husband, that he'd been sick and died, but you never said—"

"Why would I want people to know that I was arrested for my husband's murder?" Celia asked through her teeth. "When I came to Newpointe, I half expected everyone to know. The news coverage in Jackson seemed so overwhelming that I thought everyone in the world knew. But no one knew in Newpointe, and it was so good to get away from all that. Stan was the only person I told, besides Aunt Aggie, and he loved me anyway." Allie looked away, focusing on a spot on the wall. Sid kept his eyes fixed on Celia. "Allie, look at me. Sid?"

They both met her eyes.

"You know I couldn't do something like that," she said. "I love Stan. And I loved Nathan. I thought I'd never get over it. And then I was thrown in jail ..." Her face grew more crimson with each word, and she began to sob, but she managed to spill all the words out on a rush. "... and they wouldn't let me out on bond, so I was in jail for months and months ... and my parents believed the lies and turned their backs on me ... and the press wrote scathing articles about me ... and I wanted to die more than anything in the world."

"But she didn't *die*," Aunt Aggie said angrily, lifting her chin high. "They let her off, and she come here to live with me.

You know her, Allie, and you know what kind of person she is. You do, too, Sid. You know, don't you?"

Sid was shaking his head, expressionless, almost paralyzed by what she'd told him. His eyes were stinging, whether from grief over his poisoned friend's plight, or mourning over what he was learning about Celia, he wasn't sure. Was this news grounds for an arrest? If Celia wasn't his friend, would he have already read her her rights?

"Just listen," she pleaded, as if she could read the thoughts reeling through his mind. "I just want to be with Stan. I just want to make sure he's okay . . . Whatever you have to do, do it later, okay? You can wait. I'll tell you everything that happened, even get you a transcript of the depositions and the trial, whatever you want. Just let me stay here with Stan. I need to be here with him."

Sid suddenly felt very old, like one of those Van Gogh portraits of wizened age and weariness. Maybe he'd been at this job way too long. He wished he could talk to Stan and ask what he would have done if the shoe had been on the other foot. The thought of arresting Celia seemed almost as painful as the knowledge that Stan could die. If he woke up, the arrest itself might kill him.

He tried to run the facts through his mind. Arrests were made on the basis of current evidence, not past history. He didn't know yet what the evidence was, since they hadn't considered the Shepherds' house a crime scene.

Still, she needed to be questioned, not in a hospital waiting room, but at the police station where accurate records could be kept of what she said—where other law enforcement personnel who were thinking clearly could interrogate her.

"Celia, I need to take you back to Newpointe. We're gonna need to question you further."

"No!" she cried. "No, Sid, please. I have to know if he's all right! Please! You know I didn't do this!"

"Celia, let's do this easy," he said, trying to keep his voice low, despite the fact that others in the waiting room watched attentively for the gossip to take back home, and the nurse stood at the receptionist's desk, staring as if she watched some historical event unfold: *Where were you the day Celia Shepherd was hauled in?* Celia closed her hand over her mouth, half hiding, half muffling her sobs, and he hoped she wouldn't make this harder for him.

Finally, she got to her feet. Wiping her eyes with a trembling hand, she turned back to Allie. "Call his parents," she said. "They need to be here. Somebody might have to give consent for treatment." Her voice broke on a sob. "Tell them I'll be back as soon as they're finished with me. And . . . if he wakes up . . . tell him I love him." Aunt Aggie wrapped her arms around her, and huddled together, they headed outside.

As the car pulled off, Celia wailed in the backseat like a mother being separated from her young. He looked out the window and saw Allie standing at the emergency room door, staring at them, shocked, as they drove away.

Chapter Six

Allie watched through a blur of tears as the police car drove out of sight. The blue lights on Sid's squad car had a haze around them, lending to the feeling that this was a dream and nothing more. But it was real, and Allie didn't know what to do.

For a moment, she thought of getting into the car and following them to the police station, but then she remembered Celia's plea for her to call Stan's parents.

She tried to think in sequence, tried to make some sense of all the whirling facts, and finally decided to go to the pay phone.

She needed to call Stan's parents. She knew them from church. Stan's father, a retired detective, was a deacon, and his mother was the organist. They lived on Bonaparte in that beautiful little house covered with jasmine and kudzu, and they had that dachshund that barked when cars drove by.

Why couldn't she think of their names? Mr. and Mrs. Shepherd. Burt and Hortense? No, but close. Bart . . . and Hester . . . Hannah . . . Yes, Hannah!

She called for information and asked for the number, only vaguely realizing that she hadn't needed their first names, for they were the only other Shepherds in Newpointe. She wiped the tears from her face as the phone rang, and after a moment, Bart answered.

"Hello?"

"Mr. Shepherd? This is Allie Branning. I'm sorry to wake you, but I'm afraid I have some bad news. Has anyone called you yet?"

"About what? What is it, Allie?"

"It's Stan. He's taken sick and is at the hospital in Slidell. He's not doing very well."

"Sick?" His voice was more urgent now. "Sick how?"

"He's in a coma, Mr. Shepherd. I think you'd better come."

"Where's Celia?" he asked.

"She's . . . she's busy . . . all the turmoil, you know. I thought I should call." She closed her eyes and told herself that it would do no good to tell them about poison and murder and interrogations . . . not yet.

"We'll be right there, Allie," he said quickly.

She hung up the phone and pressed her forehead against the wall. Desperately, she tried to think of the next logical step. What could she do for Celia?

Jill, she thought. She could call Jill, their good friend and the best lawyer in town. Jill would know what to do for Celia. Punching in her long-distance code, she called Jill. Jill, who frequently got calls in the middle of the night from drunk drivers who needed a lawyer, picked up on the second ring.

"Jill Clark."

"Jill, this is Allie. If you're lying in bed, you might want to sit up, turn on the light, and shake the cobwebs out of your head so you can hear what I'm saying."

Jill hesitated a moment. "Allie, what is it? Are you crying?"

Allie took a deep breath and wished for a tissue so she could blow her nose. "Where do I start? Jill, tonight Stan Shepherd was poisoned with arsenic. He's in a coma."

"That's not funny, Allie. Is this one of those jokes where you shock me with some horrible story so the real one doesn't seem so bad?"

"No joke, Jill. And it gets worse. Sid Ford just took Celia in for questioning."

"*Celia?*"

"Jill, remember in the hospital earlier this year when she told us her first husband had died?"

"Yes, I remember."

"What she didn't tell us was that he had died of arsenic poisoning, and she was tried for the murder."

There was no answer on the other end.

"Jill, are you there?"

"Yes, I heard you." The words came out strained, breathy. "Allie, are you sure of all this?"

"Yes. She said she wasn't convicted, and when they let her go, she came here to live with Aunt Aggie."

"So Sid assumes that she did this to Stan," Jill said, as if talking to herself.

"I hate to say it, but it's an easy assumption."

"Easy, maybe, but not necessarily right. How long ago did they take her in?"

"A few minutes. They're on their way to Newpointe. Aunt Aggie's with her."

"Good," Jill said. "I'll be at the station when they get there."

"Thanks, Jill."

"Allie, remember something, okay? Remember the Celia we know. Don't jump to the same conclusions that Sid did. I've seen a lot of cases that aren't as they seem."

"Sure, I know. And she couldn't have done it. She loves Stan."

But even as she said the words, confusion was taking root in the back of her mind.

Chapter Seven

The fire truck was just pulling into its garage as Jill Clark parked her car in front of the adjacent police department and got out. She heard her name called and peered across the lawn. In the light from the street lamp, she saw Dan Nichols heading toward her. He was tall, six-four, at least, and built like an athlete. Even in the darkness, his green eyes were startling. As always, the heaviness in her heart lightened at the sight of him, and she waited with a smile on her face while he cut across the grass.

"Hey, Counselor," he said in that deep voice of his before he pressed a kiss on her lips. They'd grown close over the last few months, though they were taking things slow. Dan's reputation as a love-'em-and-leave-'em type kept Jill on her guard. "You didn't tell me you'd be making a trip over here tonight."

"Didn't know. Something's come up."

"Does it have anything to do with Stan Shepherd?"

"Yes, actually."

"Have they determined if it was poisoning?"

"I'm afraid so."

"Then . . . do they know who did it?"

"Not yet. They're bringing someone in for questioning."

He took a step back and regarded her shadow-laden face in what there was of the light. "You're not representing somebody who would poison a police officer, are you?"

She sighed. "Dan, I don't really think I can talk about this right now. I haven't been asked to take the case yet. But this particular person is innocent—there's not a doubt in my mind."

He frowned. "It's someone you know, isn't it? Who, Jill? I'll find out soon enough."

She thought about telling him, then decided against it. Yes, he would find out, but until she knew for sure that Celia was a suspect, the words weren't going to come out of her mouth.

Just then a squad car with lights flashing pulled to the curb, and Sid Ford got out. "I've got to go, Dan," she said. "I'll call you later."

He stood there watching as she hurried across the lawn to the car. Celia got out, followed by her Aunt Aggie, and Jill glanced back over her shoulder. Dan was standing there watching them, clearly trying to determine if Celia was the suspect. She didn't have time to worry about Celia's reputation now.

"Celia!" she said as she approached her friend with a hug. "Allie called me, and I came right down."

"Oh, thank goodness!" Celia's eyes were red and her nose was stopped up from crying. She was trembling. "Jill, I didn't do this! I didn't do it! I just want to get back to Stan and be with him—"

"Celia, I believe you. Do you want me to represent you?"

"Yes! Oh, please—"

She was beginning to sob again, and Aunt Aggie, who looked very tired, put her arm around her. "Don'tcha worry about money, Jill. I'll pay arrything."

"I'm not worried about that," Jill said, almost offended. She looked up at Sid, who looked almost as troubled as Celia. "Sid, I need to consult with my client."

"All right," he said. "Take the interrogation room."

"Let's go on in," Jill said.

As they walked up the sidewalk to the police station, Jill saw Dan standing in front of the door. "Celia?" he asked tentatively.

Jill shot a pleading look up at him. "It's all a mistake, Dan. Please don't let word get out. We'll have it all cleared up before daybreak."

"I won't say anything," he said. "Is there anything I can do?"

"Pray," Jill said as they went through the glass door.

• • •

By daybreak, Aunt Aggie Gaston looked almost as bad as Stan did lying in a coma. Though she had not been allowed in the interrogation room while Celia was being questioned, she had waited on a folding chair outside it. Stewing, she watched the buzz of minor activity in the squad room as drunk drivers were brought in, and a couple of kids arrested for disturbing the peace. One drunk driver was Mildred Bellows's husband, a fact that she stored away and decided to keep to herself. She recognized one of the kids as Lois and Jake Mattreaux's boy. He would probably call his Aunt Issie, one of the Newpointe paramedics, to bail him out so that he could keep it from his parents. Knowing Issie, she would comply. But Aggie made a mental note to let his parents know as soon as she had the chance, and to find out who the other boy was. He had probably told them he was spending the night with him, which accounted for them being out all night.

What was this old world coming to? she asked herself wearily. Kids staying out all night, husbands drinking till they almost killed someone, somebody poisoning another of her nephews-in-law . . .

The door to the interrogation room opened, and Sid came out and looked down at her. "You look awful, Aunt Aggie. Why don't you go on home and get some sleep?"

"I look awful 'cause I'm eighty-one years old."

"Not you, Aunt Aggie. You're the best-lookin' senior citizen in town, and you know it."

"Don't flatter me. I ain't buyin'. And I ain't goin' home till Celia come with me."

"Then it's gonna be a long wait, Aunt Aggie."

"Then you probably better avoid them mirrors, 'cause you won't be likin' what you see. Why you're tormentin' her this way, when all she want is to be with her husband?"

Sid looked more drained than before and leaned back against the wall opposite her. "Aunt Aggie, you know I'm not tormentin' her. I'm just doin' my job. I'm tryin' to figure out who poisoned my friend. How is he, anyway? Do you know?"

"'Course I know. I'm callin' the hospital ever' hour." She looked away, as if to end the conversation, then without looking at him, added, "Still in a coma."

Tears came to her eyes, and angry at the vulnerability, she wiped them away.

"We gotta get the prayer chain activated," Sid said quietly. "We gotta get people prayin'. Wonder if anybody's called Nick Foster."

Aggie shook her head in disbelief. The prayer chain. What a useless waste of phone calls. She had always suspected that the prayer chain was just a ruse for passing gossip, though she supposed that some of them were sincere. If it made those few feel better to think people were praying for them, she supposed there was no harm in it. And what good could Nick Foster—the bivocational pastor/firefighter—do? "Somebody called him by now, since half the fire department was at Stan and Celia's house."

"I might check just to make sure," he said.

"You don't want the prayer chain to miss this, do ya?" she asked, her wrinkled face tightening. "Fact that Celia been brought in for poisonin' her husband. Prayer chain got a *right* to know." The sarcasm was thick in her tone, and she noted with satisfaction that it seemed to sting him.

He set his hands on his hips and glared down at her with those big black eyes of his. "Aunt Aggie, do you honestly think I'm enjoyin' this? That I *liked* questionin' the wife of my best friend, and that I can't wait to tell everybody?"

"Wouldn't think it, if you listened to reason. He gon' strike again, you know. The killer. Still out there."

"I don't expect you to suspect your own niece," Sid said. "It's commendable that you'd back her up. I don't want to suspect her, either." He pushed off from the wall and started to go back into the room.

"What you're gon' do next, Sid? Drive them bamboo shoots up her fingernails? No matter how many times you ask her, the story ain't gon' change!"

"See you later, Aggie," he said.

The fact that he had dropped the "Aunt" from her name gave her some satisfaction, for she didn't want anybody who was an enemy of her niece calling her that.

She looked through the glass doors on the front of the building and saw that the sun was coming up. She couldn't believe they were still here.

Leaning her head back on the concrete wall behind her, she closed her eyes, but sleep did not come.

• • •

It was after eight A.M. when Sid and Jim Shoemaker, the police chief, finished questioning Celia. News was that Stan was still comatose, so part of the puzzle—the part only he could fill in—was still missing. When they began to leave the interrogation room one by one, Celia asked Sid, "Can I go back to the hospital now?"

"You're free to go anytime you want, but I'd appreciate it if you'd wait til we've examined the evidence they got from your house."

"What evidence?"

"The food. The dishes that were in the dishwasher. That kind of thing."

Jill, who looked as tired as the rest of them, checked her watch. "Sid, I want a copy of the lab report as soon as it's ready. Have you called to see if arsenic was found?"

"We didn't tape off their house till just a few hours ago. The evidence we collected ain't even at the lab yet. It just opened."

"Then what are you waiting for?" Jill asked. "If you really care about Stan, and if you ever cared about Celia, you'll get the evidence over there. If there's no trace of the arsenic in their food or dishes, then you'll know that he got it somewhere other than home. If you do find a trace of it there, maybe we can figure out where the food was bought. You remember how to do police work, don't you? Stan isn't the only one around here who knows how to investigate a crime, is he?"

Sid bristled. "Insultin' me ain't gon' get you nowhere, Jill. I know you're tired, but I am, too."

She blew out a frustrated breath and leaned back hard in her chair.

"Has anyone called to check on Stan?" Celia's question cut through the petty exchange and reminded them what this was about.

"Aunt Aggie has. No change."

"Maybe he needs to be in New Orleans. Maybe their facilities would be more up-to-date."

"I'm sure the doctor will have him transferred if it becomes necessary, Celia." Jill took in a deep breath. "While we're waiting for the lab results, I think my client needs to make a few phone calls."

Celia looked up at her. "What phone calls?"

"Isn't there anyone you want to call?" Jill asked. "Your parents? Your brother, maybe?"

She closed her eyes and pressed her fingertips on her eyelids. "Oh, no. It's my birthday. They were supposed to come to see me today. The first time they've ever seen my home. I was so hopeful . . ." She looked up, suddenly alarmed. "I need to call them before they leave Jackson. I don't want them to get here and find out that it's all happening again. They went years without speaking to me. It wasn't until a few months ago that we even spoke by phone. And then, yesterday, I thought we were about to reconcile completely."

Jim and R.J. exchanged looks, as if her estrangement from her family was the evidence they needed that she was a cold-blooded murderer.

"What happened yesterday?"

She groaned. "I told you, Jim, that Stan went to see them to try to convince them to come visit on my birthday. He thought it would make me happy."

"You told me he'd visited with your parents, but you didn't mention why."

"I didn't think it was relevant. My parents are John and Joanna Bradford, from Jackson, Mississippi. They own Bradford Oil."

"The rich Bradfords?" R.J. asked indelicately.

"Yes, they're the ones."

R.J. and Jim exchanged looks again. "Stan never told us you was rich," R.J. said. "You didn't seem to live no higher than any of us other police officers."

"*I'm* not rich," Celia said. "Didn't you hear me? I said that they turned against me during the last trial. They disowned me completely. Considered me dead." Angry new tears burst to her eyes as she spoke. "But I missed them. And Stan and I wanted to start a family, and I wanted my kids to know their grandparents."

Jill touched her hand, and she closed her eyes and tried to pull herself together.

"I had gotten them to talk to me, but things were still strained. Then Stan started calling them, and they listened to him. A couple of weeks ago, my brother came for a visit, and Stan asked him to help set up a meeting with my parents. He wanted my birthday to be special, so he went to see them yesterday. He got them to call me. We had a good talk, and I thought they were forgiving me—"

"Forgiving you for what?" Jill asked.

"For . . . for embarrassing the family name. For bringing shame on them. I don't know."

"So they called . . ." Jim prompted.

"They were going to visit me today—them and my brother, David, and I was so nervous and excited about it. I wanted everything to be perfect . . ." Her voice trailed off, and she wiped her eyes again. "I guess I'll have to call them and tell them, and they'll wash their hands of me again."

"I'll get Aunt Aggie to call," Jill said.

Celia shook her head. "She won't want to. Aunt Aggie's my great-aunt, and my mother is her niece. She hasn't spoken to her since the trial."

"But she can make her understand."

Celia shook her head. "No. They'll never buy it. They didn't the first time. It's taken years for them to get to the point where they'd even admit I was alive. Aunt Aggie and my brother were the only two family members who support-ed me."

"Your brother didn't have any clout with them?"

"Apparently not. He tried, but they're very proud and stub-born people."

Jill couldn't believe they could be so stubborn as to turn their backs on her again.

"Guys, could you leave her alone here and take a break until I get back from getting Aunt Aggie to make the phone calls?"

"I could use some breakfast," Jim said, standing and stretching.

"So could she," Jill said. "Why don't you get her something to eat?"

"I can't eat," Celia said. "I'm not feeling very well."

Jill sighed and waited for the two cops to leave. All of their nerves were shot, and she doubted that any of them would get any rest soon. She bent over the table and looked into Celia's eyes. "Celia, you need to eat."

"I'm queasy," she said. "If I eat, I'll throw it up. I know they said I hadn't been poisoned, and I'm sure I haven't, but I still feel sick, Jill."

"Can I get you anything?" Jill asked. "Some Pepto Bismol, maybe?"

Unaccountably, Celia closed her eyes and her face twisted and reddened as she began to cry again. She grabbed a tissue out of the box on the table and wiped at her nose. "That's what he wanted," she muttered. "Pepto Bismol. Like that would save him from arsenic poisoning, keep him out of that coma. Oh, why is this happening?"

Jill stood still, looking at her and wondering if she dared leave her alone in this state. "I'll stay here," she said softly. "I can talk to Aunt Aggie later."

Celia shook her head and waved a hand at her. "No, go. I'm fine. I need to be alone for a little while, anyway."

Jill didn't like the sound of that. She looked around the room, wondering if Celia intended to do herself harm. There was nothing in the room that she could use, but one never knew for sure. "Maybe that's not a good idea, Celia. I'll just stay."

Celia seemed to realize where Jill's thoughts were leading her. "Oh, you don't think I'm going to kill myself or something, do you? For heaven's sake, Jill, I just want to be alone to pray. I haven't had a minute alone in hours."

"Pray. Of course." Jill relaxed then and knew it was exactly what she would have expected of Celia if she'd been thinking clearly. In fact, it wouldn't hurt for her to do the same. "All right, Celia. I'll leave you alone."

Still weeping, Celia dropped her head in the circle of her arms as Jill left the room.

Chapter Eight

Jill found Aunt Aggie looking like death warmed over, and she realized how difficult it must be for a woman of her age to endure an all-nighter in a folding chair. The woman sat straight up with her purse in her lap and her feet flat on the floor, her eyes closed, as if she was sound asleep.

Jill bent over and touched her arm gently, reluctant to wake her if she slept. "Aunt Aggie?"

The old woman's eyes flew open, and she asked, "They done torturin' her yet?"

Jill shook her head. "No, they're not finished with her. We're waiting for the report to come back from the lab. In the meantime, I thought maybe you could call Celia's parents and tell them what's happened."

She gave Jill a bitterly disgusted look. "I ain't spoke one word to my niece since she turned her back on Celia, and I ain't startin' now."

"But Aunt Aggie, Celia said they were coming to visit her today, and she doesn't want them to hear about this after they get here. Please, won't you call them?"

"I'll call T-David, Celia's brother," she said. "Him I can talk to. But Celia's mama's hardheaded as a ram. I could go the rest of my life without talkin' to her, what she done to that poor girl."

Aggie got to her feet, resisting Jill's help, and started walking. "Which phone can we use?"

"Take that one," Jill said, pointing to an empty desk. "We'll use my credit card number."

Jill punched in the preliminary code, then gave the phone to Aunt Aggie. She dialed the number, rattling on as she did. "David lives in that mausoleum of a house with 'em . . . disgraceful how big it is . . . on three hundred acres . . . and he gots a whole wing to hisself. But sometimes his mama answers his line, and when she does, I just hang up . . ."

"Don't hang up this time, Aunt Aggie. Celia needs for you to do this."

Jill watched the tension on the old woman's face as she waited for the ring to be answered. When it was, she pulled her chin up and tightened her lips and said, "David, please. Well, where can I reach 'im? Yeah, Joanna, it's me." Her face was reddening, and she shot Jill a disgusted look. "No, that ain't why I'm callin'. I was glad you finally got over your bullheadedness to make up with your daughter. But Celia can't make it today, so don't come."

It was not how she would have handled it, Jill thought, irritated, but it was too late to do anything about it.

Aunt Aggie listened, her lips growing even thinner. "No, she ain't backed out, Joanna. But Stan, he's sick, in the hospital. Somebody tried to poison him."

Again, Jill's spirits sagged. There must be a better way to break the news, but delicacy had never been one of Aunt Aggie's traits.

Aunt Aggie closed her eyes, as though bracing herself for what came next, and when she opened them again Jill could see pure rage in her eyes. "No, Celia didn't do it, just like she didn't do it last time, but you never believe that 'cause you don't know your daughter. All you care about is yourself and your stupid, silly family name, which nobody cares nothin' about!"

Incredulous at how badly this was going, Jill snatched the phone out of Aunt Aggie's hand. The old woman surrendered it gladly.

"Uh . . . Mrs. Bradford? This is Jill Clark, a friend of Celia's."

"Where is my aunt?" the woman asked. Hers was a soft voice, very similar to Celia's, and she didn't sound like the shrew Aunt Aggie had made her out to be at all. "I need to talk to my aunt."

"Uh . . . she doesn't want to talk to you anymore, Mrs. Bradford. But I thought you should know that your daughter needs you now more than ever. Because of her first husband's cause of death, the police have been questioning her."

"Then they've arrested her again?"

"No. They're only questioning her." She could hear the muffled sob on the other end, something that surprised her. "I know it would help her tremendously if she had your moral support now, especially on her birthday. I'm an attorney and I'm doing everything I can to clear this up, but for now—"

"I should have known."

Jill hesitated. "Mrs. Bradford, you should have known what?"

"That this reconciliation, this reunion . . . was too good to be true." A moment of silence passed. "I had such hopes."

"You can still have a reunion."

"Is he dead?" The words seemed to come on a wave of emotion.

"No. He's in a coma."

"He was a nice man. I liked him very much. I could see why Celia loved him."

She ignored her use of past tense. "Yes, it's quite a tragedy. More so because of what Celia's going through."

"Thank you for calling, Miss Clark. I appreciate it."

Jill sat there for a moment, holding the line. "Is that all? Aren't you going to come?"

"No, I don't think so."

"But your daughter needs you."

"She has my aunt."

"Mrs. Bradford—"

The phone clicked in her ear, and Jill froze, still holding it.

"Hanged up on you, didn't she?" Aggie asked.

"Yes, she did."

"If there was a hell, it would be for folks like her."

"There is a hell, Aunt Aggie. And you don't want to wish it on your niece."

She watched as the old woman dug a handkerchief out of her pocket and dabbed at her eyes. Across the room, Sid got off of his own telephone and headed toward her.

"What did you find out?" she asked as he reached her.

He leaned over the desk, bracing himself with his hands. "There wasn't a trace of arsenic in any of the evidence we collected from the house," he said, "'cept for what Stan had … purged."

"All right, now we're getting somewhere," Jill said, springing up with renewed energy. "Sid, you have to see that if Celia had done this, there would have been some evidence."

"She didn't have to do it at home, Jill. She's experienced, remember? She knows how to cover her tracks."

"Cover her tracks?" Jill asked in a whisper, to keep from giving the gossip mill more fodder. "Give me a break! She'd have to be pretty stupid to think she was covering her tracks by poisoning her husband someplace else, with the *same* poison she was accused of using on her first husband! Don't you think she'd know that she would be the very first suspect?"

"Maybe that's what she is, Jill. Stupid. Or maybe she's just crazy. You ever thought of that? You'd better, because when I get through gatherin' all the evidence in this case, the insanity defense might be her only hope."

Before either of them knew what had happened, Aggie had leaped up and swung her purse across Sid's head, knocking him over.

"Man!" he shouted. "Why'd you do that?"

"Don't you talk 'bout my niece like that again!" the old woman shouted.

"That thing must weigh a ton!" Sid staggered back, holding the side of his head. "Whatcha got in there? Bricks? I could arrest you for assaultin' a police officer."

"You do it! Throw a eighty-one-year-old woman in jail, see what it gets you!"

He backed off, as if too exhausted to fight her anymore. "Guess this insanity thing runs in the blasted family."

Then mumbling under his breath, he headed for Jim Shoemaker's office.

Jill caught up with him and blocked his entrance. "Sid, is my client under arrest?"

"That's what I'm goin' in to talk to the chief about."

"You don't have probable cause. You don't have a shred of evidence. All you have is an unsolved case from six years ago." Sid ignored her and tried to get around her.

"Sid, *think.* Why would she tell you it was arsenic if she *wanted* him dead? It would have taken days to discover that, postmortem, if they hadn't known to test him for it. Use your logic!"

"My logic tells me she could be a few bricks shy of a full load, Jill. That maybe she tried to kill him and got cold feet at the last minute. I'll leave that to the psychiatrists. All's I know is we got a police detective layin' half dead in the hospital, and she's the only suspect we got. I don't care how blonde, how pretty, or how married she is. If she's a killer, I'm gon' lock her up."

Jill wasn't about to leave it at that. As he started into Jim's office, she followed him in.

"Jim, since you're finished questioning my client, I'm telling her she can leave," she blurted before Sid could get anything out.

"Oh, no, you don't," Sid said. "Jim, I'm gon' book her."

Jim sank back in his seat. "You can't book her, Sid. We don't have any compelling evidence or any probable cause."

Jill shot him a satisfied look, but he didn't give up.

"Jim, who else coulda done it?" Sid demanded. "Look, she's my friend, too. I've always liked Celia. But the facts just stack up against her."

"What if you're wrong?" Jim asked. "And you have to explain to Stan why you locked up his wife when he needed her most? And on her birthday, to boot."

Jill leaned over his desk. "Jim, all she wants to do is go back to the hospital and be with him. She's scared to death. Let her go. You'll know where she is."

Jim nodded and looked up at Sid. "Tell her she can go home, but not to leave town."

"What about Slidell?" Jill asked. "That's where Stan is."

"Tell her not to go farther than Slidell. And we may have to question her more later."

Sid went to a filing cabinet and leaned his elbow on it. His anger was on simmer, working up to a low boil. Jim got up, rubbing his paunch. "Sid, the investigation continues. If you show me evidence that Celia did this, I won't hesitate to lock her up."

Sid nodded and started back out the door. "I got work to do."

Jill shook Jim's hand and thanked him, then went to tell Celia the good news.

Chapter Nine

They had moved Stan to a room by the time Celia got back to the hospital, and she hurried up to his floor. Hannah and Bart, her in-laws, were in there with him, watching a television set with the sound turned low. It was as if they watched out of politeness, since it was there and they didn't know what else to do with themselves. Hannah's mouse-brown hair was mashed flat on one side, as if she hadn't teased it back into shape since being awakened in the middle of the night. Bart hadn't shaved.

Hannah sprang up when Celia came through the door. As if she'd been holding back her tears just for Celia, her mother-in-law began to cry and hugged her fiercely. "How is he?" Celia asked.

"There's been no change, Celia. Where have you been? Allie said you were filling out a police report, but we didn't know it would take all night."

A police report. Good for Allie, Celia thought. "I didn't expect it to, either." She went to the bed and leaned tentatively over Stan. "Has he been awake at all?"

"No," Bart said. "Celia, if they kept you that long at the police station, you must know something. Do you know who could have poisoned Stan?"

Her eyes were misty as she looked up at him across the bed. "Bart, if I knew . . . oh, if I only knew . . . but I don't have a clue." She touched Stan's face gently. His stubble was thick. It surprised her. It seemed to her that all of his body functions should have stopped out of respect for his state. Hair growth had no place on a face as pale as death.

Tears came to her eyes. "He's not doing well, is he?"

"No, he's not. Tell us what happened," Bart said. "Last night, before they brought him in."

She raked her hair back from her face, wishing for a shower. "He was just really sick. Throwing up, his throat was hurting, he was really weak. I thought he just had a virus or something. But then he got really sick, and he passed out, and I called an ambulance . . ." Her voice trailed off in fatigued defeat.

"Stan, wake up, honey," she said close to his ear. "Wake up. Please, honey. It's my birthday. All I want is for you to open your eyes."

Hannah was still weeping, and she pulled a tissue out of the box on the table. "Happy birthday, Celia," she said softly.

Celia wiped her eyes. "Thanks." Distressed, she breathed in a sob. "Why won't he wake up? Haven't they done anything for him? Shouldn't it be working by now?"

Bart came around the bed and pulled both women into a strong hug. "We don't know," he whispered. "The doctor isn't sure how bad this is. It may have been a lethal dose."

"He's *not* gonna die," Celia said, pulling back and looking into her father-in-law's face. "Bart, he's not. They caught it in time. They just had to."

They all held each other and wept for a long time, until finally Celia urged them to go to the cafeteria and eat breakfast. They hadn't left Stan's side since he'd been brought to the room. Reluctantly, they agreed and left her alone with him.

When they had left, she sat beside Stan on his bed, talking to him and praying over him, stroking his chest and his face. But there was no response.

She tried to imagine his eyelashes fluttering, his eyelids opening, color coming back into his face. But the image was elusive. The fear of his death was so great that it couldn't be overridden. She thought of Nathan lying dead on an emergency room gurney, how she'd flown into hysterics until they'd had to sedate her. Finally, before the coroner had taken him, they had allowed her a few moments alone with him.

People said it was easier to cope when you had closure—when you could see the death and experience the finality of it. But it had all come too soon, too unexpectedly. There was no such thing as closure. Even the shock and the sedatives hadn't helped.

Now she clung to the sound of the heart monitor testifying to the life still left in Stan's body, to the stubble that felt like sandpaper under her palm, to the feverish heat of his skin against her lips ... heat that was so much better than cold.

She dropped her forehead on his chest and sank into her sobs, feeling the comfort of him even though he didn't move. If he'd awakened, he would have held her while she cried, as he'd done so many times since he'd met her, when she'd been trapped by grief over Nathan, or her parents, or the fear of some evil still out there without name or face.

But now that evil had descended once again, claiming Stan as its next casualty. She couldn't fathom how this could happen again.

After a while, Bart and Hannah burst into the room, startling her. Their faces had changed, and their eyes shone with rage. "Why didn't you tell us?" Bart demanded.

She looked up at them, confused. "Tell you what?"

"About your first husband." The words were uttered with horror. "That he died this way."

Her face drained of all its color, and she felt the heart-deep fatigue from crying buckets of tears. "I was going to tell you."

"Then it's true?" Hannah asked. "We didn't even know that you'd been married before. Did you lie to Stan, too?"

"No," she said. "I didn't lie to anyone. Stan knew the truth. I just didn't think it needed to be broadcast all over the place. I came here to escape the gossip." She left Stan's bedside and faced them with teary eyes. "But gossip has a way of regenerating, doesn't it? Who told you?"

"Simone, the 911 dispatcher," Bart said. "We called to see if they had a suspect yet, and she said you were the only one!"

Celia sank onto the vinyl couch.

"We were good to you," Hannah cried. "We treated you like our own daughter. How could you—" Her voice broke off, and she stepped closer to the bed. "I'm gonna have to ask you to leave."

"Leave? Hannah, he's my husband. I'm not going anywhere." She got up and walked toward them, intent on making them understand. "Yes, I was married before. Nathan was murdered, this same way. Hannah, Bart, you have to understand that the same person who did that must have done this, too. They set me up last time, and now it's happening again. You have to believe me. I didn't do it."

They both looked horror-stricken and confused. "I don't know what to believe," Hannah said. "Someone tried to murder my son. Simone says that you were charged with the first murder."

"Charged but not convicted. Hannah, you know me! You know what kind of person I am! Have I ever given you reason to think I'm a killer?"

"We didn't have all the facts," Bart said. "If we'd known that you'd been accused of murdering your first husband . . ."

"What?" she cut in. "You would have stood in the way of our marriage? That's why Stan decided not to tell you. You would have judged me unfairly. I'm *innocent*."

"We can't know that for sure," Hannah whispered through her tears. "All we know is that our son is fighting for his life, and we just . . . we don't know what to think about you anymore."

"But Hannah!"

"Go home," Bart said. "It isn't good for you to be here."

"I'm his wife! I need to be here."

"But if you're involved . . ." Hannah looked so distraught that Celia felt sorry for her. She was a tigress protecting her offspring. "Celia, we need for you to go home. Just . . . keep your distance for a while. Until we understand . . . everything."

"I don't want to leave him!" Celia cried. "Please, don't make me do this! He needs me. When he wakes up, he's going to look for me. He loves me, Hannah. Bart? Don't you know that he loves me?"

"We've never questioned that," Bart said, his lips trembling. "It's just that . . . these secrets, Celia. We have to sort them all out."

She suddenly felt nauseous, and her head hurt . . . and her heart ached.

She didn't know how much more she could take. Part of her felt that if she left Stan now, he would just fade away, and she'd never see him again. The other part felt that her very presence created strife and grief and angst. Her in-laws were not judgmental people. They weren't vindictive fault-finders.

They were just scared, and she couldn't say she blamed them. If she'd had reason to think that either of them had hurt Stan, she would have reacted the same way.

Finally, she kissed her husband good-bye, and wept as she left the room.

Chapter Ten

Marabeth Simmons dialed across town to Sue Ellen Hanover at the post office, and waited on hold until the postal clerk came to the phone. She tapped her inch-long nails on her Formica desktop, and straightened the sign at the front of her desk that said "Apartment Manager."

"U.S. Post Office," Sue Ellen said, though Marabeth knew that all she'd really had to say was "hello." Sometimes Sue Ellen thought more of herself than she should, and that post office job didn't help matters.

"Sue Ellen, this is Marabeth," she said. "Did you hear the news about Stan Shepherd?"

"What news?"

Marabeth could hear it in Sue Ellen's voice, the disappointment that Marabeth would have news that Sue Ellen hadn't gotten first. She delighted in the fact that this wasn't something Sue Ellen could have read in anybody else's mail. "He's half dead in Slidell. Poisoned."

"He *what?* I'm sure I would have heard something ... Where did you hear this?"

"From Simone. I reckon she'd know, don't you? Seein' how Celia called 911 last night and all. And speakin' of Celia ... You'll never guess who they think mighta did it. Celia Shepherd! That's who!"

As Sue Ellen gasped, the door to the apartment office opened, and a tall man with sandy hair and fern-green eyes walked in. "Uh ... gotta go, Sue Ellen. I have a customer."

"But why would Celia poison her own husband?"

"Got me. Now, if you tell anybody I told you, I'll deny it. And don't let on that Simone told *me*, 'cause she'd lose her job and then where would we be?"

She dropped the phone in its cradle and looked up at the good-looking man. Suddenly, she wished she'd flossed after lunch. "May I help you?"

His grin was charming.

"Yeah, I'm Lee Barnett," he said in a voice that sounded remarkably like Elvis. "You're s'posed to be holdin' an apartment for me?"

She tried to think, but found that she was too flustered. She was too old for this, she told herself. At least twenty years older than the man ... but she'd kept her figure and had just had her hair done. Maybe he did find her attractive. Hadn't she seen an older woman/younger man relationship on *Sally Jesse* just yesterday? Nervously, she thumbed through her files. "Oh, yeah. It's apartment B-5. It's all ready for you if you'll just sign here."

He signed the lease, then glanced up at her. "Were you here when my friend chose this apartment?"

She shook her head. "No. I think our owner rented it through the phone. Musta been Monday, 'cause I'm off Mondays."

"I see."

She got the spare key off of the wall behind her and slid it across the desk, hoping he noticed her nails. "I hope you and your wife enjoy it."

He grinned, making her heart melt. "I ain't married."

"Oh." She hoped he didn't hear the delight in her voice. "When will you be moving in, Mr. Barnett?"

"Lee. Call me Lee."

Victory, she thought. He liked her.

"I'll be movin' in right now. Is the apartment furnished?"

Strange days, she thought, when a person didn't even know if the apartment he'd rented was furnished or not. "Yes, it is."

"All right, then. All I've got is a suitcase in the car. Guess I'll go on up."

She watched as he started to walk out, and she leaned forward with a smile. "You holler if you need anything, you hear?"

"Thank you. Thank you very much," he said with a wink, then left the office.

She sat back in her chair and sighed, then quickly picked up the phone and began to dial frantically. There was so much to tell, and so little time.

Chapter Eleven

"Well, *garçons*, does we order a pizza or does one o' you want to try out your hand in the kitchen?" George Broussard asked as he stood in front of the fire station's refrigerator, taking grim inventory of the sparse contents. Aunt Aggie usually brought her own groceries when she cooked for them.

"Guess we can do what every other fireman in the country has to do and learn how to cook," Mark suggested.

Dan thought that over for a moment. "Pizza," he said finally. "Maybe Stan will wake up and be okay, and Aggie'll be back cooking for us by supper."

"What a selfish thought," Slater Finch accused. Then with a grin, he added, "You think it could happen?"

The five firefighters, who'd spent most of the morning fighting a fire over at Barker's Furniture Store and had worked up some fierce appetites, erupted into a round of chuckles, but the amusement quickly faded as they seemed to collectively realize that they were laughing at their friend's expense. Stan Shepherd could really die.

"Anybody called the hospital in the last hour?" Dan asked.

Mark got up and got a glass down from the cabinet. "I just talked to Allie. She called and was told that he's still in the coma."

"Man," Slater said. "This is so bizarre. Anybody talked to Celia? She must be a wreck."

Dan looked around, but no one seemed to know anything, except maybe Mark, who didn't meet anyone's eye.

"She's probably still at the hospital. Poor kid probably hasn't had a wink of sleep," Slater continued.

Dan didn't comment.

They heard the side door open, and hoping it was Aunt Aggie, everyone got up to see. Nick Foster, the pastor of Calvary Bible Church and a fellow firefighter scheduled to come on duty tonight, hurried in. "Hey, guys," he said.

Disappointed, most of them sat back down.

"Was it something I said?"

"No, not you," Dan said. "We were kind of hoping you were Aunt Aggie."

"Hungry, huh? I don't think she'll be coming today. Not until this thing with Celia is cleared up."

Mark and Dan jerked their eyes up to his, warning him to shut up, but it was too late.

"What thing with Celia?" Slater asked.

Silence fell over the room as the men who didn't know looked around at the eyes of those who seemed to. "Nick, what you're talkin' about?" George asked, closing the refrigerator with a jolt.

It was evident that Nick knew he'd spoken out of turn, and he looked from Dan to Mark, then back to George. "Uh ... nothing. I meant ..."

"Celia's sick, too?" George asked.

"No. She's just ... upset. You know."

Slater narrowed his eyes and got slowly to his feet. "Are they suspectin' that Celia did this?"

"No, I'm sure they don't. It's just routine."

Dan rolled his eyes. The pastor was trying to tap-dance his way out of it. Dan felt sorry for him. It wasn't easy being a bivocational shepherd, and in a small town like this it was hard to know what was confidential and what was common knowledge. Nick would be beating himself up for days.

"So is Celia in jail?"

Dan decided to speak up, for he had talked to Jill earlier and knew they had let her go. "No, she's not in jail. Don't go getting all excited about this. They just questioned her about it.

But there's no evidence that she knew a thing about it. Jill's got them testing his coffee cup at work and taking food samples from the cafe he stopped at on his way out of town yesterday, and she's even got them searching Celia's parents' house in Jackson since Stan was there yesterday."

George sat slowly down in his seat. "You know, I gotta say I waked up more'n once durin' the night thinkin' how she knowed it was arsenic. How *did* she know?"

There was dead silence from Nick, Dan, and Mark. Finally, Mark spoke up. "It's probably going to hit the paper tonight," he said. "So I'll tell y'all, but I expect you to keep it under your hats. Got it?"

They all agreed.

"It turns out Celia was married before, and her first husband was poisoned to death. Arsenic. Now, that doesn't mean—"

"She killed her first husband?" George asked on a whisper.

"No!" Dan said. "See what you've done, Mark? She was acquitted."

"Did Stan know about this?" Slater asked.

"She said he did," Mark told him.

"'Course, we won't know for sure till he wakes up," Slater pointed out.

"Look what you're doing!" Dan got up, angry. "You guys know Celia. You know she wouldn't do a thing like that. Already you're doubting her."

"Dan, what we really know about her?" the big Cajun asked. "Arrybody knows she ain't been in town that long."

"She's been here longer than you have! What do you want?"

"But I growed up here," George defended. "I knew most arrybody."

"And she came so mysteriously," Slater added. "Nobody knew nothin' about her except that she was Aggie's niece."

"That was enough! We all know and trust Aunt Aggie. And besides, Celia was a sweet, soft-spoken, gentle woman, and most of us liked her instantly."

"That had a lot to do with the fact that she's one of the prettiest gals in town," Slater said. "But for all we know, she could have been a cold-blooded murderer with a pretty face. For all Stan knew, either. And now look at 'im."

Nick intervened. "Guys, please. You can't burn her at the stake before you even hear all the facts. Celia's got a sweet heart, and it isn't capable of murder. You know it, and I know it."

"Doesn't matter," Dan said bitterly. "It makes juicy gossip, so they're going to run with it. If she gets hurt in the process, who cares, right, Slater?"

Slater swung around, red faced. "Yeah, Nichols? I guess you're just feelin' all superior because you had inside knowledge. Is Jill representin' her?"

"As a matter of fact she is. And I *don't* have inside knowledge. I just happened to be outside last night when Celia was brought in. I knew better than to say anything."

"Come on," Nick said in a sterner voice. "That's enough. We don't need this!" He turned to George, then to Mark and Dan, members of his church, all of whom seemed to be seething for one reason or another. "Celia is our sister. She's part of our congregation. She needs our prayers, not our indictments."

"Then she *has* been indicted?" Slater asked.

Dan wanted to hit him. "No, you fool, she *hasn't*, so why don't you just keep your mouth shut about it?"

Nick moaned as Slater got up, and the pastor reached out and grabbed the back of Slater's collar before he could react to Dan's fighting words. "Stop it, both of you!" he shouted. "We're coworkers here, and Dan, you should know better. I'm disappointed in you!"

Dan didn't like being treated like a child, so he just turned and headed out of the room. Behind him, he could hear Slater cursing his back.

Chapter Twelve

Aunt Aggie would never have left Celia alone, but when Jill assured her that she'd canceled all of her appointments for the day and needed to spend the afternoon with Celia anyway getting all the information she could on the first trial, Aggie decided, with Celia's blessings, to go to the hospital in Slidell.

She was glad she'd gotten a few hours' sleep, at least. Now maybe she wouldn't try beating up any more cops. She grimaced at the thought of how she'd slammed her purse into Sid Ford's head. If she hadn't been an old lady who'd been up all night, he probably would have thrown her in the slammer. Being old did have its perks, she supposed.

She pulled into the parking lot of the Slidell Memorial Hospital, carefully avoiding the "senior citizen" spaces marked near the wheelchair spaces close to the door. There was no reason she couldn't walk like everybody else, she told herself. The day she surrendered to her age was the day they would bury her.

She checked with the information desk to see where Stan was and found out he was on the sixth floor. The elevator took her there, and she got off and saw the crowd of off-duty police officers, a few firemen, the preacher, and a few people she didn't know, spilling out of the waiting room. No wonder Stan didn't want to wake up, she thought. A crowd like that would keep anybody in a coma.

Bypassing them, she headed straight for his room. After all, she was his wife's aunt, so if anyone was allowed in his room, she was. She reached his door and hesitated, wondering if she had the right room. There was an armed guard standing outside it, and she wondered who had hired him. With an air of authority, she walked right past him and pushed the door open.

He reached out and grabbed her arm, stopping her. "May I help you?"

"I want to see Stan," she said, indignant. "I'm his *tante*."

"You'll have to wait," he said. "I'll check with his parents."

His parents, she thought as he stepped inside the room. The ones who threw her Celia out. She had a bone to pick with them while she was here.

She waited for his parents to invite her in, but instead, the guard came back out. "Mrs. Shepherd said to tell you to wait in the waiting room with the others."

"What you mean, 'with the others'?" Aggie protested. "I ain't one of them others. I'm flesh and blood, practically." Realizing she was getting nowhere with the guard, she pushed past him, anyway. When he tried to grab her arm again, she felt for her purse and considered using it. Jerking away, she pushed into the room.

Bart and Hannah sat side by side on the vinyl sofa next to the bed, and she consoled herself with the fact that Hannah, who was at least twenty years her junior, looked worse than she. She stood up as Aggie entered, and Aggie started to tell her to sit down and rest before she keeled right over of natural causes.

"I'm sorry, Mr. and Mrs. Shepherd," the guard said behind her as he took Aggie's arm again. "I didn't think she would be so pushy. Looks can be deceiving."

"It's all right," Hannah said, prompting him to let go of her in the nick of time.

The guard disappeared back out the door, and ignoring both Hannah and Bart, Aggie went to Stan's bedside. He still looked as white as death, and had a breathing tube under his nose. An IV ran fluid into his veins, and a cardiac machine monitored his heart rhythm. Several other machines were attached to him, but Aunt Aggie couldn't identify them. She touched his forehead, pushing the hair back from his eyebrows. He needed a haircut, bless his heart. She should have brought her scissors.

"Aggie, don't touch him. Please." Bart's voice was just above a whisper.

"Please, Aggie," Hannah whispered across her son. "We want you to wait in the waiting room."

"What you're whisperin' for?" Aggie demanded loudly. "Ain't the goal to wake him up? No wonder he still in a coma."

"Aggie, please," Hannah said again. "Don't make us call the guard back in. You really need to leave."

Aggie gaped at them, indignant. "I got as much right in here as y'all got. I love this boy arry bit as much as y'all do!"

"He doesn't need visitors," Bart whispered harshly.

"Is it 'cause of Celia?" Aunt Aggie demanded. "'Cause what you done to that girl, sendin' her home like you done . . . oughta be a law. Now you tryin' to thow me out?"

"I'll call the guard if I have to."

Aggie wondered if this was the day she'd surrender to her age—and the burial part, too—as her heart began whamming into her chest. "You oughta be ashamed!" she threw back at them. "You know my Celia didn't do this! *She* saved his life! If she wants him dead, she'd have waited to call the ambulance! Let him croak, then act like she tryin' to save him."

"She lied to us," Hannah said through her teeth.

"How? When she told you a lie?"

"It's what she didn't tell us," Bart returned. "She didn't tell us that she'd killed her first husband!"

Aggie felt the weight of her purse and wondered if she could hit them with it from across the bed. She clutched her chest, as if that would slow her racing heart, and through her white caps said, "My Celia ain't never killed a bug! She ain't *never* lied to you! She didn't tell you she was *accused* of Nathan's death, 'cause she knowed folks like you wouldn't wait for the firin' squad. You'd mow her down before the words was even outa her mouth!"

"She betrayed us," Hannah said, livid tears springing to her red eyes. "Stan may die. He's our only son!"

"Read my lips," Aggie said through her dental work. "She … didn't … do it! 'Stead of bein' mad at her, be mad at the po-leece who's stopped lookin' for the killer. He still's out there, you know, the monster what really tried to kill Stan. It ain't the likes o' me that guard needs to keep out!"

"Until the police tell us differently, we want Celia to stay away," Hannah said. "And we aren't allowing any visitors at all."

"Well, ain't that con-*ven*-ient? She been good to y'all people, and she make your son happier than he ever been. And this what you do to her!"

"Bart, do something," Hannah said.

He headed for the door and got the guard to come in. "Get her out," he ordered.

Aggie swung her purse like a lasso, aiming right between the guard's eyes. "You lay one hand on me, I'll lay you out just like him," she said, referring to Stan. "I *know* the way out." Then, straightening her dress and picking a dot of lint off of her skirt, she made her way to the door.

Just before she left the room, she turned back. "You be sorry for this one day," she said. "Destroyin' somebody never did nothin' but love your son. Someday she'll be the mama of your grandchildren."

Hannah didn't answer. She only turned back to her son.

Chapter Thirteen

He's getting away with it."

Allie looked up at Celia, who sat with her arms hugging her knees on the big four-poster bed in Aggie's guest room. She looked so small there, so innocent. And so distraught. "Who?"

"Whoever it is," she said dully. "He's ripped my life at the seams twice, and gotten away with it both times."

"He's not going to get away with it," Allie said. "Jill's working on it right now. She's doing everything she can, Celia."

Celia wasn't buying. "For at least two years after Nathan died, I was so paranoid, Allie. I kept thinking the killer was stalking me, watching me, waiting to take my life, too. For a while, I almost hoped he would."

"I remember when you first came to Newpointe," Allie said. "You *did* seem timid, quiet. I thought you were just shy. Then you seemed to get over it, little by little."

Celia sighed and rubbed her tired eyes. "I knew he was still out there. That never went away. But when I got involved in the church and met Stan, I just started concentrating more on living than dying. I think that kept me alive." She looked down at her knees, clad in faded jeans. "I trusted him so much that I told him everything. And he trusted me unconditionally. He showed me how much God loved me, because he modeled it for me." Sick grief reddened her face, and she leaned her head back on the ornate headboard.

"What if he wakes up and they tell him I tried to kill him, Allie? What if they convince him that I've had some dormant murderous instinct just waiting to jump out?"

"He won't believe it, Celia. You know better. He believed you before. He'll know you didn't do it this time. And if he wakes up, maybe he'll know where he got the poison, and the whole thing will be cleared up."

"Or maybe he'll die, and it won't matter what they do to me."

Allie got up and went to the bed, sat down beside her. Out of habit, she rubbed her hand over her round stomach. Celia's eyes followed her hand.

"We wanted to start a family, Allie," she whispered. "That's why he started talking to my parents. He wanted to make things right, so our children would have grandparents on both sides. Today's my birthday, so he went to see them yesterday in hopes of getting them to agree to come for a visit today. I was starting to think it was all behind me, all of it, that God was returning the days that the locusts ate. I was starting to think he didn't let me die all those times I asked him to, because he had something wonderful waiting. But was this what he spared me for?"

Allie wiped the tears springing to her own eyes. "I don't know, Celia."

Celia reached for a tissue next to the bed and blew her nose. "I read about all those martyrs in the Bible who walked into furnaces and lions' dens and were crucified and beaten and beheaded ... and I can't help wishing that I had some greater purpose for my suffering, too. Does it feel better to suffer for a noble cause? Does injustice carry any peace if you're standing for some divine plan?"

Allie couldn't answer. She pushed the hair back from where it stuck to Celia's wet face.

"But there isn't any grand purpose here, Allie. There's no greater good. It's all just a mistake, but even if I'm not convicted of this, there will always be people who think of me as a murderess."

She slid off of the bed and went to the window to look out on Aunt Aggie's backyard. Allie got up and followed her, and saw Chester, Aunt Aggie's gardener, pruning a pear tree.

"Maybe God's just pruning you, Celia. Sometimes bad things happen because he's just trying to prune us. Make us bear more fruit." It was not what Celia wanted to hear, she realized, but it still could have some truth.

"I feel more like all my limbs have been amputated, right down to the trunk," Celia said. She turned back around. "I'm gonna be sick."

"No, you're not. You'll get through this, Celia—"

"No. I'm really gonna be sick." Allie stepped back as Celia dashed from the room, and she winced as she heard her retching into the toilet.

Allie went in behind her and held her hair back while she bent over the commode. She should have made her eat, she thought. But Celia had complained of queasiness, and now Allie wondered again if the doctors had overlooked the poison in Celia.

The doorbell rang, and Celia looked up at her. "Don't answer it. It's Jed from the newspaper. He keeps coming to the door trying to get a statement. This'll be all over tonight's paper."

"But it might be someone with news," Allie said. "I'll go see. Will you be all right?"

Celia got up and stood over the sink to splash water on her face. "Yeah. Don't let anybody in, Allie. I can't see anyone right now."

"Don't worry," Allie said, then hurried down the stairs to answer the door.

Allie saw the man through the peephole, and instantly thought he must be a news anchor from one of the New Orleans stations. He looked like a model, though he was small in stature, with perfectly coiffed blonde hair and large blue eyes. Behind him, a photographer who'd been planted on Aggie's lawn was photographing and questioning him, but he ignored him.

"Who is it?" she asked through the door.

"David Bradford," he said. "Celia's brother."

Allie caught her breath and let him in, then quickly closed the door on the photographer. "Celia's brother," she said, smiling at him. "I should have seen the resemblance."

David shot past the small talk. "How is she?"

"Well, she's . . . hanging in there. She'll be better now that you're here. I'm so glad you came. I'll go get her."

She left him standing there and rushed up the stairs. She found Celia brushing her teeth. "Celia, you have to come. It's a surprise. I think it'll cheer you up."

"Allie, I don't feel like company. Please . . ."

"No, come on. You'll be glad you did. I promise."

Celia stepped to the banister and peered over. Her brother David was coming up, and she caught her breath. "David!"

"Happy birthday," he said. She met him halfway down and threw her arms around him, and he squeezed her so tight that Allie thought he might crush her. David was only three or four inches taller than Celia, but the similarities were so striking that Allie wondered if they were twins.

"You didn't think I'd stay away, did you?" he said, pulling her back from him and getting a good look at her.

Celia nodded and touched her brother's cheek. "It's been a long time." She looked at Allie. "I guess you've met my baby brother, Allie?"

"*Baby* brother?" Allie asked.

"She's only three years older," David said. "Celia, look at you. Have you slept at all?"

She shook her head. "How could I? Can you believe this is happening again?"

"They searched our house," David said. "Took dishes and food and looked in every nook and cranny. You woulda thought we were criminals."

Celia led him into the parlor and sank down on a couch. He took the seat across from her. "I suppose Mom and Dad were embarrassed to death."

"You could say that. And just when they were ready to reconcile. The timing . . ."

"I know," she said.

He looked around the room, got up, and ambled to a table with family pictures. He picked up one of Celia as a child, dressed in pageant dress and striking a pose. "Where's Aunt Aggie?" he asked.

"She's gone to the hospital to see how Stan is doing."

He set the picture back down. "How is he?"

"I don't know," she said. "News hasn't changed. All we can get is that he's still in a coma. His parents don't want me there."

He slid his hands into his trouser pockets and settled his troubled eyes on her. "Who would do this? It's so weird. Stan was just at the house yesterday. He looked great. And he did a great job with Mom and Dad, Celia. You would have been so proud of him. He did what I haven't been able to do in all these years. He brought them around."

"Until this morning, when they reverted back to believing the worst about me."

"They're in shock, Celia. We all are."

"Tell me about it." She rubbed her temples and shook her head. "The police questioned me for hours this morning, trying to reconstruct yesterday—everywhere Stan may have eaten. David, did he eat anything when he was visiting yesterday?"

David thought for a moment, then shook his head. "No, he didn't eat anything. Cook brought out some cookies, but if I remember, he didn't take one. He mentioned having a sour stomach. He did drink some tea, but so did we all, and it all came out of a common pitcher. The police were still there when I left. Guess they have to test every place Stan was yesterday. Isn't arsenic the poison you can get from eating almonds or something?"

"No, that's cyanide," Celia said. "Did you see him eating almonds?"

"No, but I thought maybe he had picked some up on the way home. Did the police check his car for fast-food bags or anything?"

"Yes, they checked everything."

"Well, maybe there was a receipt in there that would tell us where he stopped, what he might have bought . . ."

"They're working on tracing all those leads, but his car was pretty clean. There wasn't much to go on. It was after midnight before he got really bad," Celia said.

"Then it would have to be something he ate at home, wouldn't it? Just before he went to bed. Are you sure he didn't get up after you were asleep and eat something?"

"He didn't feel well when we went to bed. I don't think he would have eaten. Besides, they've tested the food we had in the house. *Nothing* had arsenic. No, wherever he got it, it wasn't at home," Celia said with certainty. "He got it on the road somewhere. During my trial, there were toxicology experts who said that arsenic could take up to twelve hours to work, so he could have gotten it almost anytime yesterday. But it's not a coincidence, David. Two of my husbands would not be poisoned with arsenic by accident. Somebody's trying to kill him, and we've got to find out who it is before they pull it off."

• • •

Across town, Jill Clark sat at her desk, rubbing the ache at the back of her neck as she held the phone to her ear. Someone at Judge Spencer's office in Jackson, Mississippi, had put her on hold almost ten minutes ago, but still, she waited.

While the Muzac played out an organ rendition of "Sweet Caroline," she scanned the legal pad on which she had taken copious notes at Aunt Aggie's house. Celia had easily answered all of her questions, holding nothing back. It was as if she thought that giving her enough puzzle pieces would help her to see the whole picture and quickly clear things up.

The Muzac stopped, and Jill sat up.

"Judge Spencer's office."

Frustrated, she rolled her eyes. "I was on hold for the court reporter," she said. "I'm calling in reference to a case Judge Spencer presided over. Jackson versus Celia Porter. It was six years ago."

"Hold, please."

She closed her eyes and moaned. It was so much easier to go down to the office and find it herself, but since the trial had been in Jackson, she was at their mercy. She turned the page of her notes and saw the names: Sheree Donolly and Lee Barnett. When she'd asked Celia if she'd ever had an idea who might have killed her first husband, she'd suggested these two names.

Sheree was a jilted girlfriend of Nathan's who bitterly resented Celia. Celia admitted that, if she'd been a killer, she would have gone after Celia, not Nathan. And why would she want to come back after all these years and kill Stan—someone she'd never even met? Celia had thought that too far-fetched to be true.

Still, Jill intended to check her out, see if there was any history of mental illness, any other crimes she may have been charged with.

Her eye moved to the notes she'd taken about Lee Barnett. He had been a computer programmer, upwardly mobile in his profession, Celia had told her, and she had dated him for a year. But he'd had more than one downfall. He drank too much, loved to party, and she'd caught him one too many times with another woman.

"Besides, it couldn't be him this time," Celia had said. "He's in jail."

"Jail?" Jill had asked her. "What for?"

"One of those nights he drank too much, he got into a fight and killed somebody. He was convicted of manslaughter."

"Was this before or after Nathan was murdered?"

"After," Celia had said. "Believe me, they did question him about Nathan's murder, but he'd been out of town at the time, and lots of people had seen him. A couple of years later he went to prison. I'm sure he's still there."

Jill wondered. She'd have to make sure.

The thing was, someone had set Celia up. This wasn't just about murder. Whoever did it wanted Celia to look guilty. They'd gone to great pains, twice now, to point to her.

Celia had told her about the stacks of evidence they'd had against her in the trial. Arsenic in the house, journals on her computer, in which she'd supposedly planned out the murder … When she'd told her about them, Celia had sworn that she never used that computer and that she'd never even bought an insecticide for the house, much less arsenic.

Whoever the killer was, he'd done a good job. Jill supposed it was by the grace of God that the jury had acquitted her.

"Ann Hutchins."

The voice on the telephone startled her, but she tried to refocus her thoughts. "Yes. I'm calling to order a transcript of a trial that Judge Spencer presided over about six years ago. Were you his court reporter then?"

"Yes, I was," the woman told her. "What was the name of the case?"

"Jackson versus Celia Porter," she said. "Could you tell me if it would be possible to get that transcript today?"

"I doubt it," the reporter said. "You see, I rarely transcribe my notes unless one of the attorneys asks for it for an appeal. It should take a week or two for me to transcribe it."

"No," Jill groaned. "I can't wait. I need it today. A woman's life is at stake."

The woman sighed. "Well, hold on, and I'll see what I have on it."

Again, the Muzac. She dropped her forehead against her desktop, waiting.

In just a few minutes, the woman came back to the phone. "Hello? Ma'am?"

"Yes," Jill said. "I'm here."

"You're in luck. It seems that the defense attorney requested daily copies of the transcript during the trial, so I have it all done. Would you like me to mail it to you, or will you pick it up?"

She thought over the possibilities and realized she couldn't rely on anyone to get it to her quickly enough. No, she was too anxious. "I'll drive up and get it myself," she said. She looked at her watch. It was just after noon. "I'll be there around two-thirty."

"All right. I'll have it ready for you."

She hung up the phone, trying to think. She needed several things in Jackson today, she concluded. She needed to speak to the attorney who had defended Celia in the first trial, and she needed to find out if Lee Barnett was still in prison.

Quickly, she threw the legal pad into her briefcase and locked it shut. Her secretary, Sheila, one of the angriest but most competent women she'd ever known, shot her a questioning look.

"Call Celia at Aggie's house and tell her I'm on my way to Jackson to get some things I need from the clerk of the court, Sheila. Tell her I'll call her when I get back tonight."

Sheila muttered something under her breath, but since Jill couldn't hear it, she didn't worry about it. Sheila was always muttering. The fact that she was already dialing Aggie's number was all that really mattered.

• • •

Aunt Aggie pulled her lavender Cadillac into her driveway and saw the photographer and newspaper reporter who had been there when she left. She got out of her car and slammed the big door. "Shoo! Get on outa here, Jed!"

"Aunt Aggie, can you ask Celia to give us a statement?" the reporter whined. "Just a little one? Then we'll leave."

"Celia ain't givin' you nothin'. Now leave!"

"But Aunt Aggie, if I go back to the paper without *something*, Hank'll wring my neck. You don't know him when he's mad. And this is the biggest thing that's hit Newpointe in a while. Give a guy a break, will ya?"

As he droned on, Aggie marched up the steps to her front door, turning from flashes of the camera. "Hank gon' be real mad when he has to bail you out for trespassin'!"

She reached the door, and so did the photographer. He stood poised to snap a shot when she opened the door. She reached up and unsnapped the big lens protruding from the camera's front. "You tell Hank I'll give this back when my Celia's cleared," she said. "Now get off my prop'ty 'fore I have to start playin' dirty."

The photographer whined out his complaint, but she ignored him as she pushed through her front door.

She heard voices and looked into the living room. David, her nephew, was sitting there. "T-David!" she shouted. "*Sha!* You came!"

As they hugged, Celia asked, "Aunt Aggie, how is Stan?"

"Still out," Aunt Aggie said, her face changing again. "His looney-bin folks hired a guard to stand outside his room. Threw me right out, me."

"They threw you out?" David asked. "Why?"

Aunt Aggie hesitated. "They just real careful."

"That's not it," Celia said. "They don't trust you because of me. They believe that I did it, don't they?"

"Honey, ain't nobody thinkin' rational."

"That easily, they'd think the worst about their own daughter-in-law?" David asked.

"Why not?" Celia asked as tears pressed to her eyes again. "My own parents do. Why shouldn't his?"

David looked as if he didn't know what to say about his parents' insensitivity. "You know how Mom and Dad are. Image control is a big thing with them."

Aunt Aggie watched Celia's face draining of color. "You feel okay, Celia?"

Celia laid her head back on the sofa and took a deep breath. "Aunt Aggie, do you think they would even tell us if he died?"

"Oh, they'll tell us all right. That rat Sid'll change your charges from attempted murder to murder so fast, heads be spinnin'. They'd tell us."

"What if he wakes up?" she asked. "Will they let us know that?"

"Can't say," Aunt Aggie said. "But I ain't gon' let up callin' there till he does. And he will, *sha*, don't you worry."

"How did he look?"

"Pale. Monitors hooked up to him, IV, you got the picture. Medicine's workin' on him, darlin'. It'll work. I know it will."

"I wish you believed in prayer," Celia said on a whisper. "I could use someone praying for me today."

"I b'lieve in positive thinking," Aggie said. "That's all prayer is, anyway."

"No, it's not, Aunt Aggie. It's much more than that. I need someone to pray for me, not think about me."

"I'm praying for you," David said.

Aunt Aggie tried to hide her surprise. She'd never known David to be a praying man. She'd believed him to be one of the few in the family who didn't need religion. She'd half admired him for it. He took after her, she'd thought proudly. So now he'd changed his mind?

"I appreciate that, David," Celia said. She looked up, still as pale as a Mardi Gras ghost. "Uh . . . excuse me."

She dashed out of the room to the bathroom, and moments later, Aggie heard her retching again. "That girl got some poison, too, whether they found it or not! She gon' have to black out, herself, 'fore they'll listen."

Slamming down her purse, she headed for the bathroom to help her niece.

Chapter Fourteen

Jill stared down at the trial transcript the clerk of the court had laid down in front of her. Jackson, Mississippi versus Celia Porter.

She flipped through the pages of transcript, saw the witnesses the prosecution had stacked against her. Expertly, she scanned the testimony, hoping to find the evidence they'd used against Celia. A computer journal, arsenic in the house, Nathan's affair . . .

She froze on the testimony by Celia's friend, who claimed that the week of the murder, Celia had learned that Nathan was having an affair. So, that was the motive they'd come up with, Jill thought, feeling the blood rushing to her face. Celia hadn't mentioned that.

She flipped on through and found that the alleged girlfriend was Sheree Donolly. Hadn't Celia said she was a *former* girlfriend?

She turned to the back, looking for the closing remarks that would give her a nutshell summary of the case. Instead, she found a motion for dismissal with prejudice. Apparently, the judge had complied. Celia had not been acquitted at all. Something had happened to cause the judge to dismiss, and the "with prejudice" wording of the dismissal had kept the prosecutor from trying it again.

She realized that her face was turning red and her hands were trembling as she flipped through. She looked up to see the court reporter watching her curiously. She cleared her throat. "Uh . . . thank you."

"Wasn't there something else you were looking for?"

She tried to clear her head and think. "Yes. Uh . . . Lee Barnett. I'm not sure if Judge Spencer was the one who presided over that case, but he was convicted of manslaughter a few years ago. I'm not sure of the exact date. I need to know his sentence, if he's still incarcerated, that kind of thing."

"I'll see if that was one of ours," the woman said, taking the information down. "If not, I can find those things out, anyway." She disappeared into the records room.

Jill found a chair and sank down, and began reviewing the transcript again. She started from the last page of testimony and tried to trace her way back to whatever could have caused the charges to be dropped. It was too tedious and would take too long to get to the bottom of it, so she looked for the defense attorney's name, checked her watch, then pulled her cellular phone from her purse.

She called information, got the attorney's number, then quickly dialed it.

"Summers, Stockwell, and Graham."

"Yes, uh . . . I need to speak to Robert Stockwell, please."

"May I tell him who's calling?"

"Jill Clark," she said. "I'm an attorney in Newpointe, Louisiana, and I'm representing a former client of his—she went by the name of Celia Porter. I need to talk to him about that trial."

The woman put her on hold, and within minutes, Robert Stockwell was on the phone. "This is Bob Stockwell."

"Mr. Stockwell, thank you for taking my call."

"No problem. My secretary said you were calling about Celia. How is she?"

"She's fine," Jill said. "Well, actually, she's not. You see, her husband was poisoned with arsenic last night, and she's been charged with attempted murder."

The man was dead silent, and if she hadn't heard him breathing, she would have sworn he'd hung up.

"Mr. Stockwell?"

"I don't believe it," he said. "Another husband poisoned?"

She knew the thoughts that must be coursing through his mind. Had he gotten a guilty woman off? Had he released her to kill again?

She knew her voice was too weak as she said, "She's innocent, Mr. Stockwell. I know she is. But I came to Jackson to get a copy of the transcript of her trial, and I'm a little confused about how the trial ended. I was under the impression that Celia had been acquitted."

"No, no. Is that what she told you?"

Jill honestly couldn't remember if she'd ever used that word. Maybe she'd talked around it, with words like "not convicted." She wasn't sure. "I . . . I don't think so," she said. "I may have just jumped to that conclusion based on the fact that there was no conviction. But could you clear this up for me? Why were the charges dropped?"

He seemed shaken, and hesitated for a moment longer. Finally, he cleared his throat. "About three weeks into the trial, we put a police officer on the stand who had been one of the first on the scene when Nathan's body was found. He swore that the supervising officer had made the comment that the wife is always guilty. And he had a string of other inflammatory remarks and innuendos about Celia. The jury was made up of eight women and four men, and during that testimony, you could see the anger on their faces."

"So you moved to dismiss the charges?" she asked.

"Yes. It was the perfect opportunity. The testimony had hurt the credibility of the investigation, since the man in charge seemed to want to nail her. Even the judge saw that we'd never get a guilty verdict from that jury after that, so he dismissed the charges and the trial ended."

She closed her eyes. "I wish you had let it go all the way. An acquittal would look a lot better right now."

"Afraid what the Newpointe police will think when they find out?"

Jill nodded silently. "I'm afraid they'll be as surprised as I was. One other thing, Mr. Stockwell. I noticed in scanning the testimony something about a computer journal. Could you tell me about that?"

"Yes," he said. "There were some computer files on the PC in their home. Some journal entries were made in which Celia allegedly wrote out her plans to poison Nathan because of his affair. Celia claimed she didn't even use that computer, that someone else had made those entries."

Jill let that sink in for a moment. "What can you tell me about the affair?"

"That was the motive the prosecution used. Apparently, Nathan did have a girlfriend, though, I have to tell you. I was with Celia when she first heard of this, and she was shocked. It was no act. I really didn't think she knew about it. But it came up every day of the trial. They turned it into a virtual soap opera. And when the girlfriend testified, it was quite a circus. She claimed Nathan told her the day before he died, that he'd asked Celia for a divorce and told her about his affair. Celia claims it never happened, and no one could verify if it was true one way or another." He paused for a moment, then added, "Celia should have told you these things. They're pertinent, don't you think?"

"Yes, she should have. But her state of mind isn't that great right now. She's very worried about her husband, and she hasn't slept. And I guess there could be an element of denial. It's bad enough to have your husband murdered, but while you're grieving, to be accused of that murder, and then be told that he was cheating on you?"

"Her second husband wasn't cheating, was he?"

Jill frowned. "No. Not at all."

"I was just thinking . . ."

"That maybe her toggle switch was flipped every time she faced rejection? Come on, Counselor. You knew the same Celia

I know, didn't you? Besides, she's sick with worry over her husband right now. All she can think about is getting to his side."

"He's not dead?"

"No. He's in a coma."

Silence again.

"Look, would you be willing to give me your file on that case? There might be something there that could help me to defend her."

"Certainly. I have several boxes in storage. I can have my secretary pull them and have them ready for you as soon as you can come by."

"All right. I'll be there before you close today." She paused, thought for a moment. "Look, Mr. Stockwell, I know what you're thinking. You're wondering if maybe you had her all wrong, if she really could have been a killer. But I can tell you that I've known her for the past few years, and she doesn't have this in her. That killer is still out there somewhere. He's simply struck again."

"But why? Why, after all these years? Why another of Celia's husbands?"

"That's the mystery," Jill said. "I'll let you know when I figure it out."

The clerk was just coming back as she clicked off her phone. Jill got up and went back to the counter.

"Judge Spencer didn't preside over the Barnett case," the woman said. "But I made a phone call and learned that he was incarcerated at the Rankin County Correctional Facility, just about fifteen minutes away. He was released about two weeks ago."

Jill caught her breath. *"What?"*

"That's right. He served five years, and last week—"

"Do you have an address?" she asked. "Is there a phone number for a family member I could call?"

"No, I don't think so," the woman said. "There's a former address, but this was five years ago. It's an apartment, so chances are, he won't be going back there."

"I'll take it," she said, and jotted it down.

"Was there anything else you needed?"

She couldn't think. Her heart was beating so hard that it drowned out the woman's words. "Uh . . . thank you."

Somehow, she wrote out a check for the transcript, grabbed it, and made her way back to her car. It wasn't a coincidence, she told herself. It couldn't be a coincidence.

Lee Barnett had to be the killer.

Two hours later, armed with three boxes that contained all the work Robert Stockwell had done on Celia's case, Jill found Lee Barnett's address on the map, and navigated her way to it. It was a nice apartment on the Ross Barnett Reservoir—not at all a place where she'd expect a convict to have lived.

Instead of going to the apartment where Lee was supposed to have lived, she tried the office. A woman sat at a desk, the telephone against her ear. Jill stepped inside, and the woman motioned for her to sit down.

"Yeah. Apartment 15. Yeah. Okay, I'll tell 'em."

She hung up, made a notation on her desk calendar, then looked up at Jill. "Can I help you?"

"Yes. My name is Jill Clark. I'm an attorney from Newpointe, Louisiana, and I need some information." She knew the woman didn't have to tell her anything about her tenants, but she hoped her boldness and the fact that she was an attorney would disarm her.

"Okay," the woman said. "Are we bein' sued? Are you here to give me a subpoena? 'Cause we didn't have anything to do with that fire, and the inconvenience wasn't exactly our fault."

Jill wouldn't let herself smile. "No, nothing like that. I'm looking for Mr. Lee Barnett. This was his last known address, apartment 26. Could you tell me if he's still living here?"

The woman breathed a visible sigh of relief. "Thank goodness. A lawsuit's all I need. Let me see. Nope. No Barnett in any of these apartments."

"Do you by any chance remember him? He would have been here, say, five years ago?"

"Nope. I've only been here two years."

Disappointed, Jill thanked her and left. What now?

Sheree Donolly. She needed to find and talk to the woman who claimed to have had an affair with Celia's husband. She thumbed through the transcript until she found Sheree's testimony. She'd given her address just after they'd sworn her in. She wrote the address down and studied the Jackson map. She navigated her way to the modest house in the Madison area, and pulled into the driveway.

Praying this visit would lead her closer to the truth, she went to the door.

A woman in her fifties answered. "Yes?"

Moved again, Jill thought. *Terrific.* "Hello, I'm Jill Clark. I'm looking for someone who used to live here. Sheree Donolly?"

"You're too late," the woman said. "She's in the hospital."

"The hospital?"

The woman seemed amused at Jill's surprise. "Don't look so worried. Didn't you know she was due?"

Jill felt as if she'd missed the first half of the conversation. "Due?"

"The baby. She had her baby yesterday."

Jill's eyebrows shot up. "Really? I didn't know she was pregnant."

The woman laughed. "And here I thought you were a good friend checking on her. I'm sorry ... I'm her mother. Who did you say you were?"

"Jill Clark. Uh ... Mrs. ..."

"Donolly," her mother said.

"Yes. Mrs. Donolly. Could you tell me Sheree's married name?"

The woman sighed. "Oh, she's not married, I hate to say. It's a real sore subject, but if you know Sheree, you're not surprised. She's my only daughter, but I don't approve of all she does. Still, I'm gonna enjoy that grandbaby. Sweetest little girl you ever saw. Go on up to the hospital and see 'em. I'm sure she'd love to see you."

Jill nodded, as if she'd do just that. "Mrs. Donolly, could you tell me what time of day Sheree went into the hospital yesterday?"

"Oh, she didn't go in yesterday. Went in the night before. Had hard labor for over twenty-four hours. Finally had a C-section."

Jill thanked the woman and let her think that her next stop would be the hospital, but she knew there was no point. If Sheree had been in labor on the day Stan was poisoned, she probably wasn't involved.

Lee Barnett was a much more probable suspect.

She checked her watch and saw that it was getting late. She needed to get back to Newpointe and confront Celia about the things she hadn't told her. She needed to be there in case the police pulled anything. She needed to be there in case Stan died.

Her heart sank. This was too much. She had never defended anyone against anything worse than drug dealing—except for one murder charge that was dropped within twenty-four hours. She wasn't sure she was equipped to defend Celia, and dismally, she realized that she wasn't equipped to track down Lee Barnett.

She started her car and headed back to I–55 south. She'd go straight to the police station and tell them what she'd learned. They would be getting a transcript of the trial themselves, but they probably hadn't gotten it yet. Maybe she could deflect their shock about the mistrial, then address their certainty that Celia was guilty by dropping the bomb about Lee Barnett's release. Hopefully they would take the baton and find him. Chances were, he was right there in Newpointe, watching the drama unfold.

She hoped they'd take her fears seriously, before he tried again.

Chapter Fifteen

The police station wasn't that busy this time of day, when the biggest crimes were being committed by speeding drivers on their way home from their daily commute to New Orleans. Jill found Sid slumped at his desk, and took a deep breath to sustain her. *Take the offensive*, she reminded herself. If she let Sid get the upper hand, he could probably even convince *her* that Celia was a raging murderer.

She had stopped by her office and made the police department another copy of the transcript, so that she could get the little surprises out of the way. She made her way across the room, between desks and around chairs, to where Sid sat.

"I have something for you." She dropped the transcript on his desk and plopped down wearily in the chair across from him.

"You look rough," Sid said.

"I feel rough. You don't look so good yourself."

"I did go home and get a couple hours of sleep." He sipped from a coffee mug that said something about cluttered desks being the sign of genius, and glanced down at the transcript. "Hey, where'd you get this?"

"I went to Jackson and got it."

"We were told it could take two weeks."

"No, the court reporter had it on file, because the defense attorney had requested daily copies of the transcript during the trial." She sat up rigid in the chair and locked eyes with him. It was very important that she choose her words carefully, so that the motive the prosecution had used and the way the trial ended wouldn't seem so important.

"I spoke to the defense attorney about the evidence that led to the dismissal, and he told me there had been a cop who'd said some despicable things about Celia—"

"Wait a minute." Sid's words cut her off, and he began flipping through the transcript. "Dismissal? I thought she was acquitted. That's what she said."

Jill knew she was going out on a limb, since she couldn't remember exactly *what* Celia had said. "I don't think she said that, Sid. What she told us is that she was not convicted. That was true."

She could see that Sid didn't like it. He turned to the back page of the transcript and found the motion to dismiss.

"I brought this to you so you'd be closer to clearing this up," she said. "And I also wanted to give you the name of a possible suspect that you need to check out. One of the guys questioned in the first murder was a man named Lee Barnett. He had an alibi, so the police didn't pursue it. But I find it interesting that just a couple of weeks ago he was released from prison after a five-year term for manslaughter."

Sid's bloodshot eyes returned to her. "Lee Barnett, you say?"

"Yes. Will you at least try to locate him? Find out where he was on the day of Stan's poisoning?"

Sid blew out a breath. "All right, Jill. I'll see what I can find out. But that don't explain why Celia led us to believe she was acquitted. That's important information, Jill. She coulda cleared that up any time, and you know it."

Jill knew it was true. She'd spent the last few hours fuming about that, herself. Still, she had to defend her. "She's beside herself worried about Stan, Sid. She's doing the best she can."

"To what? To cover up?"

"Look for Lee Barnett, Sid. I think that will answer a lot of our questions."

"Give me a motive," he said. "Why would this Barnett guy want to kill Stan right after he gets out of the slammer?"

"I don't know," she said. "But if you find him, maybe you'll find out."

"Don't hold your breath, Jill." He leaned up on the desk, bracing his elbows. "I know you gotta believe in your client and everything, but what if she's guilty?"

Jill didn't have the energy to fight him. She had to save it for Celia.

She headed out to her car just as she saw Dan's Acura pulling out of the Midtown fire station's parking lot. He spotted her and pulled his car over, got out, and came to her passenger door.

She smiled as he slipped in beside her.

"Hey there, Counselor," he said in that deep voice of his. Those stark green eyes had a smile in them, and he leaned over and pressed a chaste kiss on her lips.

"You smell good," she said, touching his face.

"I just showered," he told her. "We had a fire at the feed mill today, and I smelled like a smoke bomb. I'm off, so I was just about to start looking for you and see if you wanted to have a bite."

Jill remembered that she hadn't eaten at all today. She didn't have time for it, but if she took the time, maybe it would give her the energy she needed to confront Celia. "I can't spare much time," she said. "I've been in Jackson, and I really need to get over to Aunt Aggie's and talk to Celia."

"You gotta eat." He pushed a strand of hair out of her eyes. She wasn't sure why that jolt went through her every time he touched her. "Come on. We'll go to Maison de Manger and have a couple of po' boys."

Though the deli sounded like a five-star establishment to anyone not familiar with French, it was really a glorified fast-food place whose name really meant "House of Hunger." But it was one of the favorite places in Newpointe, third only to McDonald's and Burger King. "Okay," she said. "I'll meet you there."

She watched as he got out of the car and headed back to his own. A strong breeze whipped up his hair, and she bit her grin as he got into the car, flipped the visor, and finger-combed it back into place. Then he pulled the car out onto the street.

She suspected that his vanity had more to do with insecurity than pride. He hated his receding hairline. Though he'd never mentioned it to her, that seemed to be what kept him constantly looking at his reflection in windows and mirrors. That preoccupation served him well, though. She doubted he knew how good-looking he really was. His body testified to the amount of jogging and weight lifting he did, and if he wasn't aware of it, every woman in Newpointe was.

But it wasn't just his looks that attracted women, she thought. It was also his money. Dan was the only fireman she knew who owned acreage just outside of town and could afford a house that was bigger than the fire station itself. The word around town was that his father had moved heaven and earth to try to direct him into a more lucrative line of work, but Dan had a passion for fire, a passion that drew some firefighters no matter how little they got paid or how much they had to give up. His father had eventually given up and offered his blessings, along with a sizeable inheritance when he'd died two years ago. Dan Nichols would never hurt for money, which was just one more reason he was number one on the eligible list of every single woman in town. The fact that he showed any interest at all in her was a phenomenon she couldn't quite fathom.

She pulled into a parking space in front of the cafe that was perched on a bayou, and he was at her door in an instant. "Dan, have you heard any word on Stan?" she asked as they headed around to the back deck, where bullfrogs croaked and crickets chirped, and the breeze whispered through the cypress leaves.

"Nope. He's still in a coma."

She moaned.

"So what did you find out in Jackson?" he asked as they took a table.

Wearily, she set her chin in her palm. "Nothing. Every-thing. I really can't talk about it."

He looked offended, but he didn't press. "No problem. But don't expect me to tell you about the fire over at the feed mill."

She grinned, glad that she had taken the time to spend with Dan.

Chapter Sixteen

Joe's Place had a sparse crowd, and a smoky haze floated over the room that vibrated with the too-loud sounds of zydeco music. R.J. Albright sat at the end of the bar, relaxing for the first time since Stan Shepherd keeled over. He had thought of going home and falling into bed, but he'd decided that one drink might be in order just to help him unwind. He scanned the familiar faces in the room—the same ones that were here every night—and noted that there was no one here he particularly wanted to talk to.

The door opened and a stranger came in—a tall, sandy-haired guy who looked like a close cousin of Brad Pitt, only cleaner cut. After standing at the door for a moment and looking around, he headed for the bar and took a seat a few stools down from R.J.

Not too interested, R.J. went back to nursing his beer.

A newspaper lay folded on the counter between R.J. and the stranger, and R.J. saw the man glance down at the headline: Newpointe Detective Poisoned by Arsenic. He frowned and picked the paper up, unfolded it, and his eyes lingered on Celia's picture in the center of the article, next to one of Stan.

R.J. wondered if it was just his imagination or if the stranger's face drained of color.

"Where y'at?"

The man kept staring at the paper, but Joe, the bartender and proprieter, tried again.

"Where y'at, pal? You want somethin', or not?"

The man looked up into Joe's scruffy face, and for a moment, R.J. considered interpreting the Cajun greeting for him. Rapid-fire Cajun was a strange mixture of French and southern American, and not many outsiders could understand it.

"Uh . . . Gimme a beer." The man turned back to the paper, frowning as he read. Joe set a cold beer bottle on the counter in front of him, then waited for him to pay. As he reached into his wallet for his cash, R.J. saw a tattoo just under the man's shirt sleeve. It looked like a tally of some sort—four short lines and a fifth crossing diagonally through them. He'd tallied twelve.

R.J. breathed a laugh, wondering if the man kept a running score of the women in his life. The man pulled out a ten and set it on the counter. "Listen, you know anything about this case here?" he asked, pointing to the article.

Joe glanced down and rolled his eyes. "Don't arrybody? She killed her first husband, you know."

When Joe looked at him, R.J. nodded that it was true.

"When did this happen?"

"Last night. He ain't dead, though. They got him over to the hospital. He ain't woke up yet."

"And where's his wife? In jail?"

"Nope, not yet. She ain't been arrested yet."

"So she's home?"

"Guess so."

He looked back down at the article, reading the words with a little too much interest. "So where would that be?"

Joe had already turned away and was wiping the other side of the bar.

"'Scuse me," the man said louder. "Where does she live?"

Joe turned around. "Who?"

"Celia Shepherd."

Joe paused and glanced back at R.J., as if asking him if he'd heard all that. R.J. nodded.

The man saw the look pass between them and quickly tried to explain himself. "See, I know her. Or I used to. We went to school together."

"You from Jackson?" Joe asked him, growing interested now.

"That's right."

Joe leaned down on the counter. "What you know 'bout her first husband? The one died of arsenic?"

"I know she ain't a killer."

R.J. got up and hiked up his pants. Slowly, he ambled around to take the stool next to the stranger.

"R.J. Albright," he drawled, extending a hand.

The man shook. "Lee Barnett."

R.J. slipped onto the stool beside Lee, and brought his mug halfway to his mouth. "Celia Shepherd wouldn't be one o' them notches, would she?" he asked, pointing to the tattoo.

Barnett looked down at his arm, as though he'd forgotten the tattoo was there. "No, man. Those ain't for women. They're for deer."

"You shot twelve deer?"

"Fifteen, actually. But my tattoo's behind. It'd be more, but I ain't hunted in five years." He tapped the newspaper article with a calloused finger. "So do you know Celia Shepherd?"

R.J. nodded. "Stan's a good friend o' mine. Celia, too, I reckon. Downright shame."

"Is he gonna die?"

"Don't know. Hope not."

Barnett stared down at the article, reading over it again. He was still too shaken up . . . too concerned. He threw his beer back, as if trying to calm down.

"I always thought there was somethin' fishy about her," R.J. said. "She was too good-lookin' to marry a small-town boy like Stan. She looked Hollywood. We all knew there was somethin' wrong there."

Barnett stared down at the paper again, his eyes scanning the article.

"Where'd you say you knew her from?" R.J. asked.

"From Jackson," he said. "We went to high school together."

"Was she always devious?"

Barnett glanced up at him, his eyes laced with disgust. "Devious? No! She's always helpin' people. She may be a heart-breaker, but she ain't a killer."

R.J. and Joe exchanged looks. "She break *your* heart?" R.J. asked.

"Once. Long time ago." He gestured to Joe for another beer. When Joe slid it to him, he guzzled it a little too fast. "Ain't seen her in years."

"Is she what brings you to Newpointe?"

The question didn't amuse or surprise Barnett like R.J. might have expected. "I don't mess with married women. I came for the huntin'."

"She may not be married for long," R.J. said. "Not if Stan dies. And if he wakes up, he'll be smart to cut her loose."

Barnett threw back the second bottle. "Where did you say she was livin'?"

"You gonna get in touch with her?"

"Maybe. Just check on her. Give her some moral support."

"I wouldn't eat anything she fed you, pal. You might wake up dead, too."

The man's face was tense, thoughtful, as if reeling from what he'd just heard. "You don't have her phone number, do you?"

Again, Joe shot R.J. a look.

"Really, man. I need to get in touch with her. It's important. We go way back."

R.J. grinned and Barnett grinned back. Barnett had had enough to drink now that R.J. knew Barnett's talk would come a little more freely.

"Almost married her," Barnett confessed.

R.J.'s grin collapsed, and his eyes grew bigger. "You pullin' my leg?"

"Nope. We were tight."

"Oh, yeah?"

"Yeah."

"So why don't you know her number?"

He chuckled and brought his third bottle to his lips. "Been a while, and I'm new in town."

"So where you stayin', bein' so new to town?"

"Bonaparte Court apartments."

"You work in town?"

"Not yet."

"Then what brings you here?"

The man chuckled. "What are you? A cop?"

They all laughed raucously, and Barnett collapsed at his own humor. Man, he had trouble holding his liquor, R.J. thought. Three drinks and he was practically wasted.

As though the man realized it, he dug out another bill and paid Joe again, then slid off the stool. "It was nice chewing the fat with you two gentlemen," he said, "but I have an appointment."

"An appointment? It's almost dark. What kinda work you do, anyway?"

"Consultin'," he said.

"Consultin' about what?"

"Computers," Barnett said. "I'm a computer consultant. And I never let the clock dictate my hours."

"You stayin' in town for a while?" R.J. asked as he started back to the door.

"Maybe. Maybe not." He saluted them both, then hurried out the door.

R.J. set down his mug and looked at Joe. "I think maybe I need to get back over to the station and check out this fella." He paid his tab and hurried out the door.

Chapter Seventeen

Since she had gotten only a couple hours of sleep the night before, Jill was running on empty by the time she got to Aunt Aggie's house to talk to Celia. Doubts lurked like shadows in her heart, and questions shot through her mind with startling velocity. She sat in Aunt Aggie's pristine parlor, decorated with hundred-year-old antiques, delicate urns and fresh-cut flowers, and hanging plants in front of the large picture window. Celia sat in a Louis XIV chair with her back to the window. She seemed like nothing more than a silhouette against the harsh daylight, and her face captured the contrasting darkness of the room, revealing little. David sat in a matching chair on the other side of a marble-topped table. A small Tiffany lamp provided warm relief from the shadows, lighting one side of each of their faces. Still, it wasn't enough light to read Celia clearly.

"What is it, Jill?" Celia asked in a voice that revealed the fact that she'd spent much of the day crying. "You look almost mad at me. Are you turning on me, too?"

Jill shifted on the sofa and averted her eyes. "I have a few questions, Celia." The words came in a flat, metallic voice, between tight lips.

"Okay," Celia said. "Ask whatever you want. I have nothing to hide."

Jill met her eyes. "Why did you tell me that you were acquitted in the first trial?"

Celia didn't flinch. "I *didn't* tell you that."

Jill opened her mouth to speak, but an irritated, breathy sound escaped before the words did. "Celia, we all assumed it. Me, Sid . . . You didn't correct us."

Celia dropped her feet to the floor and sat up straighter. As she leaned forward, her face came out of the shadows, and the colors of the Tiffany lamp gave it warm definition. "Did you use the word *acquittal?*" Celia asked. "I don't think you did. You didn't say anything at all untrue."

"Celia, you knew what I thought."

"Why does it matter?"

"It matters because if you were acquitted of a crime, then any evidence used in that trial is irrelevant in a subsequent trial. If you were charged with Stan's poisoning, the jury has no right to even know that you'd been charged with that before. But when the trial didn't come to a natural conclusion . . ."

"Then I must be guilty? Is that it?"

"There's a difference between acquittal, Celia, and being let off on a technicality. The judge could allow that evidence."

Celia breathed a disbelieving laugh and got up. David braced his elbows on his knees and stared down at the floor between his feet. Jill watched Celia walk across the room, her arms crossed. It was a gesture that Jill was accustomed to—a defensive gesture that her clients often used. Especially the guilty ones.

"So what are you saying, Jill? That you don't believe me now that you found out I wasn't acquitted? You think I killed Nathan?"

She took a moment to consider that, then realized that she didn't—couldn't—think that. She just couldn't help being miffed that Celia hadn't been honest with her, and she needed to know the reason she had for hiding details about the case. "No, Celia. That's not it. I believe you're innocent. But you need to understand that you may be arrested for this, and if you are, your life is very much in my hands. I want to do everything in my power to help you. But that means that you have to help.

You can't leave things to my assumptions. You can't let me *think* things and not correct them."

"All right. I messed up! I wasn't thinking."

"You *have* to think, Celia. Your life, and maybe Stan's life, depend on it."

"Leave her alone," David said. "Can't you see she's upset? She's only had a couple of hours' sleep in two days, she's been throwing up, her husband's dying in the hospital—"

"Dying?" Jill asked on a whisper. "Has he taken a turn for the worse?"

"No!" Celia cried, shooting David a venomous look. "David, don't say that. He can't die."

He looked at her helplessly. "I'm just saying . . . you have enough on you without her badgering you like some half-baked criminal."

"She's not badgering me," Celia said, wearily walking back to her chair and sinking into it. "She's doing her job. It's a tough one. I'm sorry, Jill. I'll try to be more honest with you from now on. Please don't give up on me just because I didn't tell you everything."

"It's not me you have to worry about, Celia. Sid thinks he was duped, too. He thinks you were covering up."

"Why would I *do* that? I knew you'd get the trial transcript! I'm not stupid. I just had Stan on my mind, and I was so afraid of going through it all again . . ." She stopped and looked vacantly at the wall behind Jill. In her eyes, Jill saw the emotions struggling and the self-recriminations winning out. "All right, I guess I did know that you thought I was acquitted," she admitted finally, as the light from the lamp caught a tear in her eye. "But as far as I was concerned, I was. The judge dismissed the charges with prejudice. That means they can't try it again. I was off. I wasn't found guilty."

Jill reached into her briefcase and pulled out the transcript, set it in her own lap, and looked down at it. Her head was beginning to throb, and she rubbed her temples with her fingertips. "There's another thing."

"What?"

"Sheree Donolly." Jill looked up at her, gauging her reaction. Celia gave David an "I should have known" look, and he plopped back in his chair. "What about her?" David asked.

Jill kept her eyes on Celia. "Why didn't you tell me that she was having an affair with Nathan, and that the prosecution thought that was your motive for killing him?"

Jill wasn't sure if the red color on Celia's face came from the lamp or from the alarm at hearing that name again.

"Because ..." The word came out just above a whisper. "I don't think it's true."

"What? That they were having an affair? There were witnesses who said you knew about it."

"My husband loved me!" Celia's lips trembled, and she pushed her hair back from her face. "I didn't know about any affair until after he'd died. I still can't believe it, and I don't trust anything she said in that trial. Nathan and I, we had so many plans ... He wouldn't have done that, Jill. It was just a lie they used."

"You should have told me, Celia. Lie or not, I needed to know about it."

"Why? All you need is the truth, Jill. *I didn't do it.*"

Jill watched as Celia collapsed in tears, and David reached across the table and took her hand.

"Sheree and Nathan had a thing before he married Celia," David said. "Some people said it never really ended. That he only married Celia for her money."

Celia's face twisted more, and she turned to David, shaking her head. "It wasn't true, David. He loved me. We were happy."

"I know, Sis," he whispered. "They were," he went on, looking back at Jill. "At first, I kind of thought the rumors might be true, but he changed my mind. He was good to her. Our parents were crazy about him."

Jill didn't like those rumors. "What did you think, David, when you heard those things in the trial? Celia was biased, didn't want to believe them. But what about you?"

He let go of Celia's hand and looked down at his feet again, struggling with his answer.

"I need the truth, David. I know you want to spare Celia's feelings, but we need to cut to the heart of this."

David looked up at her. "I thought it was true. I had even seen him with Sheree a couple of times at the office."

"The office? You worked together?"

"Oh, yeah," he said. "When he married Celia, my dad gave him a position in our company. He was executive vice president of marketing. Couple of times, I stuck my head in his office to tell him something, and Sheree was there. Once I saw him in the car with her in the parking garage, coming back from somewhere."

Celia had heard this before, probably during the trial, so she didn't seem surprised. But she shook her head, denying it all.

"Did he offer any explanations?" Jill asked.

"Oh, yeah. Said she was trying to borrow money from him. He acted like she was bugging him to death, and he couldn't get rid of her. I bought it, at the time. But then, after all the testimony in the trial, I had to wonder."

"They were lies," Celia insisted again. "Why would those things be true, when they lied about my knowing? They said he'd asked me for a divorce just before the murder. That he'd told me about Sheree. That wasn't true. The night before he was murdered, we'd had a romantic dinner in Natchez, and we'd planned a trip to New England when the leaves changed. There wasn't any talk of divorce or another woman. They were all lies, and I won't believe them, when I already know how many other lies were set up in that whole case. Somebody out there wanted them to believe the lies, and they worked very hard to make them all sound believable."

Jill saw from the way Celia dropped her face into her hands and began sobbing that this was even more painful to her client than Jill had thought. She leaned back in her chair, too exhausted to comfort Celia. David sat there awkwardly, as if he wanted to comfort her but didn't know how. Jill wondered how *she* would feel if she found her husband dead, then was accused of murdering him, then learned that he'd been cheating on her? How would she feel if she'd had to spend months in jail, unable to get her own questions answered, unable to find the person who'd really done it?

Wearily, she got up and put her arms around the woman who was her friend, and remembered why she'd wanted to represent her in the first place. It was simple. She knew Celia was innocent.

Stooping in front of her, Jill made Celia look at her. "Celia, you have to tell me everything. But I know you didn't keep these things from me deliberately. The problem is that I'm afraid the police are going to grab this with both hands when they read the transcript. I tried to head it off by giving it to them myself, hoping they'd see that we weren't trying to hide anything. But when Sid gets finished, he's going to come to all the wrong conclusions."

Celia hiccuped a sob. "Oh, if only Stan would wake up. He would tell them. He knows I wouldn't do that. He may even know who did ... where he ate ... who he saw ... maybe something tasted funny ..." Her voice trailed off, and she covered her face again and shook her head hard. "But he may not even wake up." She rubbed her face and looked up, then touched her stomach and got to her feet. "Oh, no. I'm gonna be sick again."

She ran out to the bathroom, and Jill followed her tentatively. She stood at the bathroom door as Celia threw up. "Are you okay?" she asked after she had finished and was leaning against the wall.

"I guess."

"I think you should see a doctor, Celia. Arsenic or not, something isn't right."

Celia just kept leaning against the wall, but she didn't say anything.

Suddenly, Jill felt bone tired. Too tired to go on with this. Too tired to interpret her own instincts appropriately. "Celia, maybe I'll go by the hospital and check on Stan. But first, is there anything else I need to know? Anything at all?"

"No, Jill. Nothing."

"No more surprises?"

"Of course not." Celia led her out of the bathroom and back into the parlor. David was standing now, staring out the window, and Aunt Aggie had come in from the backyard and was waiting to see if Celia was all right.

Jill went back to the sofa, slid the transcript back into her briefcase, and snapped it shut. "Look, we'll start over in the morning, and maybe we can make some sense of all this. I really could use some sleep."

"Me, too," Celia said.

"Aunt Aggie, make her call the doctor. Something's wrong with her."

"First thing in the mornin'," Aunt Aggie said.

"I'm just gonna go on home after the hospital, okay?" Jill said, finally. "And I'll be here bright and early tomorrow." She looked at David. "Are you staying with them tonight?"

"Yes, why?"

"Because I feel better with a man in the house. We don't know who's out there, or what they want." As she said that, it occurred to her that David, with his slight build, might not be much of a deterrent. Still, his presence gave her some peace of mind.

As she stepped out into the humid night air, she took in a deep breath and wondered how this was going to end up. She hoped Celia didn't get a conviction this time. But Jill just wasn't sure that she was equipped to defend someone against murder.

Chapter Eighteen

The Wednesday night prayer meeting at Calvary Bible Church, which usually consisted only of its core group of active members, was unusually packed tonight. Allie and Mark Branning paused at the door of the fellowship hall, where supper cooked by some of the deacons' wives was being served. Every table was filled to capacity, and some of the teenaged boys were carrying folding chairs in for those in the overflow.

"Good grief." Mark stopped just inside the doorway, scanning the crowd. "I haven't seen some of these people since Easter. Are the children singing tonight?"

Though the children's musicals were always a big crowd sweller, what with all those proud parents and grandparents with their camcorders and cameras, Allie felt sure that wasn't the draw tonight. When there was drama in town, people came to church. It was the central clearinghouse for all of the gossip that had filtered its way from telephone line to telephone line.

Allie saw Dan Nichols sitting at the end of one of the tables with two seats vacant, and when he waved for them to take them, they headed toward him.

"I saved you a couple of seats if you want them," Dan said, running his fingers through his thinning hair. "The crowd really threw a wrench into supper, and the ladies are running around like chickens with their heads cut off back there trying to accommodate everybody. I already ate with Jill."

"We'll just get something later," Allie said, taking her seat next to Dan. "I'm not that hungry, anyway."

"Any word about Stan?"

Mark and Allie shot each other dismal looks before Mark spoke up. "We just came from the hospital. He's still not awake. It worries me. It worries me a lot."

"His parents are exhausted," Allie added. "I don't know how they'll get through this."

"Well, maybe tonight's prayer meeting will help them," Dan said.

"Maybe." She met Mark's eyes, but thankfully, he didn't take the opportunity to shoot Dan's hope down.

The piano on the stage at the far end of the room began to play, and Allie looked up to see Sue Ellen Hanover—the postal clerk—pounding the keys. Nick Foster got up and began leading those who had finished eating in a round of praise choruses. Since he liked to keep prayer meeting comfortable and relaxed, he held that service in the fellowship hall, where people could eat and fellowship among friends before they got down to business.

When they had finished singing the praise choruses, Nick took the microphone and began to read out the names of those who were sick, in the hospital, had special prayer requests, or had asked for intercession for friends or relatives. He seemed to fly through the names, as though he knew that the room hadn't been packed tonight for the usual fare. The fact that there were needy people out there who had requested earnest prayers, only to have them practically glossed over, bothered Allie. Nick had no business catering to the roomful of undevoted people salivating for a morsel of news.

"And now I come to the prayer request so many of you are interested in," the pastor said as if emceeing an awards ceremony. "Stan Shepherd."

The room got deathly quiet, and Nick looked up from his prayer list. His face was vulnerable, soft, and Allie could see the intense concern in his eyes. Maybe she was being too hard on him, she thought. Maybe he'd glossed over the others simply because of his desperate concern for Stan. That was understandable, even forgivable.

"I spoke to Bart and Hannah a couple of hours ago," he said, "and was told there's been no change in Stan's condition. He's still comatose, though they're administering medications to bind the arsenic in his system. When . . . if . . . he wakes up, there's potential for organ problems—kidney, liver, lungs . . . and this was quite possibly a lethal dose of arsenic. And in the case of deadly doses like that, it can act as a carcinogen, so there's the danger of cancer eventually, if he does live."

Allie hadn't realized this, and tears flooded her eyes. Mark, too, seemed to melt beside her, and he set his arm across her shoulders and pulled her closer.

"But obviously, right now, the main concern is that he wake up at all. This coma is really taking its toll on Hannah and Bart. They need our prayers for energy, and strength, and peace. And I'd like to suggest that those of us who can, enter into fasting and deep prayer for Stan. This is really in God's hands." His voice broke, and he made himself go on. "Before we go to the Lord, are there any other prayer requests?"

Allie sat there for a moment as others in the congregation were silent, apparently too moved by the depth of Stan's need to call out any new requests. But she was stunned that no mention had been made of Celia. None at all.

She felt the heat blushing to her face, and awkwardly, she got to her feet. "Nick," she called out to get his attention.

All eyes turned to her.

She took a deep breath and set her hand on her belly. Her heart pounded, and she told herself to calm down. They wouldn't respond to her anger. "Nick, I think we've left someone very important off of the prayer list. Celia Shepherd needs prayers, too. And we need to pray that the would-be killer will be found as soon as possible before he tries this again."

"I heard Celia *was* the killer," Marabeth Simmons, one of the twice-a-year members, called out. "Word's all over town that she killed her first husband the same exact way."

"Still," the postal pianist said in a pious voice, "we should pray for her mental condition, for whatever would have caused her to do such a horrible thing."

A roar went up from the crowd as members discussed with one another what kind of mental condition could lead someone to kill two husbands in a row. Astounded, Allie looked around at her friends, her brothers and sisters in Christ, *Celia's* brothers and sisters in Christ.

"Celia is not crazy, and she did not try to kill Stan!" she shouted over the noise. "You all ought to be ashamed!"

The turmoil in the room died down as everyone grew quiet.

"Are you sayin' it's coincidence?" Marabeth asked. "You think it's just a *accident* that Stan got poisoned just like that first poor man?"

"No, I don't," Allie bit out. "And neither does Celia. There's obviously a killer who's struck twice, but it isn't Celia!"

"I heard they found the arsenic in her bathroom," somebody shouted out.

"That's a lie!" Mark said, springing to his feet. "I was there."

"How come she has all them secrets?" Sue Ellen Hanover asked.

"Would any of you have spilled your guts at your new church if you were trying to escape a year of torment?" Allie asked. "She found refuge here, and she found Christ, and she's ministered in her sweet way to more of you here than I can count!"

"Thank goodness I never ate that casserole she brought me after my gallbladder surgery," Jesse Pruitt said, "or I might be dead, too."

Allie shot a helpless, astounded look to Nick, and she saw the look on his face that he wore whenever he felt he'd failed. It was warranted, she thought. He *had* failed, and her look indicted him.

Nick finally tapped the microphone. "All right, all right. Let's calm down. We can't let our prayer meeting turn into a gossip session. The fact remains that both Celia and Stan, as well as Hannah and Bart, are part of our family. We need to love and pray for all of them."

Allie sank back down, her heart hammering. Mark took her hand. She saw from the way he looked up at Nick that he, too, was disappointed that their shepherd hadn't done a better job of defending one of their wounded sheep.

"He thinks she's guilty," Mark whispered. "He's buying it with all the rest of them."

"Poor Celia," Dan whispered.

As Nick began to lead them in prayer, Allie had the disturbing sensation that the Holy Spirit was nowhere near.

She only hoped he was watching over Celia.

Chapter Nineteen

Sid rubbed his raw eyes as he read the last page of the trial transcript Jill had given him. Man, he thought, leaning back hard in his chair. If he'd had any hope before that Celia was not the killer, the transcript dashed it. In the first trial, she'd had a motive, she'd had the arsenic in her possession in the form of rat poison, she'd confessed in her computer journal ... What else did anybody need?

But if they charged her with this crime, they needed probable cause. What motive would she have for killing Stan? Being looney didn't seem to be a good enough motive. But he was sure if he looked hard enough, he'd find something. The motive always surfaced eventually.

He set his elbows on his desk and rubbed his eyes, wishing it was two strangers whose lives he was investigating, instead of his best friend and his friend's wife.

He thought of all the time he'd spent with Celia at church, all the Sunday school classes and Bible studies they'd shared, all the insights she'd offered into the mind and heart of God. He'd never had any inkling that she wasn't as she seemed, or that lurking beneath that sweet exterior was an unstable woman.

But no one had suspected Judas, either, before he'd betrayed Christ. Even when Jesus told them that one of them would betray him, no one said, "It's gotta be Judas." Instead, they pointed to themselves, and asked, "Is it me, Lord?"

He had to remember that Celia *wasn't* as she seemed. She had a past, and she had secrets, and those secrets were stacked one inside another like those little dolls that got smaller and smaller. Except her secrets got bigger instead of smaller.

"Hey, Sid," LaTonya Mason called from across the room. "I verified that info on Lee Barnett." He looked up to see the rookie cop he'd put on the case. "It's true. He got out twelve days ago. Served his full term. I tracked down his mama in Jackson, but didn't get a answer. I'll try again later."

"Okay," Sid said. "Let me know what you find out. Did you do a rap sheet on him?"

"Yep. Had a coupla DWIs, and then the manslaughter charge."

Lost in thought, Sid hardly noticed when R.J. burst through the glass door. He was out of uniform since he'd finally gone off duty, and as he bounced to Sid's desk and pulled a chair up, Sid smelled the alcohol on his breath. "Man, somethin' just happened at Joe's Place, and I don't know if it means nothin', but I thought I'd tell you."

"What?"

"There was this guy in there spoutin' off about his relationship with Celia Shepherd. Claims they used to be an item. Had a little too much to drink, and told us he'd just got to town, got him an apartment, and kept askin' us where Celia was, if we had her phone number, that kind of thing."

Sid sat up straighter and narrowed his eyes. "Yeah?"

"Yeah. And I tried to get at why he's in town, and he said he was here for the huntin'. Then he said somethin' about bein' a computer consultant. Just kept wantin' to know where Celia was, like he had to see her."

Sid stared at him, the first bud of hope beginning to blossom in his heart. Could this stranger, rather than Celia, have poisoned Stan? "Did he know about the poisonin'?"

"It was right there in the paper in front of him. Seemed genuinely surprised, but it coulda been a act. I couldn't say for sure."

"Did you get his name?"

"Sure did," R.J. said. "And I was gonna run a check on him. Name's Lee Barnett."

Sid's jaw fell open. "Are you sure?"

"Yeah, why?"

He scraped his chair back and stood up. "Only because Lee Barnett just got out of prison a coupla weeks ago, and he was questioned in the murder of Celia's first husband. You don't happen to know where he's stayin', do you?"

"Sure. He said he has an apartment over at Bonaparte Court."

Sid grabbed his keys and almost knocked his chair over.

"Where ya goin', man?"

"To pick up Mr. Barnett," Sid said. "I got a few questions to ask him."

• • •

Sid knocked on Marabeth Simmons's door at the Bonaparte Court apartments, for he knew no one would be in the office at this hour. He knew she would tell him where Lee Barnett's apartment was. There was very little that Marabeth could keep to herself, especially if she thought it was part of a police investigation.

She answered the door wearing a velveteen robe with fake fur around the collar. "Hey, there, Sid," she said.

"Hey, Marabeth. I'm here on police business. I need to know which apartment Lee Barnett is in. Do you know him?"

"Well, sure I know him," she said. "Cute as the dickens, if you don't mind my sayin' so. He ain't done nothin' wrong now, has he?"

"I don't know," Sid said. "Which apartment, Marabeth?"

"Well, he's in apartment B–5. Right up yonder." She pointed toward the man's door. Sid headed for the stairs.

"Are you gonna arrest him?" Marabeth asked. "I thought somethin' was funny about him. I was tellin' Sue Ellen over to the post office that it struck me odd that a man wouldn't know if his own apartment was furnished or not, but it takes all kinds. Don't reckon that's against any laws, though."

"No, ma'am."

"So . . . did he break some other law? Is that what you want with him?"

Sid started up the steps, and Vern Hargis—another officer who'd just pulled up in his squad car—followed him. "Thanks for your help, Marabeth."

She looked deflated that she hadn't gotten anything for the grapevine. But he didn't kid himself that she'd gone back into her apartment. He would have bet money that she was eavesdropping under the stairwell.

They went to the man's front door. There was a light on, so he hoped Barnett was home. He knocked hard.

After a moment, he heard him yelling, "I'm comin'!"

He answered so quickly that Sid thought he must have been expecting someone else. His expression crashed when he opened the door and saw the two cops. Sid wondered who he was waiting for.

"Yes?" he asked.

"Are you Lee Barnett?"

He hesitated. "Why?"

"I'm Lieutenant Sid Ford," Sid told him. "And this is Sergeant Vern Hargis. We need to ask you a few questions."

The man looked aggravated and crossed his arms with disgust. "Look, I served my time. I got out, fair and square. I ain't done anything wrong. I haven't had *time* to do anything wrong. What in the world would you have to ask me about?"

"We need to ask you about the murder attempt on Stan Shepherd's life."

His mouth fell open, and he rubbed the back of his neck as his face reddened. "Wait a minute." He took a moment to calm himself, then tried to speak again. "Look, I've never met the man. I've only heard his name. I didn't even know about the poisoning until I read it in the paper tonight."

He stepped back from the door, as if inviting them in. They went in, looked around. From the small living room, Sid could see into the bedroom. The bed was bare—no sheets or anything—and a suitcase lay open on the floor.

"I just got here today. Haven't had time to unpack or . . . buy sheets . . ." His voice seemed to trail off the further he got into the sentence. "Look, I got nothin' to hide."

"Then you won't mind coming down to the station with us so we can ask you a few questions," Sid suggested.

He breathed a nervous laugh. "Why can't you ask me here?"

"We'd rather take you to the station. It could take a while."

"Look, I don't *know* anything about the poisoning. Am I under arrest?"

"No, not at all. We'd appreciate your cooperation." As he spoke, Sid stepped over to the kitchen, glanced in. It didn't look like Barnett had even crossed the threshold.

"Is this your offhanded way of searching my apartment for somethin'?"

Sid turned back to him. "Searchin'? No, we ain't searchin'. You invited us in, remember? And now we're invitin' you down to the station."

He started to object, then stopped himself and seemed to think better of it. "All right," he said finally. "Let's go."

On the way to the police station, Sid glanced at the man in the backseat of his squad car and prayed silently that he held answers they needed. If he was the one who'd poisoned Stan, then Celia was off the hook. There was nothing Sid would like better. He would gladly eat crow and make his sincere apologies.

They reached the station, and he walked the man in. He was being amazingly cooperative, as if he feared what they might do to him. Sometimes, guilty people were too friendly, too cooperative, as if they thought their congenial manner would convince police there was no way such an upstanding citizen would break the law.

It didn't fly with Sid.

He led Lee Barnett into the interrogation room and offered him a chair. "Have a seat, Mr. Barnett. Can I get you anything? Coke? Coffee?"

"Coffee would be nice," he said. "I'm sure you know I ain't been out of prison long. Five years without alcohol, so the three beers I had tonight went straight to my head. I used to hold it better …" His voice trailed off, as if he knew he was rambling.

Vern headed out to get the coffee for him. Sid took a seat across from him, surveying the man who looked clean-cut, not at all like an ex-con. He must have gotten his hair cut first thing, he thought. A new set of clothes, new shoes.

"So what do you want to ask me?" Barnett asked when Vern brought him his coffee. He busied himself mixing in the sugar and cream that Vern had brought in little packets, but his hands trembled as he did. "You said it was about the murder attempt. I'll say again, I don't know Stan Shepherd. I never laid eyes on him."

"But you do know Celia."

"Sure. But I ain't seen her in years."

"Then what brings you to Newpointe twelve days after your release?"

He could see the struggle on the man's face. There was something to that, but Sid wasn't sure they'd get at the truth.

"I'd heard it was a nice place. I wanted to do some huntin' outside of town."

"Did you know Celia lived here?"

"Yeah. I'd heard somethin' about it. But I knew she was married."

Sid shifted in his seat. "Mr. Barnett, what were you doing yesterday?"

Barnett frowned, as if trying to figure out where they were going with this. "I was at my mama's house. That's where I been stayin'. I been veggin' out watchin' videos and enjoyin' not havin' a schedule. We didn't have TVs in there, 'cause the governor took 'em outa the jails. I had a lot of catchin' up to do."

"Was anyone there besides your mother and you?"

"Yeah, my sister took the day off work and came by, and my little niece . . . and a neighbor of my mama's came by for lunch." He looked from Sid to Vern. "Why? You need them to verify my alibi? 'Cause they will. Only I don't like gettin' my mama all crazy worryin' that her son's broke the law again. She didn't deserve it the first time. It like to killed her."

Sid made a notation on his legal pad but didn't respond to Barnett's question. "Did you leave her house at any time yesterday?"

"I went to Wal-mart and bought a couple of shirts and a new pair of jeans."

"Anybody with you?"

"No. I went alone."

"Did you, at any time yesterday, see or talk to Stan Shepherd?"

He sat back hard in his chair and stared at them as the wheels seemed to turn in his head. "I just told you. I've never seen him before. I've also never spoken to him. I wouldn't know him if he spit in my face. Besides, I was in Jackson. I can prove it. I couldn't possibly have made it to Newpointe to poison some guy and then back to Jackson in the time I spent at Wal-mart."

Sid told himself that the man could be playing innocent, pretending he didn't know that Stan had been to Jackson yesterday. "Did you talk to anyone in particular at Wal-mart who might remember seeing you there?"

The stunned look on Barnett's face told Sid that he was getting the picture. He had to realize that they were pursuing this line of questioning because they considered him a suspect. Barnett shifted in his seat, cleared his throat, rubbed his hand across the stubble on his jaw. "You people think I did it, don't you?" He leaned forward on the table, his eyes riveted into Sid's. "Why would I do that? After waitin' five years to get back into the world, why would I jeopardize everything and risk gettin' thrown back in?"

"You tell us."

"I don't believe this." He rubbed his face, thinking, and Sid watched as he seemed to search his mind for something. "I think I get it." He was breathing harder, and his face was reddening. "Yeah, I'm gettin' it now."

"What do you mean?" Sid asked.

"I think I've been had." His lips compressed, and he shifted in his seat. "Yeah, I'm sure of it."

The man was trembling as he leaned up on the table and slapped his hand on it. "Monday, the day before I'm released, I'm sittin' there mindin' my own business, when I'm told the chaplain wants to see me. So I go down to the chapel, and she tells me that some priest dropped a letter by for her to give me. And guess who it's from?"

Now they were getting somewhere, Sid thought, bracing himself. "Who?"

"Celia Shepherd." He reached into his back pocket and pulled out his wallet. "I've got it right here. You'll see." He reached into the billfold and retrieved the folded letter. His hands continued to tremble as he unfolded it. "Oh, man. It was all too good to be true. There I was thinkin' that maybe she was unhappily married and had been thinkin' about me. I had this fantasy of my comin' here and her wantin' to resume things after all these years ... Rich little Celia Bradford ..."

He pushed the computer printed letter across the table, and Sid read it. His heart plummeted. That knot in his stomach tightened. He handed the letter to Vern.

Barnett's face was getting redder, and through his teeth, he said, "Man, she lured me here so I'd look like the suspicious one, so I'd take the heat. What is my life worth, right? Just pin me with it, and she gets off scot-free. Man, I didn't do it. I ain't even heard from her in years. Not a word. And then this."

Sid looked up, not sure if he was being conned. "Where's the check mentioned in the letter?"

"I cashed it, man. It was right where the priest said it was. In the locker at the bus station. Right combination, everything."

"And this priest. Who was he?"

"You know as much as I do. The letter's signed 'Father Edmund Mueller.' Must be at one of the Catholic churches here, I guess. I never saw the guy."

Sid ran the facts through his mind. Lee Barnett had been too quick to turn this back on Celia. Was it fact, or was the truth somewhere between what he'd thought and what Barnett was telling him? Maybe Barnett wasn't the killer, but he wasn't the innocent saint, either.

"You mentioned your fantasy about Celia resumin' things. You knew she was married. Was you plannin' to have an affair with her?"

Barnett turned his palms up. "Hey, I figured I'd take her any way I could get her. I ain't exactly in the position to make moral judgments after where I've been. But I didn't see her. I just took the bait and came, and I ain't heard from her yet. I couldn't figure out why she'd want me here, in Newpointe, unless she wanted to start somethin' up with me. But now I gotta say, I think it was because she'd been plannin' this. Probably waited till my time was up. She wanted me to be here, so it would look like I blew into town to poison him. I don't believe it! What did I ever do to her to deserve this?"

A while later, Sid left the interrogation room and went to do as much checking as he could to verify the things Barnett had said. The letter was typed and could have been written by anyone trying to set Celia up, but the personal check was a little more difficult to explain. He found LaTonya Mason and got her to try to get a copy of the check from the bank, while he called Marabeth Simmons to find out who came in to rent the apartment.

"Paula Bouchillon, the owner, done it all by phone on my day off," she said. "She told me she talked to Mr. Barnett on the phone two weeks ago and that he mailed the deposit in and said he'd come by when he got here and sign the lease, which he did."

That wasn't likely, Sid thought. Two weeks ago, Lee Barnett was in jail. "Tell me about the deposit. Did he send cash, a money order, what?"

"A check, I think," she said. "Let's see. I ain't deposited it yet. No, it's right here, with a copy of the lease."

Sid's heartbeat accelerated. "Whose name is on that check, Marabeth?"

He heard papers rustling, then she whispered, "Oh, glory be! You're not gon' believe this, Sid. Oh, my. Wait till I tell Sue Ellen. Even Simone won't believe this."

"What?" Sid asked. "Marabeth!"

"The check, Sid, is on Stan and Celia Shepherd's account. I can't believe I didn't see that before, but Paula give it to me to deposit just today, and I never looked at it. What does this mean, Sid? It's somethin' to do with the poisonin', ain't it?"

Sid wiped the perspiration on his forehead and was careful not to answer her question. "Look, I'm fixin' to send an officer over right away to pick up that check. Do me a favor and put it in an envelope, and give it to the officer, okay?"

"All right, but . . . Will we get it back?"

"I'm not sure, ma'am. But that check could be important evidence. We've got to have it."

He hung up the phone before she could ask anything else and called the dispatcher, knowing that she, too, was a live wire on the Newpointe gossip lines. "Simone, I need for the officer who's closest to the Bonaparte Court apartments to go by the office there and get an envelope for me from Marabeth. I need it ASAP."

While he held, she dispatched an officer to do what she'd been told, then she came back to the phone. "Sid, what's going on? Is this about Stan?"

"Just part of the investigation, Simone. When we solve the case, you'll be the first to know."

"Do you still suspect Celia?"

"Bye, Simone." He hung up, and dropped his face into his hands. What was going on? Had Celia faked a man's voice to secure the apartment, or more likely, had Lee Barnett had access to a phone somewhere in the prison? They were allowed to make phone calls from time to time, he knew. It was, at least, possible. If he and Celia had something going, maybe he had made the call, and she had sent the check. The average person couldn't fake a bank account. At least, not from prison.

It wasn't more than fifteen minutes before T.J. Porter came in brandishing the envelope. "This what you needed, Sid?"

"Yeah, thanks." He opened it and pulled out the check. Just as she'd said, it bore the names "Stan or Celia Shepherd." In the right bottom corner was Celia's signature. He rubbed his eyes, wishing from his heart that it wasn't so.

"What's going on?" T.J. asked.

"Just more pieces to the puzzle."

"What puzzle?"

"The puzzle of Celia Shepherd. Who is she, T.J.? *What* is she?"

"I heard you'd brought somebody new in for questioning. Find out anything?"

Sid took in a deep breath. "I'm not sure yet," he said. "He wants us to think he's a Boy Scout who's in the wrong place at the wrong time. But I don't think so."

"What *do* you think?"

"I think he's a possible suspect . . . but more likely, he's Celia Shepherd's motive."

Chapter Twenty

The police chief was livid when he saw the check with Celia's signature. "I can't believe this!" Jim Shoemaker said. "All this time, I was thinking we'd made a mistake. That any minute now we'd turn up evidence that would exonerate her. But it gets smellier and smellier. A boyfriend, that check, her past . . . It all adds up to Celia Shepherd being a killer." He slammed the side of his fist into a file cabinet with a clash, then swung around. "Look, I don't want us dragging our feet on this. If Celia's the killer, let's nail her. Get a warrant to search her house again, and find whatever evidence you can. Last night you were just trying to find what had made Stan sick. This time you're collecting evidence for the grand jury."

Sid leaned back hard in his chair. "What if we're wrong? What if there really is another killer out there—maybe even Lee Barnett—and Celia's innocent?"

Jim's eyes bore into him. "Do you think she is?"

"No."

"Then let's not waste our time chasing rabbits. My experience tells me you look at the most obvious first. Celia's the most obvious suspect. If she's guilty, something in that house will tell us so."

Sid left his office and radioed for one of the squad cars to come and pick him up. Chad Avery was the first to arrive. "Where we going?" he asked as Sid got in.

"To the Shepherd house. We have to search it again."

"You got a warrant?"

"I'm stopping by Judge DeLacy's office on the way." He radioed Simone and asked her to dispatch one more evidence technician to the Shepherd house.

"We gonna be pawing through food and upchuck again?" Chad asked when he cut the radio off.

"No. This time we're lookin' for somethin' even more substantial. Somethin' that'll tell us, once and for all, that Celia Shepherd intended to kill her husband."

Chapter Twenty-One

The condition of the Shepherd's house was just as they'd left it in the wee hours of the morning. Sid Ford looked around at the kitchen, cluttered with food containers and zip-lock bags that the police themselves had left out. "We've already done a pretty thorough search through the food," Sid told the three cops with him. "This time, we're lookin' for anything that has arsenic in it. Rat poison, bug spray, whatever we can find. Chad, you take the attic. Vern and T.J., you take the garage and the utility room, then search the rest of the house with me, under sinks, in cabinets . . . I'll concentrate on the laundry room. It's not a big house, so we can lick this pretty quick if we try. Remember, whatever you find, let me know. If it's the slightest bit suspicious, it's relevant."

They dispersed to their assignment areas, and Sid began to remove the contents of the cabinets in the laundry room one by one. He checked the ingredients of each box of detergent, smelling and feeling to make sure it was what it claimed to be. Because the laundry room was only large enough to hold the washer and dryer and a cabinet overhead, he finished quickly.

He went into the bedroom and saw the bed still unmade, and Celia's robe and pajamas in a heap on her closet floor, where she'd changed clothes quickly in hopes of flying to Slidell with Stan. He went to the closet, searched the floor, and saw only a few pairs of shoes. Standing, he checked the top shelf, and saw several white shirt boxes stacked there. He pulled one down and looked inside.

A baby's knitted sweater with matching booties and blanket were folded there. Lying on top of the little clothes was a pacifier with a ribbon and clip attached. Sid frowned. Were these for a baby gift? He could think of several church friends who were pregnant, including Allie Branning. It could have been intended for any of them. He set the box back in its place and reached for the next box. This time, he pulled out an expensive white christening gown with the price tag still attached. Unusual, he thought, for Celia to give such an extravagant gift.

He groped for the bag behind the boxes and looked inside. Several rolls of yarn the color of the knitted sweater were there, along with knitting needles and several other craft items he couldn't identify. Celia had knitted the sweater, booties, and blanket herself. He whistled under his breath. It was an odd paradox, he thought, that someone caring enough to knit an entire set like that for a friend would also be a killer.

Then he realized that the baby clothes might not be for a friend at all. Maybe they had been for her. If so, if she and Stan were planning to have a baby, why would she want to kill her husband?

Troubled, he put the bag back, restacked the boxes, and stared at them for a moment. It didn't add up. But he'd seen things that didn't add up before. Crazy people did crazy things for crazy reasons.

"Sid, I got somethin'!"

Chad's voice was coming from the attic stairs in the hallway, and Sid dashed toward it. "Whatcha got, Chad?"

"Just what we were lookin' for," Chad said victoriously, and brandished a box of rat poison.

Sid felt the blood flushing from his brown face, and he rubbed his jaw roughly. As much as he'd wanted evidence, the right evidence to convict Celia if she was guilty, he realized now that, in the back of his mind, he had wanted to find something, instead, that would prove to him that she wasn't the culprit. But the evidence was there.

With his gloved hands, he took the box from Chad and examined the ingredients. Arsenic trioxide was one of the first ones listed.

"That's it," he said in a dull voice. "The smokin' gun. Man, why would she do it?"

Chad looked as thrilled as if he'd just solved the Hoffa mystery. "Anybody else find anything?"

"Not yet."

Sid bagged the poison, and kept staring at it, trying to picture a scenario in which Celia would spoon this into Stan's food, then hide it in the attic. As clear as it was, it still didn't add up.

"What is it?" Chad asked.

Sid shrugged. "Nothin'. Just thinkin' how I hate this job sometimes."

"Not me," Chad said. "When things come t'gether like this, 'at's when I know I couldn't do nothin' else."

Chapter Twenty-Two

Since Mark and Allie had not eaten at church, as they usually did on Wednesday nights, they went to Maison de Manger and ordered sandwiches. Though the place was nothing more than a deli, it was decorated like a Bourbon Street bistro. Jazz music was piped in, and on the walls were photos of Louis Armstrong and various other jazz greats with whom the owner, Eddie Neubig, had once shared an acquaintance. It was Allie's favorite place because of the crawfish popcorn she could get as an appetizer, something she craved in the wee hours of morning.

They had invited Dan to join them, and he had seemed inclined to come with them, even though he'd already eaten, when he got a beep from Jill. He had gone to call her, so Mark and Allie had gone ahead to the restaurant.

Allie was finishing off her coveted crawfish popcorn when Dan and Jill came in together. Jill looked as if she'd gone days without sleep, but she was holding Dan's hand. Allie wasn't sure she'd ever seen Dan hold a woman's hand before. He'd once told her that he didn't like to date a woman over three times, because after that she thought of them as a couple. Allie had asked him how he'd ever get to be a couple with anyone if he cut it off at three dates. He'd grinned and said that was the idea.

She realized that he and Jill were long past three dates, unless he was creative with his counting and didn't consider something like this a real date. The fact that he held her hand seemed a monumental breach of the distance Dan so arrogantly liked to keep. She didn't know what Jill was doing, but it was apparently the right thing. Maybe it was the fact that she was so busy and often so unavailable. The challenge. Maybe Dan needed to be kept on his toes that way.

"Sorry I look like I've been drugged," Jill said, dropping into the booth and sliding over. "But I wanted to see you guys. Dan told me about prayer meeting. Thanks for standing up for Celia, Allie."

"How is she?" Allie asked as Dan slipped in beside Jill.

"Not good. Her brother is with her, which cheered her up some. But she's still not feeling very well. I'm afraid the doctors overlooked something that could be wrong with her in an attempt to rule out arsenic. And of course, she's miserably depressed and sick with worry about Stan."

"He's still not awake," Dan said. "I got his mother on the phone, and she sounded really discouraged."

The bell on the front door jingled as the door swung open again, and R.J. Albright, in his tent-sized uniform, came in and went to the bar to place his order. He glanced behind him and saw the four of them sitting there. He waved, quickly placed his order, then ambled across the room toward them.

"Slow night?" Mark asked him.

R.J. chuckled. "Hardly. I'm just now gettin' to supper."

"Oh, yeah?" Dan asked. "Something going on tonight?"

It was a common question among emergency personnel. No one ever wanted to miss anything big.

"We just searched the Shepherd house again," R.J. said. He saw Jill bristling, and said, "We had a warrant, Counselor."

"Well, I hope you're satisfied now that she didn't do it. There was no arsenic anywhere in that house, was there?"

R.J. grinned as if he had a secret that he couldn't tell. "I wouldn't say that," he said.

Her face changed as she gaped up at him. "Then what *would* you say?"

"I'd probably be better off not to say nothin'," he told her.

Jill's face was beginning to turn red. "R.J., I'm Celia's attorney. I have a right to know what you think you found."

"Talk to Sid, Jill," he said. "He's headin' up this investigation. I ain't sayin' no more."

He turned and waddled back between the tables, and for a moment, Allie thought she saw Jill's heart pumping through her shirt. "Excuse me," Jill said. "I have to make a phone call."

Dan got up and let her slide out, and she hurried out the door into the night.

"What do you think they found?" Mark asked Dan.

"Who knows?"

They waited quietly, perusing the menu with their minds on that conversation with R.J., while they waited for Jill to come back in.

Out in the privacy of her car, Jill dialed the police station and got Sid Ford's desk.

"Ford," he answered quickly.

"Sid, this is Jill Clark," she said. "I understand you searched the Shepherd house tonight."

There was a slight pause. "How'd you know?"

"What did you find?" she shot back.

Again, a pause.

"Sid, so help me . . ."

"We found arsenic hid in the attic, Jill."

Her heart lurched. "In what form?"

"Rat poison," he said.

"So maybe they had mice!"

"Maybe, and I'm sure you'll make it your life's work to prove they did. But we found what we were lookin' for, Jill. Evidence. And that ain't all of it. That Lee Barnett fellow you asked me to check on? Seems he just turned up in Newpointe. Moved into the Bonaparte Court apartments. And guess who paid the deposit and the first month's rent?"

"Who?"

"Celia."

"No," Jill said. "There must be some mistake."

"No mistake, Jill. Y'ask me, your client's got some explainin' to do. You should know that we're tryin' to get a warrant right now, Jill. We got no choice but to arrest her."

"Sid, there's a killer out there laughing at how stupid you guys are!"

"All right, Jill, that's enough."

"You're right! It is enough!"

"Hey, I didn't have to tell you. You oughta be thankin' me."

She clicked off the phone and flung it across her car, screaming with frustration. How was she going to tell Celia? She wasn't sure, but she knew that she had to tell her before the police showed up to arrest her.

Feeling even more drained than before, she went back into the deli. Dan, Mark, and Allie all looked hopefully up at her. Dan slid over, and she plopped into the booth.

"Celia's about to be arrested," she said, "so I've got to get over there."

"Oh, no." Allie's face became as pale as Jill imagined hers was.

Mark and Dan stared at each other across the table.

Finally, Dan spoke. "Jill, why? Have they found more evidence?"

"Looks that way."

"They found arsenic, didn't they? That's what R.J. was hinting at, wasn't it?"

She didn't answer. "This is Celia we're talking about. There's some explanation."

"What?" Dan asked. "I mean, her first husband is dead of the same thing; there was enough evidence to indict her for it the first time—"

"An indictment is not a conviction," Jill said through her teeth, her face turning red. "She wasn't convicted, and no one has the right to try her right here in Maison de Manger because of a box of rat poison that may have been there before she and Stan even bought the stupid house!"

"Is that what she said?"

"I haven't talked to her about it." She slid out of the booth. "I've got to go."

"Hey, come on," Mark said. "Dan didn't mean—"

"I can speak for myself," Dan cut in, irritated. "Jill knows I don't think Celia did it. All I meant was that people will think she did."

"You know what?" Jill bit out. "I'm going to prove all of them wrong, and when I'm finished, I'm not sure if Celia and Stan can go on living in this town. Celia will want to go where she can depend on people, and Stan won't want to be around people who think so little of his wife."

"Hey, calm down. You're strung a little too tight right now, acting like *we're* the enemy."

"You're right," she snapped. "I'm sorry. Just ... I've gotta go."

And as they stared after her, she rushed out to her car.

"Go after her," Allie told Dan as the door closed behind her.

Dan shook his head. "No way. I didn't do anything wrong."

"She's just tense and upset," Allie said. "This whole thing is on her shoulders."

Dan muttered, "You ask me, Stan's the one we ought to be feeling sorry for. Not Jill."

"Chill out, Dan," Mark said. "I know she ticked you off, but it's not worth ruining the whole relationship over."

"What relationship?" Dan asked.

Mark gaped at Allie. "*What relationship?*" Allie repeated. "Dan, don't give us that. You've broken your three-date limit with her, and you know it."

"There you go," he said. "You take someone out more than three times, everybody assumes you're a couple. Well, we're *not* a couple. I'm still a free agent. A *happy* free agent!"

"Seem real happy to me," Mark observed.

"I'm going home," Dan said, disgusted, and slipped out of the booth.

Allie and Mark just looked at each other as he slammed out of the cafe.

Chapter Twenty-Three

The doorbell didn't surprise Celia, for the local reporters had been trying to get a statement all day. "I might have to get out my rifle," Aunt Aggie said as she got up and scurried to the front window to peer out into the darkness. Celia looked over her shoulder and saw Jill standing under the porch light. Quickly, she opened the door.

Jill was pale, tired-looking, and heavy tension lined her face. Celia stood aside to let her in. "Jill, what's wrong?"

Jill hesitated, stared at the floor for a moment, then wearily met Celia's eyes. "I'm sorry to hit you with this so late, Celia, but there have been a few developments in the case you should know about."

"There have?" Celia asked hopefully. "What?"

Jill sat down on the chair in the foyer and rubbed her eyes. She hadn't had time to apply makeup this morning, and her eyes were red and bloodshot. "Tell me about Lee Barnett."

Celia frowned. "What about him?"

"When's the last time you spoke to him?"

She shrugged. "Years. He's in jail. Killed a man in a barroom brawl."

Jill was watching her, as if evaluating her for the truth, and Celia wondered why. What could Lee Barnett possibly have to do with any of this? "He got out a couple of weeks ago," she said. "And he's in town."

"In Newpointe?" Celia asked. "Why would he come here when he just got out of prison?"

"To be close to you."

Celia's eyes narrowed and she took a step backward. "Wait. *What?* No, that's impossible. He doesn't care anything about me."

"How do you know?"

"Well, why should he? I hadn't talked to him for a year or more even *before* he went to jail."

"He called the house, though." David had heard the exchange from the kitchen and came into the foyer now, dropping the statement like a lead ball that seemed to roll around in front of them.

"When?" Jill asked.

"Several times from jail. Asked for Celia, and I told him she didn't live there anymore."

Celia gaped at her brother. "You never told me that."

"I forgot about it. I knew you didn't want to talk to him."

Celia looked troubled as she turned her eyes back to Jill. "So he got out just days before Stan was poisoned, and he came here to Newpointe? Jill, you don't think *he* poisoned Stan?"

Jill obviously didn't know what to think. "You've got to admit, Celia, that it's an awfully convincing coincidence."

"So, did the police question him?"

"Oh, yeah. Then promptly let him go."

"Let him go?" David asked. "Why would they do that?"

"Because they aren't convinced he's a suspect. They think, instead, that he was Celia's motive."

"My *what?* Where did they get that?"

"The letter."

Celia could see that Jill was watching her eyes for some reaction, waiting for a sign of guilt. But Celia was clueless. She had no idea what Jill was talking about.

"What letter?"

"The one that he claims you wrote him, telling him you rented him an apartment at Bonaparte Court and that you wanted him to come here."

Celia could feel the blood draining out of her face. She struggled for the right words, but realized she needed to sit down. "Jill, you don't really believe that I wrote a letter like that ..."

"I don't, Celia, but the police aren't so sure. And then there's the matter of the two checks written on your bank account. One written to him, and one to the apartment manager."

"No! I didn't write those checks." She got up and paced across the floor, thinking. Suddenly, she swung around to Jill. "Our checkbook disappeared a couple of weeks ago. We thought we had misplaced it, so we just started with the next set we had in the box. Stan always kept it above the visor in his car, but it was just gone. Whoever poisoned Stan must have taken it!"

Jill sighed. "Celia, they searched your house tonight."

"Again?" Her nausea reasserted itself.

"Yes." Jill's answer was clipped and matter-of-fact. "And I might as well just get it all out. They found something in your attic, Celia."

"What?" she asked. "All we've got up there is junk, old clothes, stuff like that. What did they find?"

"Rat poison," Jill said. "The main ingredient was arsenic."

Celia shook her head and began backing away. "No. That was not in my house. We've never had a problem with mice. Why would we have rat poison?"

"Celia, I thought maybe the previous owners had left it there, but I talked to Sid and he said that it was a new box. It hadn't even collected dust."

"No!" she shouted, steadying herself. "He's doing it again. He's setting me up! Just like last time with the ... the journal entries ... the computer ... the arsenic they found that time ..." She turned to the wall and covered her head, as if she could protect herself from the cruel onslaught. "This can't be. We didn't have arsenic in my attic, Jill. I would have seen it. I would have known, and I wouldn't want that anywhere near my house!" She swung around and gaped at Jill with helpless, hopeless eyes. "Jill, you believe me, don't you? He hasn't gotten you convinced, too, has he?"

"Of course I believe you," she said, but Celia could see the doubt in her face.

"What about you, David?" Celia asked hopelessly. "Mom and Dad won't believe me, but you do, don't you?"

"Absolutely," he said.

"And Aunt Aggie? I'd die if you didn't believe me. I know the evidence looks bad, but—"

"I don't care about no evidence," she said. "Don't now, didn't then. I know my niece ain't no liar."

"Then what do we do?" Celia asked, wiping her face. "We have to start with the checks and the letter. It *can't* be my handwriting. If it looks like it, it must be forged."

"The only handwriting is your signature on the checks. The letter was typed."

"Well, see? Anybody could have written it! And the check could have been forged! If someone stole my checkbook, it wouldn't be that hard. All they'd need is my signature on something else, and they could copy it. They have to start by looking for my checkbook. Whoever has it is the one."

Jill got up and began pacing across the floor. "Celia, they're getting a warrant. They're going to arrest you tonight."

She turned back to Jill and shook her head frantically. "No. They can't. Not with those photographers out there. Everyone will know." She covered her mouth and took a deep breath. "No, I've got to go there myself. Turn myself in, so they won't have to come after me. Maybe . . . maybe the judge will go easier on me, let me out on bond, if I do that."

Jill nodded. "We can do that."

"All right," she said, wiping her face with trembling hands. "Then let's do it."

Chapter Twenty-Four

Judge Louis DeLacy was a deacon in the Calvary Bible Church, the same church where Jill and Celia were members. Everyone in the congregation called him Louis, because he thought of himself as just another member of the Body, no greater than anyone else just because of the power the city had wielded him. But more important than that was the calling God had given him, the calling to mete out punishments to those who chose not to abide by the law. Normally, his job was fulfilling—satisfying, even, for he'd been responsible for keeping a number of drug dealers off the streets, disciplining drunk drivers no matter who they were, and putting away thieves and vandals.

But he couldn't remember a day when he'd dreaded his job more than today. He had been prepared for Celia's case when he'd arrived in his chambers this morning. He'd heard about Stan's hospitalization yesterday, but when he'd learned that Celia was a suspect, he'd felt sick. Both Stan and Celia were good friends, and he thought a great deal of her. She had worked alongside him to build a Habitat House for a needy family last year after their trailer had burned, and she had served on a committee that he led to raise money for a new organ. He'd had dinner at their house several times, whether alone or as part of a Sunday school class, and he'd attended Promise Keepers rallies nearly every year with Stan.

The thought that Celia would be considered a suspect for attempted murder was beyond his comprehension. Still, as Jill brought her in for her arraignment, he had to keep the emotion from his face and treat her like any other defendant. He tried to avoid meeting her eyes and focused on Jill instead, as the bailiff announced the case. He wanted to know how Stan was, but he wondered if he should address either of them personally. After a moment of thought, he decided that everyone in the room knew he was close to both women, and it wouldn't surprise them at all to know that he cared about Stan's condition.

"How's Stan?" he asked.

Celia looked up, but deferred to Jill.

"Not good," Jill said. "He's in a coma. Your honor, my client turned herself in the moment she heard of the warrant for her arrest. She had nothing to do with the poisoning. We'd like to request that these absurd charges be dropped."

Part of him reacted as a sympathetic friend who had trouble believing that Celia could be guilty. The other part of him, the part that had to keep a certain decorum in his courtroom, reacted with slight resentment.

Troubled, he rubbed his temples. "Then her plea is . . . ?"

"Not guilty," Celia said. "Absolutely not guilty."

"Judge," the prosecutor, Gus Taylor, cut in in a lazy voice, as if the whole process was so obvious that it was an insult to have to spell it out. "We have a solid case here. And we ask you not even to set bond—not for any amount—because of her past record. Her first husband died of arsenic poisoning, the same poison that's killing Stan right now."

Louis had read the account in the paper last night, but it still grieved him. This couldn't be true. It was too bizarre. What did she have? A double life?

"Your honor," Jill shot back, "I object to the prosecutor's sneaky and underhanded attempt to cast a bad light on my client by using information that is absolutely irrelevant to this case. My client has never been, nor will she ever be, convicted of any crime. Gus, were you absent the day they taught about relevance in law school?"

Louis tried to shake the troubling allegations from his mind. "She's right," he said. He cast a troubled gaze over the lot of them, from Jill to Celia to Gus, and then back to Celia again. There was more to this story, he told himself. If Celia's first husband had died of arsenic poisoning, that, indeed, was disturbing. But if there was no conviction, he could only determine that there hadn't been enough evidence. He didn't know what the evidence was here—now wasn't the time to hear it. His only purpose in this today was to set bond or deny it.

"Your honor, they also found rat poison in her attic. Its key ingredient was arsenic."

"Judge, you probably have rat poison in your attic, too, and it probably never occurred to you that it contained arsenic," Jill shot back.

He tried to think how he would have handled this case if Celia had been a stranger. Finally, he sighed. "I can't hold her," he told the prosecutor, "not with a record that's clean—"

"But your honor—" the prosecutor piped in.

"Unless she was found guilty, then any previous arrest is wiped off the slate," he said. "As far as the east is from the west, as someone said."

Jill looked at her feet and tried to suppress her grin. She doubted Gus knew who that someone was or what book it was quoted from.

"However, I can't drop the charges. I'll let you out on a hundred thousand dollars bond, Celia, but with the condition that you must not go near Stan or contact him in any way, even when he wakes up."

"*What?*" she asked.

Jill grabbed her arm to silence her. "We appreciate it, your honor."

He closed the file and handed it to the bailiff. "Next case?"

"But Louis," Celia cried, fighting as Jill tried to drag her out. "His parents won't let me see him now, but if . . . when he wakes up, if he wants to see me, I have to go. He needs me!"

Louis shot her a miserable look, then turned his eyes to the next file. He couldn't let his emotions get tangled up in this. He had to be objective. He had done the best he could.

• • •

Outside, Celia collapsed in a miserable heap on a bench against the wall, covering her head and wailing at the injustice of it all. Jill stooped down in front of her. "Celia, at least you can go home."

Aunt Aggie, who'd been sitting at the back of the court-room, had come out and was now standing over them. "Home, nothin'. Celia ain't gon' be a open target for that killer, whoever he is. She comin' back to my house."

Celia was inconsolable. "Jill, you have to do something. You have to talk to the judge. I have to go to Stan when he wakes up."

"You can't," Jill said flatly. "Not until we get this cleared up."

"Then I might as well stay here. I don't have a hundred thousand dollars, anyway."

"That's not a problem. We'll get it from a bail bondsman. Celia, you don't want to stay here. At least if you're out we can find who did this. I need your help."

"Why is God *doing* this to me?"

Jill wished she had the answers. Her instinct was to tell her to trust him, but that was easy for her to say. Jill had never been accused of murder.

Chapter Twenty-Five

*C*elia Shepherd raised the candle as she walked into the black room. *The flicker lit the room in a golden hue, and she saw the bed with the man lying on it. Her heart leapt, for she knew it was Stan, and she stepped closer, lifting the candle higher to cast the light on his face.*

But he was dead.

She had known he was dead, even though her heart had chosen to deny it. She had believed the sheer power of her will would keep him alive, that her hopes would make him fight the poison in his blood. She had prayed so hard, wailing and begging and crying out to God . . .

"Celia! Celia! Wake up!"

Slowly, she emerged from the deep abyss of her sleep, and realized that she had been dreaming. There was no dark room, no candle, no body. Aunt Aggie stood over her, shaking her, and the afternoon sun radiated through her window.

"Celia, you got a phone call. Down to the hospital. They need to talk at you." *Hospital?* Celia managed to get her eyes open and sat up, wondering when she had fallen asleep. No wonder God didn't answer her prayers, if she couldn't even forsake sleep for something so important. "The hospital?" she asked. "Is Stan awake?"

"I don't know. Come on downstairs. They been waitin' a long time. I couldn't wake you up!"

For a moment she just sat there, paralyzed, her mind reeling with dread. What if they *weren't* calling to tell her he had awakened? What if he had died, just like in her dream? Slowly, she forced herself to get out of bed. She glanced at the clock on her bed table. Three P.M. She had lain down to pray and hadn't meant to fall asleep. She went barefoot down the stairs to the one telephone at the bottom of the staircase. By the time she reached the telephone, the cobwebs had sufficiently cleared themselves from her brain, and she was beginning to cry.

Her hand shook as she took the phone.

"Mrs. Shepherd? This is Frank Dupree at the Slidell Memorial Hospital Lab. We did some blood work on you Tuesday night?"

Her heart leapt, then took a nose dive. "This isn't about my husband?"

"No, I'm sorry. Actually, it's about you. We've finished running all of our tests on you, and we thought you'd like to know that one of them came up positive."

Her mind was still on Stan's condition, groping to find its way back to the phone call. She sat down in the chair next to the telephone table. "Wait . . . what?"

"Your blood test, Mrs. Shepherd . . ."

"But they said that night that they hadn't found arsenic in my blood."

"No, there's still no trace of arsenic. But the doctor ordered several tests. It's the pregnancy test that came up positive."

Celia's breath caught in her lungs, and her hand immediately fell to her stomach. "The *what?*"

"You're pregnant, Mrs. Shepherd. That explains the nausea."

She and Stan had been trying to have a baby for over two years, and now her heart raced at the thought that it was finally coming true. She had dreamed of this moment, when she got the news and would throw her arms around Stan and call him "Daddy."

Then she wilted as she realized that her baby may never know its daddy, because Stan might not wake up from his coma . . . that even if he did, the child could be born in prison and taken from her at birth.

She suddenly felt sick again. "Thank you," she said. "I appreciate your letting me know."

She didn't know how she managed to get the phone back in its cradle and make it to the bathroom on time. When she emerged, Aggie was waiting with a worried look on her face. "What they said, T-Celia? You been poisoned, too?"

Celia shook her head. She was shaking as she raked her hand through her disheveled hair. "No, Aunt Aggie. I'm pregnant." The word choked out on a wave of tears, and Aggie's face brightened, then instantly darkened.

"Why you cryin'? Ain't that what you want?"

"I want to tell Stan," Celia wept. "I want him to celebrate with me. We've waited so long for this moment, and I don't *understand* why it has to be like this . . ."

Aggie held her and let her cry, then walked her into the parlor and set her down on the sofa. "It's gon' be awright, *sha*," she said. "I know it is. Somehow, this baby gon' make everything okay. Can you just see yourself sittin' in front of that jury with your belly out to here? Can only help in the sympathy department."

"I don't *need* sympathy. I need for them to catch the killer. I need for Stan to wake up and recover." She sat sideways on the couch, with her feet tucked beneath her, and dropped her face on the back of the sofa. "Oh, Aunt Aggie, what is he going to think when he does wake up? When he hears that his wife has been charged with his attempted murder? When he hears that he almost died of arsenic poisoning? Will he know that I didn't do it? Or will he doubt like everyone else is going to?"

"He'll know," Aunt Aggie said. "He'll fight tooth and nail to clear your name. You'll see."

She just wasn't sure. She wouldn't know until she talked to him, heard his voice, heard him defending her to those who would string her up. "Will you call the hospital and see how he's doing?"

"I just did 'fore I got you up. No change."

She groaned and wept into her hands for a moment longer. Finally, she said, "Aunt Aggie, I don't want anyone to know about the pregnancy. Not until I can tell Stan. I don't want him to read about it in the papers or hear about it from someone who thinks I did this. I want to tell him."

"Awright," the old woman said. "I won't say nothin'."

"You won't say anything about what?"

They looked up to see David standing at the doorway to the parlor, and Celia wiped her eyes and reached for a tissue in the gold tissue holder on the end table.

"Hey, David."

"What's going on, Celia? Something happened."

She blew her nose. "No, nothing. I'm just . . . a little depressed."

"Come on, Celia," he said, coming to sit next to her on the couch. "It's me. You've got me worried to death. Now, what is it?"

She looked at Aunt Aggie, and her aunt nodded, urging her to tell him. Finally, she realized that she wanted to. She wanted to share the news. At least she could tell those closest to her. She looked up at him through tear-filled eyes. "I'm pregnant."

There was no joy in his eyes as he gaped at her. "Pregnant?"

"Yes. That's why I've been sick off and on . . ." Her eyes filled again at his reaction. "David, what is it?"

"Well, it's just . . ." He got up and looked at Aunt Aggie, then turned back to Celia. "Celia, the timing couldn't be worse. Stan lying in a hospital, you being charged with his murder, a probable indictment . . ."

"I know that," she said, growing impatient. Did he really think she didn't know?

"Celia, you can't have this baby."

She looked up at him, stricken at the declaration, as if he'd made the decision and it was a done deal. "What do you mean?"

"I mean, you can't. It would be cruel to bring a child into the world in the middle of this."

She stared up at him. "David, are you suggesting abortion?"

"I'm just saying that this is going to complicate your life miserably."

"I can handle it."

"No, you can't. What do you think Stan will do when he finds out? Or his parents, for that matter?"

"Stan will defend me when he wakes up," she said with certainty. "And when I tell him about the baby, he's going to be happy."

"Right. And when they start feeding him all the lies about you, you think he's still gonna want you to have his baby? Celia, if you terminated it this time and waited until this was all cleared up and you and Stan were back together, it would be so much better."

She couldn't believe what she was hearing. Her hand went to her stomach again, and a burst of love surged through her. "God didn't make a mistake with this, David. This is my baby, and I've been praying and waiting for it."

"Did you pray to be a single mom? What if Stan dies, Celia?"

"That's enough!" Aunt Aggie got to her feet and stepped between them. "David, leave the child alone. She got enough worry."

"Aunt Aggie, you must agree with me. How can you condone this?"

"She had nothing to do with it!" Celia said, her voice rising. "It doesn't matter if she condones it or agrees with you. Neither of you has the right to decide anything for me." She got another tissue, blew her nose again. "I thought you might be happy, David."

"*You're* not even happy. When I came in here, you were sobbing, Celia. Don't tell me you weren't."

"I was crying over the circumstances. Not the baby. The baby is wanted. He or she is an answered prayer."

David seemed to realize he wasn't getting anywhere with her. He sank back onto the sofa. "It seems very romantic, Celia. But you're the one who'll be most hurt."

"I'm willing to take that chance." She wiped her face and looked down at her feet. "If you're going to support me, David,

you'll have to support me in this, too. And you can't tell anyone. Either of you."

"Why not?"

"Because I want Stan to hear about it from me."

He stared at her as if struggling with the words, then finally
gave up. "Okay, if that's what you want."

The phone rang, startling her, and Aggie went into the
foyer to answer it. "Hola?"

Celia could hear her muttering something, and she reached
for another tissue to blow her nose again. In a moment, Aggie
was back in the doorway, fairly dancing as she got out the
words. "He's awake, T-Celia! That was Allie, down to the hospital. She said he woke up!"

"Oh, thank God!" Celia got to her feet and began to weep,
harder and deeper than she had all morning. "Oh, thank God!"
She fell into Aunt Aggie's arms, then pulled David into the
embrace with them. "Oh, I can't believe it. What did she say?
How is he?"

"She wasn't sure," Aggie said. "But she knew you'd wanna
know."

"Oh, I want to see him! I want to look into his eyes and tell
him about the baby . . ."

"You have to," David said. "You have to get in there somehow
and tell him. As long as you're not there, and his family is feeding
him lies, he might believe them. You have to go see him."

"But I can't. The court order."

"Yes, you can, Celia. Stan needs to know about the baby."

He was right, she thought. She had to see him, to touch
him, to kiss him. She had to tell him about the baby, and watch
his eyes smile, and feel his arms around her. Then he would
know that she couldn't have tried to kill him. Then he would
tell them, and it would all be cleared up, and she could be with
him as the baby grew . . .

"I'll figure out a way," Celia said on a whisper. "They won't
be able to keep me away from him for long."

Chapter Twenty-Six

Stan Shepherd was still weak and felt as though he'd been dragged a hundred miles behind a pickup truck . . . then backed over. He felt so tired. So incredibly tired, but they all seemed to be so glad to see him awake that he hated to give in to the fatigue and close his eyes again.

But all the questions . . . they were asking so many, probably to evaluate whether he had brain damage. He tried to answer them, but the question he had for them seemed more pressing. Where was Celia? What had happened to him? Had they been in an accident? Was Celia hurt . . . or worse? Is that why no one wanted to tell him where she was?

"Celia," he whispered again, and his mother, standing on one side of the bed, offered him that cup of water with the straw that probed at his lips like some kind of medical instrument. He sipped obediently.

"Honey, don't try to talk."

"Stan, can you tell me your birth date? Your name and address? Your mother's maiden name?"

"Thought she said not to talk."

The doctor who stood over him wasn't amused. He was serious, so Stan tried to give him what he wanted. "April 22. Stan Shepherd. I live at 313 Burgundy Drive, Newpointe, Louisiana. Want the zip?"

The doctor smiled. "No, that won't be necessary. Detective, could you tell me the last thing you remember?"

That was a tough one. He closed his eyes and tried to think. Celia. He remembered Celia crying over him, calling 911 . . .

"I was sick."

"Yes. Do you remember when you began to feel sick?"

"I don't know." He began to get concerned and looked around the room again, taking grim inventory of the people watching him. Two doctors, a nurse, his father, his mother . . . "Where's Celia, Mom? Is she all right?"

"She's . . . not able to be here today. Just relax, darling."

He didn't like the sound of that. He turned back to the doctor. "How long have I been here?"

"Two days. You came in Tuesday night. It's Thursday now."

"Thursday? What happened to—" He tried to sit up, but realized he was too weak.

"You've been in a coma, Detective. You were poisoned."

"*Poisoned?* You've got to be kidding."

"No, I'm afraid not. It was arsenic poisoning."

Arsenic? He closed his eyes, trying to think. Arsenic. Like Nathan, Celia's first husband. Poisoned. He'd been in a coma . . . Had almost died.

His skin felt cold, damp, and he brought a trembling hand up to wipe his temples. "Where's my wife?"

Silence again.

His eyes filled. "Is she dead?"

"No, of course not," Hannah said quickly. "No, darling, nothing like that."

"Then what?" he asked, growing agitated. "Why won't anybody tell me where she is? I want to see her. She must be worried sick."

His father pushed between Hannah and a nurse, and set his hand on the railing of the bed. "Son, we don't know how to tell you this."

"Just spit it out," he snapped. "I want my wife."

"Celia's . . . not allowed to see you. There's a court order . . ."

"A court order? What kind of court would order a thing like that?"

"Son, did you know that Celia's first husband had died of arsenic poisoning, and that she was charged with that murder?"

Oh, so that was it. He closed his eyes again, racking his brain for some logical sequence of thoughts. That grogginess still hung on. Was it the arsenic, or the coma, or the damage that had been done to him? He forced his mind back to the question. Had he known about Celia's first husband?

"Yes," he said. "She told me before I married her. She told me everything. But she didn't do it, Dad."

"Son, I wish I could believe in her, but you were poisoned the same way. And there's evidence . . ."

"What evidence? I want to talk to Jim Shoemaker. I want to talk to Sid." He struggled to sit up again, and this time half made it. "Do they think she did this to me? Have they arrested her?"

"Yes," his mother said. The word, uttered with such regret, shot to his heart like an arrow, knocking him back down.

"No," he said. "How could they be so stupid? Celia couldn't—wouldn't—do this!" His breath was coming harder. "Where is she? In jail? Get her out, Dad! I don't care what it costs or what you have to do. Get her out!"

"She's out," he said. "She was released on bond."

"I want to see her!" he managed to shout. "Now!"

"That's impossible, son. Judge DeLacy ordered her to stay away from you. There's a grand jury investigation going on, and she—"

"She didn't do it, Dad! She didn't!"

"Then who did?"

He fell back and laid his hand over his eyes, trying to think. "I don't know. But I know she didn't. Give me the phone."

Bart and Hannah looked at each other, but neither made a move. "Why?" Bart asked.

"I want to talk to my wife." His voice was a barely whispered rasp now, but he wouldn't give up. "She must be scared to death. She must be humiliated. Give me the phone, Dad."

"I can't do that, Son. I have to protect you."

"I don't *need* protecting from her! At least let me call the judge. He can't make that court order hold if I ask him to let me see her. I'm a grown man."

"You're a sick man," his father said. "You're still very, very sick. You're not out of the woods yet. You have to rest, and we can't take the chance of having her finish off the job . . ."

"Give me a break!" The words came with such passion that they almost took what was left of his voice. He couldn't believe they would do this to his wife. His body begged him to give in to sleep, to rest, to recovery, but his mind fought. He had to get up and get to her, wrap her in his arms and tell her it would be all right. Then he realized that it couldn't be all right, not while the killer was still out there. What if he poisoned her, too? What if she was an open target? "Call Jim and Sid. I have to talk to them," he said. "I have to make sure that someone protects her."

"When you're rested and feeling better," his mother said. "We'll call them then."

"No, not then," he said through his teeth. "Now. Mom, so help me, if you don't, you're gonna have to tie me down to keep me in this bed."

She shot his father a distressed look. "All right," Bart said finally. "We'll call them."

"Now. Call them now."

"Okay."

He closed his eyes as Bart picked up the phone. He didn't relax until he'd heard him ask them to come. Then, finally, he surrendered to the sleep pulling at him.

Chapter Twenty-Seven

Sid had managed to get a few hours' sleep, but it wasn't enough. He rubbed his eyes and tried to concentrate on the rap sheet he'd gotten on Lee Barnett. When the phone on his desk buzzed, he picked it up, preoccupied. "Yeah? Ford, here."

"Sid, this is Bart Shepherd. Stan's father."

"Yes, Mr. Shepherd," he said, coming to attention. "How are you?"

"I'm fine. More importantly, Stan is fine. Or, he's better. He's awake."

"All *right!*" With the exclamation, he leapt out of his chair, knocking it over. Everyone in the room turned to look at him. He picked the chair up and sat back down. "Does that mean he's out of the woods? What do the doctors say?"

"They think he's on his way to recovery, though we can't be sure yet how much damage the arsenic did. He's still very weak. But Sid, he wants to talk to you. You and Jim Shoemaker. You know how stubborn he can be and, well . . ." He dropped his voice. "He's a little upset. Do you think you can come?"

"Of course. Does he remember anything? Where he got the arsenic? Who may have given it to him?"

"No, but he's adamantly insisting that Celia isn't the one."

"I wish I could be that sure," Sid said, and Bart didn't reply. "Mr. Shepherd, I'll be there as soon as I can catch up with Jim, all right? Tell him we're glad he's awake, and that it's about time."

"I will."

He hung up the phone and punched the air, then got to his feet, doing a little dance. "Stan's awake! He's awake!"

The room erupted into cheers as Sid sashayed into the chief's office. Jim was on the telephone. He looked up at Sid, rubbed his eyes, then looked again. He put his hand over the phone. "What's going on?"

"Stan's awake, man! He wants to see us!"

Jim's mouth fell open, then into the phone, he said, "I'll call you back." He hung up the phone and got slowly to his feet. "Awake? Really?" He laughed out loud and high-fived Sid. "I don't believe it."

"That's right," Sid said, still strutting. "This ain't a homicide."

"Thank God."

"We gotta go, man. He wants to see us both, if you can break away from your chiefly duties long enough."

"You bet I can. Why does he want to see us? Does he remember anything pertinent?"

"I don't know," Sid said. "His daddy called and told me he was upset about Celia. Insistin' she didn't have nothin' to do with it."

Jim hesitated, and his grin faded. "Then this isn't a social visit. He wants to see what we've got on her."

Sid stopped dancing and stared at Jim as the unpleasant task before them sank in. "Guess you're right."

Jim got his keys off of the hook on his wall. "Sometimes we've got to play the bad guys," he said.

• • •

Stan heard the voices at the door, and he struggled to open his eyes. He saw the IV bag hanging next to his bed, felt the tube under his nose supplying oxygen, heard the beep of one of the monitors next to the bed.

His gaze drifted beyond the machinery to the door where his parents were talking quietly to someone. He squinted to make them out, and saw Sid and Jim standing just outside the door.

"Sid." The word was so weak that he could barely hear it himself. He tried to raise up. "Sid."

His mother turned around and saw that he was awake, and her tired face came alive. "There he is," she said, rushing to his side. "See, I told you he was awake. Stan, Sid and Jim are here like you asked."

"Help me sit up," he said.

She pressed the button that raised the bed up, and Stan reached out to shake his friends' hands. "Thanks for comin'," he said.

"Man, it's about time you woke up, givin' us the scare of our lives," Sid said. "I don't *ever* want to have to come find you on the floor again. What do you *mean* almost dyin' on us like that?"

"Sorry, man. Call me inconsiderate."

Jim was more staid as he stepped closer to the bed.

"Chief, how's it goin'?"

"Better, now that we don't have to upgrade this to a homicide."

"You've got the wrong person," Stan said. "Celia didn't do it."

Jim looked at Sid, and Sid shrugged. "We knew you'd think that, Stan. Nobody wants to think their wife did somethin' like this."

"You know Celia. How could you think that about her?"

"Too much evidence," Sid said. "There's nothin' else we can think."

He felt his pulse speeding up, felt his breath coming harder. It seemed to have a hair trigger. "You can't call yourself my friend . . . and try to set my wife up for something like this. There's a killer out there."

Sid sighed and pulled up a chair, turned it backward, and straddled it. "Look, man," he said, resting his chin on his fists. "If you want to know what we've got on her, we'll tell you. But it ain't pretty, Stan. It's gon' hurt you."

"What hurts me is that my wife can't come to see me. That she's probably worried sick. That she's being set up for the second time."

"Do you want to hear what we've got, or not?" Sid asked.

Stan looked his friend in the eye and realized how tired the man looked. He wondered if Sid had gotten any sleep at all since Stan collapsed. Had he spent all this time looking for the killer, or simply trying to build a case against Celia? "Yes, I want to hear," he said. "What do you think you have?"

"First, and most obvious, the fact that her first husband died the same way."

"He was murdered."

"Of course he was. And she was charged with that crime."

"And those charges were dismissed."

"Only due to a technicality. You know as well as I do that guilty people get off on technicalities all the time."

He was having trouble getting a breath, and his hands were shaking. He tried to calm down. "Look, my wife is as innocent as I am. She didn't kill her first husband, and she didn't try to kill me."

"There's more, Stan," Jim said. "Have you ever heard the name Lee Barnett?"

He shook his head. "No, I don't think so. Why?"

"Because he's one of Celia's old flames. Before she was married the first time, she was involved with him. He wound up in prison for manslaughter, barroom brawl sort of thing, and he got out two weeks ago."

"So have you checked him out? Maybe he poisoned me somehow."

"Maybe. Turns out that he came to Newpointe where he had an apartment waiting. He claims that Celia sent him a letter by way of a priest—"

"*Celia?*" he cut in. "He says she wrote to him? What priest?"

"We don't know. But he says she sent him a letter saying that she had an apartment here for him, and that he could get the key in a locker at the bus station, along with a check for $200."

"He's lying," Stan said without doubt.

"Marabeth Simmons said the deal was made by phone. The check that was sent in was one of your and Celia's checks. We saw it ourselves, Stan. It wasn't counterfeit."

"Lee Barnett is a liar. I don't know where he got the checks, but I can guarantee you that Celia did not write it."

"There's more," Sid said. "We searched your house again last night, looking for the checkbook, since Celia claims she doesn't have it. Do you know where it is, by the way?"

"No," he said. "If I had it, it would have been over the visor in my car."

"We searched your car, top to bottom. Not there."

"I don't know where it is," he said. "Maybe Lee Barnett has it. Stole it and forged her name."

"It looked like her signature, Stan."

His chest tightened, and a bead of perspiration rolled into his eye. "You said there was more."

"The arsenic. We found it in your attic, Stan. A brand new box. Hadn't even collected dust. It was rat poison, sitting behind a beam in your attic."

He tried to rise up. His face grew hot with the strain. "She didn't put it there," he said. "Celia's afraid to go in the attic. It gives her the creeps. I don't think she's ever been up there. She wouldn't have done it."

"Not even to cover up a murder?"

"Why wouldn't she have just flushed it down the toilet, burnt the box? Why would she bother to go hide the box in a place she would never have gone before?"

"We don't know why she did what she did, Stan. None of it's logical."

"Think like a cop," Stan said through his teeth. "If some-one were going to set her up, he'd leave it where he knew you'd find it. Maybe it's this Lee Barnett. Go with the most obvious first, man."

"Celia's the most obvious," Sid said.

"Not to me! Not to anyone who knows her!"

His mother came to the bed and tried to push his shoulders back down. "Stan, you've got to calm down," she said.

"No!" he said, intent on making his point. "Sid, Jim, you've got to listen to me!"

Sid got up and leaned on Stan's bed rail. "Stan, Lee Barnett says she set him up so he'd take the fall when she poisoned you."

"I told you, I don't know who this guy is, but Lee Barnett is a liar."

"Maybe. He could have done all of this. But if that's the case, Celia may have put him up to it."

"No way!" He sat all the way up of his own volition and waved a shaky hand at Jim. "Jim, you get him off of her. You *tell* him that he's on the wrong track!"

His mother fought to lay him back down. "Stan, please—"

"Tell him he's wasting police hours going after the wrong person! My wife is a victim!"

Jim looked miserable. "Stan, we're exploring every avenue. We're not leaving any stones unturned."

"I don't want clichés, Jim! I want my wife. She's out there like a sitting duck, just waiting for this maniac to strike. I want her protected."

"Protected?" Jim asked. "What do you mean?"

"I mean, I want someone watching her. Twenty-four hours a day. I don't want anyone to go near her that isn't seen."

"Stan, we don't have the manpower for that. With you out—"

Stan grabbed Jim's collar and jerked his face close to his. "I've put years on this police force . . ." He stopped to catch his breath ". . . and I've never once complained about having to work around the clock to solve crimes. I've been a good detective for you, Jim, and I've put my life on the line over and over. Now I need a favor. I want my wife protected. You owe that to me."

Jim took a step back, red faced, looking at him as if he was crazy. Stan supposed that arsenic poisoning gave him more license than usual. Instead of firing him on the spot, Jim only glared at him.

Stan blinked back the mist in his eyes. "What do you want, Jim? You want me to get down on my knees?"

Sid seemed startled by Stan's passion, and finally, he turned his long, dark face to the chief. "Jim, I could watch her."

"No," Jim said. "We don't have a detective. You're the most qualified evidence technician we've got. I need you on the case."

"We could take turns. Everybody could watch for a couple of hours each day. Get twelve of us to do that, and you got the whole day and night covered. We could do it, Jim. Then, if she is guilty, we'll see who she talks to and where she goes. It could work in our favor."

Stan ground his teeth together and shook his head. "I don't believe you guys."

Jim rubbed his stomach, a habit he'd developed shortly after becoming police chief. "Stan, I'll see what I can do."

"Do better than that, Jim," Stan said, "or you'll have to find yourself another detective."

"You wouldn't quit," Hannah cut in, laughing nervously. "Stan, you love your job."

"Watch me." His tone brooked no debate. "Promise me you'll put someone on her right away."

"I said I'd do what I can," Jim said, but both Stan and Sid stared at him, waiting for more than that. "Okay," he said finally. "I promise."

Stan relaxed back into his pillow, feeling suddenly tireder than he had felt since he came out of the coma. "Thank you." He tried to slow his breathing. "One other thing. I want to see her. This stupid court order . . . Tell the judge to let her come. Tell him he can send a police escort, an armed guard, whatever. I just want to see her. I have to see her." His last words faded out on a whisper.

Sid and Jim stood looking at him as he tried to fight the heaviness in his eyelids.

Sid reached over and touched his limp hand. "I'm glad you're okay, man. Really glad. Even if you do hate my guts."

"I don't hate your guts," Stan whispered. "I hate what you're doing to my wife."

"And I hate what she did to you, if she did it."

Stan grabbed his hand and opened his eyes again. "Sid, you promise me that . . . you'll work as hard . . . to prove her innocent . . . as you're working to prove her guilty."

"Sure, man," Sid said. "Believe it or not, I don't want Celia to be guilty."

He wanted to say more, but that heaviness was too overwhelming, and his eyes wanted so desperately to close. He told himself that they would keep their promises . . . they had to. They would watch Celia, even if they thought she was guilty. She would be protected.

Knowing that, he let go and drifted back into the vortex of sleep.

Chapter Twenty-Eight

Celia stood in front of the mirror, brushing her hair up into a ponytail. She had no makeup on, and no inclination to use any, and her blue eyes were red-rimmed and bloodshot from crying. The news over the last twenty-four hours seemed to have come in waves. The things about Lee Barnett and the letter and the checks and the apartment. Her arrest. Her pregnancy. Finally, the news about Stan.

She had tried twice to call his room, but his parents had refused to put her through. They had claimed he was sleeping, which may have been true. But she knew from the chill in their voices that they wouldn't put her through even if he was awake. Who could blame them? She had been arrested for his poisoning. His parents saw her as a threat to Stan's life. Until she could prove to them—to everyone—that she was innocent, she had no hope of getting through.

Her blood pounded through her veins, and she trembled as she pulled her sunglasses from her purse and shoved them on. Would anyone who saw her recognize her? Would they know her from her pictures in the newspaper? The notorious, murderous wife?

She almost didn't care who saw her, but part of her knew that it wouldn't pay to be seen. She had a mission, and she intended to carry it out.

She grabbed her purse and started down the stairs. Aunt Aggie had gone to the fire station to cook for the men who claimed to be starving to death without her, and David was moving and shaking the oil business by phone downstairs. Maybe she could slip out without being noticed.

But David was off the phone and was sitting at the telephone table, poring over a photo album that Aunt Aggie kept there. It was futile trying to slip past him, so she stopped and looked over his shoulder.

He was staring down at a picture of them as children, sitting in a sandbox with little plastic buckets. Above that were three pageant pictures of her at age four or five, made up like a starlet and striking a pose in a thousand dollar dress with layers of petticoats. She must have been a winner, because she was wearing a tiara.

"Little Miss Southeastern Hinds County Magnolia Blossom . . . or some such nonsense. What a racket."

David nodded pensively. "You won everything. How many trophies did you have?"

"A roomful, for what it was worth. Does Mom still keep them out?"

He shook his head. "She boxed them up years ago."

Though the idea of such awards seemed so silly, they had been her identity for the first eighteen years of her life. The reminder that she'd been relegated to an obsolete memory in the attic only strengthened her resolve to go where she had to go.

He looked up at her and frowned at her ponytail and sunglasses. "Celia, where are you going?"

"Out for a little while," she said. "I just want to run a few errands, get some air."

He stared at her for a moment, then asked, "What are you driving?"

She wilted. For all her planning, she had forgotten that she didn't have her car here. It was still at her house.

"Uh . . . Well, I guess I forgot . . ."

He reached into his pocket for his keys. "Take the Beemer. No problem."

He tossed them up, and she caught them. "Are you sure it's all right?"

"Why wouldn't it be? Want me to go with you?"

She shook her head and wondered if she should tell him where she was going. It was only fair ... But then she decided against it, because he would surely talk her out of it. "No, I want to be alone."

"Okay. The court order didn't say you had to stay locked up in a house all day, did it?"

"No, it didn't."

"You're not going to see him, are you?"

"Who?"

He frowned, as if her question surprised him. "Stan, who else?"

She rallied and shook her head. "No. Not yet."

"All right then."

She left him alone and went out the back way, got into the big car that was a far cry from her little Civic. There had been a time when she had driven a Mercedes Roadster. It had been her first car. Funny how she hadn't missed it at all.

She backed out of the driveway, thankful that the photographer seemed to have left. He was probably back at the newspaper processing new pictures of Aunt Aggie's front door, and manufacturing new stories to tell the people of Newpointe about what was happening behind it.

She headed for the Bonaparte Court apartments, where Jill had said Lee Barnett was staying. She had thought about this all day—about the fact that Lee probably wouldn't hang around forever, not unless the police had warned him not to leave. She had to get to him before he left Newpointe. It was crucial.

She pulled into the parking lot of the apartment complex, found a space, then peered up at the doors and windows, wishing she had some idea which apartment he was in. No one had said.

She got out of the car and headed to the row of mailboxes beside the sidewalk, hoping to find some clue there. Most of them had last names on them, but some didn't. There wasn't a Barnett. Frustrated, she looked around the parking lot for something familiar, maybe his car ... a Mississippi plate ...

There it was, a Mississippi tag on an old silver Grand Am—the same one he'd driven when she'd known him.

It was in front of the B Building of eight apartments, so she went back to the mailboxes, found the Bs, and saw that only one of them didn't have a name. B–5. That had to be him, and if it wasn't, she'd just try another one.

She heard a door close downstairs, and Marabeth Simmons clomped down the walk back into the office. She hurried up the steps of the B Building before the woman could see her. When she was sure Marabeth had gone inside, she found B–5. Inside, she heard the sound of a radio. She knocked on the door and straightened her sunglasses.

"Yeah?" It was his voice. She would have known it anywhere. "Who is it?"

She shivered. "It's me, Lee. Open the door."

He opened it quickly, and she stared up at him. He had changed since she'd last seen him. There was a tiny scar over his top lip, and his hair was cut shorter, and he seemed stronger, more muscular, as though he'd spent a lot of time working out.

She suddenly wondered at the wisdom in coming here.

"Celia?"

She took off her sunglasses and looked up at him, wanting him to look in her eyes and know for sure that it was she he was ruining—a flesh-and-blood human who didn't deserve what was happening. "Why are you here?" she asked him through compressed lips. "Why did you tell the police all those lies about me?"

He leaned out the door and looked from side to side. "Come in," he said.

She breathed a furious laugh. "You've got to be kidding. I'm not coming in there. I want to know why you're setting me

up, Lee. I want to know why you would want my husband dead
. . . what he ever did to you . . . and I need to know if you killed
Nathan, and why . . . why you would let me take the heat for it,
why you would hate me so much that—"

"You're nuts," he cut in. "I didn't kill Nathan, and I didn't poison this husband. And *I'm* the one being set up, not you! I'll hand
it to you, Celia. I didn't know you had it in you. You're smarter
than I thought, but not smart enough to make me your patsy."

Rage filled her, and it burst out as her hand swung up to
slap his face. It surprised him, and he grabbed her arms and
jerked her against him. She lurched free.

"Get your hands off of me!"

"Hey, *you* slapped me!" He dropped his hands to his sides.
"Why did you send for me, Celia? Why me? Why not some
other chump? I never did anything to you."

"I *didn't!*" she cried. "I didn't send for you. I don't even know
who did. I don't know where my checkbook is, and I don't know
who wrote those checks, and I don't know who sent the letter, and
I don't know any Catholic priest, and *I didn't poison my husband!*"
She was weeping now, hating herself for it. She heard a door close
downstairs and wondered if Marabeth had come back out.

She stepped back out of his reach and lowered her voice. "I
just came here to tell you one thing," she said. "If my husband
dies, they can do whatever they want to with me. I won't care.
But I want you to know that I'll move heaven and earth to make
sure you pay. You won't get away with it."

He stared at her, and the confusion in his eyes registered in
her heart. A long moment of electric silence screamed between
them. "You really *didn't* send the letter or the checks, did you?"
he finally asked.

"*No!* Why would I *do* something so destructive? *I love my
husband!*"

He looked down at his feet, working through the facts. And
suddenly she understood. Lee Barnett was innocent, too.
Could it be that they had both been framed?

"Celia, you're in a lot of trouble. I guess I am, too."

"Then why don't you just leave? Get out of town? Why are you still here?"

"Because the cops told me that I couldn't leave town until they'd finished investigating. I don't want to do anything that's gonna land me back in jail. And I've got this apartment paid for for a month . . ."

"But don't you see? If you're telling the truth, they *want* you to stay here. It was planned. Whoever it is, they *want* you here, because it makes people think all sorts of things about me. Can't you stay in town but go to a hotel or something? Get another apartment?"

"Why?"

"Because a killer set you up in this one! So far he's made you play into his hands. Don't you worry about that?"

She could see that he hadn't thought of that. "Well, maybe I could move. But I don't have much money left, and no prospects for a job."

She wiped her face again and shook her head with disbelief. She didn't know why, but she believed him. She had known him well, years ago, and while he was on the wild side, he wasn't conniving. She couldn't imagine that he was lying to her now.

"What can I do, Celia?" he asked. "Tell me what to do. I could go to the police and tell them that I talked to you, that you told me you hadn't sent the letter or the checks, but under the circumstances, they'd just think I was covering for you, that we had something going."

"Don't do anything," she said. "Please, don't do anything. Just stay out of it. Don't make it worse."

She was getting a headache and starting to feel nauseous again. She thought about the baby and touched her stomach. More tears pushed into her eyes. "I have to go," she said.

"You believe me, don't you?" he asked.

She dared not admit that she did. "I don't know what to believe," she said. "Just leave me alone, okay? Don't come near me or my husband, and don't ask about me or talk about me. Don't even say my name."

"What if I find something out? Can't I call then?"

"Call the police," she said. "But you won't find anything out. He's too smart. He's too good at what he does. He knows how to nail me. I just can't figure out why someone who hated me so much wouldn't want to kill *me* instead of my husband. But I guess that would be too kind. This way he can watch me suffer." She looked up at Lee, her eyes intense. "I don't know if you're the guy, Lee, but so help me, if you are, may the wrath of God fall on you so hard that you never find a place to hide from it."

She turned and stumbled down the steps, back to her car.

•   •   •

Out in the parking lot, Vern Hargis, who had been assigned to watch Celia, saw Marabeth duck back into her apartment. He wondered what she had heard. He pulled the cigarette out of his mouth and fingered the camera in his lap, wondering why his heart felt as if it had been punctured. He'd had a remnant of doubt about her guilt, but this certainly changed his mind. From what he'd seen, it looked as if they'd had some kind of lover's quarrel. Celia had slapped him, but the intimacy in their conversation had spoken volumes. It made him sick. Sid's instincts were right, as usual. Celia was no good.

He watched her get into the BMW that must belong to her rich brother, and she sat there for a moment before cranking it up. As he waited for her to pull out, he opened the shutter door of the camera and pulled the film out. The thought of processing the pictures didn't appeal to him. But it had to be done. Cops were about solving cases, and as far as he was concerned, this one was solved.

Poor Stan.

He wondered how he would take this.

He followed her at a distance and pulled his cell phone out of his glove box. Quickly, he dialed information and got Marabeth's number. He hoped she had call-waiting.

"Hello?" she said, breathless. "Sue Ellen?"

"No, Marabeth. It's Vern Hargis. You weren't by chance on the other line, were you?" He smirked even as he asked.

"Well, yes, I was."

"So what's the scoop? I know you just overheard a private conversation."

She hesitated. "Is this police business?"

"Well, yes, it is." His tone was mocking, but she didn't seem to notice.

"Well, you're just not gon' believe who just paid a visit to Mr. Lee Barnett."

"Marabeth, I already know. What did you hear?"

"Well, they were talkin' in low voices, see, so I couldn't hear too good." She lowered her voice to just above a whisper. "But I heard her askin' him to go to a hotel. Reckon she was gon' meet him there?"

Vern frowned. "What else?"

"They were talkin' about what to tell the cops. He said he was gon' tell y'all that she didn't send the check for the apartment. I'm almost sure that's what he said. And he told her he'd cover for her, because they had somethin' goin'."

"Are you sure?"

"As sure as I can be. Vern, why aren't those two in jail? I'm not gon' be able to sleep tonight, worryin' that they'll find out I heard and come cut my throat."

"Then you'd better keep quiet about it, hadn't you?"

She didn't reply, but he knew she was weighing the cost of a cut throat versus the satisfaction of spreading the gossip. He knew she would take the risk.

When he'd hung up, he called Sid and told him the news. He only hoped Celia would head home so he could get the film developed.

Chapter Twenty-Nine

The zydeco sounds of celebration grated over the speakers in the Midtown fire station kitchen, where Aunt Aggie served blackened pork chops so spicy that the men broke out in a sweat just biting into them. She'd missed cooking for them, even if she knew that half of them suspected her Celia of terrible things. She had decided that they'd never know better if she didn't come down here to set them straight.

Ray Ford, the new fire chief, had even shown up to join them, as had some of the other firefighters who weren't even on duty. Ray planted a kiss on Aunt Aggie's cheek as she finished serving the plates. "I heard you been beatin' up on my brother, Aunt Aggie."

She didn't find that amusing. "He needed more'n me beatin' 'im. Needed a two-by-four right across the rump. Puttin' T-Celia in jail." She said it with such contempt that she fancied the bitterness dripped out of her mouth onto the food.

Slater Finch had already dug in, even before Nick Foster had blessed it. With his mouth full, he said, "How come Celia ain't Cajun, Aunt Aggie, if y'all are relatives and all?"

"Celia's mama is my baby bro's girl. He went up to the college, you know, at LSU, and got 'im a education. Tried to pretend he warn't one o' us. Married a high-falutin' gal that talked Jackie Kennedy, and he thought he was *some*-body. Celia's mama never even knowed she was half Cajun, didn't know a word o' French."

"And I thought Cajun was so genetic that the kids were born talking that way," Slater said. "But let's get real. It ain't really

French. I mean, nobody from over in Paree could understand it. Just the same, though, I didn't know a body could choose."

"Can't choose," she said. "My baby bro was born a Cajun and he died a Cajun, whe'er he liked it or not."

Junior Reynolds took a bite of the pork and began to cough and grope for his glass. Everyone watched as he choked and teared up, his face reddening. Aunt Aggie reached for a glass of iced tea and hurried around the table to give it to him.

"Too hot for ya?" she asked, handing him the glass.

"What'd you do? Poison me, too?"

He reached for the glass, but instead of handing it to him, she turned it over and dumped it into his lap. He screamed out a curse and jumped out of his chair. "What's a matter with you? Are you crazy?"

"I didn't poison nobody, and didn't nobody in my family poison nobody, and if you don't want to eat my cookin', then you get that little empty-headed wife of yours to start bringin' you a samwich. In fact, maybe y'all want samwiches. Maybe y'all can make 'em yourselves!"

The others glowered at Junior as though they might lynch him on the spot.

Nick, ever the peacemaker, got up and went to Aunt Aggie's side. "Now, Aunt Aggie. Junior was teasin' you. He didn't mean it, did you, Junior?"

Junior stood there in his wet pants, his hands innocently on his hips as he looked remorsefully at Aunt Aggie. "I got a big mouth, Aunt Aggie. I'm sorry. Please don't make me eat my wife's cookin'. And I like your pork chops. They grow hair on a man's chest. We all like 'em."

Still not amused, she marched back around the table and grabbed her purse. "Y'all can clean up after your own selves today. And I might not be back tonight, me."

"Aunt Aggie!" It was a chorus of protests, but Aunt Aggie compressed her lips and hightailed it out to her Cadillac before they quit being sorry.

The Branning's car was parked in the driveway when Aunt Aggie got home, and she figured they were inside talking to Celia. But then Celia pulled in, driving David's car, just as she was getting out.

"Where you been?" she asked her niece as Celia slid out of the BMW.

"I had to run an errand," she said. Her nose was red and her eyes glistened as if she'd just been crying.

"What errand? You shouldna been out by your lonesome, *sha*. Don't you know?"

"I had to, Aunt Aggie."

"Had to what? Where you went? Tell me, Celia."

She sighed. "I went to see Lee Barnett."

"*Coo!*" Aunt Aggie exclaimed. "He coulda hurt you. Coulda killed you! You crazy?"

"He didn't hurt me at all," she said. "I just had to confront him. Had to know what he's trying to do, why he's setting me up ..."

"And what he say?"

"He said that he wasn't." She sighed. "Aunt Aggie, I think we've both been set up. I'm not sure that he's anything more than just a pawn. But when I think how well this killer knows me, that he'd know about Lee and how we dated once, and that he was in prison, and time everything so it would look like I was poisoning Stan so I could be with Lee ... What else might he do?"

"Nothin'!" Aunt Aggie said. "He ain't gon' do nothin'." She looked up at the big house. "Reckon Allie's here. David inside?"

"Yes. He let me drive his car."

"We better go in, see if she knows somethin' about Stan."

Celia led the way into the house. There they found Allie, Mark, Dan Nichols, and David talking in the kitchen like old friends.

Aunt Aggie wished she'd made a pie this morning like she'd planned.

• • •

Celia was long past caring how she looked. She walked into
the kitchen and saw Allie and Mark sitting with David at
the table, Dan Nichols leaning against the counter. All eyes
turned to her the moment she stepped into the room, and she
met David's eyes, wondering what he'd told them.

"Hey, Sis," he said. "Did you have a good drive?"

She came in and set her purse down. "Yeah. I was feeling
kind of cooped up. Has any of you seen Stan?"

"We have," Mark and Allie said simultaneously, then Mark
went on. "He's not feeling too great, so his folks wouldn't let us
see him too long."

"Is he okay?"

They exchanged looks. "Well, I don't think he's out of danger yet," Allie said. "There was some talk about dialysis . . .
apparently some of his organs may have been damaged. But he
talked to us for a minute before his parents ran us out."

Her face grew hot. "Damaged organs? How damaged? Can
they be repaired? Could he die?"

Mark looked helpless. "We honestly don't know, Celia. We
didn't get to talk to the doctors, and his parents weren't real
forthcoming. What we found out came from the people in the
waiting room."

"Did he know about me?" she asked, feeling as fragile as a
crystal doll. "Had anyone told him why I wasn't there?"

"Yeah, he knew." Allie's tone was heavy with apology. "He
asked me about you, Celia. Wanted to know if you were all
right. That's when his parents ran us out."

Celia turned away from them as her eyes filled with tears.
"Did you tell him I didn't do it, Allie? Did you tell him it's all a
mistake?"

Allie reached for her and pulled her into a hug. "He knows
that, Celia. He loves you."

Her face twisted and she wiped at her eyes. "But did you tell him?"

"Yes. But his parents got us out so fast I'm not sure he heard. Celia, don't blame them. They're exhausted. They've been with him since the beginning, and I doubt either of them has left the hospital. Now that he's awake, they're finally going home tonight to get a good night's sleep. Maybe after that they'll see things more clearly and realize you couldn't have done this."

She let that sink in for a moment, processing it. His parents were leaving. He wouldn't have them hovering over him tonight.

Celia looked at Allie. "Allie, would you go back to see him tonight? Take him a note from me? Maybe you could even call me from his room so I could talk to him."

Allie glanced at Mark, then brought her apologetic eyes back to her. "Celia, I can't. They're not allowing visitors after his parents leave tonight."

She sank back down and tried to think. "Is someone still guarding him?" she asked.

Mark spoke up. "If I'm not mistaken, several of the guys are taking turns guarding him. Three- or four-hour shifts each."

"Who's on tonight?" she asked.

"Well, I don't know," Allie said, and Celia could see the suspicion forming on her face. "Why?"

"Because ..." She looked around at each of them. "I want to make sure he's being carefully watched. I don't want anyone sneaking in, especially if his parents won't be there."

"I know who'll be there," Mark said. "When I was up there, R.J. mentioned that Vern Hargis would be on the first shift tonight. I don't know what they consider the first shift, and I don't know who's taking over for him, but I think he'll be in good hands with Vern."

Vern Hargis. A chain smoker. He would need to take smoking breaks.

She pulled out a chair and sat down next to her brother. Dan frowned at her, as if contemplating something, and she looked up at him. "What is it, Dan?"

"You don't look so good, Celia. Are you feeling all right?"

"No, not really," she said. "I think I've had a touch of a virus. I'll be fine."

"You're pale," Allie said. "Celia, we'll go and let you lie down. We just wanted to tell you we had seen Stan, that he asked about you, that things are looking up."

"Thanks," she said.

"Are you gonna be all right?"

She nodded and wiped the tears beneath her eyes again. "Yeah, sure. I'll be fine."

"Celia, I'll check in with you a little later," Allie said. "You get some rest, okay? Jill's working hard on this. It'll be over soon."

"I hope so."

She watched as they all filed out of the room, and David led them to the door. She could hear Aunt Aggie telling them all not to rush off, but they did, anyway.

Celia sat staring at the table, trying to work out what she would do, trying to think of the pros and cons, trying to measure the consequences.

In moments, both Aunt Aggie and David were back in the kitchen. "You awright, *sha?*" Aunt Aggie asked.

She was getting tired of that question, so she ignored it. "I'm going to see him."

Aunt Aggie looked at David, and David pulled a chair out and sat down across from her. "What about the guard?" he asked.

"I'll get past him somehow," she bit out. "This might be my only chance. I have to go while his parents aren't there." She looked up at her Aunt Aggie. "The guard is Vern Hargis, Aunt Aggie. He's a chain smoker, isn't he?"

"Well, yeah, he is, but—"

"So I'll hide in the stairwell and watch until he goes out for a smoking break. I have to tell Stan about the baby," she said. "I have to tell him that I love him and that I didn't do it. I could look in his eyes and know that he believes me. I could see for myself that he's all right . . ."

"I'm goin' with you," Aunt Aggie announced.

Celia looked hopefully up at her. "You will?"

"I might can help. Let you know when Vern sneaks off."

The first hope she'd felt since she'd heard Stan had opened his eyes blossomed inside her. She looked at David. He was staring at the table, thinking.

After a moment, he met her eyes, still contemplating, working it all out. "We have to think this through, Celia. If they catch you, they'll assume that you came to finish him off. What if his parents change their minds and come back? What if a nurse comes in? What if that guard comes back before you expect him to?"

Her heart was pounding with anticipation. "I have to take the chance that his parents won't come back. But you gave me an idea. I need a nurse's uniform. If I have one, I can pretend to be a nurse. Of course, if Vern sees me, he'll know it's me. But if he's there when I come out, maybe I can get past him without looking at him."

David nodded, still concentrating. "All right, then. I'll drive you. That way I can wait in the car close to an exit, and we can drive away before anyone spots you."

"Sure you want to be an accessory?" she asked.

"Celia, you're my sister. I'll do what I can to make sure it doesn't turn out as bad as it could. Just promise me you won't take any stupid chances or get so anxious that you do something you'll regret."

"I promise." She threw her arms around his neck, kissed his cheek, then stood up to hug Aunt Aggie.

"I'll go t' Slidell and buy a uniform," Aunt Aggie told her. "Maybe a wig for me, so's I can set in that waitin' room and

Vern won't recognize me. I'll take off all my Mary Kay, and slump over like some ole lady. Get me a cane and some o' them ole lady shoes."

David grinned at her. "You're enjoying this a little too much, Aunt Aggie."

She slapped playfully at him. "You hush. We got to do it right. Now, Celia, you go on up and take a nap while I'm gone, so's you'll look purty for your husband. Don't wanna go with no swollen eyes and red nose."

Celia smiled. "Okay, Aunt Aggie. I'll do that."

She started out of the room. Behind her, she heard David say, "We're all probably out of our minds."

Aunt Aggie laughed with delight as Celia started up the stairs.

Chapter Thirty

Aunt Aggie had come home with enough paraphernalia to start a life of crime. Already she was practicing walking with the cane and a pair of brogans that, as far as she was concerned, gave the elderly a bad name. And she'd gotten Celia a nursing uniform, and had even purloined a security badge so she'd look like a bona fide employee.

"Where in the world did you get this?" Celia asked, studying the badge.

Aunt Aggie's eyes danced with delight. "I was down to the uniform shop, and a nurse come in t' try on a new uniform, and when she got undressed, she hanged her other uniform over the door. The sales lady, she warn't lookin', so I moseyed on over and seen it was for the Slidell Hospital, so I jes' unclipped the badge ..."

"Aunt Aggie, you *stole* it!"

Aunt Aggie seemed quite proud of herself. "I borried it. I plan to give it back. On our way outa the hospital, you can drop it somewhere. Somebody'll get it back to her."

She looked down at it again. The woman in the picture had red hair and glasses. "Aunt Aggie, I don't look anything like her."

Again, Aunt Aggie's eyes danced. "Look a-here," she said, digging into a bag. She pulled out a red wig and a pair of wire-framed glasses, just like the woman in the picture wore.

Celia laughed. David tried to hold back his smile, though he wasn't doing a very good job. "I think it's official now. She really is crazy."

"Vern won't recognize you. You could prob'ly even go in right in front o' him. He'd never even know."

"Maybe that won't be necessary," she said. "Maybe he'll go smoke. But if he doesn't, we'll have plan B."

"So when are we going to perpetrate this unfortunate act we're planning?" David asked.

"After visiting hours," she said. "That way I can be sure his parents will be gone."

"All right," he said.

"Oh, I forgot to tell you," Aunt Aggie said as she put the supplies back into her bag. "We got somebody outside watchin' the house."

"What?" Celia asked, her eyes shooting back up to Aunt Aggie.

"Yep. Sittin' a ways down the road, thinkin' I'm too dumb to know, but I seen him. T.J. Porter, I think. Readin' the paper when I come by, like he always parks his car on the side o' the road to read the paper."

"Do you think he's following her?" David asked.

"Prob'ly. I ain't seen him before now."

Celia dropped the badge and covered her face with both hands. "Oh, no. What if he followed me to Lee Barnett's apartment?"

"*Lee Barnett's?*" David returned. "Are you telling me that you went to Lee Barnett's?"

"Yes," she said. "Earlier when I borrowed your car."

"Are you asking for trouble? Celia, what were you thinking?"

"I wanted to look him in the eye and find out why he was doing this to me. I wanted to know if he's the one who poisoned Stan . . . and why."

He dropped his face on the table, as if giving up. "I can't believe this. It's hopeless." He raised his head back up and braced his elbows on the table. Looking at her through splayed fingers, he said, "Okay. Let's just hope that no one did see you. It won't look good, Celia. The very guy they think you tried to off your husband for, and you're seen going in his apartment?"

"No, I didn't go in."

"What in the world did he say?"

"He said he didn't do it. That he was framed, too. That someone is setting us both up."

"Yeah, right."

She sighed. "He seemed genuine. But it's hard to tell with him. I don't know him anymore. I don't know how he's changed since prison."

David went to the front window and looked out onto the street. "Well, okay, so you went to Lee Barnett's, you might have been seen ... Well, we can't do anything about that now. But we definitely can't let them follow us to the hospital. So we'll go in my car, and I'll take my suitcase out there like I'm leaving, put it in the trunk. But how will we get you in the car without him seeing?"

"We'll get in before you open the garage door. We'll duck down, and then you can open the garage and make a fuss over loading your suitcase. Since the garage is attached to the house, he won't know we ever came out."

"Yeah, that'll work."

"We can do this," Celia said.

David released a long breath, then shook his head again. "I hope Stan will appreciate it."

•   •   •

Stan was exhausted by the time his parents left that night, for a steady stream of visitors had come through to visit him. For much of the time, he'd lain there with his eyes closed, too weak to make conversation. The visitors had seemed satisfied just to see him.

Now, visiting hour was over, his parents were gone, and he felt more alone than he'd ever felt. He wanted Celia. If she were able, she would spend the night here with him, look after him, fill his loneliness. He couldn't understand why Judge DeLacy would have kept her from that.

An idea came into his mind even as defeat seemed to rush in, and he glanced over at the phone on his table. It was too far away, and he didn't think he could get up enough to reach it. If he could just get to it . . .

A nurse breezed in, carrying a tray of medications. "Are you awake, Mr. Shepherd? I would have thought you were sleeping."

"In a minute," he said. "Listen, could you hand me the phone? I can't reach it."

"Sure," she said. She rounded the bed and set the phone on his pillow. "How's that?"

"Great," he said. "Thanks."

Humming, she breezed out again.

His heart began to flutter as he picked up the phone and dialed out his home phone number. She couldn't come to him, but no court order said that he couldn't call her. He waited for the first, second, third rings . . .

Finally, the machine picked up. His own voice greeted him. He hung up.

Where was she?

Aunt Aggie's, he thought. Of course. She would have stayed with Aunt Aggie, since there was a killer out there somewhere, and she was, no doubt, depressed and upset, and Aunt Aggie would nurture and pamper her.

He dialed the old woman's number. It rang once, twice, three times. . . .

There was no machine, so he waited, thinking that they might be avoiding phone calls since they were probably getting hate calls and the press was probably hounding them. Oh, how he wished he could clear her of this quickly, so that people would leave her alone. He dropped the phone in its cradle and sank back into the pillow. He wanted so badly to talk to her. If only there was someone he could send, to ask her to call *him*.

The preacher, he thought. He could call Nick. Nick would help him. Surely, he knew that Celia hadn't done this. He could count on him. Besides, he could use a little spiritual guidance.

He dialed the number, and Nick answered on the second ring. "Hello?"

"Hey, man," Stan said, knowing he didn't sound like himself. "I hope it's not too late, but I need to talk."

"Stan?"

"Yeah, it's me."

Nick began to laugh. "You feel well enough to call me and talk? Man, our prayers are being answered, brother. I can't believe it's you."

"Believe it," he said. "Listen, Nick. I need a favor. I need you to get a message to Celia."

• • •

The plan for getting Aunt Aggie and Celia into David's car worked perfectly, and as they drove past the car parked down the street, they knew that he hadn't followed them. He was still watching the house, where lights were on, thinking that Celia was inside.

As they reached the Slidell Hospital, Celia began to tremble. This wasn't going to be easy. "How will you know where to pick us up?" she asked.

"I was just thinking about that," David told her. "What if I go in with you and find the stairwell you'll be coming down? I can park next to whichever exit you'll be coming out."

"Good idea. But you'll have to park, and we'll have to walk across the parking lot."

"I'll drop you off at the main entrance, and you head straight for the first stairwell you see. I'll meet you there after I park. And Aunt Aggie can go on up, okay Aunt Aggie?"

"I'm ready," the old woman said. Celia looked back at her and chuckled at how old she looked. She had donned her curly gray wig and glasses, and she was wearing a loose-fitting frock that she would have never been caught dead in.

"Aunt Aggie, do you think you'd look like that for real if you hadn't had that face-lift?"

"Never," Aunt Aggie said. "I take too good care o' myself."

They reached the hospital parking lot. "We'll go up and make sure which exit is closest to Stan's room," David said, as if thinking out loud, "and then I'll move the car."

He pulled up to the front entrance, and they both sat there for a moment.

"You sure you're ready for this?" he asked.

"Yes," Celia said. "I'm sure. Thanks, David. We couldn't have done this without you." She got out of the car, and Aunt Aggie got out, too. Not waiting for what appeared to be the decrepit old lady, she headed inside and around the hall behind the elevators, where she saw an exit sign. Quietly, she slipped into the stairwell there. There was an exit door right there, at the foot of the stairs, and she sat down on the bottom step and waited.

In just a few moments, David stepped inside. "Okay, let's go up," he whispered. "Aunt Aggie said Stan's in 306. We'll see how close this stairwell comes out."

They climbed three flights of stairs, then peered out the rectangular window on the third floor. "This room right across the hall is 310. I think this is as close as we'll get, don't you?" she asked.

"Probably," he said. "Okay, so you wait here, and I'll go move the car to this exit at the bottom of this stairwell. Remember, Sis, don't take long with him. Get in, say what you've gotta say, and get out."

"I will."

She watched as he trotted back down the stairs. Then she turned back to the window and waited for Aunt Aggie to come and tell her when Vern left for a smoking break.

● ● ●

The waiting room was almost empty this time of night, but no one paid Aunt Aggie any attention as she sat there where she could see right up the hall to Stan's room, where Vern Hargis had sat for the past hour reading a magazine.

He was getting nervous, jumpy, she realized, because he was shaking his foot and doing a two-fingered drum roll on his leg, and when he finally discarded the magazine and got up, she knew they were about to hit pay dirt. But where would he go?

She tried to see past him, down the hall. Was there a balcony somewhere that he could step out on? A window he could lean out of? A bathroom he could smoke in?

She saw an exit sign, and a door opened from the night. A nurse came in, holding her own cigarette pack, and Aunt Aggie's heart leaped.

"Don't you need a smoke, *sha?*" Aunt Aggie whispered under her breath.

As if he'd heard her, he looked longingly toward that exit. He seemed to consider whether he could smoke out there while still guarding the room. Her heart was hammering, and she fought the urge to yell for him to go on, smoke that cigarette, and hurry up about it.

But then her plan was thwarted when an orderly dressed in surgical scrubs ambled toward Stan's room.

"How ya doin'?" he asked Vern, and Vern nodded. The man pushed on in.

Aunt Aggie sat back in a slump, wondering what they were going to do now.

Chapter Thirty-One

Since you don't pay me overtime, you don't care if I go home now, do you?" Jill's secretary, Sheila, asked from the doorway of her office. "I mean, I could do like you and work around the clock, but like I said, I don't get overtime."

Jill didn't have time to trade quips with Sheila. She'd been going over depositions from the Nathan case and was too deep in concentration. "Sure. You can go home."

"'Cause it's after dark, you know."

"You were late coming in," Jill said, finally looking up at her.

"I figured you'd be sleeping late, since you've been working so hard."

"Even if I had, the phone would still need to be answered, Sheila, and there's lots of work to be done."

"Did you realize you didn't wear makeup today? I can't figure out if it makes you look older or younger."

Jill set her pen down and leaned back in the chair, staring at the woman. Sometimes she just wanted to throttle her . . . or worse . . . fire her. But she had done it once before only to find that there wasn't anyone else in town as qualified as she. She'd hired her back with the stipulation that she get an attitude adjustment, but apparently Sheila hadn't taken that too seriously.

"What?" Sheila asked, as if innocent of offending her boss.

"Did you expect me to respond to that, Sheila?"

"No, I was just making an observation."

"Thank you. I didn't wear makeup because I forgot. I had too much on my mind."

"Older, I think," Sheila finally decided. "Has Dan seen you like that?"

Jill turned the page of the deposition and began reading again. "Good-bye, Sheila."

The woman backed out of the room, and in moments, she heard the front door close. She was gone. Jill got up and stretched, then went in to the bathroom connected to her office and looked in the mirror. She did look awful. She couldn't believe she hadn't worn makeup, but she'd had all those questions about Celia on her mind . . . Sheila was right. She did look older. Old and unmarried. And if Dan saw her this way, he'd be even more repulsed then he'd been by her behavior last night.

She heard the door open and close again, and she went back to her desk, not wanting Sheila to catch her looking in the mirror. She didn't want Jill to have the satisfaction of thinking her comment had bothered her.

But it wasn't Sheila who appeared in the doorway. It was Sid.

"Got somethin' for you, Jill," he said.

Jill didn't want it. Whatever it was, it had to be bad news, and she wasn't up to it. She just stared at him.

He crossed the room and dropped a 5 x 7 snapshot down on her desk. "Now tell me Celia ain't guilty."

Jill looked down at the snapshot. Her face fell. It was of Celia and Lee Barnett, standing close with his hands on her arms. "What is this?"

"Your client went to see her boyfriend this afternoon," Sid said. "Because Stan made us promise to keep somebody on her for protection, Vern Hargis followed her there."

Jill frowned, studying the picture. Her heart was pounding out a dirge-like rhythm, and she wanted to cry. But that wouldn't do. "There's an explanation," she said weakly.

"Oh, yeah? Did *you* know she was goin' to see him?"

"No, but I'm sure . . ."

"That's cause she's fleecin' you, too, Jill. Wake up, woman."

Jill studied the picture and realized she couldn't see either of their faces. Just Celia's ponytail and Lee Barnett holding her. How could she have gone to see him in broad daylight, and necked with him right out in the open? Did she *want* to get caught? No, she told herself as reason took over. Something wasn't right.

She got to her feet and grabbed her briefcase with one hand and the snapshot with the other. "Excuse me, Sid. I need to go speak to my client."

"Be my guest," Sid said. "But don't eat nothin' she feeds you."

Chapter Thirty-Two

Stan was crushed when he realized that Nick had not been to see Celia since this whole ordeal had begun. He clutched the phone to his ear and tried to speak clearly. "What's wrong with you?" he asked. "You call yourself a preacher? My wife has been arrested for attempted murder . . . and you . . . you don't even visit her?"

He knew his words were too harsh, but he was too tired, too weak, to choose them any more carefully. Might as well just say what he thought. And what he thought was that Nick Foster had let Celia down.

"Stan, you're right. I should have gone. It's just that I didn't know if she wanted company . . ."

"That's lame, Nick. She needs support. Half this town probably thinks she tried to kill me. I never imagined you'd be in that half."

"I'm not! Stan, listen to me. I'll go right now. I do believe in her innocence. And you're right, I should have gone. I don't even know why I didn't. But I was working at the fire station, and then last night we had services, and—"

Stan knew he needed to calm down. His heart was beating too fast, and with all the medication being pumped into him to battle the effects of the arsenic, he couldn't afford to get too excited.

An orderly dressed in scrubs, with his surgical mask still up and his hat still on, came in and motioned for him to keep talking, so Stan didn't get off the phone.

"I'm sorry I jumped you," Stan said to Nick as the orderly went to the foot of the bed and checked his chart. He was holding an IV bag, and it hung from his finger as he flipped through the chart. "I just don't like having my wife treated like this. If there's even a chance that you believe she's guilty, or if she thinks you *think* she's guilty, so help me, Nick, I'll change churches so fast—"

"Stan, come on. I'm a preacher, not superman. I'm doing the best I can. I didn't know how to handle it. I've been praying for both of you, though. Stan, if you want me to go over to Aunt Aggie's, I will. I'll go tonight, wake her up, if you want."

"I do want," he said. The orderly came back around the bed and began changing the bag.

"So you want me to tell her to call you?"

"Yes, if the switchboard is still open. If it's not, tell her to answer it when I call. I think she and Aunt Aggie might be just letting it ring. If I don't hear something in the next half hour, I'll call her again."

"All right, Stan. Just relax, all right? I'll take care of it."

Stan hung up and regarded the bag the orderly had hung. "That bag wasn't empty, was it?"

"No, but it wasn't dripping right. I was told to change it."

Stan glanced at him. He was wearing big black glasses, and that mask made him nervous. He never liked not being able to see someone's face. "You just come out of surgery?"

The man shook his head and checked the drip. "Nope. They just made me wear the mask my whole shift tonight because of my cold. Don't want me passing any germs along."

He went back to the chart, made a notation, then started for the door. "You're all right now. Why don't you go to sleep?"

"I will," Stan said.

He lay there and let his eyes close, but as tired as he was, he didn't want to sleep. Not yet. Not until he heard from his wife. Not until he talked to Celia.

• • •

In the waiting room, Aunt Aggie saw the orderly leave the room. Vern had sat back down now and was reading that magazine again. As fidgety as he was, she finally realized that he wasn't going to smoke. He was too loyal to Stan. Celia would have to do the nurse bit and take her chances.

She got up from the vinyl sofa. Slumped over and leaning on her cane, she shuffled down the hall to the stairwell four rooms down from Stan's room.

Celia was sitting on a stair, waiting for her, and when Aunt Aggie stepped in, she sprang up. "Is he gone, Aunt Aggie? Is he smoking?"

"He ain't gon' smoke. He wants to, but he ain't gon' do it."

She took a deep breath. "Then I'll just have to pretend to be a nurse." She touched her red wig and straightened her glasses. "Will he recognize me, Aunt Aggie?"

"Not if you walk fast like you b'long there. He's readin' a magazine. I was you, I'd say hey to him and give 'im long enough to see your badge, then hurry past him. Don't look 'im in the eye. Jes' look up the hall like you're lookin' for somethin'."

She took in a deep breath. "All right. Wish me luck."

"Good luck."

She started out of the stairwell and didn't see anyone except Vern in the hall. Just as Aggie had told her, he was reading that magazine.

She walked quickly, and he looked up just as she drew near. She muttered, "Hey," and glanced up the hall.

"Hey." He glanced at her badge. Then he went back to reading.

She was inside Stan's door before she knew it.

She saw him lying there, with that IV in his arm and that oxygen tube under his nose, resting with his eyes closed, and that phone beside his head on the pillow. Who had he been talking to?

Her heart burst, and her eyes filled with tears, and she stepped closer to the bed. "Stan?"

His eyes opened, and he looked up at her.

She took off her glasses, and pulled the wig off, revealing her blonde bun. "It's me, honey."

He caught his breath and reached up for her, and she slid her arms around him and began to weep.

His embrace was weak, but his love wasn't, and as she pulled back to look at him, she saw the tears in his eyes.

"Are you all right?" he asked her.

"You're the one in a hospital bed." Her eyes filled again. "Are you in any pain?"

He ignored the question and touched her face. "They accused you."

"I didn't do it, Stan."

"Shhh, I know you didn't. We'll convince them. But you have to be careful. They're out there . . ."

"You don't know who did this?" she asked him. "You don't remember who gave you the poison?"

"Can't imagine." He wiped her tears from her face. "But we have to find out."

"We're trying. Jill's trying. But Stan, I have some good news for you. You're not going to believe this." She was crying harder and could barely speak, but she forced the words out.

"Good news?" he asked. "Good news that makes you cry?"

"My emotions are on a roller coaster," she whispered. "Mostly down . . . but this news . . ."

"What are you doing?"

Celia swung around to the voice and saw Vern standing in the doorway. "Vern, please. I just wanted to talk—"

He shot across the room and grabbed her as he called for help on his walkie-talkie. She tried to wrestle free, but before she knew it he had the handcuffs snapped on her. "Vern, please. I didn't do anything. I just wanted to talk to him."

"You're under arrest again," Vern said. "You have the right to remain silent—"

"Vern, stop it!" Stan cried. "Let her go! She didn't do anything."

More security people came in, and Celia's face was raging hot as tears ran down her face. "What do you think I was going to do? Kill him? I just wanted to tell him something. I wanted to see him!"

Some nurses and a doctor ran in. "Mr. Shepherd, did she give you anything to eat?"

"No! Let her go!"

She was screaming and wailing now, and trying to fight free. "Please. Why would I kill my husband? Why would I want to kill the father of my baby? I'm pregnant, Stan! That's what I wanted to tell you!"

"Pregnant?" The word was weak, breathless.

"His blood pressure is dropping!"

"What?" she asked. "I didn't *do* anything!"

"Who changed this bag?" the nurse demanded. "Did you do it?" she asked Celia.

"No! I don't even know how!"

"Someone changed this bag! It was half full a little while ago when I checked it. Now it's full."

"It was the orderly," Stan got out weakly.

But his words were lost in the chaos that followed, and Celia realized that something was wrong. Had he been poisoned again?

"Help him!" she cried. But Vern wrestled her out of the room. And as tears streamed down her face, she realized she might never see her husband alive again.

Chapter Thirty-Three

When Jill had failed to find Celia at Aunt Aggie's, or anywhere else, she'd been ready to erupt. She had finally given up and come home. The classical music CD piping through Jill's house calmed her spirit somewhat, though the questions of the day still churned in her mind. She made herself a sandwich in the kitchen, a dollop of peanut butter between two slices of bread, then realized that she needed something healthier, something warm. But she'd had no time to go to the grocery store, no time to do any cooking.

Again, she walked to her answering machine and checked the messages to see if Dan had called. There was nothing there. Had he forgotten her in her busyness, she wondered? Was he still mad at her for the things she'd said last night? Was he waiting for her to call him?

He certainly had a reputation for arrogance, yet she couldn't help wondering after spending so much time with him if it wasn't a reputation built on fear. Something told her that Dan was afraid of rejection and abandonment, that his detachment from women had more to do with his own insecurities than with his desire to be alone. It was an insight that had come after a great deal of thought. She wasn't sure he would agree with her. She wasn't even sure she was right.

But she supposed that she should be thankful that they had been out more than his usual three times, and that he continued to show interest. At least, he had until last night.

She went back to her briefcase and looked at the notes she had taken today when she'd visited Celia. She had been working around the clock to solve this case, racking her brain to figure out who could have poisoned Stan and Nathan. Now to learn that Celia was sneaking around, hiding things from her, was more than Jill could stand. She needed to talk to someone.

She thought of calling Allie, but she didn't want to cast more bad light on Celia. Besides, she had no business sharing the case with anyone.

She needed a friend. Just someone to eat with . . .

Deciding to swallow her pride and take a chance, she picked up the phone and dialed Dan's number. He answered quickly.

"Hello?"

"Hi, Dan. It's Jill."

She could hear the sigh in his voice. Was it relief, or dread? "Jill."

"I hope I'm not bothering you," she said. "I wanted to apologize for last night. You're right. I was strung a little too tight. I was edgy, and I shouldn't have taken it out on you."

"No, you shouldn't have."

She sat there for a moment. Was he going to make her grovel? She began to get angry. "That's what I said."

"Okay."

She sat there a little longer, holding the phone to her ear and seriously considering hanging it up. What did he want from her?

"So . . . did you get any sleep?"

The question seemed gentler, and her anger cooled a degree. "No, not really. And I've had a really rough day."

"Uh-oh. Then I guess I'd better not suggest a late dinner. We might butt heads again."

That balloon of anger seemed to deflate in her chest. "If I promise to behave better, would you go ahead and suggest dinner? I was just about to eat a peanut butter sandwich."

"You can do better than that, Jill," Dan said, all anger gone from his tone. "Let me take you out to eat."

She hesitated a moment. "It's after nine, and I don't know if I'm really up to going out. I thought maybe you could come over and I could make something—"

Before she could finish the sentence, he cut in. "You're not making anything, Jill. You've been working around the clock. I'll tell you what. I'll pick something up at Maison de Manger and bring it over. What would you like?"

She couldn't think. Her brain was too tired. "Surprise me."

"Will do," he said. "I'll see you in about half an hour."

She smiled. The night was looking up after all.

Jill spent the next half hour in a whirlwind, cleaning the mess that had accumulated in her house since Celia's arrest. She was not known for being a neat person. On a good day, she left her bed unmade, clothes thrown over a chair in her bedroom, and dishes in the sink. But in the past few days, dust had collected, dirty laundry had gathered in a heap on her bedroom floor, and stacks of unread mail spilled over her kitchen counter. She rushed as fast as she could to get the place clean before Dan showed up.

By the time he arrived, her house was passable, though not spotless by anyone's standards. They ate together, talking quietly, and she enjoyed the warmth and sustenance of the food he had brought, for she hadn't had a real meal since the last time she'd eaten with him. She'd have to watch it, she thought, or she would start associating comfort and well-being with his presence.

"So how's the case going?" he asked.

She sighed. "Not good. I'm hitting a lot of dead ends. I've spent most of today going over depositions from the first trial and making phone calls, trying to track down people who knew anything about the Nathan case. It's slow going."

He touched her hand and fondled her fingers, sending a jolt through her body. She wasn't used to affection of any kind. But she told herself that she could get used to it from Dan.

"You'll be fine," he said. "I have a lot of faith in you. Your instincts are great."

She sat there a moment, letting the words sink in. Her instincts. Weren't those what were pulling her down now? She wasn't sure whether her instincts were urging her toward trusting in Celia's innocence, or sending up alarm signals in her brain. To her, doubting Celia meant failure. Celia had been a good enough friend to her to deserve her trust.

"What's wrong?" Dan asked.

She met his eyes and wondered how much he could see. "I guess this case has just got me down."

"You're not worried, are you?"

She averted her eyes. "A little. There were some new developments today. I can't really discuss them, but it doesn't look good for Celia."

Dan frowned. "You're not starting to think she did it, are you?"

"No, not at all. Of course not."

"But what?" he asked.

"But Sid does, and that's important. It's important for me to stand behind Celia and to do everything in my power to make Sid think twice about keeping her on the suspect list. But it's getting harder all the time."

"They've found more evidence?" he asked.

She stared at him, knowing she couldn't elaborate, but needing so badly to talk. Thankfully, the doorbell rang.

She got up and hurried to it, wondering who it could be, dreading the bad news that seemed almost inevitable. She opened the door and saw Nick Foster standing there. "Nick, hi."

He looked worried, distracted, as if he hadn't come to pay a social visit. "Jill, can I talk to you for a minute?"

"Sure," she said. She ushered him in, and he saw Dan and reached out to shake his hand.

"I'm sorry to interrupt, but I'm worried about Celia."

Jill's expression changed. "What do you mean?"

He took off his glasses and rubbed his eyes. "Stan called me a little while ago," he said. "He wanted me to go by Aunt Aggie's and tell Celia to call him, because he really wanted to talk to her and they weren't answering the phone."

"Really?" Jill asked, her eyebrows rising. "That's a good sign."

"Of course it is," Nick said. "Stan doesn't think Celia had anything to do with this. In fact, as weak as he is, he had plenty of energy to lambaste me for not being there for her. And he's right. I just . . . I don't know what to think about her, Jill."

Jill understood more than he knew. She touched his shoulder gently. "Nick, we all have to keep an open mind and just pray hard for Celia."

"I know. And sometimes I really just have a hard time following the Spirit, and I wonder if I ought to even be in this profession at all."

Dan got up from the table and set his hand on Nick's shoulder. "Nick, you're a good fireman, but you're the best preacher I know. Don't start getting all down on yourself."

"The best preacher?" Nick almost laughed, but he obviously didn't find it amusing. "You haven't had much experience with them, then, have you?" He sighed. "Well, anyway, that doesn't matter. The reason I came is that I went by Aunt Aggie's, and no one's home."

"Still?" Jill asked. "Are you sure?"

"That's right," Nick said. "I knocked on the front door, went around to the back door. There were lights on in the house, but no answer. I went to a pay phone and called, still no answer. Finally, I went over to Celia's, thinking maybe she'd gone home, but there was no one there, either."

Jill frowned. "Where could they be?"

"I don't know," Nick said. "But I thought she might be over here." He glanced at the food on the table. "I guess I was wrong. I don't know what to do now. I guess I should call Stan back and tell him I can't find her."

Jill didn't like what she was hearing. She thought of Lee Barnett, then quickly tried to squelch the thought. But it hung on. Celia had already gone to see him once—what was to stop her from going again? No, certainly not. Just because Celia had gone to him once didn't mean she'd do it again. She went to the telephone and dialed Aunt Aggie's, then waited as it rang and rang and rang. No answer.

"Where could she be?"

Dan thought for a moment, then met her eyes. "The hospital?"

Jill froze. "No. No way. She knows better."

"If she wanted to talk to Stan as much as he wanted to talk to her," Nick said. "I wouldn't put it past her."

Jill closed her eyes. "It's the worst thing she could do right now. I don't think she would have tried it without talking to me first." But hadn't she gone to see Barnett this morning without talking to Jill? That had been self-destructive, but Celia hadn't cared. Right now, Celia was desperate, and she was only interested in the bottom line. Jill just wasn't sure what that bottom line was.

"Maybe I'd better call Stan and see if he's heard from her." She went to the telephone, but before she could pick it up, it rang. Quickly, she snatched it up. "Hello?"

"Jill, this is Sid Ford." The words were rapid-fire, distant, as if he was calling from a cellular phone.

"Sid, what's wrong?"

"I'm on my way to Slidell Hospital," he said. "Your girl was just caught in Stan's room."

"*What?*" Jill asked. Then rallying, she said, "Sid, don't jump to conclusions. She just wanted to see him."

"Jump to conclusions?" he shot back. "Jill, they found arsenic in his IV bag. *Somebody* put it there."

She was speechless.

"Jill did you hear me?"

"I heard you," she said.

"Use your head, Jill. Think. She breaks the court order to come there in the first place, finagles a way in usin' a disguise, and when she's caught they discover that arsenic is in her husband's bag. Nobody else could have put it there, Jill."

Jill sank into a chair. Dan and Nick stood over her, waiting to hear what was going on. "Where is she?"

"Vern's haulin' her in right now," Sid said. "But I'm goin' there to talk to Stan."

"I'll meet her at the police station," Jill said.

"You do what you want," Sid said. "But don't expect bond tonight. I've already been in touch with the judge and given him an earful. Louis is with us on this."

Jill closed her eyes.

"I thought you'd want to know," Sid said, and cut off the phone.

Jill lowered the phone but kept holding it in her hand.

"What is it?" Dan asked.

"You were right," she said. "That's exactly where Celia was."

"At the hospital?"

"Yeah. And she got caught." She didn't tell him about the arsenic. That was something that he wasn't going to hear from her. "It's gonna be another long night," she said. "I've got to get to the police station, guys."

"Of course you do," Dan said. "I'll follow you there."

She didn't have any energy to argue as she grabbed her briefcase and headed for the door.

Chapter Thirty-Four

Aunt Aggie had been sitting in the hospital waiting room when she saw Vern get up restlessly and peer into the room. She had braced herself. She knew what would come next.

And then she'd heard shouting, and security people began running to the room, and then nurses and doctors, like Stan had done one of those Code Blue things. When they had dragged Celia out of the room, crying and screaming, Aunt Aggie had been torn between beating Vern off with her cane, and taking the stairs down as fast as she could. Since Vern had gotten Celia onto the elevator before she'd made up her mind, she'd chosen the stairs.

She was out of breath by the time she got all the way down, and just as he'd promised, David was sitting in his car right beside the exit. He saw the look on her face and leaned over to open the passenger door.

"Aunt Aggie, what's wrong?"

"They got her!" She climbed into the car like a thief escaping a bank robbery. She pulled her wig off and threw it down, leaving her own white hair sticking out all over. "Come in and caught her!"

David cursed. "Where is she?"

"They takin' her to Newpointe, I guess. Maybe Slidell. Hurry 'round and maybe we'll catch up with 'em. We can follow 'em, see where they take her. But what if they see us?"

The sound of sirens began to get closer, and David shook his head. "Aunt Aggie, if they do see us, so what? *We* weren't under a court order. You and I were allowed to come here." Aunt Aggie saw several police cars pull in front of the building, and the cops got out and hustled in. "What did they do, call out the cavalry? All she did was break a stupid court order."

"The commotion!" Aunt Aggie said, dropping her head back against the seat. "You shoulda seen it! The screamin' and runnin' and wailin' and doctors and nurses . . ."

"I should have talked her out of this. Aunt Aggie, they'll put her back in jail."

"*I* shoulda talked her out of it, too. But I didn't think we'd get caught. She didn't hurt nobody."

They saw Vern leading a crying Celia out the front door and put her roughly into the squad car. Several other cops clustered around the car.

Aunt Aggie started to cry. "I got to help her. I got to go over there and tell 'em to leave her alone, that she didn't do nothin' but visit her husband . . . Give me that cane back."

"No, Aunt Aggie. I don't need my sister *and* my aunt in jail. You're not going over there swinging your cane at a bunch of cops. Now, just sit here for a minute. I think we can do more good if we follow her to the police station and try to bail her out."

"Awright," Aunt Aggie agreed. But in her heart she wasn't sure if it was the right thing to do.

● ● ●

Up in the room, Stan felt weak, disoriented, and he was having trouble breathing again, and those stomach cramps were starting. Doctors and nurses poked and prodded him, drawing blood and taking vitals, and he kept muttering, "Orderly. Not Celia. Orderly."

Someone in a lab coat stood over him, talking to the doctors and cops as if he wasn't in the room. "The IV bag was poisoned with arsenic. It also had a pinprick in it, so she must have injected the arsenic solution into the bag. Either she brought the bag in and switched it, or she injected it right here."

"No," he said. "No, you're wrong." But they weren't listening.

He tried to think what the orderly looked like. He needed to give them a description. But he'd had on that surgical mask ... said he had a cold ... and the surgical hat, and scrubs, and those glasses. He hadn't looked at him that closely, had only glanced up at him.

"Stan ..."

He looked up and saw Sid standing over him. How had he gotten here so fast? He realized vaguely that a lot had happened. Things were fading in and out, and time had slipped by. Had they medicated him? Had the arsenic damaged his brain?

"Stan, tell me what she did when she came in here."

Yes, he thought. He wanted to tell him. He shored up every ounce of energy he still had. "She told me she was pregnant," he whispered. He grabbed Sid's shirt and tugged him down. "She didn't do anything to the bag, Sid. It was an orderly. Someone came in before her ... changed the bag."

"Someone? Who?"

"An orderly. Scrubs. Mask."

Sid looked up at R.J. standing across the bed, and Stan grabbed his shirt, too. "R.J., she didn't do it."

"What *did* she do, then? What did she say?"

"I told you ... that she was pregnant. That she loved me ..." He could feel the emotions rushing from his heart straight into his face. "Then Vern came in ..."

"Stan, I know you don't think she did anything, but were you awake when she came in?"

"Yes. I was waiting for her to call."

"Call? Had you been in touch with her?"

"No, but I sent Nick ... to tell her to call me." Tears rolled down his temples.

"Are you sure you weren't asleep when she came in? She might have done something to the bag before she woke you."

"She *didn't*. Why aren't you looking for that orderly?"

Again, Sid and R.J. exchanged looks. "Stan, I don't blame you for trying to cover for your wife, but one minute you didn't have arsenic in your IV bag, and the next minute you did. She was here, man, and she wasn't supposed to be." He leaned over him and patted Stan's shoulder. "Man, I know it hurts. I know how awful this must be. But you can't deny what's happenin'. Maybe if she really is pregnant, the hormones have done some kind o' number on her brain cells. Maybe she can't even help herself. But she did it, man. It's so obvious."

He could feel the heat in his face. "She *didn't*. Where are they taking her?"

"To Newpointe. Stan, we need your help. Did she say anything else? Was she carrying anything? A purse? A bag? Did she bring anything in?"

"No. Find the orderly." The words came through his teeth, with as much strength as he could muster. "Find him, Sid. Let my wife go. She's innocent."

Again, the two cops exchanged looks. Finally, Sid nodded to R.J., who then pulled a snapshot out of his pocket.

"What's that?" Stan whispered.

"It's a picture. Evidence that Celia's involved. Stan, you told us to guard her and follow her, so we did. And earlier today, when it was Vern's shift, he followed her to Lee Barnett's place."

"Who?"

"Lee Barnett. The convict we told you about who was recently released. Her old flame. She went there to see him this afternoon. And Vern got this picture." He looked sympathetically at Stan before he handed him the snapshot. "I'm sorry, man. I don't want to show you this."

Stan felt the wallop in his heart, but he forced his hand up and took the picture. He didn't want to see it. Didn't even want to look. But he made himself.

There stood Celia in Lee Barnett's arms, right outside in broad daylight.

His heart crashed. Suddenly, he couldn't find words, couldn't think . . .

"I'm sorry, man," Sid said gently. "Stan, I'd rather be tortured than to make you look at that picture. I didn't want to show you. But tonight she came in here and poisoned you for the second time, and I'll be hanged if I'm gonna let her get away with it. And that means that I can't let you keep thinkin' that she's the victim. *You* are, man. *She's* the criminal."

"There's a reason." He didn't know how he got the thought to formulate, much less the words, but some nagging voice in the back of his heart told him it was true. "There's a reason . . . it's not the way it looks . . . It may not even be her. I can't see her face."

"It was her, Stan. Vern saw her. He followed her there, watched her go to his door . . ."

"Did he hear what she said to this . . . Barnett guy?"

"No, but Marabeth Simmons did. She heard them talkin' about checkin' into a hotel, and about what to tell the cops, and he told her he'd cover for her. Maybe they were plannin' what just happened."

Stan looked as if he'd just been walloped in the stomach.

"Did she go into his apartment?"

"No."

"They just stood outside like this, talking about murder in voices loud enough to be heard, in broad daylight?"

"No, of course not. They were talking in low voices, but Marabeth was able to make out some of it."

"Marabeth Simmons is one of the two biggest busybodies in Newpointe, and you believe *her* over *Celia?*"

"Stan, look at the picture, man. She went there. Ain't what you see there evidence enough?"

Stan stared at the ceiling, unable to speak.

"Stan, you got to listen, man."

"Get out."

Sid looked stunned by the words. "What?"

"Get out."

The nurse in the room came to his bedside, checked his blood pressure reading, then nodded to the two cops. "You'd better go."

Sid took a step back and nodded to R.J. The other cop walked toward the door, but Sid hung behind.

"Man, I don't want you holdin' this against me."

"She didn't do it."

"I think she did. And when I go, and you're layin' in here by yourself, your body tryin' to filter out that arsenic for the second time, I think you'll believe it, too. It ain't a coincidence that her first husband died of the same thing, that she was the suspect, that she was with you the first time you were poisoned *and* the second time. No coincidence, man. But I'm goin', if you want me to. Take care o' yourself, man. R.J.'s gonna be here for a while, right outside the door. He ain't gon' let nobody in without writin' their name down—doctors and nurses included."

"How about orderlies?" Stan asked through his anger. "There's one in this hospital that poisoned my bag."

"Orderlies, too. Don't worry about it, man."

Stan closed his eyes after Sid left the room, yet he fought the sleep from the drugs they had given him to combat the poison. He thought of that picture again, of his wife in Lee Barnett's arms. Was it true?

No, of course it wasn't. It couldn't be.

But pictures didn't lie. Or did they? Didn't they lie all the time? She hadn't gone into the apartment, after all.

He tried to picture Barnett's face again, and what he could see of the orderly's face. Was it the same face? Had Barnett been working with her? Could it be possible?

Tears filled his eyes as he remembered her announcement to him. A baby. Was there really a baby? What would happen to it now? Was she in jail? Was she guilty, as everyone seemed to think? Or was this all just a terrible mistake?

He didn't know, but he laid his arm over his eyes and began to sob as the confusing torrent of thoughts washed over him. What if it was true? What if his wife really did want him dead?

Chapter Thirty-Five

Nick hadn't been back home long when the telephone rang. Wearily, he picked it up. "Hello?"

"Nick?" The voice was weak, and he recognized it to be Stan's.

"Stan, is that you?"

"Yeah, it's me. Listen, uh ... something happened tonight."

"Yeah. Celia wasn't at Aunt Aggie's when I went to tell her to call you, and then I went over to Jill's and I was there when she got the call that Celia had been caught in your room."

"Yeah." His voice cracked, and Nick could tell that he was struggling with emotion. "Uh ... look man. I could use some help tonight."

Nick swallowed. "Sure. I'll do anything, Stan, just tell me what you need."

"Do you think you could come over to the hospital? Pay me a little ministerial visit?"

"Of course. I can leave right now."

"That'd be great." His voice cracked, and the silence was eloquent. "I'd appreciate that, man."

"Stan, are you all right?"

"No, I don't think so."

"Is there anything I can bring you?"

Stan was quiet again. When he finally found a word, it was wrought with emotion. "Hope?"

Nick's heart sank. Once again, he was being asked to give something he didn't possess. "I'll do what I can, buddy," he said. "I'll be right over."

Stan's parents had come back to the hospital by the time Nick got there at 10:30, and his mother had red patches under her eyes, as if she'd been weeping as hard as she'd ever wept in her life. She clucked over him like a mother hen, arranging his pillows and straightening his covers, while his father paced the room back and forth with simmering anger so intense that Nick could almost see it smoking out his ears.

Stan looked weaker than Nick had expected. Dark shadows lurked under his red-rimmed, puffy eyes, and Nick imagined that he had been weeping, as Nick himself would have done had he been betrayed in such a colossal way.

"How ya doin', man?" he said, shaking his friend's hand.

Stan's eyes immediately filled with tears again. "Mom, Dad, would you mind giving me a few minutes alone with Nick?"

His mother wiped at her own eyes. "Of course. We'll be in the waiting room if you need us."

He waited as they both left the room. Nick got a chair and pulled it up to the side of the bed, sat down, and leaned forward. "Her visit . . . was it traumatic for you?"

Again, Stan's eyes filled. "Actually, it was nice. It was right after I'd talked to you on the phone. I hung up and closed my eyes and was waiting to hear back, and there she was, with this silly wig on, and glasses, and a nurse's uniform—" His voice cracked, and he covered his face with both hands.

"What happened?" Nick whispered.

"She got caught," Stan forced out. "And then they found arsenic in my IV bag."

"Arsenic?" Nick asked. "There was arsenic in your IV?"

"Somebody put it there," he said. "And I'd swear to you it was the orderly that came in while I was on the phone with you. Only, I can't identify him. He had a surgical mask over his face, and he had on glasses and a surgical cap. Why would he come in like that, if he wasn't trying to make sure I couldn't ID him? Said he had a cold. But no one believes me. They think I'm covering for her."

"What do *you* think, Stan?" Nick asked.

Stan looked up at the ceiling. "Nick, I would lay my hand on a Bible and swear to you that my wife did not do this. But—"

That "but" was heavy and set itself down between them like a big lead box. "But?" Nick asked.

"But the picture." His mouth twisted, and he covered it with the back of his wrist.

"What picture?" Nick asked.

"The picture of her with that man. That Lee Barnett. The convict."

Nick frowned. "Wait a minute. She was with him?"

"Seems that way," Stan said. "Vern followed her. Took pictures."

Nick was stunned, and for a moment he couldn't speak. Finally, he managed to whisper, "I can't believe it."

"I saw the picture myself." He covered his eyes with the heels of his hands and balled his fingers into fists. "I don't know what's going on with her, but it's suspicious."

"But . . . the orderly. What about the orderly?"

"The hospital staff swears that everyone on shift has been accounted for, and that none of them changed the bag. But I know he was here. I saw him change it. Who *was* that and why does he want me dead?"

Nick searched his heart and all of his wisdom for an answer that would satisfy Stan, but he had too many questions himself. He looked helplessly at his friend, and shook his head. "I don't know what to say, buddy. I don't know what to do for you."

Stan kept the heels of his hands pressed against his eyes. "Tell me that my wife doesn't want me dead," he said. "Tell me that the baby she's carrying isn't going to suffer."

"Baby?" Nick sat erect. "Stan, you didn't tell me—"

"*She* just told *me*," he cried.

Nick groped for the right words, but could find none. For the thousandth time since this case had begun, he sought the wisdom of the Holy Spirit, but he still felt inadequate, useless.

"I can pray for you, Stan," Nick said, wiping his own tears. "That's all I know to do. Just pray."

"That's enough."

Nick touched his shoulder and began to pray, for answers to their questions, for peace, for truth, for healing, for restoration, for reconciliation. When the amen came, he saw that Stan was calmer. Stan removed his hands from his face and looked at him.

Nick's heart broke. His own face twisted, and he rubbed at his jaw. "I've got to be honest with you, Stan. I don't know what to do for her . . . but I know that she is still a member of my flock. Whether she's innocent or guilty, she needs God. And she needs friends."

"I don't know if there's some dark room in her brain that holds some deadly secret," Stan said, "but even if she did poison me, Nick, even if she poisoned Nathan . . ." His voice broke and his face twisted. "Even if she did those things, I still can't stand the thought of her sitting in jail alone . . ."

Nick nodded, knowing that feeling himself. "I'll go to her tonight, Stan. She may just be a lost sheep in my flock. Jesus would have searched high and low for her . . . for the one lost sheep. If she did this, there's something wrong here, Stan. Some mental illness, or something that can be explained. Or she could be totally innocent, in which case she really needs a friend."

"Help her, Nick."

Nick nodded. "I will. I'll go see her when I leave here, if they'll let me."

"And keep praying," Stan said.

"I'll keep praying," Nick promised. "It's all I can do. It's all I have." Nick wiped his eyes. "If there were a fire, I'd put it out. If there were a heart attack, I know CPR. If there were a wreck, I'd use the jaws of life. For a thing like this, I just pray."

"That's better than CPR or the jaws of life. You're doing fine, Nick."

Nick swallowed back his own emotion as he got to his feet. "Get some rest, okay? Try not to think. I'll talk to you tomorrow and let you know how my visit with Celia went."

"All right, Nick. Thanks."

Nick hated to leave him, but Stan's parents returned to the room as soon as he stepped into the hall. He got onto the elevator, let the doors close, and stood there for a long moment before pushing a button. Silently, he prayed for the power and wisdom to do the right thing.

Of its own accord, the elevator began to move, down, down, down, until the doors opened on the lobby, where someone waited to get on. He stepped off, realizing that God was telling him to move, take action, get going . . .

He headed out to his car to do *something*, hoping that it was the right thing.

Chapter Thirty-Six

W hy did you do it?"
Jill's monotone question dripped with suspicion, and Celia knew she was close to losing Jill's trust.

"Because I wanted to see him." The tears were gone. She had cried enough to fill a bayou, and now she was empty, dead, numb. She leaned on the table in the interrogation room where she'd been drilled just a few days before, and set her dull eyes on her lawyer and friend. "I wanted to tell him about the baby."

Jill's face changed. "Baby? What baby?"

"I'm pregnant, Jill."

Jill stared at her for a moment, as if not sure what to believe. "Are you sure?"

"Yes. This morning the hospital called. The blood they took the other night? It was negative for arsenic poisoning, but it was positive for pregnancy. That's why I've been sick."

The merest hint of a smile tugged at Jill's lips, and she drew in a breath. "Oh, Celia."

"That's why I went, Jill. I had to tell him. He had a right to know, and I didn't want him to hear it from the police or news-papers. It's our baby, and we've wanted it so much." Though she hadn't thought it was possible, tears stung her eyes again.

Jill contemplated that for a moment, staring at her, either assessing her sanity or her honesty. She was definitely losing her, Celia thought.

"Celia, someone poisoned Stan tonight. His IV bag had arsenic again."

Celia's heart jolted, and she straightened. "I was afraid of that. The nurse said the bag had been changed . . ."

"They think you did it."

Her face twisted as she tried to grasp some logical train of thought. "How is he? Did it get into his bloodstream? Is he all right?"

"He's okay. They don't think much got in, and they're doing what they can. He's still conscious, so that's a good sign."

"Thank God," she whispered. Then, shaking herself out of her shock, she focused on Jill again. "Did they ask him if I did it? He would tell them. I didn't touch his bag. I wasn't there long enough. Somebody else—"

"He claims there was an orderly there before you who switched the bags, but Sid isn't buying. He thinks he's trying to cover for you."

She got to her feet in the small room and looked down at her lawyer. "Why would a man cover for someone who was trying to kill him? Stan *knows* I didn't do it!"

Jill looked away. There was something else, and Celia could see her wrestling with it.

"What is it, Jill?"

Jill stood up, picked up the pencil on the table, and began tapping it on the palm of her hand. Finally, she stopped and looked her dead in the eye. "Celia, why didn't you tell me that you went to see Lee Barnett today?"

Celia wilted. "You would have gotten angry, told me it was stupid. Same reason I didn't tell you I was going to the hospital."

"I would have been right."

"I know." She dropped her face into her hands.

"They have a picture."

Celia looked up at her without much interest. "What kind of picture?"

"They had someone following you, Celia. They followed you to Barnett's apartment. They took pictures."

The fact that she'd been followed irritated her, but it didn't surprise her greatly. They had seen someone sitting outside Aunt Aggie's house when they'd left for the hospital. "So they got pictures," she said. "All I did was stand outside his door and ask him questions. There wasn't anything incriminating, except the fact that I slapped him. I guess I could be guilty of assault. But I don't think I was there for more than ten minutes."

"They have a picture of you in his arms."

"*In his arms?*" she shouted, springing to her feet. "*What?*"

Jill was silent, watching her, waiting for an explanation.

Celia didn't have one. "Jill, you've got to believe me. I was *never* in his arms. They faked the picture ... doctored it somehow. I want to see it."

Jill nodded. "I can get it for you."

"Do it!" Celia cried.

Jill opened the door and stuck her head out, and Celia heard her talking to someone. She sank down at the table and dropped her face into her hands. There was no way ... *no way* ... anyone had gotten a picture of her in Lee Barnett's arms. She had been yelling at him, had slapped him ...

Jill came back into the room, holding the snapshot. "Here it is, Celia," she said, and tossed it down in front of her on the table.

Celia picked it up and felt the heat fevering across her face. She opened her mouth, but no sound came out. After a moment, she brought her hand to her forehead. "Jill ... you've got to believe me ... I was so full of rage ... I hit him, and he grabbed me and shook me, and I told him to let me go ... He had his hands on me maybe five seconds ... *Not an embrace!* What about the other pictures? Didn't they get me slapping him? Is this all they got?"

"It's the only one they're using for evidence."

"I don't *believe* this." She sucked in a sob. "Did they show Stan?"

"I'm not sure."

She dropped her head into the circle of her arms. "What is he thinking about me? Oh, why is this happening?"

Jill sat down next to her and touched her hand, but when Celia looked up she could see the confusion in her lawyer's eyes. "Celia, I don't think they're going to let you back out. I'm going to do what I can, but I don't think they're going to set bond this time."

"You wouldn't, if you were the judge, would you?" Celia asked bitterly.

Jill didn't answer.

She raised up and wiped her eyes. "Look, Jill, if you don't want to represent me, I understand. I mean, the evidence is insurmountable. You're not even sure you know who I am."

Jill stared at her, and for a moment, Celia was sure she would take her chance to give up the case. But Jill surprised her.

"I know who you are." Tears came to her eyes, and she shook her head. "I'm confused, Celia. I don't know who's doing this, or how they're doing it. I don't know why there's been so much evidence against you. I don't know why someone would want to kill your husbands and not you—and to put you through such a nightmare yourself. I can't imagine. I don't know what Lee Barnett's part was in this. I don't know who else to trust, because I think whoever it is might be right under our nose. It scares me. But there is one thing I do know for sure. I believe you."

Celia accepted that with tearful relief. "Thank you." She tried to pull herself together. "No one else will, you know. They'll alienate you, too, just for representing me. You'll be as popular in this town as Oswald's lawyer. Are you sure you're up to it?"

"I'm up to it," Jill said. "But you might need a more experienced criminal lawyer than I. If you'd rather hire someone else, I'll understand."

"With what?" Celia asked. "I don't have any money."

"Aunt Aggie would pay."

"No, I want you. You know me. No one else does."

"Okay, then." She squeezed her hand. "Celia, are you going to be all right in jail?"

"Oh, yeah," Celia said. "No problem. Been there, done that. I can handle jail, as long as I know it's temporary. 'Course, it might not be."

The look on Jill's face told Celia that this was the first time that she'd faced such a serious case ... a case that really would decide someone's lifelong fate. She hated to give her that burden. Then she thought of Aunt Aggie, and David ...

"Where are my aunt and brother?" she asked quietly.

Jill nodded toward the door. "They're being questioned."

"Are they going to be charged with anything?"

"Not if I can help it. Something was said about accessory to attempted murder, but I think it was just a threat. Don't worry about them. I'll take care of it."

"I don't know how much more Aunt Aggie can take. She's hardly gotten any sleep lately. She's too old for this."

"She's stronger than both of us put together," Jill said with a slight smile. "And as for their putting her in jail, they'd have such a protest by the fire department that they'd have to let her back out in time for lunch tomorrow."

"I guess you're right."

"Just hold on, Celia. I'm doing everything I can, okay? You may have to stay here a night or two, but maybe we can get you out before much more time passes."

Celia had heard that before.

Chapter Thirty-Seven

The moment Aunt Aggie and David had walked into the New-pointe Police Department, they were descended on as if they were criminals about to turn themselves in. They took Aunt Aggie into one interrogation room and David into another and began to question them separately about the incident. Aunt Aggie was livid.

"Yeah, I helped her sneak in the hospital, and I helped her get in that room, and if you wanna lock me up for that, then I ain't fightin' you."

Vern Hargis shot a look at Chief Shoemaker. "We just want to know what happened, Aunt Aggie."

"I tole you already. She wanted to see her husband!"

"But the judge told her not to. There was a court order."

"Aw, she don't care about no court order. She missed her husband. He's layin' in the hospital dyin', he finally come awake, and she want to see him. You bet I'm gon' help her."

Vern rolled his eyes. "Aunt Aggie, there was arsenic found in his IV bag. Celia tried to kill him again."

Aunt Aggie's heart tightened into a fist, and she shot to her feet. "Celia didn't poison him! I don't know who did, but Celia didn't."

"Aunt Aggie, you have to admit—it's hard to believe it was just a coincidence that he was poisoned a second time when she just happened to be there."

Aunt Aggie's mind raced. The answer was there—she had seen so much as she'd sat there waiting for Vern to go take a smoke. Suddenly, it came to her. "That orderly had a bag with 'im! He was carryin' it just as plain as day. Just a few minutes 'fore I went to get Celia! Vern, don't you remember? Didn't you see 'im? And Celia, she was empty-handed."

Vern looked troubled. "I'm not sure, Aunt Aggie. There was an orderly, but I didn't see him carrying anything."

"Why'd he have his mask on, then? That hat? I didn't think of it then, but he was the killer! Vern, if you'da stopped him, we'd have 'im now!"

Jim got to his feet. "That true, Vern? Did you check that orderly's identification?"

Vern shifted uncomfortably. "I saw it, Jim. He had a badge on. I didn't stop him and examine it, but ..." He looked up at Aunt Aggie. "Celia was wearing a badge, too. Where did she get it?"

"I took it," Aunt Aggie said, lifting her chin proudly. "Stole it myself right offa somebody's uniform at the uniform shop today."

The two men looked at each other again as if they didn't believe a word she was saying. "Whassa matter, you don't think a ole lady can steal?"

"We didn't think you were a thief, Aunt Aggie. Sue us."

Aunt Aggie wished she had her cane with her so she could knock them upside the head. "I wanted to help her. She deserved to see Stan. She had stuff she needed to tell him."

"Stuff about the murder attempt?"

"No, nothin' about no murder attempt! She don't know nothin' about no murder attempt!"

Vern was getting impatient. "Aunt Aggie, we need your cooperation. We need you to sit down and relax, and quit ranting and raving."

"Rantin' and ravin'? You ain't seen nothin.' You got my Celia locked up in jail like she some half-baked killer, and you think I'm rantin' and ravin'?"

"Aunt Aggie, I don't want to have to lock you up with her."

"Do it!" Aunt Aggie challenged. "Go ahead, lock me up." She held out her wrists for them to cuff, but they only looked amused. It made her madder than ever.

"Aunt Aggie, we're not locking you up. However, we have to inform you that you are an accessory to a murder attempt."

"Accessory? You don't know what you talkin' about. Alls I did was sit in a waitin' room and tell my Celia when she could come in. You're just mad cause you didn't recognize her when she come through."

"Yeah, I'm mad," Vern said. "I'm mad that she poisoned him right under my nose. Call it a vendetta if you want to, but I'm gonna make sure that she goes down for it."

Aunt Aggie kicked a chair, hurting her foot, but she would have died before she would let them know it.

"Tell us about David," he said. "What was his part in all this?"

"He drove the stinkin' car," she said. "Dropped us off, come in to see where we'd come out, then sit there and waited at that exit."

"Then he's an accessory, too," Vern said.

"It wasn't against no court order for me and David to be at that hospital," she said. "We didn't break no laws."

"It's against the law to poison a man twice."

"Didn't nobody I know poison Stan!" She could feel her blood pressure rising, ready to explode out the top of her head. "If we're accessories, then you're one, too, Vern. You let the killer walk right in and change that bag, without so much as readin' his badge. Y'ask me, you might be in on this whole thing your own self."

"Oh, for Pete's sake ..." Vern muttered. He threw his pen against the wall and stood up, aggravated beyond measure. "I'm gonna let her go, Jim. She's just wasting our time."

"And Celia? What you gon' do with her?" Aunt Aggie asked.

"She's staying," Jim said. "The judge would be crazy to let her out again."

"Then I'm stayin', too."

Vern gaped at her. "No, you're not, Aunt Aggie. You're going home, if I have to take you myself."

"You can't let a criminal like me back out on the streets," Aunt Aggie said. "Not when I could go around accessorizin' more murders, stealin' and whatnot."

"Aunt Aggie, I'm not locking you up! Go home!"

She sat back down and put her purse stubbornly in her lap, determined not to move. "Then I want to press charges."

"Against who?" Vern shot back.

"Against me. For stealin' that badge. I confess. Go get one o' them court reporters in here and I'll give 'em my statement."

Jim began to chuckle with frustration. "Aunt Aggie, we're not going to lock you up for stealing a badge."

"Why not? What kinda po-lice department you call this? If you can't get locked up confessin' to a crime . . ."

"The judge wouldn't give you more than a slap on the hand for stealing a badge off of a uniform."

She could feel her face reddening, and her heart hammered with anger. She got up and looked Vern squarely in the eye. "What about assaultin' a po-lice officer?"

Jim chuckled again, but Vern didn't find it funny. "Aunt Aggie, you don't want to do that."

"Why not? I done it before. Ask Sid Ford if I ain't."

Jim nodded confirmation, and Vern rolled his eyes. "Aunt Aggie, I told you. Go home."

"Make me."

Vern's face twisted with disgust. "What are you? Six years old? Give it up, Aunt Aggie! You can sit in here all night if you want. I'm through with you." With that, he turned to leave.

Aunt Aggie couldn't think of anything she hated worse than not being taken seriously. Suddenly, she decided to make sure she got her way.

She swung her purse in a circle from its handle, just like a lasso, then sent it flying across the room. It hit the back of Vern's head, and he swung around, his eyes livid. "Are you crazy?"

"That's twice now I assaulted a po-lice officer. Add that to stealin', and accessorizin' murder, and you got plenty o' reason to lock me up. I *demand* to be locked up!"

Vern's nostrils were flaring, not a pretty sight. "Demand? You demand it? All right, Aunt Aggie. I'll lock you up. But you won't be in the cell with Celia, if that's what you hoped. You can both sit there alone and think about what you've done."

Aunt Aggie wasn't afraid. She'd been in the women's part of the jail to visit people before, and she knew that there were only four small cells. If she and Celia weren't roommates, at least they could talk to each other, and she could make sure she was all right. She held out her hands to accept the cuffs. "I'm ready."

Vern looked as if he could scream. "I'm not cuffing you, Aunt Aggie."

She was a little disappointed. Something about walking through the police station in handcuffs appealed to her. The uproar it would cause, the rumors, the outrage . . .

He opened the door and took her arm, led her out. David was waiting for her.

"They lockin' me up," she yelled to him, louder than she needed to. "Throwin' me in the pokey."

David's jaw fell open. "You've got to be kidding. For *what?*"

Vern seemed too embarrassed to answer, so Aunt Aggie obliged. "Assaultin' a po-lice officer. Couldn't get 'em to do it for nothin' else."

David turned his outraged eyes on Vern, then on Jim Shoemaker. "This is ludicrous! What is the matter with you people? Locking up my sister, and now my eighty-one-year-old aunt? Are you absolutely out of your minds?"

Jim's amusement had passed, and he was beginning to lose his patience. "If you want to make it a threesome, we can oblige you, too."

"*None* of us did anything!" he shouted. "My sister is being framed. And Aunt Aggie ... well, give me a break. You know what she wants. She's looking out for my sister, but for crying out loud, she doesn't need to go to jail, too. Look, I'll just take her home, and—" He reached for her, but Aunt Aggie jerked back from him.

"David, so help me, I'll wallop you, too, if you interfere. Justice is bein' served. I got to serve my time."

David's face was crimson. "You've done some crazy things, Aunt Aggie, but this beats everything."

Aunt Aggie couldn't help smiling. "It does, don't it? How 'bout that? Now you run on home. If my fire boys call to see where I am, you tell 'em I can't cook for 'em till they let me outa jail, now, you hear? They'll understand."

David looked at Vern with disgust. "They'll tar and feather you. They'll raid the place to get her out."

"I'll take my chances," Vern said, then pulled Aunt Aggie into the hall leading down to the basement where the jail cells were.

Chapter Thirty-Eight

Though it was getting late when Jill left the police station, she walked next door to the fire station to see if Dan was working. She found him in the weight room bench-pressing, and stood at the door watching him for a moment before he saw her.

She didn't know why she was here, really. She should be able to handle this. She'd had difficult cases before. Granted, none of them had left her client's life hanging in the balance. And she'd never had so many surprises in a case, surprises that shouldn't have been . . .

But she did believe Celia. She did.

Tears pushed into her eyes, and she sniffed. Dan heard her and looked up. "Jill." He got up, as if self-conscious about what he was doing, and wiped his face on a towel. "I didn't know you were here. It's late."

She shrugged. "Yeah, I was just at the police station. Thought I'd come see if you were here."

"You're upset," he said, looking into her eyes. "Come sit down. Tell me what's wrong."

She let him lead her to a folding chair, and he took the weight bench across from her. "Nothing, really," she said. "I just . . . uh . . . I'm having some problems with Celia's case. I don't know quite what to do."

"Has something happened?"

She contemplated telling him. How much was attorney-client privilege? How much was guaranteed to be in the paper tomorrow, anyway? How much would the fire department know in just the next few minutes when the cops started talking?

"Celia's back in jail."

"What? Why?"

She got up and walked across the room, picked up a small barbell, set it back down. "She broke a court order and went to see Stan tonight. It just so happens that, after she got caught, they discovered that someone had injected arsenic into his IV bag."

Dan got slowly to his feet, his mouth open.

"He's okay. I mean, this new poison didn't have much time to get into his system. They caught it in time."

"Jill—"

"I know," she said, stemming his response. "I know how it looks. Believe me . . . I know. She's in jail. They probably won't let her out. And I don't know how I'll fight this."

Forgetting the sweat he'd worked up, he put his arms around her and pressed her head against his shoulder. She rested in that embrace, thankful that something had the power to bring her that much relief, that much comfort.

"What is she saying?" Dan asked.

Jill pulled back and looked up at him. "That she didn't do it. Even Stan . . . he's saying that an orderly came in before her and switched the bags . . . Sid is convinced he's covering for her. But that doesn't make sense. She would know she'd get caught. Why would she do that?"

"It's an awful coincidence, Jill," he said. "For this person to come in and poison him again, and it just happens to be right before she comes? That's hard to buy."

"She didn't do it." The words were said so weakly that she hardly believed them herself. "She didn't, Dan. It may look like it to everyone else, but not to us."

He let her go and sat slowly down. "I want to believe her. I know what it's like to have people accuse you because of how things look. This town is bad about that. I haven't forgotten how they almost strung me up. You were the only one who believed in me."

"I may be the only one who believes in her. But I have to."

He met her eyes. "What if you're wrong?"

"Then I'll be wrong. But she's my friend, and now she's my client. I have to get rid of whatever doubts I have."

"Then you admit you have some?"

She looked at him for a long moment. "I don't want to, Dan. I don't want to have doubts about my friend. I look in her eyes, and I believe her. But then when I walk away, and I start adding things up . . ."

"You start to realize you're human?"

"I haven't got time to be human," she said.

Chapter Thirty-Nine

Issie Mattreaux hated to be stood up. She sat alone at the bar at Joe's Place, nursing a glass of wine and feeling sorry for herself. She might have known the guy who was meeting her here wouldn't show. She'd met him on one of her calls today, when he'd found his cousin in a hypoglycemic coma. He had called 911 and had been impressed when she so easily revived the patient with glucose. She'd spent the next half hour bantering with him, and when he'd finally asked her out, she'd had high hopes. He'd had to work late, so he'd asked her to meet him at ten o'clock. But it was already eleven, so he was an hour late, and she knew better than to kid herself any longer.

From the corner of her eye she noticed a man across the room looking at her, and she turned and met his eyes. He wasn't bad looking. In fact, he looked better than most of the men who frequented this place—even better than the guy who'd stood her up. She smiled at him; he smiled back. After a moment, he got up and came to claim the stool next to her. "Buy you a drink?" he asked.

She lifted hers slightly. "Got one."

He smiled. "Can I buy you the next one?"

She considered that a moment, then lifted her glass and finished it off. "Sure."

He grinned and waited for the waiter. "How about another one for the lady?"

Joe seemed to sneer at him, and Issie frowned. It wasn't Joe's way to be rude to his customers. There must be something wrong. She glanced up at the man. "I'm Issie Mattreaux," she said.

He nodded. "Lee Barnett."

The name sounded familiar. She ran it through her mind, trying to process it. "You new in town?" she asked.

"Yeah," he said. "Just been here a few days."

Suddenly it came back to her. The gossip at the fire station, about the man in Celia's past. No wonder Joe was giving him the cold shoulder. Joe brought her the drink and she thought of refusing it, but then decided she needed it. "I've heard things about you," she said, bringing it to her lips.

"Yeah," he said. "I guess everybody has, but they're not true."

She looked up at him. "How do you know what I've heard?"

"Because they're sayin' that I had somethin' to do with Stan Shepherd's poisonin', and that I'm involved with his wife."

"Aren't you?"

He sat there a moment, as if contemplating the question. "Tell you the truth, I'm not sure."

"Not sure? That's interesting."

"Well, see, I thought I was. I thought there was this letter from her, and a check . . ."

He'd had too much to drink, she could tell, because his speech was slurred. She wondered how many he'd put away.

"But I don't think she wrote that letter, and I don't think she wrote those checks."

"Then who did?"

"Got me. That's the ten million dollar question. Matter of fact, it could be a life or death question."

"If you're not involved with her, then how come you're staying around town?" she asked.

He shrugged. "They won't let me leave till the investigation's over. But I'm tellin' you, I didn't do anything."

Something told her to get up and leave, to walk right out, but she was lonely, and she had nothing to do at home. She decided to stay. What could it hurt? She took another drink of her wine, set it down, ran her finger along the rim.

"You a friend of Celia's?" he asked.

"I know her."

"What about Stan?"

She nodded. "Yeah, I know him better. I'm a paramedic. I work with him from time to time."

"Paramedic, huh? So you go around saving lives?"

The question irritated her. "Sometimes. I almost lost Stan Shepherd." She regarded him, watching for his reaction. He was handsome, just the type she could picture Celia dating years ago. She wondered if there really was anything between them. Something about that possibility piqued her interest in him. She wasn't sure why that was, didn't want to explore it. But when a man had an attractive woman interested in him, he seemed more valuable in her eyes. As if to counter her attraction, she said, "So I hear you were in prison."

He swiveled on his stool and looked out over the crowd. "Not the kind of thing I like for a girl to know about me the first time I meet her, but yeah, it's true."

She sipped her drink. "Got involved in a barroom brawl and killed somebody?"

"Word travels fast."

She picked a fish-shaped cracker out of the bowl on the bar and nibbled on it. "So if you could kill somebody in a bar, what would keep you from killing somebody with poison?"

"Prison," he said simply. "The best deterrent I know. I'm not going back."

She finished off the cracker, took another sip, then glanced at him again. "It's just suspicious, you know. You being here, where Celia is. Showing up right around the time Stan was poisoned."

He leaned his elbow on the bar and lowered his voice. "I think it was supposed to be suspicious," he said. "That's what this is all about. We're both being framed."

"She's the one in jail," Issie pointed out. "You're sitting in a bar hitting on me."

He pulled back a little and grinned at her. "Hitting on you? I thought I was making conversation."

A grin tugged at one side of her lips. "You bought me a drink, didn't you?"

He laughed softly. "Yeah, I bought you a drink."

"That usually means that you're being hit on."

"Yeah, well, I've been out of circulation for a while," he said. "I don't know the rules anymore."

She breathed a humorless laugh. "Oh, you know the rules. Who are you kidding?" She was playing with him, she realized, and she wondered if she had had too much to drink, herself. But there was something about his eyes. Something exciting, something fun, a thrill she hadn't had the opportunity to experience in a long time. The forbidden.

He seemed to read her thoughts. "This place is awfully smoky," he said in a deep voice too close to her ear. "What do you say we go someplace else?"

"Someplace like what?" she asked innocently.

"I don't know. You tell me. You're the one who knows Newpointe."

Her senses came alive as she thought of the possibilities. They could go to Maison de Manger and get a bite, or they could go for a walk along the bayou behind the fire station. Or they could drive down to Lake Pontchartrain, or go to her apartment, or his ...

She'd heard about his apartment, that Celia had set him up there, and she wondered what it looked like. Then her common sense ruled that out, and she realized that it was stupid. She couldn't be caught alone in an ex-con's apartment, not when he was suspected of murder, no matter how much she'd had to drink.

"I think I'll just stay right here," she said.

He grinned again. "Okay. I'll stay here with you. It's safer. I can't attack you if we're in a crowd."

She grinned. "You couldn't attack me, anyway."

"Tough guy, huh?"

She nodded. "I can hold my own." It was true. She'd had self-defense training, and was stronger than she looked. More than a dozen times lately she'd had to lift an unconscious grown man onto a gurney. She felt quite sure she could fight one off if she had to.

"If you're so tough, then why are you so afraid to go anywhere with me? It can be someplace public, you know."

"I know." She winked. "But I think I'll stay right here."

"Okay," he said. "Maybe we can get to know each other even in all the smoke and noise."

"Do you like to dance?" she asked.

He grinned. "Haven't done it in five years. There weren't many cotillions in prison, but we can give it a whirl."

She set her glass down. "All right," she said. "Let's have at it."

Chapter Forty

There were only four small cells in the women's portion of the Newpointe city jail. They were each five by ten, with a small cot with a flat mattress, and a sink and commode behind a partition. Celia lay on her cot, fighting her nausea. She didn't need that sick feeling on top of the despair closing in on her, but it was there, nonetheless, reminding her that there was a baby involved, that this was no longer just about her life and her integrity. Now she was also defending her child.

She got up and went to the sink, bent over, and splashed water on her face. At least the sink was clean. It could be worse. The commode, too, had been recently cleaned, and a sterile smell wafted in the air.

She sighed and sat back down on the bed, wishing for something to occupy her mind, to keep her from thinking of the horror on Stan's face as they had dragged her out of his room. He still loved her; she knew that without a doubt. But she wasn't sure he believed in her anymore, not after someone had poisoned him.

But didn't he know that it wasn't her? He had to.

She tried to rest in that knowledge, but it was difficult.

The door to the hall opened, and she heard footsteps. Were they coming for her? Had Jill maneuvered a way to get her out this time?

"T-Celia?" It was Aunt Aggie's voice, and Celia sat up and looked through the bars.

"Aunt Aggie?" She saw Vern ushering the old woman past. "Aunt Aggie, what are you doing?"

"I'm locking her up," Vern said.

Aunt Aggie was smiling, as if she were the victor. Celia realized her aunt had given them reason to incarcerate her so that Celia wouldn't be alone. Horrified, she tried to appeal to Vern. "Vern, this is ridiculous. Aunt Aggie, I can handle this. I've done it before. Now go home."

"Too late," Vern said.

"What did she do?" Celia demanded.

"Knocked me upside the head, for one thing," Vern said.

"I deserved to be locked up," Aunt Aggie said proudly. "I'm a thief, and I'm dangerous."

"Dangerous? Come on, Vern, she's eighty-one years old."

"She asked for it, Celia." He opened the door in the cell next to her and pushed Aunt Aggie in. "If there was some way I could put her in a different section of the jail, I would, so you two couldn't talk. But we got regulations, and this is the only place we keep the women."

Aunt Aggie walked into her cell and sat primly down on her cot. He slammed the bars. "Good night, ladies," he said.

Aunt Aggie's eyes were intent on Celia through the bars. Celia gaped at her as Vern left the area.

"Aunt Aggie, what in the world are you up to?"

"I didn't want you bein' alone down here," the old woman said. "I couldna slept tonight. Couldn't bear it."

"Aunt Aggie, I'm fine."

"Well, I'm fine, too. Now we'll be fine together."

Celia's throat filled with emotion over the lengths her aunt would go to protect her. "Aunt Aggie, you don't deserve to be here."

"And you don't either."

"But I can handle it."

"So can I."

Celia shot her a frustrated look. Aunt Aggie stood up and leaned her head on the bars. "Look, *sha*. I can't do nothin' about it now. I'm here and you're here, and we're both here for the night. Can we at least make the best of it?"

Celia reached through the bars and held her aunt's hand. "I love you, you crazy thing."

"I love you, too," Aunt Aggie said matter-of-factly. "Now what can I do for you?"

Celia almost laughed. "Aunt Aggie, short of naming the killer, there is *nothing* you can do."

"Well, I can't do that," she said. "But I knew you'd wanna talk to Stan. I can help you with that."

"Talk to Stan?" she asked. "How can I do that?"

Aunt Aggie looked as if she had a delightful secret. "What if I told you I had a phone with me?"

"Aunt Aggie, that's impossible. You came in here empty-handed. They had to have checked your purse in."

"Don't mean I can't hide no phone."

Celia's eyes twinkled. "You can't be serious. You smuggled a telephone in here?"

"There're advantages to age, you know. They don't dare frisk an old lady."

Celia couldn't help laughing. "Oh, Aunt Aggie."

"I ain't promisin' you can get through. I don't know when the switchboard closes, but you can try." She pulled up her skirt, pulled out the elastic band on her panty hose, and fished out the cellular phone tucked down in them.

"Aunt Aggie, you amaze me."

"I amaze myself, *sha*." She thrust the phone through the bars.

"What if we get caught with this? It's not gonna look good."

"Then don't get caught. Just make the call and hurry it up."

Celia looked at the phone, almost reluctant to take it. But it would be wonderful if she could call Stan, just to see if he was all right, and to tell him once again that she had had nothing to do with the poisonings, and tell him again about the baby. Her hands trembled as she took the phone, flipped up the top, and dialed information.

"No need to do that," Aunt Aggie said. "I know the number. I been callin' it enough since this whole thing started."

Celia dialed the number Aunt Aggie called out, then brought the phone to her ear and waited.

"Slidell Memorial Hospital, may I help you?"

Her heart leapt. "Uh, yes, could you connect me to Stan Shepherd's room, please?"

She waited for the woman to tell her that the switchboard was closed, that it was too late, but she didn't. Instead, the phone began to ring.

"They connectin' you?" Aunt Aggie asked hopefully.

Celia's eyes were wide as she waited. "Yes."

After a couple of rings, someone picked up the phone. "Hello?"

It was his mother, and for a moment, she thought of hanging up. But she needed to talk to him, and it was worth whatever chance she had to take. "Hannah?"

Hannah hesitated. "Yes?"

"Hannah, it's me. Celia. Please don't hang up! I need to talk to Stan . . . Please."

Hannah's voice was tight as she answered. "He has nothing to say to you, and if you call here again—"

"Stan knows I didn't do it. He saw me there. I didn't change his bag. He knows. Please, Hannah. Just let me talk to him for a minute. Tell him it's me."

There was silence. She closed her eyes and prayed that Hannah was giving Stan the phone. Finally, Hannah said, "He saw the picture of you with that man, Celia. His eyes are opening. He doesn't have anything to say to you."

"That picture . . ." Her voice broke off, and she groped for words. "It wasn't what it seemed, Hannah. Please . . ." She sobbed, then tried to rally. "Is he all right? Did much of the poison get into his system this time? What are the doctors saying?"

The phone clicked in her ear, and she realized that Hannah had cut her off. "Hannah, don't hang up!" But it was too late.

She handed the phone back to Aunt Aggie, dropped onto the cot, and covered her face with both hands. "Oh, Aunt Aggie. I've lost him. He believes them! He believes them!"

Aunt Aggie took the phone back and tucked it into her skirt. "He don't believe 'em, *sha*. Don't you believe his mama."

"No, Aunt Aggie," Celia said. "They showed him the picture. He thinks I'm trying to kill him!" Celia curled up into a fetal position, her face still covered, and sobbed into her hands. "Oh, Aunt Aggie, what am I gonna do? What am I gonna do?"

But Aunt Aggie was uncharacteristically speechless as Celia wailed out her pain.

Chapter Forty-One

In the hospital, Stan covered his eyes with his wrist, and his mother leaned over him. "Honey, are you all right?"

He shook his head. "I wanted to talk to her, Mom."

"To what end?" his mother asked. "Stan, she's dangerous. Physically and emotionally. I don't want you listening to her lies. Look at you. You didn't even talk to her, and you're all upset."

He took in a ragged breath and wiped his face roughly. "It's been a long day, Mom. A lot's happened."

"I know it has, Stan."

He closed his eyes and pretended to sleep, but he knew sleep wasn't going to come tonight. It was too hard. How could Celia have betrayed him? And was it true about the baby, or had she lied to further manipulate him? What was going on with her? How could he have been so blind?

He thought again of that picture of her in Lee Barnett's arms and fought the despair.

His mother picked up the phone and began to dial. He wiped his face and looked up at her. "Who are you calling, Mom?"

"The Newpointe police. I'm going to tell Sid Ford that Celia called. I thought she was in jail."

"No, Mom," he said. "Don't tell him."

She looked at him as if he was crazy. "I certainly am."

With all his effort, he pulled himself up, reached for the telephone, and took it out of her hand. "Hang it up, Mom," he insisted. "Now."

She hung up the phone. Deflated, she headed into the bathroom to get ready for sleep.

Stan realized that his mother had every right, every reason, to report the phone call. But as it was, he couldn't stand the thought of Celia sitting in that jail cell. He had long thought that they needed to do something to improve the women's portion of the jail, but it was rarely used. He'd never had anyone he cared about down there before. Now something inside him ached at the thought that she was sleeping on that thin mattress, using that toilet, that sink . . . He hoped someone had had the presence of mind to clean it before she'd gone down there.

Then he wondered why he cared. If his wife had truly tried to kill him, shouldn't he hope the worst for her? No, somehow he couldn't. His heart ached. It was broken into tiny pieces, and he doubted he would ever put it back together again. How would he ever trust again? How would he ever believe? Marriage was supposed to be for better or for worse. Had things been so bad, against his knowledge, that she hadn't been able to endure it? He tried to relax the torment from his face, to hide it from his mother as she came out of the bathroom, so she would leave him alone. But part of him didn't want to be alone.

He'd never felt more alone in his life. And he wondered what the cost would be of continuing to love Celia, especially if he didn't believe her.

Chapter Forty-Two

The police station was still buzzing at eleven-fifteen when Nick showed up to see Celia. Phones were ringing and printers were printing. A drunk man yelled curses to a cop who was booking him, and a woman with a black eye and bloody mouth sat at a cop's desk wailing that she couldn't press charges against her husband.

Nick's soul swelled at the depravity of his own generation, and he clutched the Bible in his hand, wishing he'd brought one for each of them. Reminding himself of his purpose for coming, he scanned the desks for Sid Ford. There he was at the back of the room, talking to Jim Shoemaker. He wondered if those men ever slept.

He cut between the desks and made his way back. "Sid," he said, hating to interrupt.

Sid glanced back at him. "Oh, hey, Nick. How ya doin'?"

"I'm interrupting," he said, shaking both of their hands. "Sorry, Jim. Do you mind if I talk to Sid for a minute?"

Jim told Sid to come into his office when he'd finished with Nick, and he left them alone.

"Sid, I need to see Celia," Nick said in a quiet voice.

Sid shook his head. "Sorry, man. It's after visitin' hours."

"Please, Sid. Stan asked me to come and see her. It's spiritual business that I need to take care of."

"I'm sorry," Sid said. "We ain't makin' no exceptions."

"Sid, I'm your preacher. You can help me out just this once. Bend the rules a little."

"No way, man. We been jerked around enough tonight."

"Jerked around? You think I'm jerking you around?"

"Yeah, I think you are," Sid said. "I think you're pullin' rank on me."

"Rank? We're not even in the same department."

"Rank with the Lord," Sid said. "Just because you're my preacher, I'm s'posed to bend the rules."

"Sid, if it was you in jail, you'd want me to visit."

"If it was me in jail I would deserve a visit," he said. "You can come back tomorrow when it's visitin' time. But right now we need to let her and Aunt Aggie stew."

"Aunt Aggie?" Nick asked. "*She's* in jail?"

"Yeah," Sid said defensively. "And don't you get on my case about that. Second time she assaulted a police officer, they threw the book at her."

"An eighty-one-year-old woman?"

"You got a problem with that?" Sid threw back.

Nick saw that he wasn't going to get anywhere with him. "All right, Sid, look. If you won't let me visit, at least take this Bible down to her. That's the least you could do. She has the right to a Bible."

Sid took the Bible, as if he knew Nick was right. "I'll get it to her when I got time."

"No, Sid," Nick pleaded. "Do it now. For Stan. He wanted me to come and see about her, make sure she was all right. If you won't let me in, at least, for his sake, take her the Bible."

"All right, but I gotta tell you somethin', Preacher. I'm gettin' sick and tired of all this. I don't like folks poisonin' my friends. When you start tryin' to kill a police officer, I take it real personal. And I ain't fixin' to coddle Celia Shepherd, or even her demented aunt, for that matter."

"I'm not asking you to coddle them, Sid. I'm just asking you to give them what they're entitled to."

"Aunt Aggie don't want no Bible."

594

"No, I realize that. But Celia might. Please, just get it to her right away."

Sid rolled his eyes, but he started back to the basement door.

"Are you taking it now?" Nick asked.

"What does it look like?" Sid shouted.

Nick had to be satisfied with that, and finally, he turned and left.

He walked out of the police station, looked up at the stars, and wondered for the thousandth time what he was doing being a preacher. Silently, he asked the Lord what he could do for Stan, Celia . . . if he should do anything. He started to go back to his car, but the night was cool and serene. In the midst of all this turmoil, it was a welcome relief.

He decided to walk for a few minutes, and he set out past the fire station, down to the corner. Across the street, he saw Joe's Place. He could hear the music spilling out of the doors. The parking lot was full.

Many of the patrons were part of his flock, but he'd had little impact on their nighttime behavior. He wondered what he could do, what he could say, to make them understand that life wasn't found in the confines of a smoky bar.

The door opened, and a triangle of light spilled out along with a cloud of smoke. He saw Issie Mattreaux coming out with a man swaggering behind her. Something drew him across the street, and he stood at the edge of the parking lot, watching, listening—his nerves on red alert.

• • •

Issie had every intention of letting Barnett come home with her, even though it was against her better judgment. He'd had too much to drink, but so had she. The alternative choice of going home alone was too boring to consider. Lee Barnett could add some excitement to a stressful but mundane existence. Besides, he was a good-looking man, and any woman in town would have thrown caution to the wind for him. She was sure of it.

She opened her car door and tossed her purse in, then turned back to the big, virile man with romance on his mind.

"So . . . you wanna come to my place, or do I come to yours?" the man muttered as his lips hovered over hers.

"Maybe I'll come to yours," she whispered. "That way I won't have to throw you out when I'm tired of you."

He chuckled under his breath. "You won't get tired of me."

As if to prove it, he leaned in to kiss her, but almost lost his balance. She caught him, and he grabbed both her shoulders and gave her a punishing kiss.

Issie tried to push him away. Too many people could come out of the bar and see her with Barnett, and by tomorrow, rumors would fly. No, she preferred to show her affections privately.

She tried to break free, but he wouldn't be deterred. Turning her head to break the kiss, she said, "Not here, Lee. Not now."

"Why not?" He tried to put her into the car, but she kept pushing him away.

"Someone will see us."

"So?"

"So . . . I said no!" Her voice was getting louder. "Stop it!"

She heard footsteps on the gravel, and someone grabbed Barnett by the back of the collar, pulled him away from her, and flung him to the ground. Issie realized her "rescuer" was Nick Foster.

"Nick!"

Nick left Lee lying disoriented on the ground and swung around to her. "Are you all right?"

"Yes," she said. "He was . . ."

"Who do you think you are?" Barnett called out from the ground.

Nick spun around. "I was about to ask you the same question."

Suddenly, Issie felt ashamed that the preacher had seen her in such a compromising position. She decided to play the victim.

"He had a little too much to drink," she said, feigning distress. "I should have known better than to walk out to the parking lot with him by myself." She looked up at him, widening her eyes as innocently as she was able. "Thank goodness you came along."

Barnett staggered to his feet and brushed off his jeans. "Look, I don't want any trouble. I just met Issie here in the bar, and we were havin' a couple of drinks. I walked her out to her car . . . no big deal." He shot Issie a look. "You didn't tell me you had a boyfriend."

"He's not my boyfriend," Issie said, unable to meet Nick's eye.

"What is he then? Your father?"

She could see that the barb stung Nick. He was a little older than Issie. But not old enough to be her father.

"I'm actually her preacher," he said.

"Preacher?" The man's eyebrows shot up as if he was impressed. "You really a preacher?" Suddenly, it seemed he'd forgotten that the man had just flung him to the ground. He took a drunken step toward him. "You know a priest around here named Mueller? Edmund Mueller?"

Nick frowned, wondering what in the world he was talking about. "I don't know any Mueller."

"Oh, yeah, you got to," he said. "A priest. Don't you preacher types hang together? You gotta know him. He came to visit me. Celia Shepherd's priest."

Nick shook his head. "*I'm* Celia's pastor, and my name is Nick Foster."

Barnett squinted at him for a long moment. "You sure?"

"Yeah, I'm sure."

Barnett looked thoroughly confused, and he stood there a moment, looked down at his feet, and shook his head.

"Who are you?" Nick asked.

Barnett kept staring at his feet, and Issie became slightly annoyed that he'd forgotten her so easily. Instead, he seemed to be struggling to understand something about some nonexistent priest. The perplexity and vulnerability on his face revealed something almost sad. It reminded her of herself.

"Who is he?" Nick asked her.

Issie took a deep breath. "Lee Barnett. The one they're saying is involved with Celia."

Nick's face seemed to drain of color, then quickly redden again. The flashing neon sign in front of Joe's Place seemed to punctuate his surprise.

"Look, you just go on home," Nick told the man, "and I'll make sure Issie gets home all right."

"Yeah." Barnett still seemed confused. "I'd appreciate that." He tapped his pockets, presumably for his keys, and began to wobble away.

The ease with which he dismissed her stung Issie, and biting back the feeling of rejection, she got into the car and closed the door. She turned the key to start it, but Nick knocked on the window and motioned for her to wait. Time for the sermon, she thought, cutting the car back off as Nick came around to the passenger side.

Nick got into the car and sat there for a moment, not sure what to say. Should he be a preacher now, or just a man? Or was there really any difference in the two?

Issie seemed self-conscious when she met his eyes. "I really appreciate your coming along, Nick. I always think I can handle things. I'm not exactly a wimp, but he was coming on a little strong."

Nick stared at her. Her face was lit only by the red neon lights on the front wall of Joe's Place. "What are you doing, Issie?"

"What do you mean?"

"I mean, what do you want? What would make a beautiful woman who has everything going for her come here every night alone, drinking and picking up strange guys?"

He could see her visibly wilt beneath the words. He hated it. He'd much rather use words that built her up, but he couldn't find any at the moment.

"Nick, just because I don't have the same values and beliefs that you have, doesn't mean that I'm some kind of terrible person. There's a thing called tolerance, you know."

Nick shook his head. "Some things shouldn't be tolerated."

"Oh, yeah?" she asked. "Like what?"

"Like promiscuity. Drunkenness. Explaining away your sin as if it was something that happens to you instead of something you choose."

He could see that she didn't take that well.

Her mouth fell open, and she tried to speak but failed. After a moment, she rallied. "Come on, Nick. If I wanted a sermon, I'd go to church."

"I'm sorry," Nick told her. "I didn't mean to preach."

"I guess you can't help yourself."

He sat there for a moment, wondering if he could. Was his preaching really a calling, or was it something *he* had just wanted to do in his zeal for Christ? Maybe it was one of those plans he had made, *then* asked Christ to come along, instead of waiting for the calling itself. He had been so sure at first, but now he wasn't sure.

"Don't you ever feel like letting your hair down?" Issie asked. "Just kicking your shoes off and drinking a little and dancing until the cows come home? Haven't you ever just wanted to spit out a couple of cuss words and follow your feelings?"

Nick thought back over his youth, when he had done all of those things. It had been an empty youth, and he hadn't really felt alive until the day he'd found Christ. "I have temptations," he said, "because I'm human. It goes with the territory. And sometimes I follow those temptations, and I sin. But you know what happens to me when I do?"

Issie rolled her eyes. "You get struck by lightning."

"No," he said. "Worse. I feel horrible about myself. I can't rest until I've repented."

"Oh, of course." Issie seemed amused. "That guilt thing that you right-wing extremists have. You love guilt."

He was saddened by the label she used like a weapon, as if she hoped it would wound him.

"It's like you think guilt will absolve you of everything."

"Oh, no," Nick said. "You've got us all wrong. Guilt doesn't absolve us of anything. And if we feel guilt, it's because we're guilty."

"Guilty? Just because you stumble now and then? Nick, give yourself a break. If nobody's hurt—"

"Nobody's hurt?" he asked with disbelief. "A man died because I stumble, Issie. He gave his life so I wouldn't have to drown in guilt."

Issie seemed lost for a moment, but then he saw the understanding dawn in her eyes. "I thought Jesus said he came to save the world, not condemn it."

"That's exactly what he said. And that's what he did, when he died for me. He saved me. See, I was already condemned, when I was going to bars every night, when I was promiscuous ..."

Those big eyes widened again. "You?"

"Me. I was condemned then. Without Christ, everybody's condemned."

"Oh, yeah," she said sarcastically. "Right straight into hell."

Nick shook his head. "I wish you believed it."

"Why?" she asked angrily. "Why do you care?"

His eyes drove deep into her, and she shifted with discomfort. "I care because I can see your potential, Issie."

"Potential? For what?"

"I see you in emergencies," he said. "I see you when you save people's lives. I see the way you throw yourself into your work as if every case was your only case, as if every person you're called to help is a life-or-death situation. I see goodness inside of you, Issie."

"Yeah, right," she said. "And what else?"

"I also see self-destruction, and I don't know where that comes from."

"And sin?" she mocked.

He thought about that for a moment. "You remind me of myself."

"Yourself?" she asked. "Oh, please."

"That's right. Ten years ago, before I knew Christ, I was just like you."

She stared at him for a moment, her expression heavy with a million thoughts. "I think it's nice, Nick, that you were able to turn your life around and find a purpose for it. I think it's great that you don't have to feel that guilt anymore. And I'm glad that you have the discipline not to fall back into the lifestyle you had. But I'm not like you."

"Thank goodness," Nick said.

A moment of smothering silence followed, but finally, she smiled slightly. "Actually, I would think that if I could be like you, it would be a nice thing to be." She sighed and averted her eyes. "A lot of ladies in town are vying for you, Nick. You and Dan Nichols."

He laughed, embarrassed. "That's ridiculous."

"Ridiculous? I think you know better than that."

"But you don't agree with them?"

Her smile was too pretty for his own good. "It's not that I don't agree with them. It's a question of type."

"Yeah, I guess the preacher's the last person in the world you'd ever be interested in."

"And I guess a party girl like me couldn't be farther from your dream of the perfect woman."

Their smiles faded, but neither of them refuted what the other had said.

"Want me to follow you home?" he asked.

She shook her head. "Better not."

"What if that Barnett fellow shows up tonight?"

"I didn't tell him where I live."

"Be careful of him," he said. "We don't know his part in Stan's poisoning. He could be the killer."

"I'm aware of that."

"Then what were you doing with him?"

Her expression fell. "Tell you the truth, I don't know," she said.

He could see the darkness in her soul, the despair, the loneliness, and he wondered what had caused it, where it had come from. Part of him understood what it was in her life that drove her to the bar every night. He had experienced it himself, working as a firefighter. They had thankless, dangerous jobs, with fierce stresses and little pay. They saw things others didn't have to see, and went home with the nightmares. It was tough when you had to go home alone. He knew.

He wished she had something more than Joe's Place to sustain her.

"Well, guess I better go," he said.

"Yeah." She started her car. "Hey, listen. Thanks for the rescue. And thanks for the sermon, too."

He smiled. "Anytime. But I'm best on Sunday mornings."

She breathed a laugh. "Well, maybe some day I'll get around to coming."

"If you have absolutely nothing else to do?"

"Something like that."

He opened the door and got out. "Lock up, okay?"

"Will do."

He backed up from the car and waited until she did it, and slowly ambled back across the street to where his car was parked. Why was it that Issie Mattreaux kept popping up in front of him? There were dozens of women in town who frequented bars and nurtured their promiscuity as if it were a religion that would bring some meaning to their lives. Why was it that she had such an effect on him? He didn't know, but he decided that it was wrong. She was not for him, and he needed to get her out of his mind.

He got into his car and watched as she pulled out of the parking lot and headed home. Before he cranked his car he said a prayer for her protection, a prayer for her rescue. The rescue of her soul.

Chapter Forty-Three

Shortly after the lights in the Newpointe jail went off, Aunt Aggie fell asleep. Sleep was a luxury not available to Celia, however, for as much as she would have liked to drift into a never-never-land of rest and dreams, she was unable to turn off the thoughts that kept her awake. If what Stan's mother had said was true, Stan had turned against her. He had decided to believe the lies.

Crushing despair almost smothered Celia as she lay curled up on her cot. A memory came back to her, vividly clear and precise, of another cell and how she had longed for an extra blanket and wished for an escape. It was almost too similar to be true. Her husband had been murdered, her family had turned against her, and someone was trying to frame her for something she had not done.

The difference was that, the first time, she'd had nowhere to turn. Through grace, God had shown her where to turn this time. But it was so hard doing what she knew she should. It was difficult to put her life in God's hands, when she had no idea why he'd allowed such a travesty of justice again, what good he could make come of it, and how he could ever use her for his kingdom again with this stigma attached to her.

The door to the hallway opened, spilling in some light from the stairwell, and she glanced over at Aggie, thinking that probably David had convinced the judge to set bail. Thank goodness the old woman would not have to stay. The overhead light flicked on.

She sat up as Sid Ford paused at her cell instead of going to Aunt Aggie's.

"I got somethin' for you," he said in a quiet, though grudging, voice.

Celia stood up, feeling weak. "What?"

"A Bible," he said. "Nick Foster came by and wanted to see you, but it was past visitin' time. I told him I'd bring you this Bible anyway."

She looked at the Bible in Sid's hand and slowly walked toward him to take it through the bars. "Thank you, Sid," she said.

He couldn't look her in the eye. "No problem." He glanced over at Aunt Aggie. "She all right? She ain't dead or nothin', is she?"

"No, she's just sleeping. She's very tired."

"Ain't we all?"

He started away from her, and she stepped to the bars, wrapping her hand around one of them. "Sid?"

He stopped but didn't look back at her. "Yeah?"

"I really appreciate the Bible. I needed it more than anything tonight. Would you mind leaving the light on so I can read it? It's just us here, and Aunt Aggie's sleeping soundly. I'd really like to read, if it's not too much trouble."

He didn't say anything, just walked through the door and closed it behind him. But the light didn't go back off.

Celia went back to her bed and looked down at the Bible in her hands. It was a godsend, she thought. An answered prayer. She was so thankful for it, but she didn't know where to begin to find the sustenance and comfort she knew waited for her there. She wished she'd spent more time studying God's Word.

She pressed the Bible against her heart, pulled her knees up, and pressed her forehead against them. "Oh, Father," she whispered. "You and Aunt Aggie are the only ones who aren't doubting me right now." She squeezed her eyes shut from the onslaught of tears. "Lord, you know what's going on," she whispered. "You know I didn't poison Stan. You know I love him. You know I'm innocent. Father, show me what to do. Show me how to fight this battle. Show me how to find peace and trust that you will deliver me from this evil." She wept as she prayed, her very heart uttering the words that her mouth could not say, and she felt God listening. His comfort embraced her like loving arms, and she wept, without words, without question, without answers.

Suddenly, the word *Jehosaphat* came to her mind. She opened her eyes and leaned her head back on the wall. "Jehosaphat," she whispered. "I don't even remember who he is." He was in the Old Testament. A king or something, but what had he to do with her?

She drew in a cleansing breath and decided that maybe God was speaking to her in his soft, still voice. Maybe she needed to read the story of Jehosaphat again. She looked into the concordance, found him listed, and turned to 2 Chronicles. She read how faithful Jehosaphat was as king of Judah, how he sought the God of his father, how he followed his commandments. She read how God had blessed him, raised him up, made him prosperous, how he had great riches and honor. How he established a God-fearing government and brought his people back to the Lord.

Still not certain how this applied to her, if at all, she kept reading, hungrily searching the Word, burying herself in the sustenance of it, the goodness of the story, the love inherent in the plot. She read how the sons of Moab and the sons of Ammon, and the Meunites, came to make war against Jehosaphat. And how he was afraid, because of their numbers. Suddenly, her heart began to pound harder. God was showing her another man who'd had a battle to fight, a battle that seemed impossible. He hadn't known how to fight, either. She read further and saw that Jehosaphat turned to God, and not to the counsel of men, and how he trusted in God. Then she came to chapter 20, verse 15, and she read the words that the Lord gave to the king, the words that sealed his strategy and gave his nation peace.

"Do not be afraid or discouraged because of this vast army. For the battle is not yours, but God's."

Her heart jolted, and her eyes filled with tears again. She sat staring at the words, soaking them in, breathing them, letting them seep into the pores and the chambers of her heart.

"Do not be afraid or discouraged ... the battle is not yours, but God's."

She looked up at the ceiling as if she could see the Lord through the beams. The battle wasn't hers. She hadn't invited it. Had done nothing to deserve it. She had not entered into it willingly. She had been thrust into it. And now God was telling her that she didn't have to claw and fight her way out. It was the Lord's battle.

A tremendous peace fell over her, and she began to weep, this time not of despair but of joy and the comfort that only the Lord could provide.

The battle is not yours, but God's. What wonderful words. What a bountiful provision. If the battle was not hers, then she need only wait. The Lord would provide somehow. He would reveal the truth.

She read on and saw how God had delivered Judah from the hands of their enemies, how Jehosaphat praised God and said, "Give thanks to the LORD, for his love endures forever."

That was what she would do tonight.

The lights flickered and went out, and Celia sat in the darkness for a moment, letting her eyes adjust, but no fear came upon her as she had expected. Aunt Aggie still slept in her cell, and Celia stayed on her bed, her Bible in her lap. Though she could no longer read it, she touched the pages as if life emanated from them. "The word of God is living and active. Sharper than any double-edged sword, it penetrates even to dividing soul and spirit, joints and marrow; it judges the thoughts and attitudes of the heart." The verse Stan had taught her years ago played over and over in her mind. He could judge her intentions, her thoughts, and he knew she had no murderous intent. He could also judge others' hearts. He knew who the killer was. He knew who had doubted her wrongfully. He knew how this would turn out. He knew what she would endure. But there would be a purpose, because she belonged to him.

She didn't intend it, didn't plan it, but suddenly a soft chorus came from her mouth, and she began to sing and praise God. Softly, but with all her heart.

In the darkness, Celia could see Aunt Aggie beginning to stir, and she sat partially up and looked at her niece through the bars. "Celia, you okay, *sha?*"

"I'm just fine, Aunt Aggie. Just fine."

"What you singin' about?"

"I'm sorry I woke you."

"You singin' about Jesus?" Aunt Aggie asked.

"Yes."

She couldn't see her in the darkness, but she could imagine Aunt Aggie rolling her eyes and shaking her head with what she considered the futility of it all. Poor Aunt Aggie.

"Oh, Aunt Aggie, something wonderful happened."

"What is it?"

"Sid Ford brought me a Bible. Nick Foster sent it. And I was praying and asking God for a sign, and he led me to a passage that told me the battle is not ours, but God's. Isn't that wonderful?"

Aunt Aggie's silence indicated how perplexed she was. She wouldn't see why this was wonderful at all. Celia almost laughed.

"Don't you see, Aunt Aggie? It means I don't have to fight. God knows I'm innocent. He's gonna take care of me and my baby. So I was just sitting here singing a praise song to God."

Aunt Aggie, once again, was at a loss for words. The darkness punctuated the silence between them. Finally the old woman said, "I'm glad your religion is givin' you some comfort."

Celia knew Aunt Aggie thought that was all it was. A false assurance that she put in some meaningless context of rules and circumstances that had no life to them at all. Again, she began to sing.

Aunt Aggie was silent at the end of the chorus. But Celia was smiling. "You'll see, Aunt Aggie. God's going to deliver me through this."

"I know you're gon' be all right," the old woman said. "I don't think God's gon' have nothin' to do with it, but you'll be all right if I got anything to say about it."

"The battle's not yours, either, Aunt Aggie," Celia said. "It's not Jill's, and it's not David's, and it's not mine. The battle is the Lord's."

"Well, if you don't mind, I'm still gon' keep payin' Jill to do what she can," Aunt Aggie said cynically.

Celia heard the sheets rustle as the old woman lay back down. But Celia wasn't finished praising the Lord. Quietly, softly, she began to sing again.

Chapter Forty-Four

In Slidell, Stan lay awake in the darkness of his hospital room, watching his mother sleep on the vinyl couch beside him. He closed his eyes and tried to pray. But he kept seeing the picture of Lee Barnett holding Celia, hearing her cry out that she was carrying his baby, hearing Sid and R.J. telling him how certain they were that Celia had tried to kill him.

"Lord, I don't know what to think," he cried out in his heart. "Tell me what to think. Tell me what to believe."

She was sitting in a jail cell, and the thought haunted him. Even if she was a murderer, cold-blooded, evil, he still couldn't stand the thought of her in jail. He wondered if Nick had gotten in to see her, if he had taken her the Bible. He wished he could have spoken to her when she called, heard her out. Maybe something she said could have brought some explanation, some understanding. There were so many "should have's", so many "if only's." He couldn't sort them all out.

He closed his eyes and let the tears seep down his temples and into his hair. He didn't know what was going to become of him after all the damage from the arsenic was assessed. He didn't know if he would ever be the same. His marriage certainly would not. The injustice of it all, the tremendous betrayal, the despair that seemed so smothering overcame him, and again his heart cried out to God. "Tell me what to do, Lord. Tell me what to do."

The words he had learned as a child in Bible drill came back to him. "Trust in the LORD with all your heart and lean not on your own understanding."

Was that the answer? Was the Word of God speaking to him, reminding him what he was to do? Hadn't he known it all along? All he had to do was trust in the Lord with *all* his heart and lean not on his own understanding. Maybe that was the mistake he was making. But how did one keep oneself from trusting his own understanding when things seemed so clear? He didn't want her to be guilty, but he couldn't imagine that she wasn't. Not now. Not after what he had seen. Not after what he had been told. Still, he couldn't stop loving her. How did one end a love that had been such a vital part of his life for so long?

Trust in the LORD with all your heart and lean not on your own understanding. The words played like a recording in his mind, over and over and over. Yet he was not able to let go of his own understanding. Not yet.

Chapter Forty-Five

Thoughts of Jill woke Dan early the next morning. He didn't like waking up with a woman on his mind. It wasn't like him. He didn't know what it was about her that had gotten under his skin, but he decided that he needed to see her.

It was seven A.M., but he tried to call her at home. There was no answer, only her machine. He hung up without leaving a message. Maybe she was at work.

He dialed the number of her office, and the machine picked up. Her secretary wasn't in yet, but maybe Jill was there, working away, ignoring the telephone. He decided to leave a message.

"Jill, this is Dan. Are you there?" He waited a second, and the phone clicked.

"Hey, Dan. I'm here."

"Oh." Suddenly, he wasn't sure what he wanted to say. He felt ridiculous having tracked her down like this, like it was some emergency, when all he wanted was to talk to her. "I didn't think I'd catch you there this early."

"Did you try me at home first?" she asked.

He hated to tell her that he had. It wasn't his style to track women down, like one of those desperate on-the-prowlers whose very existence seemed to hang on the affections of beautiful women. "I was just calling to see if you'd like to have breakfast." It was the first he'd thought of it, but he had to come up with something.

"Breakfast?" She hedged. "Uh . . . Dan, I'm a little busy right now."

"Busy?" This was the first time a woman had been too busy to spend time with him. He hesitated, trying to come up with a response. "Of course you are. I figured you were. Maybe another time." He waited for her to tell him when, to give him a rain check . . . maybe lunch. But she didn't.

"Dan, I'm just really swamped right now. I'm trying to gather my thoughts before I face the judge this morning. I'm doing everything I can to get Celia out. Then I wanted to run to the hospital in Slidell to see Stan. I just heard he's having dialysis today to flush his kidneys of the toxins. It's gonna be a busy day."

"I understand," he said. "No time to eat."

She seemed preoccupied, distant. "Look, we'll catch up with each other later, okay?"

"Sure," he said. "No problem." He hung up and felt as low as he'd ever felt in his life. This was exactly why he avoided serious relationships. He hated the rejection. Hated the groveling. Hated the feeling that he wasn't good enough. He hated the memories it brought back of his childhood.

He tried to push the thoughts out of his mind as he went up to his bedroom and changed into his running clothes. But he couldn't forget that smothering feeling of rejection. His parents, too busy to spend time with him, leaving him with a nanny while they shuttled off to Aspen to spend Christmas. His parents entertaining and making him stay upstairs, so they wouldn't be disturbed. His parents shipping him off to camp for the summer, a ritzy, cushy camp for rich kids whose parents didn't want them around. No, he hated that feeling of rejection, and he wouldn't tolerate it again. He hated that feeling of having to garner someone's approval, someone who hardly even cared that he existed. No, he wouldn't endure that again, not for any price.

He decided not to brood. Instead, he ran five miles, pushing himself past his own limits, forcing the poisons of rejection out of his system. He didn't know what he was so agitated about. He'd never declared his love to Jill Clark, and she'd never declared hers to him. Though people had started to speak of them as a couple, there was no exclusivity, no "understanding." If things just faded out, no one would think less of him. That was the way relationships worked with him. They would just think that he had grown tired of her and decided to move on.

Was he really that pompous? he asked himself as he got back home. Was it really his pride that was eating at him, rather than his disappointment that things were ending this way? Yes, he admitted. But knowing it didn't change things. Prayer was what he needed, he realized with a jolt of humility. Prayer and a shower.

He chose the shower first and put the prayer off until later.

Chapter Forty-Six

Judge Louis DeLacy had released Aunt Aggie early the morning after her incarceration, as soon as he was told how she'd wound up in jail. He was not about to allow her to spend another moment there, he said. She was tearful as she left Celia in the jail cell, promising to visit as often as they would allow her to.

Celia's peace remained, and manifested itself as compassion for Nick when he finally got in to see her. He looked tired and uncertain, and she saw the doubt about her in his eyes. She realized vaguely that if she had seen that look in his eyes yesterday, she would have been crushed. But today, she knew better than to blame him. She hugged him as he came into her cell, and pointed him to the only chair in the room. She sat across from him on the cot.

"I know what you must be thinking, Nick," she said. "I know everybody in town must think I'm absolutely guilty. I mean, how could I not be, with all the evidence against me?"

"I don't think you're guilty, Celia," Nick said weakly.

It was obvious that he was lying. She hated seeing him in this position, and almost wished he hadn't come. "Don't lie, Nick. Not for me."

He drew in a deep breath, and his face changed. Suddenly, she saw the real Nick, the one who wasn't acting, the one who was honest even when it hurt. "Okay, Celia," he said. "I'll be straight with you. I don't know what to think about you anymore."

She had believed she was ready for that, but when they came, the words still stung her. "Why would you think anything other than what you've always thought?"

"Because I haven't always known the whole story."

"Yes, you have," she said. "What you haven't known is all the old allegations. But they weren't truth. What you've known about me is truth."

She could tell that he struggled between his ministerial facade and the humanity within him. It was what she loved about Nick—the fact that he was so spiritual, yet so human ... so close to God ... yet so like herself.

"I have to ask you something," Nick said.

"Anything, Nick. I don't have any secrets."

"Well, you seem to have had some. A lot of things no one knew about you until all this blew up."

"I understand how that could make you suspicious," she said. "But you've got to understand that I had a right to start fresh. I was wrongly accused. I didn't need to drag that around for the rest of my life. If I had done something wrong to deserve that, fine. But I didn't. So I left it behind me and I pressed on."

"I can see that," Nick said. "But the question I want to ask you is more immediate, and even more personal. It's about Lee Barnett."

"What about him?" she asked.

His eyes were direct, probing, as he asked the question. "Why did you go see him yesterday?"

Her heart jolted. How had Nick found that out? Had the police been talking out of turn? Had they been gossiping her business all over town?

"How did you know about that?"

"Stan told me."

Her heart crashed, and despair hovered over it, waiting for an opening so it could move in and fill her with the darkness she'd stumbled through yesterday. But then she told herself that it was no surprise. She knew he had seen the picture.

It was still the Lord's battle, not hers. The realization enabled her to hold the despair at bay.

"Nick, I'm gonna tell you what happened yesterday, and I'm not telling you to defend myself, because I'm innocent and I don't *need* to defend myself. But I want you to know the real story."

Nick waited.

"I went to Lee Barnett because I wanted to find out what he was up to," she said. "I didn't step one foot in his apartment. I didn't touch him except to slap him once when I got so angry that I couldn't hold it in any longer. He grabbed me and shook me, and that must be when Vern snapped the picture. Now, if anyone wants to know the truth about that encounter, I suggest they go to Vern and ask him what he saw before and after that embrace. Put that picture in context. Ask him to see what else is on that film. Look at our faces, Nick."

Nick was quiet as the words sank in. He seemed to be listening, seriously wanting to believe her. She desperately wanted him to.

"Nick, please tell Stan the truth. He must know in his heart that I didn't do this."

Nick looked down at his feet, and she could see that he still struggled with what to believe about her.

Her expression crashed. "Nick, I am so sorry for you."

"For me?" he asked.

"Yes," she said. "When this is all over and I've been acquitted of any guilt, and you see how hard someone has worked to set me up, it'll be one more time when you beat yourself up for not doing the right thing."

He sat there, his face vulnerable, exposed. She knew what was going through his mind. He had to be thinking about all the times he had failed. All the inadequacies, all the mistakes. It was what made him such a good preacher . . . and what made him so human.

"I'm gonna forgive you, Nick," she whispered. "And when you feel guilty for doubting me, I want you to remember that, if it weren't for your teaching, I may never have come to Christ. Yes, Stan led me, but you closed the deal, Nick. I'm tremendously grateful to you. So when you find out that I'm innocent, that everything I've said is true, and you get mad at yourself, I want you to remember that what you did for me five years ago was a whole lot more important than this."

Nick's eyes filled with tears, and he set his elbows on his knees and cupped his face in his hands. Finally, he looked up at her. "Celia, I love you. I want to believe you. I want to know that you know Christ, that all of this has not been a terrible act. Because if it is, then my judgment is horrible and my discernment is pretty lousy. I need to believe you."

"Then do it," she said. "Believe me."

He looked into her eyes, long and hard, and she knew that in his mind he probably prayed for eyes like God's eyes, to see into her and know if she lied. And suddenly she realized that God had told him in words that she had not been able to utter that she was innocent.

The tension in his face melted away, and more tears filled his eyes. He seemed to straighten, and his eyes were softer as he regarded her. "I believe you, Celia. I do."

"Then help Stan to believe me," she said. "Please Nick. I need you to help Stan believe me."

"I'll do everything I can," he told her. "I promise."

She gave him a hug, and he started to get up. "Nick? Tell him to trust in the Lord with all his might. And then he can trust in me."

Nick nodded and left her alone.

Chapter Forty-Seven

The dialysis did wonders for Stan, making him feel better than he'd felt since he'd been poisoned. It seemed that no major damage had been done to his organs, though the arsenic had taken its toll on him, and it would be weeks, maybe months, before he was restored to his former energy level.

They released him from the hospital with strict orders for his mother, who was going to care for him at home. Because his parents were sensitive to his need to return to some form of normalcy, they decided to move into his own house with him so he could sleep in his own bed and be surrounded by his own things. Newpointe police officers would continue their rotational guard of him.

Nick caught him in the corridor as they wheeled him out in his obligatory wheelchair. Stan's father tried to intervene, but Stan insisted on a moment with him alone. Nick wheeled him back into his room and sat down in front of him. "I spoke to Celia this morning," he said. "Stan, I know things look grim for your marriage, but I want you to reconsider your trust in her."

Stan almost laughed. "This is a role reversal, isn't it? Last time we talked, I was the one telling you to stop doubting her."

"I did doubt her," Nick said. "You were right. But when I met with her, I could tell that she wasn't lying. She's not guilty, Stan. You've got to trust her."

He closed his eyes. "How is she doing?"

"She's good," he said. "Better than I could have imagined. She said to tell you to trust in the Lord."

Stan's eyes came open. "Trust in the Lord?" he asked. "Is that exactly what she said?"

"Yep. Exactly."

Stan remembered the verse the Lord had given him just last night. *Trust in the Lord* . . .

It sounded like something Celia would say. That childlike faith came so easily to her. That bottom line that made it a done deal, even when others would have sought counsel and groped around for meaning and understanding. Celia didn't need much. A simple verse of Scripture.

"I know you can't get around much," Nick said. "But if you felt like going to visit her later, I could take you. We could put you in a wheelchair and you wouldn't have to walk . . ."

Hope blossomed with the idea, but then the image of her in Lee Barnett's arms—that irretractable image that would not let go—stopped him. "I'll think about it."

Nick gave him a skeptical look.

"No really," Stan said. "I just need to pray about it. I need to think."

"All right." Nick took his hand, shook it firmly. "Get some rest, okay? I'll be praying for you. And if you need me, anytime, man, I'm there."

The sight of his house as they pulled into the driveway brought a fresh onslaught of grief. Stan sat in the front seat of his father's car, wishing he could go in and find Celia waiting there, as she always was, full of news about her day, fluttering around him trying to help him unwind from whatever case he'd been absorbed in. The thought that he may never have that again was too much to bear. For a moment, he made no move to get out of the car, just sat there, staring at the door from the garage into the kitchen.

He tried to grapple with the logic of avoiding her. If he did, wouldn't he be sealing his fate, discarding his marriage, throwing her to the wolves? And what if she really was innocent? Could he live with himself if he'd turned against her?

Maybe Nick was right. Maybe he did need to see her. If he could just touch her, look in her eyes . . . he would know the truth. He knew he would. He'd been lied to countless times during his career as a cop, and his detective instincts hadn't been damaged by the arsenic. He would know, if he saw her. It would be obvious to him.

He got out of the car, staggering slightly, and his mother helped him walk to the door. "You sure you don't need the wheelchair, hon?" she asked.

"I'm sure. I can make it."

T.J. Porter was the guard on duty, and he parked his squad car out front and carried his bag in as his father pulled the wheelchair out of the trunk of the car. He waited as he gave his mother the key, and she unlocked the door leading in from the garage. It opened, and he stepped inside, his eyes scanning the kitchen, which was still in disarray from the investigation. Slowly, he walked through the kitchen into the living room.

"What's that?" his mother asked, and he followed her eyes to an envelope on the floor right inside the front door. "Looks like someone slipped it under the door." She picked it up, and her face changed. "It's addressed to Celia."

Something hardened in his chest as he took it, and he sank onto the closest chair and sat down. His hands trembled as he opened the envelope and pulled out the paper. He scanned the typed print, then shot a look at the bottom, to the signature of Lee Barnett.

His heart plunged again, and he began to read.

"Dear Celia," it said. "I look forward to being with you as soon as things are worked out. Please call me as soon as you have the chance. I miss you, and I love you. Lee Barnett."

Stan tossed the letter on the table next to him and dropped his face in his hands.

His father was just coming in, and his mother picked up the letter. "Bart, it's from Lee Barnett," she said. "For Celia."

Silence stood like a lethal gas around them, as all eyes turned to Stan. He began to weep.

His mother's eyes were full of tears, too. "Let's get him to bed," she said.

His father came over and pulled him up from the chair. Stan did as they wanted him to do, for he had no energy to fight them.

Chapter Forty-Eight

Stan awoke in his own bed several hours later. He could smell Celia's scent on the pillow next to him, and the fragrance sent sweet relief washing over him. Groggy, he turned over and slid his hand to her side of the bed, reaching for her, but the coldness of the sheets jolted him back to reality.

That image of her with Lee Barnett filled the big screen of his mind again, and the words of the letter echoed. Barnett had told her he loved her, as if the two of them had exchanged those words many times before. But when? How could she have been carrying on an affair without Stan's knowing it?

Something didn't ring true. The note slipped under the door was enough of a red flag. If, indeed, Celia had been seeing Lee Barnett, wouldn't he know that she was staying with her Aunt Aggie? Why would he have slipped a note under their door, unless he knew that Stan would be the one to find it?

Why would Celia have killed her first husband, why would she have tried to kill him, why would she claim she was pregnant, why would she have an affair with a man barely out of prison, why would she have lied all these years about her love for Stan? What would she possibly have to gain? None of it made any sense.

He got up and walked weakly into the living room. His father was sound asleep in his recliner. Some World War II movie was playing on the television. His mother had lain down on the couch and was sleeping. He felt sorry for them. They hadn't gotten much sleep lately, and the one night they had tried to go home to rest they had been called back because of the second murder attempt.

Stan decided not to wake them. He sat down in an easy chair adjacent to the couch. The letter was lying on the table next to it, and he picked it up and read it again. He thought of the explanation Celia had given—that someone had written a check and sent it to him, that there was a letter that she had not written, that it had her signature. It was typed, just as this one was. Why would he type it?

The possibility suddenly occurred to him that he could go straight to the source—look in the man's face and ask him those questions. Wouldn't he know if the man wanted him dead? Wouldn't he be able to see if there were lies in his eyes? As a detective, he was more astute than most. His instincts paid off well. Maybe he would be able to tell.

The cops who were working on the case now were passionately involved, because he was the victim, their one detective, their friend, their brother. Someone needed to be equally passionate on the other side. Celia had no one. Not even him.

Maybe, just because of the years of happiness she had brought him, he owed it to her to go to Barnett and see what he could determine.

He quietly went into the foyer and slipped out the front door. T.J. Porter was sitting on a lawn chair beside the front door. He got up as soon as he saw Stan. "Stan, should you be up?"

"I'm okay," he said, already out of breath. "Look, I need a favor."

"What favor?"

"I need for you to take me somewhere."

"Where?"

"I want you to take me to the Bonaparte Court apartments."

T.J. looked at him like he was crazy. "Stan, sit down."

Stan sat with relief in the folding lawn chair and looked up at the huge man.

"Stan, this isn't a good idea, man. You don't need to be out. You just got out of the hospital. You can barely walk."

"I can make it. Just get me there."

"Why? What purpose would it serve?"

"Nothing illegal," Stan said. "I want to talk to Lee Barnett. I want to look him in the eye and talk to him."

T.J. ran his fingers through his hair and shook his head. "I can't do it, Stan. I'm sorry."

"Why not?"

"Because I've been told to guard you."

"You weren't told to imprison me, you were told to protect me. Now, you can go along and protect me."

"But Sid said—"

"I don't care what Sid said. I'm still on the police force. And Sid is my subordinate. So are you."

"But Stan, you can't pull rank when you're so sick. You're not on active duty right now."

"I don't recall taking a leave of absence. I'm on sick leave. That's all. Now, I order you, as your superior, to take me where I want to go."

T.J. looked miserably divided. "What about your parents?"

"My parents are fine," he said. "It's me the killer's after, not them. As long as you're guarding me, you're doing your job."

T.J. breathed a heavy, defeated sigh. "All right, Stan, get in the car."

Stan went to the car, opened the door, and sank into the front seat. T.J. got in on the other side and pulled out of the driveway. "Did you tell your folks?"

"They're sleeping," Stan said. "I'll be back before they even wake up."

He leaned his head back on the seat and closed his eyes as T.J. drove. Silently, he prayed that he would be able to see clearly what was going on. If his wife was an adulteress, he needed to know. If she was a killer, he needed to know that, too. If Lee Barnett had anything at all to do with this, he had to see it.

It took only ten minutes to reach the Bonaparte Court apartments on Rue Matin, and T.J. pulled into the parking space closest to Barnett's apartment. Stan gave him a look. "Do you know which apartment it is?"

"Right there," T.J. said, pointing to the one on the second floor. "B–5. We've been patrolling it at least hourly. Stan, I don't know how you'll get up those stairs."

"Don't worry about it," Stan said. "I'll make it."

"I'm coming with you."

Stan thought that over for a moment, then decided it probably was a good idea. "Yeah, if I'm facing my killer, then I probably do need an armed guard."

T.J. got out, came around to the passenger side, and helped Stan out of his seat. "Stan, it won't be easy getting you up those stairs, buddy."

"I can do it," Stan said. "Just give me a little time."

He took the steps one at a time, stopping to rest on each one. T.J. put his arm around his waist and helped him up the final few steps. He was sweating and had to stop to catch his breath before they got to the door.

"You sure you want to do this, buddy?" T.J. asked.

"I'm sure."

They reached the door, and T.J. rapped hard on it. For a moment, there was no answer, then a muffled, "Who is it?"

"Po-lice," T.J. said.

Stan shot him a look. "You didn't have to tell him that."

"That's exactly who we are," T.J. said. "Best way to get him to open the door that I know of."

"Or to make him run out the back window," Stan said. But there was no need to worry. The door opened and Stan found himself facing Lee Barnett for the first time. He stared at the man. His hair was unwashed, his face unshaven. Dark shadows defined his bloodshot eyes, as if he were hung over. He wasn't wearing a shirt, and Stan saw the tally marks tattooed on his arm.

Could Celia really be involved with a man like this?

"Yeah, what do you people want now?" Lee asked.

"My name is Stan Shepherd," Stan said.

Lee's face changed and his eyes opened wider. "You're outa the hospital?" he asked.

Stan gazed intently into his eyes, looking for some sign of evil. Was this the orderly in the surgical mask and glasses? He wasn't sure. "Yeah, I'm out. I want to talk to you."

"Is this police business?" Barnett asked. "Or personal?"

"A little of both," Stan said.

Barnett backed up from the door. "Well, I guess you oughta come in, then," he said. Stan looked at T.J., who seemed a little uncertain about whether they should go inside. T.J. patted his weapon, then nodded that it was probably all right. The two men went inside.

Barnett nodded toward the couch, and Stan gratefully sank down. "I thought you were practically dead," Barnett said.

Stan nodded pensively. "Somebody would like to see me that way."

"Sounds like it." Barnett took the seat across from them. "I think I know why you're here."

Stan waited. Often silence was the best catalyst he knew to get someone talking.

"You're here to ask if I'm the one who poisoned you."

Stan waited for him to go on, to hang himself.

"Well, I'm not." He said the words without flinching, without averting his eyes. He looked intently at Stan, as if determined to make him believe.

Stan reached into his back pocket and pulled out the envelope that he'd found under the door today. "You know anything about this?" he asked.

Barnett eyed the envelope, and so did T.J. "No, what is it?"

His response seemed genuine, but Stan watched him nonetheless, waiting for some flicker of deceit. He pulled the letter out. "It's a letter to my wife. Has your signature on it."

Barnett got up, grabbed the letter, and peered down at it. "Now how would I have typed this? And anyway, that isn't my signature. I don't write like that."

Stan watched him carefully. "Can you prove you didn't write it?"

Barnett held his hands up. "Can anybody prove anything? All I can tell you is that I don't have a typewriter *or* a computer. How would I have printed this out? You can search this apartment high and low. I don't have that much stuff here, anyway."

Stan nodded to T.J. and the big cop got up and began to go through the rooms, looking for some sign of a typewriter or computer.

"I'll tell you somethin' else," Barnett said. "I can guarantee you that's not my signature." He pulled out a driver's license that had been issued the day after he'd gotten out of prison, and handed it to Stan. "See, that's my signature, right there. Nothin' like the one on that letter."

"Then who wrote this and why did they put it under my door?"

Barnett almost laughed. "Don't you see? It's just part of the game they're playing."

"Who's playing?"

"Whoever this is that's tryin' to set me up." Barnett was beginning to break out in a sweat, and he leaned back in the chair. "Look, I understand where you're comin' from. You're the one who almost bought the farm, and you're prob'ly not feeling so good right now. But I didn't have a thing to do with this, and neither did Celia."

Stan might have predicted that Barnett would defend her, but it still hurt. He sat for a moment, trying to compose himself, trying to fight the emotions overcoming him. He was a cop, he told himself, and he was here as a cop, no matter how he felt.

"She came here yesterday," Barnett said matter-of-factly. Stan wondered why Barnett would volunteer that if, indeed, anything was going on. "She was mad as a hornet. It was the first time I'd seen her since before I went to prison, and she looked awful. She was furious at me, man, and I could tell just from lookin' at her that she didn't have nothin' to do with poisonin' you."

Stan kept staring at Barnett. "What about the letter she sent you? The checks?"

"Apparently it wasn't her." He got up and paced around the floor. "Some fictitious priest named Father Mueller brought the letter to the prison chaplain. I ain't been able to find him, and now I'm wonderin' if it wasn't the killer himself."

T.J. came back in and shook his head. There was nothing with which Barnett could have typed the letter. That didn't rule out one of those all-purpose office shops. There wasn't one in Newpointe, but he could have gone to Slidell or New Orleans.

"Look, man, there wasn't a happier guy alive than I was a coupla weeks ago when I got that letter and those checks and thought they were from Celia. I tell you what, talk about redemption. I thought maybe there really was a God, and he had sent Celia to rescue me. But then I got here, and everything started breakin' loose, and I realized that I'd been had, that some jerk out there didn't care if a ex-con got blamed for doin' somethin' he hadn't done. And, to tell you the truth, when I first realized I'd been set up, I thought Celia set me up. I thought she'd probably tried to off you, then pinned it on me since I was convenient. But yesterday when she came to see me, I knew better."

"Did she come into your apartment?" Stan asked.

"No, of course not. She wouldn't be that stupid. Don't forget I just got out of prison. She wouldn't trust me."

Stan's mouth trembled slightly, and he pulled the snapshot from his pocket and stared down at it. Then he held it up where Barnett could see. "Explain this."

Barnett took the picture, squinted down at it, then began to laugh. "Oh, this is priceless."

Stan couldn't find the humor.

"I musta held her for a split second, right after she slapped the fire outa me. It was in self-defense, man. I can't believe this guy got that picture at exactly that moment. He's a master. He'd get rich as a paparazzo." He studied it with a look of amusement. "Come on, man, give me a break. Look at my face in the picture. It's not exactly tender."

"I can't see much of it," Stan said. "I can't see any of hers."

Dismissively, he thrust the picture back at Stan. "Well, if you *had* seen hers, you would have seen that she was cryin' and her face was beet red. Let me tell you somethin'. She can pack a wallop when she wants to."

Stan would have found that amusing, if it hadn't been so sad. He knew all too well how much of an emotional wallop she could pack. He stared down at the picture, then looked at the letter and back up to Barnett. "You know there's no law against having an affair with another man's wife," he said. "You can't go to jail for it. If you're having an affair with my wife, I need to know that now. I need to know whether my wife is involved in this in any way."

Lee Barnett gaped at him. "And you claim to love her?"

Stan didn't appreciate the question.

"No, really, I mean it, man," Barnett said. "You're the guy who's supposed to love and cherish her, right? I mean, you married her. You've lived with her all this time. You know her better than anybody else. But here I am, ain't laid eyes on her in years, and I see her one time and I know for sure she's tellin' the truth. Man, if she ain't after an affair, maybe she ought to be."

If Stan had had more strength, he might have lunged for him, but there was too much truth in the words.

"Look, I know there's evidence. Apparently, there's evidence against me, too, and you're holding two pieces of it in your hands. But I can swear to you that that don't mean a thing. I ain't foolin' around with your wife, she ain't in love with me, she didn't poison you, she didn't set me up, she didn't come here to have a secret rendezvous with me yesterday, none of those things. But somebody wants to kill you, man. And I don't know why, but he wants it to look like Celia did it, and he wants it to look like she did it for me." He chuckled slightly. "If it weren't so scary, I might be a little flattered."

"Flattered?"

"Yeah, that the cops would think that somebody could care enough about me to kill her husband over me."

Stan's eyes narrowed as he tried to process that admission.

"Trust me, detective. There ain't nobody in the world who would do that for me. And nobody in the world I'd go to prison for, either."

Every instinct in Stan's body told him Barnett was being straight with him. He'd always trusted those instincts. He had no reason not to trust them now. He got to his feet and nodded to T.J. T.J. started across the room to the door.

"I appreciate your time," Stan said.

"You believe me, don't you?" Barnett asked.

Stan didn't want to commit himself. "I'll think about it all."

"Think about it hard," Barnett said. "Look, I ain't in love with your wife, but I don't much like the idea of her sitting in jail for something she didn't do. It just ain't right. I had to go to prison for something I *did* do, and it was bad enough. I can just imagine what it would be like if you were innocent."

He held the door and turned to T.J. "Hey, do I have to stay in town? I was told I couldn't leave town, but I'd really like to get back to Jackson. I don't know anybody here, and I'm not havin' good luck, and it's not where I want to be."

"You'd better stick around, buddy, until you're told you can leave."

"Terrific. At first, I thought it wouldn't hurt, that the apartment was paid for, so who cares? But I don't like it here. It's a hostile environment, and I'm not getting very far. Maybe I oughta take Celia's advice and stay in a hotel or somethin'. I feel like a sittin' duck. I just ain't got any money to pay for nothin' else."

Stan turned around at the word *hotel* and stared at the man. Hadn't Marabeth Simmons mentioned them talking about a hotel? Maybe it had been in that context.

Stan sighed and started down the stairs.

Barnett stepped outside of his door. "Hey, you take it easy now. That arsenic, it ain't nothin' to play with."

Stan stopped on the steps and turned around, looked up at him again. "Did she tell you she was pregnant?"

Barnett's eyebrows shot up in mild surprise. "Who? Celia? *Pregnant?*"

He studied the man's eyes for some sign of deceit, but again, the most he could find was indifference. "Yeah, Celia."

"No, is she?"

Stan didn't answer, and finally, he turned away again. He took the remaining steps down, carefully. When he reached the bottom, he looked up. Barnett was leaning against the rail, staring down at him with a slight frown as if worried he might fall. He nodded good-bye and Barnett gave him a half-wave before going back in.

Stan got into the car, and T.J. went around to the driver's side and cranked it up. "So what do you think?" T.J. asked.

"He didn't do it."

T.J. rolled his eyes. "Then how do you explain all the evidence that says he was involved?"

Stan stared at his friend. "I think he just explained it."

"And you believe him?"

"I'd stake my whole career on it. And my marriage."

"Are you sure, Stan?"

"She's innocent." His mouth twisted. He put his hand over his face and wept into it.

T.J. reached out and touched his shoulder. "You okay, man?"

"No, I'm not okay. My wife is in jail because of something she didn't do, and for a little while, I believed she did it. I can't believe I bought into it. Whoever's doing this, they're evil, and I played right into their hands."

"Man, don't go off the deep end. You don't know for sure that Celia's innocent."

"Well, until I know for sure she's guilty, I'm gonna believe she's innocent."

T.J. sat there for a moment, letting the car idle. "You ready to go home, buddy?" he asked.

Stan shook his head. "I'm not going home."

"Man, you're sick. You need to be in bed."

"Take me to the station."

"The station? What are you gonna do? Go back to work?"

"No," Stan said. "I'm gonna visit my wife."

Chapter Forty-Nine

The noise in the police department came to an abrupt halt as Stan stepped through the door. All eyes seemed to turn to him, even those of the criminals being booked. Sid Ford got to his feet and began to laugh as his eyes misted over.

"Man, *there* you are! Your folks was worried sick about you. What you doin' here, man? You s'posed to be in bed."

"They let him out," T.J. said, "and now he's trying to investigate this crime himself."

Sid approached Stan and shook his hand as if he were fragile. "Man, you need to be at home in bed. You need to let us take care of this. We're gettin' to the bottom of it. Let me call your mama back and tell her you're here."

"You're on the wrong track," Stan said weakly, "but we can talk about that later." He tried to catch his breath. "Right now I came for another reason."

"Another reason?" Sid asked. "What?"

T.J. shot Sid a look. "He wants to see Celia."

"No, man!" Sid took a step back, shaking his head. "You don't wanna do that. That's gon' be too hard on you! You know it is."

"I want to see my wife," Stan said. "You can't stop me."

"Man, there's a court order sayin'—"

"There's not a court order telling *me* to do anything," Stan said. "If I want to see my wife, I can. Sid, I don't think you want me to pull rank on you."

Sid held his hands out to stem the threat. "Man, you don't have to go that far. I'm just tryin' to protect you."

"I'm sick of people trying to protect me in the wrong way. My wife doesn't deserve to be locked up. I want to see her."

"You ain't gon' talk us into lettin' her out."

"I know that," Stan said. "Just take me to the jail."

Sid rolled his eyes, as if he couldn't believe he was being asked to do such a ludicrous thing. But finally, he led him to the basement.

Stan stepped carefully down the stairs, stopping every few steps to catch his breath. Sid reached the door to the women's jail before he did, so he tried to hurry the rest of the way down.

"Sure you're up to this, man?" Sid asked. "You don't look good."

"Yeah . . . I'm fine . . ."

Sid opened the door and Stan stepped in. He looked from one cell to the next, but didn't see Celia. Then he heard a gut-wrenching sound from behind the partition surrounding her toilet. Celia was throwing up.

Stan stepped up to the bars and looked into the dimly lit cell. A Bible lay open on the cot, and her shoes were beside it. He heard her retching again, then the toilet flushed.

"She throwin' up?" Sid asked.

Stan couldn't answer, for there was a lump of emotion the size of Texas in his throat. Had she been sick like this the whole time? Didn't anyone care? Suddenly, a fierce, protective instinct came over him. "Open the door," he ordered Sid.

"Stan, don't you think you better talk to her through the bars? I mean, we ain't talkin' about somebody stable."

"Open it," he said again.

Sid registered his disapproval with a loud sigh and opened the cell. "I'm waitin' right by the door, man. Holler if you need me."

But Stan wasn't listening. Weakly, he headed across the cell and stepped around the partition. Celia was on her knees in front of the toilet, and as he stepped up behind her, she began retching again. Stan leaned over her, gathered her hair, and pulled it back out of her way.

As soon as she was able, she looked up to see who had come to her aid. Surprise widened her eyes, and the gray color of her complexion quickly flushed with pink tones. She got to her feet, and as tears flooded her eyes, whispered, "Stan?"

He hadn't expected to be so overcome with love, not after all the doubts, but his eyes filled with tears and he pulled her to her feet. "Are you all right?" he whispered. "Let me help you."

He led her to the sink and she bent over it to rinse her mouth out, then fell back into his arms. She wept against his shirt, her body shuddering. After a while, she managed to whisper, "I'm fine now." She pulled back and looked up at him. "What about you? You look terrible, honey. You need to be in bed." She touched his cheek. "You've lost weight . . . and you're skin . . . it's yellow. Why are you here? Why aren't you in bed?"

"I had to see you." He felt himself wobbling unsteadily, and she led him to the cot and made him sit down. She sat next to him, sideways so she could face him, and he combed his fingers through her hair as remorse and shame welled up inside him and filled his eyes with tears. "Can you ever forgive me?"

"Me?" she asked. "What for?"

"For doubting. They showed me that picture, and told me about Lee Barnett, and the arsenic in the attic, and all the other stuff, and I bought into it, Celia. I'm so sorry."

Her face twisted and grew redder. "How do you know they're not right?"

"Because . . ." He wiped his face with a rough hand. "None of it makes any sense. I look at you . . . and I know who you are . . ." His voice broke off and he embraced her again. "Please forgive me."

"I do," she whispered. "Of course I do."

"Who did this, Celia?" he asked. "Who could it be?"

"I don't know," she said. "I've racked my brain for years, even before you were poisoned. I have no idea. I really don't. I suppose it could be Lee Barnett, but it didn't seem like it was, when I went to visit him. I can't understand his motive, if it's him. Why would he do something that would land him right back in prison? It doesn't make any sense."

He shook his head. "No, I don't think he did it. I just went to see him myself."

Her eyebrows rose. "You did?"

"Yes. I think he's being used somehow." His eyes took her in, drinking in her beauty, her sweetness, and he touched her face. "Celia, the other night when you came to the hospital, you said something."

She smiled slightly. "Yes."

"About a baby?"

Her tears spilled over again. "Mm-hmm."

"That's why you were throwing up?"

She nodded.

His mouth trembled. "When did you find out?"

"Remember, I had been nauseated for a few days, even before you were poisoned. That night they took blood samples from me, determined I wasn't poisoned, so I didn't know what it was. But a couple of days later, they called and told me that I was pregnant."

Stan's face twisted as new tears reddened his eyes. "An answered prayer," he said. "Funny, I never dreamed it would be answered quite this way."

"Me, either," Celia said. "But it's gonna be all right."

"How can you say that? They think you tried to kill me."

"But *you* don't think I tried to kill you, and that's the most important thing," she said. "Stan, God already knows who's doing this. It's gonna be all right. I promise."

"But I don't want you in here," he said. "I don't want you in jail. This place was built for criminals, not for my wife."

"I know how you feel. I'd feel the same way if you were in here. But Stan, it's really okay. I'm spending all my time soaking up the Bible. I needed this time. As long as I'm in here, I'm safe, and maybe you are, too. If somebody's trying to set me up, they can't do it while I'm in jail."

He breathed in a deep shuddering sigh. "Celia, I would have done anything to keep this from happening."

"So would I," she said. "But right now all we can do is try to figure out what's going on. The best thing you can do for me is to get plenty of rest and get well. We're gonna have a lot to do over the next nine months."

He laughed softly. "Yeah, I guess we are." He thought of the nursery they were planning to add on to their little house when she got pregnant, how he was going to do most of the work himself. The wallpaper they'd picked out, the little sleigh crib they had their eye on . . . He thought of all the decisions—pink, or blue, or yellow, or green . . . He thought of that camcorder he was going to have to buy . . . and then he thought of the fact that his wife might have to stay in jail until the trial that could take forever to come about. That this baby could come home from the hospital without its mother. He couldn't stand the thought.

"Look at me, Stan," she whispered. "We've got to trust in the Lord. He gave us this baby. He's not going to forsake us now. David said the timing was all wrong, that it wasn't fair to the child, that I should have an abortion, like that would be more fair—"

"An *abortion?*"

"He doesn't understand. He doesn't know that God's timing isn't flawed. But this is our baby, no matter how or when God gave him to us."

He pressed his forehead against hers and closed his eyes. Again, her simple faith astounded him. He had once believed he had that kind of faith, but now he wasn't so sure. She slid her arms around his neck again, and he held her as tightly as his weakness would allow.

Finally, Sid ambled back to the cell door and rapped on the bars. "Come on, Stan. I can't stand here all day."

"Then leave us," Stan said.

"I can't do that, man."

Reluctantly, Stan got up and kissed his wife, wiped the tears from her face. "I'll be back soon, and I'm gonna have some answers," he said.

"Remember one thing," she whispered. "The battle's not ours, but the Lord's. He'll fight it for us."

Her faith had always been so absolute, and now he found himself grateful for it. She was right, and in the deepest part of his soul, he knew it was true.

Walking away and leaving her in that cell was the hardest thing he had ever done, but he vowed as he did that he would get her out as soon as God permitted.

• • •

Sid walked Stan and T.J. back out to the car and helped him get in. "You get back on home and rest now."

Stan knew that he'd pushed the limits of his energy level, and the only thing he could do was go home and collapse in bed for a while. But as he rested his head on the back of his seat, he looked up at Sid. "I'm calling a meeting for tonight."

Sid frowned. "A meeting? What you mean, man?"

"A meeting," Stan repeated. "My house, seven o'clock." His words were heavy, labored.

"Who you want at this meeting?"

"You, Vern, Jim, Jill, Gus, the prosecutor, and whoever else is involved in this case in any way."

"Man, you can't get involved in this. You're too close. It's too personal."

"Consider it an interview as part of the investigation," Stan said. "Your star witness wants to talk. Will you be there, or won't you?"

"Yeah, I'll be there, but I can't speak for nobody else. I mean, Vern ..."

"Tell him to bring the rest of the snapshots he got from following Celia yesterday. I want to see every last one of them."

Sid shrank back. "What you tryin' to do? You tryin' to get in the way of this investigation?"

"Nope. I'm trying to see that it's done right."

"Man, he was straight."

"Well, it's funny that he'd pick that one shot out of the entire meeting."

"What do you think, man, that he's in on some kinda conspiracy to cover up? You suspectin' me, too, now?"

"No."

"Man, you know we're good cops. You know we're doin' a good job."

"All I know is my wife is sitting in jail for something she didn't do. My house. Seven o'clock." With the last bit of energy he had, he pulled the door shut. Sid straightened and stepped back on the curb.

"Home?" T.J. asked.

"Home," Stan said.

"Man, your parents called the station two or three times to see what you were doing and when you're coming home."

"I'm a big boy," Stan said. "They'll get used to it."

He sank his head back onto the neck rest and thought how weary he was of all these people who didn't have a clue. He only hoped he could set them straight before much more time passed.

• • •

Jill was in her office when Stan called. She could hear the weariness in his voice, but he pressed on, nonetheless.

"Jill, I'm calling a meeting at my house for tonight at seven o'clock," he said.

Jill frowned. "A meeting? What for?"

"I want everybody who's involved in this case to get together. I just came from seeing Celia. I also saw Lee Barnett today."

"Stan! Aren't you supposed to be in bed?"

"Things have to be done, Jill. They're botching the whole investigation. Can you be there or not?"

"Of course, Stan. Of course I'll be there. You saw Celia? Stan, did you two talk? Do you—?"

"I know she's innocent," he said. "I want to get her out as soon as possible."

"So what's this meeting about?"

"We're going to put our heads together and figure out what's going on," he said. "And then we're going to make a plan."

"What kind of plan?"

"I don't know yet," Stan said. "But something to draw the killer out. We've got to figure out who this is before Celia has to suffer anymore."

Chapter Fifty

Stan was feeling weaker than ever when seven o'clock rolled around. His mother fussed around him as if he were a child. She had come close, at least twice, to calling everyone and canceling the meeting. But when he'd been adamant to the point of asking her to leave if she couldn't tolerate his actions, she'd settled down.

Now he sat with his feet up in the recliner in his living room, his head resting back on the chair. He'd had little appetite, though he'd forced himself to eat something, just so his mother would be satisfied.

When the doorbell rang, his mother answered. Jill breezed in. "Am I the first one here?"

"Yes," Hannah said. "Jill, I wish you could talk him out of this. It's madness. He's not up to having people over ..."

"Mother!" Stan snapped, and she decided to shut up and leave the room

Jill stood in front of him, looking down at him with concern. "Stan, how are you feeling?"

"I'm okay."

"We really don't want you to wind up back in the hospital. We're so thankful that you've been able to come home."

"I said I'm okay."

His tone warned her to change the subject, so she set her briefcase down and took the seat next to him. "I went by a little while ago to see Celia."

His tone changed. "You did?"

"Yeah. Her spirits were so much higher than the last time I saw her, thanks to your visit today."

Stan's mother reappeared from the kitchen, a horrified look on her face. "Stan, you went to see Celia? In *jail*? Is that where you were?"

"That's right."

"Stan, what were you thinking?"

"That I wanted to visit my wife."

Thankfully, the doorbell rang again before Hannah could react, and flustered, she went to open it. Sid Ford walked in, followed by Vern and Chief Shoemaker. A few minutes later, Gus Taylor, the prosecutor, showed up.

"We're all here," Sid said. "What you want to talk about?"

He invited them all to sit, then he dropped his footrest and forced himself to sit up straight. "The reason I called this meeting," he said, "is that there are some things we all need to get to the bottom of."

Trying to take the lead, Jim shifted in his seat. "Stan, I know that things are hard for you right now. It must be terrible to be told that your own wife may have been involved in your murder attempt. But you gotta know that we're doing everything we can."

"No, you're not," Stan said matter-of-factly. "I know absolutely that you aren't doing everything you can. The only thing you've managed to do so far is to torment my wife. There's still a killer out there, and nobody's doing a blasted thing to find him."

"Stan, we've got a ton of evidence," Gus said.

"Yeah, let's talk about that evidence," Stan said, breathing hard. "Vern, that meeting you saw between Barnett and my wife. Tell us about it, why don't you?"

Vern looked uncomfortable. "Well, you know, I was followin' her like I was told. We were doin' it 'cause you asked us to."

"Don't change the subject. Just answer the question."

Vern looked offended. "Well, I didn't know I was in a courtroom."

Stan's eyes drilled into him, waiting for him to answer.

"Just what I told you. I was followin' her, she went to visit Lee Barnett, and I took some pictures."

"I want to see the rest of the pictures on that roll of film," Stan said.

"I told him to bring 'em," Sid said.

Vern pulled the pictures out of his pocket and shuffled through them. "There aren't any that are very helpful in the case. I don't know why—"

"Just give them to me," Stan said. Jill got up and moved her chair closer to him as he flipped through them. It was all so clear, in context. He could see the fury on Celia's face now, the tears, the hands balled into fists. He could see her talking through her teeth in outrage. He could see the blurred arm as she slapped him . . .

"Vern, Sid . . ." He took a long breath and tried to steady his voice. "Why didn't you flash any of *these* pictures in my face when I was in the hospital? These pictures that would have shown that she didn't go there for some kind of romantic tête-à-tête."

"I showed you what I considered evidence, Stan."

Sid shook his head. "Man, I saw them pictures before. They don't mean nothin'. So they could have been havin' a fight."

"Or she could have gone there for the very reason she said she did," Stan said. "To pin Lee Barnett down about what he's doing in town and whether he tried to kill me. These pictures bear that out."

"You don't find it the least bit suspicious that she went to him in the first place?" Gus asked.

"Stan, I know this is the last thing you want to believe," Jim threw in. "I know it's as painful as all get-out. But you're not thinking clearly. You're sick, and you're hurt, and if you were back at work doing this same investigation on somebody else's attempted murder, I guarantee you you'd make the same assumptions they've made."

"I wouldn't do the smorgasbord approach to collecting evidence," he said. "Picking and choosing a little here ... a little there ... disregarding all the evidence that doesn't support my theory. That's shoddy police work, Jim, and you know it."

The plump man got up, unable to stay seated. He rubbed his belly as if it burned and paced across the room. "Look, Stan, I've taken a personal interest in this case because it's you. You know I don't usually get involved in investigations. But somebody tried to kill a police officer, and I'll be cursed if I'm not gonna follow the most obvious trail, no matter who that leads us to."

"I feel the same way," Gus said.

Jill sprang to her feet, facing off with him. "What if the most obvious trail is just that—obvious—because someone wants it to be? Gus, what if the killer has some perverted reason for wanting to see Celia locked up for the rest of her life? I mean, he's done it once before already, but she got off. What if he's carefully laid a trail—the arsenic in the attic, the checks to Barnett, the letter from Celia."

"And the letter left under my door today," Stan added.

"What letter?" Sid asked.

Stan spoke up. "The letter that was signed Lee Barnett, only it wasn't his handwriting."

"Maybe it was a for-real letter, man. Let me see it."

"No," Stan said. "Just think, Sid. You know Celia. Does she seem stupid to you?"

"No. I can't say she does. A little looney, maybe, in light of all this, but not stupid."

"Then why would she do such stupid things? Why would Barnett?"

"Man, you don't wanna go there. Barnett's so stupid that he gets drunk at Joe's Place every night and spouts off at the mouth about everything in his head. Tried to pick Issie Mattreaux up last night. Everybody who was in Joe's Place is talkin' about it. That's how stupid he is."

Stan didn't know how to counter that. If Lee Barnett could have proved to have some self-control, some savvy, some sense, maybe they would listen. But Barnett obviously wasn't helping any.

Jill looked down at him, as if waiting for a comeback, but he found himself without one. What now? Where did they go from here?

"Look, I have an idea," Jill said, turning back to the others. "It's the best one I've been able to come up with to draw the real killer out, and if it's Celia, even prove that it's her."

"Celia?" Stan shot back. "You're her lawyer. You're supposed to believe her!"

"I do," she shouted over him. "Just listen. This will satisfy everybody. Those of us who think she's innocent will be able to identify the real killer, and those of you who think she's guilty will be able to prove she is if she is."

"What?" Gus asked skeptically.

She sat down, and looked down at her feet, and Stan became aware that she wasn't at all sure of her idea. Still, she went on.

"It's kind of far-fetched, but just hear me out, okay?"

"Shoot," Jim said. "We don't have to go for it."

"No, you don't. Not unless you're serious about doing the right thing." No one said anything in response, so she leaned forward and went on. "For the moment, let's assume that Celia is innocent, and that there's a killer out there trying to set her up for a second time. He can't act while Celia's in jail, right? I mean, if he attempts to kill Stan again while she's locked up, it's clear to everyone that she couldn't be the culprit. Am I right?"

The others in the room looked at her with dull eyes. "We're not letting her out, if that's what you're getting at," Gus said.

"Just listen," Jill went on. "On the flip side of that, if she were by some chance guilty—"

Stan groaned and shook his head.

"—then she still can't act until she's out. So either way, we'll never be able to be absolutely sure who the killer is as long as she's in jail. Now, I know that Celia has to stay in jail, that she's been denied bond. Believe me, I realize that. But there is one scenario in which she could be let out for a couple of days. If she had a death in the family, the judge would probably let her out for the funeral."

"You gon' kill somebody in her family so she can get out for a day?" Sid asked.

Jill shot him a murderous look. "Right, Sid. I thought we'd just shoot her mother so we could get on with things. Give me a break."

"Well, what else are you suggestin'?"

"I'm suggesting that we *stage* someone's death. Specifically, Aunt Aggie's. That we make it look like Aunt Aggie had a heart attack and died. Do the obituary, get a coffin, have a funeral, the works. The only people who would know about it are those of us in this room, Aunt Aggie, and the judge, who would have to agree because I couldn't lie to him."

"Aunt Aggie's on Celia's side. She'd do anything to get Celia off."

"That's because she's certain she's innocent. If I told her this would prove it, and draw out the killer, I guarantee you she'd go along with it. But just in case, you could post a guard to be with her twenty-four hours so she doesn't tip Celia off."

"I don't get it," Stan said. "How would this help?"

"If we could get her out of jail for one night, and make sure word got out, then it's possible the killer will try again. It would be his perfect opportunity to seal her fate. Or, if it's Celia, and she's dead set on killing Stan, as you seem to think—so desperate that she would have gone into his hospital room and changed his IV bag, knowing she'd get caught—then she'll try again. Either way, we win. When the killer strikes, you'll have people there waiting for him ... or her."

There was dead silence in the room as each of the men contemplated the idea. Finally, Sid spoke up. "What about Stan? How does he figure into all this?"

"We'd hide him," she said. "Use a decoy. Put somebody in his bed, fill the house with guards. Tell people he's not well enough to attend the funeral. Celia still couldn't go near him because of the court order. Meanwhile, he would be safely hidden where no one could get to him."

"So we're gonna scam the whole town?" Jim asked. "Make them all think Aunt Aggie died? The mayor'll have my hide. The fire department'll tar and feather us when they find out the truth. Not to mention how Aunt Aggie'll react."

"Aunt Aggie loves Celia," Stan said. "She'll do anything to help her. But I'm not so crazy about Celia having to grieve Aunt Aggie's death. She's had too much on her, and now there's the pregnancy. I don't want her to face any added stress."

"Pregnancy?" Gus asked. "What do you mean—"

"My wife is pregnant!" he said. "And if you baboons weren't so intent on this witch hunt, you'd have noticed that she's throwing up constantly."

Jim looked at Sid. "Did you know about this?"

Sid shrugged. "Not till this afternoon when I saw her barfin'."

"She said something about it yesterday," Vern said. "When I was dragging her out of his hospital room, but I figured she was just blowing smoke."

"I just found out yesterday, myself," Jill said. "She asked me to keep it to myself so the media wouldn't have a field day with it."

"Why wouldn't she want the press to know, if it's Stan's baby?" Vern suggested. "I mean, if she has nothing to hide—"

"Vern?" Stan cut in.

"Yeah?"

"Why don't you shut up?"

Vern looked wounded.

Stan turned back to the others. "As I was saying . . . she'd grieve. Hard. I don't want her to have to go through that."

"Celia will be all right," Jill assured him. "Please, Stan. It's the only answer I can see, unless the killer does something on his own to convince these guys that it's not Celia. You got any better ideas?"

Stan didn't. He rubbed his eyes, wishing God would miraculously expose the criminal and relieve Celia of all of this. But maybe that wasn't how God intended to work.

"What do you say, guys?" she asked.

Jim looked from Gus to Sid. Gus nodded, and Sid shrugged. "Talk to the judge, Jill," Gus said. "If Louis goes along with it, I will."

"I'll talk to him tonight," she said. "I'll go to his house." She looked back at Stan, her eyes dancing. "I think this will work, Stan."

Somehow, Stan thought the solution might just cause more problems.

Chapter Fifty-One

Judge Louis DeLacy paced across the brick floor of his country kitchen, his hands crammed into the pockets of his baggy jeans. He stared down at the brand new Nikes he wore, frowning as he listened to Jill's plan. He didn't react until she had finished.

Finally, he shoved up the sleeves of his sweatshirt and focused on her.

"I like Celia," he said. "I've been sick about having to put her in jail. And with what you've told me about her pregnancy ..." He shook his head and ran his fingers through his salt and pepper hair. "I don't like having a pregnant woman in jail. It's a touchy situation. But I have to be objective, Jill, and I can't make special exceptions for people just because I know them or go to church with them."

"Louis, I'm not asking you to make a special exception," Jill said. "I'm asking you to do what you'd do for anybody who's in jail and has a death in the family. It's routine for you to give weekend passes for funerals."

"I give weekend passes to those who have to go out of town to attend the funeral," he said. "And it depends on the crime. I don't give them to people charged with attempted murder."

"Celia is not a murderer, Louis. You know that. I'm just trying to prove it. Trust me. I won't let her out of my sight. And the cops aren't going to let her out of their sight, either. You know she can't do anything. But if we're lucky, we can prove whether she's innocent or guilty."

He went to the coffee pot that had just finished perking and poured it into two cups. He handed one to Jill and sipped thoughtfully.

"I could let her out for the funeral," he said, "but as for spending the night, I just don't think that's necessary."

"None of it's necessary, since no one's really dead. That's the whole point! If she doesn't spend the night, then it's not likely that the killer is going to strike. If she's only out for a two-hour period . . . don't you see? He has to do something that can be blamed on her."

"But what excuse can I give for letting her out overnight when the funeral is right here in town? There'll be an uproar."

"Since when did you care more about what people think, than about justice?"

Louis shot her a look. "This isn't about justice. It's about a deception."

"It's about a deception that *leads* to justice," Jill said. "We're trying to make sure the real killer is found." Abandoning her coffee, she got up and moved closer to him. She leaned on the counter next to him and lowered her voice for impact. "Louis, I believe with all my heart that Celia is innocent and that the killer is out there, waiting for another chance to set her up. Stan believes it, too, and it's his life that's at stake. Come on, Louis, please. If you've ever trusted me, if you've ever seen any wisdom at all in me, if you've ever believed that I have good instincts, *and you know I do*, please trust me on this."

He puffed his cheeks and blew out his frustration. "So what day are you proposing to do this?"

Jill's heart leapt. Was he about to grant permission? "As soon as possible. We'd have to set it all up with Aunt Aggie, get everything in place. Maybe tomorrow?"

He thought for a moment longer, then breathed a laugh. "Aunt Aggie'll never go for it. Who would? Who would want to convince the whole town that they're dead when they aren't?"

"She'll get a kick out of it," Jill said, her eyes dancing. "Come on. If she doesn't go for it, we won't do it. But I'll convince her."

Louis grinned and turned back to the counter to shovel some sugar into his cup. "Somehow I think you could."

Her eyes sparkled. "Then you'll agree to it?"

Again, silence passed as he considered it. "I guess so," he said finally. "I don't know any other way to put an end to all this craziness. Let's just hope it works."

After getting Louis's order for Celia's weekend pass, Jill headed for Aunt Aggie's house. David answered the door.

"Hi, David," Jill said, walking into the house. "Is Aunt Aggie here?"

"Sure," he said. "She just got back from the fire station." He stuck his head in the kitchen and called for her, then turned back to Jill. "Any news?"

"No," she said, as though disappointed. "None at all."

"I saw Celia a couple of hours ago," he said. "She seemed okay. Apparently Stan's on her side now."

"Yeah, it really buoyed her spirits."

Aunt Aggie rustled in wearing a hot pink wind suit. "Jill, come in. You got news?"

"No, Aunt Aggie. I'm afraid not." She considered telling both of them about the plan, but somehow feared that David, the more practical of the two, might not go along with it. She couldn't take that chance. "Listen, I was just at Stan's a little while ago, and he would like to see you, if you have time."

"Stan? Sure I got time," Aunt Aggie said. "He wanna see me now? This late?"

Jill looked at her watch. She hadn't realized it was almost nine. "Now would be good, if you have some time. His sleep schedule's a little messed up. I figure we can humor him if you're not too tired."

"Lemme get my purse." She headed back into the kitchen, then reemerged quickly. "David, I won't be long."

"So what he wanna talk to me about?" Aunt Aggie asked as they headed out to the car.

"About Celia," Jill said.

Aunt Aggie got in and Jill went around to the other side. "'Course about Celia," the old woman said. "But what? Is somethin' happenin'?"

Jill pulled out of the driveway and looked over at the woman who waited so anxiously to hear what was going on. "Actually, Aunt Aggie, I lied to get you out of the house. We're not really going to see Stan. I had something I needed to discuss with you, and I didn't want to do it in front of David."

"What you got to say to me you can't say in front of T-David?" Aunt Aggie asked.

"Oh, it's not David. It's just that I promised this would be very secretive. We have a plan, Aunt Aggie."

"A plan?"

Jill pulled her car over to the side of the road and regarded the old woman. "Aunt Aggie, I've thought of a plan that will draw the real killer out and clear Celia. There's just one catch. I need your help."

"You got it," the old woman said. "I'll do anything it takes to find out who that killer is and clear my Celia."

"I thought you would," she said. "But it's a lot to ask. An awful lot."

"I *said* I'd do anything."

Jill braced herself. "You're gonna have to die."

The look on the old woman's face would have been comical if they hadn't been dealing with such a serious subject. "Say what?"

"Not really die," Jill clarified. "Just *pretend* to die."

"I'm sorry, Jill, I ain't follerin' you."

She tried to think of a better way to explain it. "Aunt Aggie, what we need to do is to pretend that you've died suddenly of a heart attack. All we have to do is tell key people at Joe's Place, the fire department, and the beauty shop, and the next thing we know it'll be all over town. We start making funeral arrangements, get a coffin—"

"Wait a minute!" Aunt Aggie shrieked. "You're scarin' me."

"I know, Aunt Aggie," Jill said, softening her voice. "I'm just trying to get to the good part."

"Thank goodness you don't think *that's* the good part."

Jill almost laughed. "Aunt Aggie, the judge is going to give Celia a pass for two days, one night. When she gets out, we're counting on the killer coming out and trying to make another attempt that Celia can be blamed for, at which point, we'll have plenty of police officers waiting to arrest him. The flip side is that *they* believe *Celia* did it. They figure that if she had any intention of killing Stan, she'd probably try it while she had the chance."

"She didn't kill nobody!"

"I know that, Aunt Aggie. And the truth is, she'd be stupid to try the two days she's out of jail, but they're thinking she's crazy, anyway, and she might try. Anyway, I've convinced them to try this. It's the only answer."

"Well, we ain't gon' tell Celia I'm dead, are we?"

"Yes, we are."

"No! We can't do that. It'll break her heart. No, I won't let you tell her that."

"Aunt Aggie, she has to believe she got a bona fide weekend pass or no one's gonna believe that she's really innocent. We have to let them think she has the opportunity to act, and if she's a murderer, she really will. What I know will happen is that the real killer will realize this is another opportunity to make it look like Celia did it, and he'll act. We'll be able to catch him, Aunt Aggie. Once and for all."

Aunt Aggie thought about that for a moment. "So you say they gon' be a funeral?"

"Yes. The whole works. We have to make it look real."

She sat staring out into the night for several moments. "I want to go to the funeral," she said.

Jill frowned. "Aunt Aggie, you can't be there. It's your funeral."

"I want to hide someplace and watch," she said. "I always wondered what my funeral'd be like. Want to see it for myself."

"Aunt Aggie, that's ridiculous. I don't think you want to be there and see Celia crying and the firemen grieving—"

Aunt Aggie's chin came up. "I ain't doin' it 'less I can be there."

Jill gaped at her. "Aunt Aggie, are you serious?"

"Serious as a heart attack," Aunt Aggie said. "That is what I'm gon' have, ain't it? A heart attack?"

Jill almost chuckled. "I guess." She sighed. "Well, if you insist, I guess it's okay to have you there, provided we let Sid and Jim know. And you can't tell anyone, do you understand? Not even David. Not Celia's parents. Nobody. They have to all think you're dead."

"When can I come back to life?" she asked.

"As soon as the two days are up, we'll announce to the world that Aunt Aggie's alive. It'll be like a resurrection. People will be so happy they'll be rejoicing in the street. The fire department will probably shut down in celebration."

Aunt Aggie grinned. She liked that idea. "It will be a surprise, won't it?"

"Absolutely."

"Maybe people start 'preciatin' an old woman."

"Without a doubt," Jill said.

Aunt Aggie looked up at her with playful eyes. "Well, let's get to it," she said. "My heart's startin' to feel a little weak."

"Good, Aunt Aggie," Jill said. "By this time tomorrow it should give completely out."

Chapter Fifty-Two

The sting was set up by the following day, and Aunt Aggie was told that her time had come. Jill had hoped to have her drop dead in a private place, where she could be pronounced dead without the aid of firemen, police officers, and paramedics, who could tell in a moment that there was nothing wrong with the old woman, who had more strength and energy than the average thirty-year-old.

Jill had visions of calling the funeral director and telling him that they needed a coffin and funeral arrangements, but that she would take care of the body herself, thank you very much. It almost seemed funny now that she had ever believed she could pull this off. Finally, Sid Ford convinced her to bring the funeral director in on the sting. There was just no way around it. Otherwise, Aunt Aggie would be found out the moment the mortician found a pulse.

To make matters worse, the private death that Jill had envisioned threatened to go no further than her imagination, for Aunt Aggie had visions of much grander things. She wanted to drop dead in the town square, on the corner of Jacquard and Purchase Streets, have a huge fuss made over her, and have all the protective services show up on the scene. She wanted to go out with red and blue lights flashing around her, sirens blaring, and wailing and gnashing of teeth. It had taken some doing for Jill to convince her that they could never pull that off.

"You can't will your heart to stop beating for show, Aunt Aggie," Jill reminded her. "The paramedics will know you're not in arrest."

"Aw, I could die on the way to the hospital," Aunt Aggie said. "Nobody'd know no different."

"The paramedics would know," Jill insisted. "You really can't fool them."

"I can die in the hospital, then!"

"Aunt Aggie, you'll be surrounded by doctors. They're not stupid. They know when somebody's dead!"

Aunt Aggie looked as if Jill was spoiling all her fun. "Well, then, what you wanna do? Jes' have me die quiet without nobody knowin' about it?"

"Aunt Aggie, *everybody* will know about it. That's the point!"

At long last, she had convinced Aunt Aggie to die in Slidell, presumably on her way to a doctor's appointment regarding the chest pains she'd been having. That way, the paramedics of Newpointe couldn't ream Jill about not calling them in to help. They could all assume they *had* called an ambulance and tried to revive her. Sid even managed to bring a discreet Slidell surgeon in on the scam to pronounce her dead. The mortician, who served as the town's medical examiner as well, took care of the death certificate. No one knew any better, and they had managed to evade any direct questions about the death. Now it was time to tell Celia.

Jill went to the police station and paced in front of the door down to the jail, trying to think of the words she would use, the level of emotion she would muster. How could she spare Celia any more pain than necessary? She shook her head. It just wasn't possible. She tried to think of the realistic order in which they would have done things, had Aunt Aggie really died. She would have told David, first of all. He was the one staying in her home, expecting her to return. She hadn't done that. She caught her breath and decided that she was messing this up already. Quickly, she started back up the stairs and across the police room to the front door.

Sid stopped her. "You done it already?"

"No," she whispered. "I just remembered that I haven't told David. I've got to do this right or it won't look real."

"You ain't wimpin' out, are you?"

"No, of course not," she said. "I'll be back shortly."

He nodded and looked toward the door to the basement jail cells. "Man, I don't know about you, but I'm a little nervous."

"Yeah, I am, too," Jill said. "This feels really wrong, even though it was my idea."

"Yeah, and pretty soon you got to lie to the preacher."

Jill felt nauseous. "Look, I'm gonna go tell David, and then I'll bring him back here with me, to break the news to Celia, all right?"

"Okay," he said.

"Hopefully we can hold off letting anyone else know until they've been told."

Jill hurried out to her car, cranked it. Dan Nichols was outside washing the pumper, and he looked over at her and waved. She gave a distracted wave back.

He ambled over to the car, but she cranked it anyway, too preoccupied to talk.

"What's goin' on?" he asked.

She couldn't look him in the eye.

"Are you okay?"

"Yeah, I'm fine. Look, I've got some stuff I've got to take care of. I'm kind of in a hurry."

He looked crestfallen, then quickly rallied and that prideful look passed over his face as though he couldn't care less. "Sure, whatever. Talk to you later."

She rolled up the window and pulled out of her parking space, her heart sinking further. How many lies would she have to tell before this weekend was over? She didn't know if setting Celia free was going to be worth it all. Was it ever right to lie?

She headed to Aunt Aggie's house and pulled into the drive-way. The old woman's Cadillac was still parked in the parking lot at Jill's office. David was here, though, probably waiting for Aunt Aggie to get home. Again, she felt nauseous, but she pushed it away. A lawyer's job was never easy, never cut and dried, never particularly clean. It had been her idea, after all. Whispering under her breath, "Lord forgive me," she got out of the car and headed to the door. Tears were coming to her eyes already, and it was no act. She couldn't believe she was about to hurt so many people.

The pain they were going to feel was already welling inside of her. Again, she pushed it down and knocked on the front door.

• • •

David was stunned by the news. For a moment, he just stared at Jill, his face a portrait of shock. He looked around him, as if he didn't know what to do with himself. "I can't believe this."

"I know. It was a shock to us all." Jill hated herself as she muttered the words, but decided she was going to join the Newpointe theater as soon as all this was over. She was a natural.

"They didn't try to revive her? Give her CPR? Anything?"

"They did," Jill said. "David, her death was instant. She didn't respond."

"But they could have defibrillated her. They could have done something!"

She looked at her feet. "It was too late."

David sank back into his chair, his eyes glazing over.

"David, I really hated to come and tell you this," she said. "I guess since Celia's in jail, you're the one who's going to have to make all the arrangements."

He just looked at her, his eyes vacantly searching her face. Did he suspect that she was lying? If he did, she would have to confess, tell him the truth. But that could be a mistake. The fewer people who knew about the sting, the better it would work out.

"Look, I'd be happy to handle all the funeral arrangements for you."

"No," he said. "No, I can do it." He shook his head and looked at the telephone. "I guess I need to call my parents."

"Of course," she said.

He got up. "So many things to do. Where should I begin?"

"I guess with the funeral."

"All right. Do they have her … her …"

He struggled with the word "body," and Jill relieved him of it. "Yes, they have her there now."

He closed his eyes. He was getting pale. She wondered if he could manage this alone. "Well, I guess I'll call them, make an appointment. I guess that's what you do when this kind of thing happens." He sank back into his chair again. "I never thought Aunt Aggie would die. She seemed so invincible."

"None of us is invincible," she said.

He glanced over at her. "Have you told Celia?"

"No, actually, I was hoping you would go with me to do that."

He rubbed his face with both hands, then his eyes, and looked at her over his fingertips. "Yeah, I guess that would be best, wouldn't it?"

He drew in a deep breath and got to this feet. "It was all that rich cooking, you know. That's what did it."

"Aunt Aggie seemed healthy."

"But that rich cooking. I've tried to tell her for years."

Jill looked down at her hands.

He shook his head, then slapped his hands on his thighs. "Well, I guess we'd better tell Celia before somebody else does."

"Yeah. I don't think too many people know yet, but we don't want her to hear it from anyone else."

"She won't even be able to come to the funeral. This is just too much."

"I've already spoken to the judge. He's going to let her have a weekend pass," she said. "They often do that in the case of a funeral."

"Yeah, but with a murder charge?"

"I convinced him."

"Well, that's something." He looked around the room as if trying to collect his thoughts, then shook his head sadly. "Let's go and get this over with."

Chapter Fifty-Three

Jill saw the look of apprehension on Celia's face as she and David waited for the jail door to be unlocked. So far, her performance had been Oscar caliber, she told herself. David had bought into it, and already Celia looked as if she were fighting Armageddon in her heart. Did she think she'd brought her news of the end of the world?

Tears were already welling in Celia's eyes, and she took a step back.

"Celia, we have something to tell you," Jill said.

"No," she said, sucking in a sob. "No, don't."

"Celia—"

"It's Stan, isn't it?" Celia blurted.

Relieved that the news at least wasn't as bad as that, depending on one's perspective, Jill shook her head. "No, honey, of course not. Stan's doing fine. In fact, they can't keep him in bed."

It was as if a black cloud suddenly floated away and the sun shone through again. She let out a huge breath of relief and the tears began to roll down her cheeks. "From the looks on your faces, I thought you were going to tell me he's dead. I just don't know what I'd do ..."

Jill hated to bring that cloud back, so she focused on the floor, trying to find the words she had rehearsed earlier today. Somehow, they seemed inadequate and cruel.

The shadow passed back over Celia's face. "What is it?" She turned her eyes from Jill to David. "David, something's wrong. What?"

David drew in a deep breath. "Celia, I don't know how to tell you this."

"Just say it," she said, almost angrily. "Spit it out. What's going on?"

"It's Aunt Aggie," Jill said.

"Aunt Aggie?" Celia repeated. "What—"

"Aunt Aggie died this morning."

"NO!" The word came out of her with such power that Jill took a step backward. Celia covered her head with her arms and began to wail as she fell down on her bed.

Tears burst into Jill's eyes. She had never hated herself so much. She went to the bed and tried to put her arms around Celia, but the small woman was moaning and sobbing and curling up into a ball, as if stretching to her full height was just too painful after such a blow.

"I'm sorry, Celia," Jill said over the moans. "So sorry."

Celia unfolded then and threw her arms around Jill, and clung to her as her body racked with pain.

"What happened?" she managed to squeak out.

David came closer to the bed, but looked awkward, inadequate. Jill realized that he, too, was grieving, and that this was probably just as hard for him. "She probably died the best way she could, Celia. She just had a heart attack and was dead instantly."

Celia let go of Jill and turned on her side, pulling her knees up to her chest as her arms covered her head again. A sound like that of a wounded animal came from her throat, and Jill almost considered backing out of the charade. Could she really go through with this and cause Celia such pain?

Suddenly Celia sprang up and slid off the bed, rushed to the toilet behind the partition in the cell. Jill heard her heaving into the commode. She followed her in and tried to help her.

When Celia had stopped throwing up, she sat on the floor and leaned back against the cold concrete wall. "It's my fault," she wept. "It's just as if I killed her myself."

Jill got down on her knees next to Celia and put an arm around her. "What do you mean?"

"It was the stress of all this stupid stuff! She couldn't take it. We thought she could take anything, but all the stress . . ."

She might have known that Celia would blame herself, but she hadn't anticipated it. "Celia, you couldn't do anything about that. None of this is your fault."

"She just . . . can't be gone! She . . . can't be!" Jill held her again for a long moment, and finally she got her to her feet and walked her back to the bed. David was leaned back against the wall now, hands in his pockets, looking as dismal as Celia seemed to feel.

"We've managed to get you a weekend pass for the funeral," Jill said finally. "David's making all the arrangements, but they're letting you out tomorrow. You can go to the funeral, spend the night at Aunt Aggie's, then come back the next morning."

The word *funeral* seemed to plunge Celia into deeper grief, and she lay back down and hugged her pillow to her face.

"You have to stay with me the whole time," Jill went on. "I swore to Louis that I wouldn't let you out of my sight."

Celia's shoulders shook as the pain rampaged through her.

Finally, she moved the pillow and turned on her back, looked up at the ceiling with wet, red eyes. "How's Stan taking it?" she whispered.

Jill looked at her vacantly for a moment. "I haven't told him yet. I wanted to tell you first."

She nodded. "Just break it to him easy, okay? He loves her, too, and he's suffered so much . . ." She broke down again, and finally, David came closer to her cot, as if trying to find a way to comfort her. Celia raised up and met him halfway. The two hugged.

"It's gonna be okay," he whispered.

"No, it's not," Celia muttered as she wept against his shoulder. "Aunt Aggie wasn't a Christian."

David didn't seem to know what to say to that.

After a moment, David let her go. "I have a funeral to arrange," he said. "You have any special requests?"

Celia couldn't answer.

"Maybe some of the firemen could speak about her?" Jill suggested. "They loved her so much."

"That's a good idea," David said. "We'll do that. Any special music?"

Celia threw up her hands. "I don't know."

"We'll think of something," Jill said.

"I want Nick to do the funeral," Celia offered suddenly. "She didn't have her own minister, and he knew her best."

"That's what I was thinking, too," Jill said.

She gazed at Celia, wishing she could ease some of the pain. But what would she say? *She'll only be dead a couple of days, Celia.* It was all ludicrous, yet it had to work.

As they left, Jill looked back over her shoulder through the bars that locked her friend in. Celia was on her side, clutching the pillow and weeping her heart out. Silently, Jill prayed that this cruel deception would somehow turn out for good.

• • •

When they had gone, Celia buried her face in the pillow as great sobs tore through her. She tried to pray, but the despair was too great, the grief too intense. She felt as empty and limp as a rag doll with no stuffing as she approached the throne of God. She had nothing to give, and no words to say. What did one say to the Lord about a loved one who didn't believe? She had failed. She had let Aunt Aggie down.

Why hadn't she tried harder to lead Aunt Aggie to Christ? Why hadn't she convinced the old woman of what she needed to do before she died? Why had she believed there was plenty of time left? But at the foot of that cross where her Savior hung for her failings, she found no condemnation, no judgment, no accusation. Instead, she felt the warm arms of God around her, holding her, whispering soothing words in her ear, letting her weep out her heart, offering his comfort. It was a phenomenon she hadn't experienced many times in her life. Usually when she went to God, she had supplications, petitions. Usually, she had problems and urgent requests. Hardly ever had she come to him speechless, without a word that she could offer, without anything of herself to give, without anything to ask. It was too late; Aunt Aggie was gone. What more was there?

Miraculously, God's comfort led to sleep, and she dozed on the flat mattress, numbing herself to the pain of Aunt Aggie's death.

Chapter Fifty-Four

The visitation for Aunt Aggie was at the Cain and Addison Funeral Home the night before the funeral, and Aunt Aggie insisted upon attending. Jill tried to talk her out of it, but the old woman would not be swayed. She wanted to see how people would take to her death, she said. She wanted to see who her real friends were.

The funeral director, who was in on the sting, was able to change her mind, however, for he had no place adequate to hide her where she could see and hear what was going on, without being seen and heard herself. Finally, she convinced Jill to set up a camcorder in the room, stuffed in a spray where no one could see it. Jill promised that if Aunt Aggie stayed away, she'd show her the video the moment visitation was over. Aunt Aggie had reluctantly agreed.

Now Jill sat with the old woman as they played back the hardest two hours of Jill's life, during which David and his and Celia's parents, along with various and sundry other relatives that no one in Newpointe had ever seen before, stood shaking hands of well-wishers and teary-eyed friends. Aggie stayed in Jill's house with her, and no one knew she was there. Outside, Vern sat in his unmarked car, watching to make sure Aunt Aggie didn't slip away to fill Celia in somehow.

"I can't believe they don't have no open casket," Aunt Aggie said. "Woman who preserves herself good as me at my age oughta have a viewin'."

Jill wondered if the woman had finally gone senile. "Aunt Aggie, if we opened the casket, they'd see that you weren't there."

Aunt Aggie's eyes danced with the possibilities. "I could be there," she said. "Matter of fact, that might be the best way t' tell what's goin' on. Lay up in that coffin and hear what folks is sayin' 'bout me."

"Aunt Aggie, they could see you breathing. What if someone touched you and you were warm?"

"I ain't been warm in ten years," she said. "I freeze to death most times. Ain't the circulation, though, cause these arteries ain't got no clogs. It's just my tempa-ture. Feel of me, see if that don't feel like death."

Jill took her hand and confirmed that it was, indeed, cold. "Aunt Aggie, what am I gonna do with you? I promise, at your next funeral, we'll open the casket."

Satisfied at that, Aunt Aggie sat back and watched some more of the video. The firemen were coming in with red eyes and noses, not knowing what to say to the people they'd never met before who represented Aunt Aggie's family. "They shoulda let Celia out for the visitation," she said. "So's I wouldn't be mourned over by a bunch of mealymouthed, greedy souls. Ain't seen most o' them in fifteen years. Ain't heard from 'em in ten. That one right there, old bat, she's my sister-in-law, Celia's *grandmere*. Turned away from Celia when all the others did. Crazy as a loon now, though. Don't know a shoe from a hat. What'd they do? Parked her in a nursin' home, waitin' for her to die. Don't know why they even brang her here."

Jill looked at her, stricken. She had wondered who the old woman was with the vacant eyes, and now she was disappointed to see how detached Aunt Aggie was from all of them. "Don't you care, Aunt Aggie? Haven't you missed her? Your own sister?"

"Nope. I hold grudges, Jill. I'll hold this one till I die."

Jill gazed at the screen. "I always wanted a sister."

The old woman grew quieter. "Still wish Celia was there."

"We talked about it, and didn't think it was appropriate, even if they had let her out a day early."

"Not appropriate to come to her Aunt Aggie's visitation?"

"Of course it would be appropriate for her to attend under any other circumstances, Aunt Aggie, but since half the town thinks of her as a killer, she just didn't think it would be very comfortable. Besides, she's really torn up about your death. It would be hard for her to be there."

Reminded of her niece's grief, Aunt Aggie's eyes misted over. "Bless her heart. I hate to put her through that."

"I hate it, too. Oh, boy, you have no idea how I hate it. The lies, the deceit . . . it's not my thing."

As the last of the visitors left the room, she heard the voices of the relatives that remained behind, milling around the small room. She heard the low voices of Celia's parents, and then David came over and put his arms on both their shoulders, hugged them tightly. Celia's mother was crying quietly.

"You'd almost think they *cared* I was dead," Aunt Aggie said. "But they're jes waitin' for probate."

"Do you think?" Jill asked.

"Can't be nothin' else," Aunt Aggie said. "They never picked up the phone to call me when I was alive."

Jill grinned at her use of the past tense. "It seems to me that you wouldn't have taken it real well if they had. Don't forget I was there the last time you spoke to Celia's mother. I wouldn't want to get on your bad side, Aunt Aggie. You do have a bite."

Aunt Aggie pshawed. "Aw, that's only 'cause I can't stand her."

Jill watched the woman in the video crying harder. "She obviously does care about you. Maybe she's not such a bad person."

Again, she harrumphed. "She's selfish and mean-spirited, and she don't care nothin' about her daughter. That says it all to me."

"What about when she was younger, before she had children? Did you two get along then?"

Aunt Aggie grew pensive, as if trying to remember. "We did," she said. "She was a cute little ole thing, and I loved her.

It wadn't till she turned her back on her own kin that I turned my back on her."

She watched as the camera recorded her niece and her husband wiping their eyes and crying quietly. "She's pretty," Jill said. "I can see where Celia gets her looks."

"Purty on the outside, maybe," Aunt Aggie said. "That's about it."

"You know, she didn't have to come for the visitation *or* the funeral. She didn't have to stand there listening to all the well-wishers. She could have just shown up at the last minute before the funeral, paid her last respects, and left."

"I tole you why she's here. Probate."

Jill didn't want to be quite that cynical. "Maybe David made her realize how much she needed to be here. Maybe he's working on a reconciliation between them and Celia."

"Maybe," Aunt Aggie said. "Reckon he's a good boy, after all."

"After all?"

"He's a little greedy. Cares a little too much about money. Means too much to him, all them things. Money never did make me no better 'n nobody else, but don't ever'body know that."

"Maybe now that you're supposedly gone, and everybody's grieving and hearts are broken, maybe this will be the start of something new. Maybe Celia's parents will come to see that she isn't guilty, and they'll reconcile, and you can let go of your grudge and forgive them . . ."

"I ain't holdin' my breath," the old woman said. "I wouldn't advise you to."

Chapter Fifty-Five

Celia avoided the second visitation that was held before the funeral the next morning. She was released from jail a couple of hours before, and went to Aunt Aggie's house to shower and change. The sight of the old woman's things—everything she loved—created a fresh void in her heart. She ached with the pain of it.

David was there with her, and Jill was staying in one of the guest rooms. Already, dozens of friends had brought food over, and the firemen had contributed greatly to the wealth of culinary delights. It seemed that they had appreciated her cooking for them so much, that now in her death, they felt they owed it to her to bring food for them. She wondered if they had realized that she was getting out of jail for the funeral, or if they expected David to eat it all alone, since her parents were staying in a hotel.

She wept in the shower as she got ready for the funeral, then threw up in the toilet as she got out. This grief wasn't good for the baby, she thought.

She looked in the mirror and saw how pale she was, saw the dark circles under her eyes. People would look at her and think she was certainly a murderer. If only Stan could be there. But that was one of the conditions of her release. She could have no contact with him while she was out. The idea upset her terribly. But there was nothing that could be done. Besides, she'd been told that Stan needed to rest, that he had no strength or energy to come to the funeral, anyway. She remembered how he had come to her cell just yesterday, how weak and breathless he'd been. She hoped he wasn't taking the death too hard.

She went downstairs and saw David pacing across the living room floor, back and forth, back and forth. It had been a trying time for him, she thought. He'd lost almost a week of work already, no small feat in a job as high-pressured as his, and had stood by her wholeheartedly now for Aggie's death. He'd had to take care of all the arrangements, all the food being delivered, all the flowers, all the well-wishers. She wondered if it was taking its toll on him.

"David, you look tired," she said from the staircase.

He turned back to her, stared at her for a moment. "*You* look like death warmed over. Are you sick again?"

"Just a little. It'll pass. It always does."

"You know, this isn't going to be easy," he said. "You have enough stress with the funeral and Stan and the murder charges, without all this nausea. Celia, I know you hate it when I bring this up. But be realistic. Think of your health. I checked, and I found out that Newpointe has a Planned Parenthood clinic."

She was too tired, too depressed, to realize what he was suggesting.

He sighed. "They could see you today, Celia. I could take you there, and at least that part of this ordeal would be behind you. You wouldn't have to worry about what was going to happen to a baby that might be born in prison . . ."

She stared at him, stricken, as if he'd just poured alcohol on an open wound. She touched her stomach. "David, this is your niece or nephew. How could you suggest that to me again?"

"Celia, a person can only take so much. You may think you're Wonder Woman, but you're not."

"I'm stronger than you think," she said. "And I trust God with this baby." Her mouth quivered with the words, and she turned back to the table to get her purse together. She swallowed a sob, then whispered, "Not another word about that, David. Not one more word."

He looked as if he didn't know if he could agree to that. "All right. I just hope you don't start throwing up at the funeral. It's going to be very hard, once you get there with the family—"

"I know," she told him. "I'm gonna get there, and Mom and Dad will either ignore me completely or comment on the gall it took for their killer daughter to show up for their aunt's funeral."

"They won't," he said. "I've already talked to them."

"Oh, then you expected it to happen, too?"

"Well, the thing about where you were gonna sit at the funeral . . . all that stuff."

Her expression crashed. "You mean they didn't want me to sit with the family at the funeral?"

He hesitated, as if he hadn't meant to spill the beans. "Look, I nipped it in the bud, okay? I let them know that you had more of a right to be there than they did. You were her favorite."

"I wasn't her favorite," she said. "I was just the one who needed her most."

"Yeah, Aunt Aggie was real big on need. She liked the way you needed her."

She didn't want to think about how adept Aunt Aggie had been at filling those needs.

Jill came down the stairs, dressed in black and wearing makeup for the first time in days. "Ready to go?" she asked.

Celia nodded and opened the door. Immediately, she was assaulted by a reporter and a photographer who stood on the front lawn. Quickly, she pulled back into the house and closed the door. "What are they doing here?"

"They must have heard you were getting out," David said. "They were at the funeral home last night, snaking around asking everyone questions about their opinions of these murder attempts."

"You're kidding! People were talking to them? My friends?"

"Celia, I don't know if you still have any friends in this town. Not any real ones, anyway. And yeah, a few were talking to them. It's in the paper today."

"Oh, no. Where is it?"

"You don't have time to read it," Jill told her. "Come on, Celia, we're just gonna have to walk through them. Just hold your head up and ignore them."

David opened the door again. She stepped out onto the porch. The camera began to flash again, and she turned her head and started toward the car.

"Celia! Is it true that your aunt died of arsenic poisoning?"

She swung around. *What?*

"Is it true that arsenic killed your aunt?"

She looked at David, then at Jill, as if wondering if the suggestion bore some truth. "No!" Jill said. "She died of a heart attack."

"That's what we were all told, but rumor has it that they're just calling it a heart attack to cover for the arsenic."

"And of course you're suggesting that I did it?" Celia asked.

"Did you?"

Amazed, she got into the car, slammed the door behind her, and locked it. David got in on the other side. Jill went to her own car.

"How could they think I could kill my poor dear aunt with arsenic?"

"Well, they think you killed your poor dear first husband with arsenic."

He was irritable, she could see, and she wrote it off to fatigue and stress. He'd had enough of this, and he hadn't deserved any of it. In the back of her mind, a niggling thought came. What if David was doubting her, wondering if she was guilty, questioning his support of her?

She wept silently as they drove to the funeral home and parked in the back. Already, the parking lot was full. Jill got out of her car and walked in with them. When Celia stepped into the hallway, she saw the dozens of people standing there. They all turned to look at her when she came in. She saw faces that used to be friendly, but this time they were hostile, and they turned away and began whispering. Jill gave her a hug and joined the crowd. Celia followed David into the family room, but was immediately confronted by her parents sitting on a bench across from the door.

She stopped cold. Their eyes met, and she felt the chill from both of them. "Mom, Dad?"

"Hello, Celia," her mother said, and her father only nodded.

It was as if they were strangers, she thought, as if her mother had never changed her diaper, patched her skinned knee, sung her a lullaby when she couldn't sleep. It was as if her father had never taught her to ride her bike or tie her shoes, or helped her with her geometry. As if her mother had never delighted in taking her shopping, or teaching her to put on makeup, or brushing her hair. She turned away, not willing to give them the satisfaction of seeing her cry. There were other relatives in the room, relatives she had seen occasionally over the years, and they, too, looked at her as if she were a malignancy in the midst of their family.

She thought of running back out into the hall, but she couldn't face those people again. She was trapped.

When Nick came in, he shot straight to her. "Celia, how are you?"

Relief flooded over her like a soothing tide. She reached out and hugged him desperately.

"I'm so sorry," he whispered in her ear. "So very sorry."

She turned her wet face up to him. "The worst part is that she didn't know Christ," she whispered. "I didn't work hard enough to lead her to him. I thought there was plenty of time."

"So did I," Nick said. "Believe me, I haven't slept a wink since I heard about her death. I've been beating myself up like you wouldn't believe. Don't do that to yourself. The truth is, it was her choice. We both tried."

She sucked in a sob. "But it's so tragic."

"That it is," he said. "This is gonna be the hardest funeral I've ever done."

He hugged her quickly again, then whispered in her ear. "Stan said to send you his love."

The words were like an injection of hope and promise, of joy and peace, and even comfort. "How's he doing?"

"He's doing well," he said. "He's really tired and weak, and the doctor apparently advised him to stay at home. I hear he got out a little too much yesterday and was seen around town a couple of places. It must have taken a lot out of him. The doctor warned him that he was gonna put him back in the hospital if he didn't start taking it easier." He looked at her with concerned eyes. "How are you doing?"

"I'm fine," she said. "Just a little tired. And my family . . . well . . . they're not too thrilled to have me here."

"Yeah, I know. I've kind of encountered that, already."

She hated the fact that her own preacher had to know of her family's indifference toward her. Nick let go of her and stepped toward her parents. "If you're all ready, the music has begun and all of the congregation are filtering in. If you don't mind, I'd like to lead us in a prayer."

Her parents were not praying people, she knew, but in a time like this, she supposed that everyone prayed. She wondered if they ever prayed for her.

They formed a circle, but it was a broken circle. No one was bound by held hands. Even their eyes did not meet. Nick led them in a prayer that was short, but poignant, and Celia found herself crying again, harder. She didn't know when the tears were ever going to end.

When it was time, they walked into the chapel and took their places in a secluded section of the room where people couldn't stare at them. She was thankful for that. She sat at the end of the row, next to David, with no one on the other side of her.

She wished for a Kleenex. Had Stan been here, he would have had some in his pocket. He always remembered to bring them to funerals and weddings, because he knew how easily she cried. He would have held her close and reminded her that she was loved. He would have helped unwind the knots in her stomach, and nursed the bruises on her heart. He would have made the pain easier to bear.

But he wasn't here, and no one had brought Kleenex for her. No one held her hand. No one offered comfort.

So she returned to the silent, strong arms of the Creator who'd comforted her last night in places too deep for human love to reach. And in his arms, she found hope and peace where she'd been certain there was none.

Chapter Fifty-Six

From up in the closed-off balcony of the funeral home that smelled like rotting wood and dust, Aunt Aggie sat watching the funeral. She had to sit at the back, in the shadows, so that Nick could not see her from the pulpit. Sid Ford stood by the balcony door, presumably to keep anyone from coming in and spotting Aunt Aggie, though Aggie felt sure he was mostly there to keep her under control, in case she got a notion to yell something down to the mourners. She had been here for hours, for they didn't want her to take the chance of being seen coming or going.

She could see the congregation through a lattice railing, though they couldn't see her. She could see the uniformed firemen designated as pall bearers sitting in the front row, and the others scattered around the room, wiping their own eyes. Someone from Celia's church sang a hymn that Aunt Aggie couldn't identify. She wondered if Jill had suggested it.

Mark Branning got up to say a few words, and Aunt Aggie leaned forward, listening hard. She didn't want to miss a syllable.

Mark wiped his eyes as he reached the podium, and he was quiet for a moment, as if trying to find his voice. "We all at Midtown fire station loved Aunt Aggie," he said. "She was one of the sweetest, most caring women we've ever known, and she was a heck of a cook."

She heard some soft chuckles around the room, and she smiled.

"Aunt Aggie didn't put up with much, but she was fiercely loyal to the people she loved. I respected that about her. I'm gonna miss her." His voice broke. "There's gonna be a huge void in this town. But I wanted to tell a few stories about the Aunt Aggie that I knew. Last summer, Aunt Aggie ..."

She heard a commotion somewhere in the congregation beneath her, and Mark's voice faded out. She fought the temptation to get up and lean over the balcony railing to have a look. Instead, she stood up in the shadows, straining to see. Several people were standing up, and she couldn't see who they were hovering around. Someone was sick.

"Uh ... excuse me." Mark's voice rippled with panic. "My wife ... will someone call our doctor, please?"

Mark dashed from the podium, and Nick took his place. "Allie seems to be in labor," Nick said. "We need to get her to the hospital."

Aunt Aggie caught her breath. Allie Branning had the gall to go into labor during her funeral? Couldn't she have waited just another hour? She wasn't due for another month, after all. She pushed the resentment back down, then told herself that was ridiculous. When a baby was ready to be born, it was ready to be born. Couldn't nobody stop it.

She saw Mark walking her out a side door, saw several people run out with them. Aunt Aggie sat back down, trying not to resent being upstaged.

After a few minutes, the crowd's roar died down, and Nick took over. "Well, I guess Mark won't be making those comments, after all. But I have some things to say. Aggie Gaston was a woman unlike any woman I've ever known," Nick began. "Everyone in town called her Aunt Aggie, though only Celia Shepherd was related to her."

Aunt Aggie smiled. It was brave how he'd mentioned Celia's name, even though he knew a murmur would follow. And it did.

"Aunt Aggie was a giver. She was one of the kindest, gentlest, most giving people that I've ever known. Twice a day, she brought meals to the firefighters on duty at Midtown. Why? Because she thought they needed what she called 'good eats.' She led a long, prosperous, contented life," he said.

She could see how carefully he was choosing his words. It was hard for a preacher to preach a funeral for someone who didn't believe. She almost felt sorry for him. Too bad they couldn't have had the sense to find an atheist to preach her funeral. Either an atheist or a liar, who could pretend they'd all see her again someday in heaven, if that's what they wanted to hear. But she supposed that wasn't done.

She wondered if this was gonna be one of those times when Nick was gonna look everybody in the eye and tell them what a pity it was that Aunt Aggie wasn't going to heaven. Would her death become the launch point for a fire-and-brimstone sermon?

"I wish Aunt Aggie could have known the abundant life offered in Jesus Christ," he said solemnly. "'Cause I think she would have been a glorious servant for the Lord. With her giving spirit, and her love for so many people, and the wisdom that came with her age, and her inner beauty—not to mention her outer beauty. I know that she could have made great strides in the kingdom of God."

"There he goes," she whispered to herself. The God stuff had to come sooner or later, she supposed.

"Her greatest sorrow in life," he said, "was when her dear niece Celia was accused of attempting to kill her husband. But Aunt Aggie needn't have worried," Nick went on, "because Celia has the peace of the Lord. And even though she was sitting in a jail cell all alone, she had the joy of the Lord, because she was in tune with him, and he was speaking to her.

"When I first heard about all the stuff with Celia and Stan," he said—as if he was talking to a room full of close friends—"I thought that it was possible that Celia was guilty. But then I went to see her, and I saw the Holy Spirit in her eyes, in her face, and I saw Jesus in her heart and in her attitude. I saw peace, the kind that someone who's entered into a new level of spirituality can attest to. I saw a woman who knew God and, despite the circumstances, was trusting him." He looked around at the other faces in the room. "I wish Aunt Aggie had trusted God, because he loved her dearly. I wish she had known how precious that love of God can be." His voice broke, and he looked down at his notes. He was having trouble going on.

Aunt Aggie watched, captivated. Something in her heart deflated, and she wished she hadn't come. Jill had been right. It was crazy. What had she expected? She had wanted grief . . . didn't everybody want to know they were missed when they died? But she hadn't quite expected the grief that had to do with her religious beliefs—or lack thereof. A heavy weight came over her, making her feel suddenly very, very old and very tired. The finality of this whole death business began to dawn on her, and she realized many of the tears being shed in the room were not because she was such a wonderful person, but because she didn't believe in God. She thought of standing up and shouting out to everyone in the room that death hadn't conquered her yet, and that it didn't matter if she believed, that she was happy, and she was good, and she was a philanthropist and generous with everything she had, and that she met people's needs when she saw them. What more did they want from a person?

But she didn't. She sat quietly, as she had promised she would, because she wanted so much for Celia to be cleared. Still, she felt a tightness over her chest, and wondered if she died right here, right now, if they'd let this dismal funeral suffice. Was this all there was after a life well-lived?

She saw Celia sitting at the end of the family pew, being shunned by the rest of them. She couldn't wait to give Celia's parents a piece of her mind when she resurrected, tell them what she thought of them, coming to her funeral and acting all mournful, then treating her Celia like a leper.

Soon the funeral was over, and she realized that Nick hadn't had much good news to offer the crowd on her behalf. He couldn't tell them that they would see her again, because he didn't know that they would. She thought it probably would have been nice for him to say anyway.

It was she who felt the worst, sitting here, viewing something that most people never had the chance to see. She wasn't enjoying this like she thought she would. In fact, she was ready to go home, to try to wipe out of her mind all the things she had seen and heard here today. But she couldn't leave. She had to sit through until the end, hear every word. It had been her choice, after all.

She glanced at Celia again and wished her little heart wasn't breaking over some imaginary spiritual condition that Aunt Aggie had never understood. And then she thought of Celia that night when Aggie had been in jail, too, singing a hymn, telling her that things were going to be all right, as if she'd forgotten she'd been accused of trying to kill the man she loved most in the world. Aunt Aggie just couldn't fathom it. Either Celia was stupid, or she had been brainwashed so deeply that every fiber of her own being believed in the things she said she believed. And suddenly, Aunt Aggie realized that it wasn't with every fiber of her being that she believed there wasn't a God. The idea of God was just something beyond her grasp, something she had never experienced before, something she thought was a bunch of hooey. For the first time, it occurred to her that these people, who were crying at her funeral because they thought they'd never see her again, might know something she didn't know.

She wiped at a tear in her own eye, surprised that she would cry at her own funeral, when she'd expected to laugh her head off. She hoped Jill would come quickly to get her after the service. She didn't know how much more of this she could take.

The funeral broke up, and in moments, Jill was in the balcony with her. "Aunt Aggie, the funeral director said there's a van out on the side with blackened windows. He's gonna be driving it, and you can sit in the back if you want to go to the burial site."

She shook her head. "No, I think I've had enough."

"Really?" Jill asked. "Well, I thought you'd want . . ."

"No, never mind. I'll jes' stay here and wait till you come back."

"All right. It shouldn't be that long. Just stay right here and don't come out, and no one will see you. Sid is staying with you."

Jill ran back out, and Aunt Aggie could hear below her as everyone filed out of the room, talking quietly, no doubt, about the tragedy of her death and the scandal of Celia's plight. She stared down at that pulpit where Nick had done her eulogy. This was good experience, she told herself. As soon as she came back to life, she was going to write her own eulogy, maybe videotape it, so nobody would have to endure the likes of this again. Yes, it was a very good experience, she thought. She just wasn't sure why it didn't feel so good.

Chapter Fifty-Seven

Lee Barnett was the first person Issie saw when she walked into Joe's Place that night. She told herself that she hadn't gone there to see him, that she just wanted a drink to unwind after the funeral, but that didn't explain the elation she felt when he spotted her and patted the empty stool next to him. She felt like the high school cheerleader who had a crush on the town's bad boy.

As she took the stool, he ordered her a glass of wine, the same brand she'd been drinking the other night. "How's it going there?" he asked.

"Fine," she said, trying to seem nonchalant about seeing him.

He grinned. "Don't pretend you're not glad to see me. You know you are. I could see it in your face when you came in."

Something about that bold appraisal charmed her. "You're pretty confident for somebody in a lot of trouble."

"I'm not in trouble," he said. "Haven't you heard? I met with Celia's husband. Convinced him I'm a Boy Scout. 'Cause I am, you know."

She smiled. "Yep. That was my first thought about you. A real Boy Scout. Especially the other night when my preacher had to rescue me from you."

"Another few minutes, and I'm the one would've needed rescuing," he said.

She started to tell him he had a lot of gall, but she hadn't exactly been fighting him off. Besides, she liked gall in a man.

She sipped on the wine Joe put in front of her, and decided to change the subject. "So did you hear about Aggie Gaston?"

"Who?"

"Celia's aunt. She died. She was buried today."

"Arsenic poisoning?" Lee asked.

Issie frowned and shook her head. "No, she had a heart attack."

Lee nodded. "Good."

"Good?"

"I mean, I'm glad it's not arsenic. There's a little too much of that going around, if you know what I mean."

Issie supposed he was right.

•   •   •

Across the crowd of people, R.J. sat at the back table pretending to read the paper. He knew he wasn't fooling anybody. Lee Barnett had seen him come in, and he knew he was being watched. Still, he kept up the pretense, if not for Barnett, then for everyone else in the room. His cellular phone vibrated, and he pulled it out of his hip pocket. "Albright."

"Where are you?" It was Sid's voice.

"Joe's Place."

"Albright, are you drinkin' on the job?"

"No," he said, shoving the empty beer bottle across the table as if Sid could see through the phone.

"Where's Barnett?" Sid asked.

"Right here. Got my eye on him. Thing is, he knows I'm watching him."

"Well, that's a big help."

R.J. bristled at the sarcastic tone, as if he didn't have enough police savvy to do the right thing. "I was just fixin' to leave," he said. "You don't have to tell me how to do my job, Sid. I think I can handle it."

He clicked off the phone and dropped it back in his pocket, then left the paper on the table and got up to leave. Barnett, who was bantering flirtatiously with Issie Mattreaux, winked at him as he left. R.J. felt like throttling him. He didn't like being taunted, even silently. He went out across the street and headed to his car parked in the police parking lot. He could see the front door from there. With the aid of his binoculars, he could watch Barnett come out, then follow him to wherever he went. *Fun detail,* he thought sarcastically. It was going to be a long night.

• • •

Two hours later, Lee Barnett had had too much to drink. Once again, he'd passed his limit, and he knew it. But he was doing so well with Issie Mattreaux. The knockout brunette was laughing and flirting, and he knew that he had a much better chance of getting her to go home with him tonight than he'd had the time before, and he'd been really close then.

He leaned into her, too close, he knew, but she allowed it. He reached out and stroked her arm.

"Hands off," she said in a teasing voice. "I'm not into public displays of affection. The town's already buzzing about Issie spending time with Celia's ex-con."

"How about private displays?" he asked against her ear.

She didn't say no, so he took that as a yes.

"Come on, Issie. Who are you kidding? You know you want to go home with me."

"You're awfully cocky for somebody who'd let a preacher knock him down."

She was still teasing, but he was less amused. "Hey, I can take on the preacher."

"Yeah, if you're not drunk, maybe."

"I ain't drunk," he argued, sliding one hand under her hair to cup the back of her neck. "I'm in love."

She laughed then. "In love? Is that what you call it?" She took his wrist and removed his hand.

He grinned. "If you don't want me touchin' you in public, then let's go someplace private. I'm gettin' tired of these games."

"I'm thinking about it," she said.

He put his heavy arm around her and pulled her too roughly against him. He knew instantly it was a mistake because she fell off her stool with a clatter. Quickly, he helped her right herself and she got back on the stool. The look on her face had changed.

"I'm sorry," he said, stroking her back. "I didn't mean—"

"I think she told you to let her go."

The voice of the man sitting next to Issie thundered over his own voice, and Barnett didn't like it.

"Stay out of this, pal. This is between me and the lady."

"You ain't treatin' her like much of a lady," the guy said.

Issie looked over her shoulder and tried to calm the guy down. "It's okay, Billy, I can handle it."

"Yeah, she can handle it, *Billy*," Barnett said, jerking her against him again to make his point.

Billy dove from his stool, and his fist came across Lee's jaw, knocking him back against a table. The people around it stood up, and a woman screamed.

Humiliated, Barnett got to his feet and lurched for the guy. But Billy was ready for him, and they wound up on the floor, wrestling like children. Barnett found himself with his thumbs against the guy's throat, and it brought back a memory. A memory of something that had landed him in prison for five years. Quickly, he let go of his neck.

He hadn't realized how long he'd been struggling with the man until the door burst open and the cop who'd been there earlier came in. He broke up the fight and pulled Lee to his feet. "You're under arrest, Barnett," he said. "You have the right to remain silent . . ."

"No, man!" Lee said. "I ain't goin' back to prison. Man, I served my time. I didn't do nothin'. I was sittin' here mindin' my own business."

"Save it for somebody who's interested," the cop said and dragged him out of the establishment in handcuffs.

As the cop half-dragged him across the street to the jail, Lee thought how ironic all this was. He couldn't believe it. It was just too stupid to be true. *He* was too stupid to be true.

After they'd booked him and thrown him in the jail cell, he stood nodding his head. Yep. He deserved to be exactly where he was. He kicked the cot, almost breaking his foot, then hopped around cursing venomously until the others in the jail began cursing back at him.

Chapter Fifty-Eight

While Aunt Aggie spent the night in hiding, Jill stayed in Aunt Aggie's house with Celia. David had decided to have dinner with his parents before they headed back to Jackson.

Still fully dressed, Jill lay in the guest room next to Aunt Aggie's room, where Celia was going to sleep tonight. Every muscle in her body was tense as she waited for her plan to work. The killer had to strike tonight. If he didn't, she didn't know what she would try next. She checked her cell phone to make sure it was still powered, and wished Sid would call.

It was already past midnight, and Jill could still hear Celia weeping in the bedroom. The pain Celia was going through broke Jill's heart. She hoped the joy of seeing her aunt revived would be enough to make Celia forgive her. The forgiveness would come hard, though, if her plan didn't work tonight.

The cell phone vibrated, and she bolted upright. Maybe they had caught the killer already. Maybe it was over. Quickly, she clicked it on.

"Jill?" It was Sid's voice.

"Yeah, it's me," she whispered. "What is it? Has anything happened?"

"Nothin' here," he said. "But somethin' else I thought you might be interested in."

"What?"

"Lee Barnett. He got arrested tonight at Joe's Place. Seems he had too much to drink and got in a fight. Disorderly conduct."

"Oh, no!" she whispered. "Sid, what if he's the killer? He can't make a move if he's stuck in jail! The whole sting could blow up in our faces if the killer's not free to strike."

Sid wasn't buying. "We ain't callin' this off, Jill. He's in jail and I can't do nothin' about it."

"You can let him back out," Jill said through her teeth. "Sid, *think!* You're messing this whole thing up!"

"I didn't mess nothin' up. He got arrested fair and square. Remember, most of my cops ain't in on this sting."

She began pacing the floor. "I know that," she whispered harshly. "But isn't there someone who could go bail him out? Without him, we're in serious trouble here."

"Jill, I'm tellin' you, your client is our killer. She's the only one we gotta watch."

"Celia is in Aunt Aggie's room crying her heart out. She's not going anywhere. Do you realize we only have tonight? Please, Sid. You know the judge'll go along with setting bail to keep the sting from being sabotaged. I'll call him myself."

"You gon' have to," Sid said, "'cause I ain't callin' him. I don't like this."

"Well, you don't have a choice! As long as somebody meets bail, that guy's out on the street where he can do the harm we need for him to do."

Sid moaned.

"You let me know the moment something happens," she said. "By the way, where is Stan?"

"Took him and his folks and Aunt Aggie to my house. Nobody knows. We took every precaution. I'm at Stan's. His and his parents' cars are still here. No reason for nobody to think he ain't in here, sound asleep."

"All right," Jill said. "Let me know the minute something happens." She went out into the hall and peered into Aunt Aggie's room, just to make sure Celia hadn't overheard. Her client was sitting in the dark on the pillowed window seat, gazing out into the stars. She was still crying, but she was quieter now. Jill wished Celia would fall asleep.

She went back into her room and quickly dialed information to get Louis DeLacy's phone number. It rang several times before he answered. "Hello?"

The judge had been sleeping, but Jill didn't let that stop her. "Louis? Jill Clark. We have a problem."

"What problem, Jill?"

"They've arrested the major suspect—other than Celia—for disorderly conduct."

"What? Of all the cockamamy . . ."

"He's in jail, Louis. I need for you to set bail so somebody can get him out. I'll pay it myself. Just please, help me. If he isn't out, we'll never know if he's the real killer."

"Oh, for heaven's sake. I'll set it at fifty dollars, Jill, and I'll go to the police station right now and take care of it. But I can't bail him out. That would look too suspicious. And I don't want you leaving Celia."

"I'll find someone to do it. Thank you, Judge."

She hung up and punched out the number for Midtown station. She hated calling the fire department this late at night, when the guys were probably asleep, but it couldn't be helped.

"Midtown fire station," someone said.

She hesitated. "May I speak to Dan Nichols, please?" she whispered.

The man didn't hear her well enough. "Excuse me?"

"Dan Nichols," she repeated just above a whisper.

A few minutes passed, and finally, a groggy-sounding Dan came to the phone. "Hello?"

"Dan, it's me," she said.

"Jill? I can hardly hear you. Where are you? Are you all right?"

"I'm fine," she said, "but I need a favor."

He paused. "Jill, what's going on?"

"Please, will you just do me a favor? This is very serious. I need for you to do me this favor without asking any questions, I need for you to do it as soon as possible, and I need for you to keep quiet about it."

"What is it?"

"Lee Barnett was arrested tonight for brawling at Joe's Place. His bail is going to be set at fifty dollars. I need for you to give it about twenty minutes, enough time for the judge to officially set bail, then go get him out. I promise, I'll pay you back with interest, and I'll explain everything for you tomorrow. But I need for you to do this."

Again, there was silence. "Jill, why would you help him? Where are you?"

"I can't explain right now. Please, trust me. This is very, very important."

"Since when have you been Lee Barnett's advocate?"

"I'm not. Please, Dan, will you trust me and do it? Can I count on you?"

He hesitated again. "I guess so, Jill, but tomorrow I would like to hear the story."

"I promise you will," she said. "And trust me, it's a doozy."

Chapter Fifty-Nine

Dan Nichols paid the bail, then waited around for Lee Barnett to emerge from jail. When he did, he looked as mad as a rabid dog.

The cop who brought him up pointed him to Dan, and Barnett swaggered over. "You the one bailed me out?"

"That's right," Dan said.

"I owe you," he said. "I just don't have it right now. I haven't gotten a job yet."

"Don't worry about it." Dan started walking toward the door, unwilling to get too chummy with the man who might very well have poisoned Stan. What Jill was up to was beyond him.

"Hey, I appreciate it, man! Nice to have a friend in town."

Dan glanced back and started to tell him that he wasn't his friend, but he decided to leave it alone. Instead, he just headed back to the fire station.

• • •

From where he was parked outside, R.J. watched Barnett walk back across the street to Joe's Place, where his car was parked. He couldn't believe the judge had set bail already, and to make matters even worse, he'd been assigned to follow him again. R.J. didn't see the point, if every time he arrested a guy, they let him go. He supposed if they wanted to waste his time, it was their prerogative.

He watched him pull out of the parking lot, and realized he could bust the guy again for drunk driving, if he wanted to. But he didn't. He watched him drive in a roundabout way through Newpointe, as if he couldn't remember which way would take him home. R.J. followed him as he drove through town, waiting for him to make a move.

They came to a busy intersection at the corner of First Street and LaSalle Boulevard, and a car got between them as the light turned red. R.J. tried to keep his eyes on the taillights of the Grand Am, but soon he lost sight of it. Had he gone left or right? He honestly didn't know.

He cursed and gunned his engine as the light turned green. He passed the car in front of him, cursing again, and tried to catch up to Lee Barnett. But it was too late. Barnett was out of sight.

Chapter Sixty

Sid began to get nervous as he sat in the dark in Stan's bedroom. If they could anticipate how the killer would strike, it would be so much easier. But so far, the only method had been poison. Would the killer come in and try to inject more poison into Stan, or would they bring a gun this time and just shoot him outright? He didn't know what to be prepared for.

Police officers were staked in the trees all around the house where they could see anyone who approached the house the moment he arrived. But they had to catch the killer in the act or there would never be a conviction for anything more than breaking and entering. They had to be able to prove they had the right person.

He looked over at the bed, where they'd put a dummy under the covers. In the dark, it looked as if someone slept there. He hoped that all they'd gone through in the last two days was not in vain. He hadn't been crazy about this idea at first, but it had grown on him. And as they'd planned out the farce, he had begun to hope it would work. If Celia was the killer, and he felt sure that she was, they would be able to prove it unequivocally tonight, to everyone, including Stan.

His telephone—which he brought instead of his radio because of the noise level that would alert any intruder—vibrated on his hip, and he grabbed it up and put it to his ear. "Yeah?" he whispered.

"Someone's coming," one of the guys outside said. "We almost missed them. But whoever it is is on foot, headed toward the house from the woods behind it."

"Is it a man or a woman?"

"Hard to tell. They're wearing a black ski mask."

Sid closed his eyes and hunkered back against the corner. "Are they armed?"

"Can't tell. Whoever it is is almost to the house."

Sid aimed his weapon, waiting.

He got up and went to the door of the bedroom, where he could see the back door. There was no sound, none at all, and he waited for a scratching or breaking glass, anything that would indicate the door was being broken into. Instead, the door came open easily, as if the intruder had a key.

It *had* to be Celia!

He sank back into the bedroom, waiting. What would she do next?

But the prowler didn't come toward the bedroom. Sid waited as agonizing moments ticked by. He heard nothing. If people had truly been asleep in this house, no one would have been awakened. He inched to the door again and peered out. There was no sign of whoever had come in. The uncertainty of what was going on made him very nervous. Should he leave the bedroom and find the person, wherever they were hiding? Should he go ahead and make an arrest? If it was Celia, wouldn't this be enough evidence to convict her, or would she just convince the judge that she had come into her own home not meaning any harm?

Something told him to sit still, not to move.

Then he heard the slight squeak of the back door opening again. He inched back to the casing and saw the person stealing out. Quickly, he grabbed his phone.

"She's comin' back out! Don't let her get away!"

"Did she try anything?"

"Nothin'. Didn't even come in the bedroom. Man, somethin's up, but I don't know what."

"Did she plant a bomb . . . start a fire?"

"I don't know, but I ain't likin' this. Just grab her. Don't let her get away, whatever you do! I'll be searchin' the house."

"I'm on it." He heard the phone click off and looked out the window. His phone vibrated again.

"Chad's in pursuit, but she took off through the woods. Chad's followin' on foot, and we have some patrol cars comin' out on the other side."

"How did she get away?" Sid yelled into the phone.

"Just went the other way. We weren't expectin'—"

"You *idiots!*" Sid screamed. "Catch her or all your jobs are on the line." He flicked on the lights and began to go through the rooms one by one, looking for anything that might look suspicious. There was no fire, none that he could detect, no smoke of any kind. He began to sweat. It was hot in here, getting hotter. Why was the heater on?

He went from room to room with his gun, looking around, desperately trying to determine what the intruder had done. In the living room, he began to smell gas. Slowly, he walked to the fireplace, where the smell was strongest. There was a gas starter in the bricks, and he pulled his latex gloves out of his pocket, put them on quickly, and tested the chrome key. It had been turned on full blast, letting gas flow through the air. Whoever might have been in the house sleeping would never have woken up.

So there *had* been a murder attempt!

He ran outside. "All right, we've got an attempt," he said. "She turned on the gas starter in the fireplace, tryin' to kill everybody in the house with gas poisonin'."

"You gotta be kidding."

"Don't go in there. Call the fire department."

"Maybe we could get fingerprints on the starter's key, or on the door."

"First we gotta catch her, and we gotta do it now."

R.J.'s unmarked car screeched up to the curb, and Sid jumped in. R.J., who'd been out looking for Barnett, had heard all the commotion on the radio and decided to come this way.

"Man, turn this thing around and go to the street behind them woods!"

"What's goin' on?" R.J. asked. "I heard somethin' about gas leaks and Celia runnin' through the woods. How'd she get away with the place surrounded?"

"Ask *them*," Sid said, disgusted. "Just step on it."

R.J. turned his blue light on and hurried around the streets until he came out on the other side. Already, four police cars were parked there with blue lights flashing. The canine force was out, and he could hear their two dogs barking as they hurried through the woods. He got out of the car.

"Hey, Sid, we got something!" someone called, and he hurried over.

There was a BMW parked there, pulled slightly in among the trees.

"This car has to belong to the person involved."

Sid's heart lunged. "That's Celia's brother's car. That's what she's been drivin' since all this started."

The cops all stared at him, as if they didn't want to hear it. "Come on, man. We gotta find her."

"Well, did you call to see if she's slipped away from Jill?" R.J. asked.

"No," Sid said, kicking himself. Quickly, he dialed the number. Jill answered the phone. "Yeah?"

"Jill, it's Sid."

"Has something happened?"

"Sure has. Look, has Celia left the house?"

"No, she's still in Aunt Aggie's room."

"All right, do me a favor. Get up, go to her room, talk to her. I want to make sure you see her face-to-face."

"Why? You think I'm hearing a tape recording of her crying or something? I hear her, Sid."

"Jill, just do it!"

He listened to the silence for a moment as she went to the other room. He heard her calling, "Celia?"

In reply, he heard Celia's voice. "Yeah?"

"You okay?" she asked. "Can't you get to sleep?"

"I'm okay. Don't worry about me."

"All right." Silence again as Jill went back to her room. "Sid, she's fine. You heard her," she whispered.

Sid turned back to the BMW. "Then do you have any clue where David is?"

"David? Well, he had dinner with his parents, then came back and went to bed."

"Go look in his room, Jill. I need to know where he is."

"Okay." He heard her knocking on the door, and calling out, "David? David, it's Jill. I need to talk to you." No answer.

Then Sid heard Celia's voice again. "Jill, what is it?"

"I need to talk to David," she said. "It's very important. He's not answering."

"Maybe he's sound asleep."

Jill banged again loudly. "David! Wake up!"

Still no answer. She opened the door. The bed was still made up, and the clothes he'd been wearing lay in a heap on the floor. David was gone.

"Where is he?" Jill asked Celia, panicked.

Sid heard the silence, then, "I guess he went out again. Must not have wanted to wake us up."

Jill was breathless as she came back to the phone. "Sid, he's gone." She ran to the back door and looked in the garage. "His car's gone, too."

"That's what I thought," Sid said. "Jill, I think we may have found the killer. And you're right. It ain't Celia."

• • •

Celia stood in David's room as Jill finished her phone call. From the panic in her friend's voice, she knew Jill thought that David was the killer. But that was ludicrous. He was her brother, and he loved her. He had done nothing but support her through this whole ordeal.

She went to the bed and picked up the photo album that lay there. It was the same one she'd seen him studying the other day. She opened it and saw a page full of her baby pictures. Her parents held her like a pageant trophy and smiled with such pride and delight that no one would have dreamed that they'd someday disown her.

She turned the page and saw herself at three, dressed in a flowing white gown with baby's breath in her hair, holding her newborn baby brother. It seemed more a picture of her than of him. She scanned the snapshots one by one, noting the way the camera zoomed in on her, leaving him as an afterthought.

She thumbed past the pageant years, where she was pictured in a fortune's worth of dresses and tiaras. David appeared in some of them, always to the side or in the background, sulking while she hammed it up. She wondered why he seemed so interested in those pictures now. They couldn't hold fond memories for him. She wouldn't blame him if they drew out resentment and bitterness in him.

But enough to kill? No, she thought. That was ridiculous. Whatever Jill was so upset about, it couldn't be that.

But a chill came over her as she realized that something wasn't adding up. If he was resentful and nursing childhood wounds, why did he act like the loving brother who would stick by her through thick and thin? Why had he put his workaholism aside to spend a week with her in her time of need?

She saw his briefcase lying on a table, and something compelled her to open it. She saw the usual items—his laptop computer, some paperwork that meant nothing to her, a day planner. She unzipped the pocket on the side and pulled out three pens. On the other side, she saw various notepads and Post-it notes haphazardly stuck down in the pocket. She pulled them out, but as she did, her fingers brushed something under the lining. She pulled it to see if there was another pocket. The lining came free . . .

She slid her fingers into the opening and pulled out what was hidden there.

Her heart froze.

It was the checkbook she'd been looking for.

She tried to catch her breath, but her chest seemed too heavy. She stumbled out of the room as her mind raced. It made no sense. David wouldn't—*couldn't*—have poisoned Stan.

She heard Jill in the kitchen talking to Sid in a panicked voice. Something about gas leaks and David's car in the trees . . .

Her heart sprinted as she tried to think. Had something happened to Stan?

She managed to move herself into the kitchen, just as Jill hung up.

"Is Stan all right?" she rasped.

Jill turned back to her, and her face changed. "Celia, you look awfully pale. Sit down." Celia did as she was told, but she kept her eyes fixed on Jill. "He's fine," Jill said. "But there was another murder attempt, Celia. They're looking for David."

Celia looked down at the checkbook in her trembling hands.

Jill saw it. Gently, she took it out of her hands and opened it. "Celia, where did you find this?"

Celia frowned, desperately trying to think of a reason why David would have had it. "It was . . . in his briefcase . . . hidden in the lining . . ."

Jill's eyes widened, and slowly, she stooped in front of Celia and looked in her eyes. "Celia, I know this is hard for you. But I think your brother may be the killer."

"No," she said, beginning to cry. "There's an explanation. I know there is. You can't jump to conclusions. Maybe . . . maybe someone put it there, to set *him* up."

Jill lifted Celia's chin and made her look at her. "Celia, David and Aunt Aggie were the only two who knew when you'd be at the hospital when the IV bag was changed. David was there the whole time. He was with Stan the day he was poisoned. He had the checkbook."

"No!" Celia got up and pushed past Jill, shaking her head frantically.

Jill was red-faced as she clicked her phone back on and dialed. "Sid, it's me. Listen, you're not going to believe this."

Celia couldn't listen. Sobbing, she ran out of the room as Jill told Sid that David was a killer.

She went to Jill's purse, which sat on a chair in the parlor, and pulled out her keys. Quietly, she went down the hall to the back door and slipped out. She got into Jill's car, cranked it, and pulled out of the driveway before Jill even knew she was gone.

Chapter Sixty-One

Fighting back his panic, David ran through the thick woods behind Stan's house, tripping over vines, swiping at spider webs and hanging moss. A bayou cut between him and his car, and he tore through the brush and the brambles, ducking under limbs and leaping over fallen branches, until he reached the edge of the bayou. He plunged into it, hoping the water would throw the dogs off his scent, but the murky water wasn't deep enough. It only reached his waist, and his shoes clung to the mud bottom like suction cups, slowing his progress across. He couldn't see where he was going, and a tree branch stopped him, knocking him back, but he rallied. Knocking the Spanish moss out of his way, he sloshed through the murky water, trying to follow the bayou to Clearview Street, where a bridge crossed. Maybe he could hide under the bridge until they gave up on him, or until the dogs got to him first.

Behind him, he could hear them closing in, and he thought of diving under and swimming, but the water was too muddy and dark, and it wasn't deep enough. He shivered at the thought of alligators lurking nearby, watching him though he couldn't see them, or snakes curling through the water, wrapping around his legs . . .

He saw a flashlight beam up ahead, and he tried to turn back, but there was another one to his right and another one behind him. The dogs, held back by their leashes, howled and barked as they led the cops straight to him.

He took a deep breath and plunged under water and began to swim with all his might along the bottom of the bayou.

When he came up for air, the dogs sounded farther away. He forced himself to go under again. He swam until it got too shallow, then sloshed up onto the grass of the bank. The sirens sounded miles away now. He saw the lights of a house and headed toward it. A man's bicycle was parked on the patio.

He kicked at the stand, flung his leg over, and took off into the night, pedaling the bicycle as fast as he could as the sirens grew farther away. They were still looking for him in the bayou. If he could just get out of these wet clothes and call the police to report his car stolen, he knew he could still make them think that Celia was the one who'd broken into Stan's house tonight. They had believed everything else he'd thrown at them.

He reached the Bonaparte Court apartments and looked up at the apartment he had rented for Lee Barnett. The light was off—Barnett wasn't home. Perfect. He parked the bike under the stairwell and hurried up the steps. He pulled his keys from his wet jeans pocket and found the apartment key. He was glad he'd had a copy made.

He opened the door and slipped inside, paying no heed to the mud he left on the carpet as he headed for the bedroom. He turned on the light and saw Barnett's suitcase lying on the floor in the corner, near a pile of dirty clothes. He dug through and found a pair of jeans, then discarded them. They'd never fit. Barnett was taller and broader than he.

He found a pair of gray gym shorts and a T-shirt. Good enough. Quickly, he stripped of the wet clothes, left them on the floor, then hurried into the shower. He rinsed the mud and muck off of his skin, and quickly shampooed the bayou out of his hair. He got out and dried off, then got dressed. The clothes fit fine.

He picked up Barnett's blow dryer and dried his hair, then ran back to the suitcase for socks. He pulled them on, carefully avoiding the wet, muddy places on the carpet. Shoes, he thought, looking around. He needed shoes.

A pair of Nikes lay on their sides beside the bed, like a gift waiting to be worn. He slipped them on. They were a size too big, but they served the purpose.

He grabbed a towel and hurried out the front door, grinning as he ran back down the stairs. He wiped off the seat on the bike, dropped the towel, then took off into the night. Now all he had to do was get to a phone and report his car stolen. He'd claim that Celia and Lee Barnett took it and left him stranded, that it had taken him this long to get to a phone to report it.

They'd buy into it, because it was evidence. And everybody knew that evidence superseded common sense. And when they came to check out Lee Barnett's apartment, they'd find the wet, bayou-soiled clothes. There was only one conclusion they could jump to.

He laughed as he rode down Rue Matin and turned onto Jefferson Avenue. The Newpointe Inn, where his parents were staying, was up on the left, so he pulled into the parking lot, abandoned the bicycle, and dashed inside. He rode up on the elevator, then ran down the hall to their room.

He banged on the door, knowing he was waking them up.

"Who is it?" his father asked through the door.

"David," he said. "Let me in, Dad."

His father opened the door, and he hurried in, breathless. "You're not gonna believe what she's done now," he said as he headed for the phone. "She stole my car. Celia and that ex-con. Left me out on the street. I had to walk all the way here."

"What?" his mother asked, coming out of the bedroom as she tied the belt of her robe.

He held up a hand to stem their outbursts, and waited as 911 answered.

"911, may I help you?"

"Yeah, this is David Bradford. My car was stolen a little over an hour ago. My sister, Celia Shepherd, took it and left me on the street. I had to walk to a phone." He paused, waiting for the dispatcher to recognize his name. Surely they had an APB out on him.

"Mr. Bradford, where are you right now?" the woman asked.

"I'm at the Newpointe Inn, in my parents' suite. Look, I don't know what she might do. She said she was going to finish off her husband. Oh, and Lee Barnett was with her. I've been defending her, but I can't anymore. She's crazy. She even mentioned something about coming after our own parents, that it was time they paid for disowning her ..."

His parents gasped, and his father put his arms around his mother to comfort her. They were scared to death, buying the whole thing hook, line, and sinker.

The dispatcher put him on hold, and he could imagine how they were tracing the call to make sure he was where he said he was, how she was relaying the conversation to someone who would weigh what he'd come to believe against the evidence. Again, the evidence would rule.

"We'll have an officer there shortly, Mr. Bradford," the woman said. "Do not leave."

"Oh, I'm not going anywhere. But maybe they ought to start looking for her before she kills Stan. There's no telling what she might do."

He hung up and got to his feet. His parents were gaping at him, horrified, and his mother was crying. He went to hug her, like a dutiful son. "It's okay, Mom. The police are on their way. Dad, do you still keep a gun with you when you travel?"

"Just a small caliber pistol," he said. "But yes, it's in my bag."

"Go get it," he said. "We might need it if Celia gets here before they do."

His father disappeared into the bedroom, and Joanna began to weep into her hand. "What's gotten into her? She seemed so rational at the funeral. I started to think that ... maybe ... she wasn't really—"

"She can turn it on and off, Mom. I've been with her all week, and you wouldn't believe the desperate, crazy mood swings. It's like Dr. Jekyll and Mr. Hyde. She's sick."

His father came in with the gun, and David took it from him and put it in the waistband of his gym shorts, then pulled the T-shirt out to hang over it. "I'll have it, just in case I need it."

Someone knocked on the door, and his mother made a frightened sound and backed against his father. David went to peer out the peephole. "It's the cops," he said, and both of his parents dropped onto the couch with relief.

Chapter Sixty-Two

Lee Barnett pulled his car into a parking space near his apartment and realized that he was parked crooked. He didn't care. He could straighten it out in the morning. Right now, he needed to get to bed and sleep off the booze he'd put away before he was arrested.

He had been too drunk to find his way home, and he'd spent the past hour just driving around town trying to figure out which way to go. Once, he'd run his car off the road into a small ditch. It had taken him twenty minutes to get it out, with the help of a couple of teenagers who'd pushed it while he'd steered it back onto the road.

Now he was here, and he slapped at his pockets for his keys, then remembered they were still in the ignition. He laughed at himself, then got out and staggered toward the steps. He made his way up and went in, turned on the light, and saw the muddy prints across his living room carpet. In his drunken state, he thought he had made them.

He went into the bedroom and failed to notice the wet clothes on the floor. Instead, he stepped out of his shoes, cursed at the wet carpet, and fell onto the bed. He closed his eyes, thankful that he'd finally made it here.

The doorbell rang, followed by a loud knock, and he heard someone shout, "Police, open up!"

He frowned and sat up. What did they want with him now?

He cursed again, got up, and stumbled for the front door. He threw it open. "What?"

"We have a warrant to search your apartment," the cop said.

He stepped back from the door as they came in. "Wet carpet," someone said, and Lee found a chair and dropped into it.

"The clothes are here!" someone shouted from the bedroom. "This is exactly what he was wearing."

He looked up as one of the cops began to handcuff him. "Mr. Barnett, you're under arrest. You have the right to remain silent—"

"You already did this tonight. I got bailed out, remember? I can't get arrested twice for the same fight, can I?"

But the man just kept reading him his rights as they led him out to the police car.

Chapter Sixty-Three

Sid shook his head, puzzled by the news of the theft of David's car and Lee Barnett's arrest. He'd had it figured out, and now, in just a few minutes' time, his theory had been shot all to pieces.

Still, he decided that Stan might not be safe. He headed to Jill's house, where Stan and Aunt Aggie were staying. While he drove, he called Jill back.

"Hello?" She sounded shaken, anxious.

"Jill, I'm on my way to see Stan and Aunt Aggie. I ain't sure what's goin' on or if we got the right man. One minute I'm sure it's David, and then we find David calmly sittin' in his folks' hotel room with some story about a car theft that Celia and Lee Barnett perpetrated, even though I know Celia's there with you."

"She's not," Jill cut in.

He didn't hear. "And the next minute we're findin' wet clothes in Lee Barnett's apartment, even though the guys at the station say that right now he's wearin' the same thing he had on when he was arrested earlier tonight—"

"Sid, I said she's not here."

His words ground to an abrupt halt. "Who? Celia? Jill, where in the world is she?"

"She left. Took my car, while I was talking to you. I just realized she wasn't up in her room."

Sid felt the heat of a volcano prickling through his skin. "Jill, are you sure you ain't been lyin' to me about her bein' there? Cause if what David says is true—"

"It isn't true, Sid!" she shouted. "She was here! But she found that checkbook, and heard that David had gotten away, and she just left!"

"I don't believe this. She sure don't make it easy to clear her."

"Sid, listen to me. David's doing it again. He's getting away with it. If you found the wet clothes in Lee Barnett's apartment, couldn't he have put them there? I mean, if he's the killer, he'd have the key to that apartment. He'd be the one who rented it in the first place!"

"That's far-fetched, Jill. I ain't buyin'."

"But he had the checkbook, Sid. And he's saying that Celia and Lee Barnett stole his car? Lee was in jail, and then someone was following him, weren't they? They would know if he'd gone and turned on the gas starter at Stan's house."

"R.J. lost him," Sid said. "There was about an hour there when we didn't know where he was."

"And you believe that in that time he went home, changed clothes, picked up Celia, stole David's car, broke into Stan's house, waded down the bayou, went home, and changed back into what he'd been wearing before? Come on, Sid!"

"All I know is that David Bradford ain't wet. He's sittin' in his folks' hotel room dry as a bone. The guys just took the report of the stolen car and left him. I talked to 'em myself."

"They left him there? Are you telling me that he's free to go back out?"

Sid realized that probably wasn't the wisest thing, after all. He was confused. He didn't know what to think. "Look, I'm at your house. I'm gon' go in and talk to Stan. Maybe he can help me sort all this out. Meanwhile, I'm gon' have to put an APB out on Celia. You say she's in your car?"

"Yes, although I can't see how that could be, if she stole David's car."

"Maybe she stole your car because she couldn't go back to David's, since we'd found it."

"Sid, for this to be true, I'd have to be lying about her being with me all night. Are you calling me a liar?"

"She's your friend, Jill. You're tryin' to keep her outa trouble."

"I'm not a liar, Sid!"

Sid cut the phone off and dropped it on his seat, then got out of the car and dashed to the front door.

• • •

Stan answered the door, and saw Sid standing there. "What's going on?" Stan asked. "I heard sirens over an hour ago. I tried to call the station to find out what was going on, but I got put on hold—"

"Somebody broke into your house and turned on the gas starter in your fireplace, so you'd die in your sleep."

Stan's eyebrows lifted. "And you were there, right? Caught him?"

"No," Sid said. "We botched it up, man. Whoever it was got away. We found David Bradford's car on the other side of the woods, and thought sure it was him. And Celia claims she found the checkbook in his briefcase, but she's disappeared, and I don't even know if Jill was tellin' the truth about her bein' at Aunt Aggie's all night, and David's reported his car stolen, claimin' Celia and Lee Barnett took it, and we found wet clothes in Barnett's floor, even though he really couldn't have had time to do all this since the time he was in jail for the bar fight . . . and whoever the killer is would have a key to Barnett's apartment anyway . . ."

"Wait a minute," Stan said, cutting him off. "David said that Celia and Lee Barnett stole his car?"

"Yes," Sid said.

He backed off, trying to think. David had the checkbook. David's car was at the scene of the crime. David had lied about Celia stealing his car.

"What is it?" Aunt Aggie called as she came up the hall in her robe. "Somethin' happened?"

Sid nodded, but Stan grabbed his arm and made him look at him. "If David said that, Sid, then he's the killer. Celia didn't do it."

"But man, I don't know where she is."

"The question is, where is David?"

"He's at the Newpointe Inn, with his folks. Two of the boys took the stolen car report and left him there."

"Left him there? Just like that? Sid, are you crazy?"

"They arrested Barnett. Celia's missin'. All the evidence points back to—"

"Sid, there is evidence, and then there is evidence." He tried to catch his breath. "You're falling for all of it, just like he wants. You aren't using your head. Think! He got away and had to change clothes so he could refocus the suspicion. He had a key to Barnett's apartment! He had to go somewhere!"

"But it's too far-fetched. It ain't as obvious . . ."

"Sometimes evidence can be too obvious, Sid!" Stan shouted. "Come on. We've got to get to the Newpointe Inn. If it's David, he's not going to stay there for long. And if Celia's out there somewhere, she's probably looking for him. If she gets to him before we do, her life is in danger."

"Or his," Sid said.

Stan grabbed his gun and shoulder holster, which had been lying on the table, jerked the keys out of his friend's hand, and headed for the door.

"Wait up, you!" Aunt Aggie shouted. "I'm comin' too."

"You can't, Aunt Aggie," Sid said, hurrying out the door. Stan went to the driver's side. "Stan, you can't drive in your condition. I'll drive. Just wait up."

Stan grudgingly gave him his keys back and got in on the passenger side. Aunt Aggie ran out behind them and jumped into the backseat.

Sid stopped her from closing the door. "No way, Aunt Aggie. Get out!"

"You gon' drag a ole lady outa the car?" she challenged.

"If I have to!" Sid shouted.

"Shut up and get in the car!" Stan yelled. "Celia's life is in danger!"

Chapter Sixty-Four

Celia drove aimlessly, looking for David. If he'd gotten away without his car, he must be on foot. Maybe she would spot him.

But after some time, she realized that she wasn't going to find him. He was too good at this.

She sobbed into her hand, unable to believe that her brother was a killer. She didn't understand. Why would he do it? Why would he have killed Nathan six years ago? Why would he have set her up? Why, after all this time, would he have poisoned Stan? It made no sense at all.

She thought of her parents, who had shunned her at the funeral. He had eaten dinner with them tonight. They were still at the Newpointe Inn.

She didn't know why, but she decided to go there, to confront them.

Her hands trembled as she parked Jill's car in the parking lot and hurried inside. She stopped at the desk and asked for her parents' room number.

"I'm sorry, but I'm not allowed to give that information."

"Please," she cut in, beginning to sob again. She dropped her face, tried to cover her mouth. "Look, they're my parents ... the Bradfords. I need to see them ..."

The woman looked like she felt sorry for her. "Look, I'm not supposed to do this, but if they're your parents ..." She checked her computer, then turned back to her. "They're in 305."

"Thank you." Celia headed for the elevator.

She rode up, wiping her face and trying to decide what she would say to them when she saw them. Should she tell them that she suspected David? Would they even believe her? Would they know where he was?

She got off and found their door. She took a deep breath and knocked.

She heard voices inside, and knew someone was looking at her through the peephole. Would they pretend they weren't there, and hope she'd go away? She pressed her forehead on the door. "Mom ... Dad ... please let me in. I have to talk to you."

The door opened, but she saw no one there. She pushed into the room, and turned to see who stood behind the door.

David grabbed her arm and closed the door behind her. She screamed, but he threw his hand over her mouth. "I have a gun," he told her in a whisper. "Don't scream again."

She swallowed as he let her go, and turned around to see the pistol he held pointed at her.

"David, why are you doing this?" she cried.

"Mom, Dad," he called into the bedroom. "It's okay."

Her parents came out with looks of terror on their faces. They looked at Celia, then at the gun he held on her.

"Be careful, David," her mother said. "That thing could accidentally go off."

She couldn't believe her ears. "Mom? Don't you see what's happening?"

"Don't talk to her, Mom," David said. "Just get out. You and Dad get out of the room where you'll be safe. Call the police and tell them she's here."

Suddenly, it was all so clear to her. David was the killer. And he had convinced her parents that she was. "Mom, Dad! It's him! He did all this!"

Her parents wouldn't listen. Instead, they opened the door and fled out into the corridor.

The door swung shut behind them. "Why, David?" she asked him. "Why?"

He laughed. "If I shoot you, I can claim we were fighting over the gun, and it went off. I've convinced Mom and Dad that you're certifiable. I'll convince the police, too. Even Stan will believe me when it's all over."

"But . . . I don't understand. What did I ever do to you? Why do you hate me so much?"

"Why?" He laughed again. "I didn't hate you, Celia. I hated the way they felt about you."

"Who? Mom and Dad?"

"You were their trophy child," he said. "I was invisible."

She backed away, trying to make it to the door. She turned the knob, but he came closer with that gun.

"David, that wasn't my fault. I didn't mean to make you feel that way. I loved you . . ."

"And then you grew up, and there you were with your husband taking an executive position in the company . . ."

"You got one, too," Celia said. "Dad didn't overlook you!"

"He didn't value me, either. You were gonna get the lion's share of the inheritance, like you got everything else."

"Then why didn't you kill me?" she demanded on a sob. "Why did you kill him? Why did you go after Stan?"

"Because," he said through his teeth, "if I'd killed you, you'd have been a martyr. They would have built a shrine to you. Started a foundation. Grieved over you so hard that I still would have been invisible!"

"But David, it wasn't that way—"

"You have no idea how it was. But it changed, Celia. As soon as they thought you were a murderer, I wasn't invisible anymore. You weren't the trophy child; you were the embarrassment. And then the whole inheritance was mine, and I was the one who was going to take over the company some day . . ."

She couldn't speak. Sobs rose up in her throat as her heart broke.

"Then Stan started working on them about your birthday, and I saw them starting to pull out your pictures again, and I knew that they were going to forgive you. I had to remind them what you really were. I had to make you a murderer again." He stepped closer to her, ran the barrel of the pistol across her throat. "But you know what? If I kill you now, you won't be a martyr. It won't hurt them a bit. You're a threat. An embarrassment. They'll be glad you're finally gone."

She dropped to the floor, trying to sob silently. "David, I'm pregnant. I'm carrying your niece or nephew. You couldn't kill me, could you?"

He bent over her. "I can't let another trophy child be born. It would ruin everything."

She wailed out a sob, and he yanked her to her feet.

"Now, here's how we're gonna do this." He took her hand and closed it around his hand—the hand that held the gun. "We're going to struggle for the gun, Celia. And it's going to go off. And you're going to die, but they'll see the gunpowder on your hands, and they'll believe the evidence."

"No," she cried, trying to pull her hand away. "No!"

He grabbed her wrist and made her hold the gun, and suddenly, she realized that if she didn't fight back, if she *didn't* struggle, he was going to kill her. She closed her hand around the gun, and tried to raise it up, but he was stronger, and he overpowered her. He turned it in to her, but she pushed it away with all her might and prayed with all her heart.

Chapter Sixty-Five

Stan saw Jill's car parked at the Newpointe Inn. "There's Jill's car," he said, as Sid double-parked behind it. "That means Celia's here. And she's in trouble."

He got out of the car, and Sid and Aunt Aggie got out behind him.

Stan saw Celia's parents standing at the front desk, talking frantically on the phone. They saw him and spun around. "Where's Celia?" he demanded.

"She's up in the room with David. We're calling the police." Joanna looked up at Sid. "It's okay, though. David's got a gun."

Stan didn't know he had such energy left in him as he bolted for the open elevator. Sid jumped on as the doors began to close, and he heard Joanna scream as Aunt Aggie came into the lobby.

The elevator opened, and Stan shot into the hall and ran to 305. He was out of breath and soaked with sweat, and felt as though he might pass out. As he ran, he pulled his weapon out of his shoulder holster.

Just as he reached the door, a gunshot shattered the silence. He bolted into the room and saw David and Celia struggling with the gun. David was overpowering her, pointing the gun at Celia's chest.

Stan aimed and pulled the trigger.

David flew back against the wall, then slid down into a heap on the floor.

Celia screamed and collapsed on the floor, holding her head with both hands and rocking back and forth. Stan went to her side and pulled her into his arms.

She couldn't stop screaming.

Sid looked stunned as he came into the room. He turned back to Celia and Stan, then looked at David.

Stan heard people running up the hall, and Vern and R.J. burst into the room.

Celia's screaming stopped and became desperate, gasping sobs instead.

"Get the paramedics up here," Sid told them. "She may be hurt." He went over to David, took his pulse. "He's dead."

"Nooo!" she wailed. "Noooo!"

Stan only held her, trying to comfort her, trying to whisper soothing words into her ear.

Issie Mattreaux and Steve Winder ran in with a gurney and laid it down beside Celia. "Celia, are you hurt?"

She was shaking and sobbing, and Stan wouldn't let her go. "She's pregnant," he said. "In her condition, this kind of thing . . ."

They pried his arms off her and tried to examine her, but she couldn't calm down. "Let's get her out of here," Stan told them, helping her to her feet. "Come on, baby, let's go downstairs."

Still wailing, Celia let him walk her out.

Chapter Sixty-Six

It took over an hour for Celia to calm down, but Stan wouldn't let them give her a sedative for fear it would harm the baby. Since he didn't feel sure enough that their own home was safe, he took her back to Aunt Aggie's house. There he tucked her into bed then lay beside her, holding her.

She didn't yet know that Aunt Aggie was alive. Her aunt and parents had been in a police car, out of harm's way, when they'd brought her through the lobby. She had been so distraught at the time Stan had decided not to tell her then. He'd been more worried about getting her to the hospital to make sure she was all right.

Now, he wondered if it was time to tell her. Maybe the news would pull her out of her despair. He knew that Aunt Aggie was downstairs with Jill and Stan's parents, chomping at the bit to come up and comfort Celia.

"Celia, honey, look at me," he whispered.

She turned her swollen, red eyes to him, and he thought he would do anything in the world to put some joy back in those eyes. "Honey, there's something I have to tell you. Some good news."

He knew she couldn't imagine any news being good after what had happened tonight. "What?" she whispered.

"Well, while you were in jail, some of us tried to come up with a plan to draw out the killer," he said softly. "We had to figure out a way to get you out of jail so he could strike again. We knew he couldn't do something and blame you if you were in jail."

She was listening carefully, trying to follow him.

"So . . . we had the idea that . . . if there was a death in the family . . . there'd be a good reason for you to get out . . ."

She frowned and sat up slowly, staring at him. He sat up, too, and framed her face with his hands. "Celia, Aunt Aggie isn't really dead."

She caught her breath, got up, and gaped down at him. "Stan, this isn't funny."

"It's not meant to be. Honey, she's alive. She's downstairs."

She bolted to the staircase and tore down the stairs. Stan followed her.

"Aunt Aggie!" she called, and suddenly the old woman came out of the kitchen and ran into her arms.

"I ain't dead, *sha!*" Aunt Aggie said, bursting into tears. "It was just a hoax to draw the killer out. We didn't know it was gon' be David."

Celia began to weep again, clutching her as if she'd never let her go. Hannah and Bart came out of the kitchen and watched quietly, and Jill came, too. They all watched as Celia crushed the old woman against her and cried out what was left of her tears. Finally, Celia stepped back and looked around at all of them. "I want to know whose idea this was!" The words came out through her teeth, and her face was red as she looked around at them. "Who decided to tell me my Aunt Aggie was dead?"

Jill stepped forward. "It was my idea, Celia. It was the only way I could think of to—"

Celia slapped her face. Jill brought her hand to the print on her cheek and took a step back. "Celia, I'm sorry. So sorry."

Celia fell into Aunt Aggie's arms again. "It ain't her fault," Aunt Aggie told her. "If it weren't for her, you'd still be in jail. And David, he'd still be foolin' all of us. Stan might be dead . . ."

Stan stepped forward and touched Celia's shoulder. "Honey, I know you feel betrayed . . ."

"Everybody betrayed me!" she cried. "Everybody!"

She let Aunt Aggie go and fell back into his arms. He held her, stroking her hair, squeezing her against him.

Slowly, his parents stepped up to her, touched her hair tentatively. "Celia, we hope you can forgive us someday," Hannah said.

Bart was beginning to cry himself. "We're so sorry."

She stepped out of Stan's embrace and looked at her in-laws through teary eyes. For a moment, he thought she might slap them, too, but instead, she just reached out for them. They hugged her desperately.

After a moment, she turned back to Jill. She looked at her, shaking her head, then reached out for her, too. Jill hugged her like a sister. "Oh, Celia," she whispered.

"I'm sorry I slapped you," she said. "I should be thanking you . . . for sticking by me."

"It's okay," Jill whispered.

"Let's get you some eats," Aunt Aggie said when the two women had let each other go. "You eatin' for two now. And this has been a rough night. Got to calm you and the baby down, let him know arrything gon' be awright."

Celia laughed for the first time in a long time and followed her aunt into the kitchen.

After she'd eaten Aunt Aggie's cooking, the pall that had hung over Celia seemed to be lifting. Aunt Aggie sat across the table from her and Stan, and Celia just stared at her. "Aunt Aggie, there's something I have to say to you," she said.

Aunt Aggie touched her hand. "Say anything you want to."

She breathed in a deep sigh. "Aunt Aggie, when I thought you were dead, I couldn't even take comfort in knowing I'd see you again when I die, because we're not going to the same place, Aunt Aggie."

Aunt Aggie's face changed.

"Aunt Aggie, I'm not gonna leave you alone until you love Jesus like I love him. I'm sorry, but I just can't. You're gonna have to get used to me harping on you all the time, because I don't ever want to have to go to your funeral again and sit there despairing that you never knew him. And beating myself up with guilt because I didn't work hard enough. God's given me another chance, and if it kills me, I'm gonna use it."

Aunt Aggie didn't know what to say to that. "You do what you gotta do, darlin'," she said. "Don't mean I'm gon' listen."

"You're a stubborn woman, Aunt Aggie." She got up and went around the table, and hugged the old woman again. "But I love you. And I don't want to lose you again."

Stan couldn't help smiling at the joy he saw on his wife's face as she held her dear Aunt Aggie.

• • •

Aunt Aggie slept until almost noon the next day, so exhausted was she from the ordeal of the night before. When the doorbell downstairs rang, she pulled herself out of bed, slipped on her robe, and looked out the window to see who it could be. Had anyone found out that she was alive yet? Was it time for the party to begin?

And then she saw the Bradford's BMW parked out front. She opened her door quietly and walked out to the staircase, listening. If they had any cross words to say to Celia, they would have her to answer to.

Instead, she saw something that surprised her.

Celia stood at the door, staring at her parents. "Mom? Dad?" she asked hesitantly. "Come in."

Aunt Aggie thought that Celia was a better person than she was. She would have thrown them out the minute she laid eyes on them.

They came into the house and Celia closed the door. Stan was behind her in a moment, watching with anticipation.

Joanna's face twisted with emotion, and tears came to her tired, puffy eyes. "Celia, we need to ask your forgiveness.

We're so sorry for the way we've treated you all these years. We want to explain, but there isn't a good explanation. Not one that can make up for six years when we should have been there for you. Can you ever forgive us? He told us such lies ... and we believed him. We believed all of it ..."

Tears rolled down Celia's face.

"We don't have a right to your forgiveness," her father went on. "But we need to ask. We had to let you know that we know David was guilty. We should have seen it."

Celia wasn't able to speak. She just put her arms around both of her parents, and they clung to her and wept.

From her place at the top of the stairs, Aunt Aggie wiped her own eyes.

"I'm gonna have a baby," she heard Celia tell her parents.

"We know," her mother said. "Aunt Aggie told us last night." She let her go and patted her daughter's stomach. "We're finally gonna have a grandbaby. To think we almost missed it."

"You didn't miss it," Celia said. "You're just in time."

Aggie watched, overcome, from the top of the staircase. Slowly, she sank down onto the top step and leaned against the post. What she had just witnessed was so different from what she would have done, and yet it was so sweet.

Was this something God had enabled Celia to do? Was this the empowerment Celia had spoken of? Was that what kept prodding Aunt Aggie now, ever since the funeral?

The battle is not yours, but God's. Wasn't that what Celia said God had told her that night in jail? And hadn't it turned out to be true? If there was a God, he'd worked it all out. He'd won the battle, so Celia had won. But remembering their night in jail, Aggie realized that Celia had won before they'd determined David to be the killer. She had peace and joy, even in the worst of circumstances. How could that be?

She didn't know, but she did know that it was too hard to admit she was wrong after so many years. She could fake it, she supposed, for Celia's sake. She could go downstairs and tell Celia that she had accepted Jesus, that she had changed, that she would go to church with her now, just so Celia wouldn't cry and worry.

But that wasn't Aunt Aggie's style. She may lie about death, but she wasn't going to lie about anything like that. Still, she wondered if, indeed, there was a God, working on her soul right at that very moment, pulling her to him. She didn't know if she had it in her to confess, to repent of all the things she'd never thought of as sins. She'd always fancied herself a good person. One who did the right things.

But if there *was* a God, then in his eyes, she must be an awful disappointment.

She got up and went back into her room, wiping away the tears. She hardly ever cried. Hadn't done it in years before this whole mess had started, but in the last few days it seemed that the fountain wouldn't stop flowing. Her tears were never going to end.

She sat down at the secretary in her bedroom, stared down at the wood grain. Was the Lord speaking to her? Was he the one putting this heaviness in her heart, this emptiness in her soul, giving her this hunger that she didn't know how to fill? Was it him, or just the circumstances, the emotion, of the last few days?

She didn't know. All she did know was that when she looked at herself in the mirror, she didn't like what she saw so much anymore. She wondered what God saw.

And then she realized that, for the first time in her life, she was thinking of God as if he were real. She didn't know how to take that.

She began to cry even harder, and put her wrinkled hands over her face, wishing that none of this had ever happened, that she'd never been convicted, that she'd never had to break her niece's heart. She'd never planned to have to look God in the face, but she supposed if Celia was right, she would have to someday, when every knee would bow and every tongue confess.

Wasn't that what Celia always quoted? "Even you, Aunt Aggie,"
she had told her once. Aunt Aggie hadn't believed it then. Now,
she thought maybe it was true. One day, her knee would bow.
One day, her tongue would confess. It was her choice whether
she did it too late.

Slowly, she got off her chair and got down on her knees. It
wasn't a comfortable place to be. She figured her bony knees
would be bruised when she got back up, and she might limp for
a while. But she stayed there, as tears rolled down her face, and
she folded her hands together like a child in prayer and looked
up at the ceiling.

"I don't know who you are or what you want with me," she
said. "But I'm startin' to think that maybe you're really there.
And if what Celia says is true about you, well, then I reckon I
oughta listen." Her voice broke and she sobbed against her
hands. "I guess what you see down here's a mighty wretched
person. I can't do nothin' about the past, but I can tell you how
sorry I am. And I can start from today. That's what Celia says
you do anyhow. Just start folks right where they are."

She closed her eyes and shook her head as sobs tore from her
throat. "Oh, Jesus, don't ever make my Celia have to grieve like
that again. Help me know you before my time really comes."

It was at that moment that the gentlest peace she'd ever
known in her life washed over her, and Aunt Aggie looked at
the ceiling, frowning, wondering why in the world he would
answer her prayer—the first one she'd ever prayed. But he had.
And just as clear as she knew her heart was still beating, she
knew that Jesus had accepted her prayer.

Something was different now. Something had changed.

She thought of running down to tell Celia what she had
done. But some part of her wanted to be alone with him just for
a little longer, to bask in that comfort and that peace, and especially that love. She had loved many people in her life and had
received love from many others. But never had she experienced

a love quite as grand as this. She wasn't ready to break the moment. She didn't know how this Christianity thing worked. She supposed she'd have to start going to church now to find out. But for now, she just wanted to bask in the love that God was showering over her. For now, she just wanted to spend a little more time with him.

Chapter Sixty-Seven

Dan Nichols stood at the nursery window, looking in at the little baby with the sign that said "Branning" on its crib. His heart ached at the thought that his best friend had fathered that child. This tiny, fragile human being would be completely dependent on Mark and Allie to take care of him. Part of him longed for that kind of responsibility, that kind of a challenge. But another part knew it was never to be. Not Dan Nichols. He'd had poor parenting. He would probably make a horrible father.

That is, if he ever got to the point of marriage in the first place. This relationship with Jill had about done him in. He had decided long ago, when he became an adult and quit trying to please his parents, that he never wanted to be in a position of vulnerability again. He never wanted to allow anyone else he loved to hurt him. Therefore, he had tried not to love, and it had worked for most of his life. But over these last few days, he'd realized that Jill had made him vulnerable again. He didn't like it. Not one bit.

"Dan?"

He turned around and saw Jill standing behind him, as if his own mind had conjured her up. Celia and Stan were with her. Stan was in a wheelchair, and Celia pushed it toward him. Instead of greeting Jill, he went right to Celia, gave her a hug. "Celia, you look great. It's so good to see you out." He slapped hands with Stan. "Man, you're looking good."

"I could have walked," Stan said, "but my wife insisted on the wheelchair. She thinks I've been overdoing it. I'm trying to humor her."

"Yeah," Celia said. "I appreciate it. Is this their baby?" She stepped up to the glass and looked in.

"Yeah, that's him."

"We're gonna have one of our own, you know," she said, her eyes dancing.

"That's what I heard," he said. "You know, maybe if you go in there and talk to Allie, she'll call them to bring the baby in, and you can hold him."

"Do you think so?"

"Sure. If they let me, they'll let anybody."

"You held the baby?" Jill asked.

At last, he let himself look at her. "Yeah, I did."

Electricity sparked between them, and he made himself turn away.

Stan didn't seem to notice. "I hear you played a part in our little sting last night."

"Yeah, without even realizing it. By the way," he said, glancing at Jill, "you owe me fifty bucks."

She smiled tentatively. "I sure do. I'll write you a check before we leave."

"No problem."

Celia and Stan headed for Allie's room, but Jill hung back, looking up at him with searching eyes. But he didn't want her to see into him.

"You're mad at me," she said. "Is it about Lee Barnett?"

He frowned and shook his head. "No. Why would I be mad about Lee Barnett?"

"Because I was so short with you last night? And the time before that, when I saw you? And when I avoided you at Aunt Aggie's funeral? I'm sorry, Dan, but I was having so much trouble with that lie about Aunt Aggie . . . I couldn't look you in the eye. And the stress of the last few days . . ."

He raised a hand to stem her excuses. "No problem. I understand."

"Look, I was hoping that maybe we could go out to dinner later. I could catch you up on everything. I tried to call you, but you weren't home."

He wondered if she thought he was a charity case or something. *Poor guy. Throw him a crumb here and there, and maybe he won't look so forlorn.* He tried to harden his expression. "No, I've got plans for tonight."

She looked disappointed. "Tomorrow?"

"No, I've taken a few days off. I'm going deer hunting."

"Deer hunting? Oh ... well, then, when you get back."

He hesitated and looked at the baby again. "We'll see." His refusal to commit seemed to startle her, and she touched his arm. He wished that his pulse didn't speed up at such a simple gesture. It made him furious at himself.

"Dan, you *are* mad at me."

"No, I'm not, Jill," he said. "I'm just busy."

"Like I've been busy," she said. "Look, I know I've been distant and unavailable, but I've been under so much pressure. I didn't know which end was up. If I've been short with you or didn't seem to want to spend time with you, it was because my friend was hurting so badly and I wanted to help her."

"You did a good job," he said honestly. "You really did. I'm glad she had you in her corner."

"But?"

He couldn't look her in the eye. "But I'm not the kind of guy who really hooks up with one woman very long, Jill. You know that about me."

She kept staring at him, and he wondered what was going through her mind. Was she buying it?

She looked down at her feet, swallowed. "Well ... I'm not really one to beg," she said, her voice quivering slightly. "I mean, if you're not interested, you're not interested. I just thought we had something going."

She cut her words off, and he could see her mentally kicking herself, as if she didn't expect herself to be saying such things. "Look, we're friends," she said quickly. "We don't have to explain these things to each other. If we don't want to date, we don't want to date. It's not going to ruin our friendship. Right?"

"Right," he said, wishing she would beg just a little. They stood side by side, staring at the baby, because it wouldn't do to look at each other. It was as if the sight of that tiny little life kicking in that crib had something to teach them, something about life that neither of them could understand. But Dan had a sinking feeling that it was not a lesson he was ever going to learn. Those lessons were for people like Celia and Stan, Allie and Mark ... people who weren't afraid to love and lose. People who had the stamina to risk rejection and come out on top.

The nurse came to get the baby, and holding its little wrist, made it wave bye-bye to them as she took him to his mother. He stole a look at Jill as the baby was taken away. Her eyes were misty, soft, and he wondered if the sight of that child did the same things to her heart that it did to his.

She began to dig into her purse, pulled out her checkbook, and wrote out a check. She tore it out and handed it to him. "There you go. I really appreciate your help last night. I thought Lee Barnett was the killer. When they arrested him for a barroom brawl, I thought our whole sting was over. We had to get him back out there so he would be free to make a move."

"Whatever happened to him?"

"Oh, the judge figured he'd been through enough, what with all the ways David had manipulated him. He dropped all the charges against him and told him to go back to Jackson."

Dan nodded but couldn't seem to find his voice.

She looked up at him. "Well, guess I'll go see Allie. I'll see ya."

"Yeah," he said. "See ya."

Dan watched until she disappeared around the corner. His heart felt like a broken balloon on the bottom of his chest cavity, yet part of him felt some relief at breaking those ties. Was it that easy? he asked himself. No, his heart told him it wasn't. But he would get over it in time. It was his choice, after all.

• • •

In Allie's room a few minutes later, Celia and Stan sat on the vinyl couch and held the baby that squirmed in their arms, his alert eyes focused on Celia. Stan enjoyed the baby, but he was more captivated by the look of pure joy and excitement on Celia's face. "Oh, Allie, isn't he a miracle? Isn't he just the most wonderful thing?"

Allie's smile was radiant. "I'm so excited about your news, Celia."

"Yeah, and to think I don't have to go through my pregnancy in prison."

Mark shook his head. "Man, that was the worst. Just the worst. And I'm so glad Aunt Aggie's not dead, 'cause I really blew her funeral."

"She called me this morning," Allie said, "and gave me heck for upstaging her."

They all chuckled. "You know," Celia said, "I think Aunt Aggie's coming around. I think the Holy Spirit convicted her through all this. I don't know what will come of it, but I know God's working on her."

"He's working on all of us," Allie said. "Wouldn't you say that's true?"

Celia smiled and nodded her head as the little baby squirmed in her arms. She met Stan's eyes and nodded. "Oh, yeah. We're all just works in progress, aren't we? Someday we'll all be people God's proud of."

"Someday," Stan said.

But he couldn't help thinking that God was already proud of his wife.

Afterword

W hy do people always let you down?"

One of my children asked this question after her heart had been broken, and I wanted to leap to the defense of the human race. "They don't always let you down," I wanted to say. "Some people are reliable and dependable. Some people are good and won't hurt you."

But I stopped myself, because I realized that this could be one of the greatest life lessons she would ever learn. The truth is, every human on the face of the earth has the ability to let someone down. Everyone is capable of breaking a heart. It's our nature. There is no one who can live up to another's expectations a hundred percent of the time.

No one but Christ.

So I told my child that we are not to put our hopes in people, but in Christ, who would never, ever let us down.

To some people, that's good news.

To others, it's like saying we can count on the tooth fairy. To them, Christ seems so far removed from reality, that they think reaching for him would be like reaching for thin air.

But they would be wrong.

You see, Jesus knows of our heartbreaks. His heart broke when one of his twelve closest friends betrayed him for thirty pieces of silver, and when the rest scattered to avoid arrest. His heart broke when he heard Peter, one of his most trusted confidantes, swearing he didn't even know him. His heart broke when he hung on that cross between thieves and heard the soldiers mocking him and knew he had done nothing for which he should be executed. His heart broke when the thief next to him cursed him and challenged him.

But that must have reminded him why he was here. He had come to earth for the sins that caused all of those heartbreaks. In the book of Hebrews, we're told: "In bringing many sons to glory, it was fitting that God, for whom and through whom everything exists, should make the author of their salvation perfect through suffering. Both the one who makes men holy and those who are made holy are of the same family. So Jesus is not ashamed to call them brothers" (Hebrews 2:10–11).

Because of Christ's suffering, he not only understands our suffering, but he has such an affinity with us that he can call us brothers. To me, that's wonderful news! That tells me that no matter who breaks my heart in this life, or who lets me down or deceives me or rejects me or betrays me . . . I'll still have an anchor. Jesus understands, and he will never break my heart.

Oh, if you don't know him, what joy you are missing! Let his suffering and heartbreak change your life today. Accept the love he offered you when he gave his life for you. Focus your life on him, and he will never let you down.

"The Lord himself goes before you and will be with you; he will never leave you nor forsake you" (Deuteronomy 31:8).

God bless all of you!

Terri Blackstock

Last Light

A Restoration Novel

Terri Blackstock,
#1 Bestselling Suspense Author

Today, the world as you know it will end. No need to turn off the lights.

Your car suddenly stalls and won't restart. You can't call for help because your cell phone is dead.

Everyone around you is having the same problem ... and it's just the tip of the iceberg. Your city is in a blackout. Communication is cut off. Hospital equipment won't operate. And airplanes are falling from the sky.

Is it a terrorist attack ... or something far worse?

In the face of a crisis that sweeps an entire high-tech planet back to the age before electricity, your family faces a choice. Will you hoard your possessions to survive — or trust God to provide as you offer your resources and your hearts to others?

Yesterday's world is gone. Now all you've got is your family and community. You stand or fall together. Like never before, you must rely on each other.

But one of you is a killer.

Number one bestselling suspense author Terri Blackstock weaves a masterful what-if novel in which global catastrophe reveals the darkness in human hearts—and lights the way to restoration for a self-centered world. *Last Light* is the first book in this exciting series.

Softcover: 0-310-25767-0
Audio CD, Unabridged: 0-310-26880-X

Pick up a copy today at your favorite bookstore!

ZONDERVAN®
.com

Night Light

A Restoration Novel

Terri Blackstock, #1 Bestselling Suspense Author

In the face of a crisis that sweeps an entire high-tech planet back to the age before electricity, the Brannings face a choice. Will they hoard their possessions to survive — or trust God to provide as they offer their resources to others?

Number one bestselling suspense author Terri Blackstock weaves a masterful what-if series in which global catastrophe reveals the darkness in human hearts — and lights the way to restoration for a selfcentered world.

An era unlike any in modern civilization is descending, one without lights, electronics, running water, or automobiles. As a global blackout lengthens into months, the neighbors of Oak Hollow grapple with a chilling realization: the power may never return.

Survival has become a lifestyle. When two young thieves break into the Brannings' home and clean out the food in their pantry, Jeff Branning tracks them to a filthy apartment and discovers a family of children living alone, stealing to stay alive. Where is their mother? The search for answers uncovers a trail of desperation and murder ... and for the Brannings, a powerful new purpose that can transform their entire community — and above all, themselves.

Softcover: 0-310-25768-9
Audio CD, Unabridged: 0-310-26921-0

Pick up a copy today at your favorite bookstore!

True Light

A Restoration Novel

Terri Blackstock, #1 Bestselling Suspense Author

The darkness deepens in a world without power.

But, daring to defend a young outcast, one family strikes a light.

In the face of a crisis that sweeps an entire high-tech planet back to the age before electricity, the Brannings face a choice. Will they hoard their possessions to survive—or trust God to provide as they offer their resources to others?

Number one bestselling suspense author Terri Blackstock weaves a masterful what-if series in which global catastrophe reveals the darkness in human hearts—and lights the way to restoration for a self-centered world.

Now eight months into a global blackout, the residents of Oak Hollow are coping with the deep winter nights. But the struggle to survive can bring out the worst in a person—or a community.

A teenager has been shot and the suspect sits in jail. As the son of a convicted murderer, Mark Green already has one strike against him. Now he faces the wrath of all Oak Hollow—except for one person. Deni Branning has known Mark since high school and is convinced he is no killer.

When Mark finds himself at large with a host of other prisoners released upon the unsuspecting community, Deni and her family attempt to help him find the person who really pulled the trigger. But clearing Mark's reputation is only part of his battle. Protecting the neighbors who ostracized him is just as difficult.

And forgiving them may be the hardest part of all.

Softcover: 0-310-25769-7
Unabridged Audio CD: 0-310-26922-9
Audio Download, Unabridged: 0-310-26948-2

ebook:
 Palm™ Reader: 0-310-27484-2
 Adobe® Reader: 0-310-27474-5
 Microsoft Reader®: 0-310-27477-X
 Mobipocket Reader™: 031027480x

Pick up a copy today at your favorite bookstore!

Read an excerpt from

TRUE LIGHT

BOOK THREE OF THE RESTORATION SERIES

TERRI BLACKSTOCK

THE BUCK FELL WITH THE FIRST SHOT, AND ZACH EMORY couldn't help being impressed with himself. From his deer stand, it looked like an eight- or ten-pointer. If the weather stayed cold, he'd be able to make it last for several weeks' worth of meals.

He climbed down from his deer stand and pulled up the collar of his jacket. It was so cold his ears were numb, and his fingers had begun to ache. But it was worth it. Even in the pre-outage days, Zach had spent many mornings sitting in a deer stand freezing to death, just for sport. Now it was a matter of survival.

He jogged toward the animal that lay dead twenty yards away. His brother Gary would be crazy with envy. They had a competition going, and Gary was two up on him. Zach hoped Gary had heard the gunshot and would come to help him move the deer. It would take both of them to lift it into their rickshaw.

He bent over the buck. Ten points. And a perfect shot right through the heart. His dad would finally be proud, and if he was lucky, his mother would drag herself out of bed to get a look.

He heard footsteps behind him and turned to see a man emerging from the trees, walking toward him. Zach squinted, trying to place him. He'd seen him before, but he couldn't remember where.

"Did I score or what?" he asked as the man came closer. "He's a ten-pointer. Got him in one shot, right through the ticker!"

The man didn't look like he'd come to celebrate. He stopped about thirty feet away ... and raised his rifle.

Was he going to shoot? Zach's hands came up, as if that would stop him.

The gun fired—its impact propelling Zach backward, bouncing him onto the dirt.

two

THE BUILDING SMELLED OF MOTOR OIL AND GREASE — A SCENT Deni Branning associated with progress. A symphony of roaring engines brought a smile to her face as she rolled her bike inside. Oh, for the days of noise pollution and hurry — of bumper-to-bumper traffic, honking horns, blaring radios, and twenty-four-hour TV.

All over the large warehouse, mechanics and engineers with black-stained fingers worked at converting engines. The building had been purchased by the feds a few months ago, when they instituted the draft. Instead of drafting soldiers, the government had conscripted all of those with experience as mechanics. Later, they'd added others to the conscription list: electricians, scientists, and engineers. Many of them were allowed to live at home and work in the local conversion plants, but others had been sent across the country to serve where they were needed.

Pushing down the kickstand on her bike, she reached into her bag for her notepad and looked around for someone in charge. She saw Ned Emory, from her neighborhood, standing nearby with a clipboard, instructing a group of mechanics with a disassembled engine laid out in front of them. She headed toward him.

"Excuse me," she yelled over the noise. "Mr. Emory?"

He turned. "Yeah?"

She could see that he didn't recognize her, even though his son Zach had been close friends with her brother for years. "Deni Branning. Jeff's sister?"

Recognition dawned in his eyes. She reached out to shake hands with him, but he showed her his greasy hands. "Better not shake. What brings you here?"

"I'm writing an article about your work here. Do you have time for an interview?"

As if he hadn't heard her, he turned back to the men, barked out some orders that she couldn't hear, and started walking away. Glancing back over his shoulder, he said, "I heard the newspaper is back up and running. They hired you, did they?"

She caught up to him and tried to match his steps. "That's right. the *Crockett Times*. They liked what I'd been doing on the message boards around town. This'll be the cover story for next week's issue."

He didn't seem impressed, so she pulled out her big guns. "You guys are like rock stars. Everybody wants to know what you're up to."

Pride pulled at the corners of his mouth, and she knew she'd struck a chord. "Sure, I can give you a few minutes. What do you want to know?"

He started up a staircase, and she blew out her frustration as she followed him. "Is there someplace we can sit down?"

"I don't have time to sit down." He reached the top of the stairs and headed across the concrete floor to an area where a dozen mopeds sat in various stages of completion. "Hey, Stark! I need at least four of these done by the end of the day. Get Bennett over here to help you."

Deni's gaze swept over the bikes. "Wow. How can I get one of those?"

"You can't. They're not for the private sector." He was walking again, but she hung back, unable to tear herself away from the coveted mopeds. She stepped toward one and touched the seat.

He turned back and gave her an impatient look. "Do you want to do the interview or not?"

She shook off her longing and forced herself to focus. "Of course."

He led her past a table filled with generators, and again, her longing kicked in. "Do those work?"

"They do after we harden them against the Pulses."

Her heart quickened. If they were making hardened generators here, it wouldn't be long until they actually had electricity. Could there really be lightbulbs at the end of the tunnel?

"When will those be available for the public?" she asked, catching up to him again.

"Our illustrious supernova will burn out before we can finish supplying the hospitals. They're priority number one for the generators right now. Without robotics, assembly lines—electricity, for that matter—we have to do everything by hand, one at a time. And even if we could produce enough for the public, there's one missing ingredient."

"Gasoline," she said.

"You got it." He reached a series of offices with glass walls, overlooking the work on the floor below them. "We can't get enough gas without operating tanker trucks, and once we get it here, we don't have electricity to work the pumps."

She was well aware of the chain of problems. "But aren't you guys all about creating work-arounds?"

"Right now we're just trying to help critical services operate. Like I said, the star will likely burn out before we get caught up with that. Then we'll shift our objectives from sustaining to rebuilding." He headed into one of the offices, dropped his clipboard on his desk, and motioned for her to take a seat.

As Deni sat down, something outside the glass caught Ned's eye, and Deni turned to follow his gaze. Someone was running up the stairs.

Ned frowned as his son Gary came running toward his door. "Dad, Zach's been shot!"

"*What?*"

Deni caught her breath and got to her feet.

"We were hunting at the Jenkins's place. I heard some gunshots and ... when I found him ..."

"Is he dead?" Ned blurted out.

"I don't think so. I got help and somebody went to get an ambulance. They're taking him to University Hospital."

Ned grabbed his son's shoulders. "What condition was he in when they took him?"

Gary trembled as he raked his hands through his hair. "There was blood all over his shirt ... front and back."

Deni's heart stopped. Her brother's best friend ...

Ned raced out of the office and hurried down the stairs, Gary on his heels. Deni followed them as far as the top of the stairs, then waited there as they hurried through the building. All the engines went quiet, and everyone stared as Ned ran to a beat-up Buick. "The keys!" he shouted. "Where are the keys?"

Someone tossed them to him, and he got in and started the engine. Gary jumped in beside him. Two guys pulled up the garage door and the Buick rumbled out.

Deni muttered a prayer for Zach as they drove off—and then a thought struck her. Jeff, Deni's brother, sometimes hunted with Zach. Could they have been together? What if he'd been hurt too?

She had to get to the scene of the shooting. She ran downstairs, grabbed her bike, and pedaled out behind them.

three

"ZACH? ZACH, CAN YOU HEAR ME?"

Zach tried to open his eyes, but they were glued shut. Something was shaking and bumping him—and with each jolt, pain exploded through him.

"Zach, we're getting you to the hospital, okay, buddy? Stay with me."

Was he in an ambulance? How long had it been since he'd been in a running car? Weeks? Months? Years? His brain couldn't find the answer.

He tried to breathe, but something was crushing his chest. Drowning ... choking ... gurgling.

Something sliced through his throat. "We're gonna help you breathe, buddy. Hang on, we're almost there."

He couldn't breathe. Gagging. Smothering. Gasping.

The ambulance jerked to a stop, people all around him yelling, probing, pushing.

As they rolled him into the building, Zach knew he was dying.

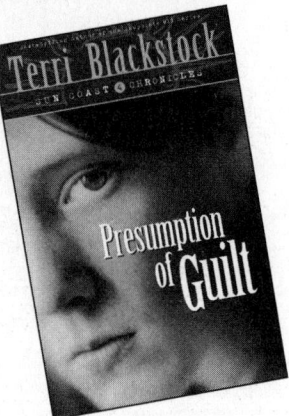

Cape Refuge Series

This bestselling series follows the lives of the people of the small seaside community of Cape Refuge, as two sisters struggle to continue the ministry their parents began—helping the troubled souls who come to Hanover House for solace.

Cape Refuge
Softcover: 0-310-23592-

Southern Storm
Softcover: 0-310-23593-6

River's Edge
Softcover: 0-310-23594-4

Breaker's Reef
Softcover: 0-310-23595-2

Pick up a copy today at your favorite bookstore!

About the Author

*T*erri Blackstock is an award-winning novelist who has written for several major publishers including HarperCollins, Dell, Harlequin, and Silhouette. Published under two pseudonyms, her books have sold over 5 million copies worldwide.

With her success in secular publishing at its peak, Blackstock had what she calls "a spiritual awakening." A Christian since the age of fourteen, she realized she had not been using her gift as God intended. It was at that point that she recommitted her life to Christ, gave up her secular career, and made the decision to write only books that would point her readers to him.

"I wanted to be able to tell the truth in my stories," she said, "and not just be politically correct. It doesn't matter how many readers I have if I can't tell them what I know about the roots of their problems and the solutions that have literally saved my own life."

Her books are about flawed Christians in crisis and God's provisions for their mistakes and wrong choices. She claims to be extremely qualified to write such books, since she's had years of personal experience.

A native of nowhere, since she was raised in the Air Force, Blackstock makes Mississippi her home. She and her husband are the parents of three children—a blended family which she considers one more of God's provisions.

Three ways to keep up on your favorite Zondervan books and authors

Sign up for our *Fiction E-Newsletter*. Every month you'll receive sample excerpts from our books, sneak peeks at upcoming books, and chances to win free books autographed by the author.

You can also sign up for our *Breakfast Club*. Every morning in your email, you'll receive a five-minute snippet from a fiction or nonfiction book. A new book will be featured each week, and by the end of the week you will have sampled two to three chapters of the book.

Zondervan *Author Tracker* is the best way to be notified whenever your favorite Zondervan authors write new books, go on tour, or want to tell you about what's happening in their lives.

Visit *www.zondervan.com* and sign up today!

ZONDERVAN®

ZONDERVAN.com/
AUTHORTRACKER
follow your favorite authors

We want to hear from you. Please send your comments about this book to us in care of zreview@zondervan.com. Thank you.

ZONDERVAN.com/
AUTHORTRACKER
follow your favorite authors